To Pete

great affection —

Jim

UNDERSTANDING AMERICA

UNDERSTANDING
AMERICA
THE ANATOMY OF AN
EXCEPTIONAL NATION

PETER H. SCHUCK AND
JAMES Q. WILSON, EDITORS

PUBLICAFFAIRS
New York

PublicAffairs books are available at special discounts for bulk purchases in the U.S. by corporations, institutions, and other organizations. For more information, please contact the Special Markets Department at the Perseus Books Group, 2300 Chestnut Street, Suite 200, Philadelphia, PA 19103, call (800) 255–1514, or e-mail special.markets@perseusbooks.com.

Designed by Pauline Brown

Text set in 11.5 point Bembo by the Perseus Books Group

Library of Congress Cataloging-in-Publication Data

Understanding America : the anatomy of an exceptional nation / eds., Peter H. Schuck and James Q. Wilson. — 1st ed.
    p. cm.
  Includes bibliographical references and index.
  ISBN 978-1-58648-561-0
  1. United States—Civilization--1945- 2. National characteristics, American. I. Schuck, Peter H. II. Wilson, James Q.
  E169.12.U479 2007
  973.918--dc22

                                                2007042142

First Edition

10 9 8 7 6 5 4 3 2 1

To the memory of Nelson Polsby:
a seminal scholar, renowned teacher,
and cherished friend

Contents

Part Two
AMERICAN PUBLIC POLICIES

Part Three
A LARGER PERSPECTIVE

Preface

The stakes in understanding America could hardly be higher. For better and for worse, America is the 800-pound gorilla in every room in the world. When it has an itch, the world scratches. When it gets a cold, the world sneezes. Its actions—and its failures to act—often send ripples around the globe. For some, it is a model for other societies to emulate. For others, it is one to avoid. Unless Americans gain a sophisticated understanding of the nation's political institutions, cultures, and policies, they will be poorly positioned to think and act as effective citizens. Unless our observers from abroad acquire this understanding, they will be ill-equipped to comprehend the American systems and policies that are inexorably shaping their lives.

All the more astonishing, then, is the absence of any authoritative, up-to-date, accessible, comprehensive, and single-volume account of American institutions, cultures, and policies. Should American or foreign readers want to learn how and why these institutions, cultures, and policies are distinctive from those in other advanced liberal democracies, how they work (and don't work), which social forces are operating to transform them, what major challenges they face in the future, and how those challenges might be addressed, they will be frustrated and disappointed.

This book seeks to fill that void, to explain America to itself and to its foreign observers. Some sort of explanation is clearly needed. Today, American politics often seem to be polarized between those who see this country through the eyes of either a hard-core liberal or a rock-ribbed conservative. Just how deeply this polarization accurately represents the thinking of most Americans is unclear. Some political scientists such as Morris Fiorina believe that we are not deeply polarized, while others, such as Alan Ambramowitz, argue that we are. What is very clear, however, is that Congress, interest groups, and the mass media are divided into two camps that disagree about almost everything. For Americans marinating in their own society, a clear understanding of its nature and distinctiveness remains elusive.

Our friends in Europe, Asia, and Latin America see America from a distance, but that perspective yields little insight. All of them see the American nation as a superpower, but many suppose that it is one managed by some strange combination of a vulgar popular culture, a rigid and intolerant religious revival, a bullying military establishment, a ruthlessly predatory capitalism, and a callous indifference to the plight of poor people.

It is a bit odd for any nation to be deeply divided, witlessly vulgar, religiously orthodox, militarily aggressive, economically savage, and ungenerous to those in need, while maintaining a political stability, a standard of living, and a love of country that are the envy of the world—all at the same time. To do all these things at once, America must indeed be unusual. Or even, as Alexis de Tocqueville said a century and a half ago, exceptional. Of course, Tocqueville meant something else by American exceptionalism: he was trying to explain to his European friends what this new phenomenon, democracy, meant in practice. Nobody then knew what it meant to live in a country where equality of condition was so widespread and where the common people actually ruled themselves. Tocqueville, himself an aristocrat, spent nine months in this country trying to understand what "the great democratic revolution" was all about. He thought it rested on individualism, a quality about which he had mixed feelings. The many subsequent discussions of American exceptionalism have focused on one or another aspect of the society, such as the absence of a strong socialist movement or the preference for a weak state, but have not analyzed, as our authors do here, the many specific manifestations of American exceptionalism in a wide range of institutional and policy domains. Never before has the debate over American exceptionalism been so firmly grounded in detailed social scientific findings. We consider this to be a major and, well, exceptional contribution of this volume.

Americans have embraced democracy even as they complain endlessly about its problems. And democracy has spread throughout the world, so much so that only a few ideologues, tyrants, or reactionaries now denounce it. But foreigners find American-style democracy lacking in many good qualities. Americans may proudly think of their nation as exceptional, but many foreigners roll their eyes and complain that Americans often deviate from the democratic ideal.

To them, Americans are exceptional all right: exceptionally vulgar, exceptionally materialistic, exceptionally imperialistic, exceptionally clumsy, exceptionally unfeeling, and exceptionally self-centered. Beneath the surface, these complaints sometimes seem unduly harsh. After all, Americans may be vulgar, but our music, books, and films dominate the global cultural market—and not just at the low end. Americans may be materialistic, but our material goods—blue jeans, iPods, and computer programs—are eagerly consumed everywhere. America may seem imperialistic, but most of the people in Europe, Bosnia, Kosovo, Kuwait, Taiwan, Israel, and Iraq wanted to be assured that in their hour of need, American military might was available to help them. Americans may be clumsy, but a superpower seeking to pacify a convulsive, often hostile world is bound to stumble at times. Americans may prefer a welfare state more limited than Europe's, but they are extraordinarily philanthropic toward the poor. Americans may be self-absorbed, but who isn't?

As editors, we think that American scholars can help both Americans and our foreign observers to understand this country better. We have asked some of the very best experts in our nation to write, clearly and without jargon, about almost every important aspect of American life, and a leading European commentator to reflect on how the United States is viewed there. These talented authors possess diverse political perspectives. At the end of the book—after their chapters on American institutions, culture, and public policies—we briefly summarize their leading ideas in order to help the reader understand precisely how and why America is exceptional, and what this means both for Americans and for a world that, like Tocqueville, finds America endlessly fascinating and deeply enigmatic.

—Peter H. Schuck and James Q. Wilson

Part One
AMERICAN INSTITUTIONS AND CULTURE

CHAPTER 1

The Political System

Nelson W. Polsby

The late Nelson Polsby, a leading scholar of American politics, explains why American democracy is different from democracy in almost any other nation. The Founders created neither a system where a president rules nor one where a parliament governs, but one where the president, Congress, and the courts share power in ways that make change difficult; where independent states run much of what the whole government does; and where a Bill of Rights sets great limits to what any government can do.

OVER THE LAST HALF CENTURY, THE AMERICAN POLITICAL SYSTEM has experienced very substantial changes. These changes have re-modeled the presidency, Congress, and the national political parties without disturbing certain basic features of the political order that have distinguished the American system from the rest, mostly during its existence under a constitution over two hundred years old. The enduring features are a separation of powers, federalism, and a strong form of judicial review associated with an explicit Bill of Rights.

Separation of Powers

The separation of powers refers, in the first place, to the assignment in the original document of legislative, executive, and judicial functions to different institutions, separately constituted. These institutions are required by the rules laid down in the document to share in policymaking, and thus are continuously mutually account-able, each to the others.

The Framers of the Constitution were well aware of what they were doing. In *The Federalist,* the authoritative commentary by three Founders, James Madison says:

> [T]he great security against a gradual concentration of the several powers in the same department, consists in giving to those who administer each department the necessary con-stitutional means and personal motives to resist encroach-ments of the others. The provision for defense must in this, as in all other cases, be made commensurate to the danger of attack. Ambition must be made to counteract ambition. The interest of the man must be connected with the consti-tutional rights of the place. It may be a reflection on human nature, that such devices should be necessary to control the abuses of government. But what is government itself, but the greatest of all reflections on human nature? If men were angels, no government would be necessary.[1]

Checks and balances were built into the structure of the gov-ernment from the beginning. Congress cannot ordinarily enact laws without a presidential signature. Presidents cannot ordinarily ap-point major subordinate officials without senatorial advice and consent. Presidents appoint judges, but only with senatorial confir-mation. The entire business of government, formally organized hier-archically under the president, cannot run without appropriations that must be annually enacted into law by Congress and originate in the House of Representatives. Members of Congress are elected to office each in his or her own constituency, in aggregate covering the entire map—the same map that provides the presidential electorate. So both elected branches answer periodically to the same popula-tion overall, but at different time intervals and organized into their own electorates. And between elections, presidents and members of Congress must answer to one another if their work is to be done.

What the Framers created was therefore emphatically not a presidential system, where the chief executive rules more or less alone; nor was it a parliamentary system where the "government" arises via party organization from a relatively passive legislature. Rather, they created a system in which president and Congress, as separate entities, must cooperate in the making of laws and in practice actively compete in exercising influence over the subordinate agencies of the permanent government.

Over the last half century, the presidency has greatly expanded in its powers and responsibilities. The main stimuli for this were two world-shattering events: the Great Depression and World War II. Both focused demands upon the president and led to the creation of an administrative apparatus responsible directly to the president that could guide presidential supervision of the permanent government and mediate relations with Congress. Over a very short period of time, American involvement in foreign affairs—a president-dominated policy domain—evolved from peripheral and sporadic to central and constant. The news media focused more and more on the single individual at the center of national government.

Before World War II, it was much harder to discern a difference between the executive branch of government and the presidency, mostly because the preexpansion presidency was so organizationally compact. No Executive Office of the President to speak of, no phalanx of undersecretaries and assistant secretaries appointed from outside the bureaucracies to watch over executive departments. As late as Franklin D. Roosevelt's administration, Joseph Alsop remembered, "[T]here literally was no White House staff of the modern type, with policy-making functions. . . . There was a secretarial camarilla of highly competent and dedicated ladies. . . . But that was that; and national policy was strictly a problem for the President, his advisers of the moment (who had constant access to the President's

office but no offices of their own in the White House), and his chosen chiefs of departments and agencies." Until the 1930s, the budgets for the executive branch were prepared in the several agencies,
collected in the Treasury Department, and sent over to Capitol Hill
to start the annual appropriations process without routine presidential supervision. In the next stage, starting in 1939, a Bureau of the
Budget was established, to be located in the Executive Office of
the President, but not until the administration of Dwight D. Eisenhower in 1953 was the bureau headed by a political appointee who
had not been a civil servant. Now political appointees have infil-
trated the Office of Management and Budget (the Budget Bureau's
successor) two or three levels down, and they run an agency on the
president's behalf that monitors budgets and regulations originated
in the bureaucracies at arm's length so that they conform to presidential priorities.

The Great Depression (1929–1940) sparked an increase in demands for presidential initiatives, but a famous plea that "the President needs help" and its associated proposal for professional White
House staff at first went largely unheeded by Congress. It took
World War II to create a presidential branch, dealing with the mobilization of the domestic economy for war and fighting the war itself. After World War II, the scope of presidential responsibilities did
not revert back to its prewar scale. Instead, notably in the fields of
strategic intelligence, defense, and economic and fiscal policy, presidential business grew, followed by political appointees from outside
the permanent government and the appearance of officials that
Richard Neustadt called "in-and-outers" (most of whom stay in office for an average of only two years). These officials, who now can
regularly be found in most cabinet-level agencies at least as far
down as the assistant secretary level, and usually below that (General
Counsel, deputies to assistant secretaries), constitute today's presidential branch. The imposition of the norm of democratic accountability by means of an organizationally fortified—and consequently

somewhat isolated—president's imprint on bureaucratic behavior thus came in fits and starts to the executive branch, mostly in the last half of the twentieth century.

Since the agencies of the executive branch exist within a constitutional separation of powers, their appropriations and the laws establishing their programs must come through Congress. As the presidential branch grew in the post–World War II era, Congress discovered a need to assert its independent influence over the permanent government. An astonishing burgeoning of congressional staff took place over a very short time in the 1970s, evidently in direct response to a perceived competitive disadvantage in the struggle to influence the bureaucracies imposed on Congress by the presidencies of Lyndon Johnson and Richard Nixon.

Starting with the Johnson administration, and accelerating with the Nixon presidency, a great many of the underlying facts and numbers on which day-to-day legislating depends, and which used to be supplied routinely to Congress by the executive branch, became subject to presidential political spin. Mistrust of the presidency, known in Johnson's day as a "credibility gap," began to develop on Capitol Hill along a broad front, and not only with respect to the Vietnam War. Soon after, Congress felt the need of its own access to information and completely changed its pattern of staffing.

The sheer numbers are staggering. Two entirely new congressional agencies were created: the Office of Technology Assessment (1974) and the Congressional Budget Office (1975). The CBO in particular had an almost immediate impact. Staffed by nearly two hundred economists and other professionals, the CBO's budget estimates quickly developed a reputation for realism that overshadowed the increasingly partisan and massaged numbers of the Office of Management and Budget (OMB). Very soon it became commonplace in Washington practice to conduct bipartisan or non-partisan discussions of live economic issues using CBO, not OMB, numbers.

Between 1960 and 1980, the staff of the Congressional Research Service of the Library of Congress was increased fourfold; and the numbers of employees assigned to the House and the Senate, to individual members and to committees, jumped comparably. By 1985, roughly twenty-five thousand staff members worked for Congress. This includes only the Congressional Research Service component for the Library of Congress, and only the third of the General Accounting Office employees who work directly for Congress. In 1957, 2,441 staff were employed by House members and 1,115 by senators; by 1985, those numbers had turned into 7,528 and 4,097, respectively. In 1960, 440 staff were employed by House standing committees and 470 by Senate standing committees. In 1985, those numbers had become 2,009 and 1,080, respectively. The growth in a couple of short decades was remarkable. The growth in another measure is even more remarkable: In the forty years from 1946 to 1986, while the consumer price index rose 450.8 percent, appropriations to the legislative branch rose 2,859.3 percent.

An inspection of the year-to-year figures shows double digits in the growth of appropriations for congressional operations after Lyndon Johnson's 1964 landslide, continuing right through the Nixon era. There is no sure way to quantify the attitudes of mistrust that appear to have caused these figures to skyrocket when and as they did, but it is possible to speculate about the causes of the creation of a legislative bureaucracy after so many years in which the legislative branch found it possible to live comfortably with a comparatively thin roster of professional staff. Loss of comity with the executive branch, driven by the development of a greatly augmented presidential branch of government, is by far the most plausible explanation.

Under the old dispensation, congressional staff were professional at looking after the political needs of members, mixed in, in exceptional cases like the House Appropriations Committee, with some attention to oversight of the executive. On the whole, service on congressional staff did not require much interest in or competence at public policy analysis, much less political innovation. Expertise came with long years on the job rather than as the result of professional training. Today while the numbers of professionals employed by Congress has burgeoned, their average age has shrunk, and they now come to Capitol Hill with professional credentials. Many more of them—not just in absolute numbers, but as a proportion of the whole—focus on policy and on promoting their employers' interests through the advocacy or adoption of public policy positions. This is most noticeable in the Senate where individual senators are stretched so thin by the multiple responsibilities of their committee work that it is largely impossible for them personally to keep track of everything. Their staff members do it for them, and in the process not infrequently engage in sophisticated forms of political entrepreneurship in their principal's behalf. Sometimes a staff member's duties extend not only to seizing and promoting a policy position or making or adopting an issue in behalf of his or her principal, but also engaging the interest and approval of the principal as well.

Staff members with these extraordinary opportunities to affect public policy tend not to devote their lives to congressional service as so many of their predecessors did, but to job-hop around the policy subcommunities on which they are making a mark. So not only are congressional staff different today in their sheer numbers, but they are also different in their training, their career expectations, and the ways in which they define their jobs. Collectively, they far more resemble their counterparts in the political entourages of the presidential appointees who run the federal agencies of downtown Washington than they resemble preceding generations of staff members on Capitol Hill. They have brought increased capability, overall, to Congress to deal substantively with policy and they have done much to provide a link between Congress and the increasingly specialized and professionalized worlds of policymakers, policy advisors, lawyers, and foundation, university, and think tank personnel who make up the various policy subcommunities of Washington and throughout the United States. There was a time—not long ago—when Congress, and congressional staff, stood aloof from the communications networks maintained by these policy subcommunities. This is no longer true.

In addition, Congress's two-time resort in recent years to the hitherto moribund mechanism of presidential impeachment indicates its recognition of the growth of an expanded presidency. The proliferation of bureaucratic leaks can be seen in a similar light.

Richard Neustadt, who served as a junior civil servant in the Bureau of the Budget during the Truman administration, wrote an influential book called *Presidential Power* (1960) in which he argued, with great vigor, that the president has political interests in the policymaking process that only he himself can protect. A corollary of this axiom is that the various agencies of the permanent government, the executive branch, also have interests of their own, created by the laws and programs they are assigned (sometimes were created) to administer and by the existence of clientele out in the general population served by or regulated by these laws.

If the president, formerly the main ally and patron of the bureaucracies, now operates from inside a bubble created by his occupation of the presidential branch, and in effect withdraws from an obligation to protect agency interests, how do the agencies assert and protect these interests? One approach is the invocation of norms arising from professional practice and expertise, embodied in the occupations that so many civil servants (economists, lawyers, statisticians, diplomats, career military personnel, scientists, and so on) bring to government. This includes refusal to cook the books and leaking to the news media that professional advice is not being followed by presidential branch political appointees. A second avenue is to appeal to Congress. This activity has been dignified by a semiformal designation in the literature of public administration. It is called an "iron triangle." The classic iron triangle consists of a three-way alliance among interest groups, congressional committees, and bureaucratic agencies and derives its notoriety from the exclusion of the president and his branch. Typically, agencies share clientele (e.g., farmers) with the congressional committees (e.g., agricultural committees) assigned by the organization of Congress to monitor and appropriate for them. So communicating with congressional staff is one indirect way to mobilize clientele. And, of course, clientele can on occasion be mobilized more directly. When the political head of the Food and Drug Administration refuses to authorize a morning-after contraceptive pill deemed safe and effective by the agency's medical advisory board, the ensuing leak pits potential clientele of the agency against the electoral "base" being protected by the presidential branch. In the American political system, interest group politics proceeds not only outside the government, mobilizing voters and making demands on candidates for elective office, but also inside the government, and is frequently expressed through administrative and bureaucratic activity, as in the creation and normal operation of iron triangles (and, in later terminology, "issue networks").

Most nations have governments that employ chief executives, and virtually all have legislatures, but the American Congress has no close counterpart anywhere in the world in the autonomous power that it exercises as a collective entity. This means that detailed knowledge of the wiring diagram of the American national legislature is required to resolve uncertainty about how to assess any particular manifestation of congressional opinion. For unlike the parliaments with which so many observers of modern democracies are familiar, the Congress has a highly consequential internal structure. And this is true, but true in different ways, for both the House and the Senate.

In bicameral national legislatures of democratic nations, the more numerous, more representative body (often the "lower" house) is usually by far the more important. Nobody leaves the House of Commons to enter the House of Lords in the United

Kingdom in order to seek power. At least one recent prime minister (Alec Douglas-Home) had to travel in the opposite direction to lead his party and the government.

In the United States, while as collective entities the House (with 435 members, allocated to the states roughly proportional to each state's population) and the Senate (with 100 senators, 2 per state regardless of population) are more or less equivalent in their powers and in their overall influence on public policy, the Senate gets more public notice. Its smaller size permits a more flexible mode of operation and gets senators more national publicity. Its internal rules are more accommodating to individual members. In recent decades, changes in the presidential nominating process have encouraged many senators to think of themselves as potential presidential candidates. With six-year intervals between elections, they have the time to cultivate national constituencies, not merely those tied to their home states. They exploit lax rules of debate (e.g., germaneness to pending business not necessary) to seek publicity. They have very large staffs, capable of supporting the capture of highly visible issues by those senators eager to make a national impact.

During the last fifty years, the Senate has become a more nation-regarding and outward-looking institution, and a less a state-regarding and inward-looking institution. Senators now interest themselves in constituencies beyond those mobilized exclusively in their home states as a matter of course, and seek to influence national policy based on the assumption that it is politically useful to them to achieve national recognition and national resonance in their work. This sea change in the expectations of senators and in the way they do their work, and therefore in the role of the Senate in the political system, has in large part been driven by a fundamental change in the career prospects of U.S. senators that occurred in the early 1950s as the result of the arrival on the scene of national television.

There is, as it happens, a good baseline from which to measure the transformation of the Senate. William S. White, congressional correspondent of the *New York Times,* published a book in 1957 entitled *Citadel,* which at the time was accepted as capturing the spirit of the place—the prevailing institutional ideology, in effect—as it had been handed down and as he experienced it. What White described was a rather stuffy and comfortable club, complete with leather chairs, snoozing members, obsequious attendants, cigar smoke, and bourbon, run more or less exclusively for the benefit of a smallish number of elderly and important men. Internal norms of clubability were what mattered, White argued. Ideology did not matter, although it seemed to be coincidentally the case that the most significant people in the place, the old bulls who constituted the "inner club," as White called it, just so happened to be conservative, mostly southern, and ill disposed toward much of the New Deal, though not the part, presumably, that sent resources to southern farmers or invented tax breaks for the oil industry. And they tended to be against the advance of civil rights, sometimes immoderately so, even though the institution was alleged to prize moderation. White made the claim that the more progressive senators—therefore outsiders—tended to give offense primarily because of their lack of deference to the collegial norms of the place and not because of the substance of their views. One could not do well in the Senate by publicity-seeking, he argued, or by running for "other" offices—presumably the presidency.

White argued that in its essence the Senate of those days was fulfilling its historic constitutional purpose of "cooling the legislative tea" by providing a calm and skeptical and carefully deliberative counterweight to an allegedly more impulsive House of Representatives and a demonstrably more innovative and demanding presidency. What he described, however, was in large measure the successful pursuit of parochial interest, sometimes clothed in statesmanship, sometimes not. The southerners who ran the place, insofar as they actually did so, attended with great care to the local prejudices of the small and lily-white electorates that sent them to Washington. No doubt they were obliged to do so in order to stay in the

Senate, but nevertheless ease of reelection was a clear prerequisite enabling the more talented among them to adopt an interest in broader concerns, such as foreign or military affairs (Richard Russell, J. William Fulbright), or health care (Lister Hill).

On the whole, the descriptive accuracy of White's portrait was uncritically accepted by a great many of those journalists and biographers who wrote about the Senate during the 1960s and even thereafter. Magazine profiles of senators of that era commonly attempted to assess whether the subject was "in" or "outside" the "inner club," and one writer once went so far as to publish what he advertised as a guess at a comprehensive list of the "club's" members. By the time *Citadel* was published, however, two forces were transforming the Senate radically. One was television, and the other was Lyndon Johnson. Television, it appears, made its impact very suddenly indeed on the U.S. Senate. In March of 1951 a senator who had not much weight in the institution, Estes Kefauver of Tennessee, became an overnight media star as the result of the daytime broadcast of hearings of his committee's investigation of organized crime. Kefauver went on to run in the 1952 presidential primary elections—very successfully—and more or less on the strength of his lucky burst of publicity he became a factor in the presidential nominating politics of the Democratic Party for the rest of his life.

From the 1950s onward, senators began to maneuver themselves toward active roles in presidential nominating politics in wholesale lots, if they could manage it. Some of them simply used the Senate as a publicity springboard from which they could launch themselves. Kefauver and, more successfully, John Kennedy pursued that strategy. Others, following the early lead of Arthur Vandenberg, Robert A. Taft, and, notably, Hubert Humphrey, sought to use their position in the Senate to pursue national policy goals in a way that would commend themselves to the state party leaders who in those days controlled the presidential nominating process. In short, they began to invent the Senate as an arena within which and not merely a platform from which one could launch a presidential bid.

Lyndon Johnson's ambitions and opportunities led him to this within-which strategy. Under the patronage of elders of the old inner club, he became the Democratic leader of the Senate midway through his first term as senator. He managed the business of his party in the Senate in part with an eye toward national office—refusing, for example, to join in overtly opposing civil rights initiatives by southerners who put him into the leadership.

Johnson's energetic leadership of the Senate also greatly changed the institution itself. Decisions by consensus of senior members were replaced by the accretion of powers, large and small, in Johnson's own hands. Ralph Huitt, Joseph Clark, and other students of that era have left us a picture of a body that was being explicitly managed by an assiduous, compulsively driven leader anxious to make a record and advance his career by coordinating as many different things as he could reach within the institution.

By the time Johnson ascended to the vice presidency in 1961, the old citadel had largely disappeared. Senators were in no mood to continue the highly centralized pattern of leadership that Johnson had imposed on the institution. It was considered by senators to be a great virtue that Mike Mansfield, Johnson's successor, vastly preferred a lighter touch on the reins. But the Senate did not return to the closed collegial pattern of the old inner club. The goals of senators had in the meantime perceptibly shifted. A senator (Kennedy) was in the White House—the first one directly elected to the presidency since Warren G. Harding. He had beaten a former member of the Senate (Nixon) in the general election as well as several in the prenomination period to get there. And a senator (Johnson) was vice president. Ten senators at least—Russell, Kerr, Lodge, Johnson, Kefauver, Kennedy, Taft, Vandenberg, Symington, and Humphrey—had seriously contended for the presidency over those nomination cycles.

Aiding this institutional change were changes in the presidential nominating process that converted a system reliant on brokerage among state party leaders into a system heavily reliant on primary elections, hence primary electorates, and the national news media. Senators, adapting to the new structure of opportunity, have in short increasingly used the Senate as an echo chamber that could help them influence national policymaking.

Whereas the Senate is run rather like a carpool, solicitous of individual members, the House is more like a bus line, much more formally scheduled and controlled by its leadership. An important change in the House took place over the last three decades as a result of a very complicated social process. For over one hundred years after the Civil War (1861–1865), with minor exceptions, the southern quadrant of the country sent nothing but Democrats to Congress. Bitterness over Reconstruction made the party of Lincoln untenable for ambitious southern politicians, although the ideological sympathies of a great many of them as time went along were far closer to the national Republican Party than to the national party of the New Deal, Fair Deal, New Frontier, and Great Society. So for a century, inside the House Democratic caucus, there was a sizeable group—sometimes as much as a third of the whole caucus—of conservative southern Democrats or "Dixiecrats," often holders of safe seats with small, homogeneous, non-poor, and of course white electorates. Under seniority rules governing committee service, many Dixiecrats led committees. Dixiecrats plus Republicans frequently made *de facto* majorities in years after Republicans did well in the biennial House elections.

So for the recent half century or so (1940–1990) that Democrats nominally controlled the House, the majority of the majority party could not readily control policy outcomes. These depended on who sat on which committees, and subcommittees, and not only substantive subcommittees but also appropriations subcommittees. Each of these units of the whole had its own political configuration.

In some the members were dominated by staff and in some vice versa, or the chairman counted for more than usual, or the most significant alliance ran between the Democratic chairman and senior committee members of the Republican Party. Distributions of members on committees and subcommittees by age, by ideology, and by constituency, whether homogeneous or diverse in each dimension, yielded up different substantive policies from subcommittee to subcommittee and from year to year as these features of the membership evolved and changed.

This fifty-year regime in the House was characterized overall by a standoff between two grand coalitions of nearly equal size that cut across party lines: One side was dominated by mainstream Democrats and also included a small number of liberal and moderate Republicans, mostly from the northeastern states. The other was the so-called "conservative coalition" of Republicans and Dixiecrats.

In the last third of the twentieth century, the Dixiecrats began to disappear from Congress. In their place, throughout the South, Republicans, no less conservative, began to be elected to Congress. This trend changed a pattern of partisan affiliation that had persisted for a century. It was brought on by a significant change in the populations of the southern states. Affluent Republicans, many of whom had spent winter vacation time in the South, began to migrate from the North and establish permanent voting residences. The presence in former Confederate states of Republican retirees and others attracted by post–World War II economic development changed the odds for success of local conservative Democrats who wished to align themselves with the national party more congenial to their ideological views, and so Dixiecrats began to convert to the Republican party, especially in southern cities and suburbs. An important catalyst for this political change was the advent and rapid spread in the mid-1950s of residential air conditioning, which made year-round southern residence much more attractive to northern migrants. All the other elements for political change had been in place for many years, but not until air conditioning was established did the party balance change.

Two civil rights acts in the mid-1960s enfranchised African-Americans in the South. They voted overwhelmingly Democratic. What needs explaining, however, is not the Democratic vote but the Republican vote, some of which was supplied by converted Dixie-crat voters who disliked finding themselves less influential in their own party. The rest were Republicans arriving from the North once air conditioning in the 1950s made year-round habitation in the South tenable.

This development caused the disappearance of Dixiecrats from the House Democratic caucus in Washington and changed the chemistry of the House Democratic party. So long as a large fraction of the House Democratic party was Dixiecrat, the party had little prospect of mounting a sustained program of action reflecting mainstream Democratic values. The caucus was unusable and un-used as a mechanism for enforcing policy.

Committee chairmen captured a great deal of autonomy in this era. In well-run committees, alliances were quite common between Democratic chairmen and Republican ranking members. Legisla-tion was crafted to reflect cross-party consensus and comity, and cooperation across party lines was common. But when the Dem-ocratic caucus began ideologically to unify around mainstream Democratic sentiment, chairmen were put on notice that they would have to pay more attention to rank and file committee members of their own party and withdraw from bipartisan al-liances. In an unprecedented bloodletting after the election of 1974, three chairmen were deposed by the caucus. Most other chairmen got the message and a seismic shift took place in which the leaders of the House Democratic Party, as the instrument of the caucus, took power away from committee chairmen.

This left many senior Republicans on committees high and dry. They had shaped their careers around influencing the legislative process in alliance with senior Democrats. The disappearance of the

Democrats from this alliance made the senior Republicans vulnerable to Republican members—not necessarily more conservative than they were—who proposed a strategy of warfare to discredit the Democratic management of the House as a means of undermining the half-century-long Democratic majority. The idea was not to cooperate, or even to legislate, but to take control. This strategy prevailed narrowly in the Republican conference, and in the 1990s, when the Republicans won a majority of seats in the House, it legitimized a large number of changes in House procedures.

Republicans in the House had always been more ideologically unified than Democrats and more comfortable with hierarchical organization. When they got their chance to run the House after the elections of 1994, their new Speaker, Newt Gingrich, seized the opportunity to further undermine seniority and selected committee leaders according to partisan programmatic criteria. By then bitter partisanship had replaced bipartisan comity as the prevailing spirit in Congress, and so it has remained since.

The president is the most interested observer of Congress and its most devoted lobbyist. Congress, despite its full complement of internal institutional imperatives, must nevertheless somehow coordinate its activities with the president. Hence, significant changes in the presidency over the last fifty years have had a great impact on Congress. Of these, two have had the greatest importance. The growth of a formally designated congressional liaison service—a staff of full-time professionals in the White House that deals exclusively with Congress—is the less significant of the two. More important has been the capture of certain executive agencies by the presidency—notably the Bureau of Budget, now the Office of Management and Budget—that once provided more or less neutrally competent ad hoc service to the legislative branch.

Federalism

Just as there are nations other than the United States with constitutionally given separations of power, there are also devolved federal systems other than the American one. Federalism interacts with the separation of powers, as well as making its independent contribution to the organization of the system. As an independent factor, federalism means at a minimum that separate account must be taken of autonomous centers of power in each of the fifty states and the District of Columbia. Schooling, transportation, and the maintenance of public order are examples of policy domains that cannot possibly be understood without a disaggregated look at the activities, policies, decisions, and inclinations within each of the fifty states.

The federal structure of the American political system also contributes importantly because of the way in which federalism underwrites the American party system. A significant reason that Americans make do with only two major political parties, unlike voters in other much smaller western European countries, who are accustomed to what they perceive to be a far greater range of partisan choices, is because each of the two American major parties is in most respects a loose coalition of state parties. These coalitions are not structured alike. Democrats are primarily a mosaic of interests making claims on government; Republicans are bound together much more by ideological agreement.

Americans find it possible to express many aspects of their political diversity by virtue of the fact that party structures are based primarily on local authority, and nominations to public office are locally made and sustained. Thus the American political system embraces not only in its national aspect a two-party system, with its two parties differently constituted, but also in its devolved aspect close to a one-hundred-party system. It is necessary to hedge on the exact number because of the anomalies of local political cultures: Nebraska, for example, maintains a state legislature that is not only unicameral but non-partisan. In some parts of the country, public officials run unopposed because of the weakness of opposition political parties. On the whole, however, it is possible to speak of Vermont Republicans and Vermont Democrats, and to compare and contrast them with Democrats and Republicans from South Carolina, Montana, New Jersey, and so on.

States and regions have their own distinctive political cultures arising from the peculiarities of their original and subsequent settlement, their historic and contemporary economic interests, and the local political institutions that have emerged in their varied climates and soils. These cultures, these institutions, send to Congress widely varying representatives who in turn participate in the system of separation of powers, thus linking two of the most prominent elements of the American political order, the separation of powers and federalism.

Judicial Review

On top of these two is the peculiar institution of judicial review, a process by which judges appointed to serve during good behavior—that is, until they retire or die or are impeached—interpret the laws and the Constitution and make final determinations about the legality of government acts. Opinions differ about the grounds upon which judicial review can be justified. It seems to be relatively clear, in any event, that the existence of such an institution is unavoidable once a Bill of Rights comes into being. These first ten amendments to the Constitution, ratified in 1791, contain plain texts mostly prohibiting Congress from acting so as to impair various enumerated rights reserved to inhabitants of the United States or (in a later clarification) the states. Who but the courts, empowered to hear and settle cases and controversies under the Constitution, were in a position to listen to complaints and adjudicate between differences of opinion on the subject of whether Congress had in any given instance violated these rights?

Thus, from this perspective, a Bill of Rights carries with it an entailed structural consequence; it brings into being a strong form of judicial review. This structural feature in turn carries a great deal of baggage in its train. It inflates the importance of judges in the system.

It makes the lawsuit a preferred method of resolving issues of status—rights and obligations—as between government and citizen and citizen and citizen. It empowers lawyers as intermediaries of choice for settling claims.

By 1836 our visitor Alexis de Tocqueville could exclaim over the richness and the obtrusiveness of the American legal culture, the prevalence of lawyers, and litigation. And so it has remained. Matters that are settled either by custom or by informal operations of the status system in some political systems are settled by litigation and the explicit rendering of written opinions in the United States.

This seems, somehow, entirely apt for a system in which newcomers to local populations and to citizenship—immigrants from abroad, internal migrants, the newly enfranchised—have played such a large part and in which relations among socially heterogeneous elements must be peacefully maintained and more than occasionally negotiated and renegotiated. The rigid social separations of a caste or a well-settled status system might have worked in some circumstances to order the relations of a heterogeneous people, but not in the presence of a Bill of Rights, especially once it extends to cover all inhabitants. Under such a regime, the emergence of legalism as a means of introducing changes and adjustments (and not merely red tape) into human relations seems, if not inevitable, at least likely.

Thus no fewer than three significant features of the operating American political system are expressed at the very core of the Constitution. All three can be found in some form or other in other political systems, but not, I think, all three together. And each gives rise to further anomalies that have been institutionalized in important ways: the separation of powers to a uniquely powerful Congress, federalism to a devolved and variegated hundred-party system, and the Bill of Rights to an advanced form of legalism as a method of ordering relations in the society.

Complexity and Intermediation

It seems almost unnecessary to argue that very great complexity is an emergent property of a political system thus designed and evolved. The complexity of the American political system may as well be directly acknowledged, however; it is, after all, frequently the complexity of the system that stymies proposed reforms based on false analogies with simpler systems.

Perhaps the classic such case is the perennial barrage of complaints about American national elections that they go on too long and are too expensive. What is needed, it is frequently said, is a national election on the British model where expenses are tightly controlled and the whole thing takes at most six weeks. Advocates of this particular set of reforms may overlook the fact that American elections require long ballots—indeed in some localities very long ballots—to accommodate all the electoral contests that take place concurrently with presidential elections and that British parliamentary elections, with one contest per constituency, can be accommodated on very short ballots. To simplify elections entails simplification of the underlying government that elections serve to populate. Complexity in democratic government—among other factors—requires complex electoral arrangements, and American government is both—approximately democratic and complex.

There is also the problem of weak parties that choose candidates for public office in highly decentralized nomination processes to large numbers of offices. Often, this means contested primary elections that require time and money to settle, sometimes a great deal of both.

Another point along the same lines is perhaps less obvious, but equally consequential. This has to do with the sheer size of the decision-making community in American government. One way to grasp the elemental force of this point is to pose the issue as an ambassador's problem. An ambassador newly arrived in most of the world's capital cities can, over a reasonable length of time, get to know virtually everybody who is instrumental to governmental decision making. Even in the most advanced and civilized democratic nations, there is a not-too-large group of parliamentarians and civil servants who, to all intents and purposes, run the country. In authoritarian regimes, of course, the number of key actors is much smaller.

In the United States, that number is dauntingly large. It is large in part because policymaking is not contained within the government, or even within the interplay between the two political branches of government, but spills out into a great variety of intermediary organizations: think tanks, law firms, and interest groups. And this is only to speak of the national level, not the fifty states. Different policies, from public housing to military procurement to the management of trade deficits, activate different congeries of political leaders, congressional staff members, bureaucrats, lobbyists, and interested bystanders. Over relatively short periods of time, occupants of these varied roles change jobs, and new people are rotating in all the time. The idea that a new ambassador could get to know all the American players that matter to his country in any reasonable time seems very doubtful.

It is, of course, not merely the responsibility of newly arrived ambassadors to keep track of the players in American policymaking. In a separation of powers system, players are obligated to keep track of one another, and of the ongoing state of policymaking in the arenas that interest them. For subject matter specialists this is not an impossible job. For generalists, it may be. In any event, the very size of American policymaking communities frequently requires recourse to means of internal communications unheard of in nations with smaller decision-making populations, namely, publication in the national general circulation press (as well as in trade papers) as a device for sending messages among political leaders. This means that a rich menu of information about proposed, tentative, and internally contested governmental action is regularly available in Washington to observers who can afford the price of the daily newspapers. It means also that many policies that become publicly known do not necessarily become the law of the land.

These are some of the consequences of the complexity and size of the American policymaking community: complicated elections and policymaking in the open, both processes importantly mediated by news media that are themselves far more integral to elite political behavior than is commonplace abroad. If American bureaucracies were stronger and less porous, and less formally responsible to an in- dependent legislature, then the intermediation at the elite level of news media in public policymaking would be less possible and cer- tainly less consequential.

Thus some of the salient features of the contemporary Ameri- can political system are:

1. A presidential branch increasingly separate and distinct from the executive
2. Competition between presidency and Congress for in- fluence over the permanent government
3. A singularly important legislative branch, capable of forging alliances with interest groups
4. A one-hundred-party system, based in the several states, providing for some of the variation in representation that in other electoral systems is supplied by multiple national parties
5. A strong form of judicial review that underwrites fre- quent recourse to litigation and reliance on lawyers in or- dering relations among citizens and political institutions
6. A very large population of decision makers in many pol- icy areas and reliance on the national news media to send signals among them

None of these institutional features are exactly as prescribed by the Framers of the Constitution, yet reflect in important ways the constitutional framework as various forces of history have been expressed through the political activities of the large and heterogeneous American population.

CHAPTER 2

Bureaucracy

Donald F. Kettl

In many democracies, the bureaucracy makes most of the important decisions, but in America, as political scientist Donald Kettl shows, federal bureaucrats must share power with state ones, try to manage affairs by working with private organizations, and are heavily influenced by court decisions. And because the president and Congress share power over administrators, we have many political appointees that each elective branch tries to use in order to direct daily affairs.

IN *THE FEDERALIST,* ALEXANDER HAMILTON CALLED THE JUDIciary the "least dangerous branch." The Founders had carefully limited the power of the courts by putting appointment of judges, and even the very structure of the judicial system itself, under the shared control of the executive and legislative branches. There was no need to fear an imperial judiciary, Hamilton argued, because the president and Congress would prevent it.

Left unsaid was what the *most* dangerous branch might be. For a group of revolutionaries who had just driven out the army of King George III, it scarcely needed to be defined. What the Founders feared more than anything was an executive so strong as to undermine the liberty that had been so dearly won. The focus, of course, was on the president, for the unique American system of checks and balances was really a system to limit the president's power. Congress was the first branch, the repository of the people's power. There might be a risk of "excessive democracy," but it was not a risk of tyranny (except over minorities). The judiciary's power was sharply limited. It was the president who presented the greatest risk to the new nation, the Founders feared, and it was the president whose power most needed to be checked and balanced.

The risks of presidential power, of course, lay not in the power of the presidency but in the governmental apparatus the president would control. However, the Constitution gave the president relatively few direct powers. The president could wage war but not declare it, spend money but not appropriate it, nominate officials but not confirm them, administer laws but not pass them. In fact, the president's domain was fairly limited: he could issue pardons, receive ambassadors (and thus recognize foreign countries), and report from time to time on the state of the union. The real power of the executive lay in the president's ability to leverage the power of the bureaucracy, especially in armed forces and in the civilian governmental apparatus. And in the early days, Congress was not even sure it wanted to allow that. In 1789, James Madison won a narrow vote in the House to permit the president to remove government officials. Had the vote failed, Congress (or at least the Senate) would have had to confirm all removals as well as all appointments.

The puzzle over government power, especially in the bureaucracy, frames the ultimate paradox of the American Constitution. The *most* dangerous institution was the executive's bureaucracy, but the Founders did not much discuss it. Neither the Constitution nor *The Federalist* says anything about it.[1] The nation's key documents are much more explicit about the role and power of the other institutions; the bureaucracy's power lies largely in what is unsaid. Bureaucracy is the great residual of national ambition and governmental power, the strength that was required to build the nation.

Of course, one of the most confounding truths about American bureaucracy is that it is not a single entity. Administration occurs throughout the American intergovernmental system. Local governments provide most of the front-line services, including police and fire protection, emergency medical response, education, and sanitation. State governments run prisons and state universities, as well as most of the highway systems. The federal government provides for national defense, homeland security, social insurance programs, air-traffic control, and a vast array of other services. But the dividing lines are never neat or clear. Responsibility for managing most government services spills over intergovernmental boundaries. Thus, the meaning of "bureaucracy" varies with the level of government and, because of the blurry boundaries between the levels, the cross-pressures on bureaucracy are enormous.

Moreover, even within each level of government, the bureaucracies differ widely in culture, structure, function, and political setting. The FBI is a very different place than the Environmental Protection Agency. Police officers and fire fighters share first-response duties, but the differences run so deep that sometimes even fistfights break out at the scene of emergencies as departmental officials argue over who is in charge. At the federal level, NASA and the Department of Energy have cultures heavily focused on engineering. The Department of Labor focuses on helping people find work; the Department of Commerce concentrates on those who employ them. The Department of Health and Human Services is a complex amalgam, with some bureaucrats working on disease prevention and others seeking to help people escape welfare. Organizational culture helps define what bureaucracies are. Trying to develop general characterizations about it within the vast and complex American bureaucratic apparatus is impossible.

One of the most notable features of the United States is its sheer, exhilarating, and confounding diversity. American bureaucracy reflects all these elements, and that makes it difficult to characterize the nation's bureaucracy as a whole. Nevertheless, several central themes run throughout this important institution, and none is more important than the place of bureaucratic power in American democracy.

Bureaucratic Power

Despite their experiences with the English king, the Founders quickly if reluctantly concluded that the nation needed a strong bureaucracy. In the nation's first years, until the Constitution took effect in 1788, the Articles of Confederation proved constantly lacking. The revolutionary commander, George Washington, won the war in spite of the weak power it gave him. In the first postrevolutionary years, rebels in Massachusetts threatened insurrection, and security on the frontier was a constant worry. Commerce between the states was ragged, and European powers hungrily eyed the fledgling nation. The Articles of Confederation failed primarily because it lacked administrative muscle. It was clear that the new United States needed a more robust government if it was to survive.

But having chased away the British king, the Founders did not want to risk repeating the problem by creating *too* strong a bureaucracy. So they dealt with the issue in yet another of the remarkably clever maneuvers of the nation's Constitution writing. They created a new government that was more powerful than under the Articles, but they left the scope of power largely undefined. The Founders seemed to have assumed that the bureaucracy would be a natural, even inevitable element of the government they were creating. They also seemed to conclude that, when it came to defining the power of the bureaucracy, the less said the better.

Just how strong bureaucratic power ought to be was a constant source of conflict in the nation's first decades. Bitter policy disputes (heavily spiced by deep personal conflicts) cost Alexander Hamilton his life in a duel with Vice President Aaron Burr, whose political career was truncated soon afterwards. Congress created, and then abolished, two national banks. However, by the time of the Civil War, the issue was evolving from *whether* government ought to be powerful to *where*—in the national government or in the states—the power ought to lie.

The Civil War largely settled this question and also opened the door to a vast expansion of bureaucratic power. As they spread west, Americans discovered a sense of manifest destiny, a hunger to conquer the continent and improve their lives. With that growing ambition came a greater taste for public action, first to tame the land and then to provide more services. With more public action came the inescapable need for a well-built bureaucracy with sweeping powers, a system that would have stunned most of the nation's Founders. In time, that led to expanded local services, including schools, police, fire, mass transit, and efforts to reshape the cities. It led to programs to provide social security and health care for the elderly, to improve the environment, to develop energy, to create jobs, and to spur commerce at home and abroad.

American government—and, especially, American bureaucracy—expanded with each major war, even in those parts of the government that had little to do with fighting the war. Once the wars ended, government shrank only modestly in size. The "war to end all wars" helped feed the growing American appetite for public action. The taste of victory led quickly to the bitter aftertaste of the cold war. There was no big "peace dividend" after the Vietnam War, and the "war on terror" promises to create continuing demands for defense spending. On both domestic and international fronts, American bureaucracy has gradually blossomed, rarely scaling back its size.

Over time, however, the fundamental puzzle has been how best to empower the bureaucracy to be effective while limiting its power so as not to jeopardize individual liberty. Even hundreds of years later, the nation's revolutionary heritage remains an unshakable hold on its political culture. Taught in school about the bravery of colonists who snuck aboard a ship in Boston harbor to defy the king and toss tea overboard, Americans retain a strong antigovernment streak. But like people everywhere, they have high expectations about their government and, especially, about what services their government can provide to them. Thus, Americans share many of the tensions that exist elsewhere between citizens and their governments—but with a twist born of the fact that the nation came into being by throwing off imperial power.

Magnifying those tensions are the delicate institutional arrangements born of the nation's revolutionary past. In the parliamentary systems that dominate much of the rest of the world, the bureaucracy is an appendage of the ruling party. Citizens elect parliamentarians. The party with the most seats forms the government, in coalition with others, if necessary. The party's leader becomes the prime minister and appoints the government's ministers who, in turn, run public agencies. Although relationships between the permanent government and the ministers often are contentious, the voters expect that the government they elect will in fact run the government. In the United States, by contrast, the links between voters, officials, and bureaucratic institutions are multiple and often conflicting. While Americans might expect that *someone* is in charge of the administrative system, they also like the fact that the constitutional separation of powers provides multiple sources of influence over the administrative system. They tolerate bureaucratic power because they know there are so many ways of shaping and harnessing it. But as much as any people on earth, they savor their right to complain about it.

ADMINISTRATIVE ROLES AND POLITICAL POWER

A handful of principles shape the exercise of bureaucratic power in the United States. First, the bureaucracy has *only* the power authorized by law. This principle defends the primacy of the people: through elections, the people grant power to elected officials as outlined in the Constitution; through the balance of powers in the Constitution, the president and Congress agree on laws. Meanwhile, the courts seek to keep balance among the players. The bureaucracy administers the law, and thereby gains power, but it can only do what the law specifically authorizes. That inflexibility sometimes creates complaints about bureaucratic unresponsiveness, but that is the foundation of bureaucracy in the democracy. In fact, a long-standing law, the "antideficiency act," prohibits administrators from spending any money not specifically authorized by law. That has led to the occasional, bizarre theater of federal officials being sent home and their offices being locked when Congress and the president fail to agree on a new budget. Except for emergency services, the antideficiency act forbids administrators from performing any official duties—even sitting at their desks and using government-funded electricity. Without an approved budget in place, administrators have no authority to do anything.

Second, the bureaucracy *must* exercise the power the law conveys. Not only are administrators forbidden from doing what the law does not permit, but they are also required to do what the law says. They have discretion in *how* to do their job, but they legally have no discretion about *whether* to do so.

Thus, bureaucratic power flows from the people through elected officials and the major political institutions to administrators. That conveys substantial muscle to the bureaucracy. The principle of delegated authority holds administrators accountable for how they exercise that power. Of course, American administrators—like those everywhere—hold vast reservoirs of power in how they interpret that delegation. Administrative discretion provides police officers flexibility in deciding just how strictly to enforce the laws on speeding, and air-traffic controllers in determining how best to bring planes in for safe landings. Their professional training and skill magnifies that power and creates the potential for abuse. But at the foundation of their role lie the principles of delegation and accountability to balance the necessity of bureaucratic power with the insistence on democratic control.

Despite these elaborate controls, the growth of American bureaucracy has never been easy, especially in comparison with the administrative apparatus of Europe. Americans tend to love their public services (at least the ones that affect them). They tend to have little respect for bureaucratic institutions in general, and "bureaucratic" is a universal pejorative for red tape and unresponsive service by government officials. Citizens—and their elected officials—have long wanted a large cafeteria of services, but they have resented paying taxes. They tend to appreciate their local firefighters and police officers and teachers, but they condemn "faceless bureaucrats" who spend money without appearing to deliver value. The tension between an ambition for governmental policies and a loathing for the large institutions charged with pursuing them is one rooted in the nation's very founding. It is one that continues to lie at the core reality of American bureaucracy. It creates constant tension for which no equilibrium has yet been found.

The Civil Service

America's search for that equilibrium has long focused on the civil service system. Like governments everywhere, the American civil service seeks to build institutional capacity to do the government's work. At the federal level, the civil service system dates from 1887, following the assassination of President James Garfield by Charles Guiteau, who was angry at not having received a federal job. The assassination highlighted a growing issue for reformers. The nation's Progressive movement sought a government that was more powerful and more efficient, but also more responsive to the people. The Progressives concluded that the wholesale changes that often came in public employment with shifts in presidential administrations were undermining government's performance, because itinerants did not stay in the job long enough to develop expertise. They believed that the government needed a robust career staff that could build institutional capacity for determining the best way to do government's work. And to ensure that a more powerful bureaucracy would not threaten individual liberty, they made the career staff accountable to elected officials and to political appointees at the top of executive branch agencies. From those principles grew the modern American civil service system.

The Progressives found themselves at the intersection of deep historical pressures: to use government jobs to reward friends, and to make sure that the most competent employees did the people's work. Andrew Jackson campaigned for the presidency in 1828 with a pledge to drive the supporters of John Quincy Adams out of public jobs. Long tenure in office, he claimed, had made them lazy, lax, and arrogant. "Rotation in office," he said, was a far better way of staffing the government. He argued that government ought to be democratized and that public jobs ought to be open to a far broader collection of individuals. The pledge of democracy quickly translated into the reality of patronage, with jobs awarded to the president's allies and friends. One supporter, Senator William L. Marcy, famously coined the phrase, "To the victor belong the spoils," and the "spoils system" label was born. In fact, the use of government jobs to edge out political rivals and shore up political support dates from the first major presidential transition, when the third president, Thomas Jefferson and his Democrat-Republicans, took over from the George Washington–John Adams Federalists following the 1800 election.

But Jackson and his supporters raised it to an unprecedented level. Conservatives worried about the reign of "King Mob" and the risk that too much democracy could undermine the republic. In the years that followed, tens of thousands of enthusiastic supporters converged on Washington following every election to seek jobs. There were always far more supporters than jobs, so disappointment was inevitable—and sometimes deadly, as witnessed in the case of Guiteau's decision to use a gun to settle the score.

The creation of the American civil service was part of the broad Progressive reform movement of the late nineteenth century—an unusual strategy of seeking a new balance between democratic responsiveness and competent government. Reformers believed that the nation could no longer afford to lose experienced, talented employees following every election. At the same time, they did not want to raise the bar of government service too high. Their goal was to create a permanent bureaucracy, staffed with highly competent employees but structured to make the bureaucratic service politically responsive. The civil service thus not only came to define the way the nation staffed its government. It became a fresh strategy for balancing politically accountable government with the reality of a strong, powerful bureaucracy.

ELEMENTS OF THE AMERICAN CIVIL SERVICE

The civil service system builds on policies for position classification, compensation, and staffing. It begins by defining the jobs required to accomplish a public bureaucracy's task. Experts assess the knowledge that the position requires, the responsibilities it entails (including whether the individual will have to supervise others), and the complexity of the task. The nature of the job defines the salary that an employee receives. Pay depends on what public officials know, not who they know; technical knowledge and longevity in service define an employee's place in the pay grades. Public bureaucracies staff these positions through competitive exams, which seek to find the best qualified individual for each position. Promotion is by merit.

Unlike the bureaucracies of many other nations, the American bureaucracy has open entry, in policy and in fact, to public employment. That contrasts sharply with the French model, in which the top officials—the *"grand corps"*—come from the top graduates of L'Ecole Nationale d'Administration. Most of these graduates, moreover, come from the upper middle class. In the United Kingdom, the most prestigious universities provide the principal entry into the public service, especially the fast-track positions that supply future leaders. In many nations, the elite—in both class and education—dominate government jobs, especially the top positions. That is far

less the case in the United States. The civil service system was designed to end wholesale "rotation in office" with every election, but
there remains a deep and fundamental commitment to broad representation in the public service.

The American tradition of hiring through civil service tests,
though fundamentally challenged by the shifting demands of the
government workforce and the difficulty of assembling good tests, is
a testimony to the government's significantly greater openness to
anyone who chooses to make a government career. In fact, the civil
service is one of the most broadly representative workforces in
American society. In 2004, the federal executive branch's workforce
 was 44 percent female and 31 percent minority. White males continued to dominate heavily the very top of the government service,
but minority representation at higher civil service levels (grades 14
and 15 in the "general service") increased from 13 to 19 percent of
all workers from 1994 to 2004. At the senior level, the increase was
from 10 to 14 percent.[2] In contrast, in the United Kingdom, women
accounted for 52 percent of the national government workforce in
2004. Minorities were 8 percent of all workers and 3 percent of
workers in the highest grades.[3] Thus, while women remained a bit
less represented in the U.S. federal workforce than in the population
at large and in the British government, minorities had far stronger
representation in the American national government than in the
United Kingdom.

Distinctly American values have long shaped the nation's views
about the public service, as Herbert Kaufman explained: neutral
competence, executive leadership, and representativeness.[4] America
has sought *neutral competence,* to create a bureaucracy both highly
skilled and insulated from partisanship. This is not a quest to make
the bureaucracy unaccountable. Rather, it is an effort to ensure that
administration does not develop a partisan bias. *Executive leadership*
seeks strong and effective top-level officials to ensure sound implementation of national policy. *Representativeness,* the oldest of the

values, seeks to ensure that public employment is open to a broad range of citizens. It also seeks a public service that broadly reflects the population as a whole, so that the actions of the bureaucracy are more likely to be responsive to the people.

That has led to a recurring theme of separating policy from administration. Woodrow Wilson championed the notion in a famous 1887 paper, "The Study of Administration," and the notion preoccupied the study of American public administration for much of the next century.[5] While many scholars tried to parse the debate in a way that would permit the creation of a sharp line, Wilson's point was more subtle: to find a way to move away from the problems of competence and capacity that came with "rotation in office"; to professionalize government service; but to recognize that with a more effective bureaucracy came risks to democratic control, so accountability had to be a fundamental goal. Analysts have long since recognized that no firm line can be drawn between policymaking and its administration, but the very discussion contrasts sharply with France, where there is constant debate about whether top administrators not only implement but also effectively make public policy.

Administrative Constraints

The civil service system deeply embodies enduring American values. Critics have long complained, however, that its workings limit operating flexibility, especially in motivating employees and providing the flexibility needed to accomplish rapidly changing governmental tasks. Indeed, many federal agencies have made efforts to break out of the system. When management problems plagued the Internal Revenue Service, the air-traffic control system, and homeland security, elected officials created separate systems that began breaking down the historical cohesion of the nation's civil service policies.

Governments in the United States employed 23 million persons in 2005, most of whom (82 percent) were at the state and local

Figure 2.1   Trends in Government Employment

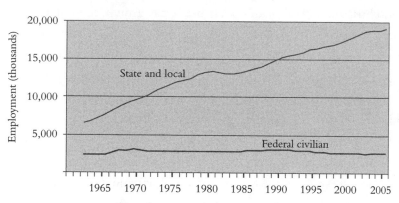

SOURCE: U.S. Office of Management and Budget, *Budget of the United States Government, Fiscal Year 2007: Historical Tables* (2006), Table 17.5.

level. In fact, most of the growth in government employment over the last generation has been at the state and local levels. As the population has grown, these governments have hired more teachers and police officers, firefighters and street workers. Federal government spending has increased substantially, but most of that spending increase has come through entitlement programs, including social security and health care programs such as Medicare for the elderly and Medicaid for poorer Americans. It has been relatively easy for the federal government to grow without increasing employment proportionately.

The same has not been true for state and local governments, which are responsible for most front-line services (see Figure 2.1). Most of the federal government's employees work outside Washington. In fact, 85 percent of its employees work beyond the Washington metropolitan area because, of course, most of the federal government's work is done outside the capital.[6] Finally, there is the large—but largely uncounted—number of individuals who work for contractors in the private and non-profit sectors that increasingly do much of government's work. As we shall see later, expansion of this area has fueled much of the growth of government. Thus, while American government has grown, the federal bureaucracy has not (with the notable exception of the federalization of airport security workers following the September 11 terrorist attacks). The real growth of government, at least as measured by the number of public employees, has come at the state and local levels, and in contractors supporting government's work.

Americans' deep antipathy to bureaucracy tends to blind them to a surprising fact. Compared with the world's major democracies, the extent of American government employment is about average. It is about the same as the size of government employment in Ireland, Italy, and Portugal. It is a bit larger than in the United Kingdom, significantly larger than in Greece and Korea, but far smaller than government employment in Finland, Hungary, and France (see Figure 2.2).

Figure 2.2   Government Employment as a Share of Total
Employment

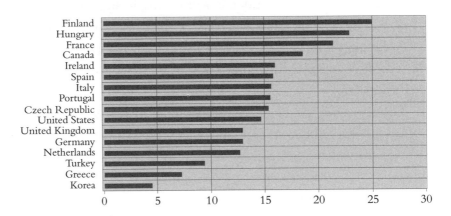

SOURCE: Organization for Economic Cooperation and Development, "Share of Public Employment to Total Employment" (2001), at www.oecd. org/ dataoecd/37/43/1849079.xls.

The Political Environment of American Bureaucracy

The United States is typical in its reliance on civil service systems and in the size of its government (measured by the number of public employees). The truly distinctive characteristics of American public bureaucracy lie in the complexity of the nation's administrative system and in the bureaucracy's peculiar interconnection with the political system.

The president does not have the same position with respect to the nation's executive branch employees that a private sector chief executive has over a company's employees. Through the legislative process, Congress controls the structure of federal agencies. It sets the budgets under which they operate, as well as the size of their staffs. The president, of course, can (and does) propose legislation and has strong bargaining powers in dealing with Congress. The courts have independent authority to oversee, and sometimes overturn, administrative actions. But the central reality of the federal bureaucracy is that, despite the president's common title of "chief executive," the bureaucracy is far more the creature of Congress. There is no better metaphor than what a visit to a cabinet secretary's office during the Clinton administration revealed. Tucked behind the ceremonial office, in a small hideaway, the secretary kept a treadmill to get exercise and work off tensions. The treadmill was in a window facing the dome of the Capitol, with the House and Senate clearly visible. The secretary's daily reality was much more a product of running on that treadmill toward Congress than of efforts to work with the White House and the president's advisers. The president's staff is too small and the president's political agenda is too focused to permit much executive coordination from the center. Congress and, especially, congressional committees, frame much of the political reality of bureaucracy.

Add to that the powerful role that interest groups play in bureaucratic politics. Not only does the fragmented nature of Congress create administrative fragmentation, but so, too, does the array of interest groups. There are few public services for which there is a broad political constituency. Even for those services designed to protect all citizens, like national defense, there are some interests that care far more deeply than others, like defense contractors where jobs and profits depend on government spending. Most public programs have relatively narrow political constituencies. Following these relatively narrow issues are relatively specialized media reporters. The result is often a hyperfragmentation of administrative agencies, the governmental institutions (like congressional committees), and highly specialized constituencies, all along individual issues. The issues tend to be matters about which some forces care very deeply and most others barely care at all. That further confounds the difficulty of creating any central chief executive role and focuses the attention of public bureaucracies into relatively narrow niches that match the driving political realities. The result is a collection of "issue networks" that define American bureaucracy.

These issue networks have two important implications for bureaucracy. One is that they create a substantial reservoir of political power. In a legal sense, administrators' power depends on responsibilities delegated through law. In a political sense, their power also depends on the constellation of political forces that support their actions. Administrative agencies with powerful allies among interest groups and congressional committees can win funding increases and protection from attack. Those with weak friends can struggle. Administrative power, not surprisingly, has both a legal and a political face.

The other implication is that these issue networks tend to fragment bureaucratic power. There is really no such thing as "the bureaucracy." The administrative apparatus is splintered among government's vast array of functions and by the political supporters who line up behind them. The executive branch tends to mirror the jurisdictional lines of congressional committees far more than any executive plan of administrative efficiency. Committees in action are usually subcommittees at work. Those subcommittees have jurisdiction over the programs that government agencies administer, their budgets, and the number of employees authorized. Senate committees play the key role in Congress's confirmation of presidential appointees to lead cabinet agencies and their major components. Because power in Congress is so highly fragmented, so is its attention to public bureaucracy. And because other major elements of political power follow congressional jurisdictions, that means that the political realities for public bureaucracy produces a highly fragmented perspective as well.

Coordination problems plague complex organizations everywhere. The fragmentation of American political culture—and especially of Congress—multiplies the problem of administrative coordination. For political forces seeking to influence administrative action, however, the fragmentation is a blessing. It creates multiple points of access to the administrative system, and that makes it possible to short-circuit the often cumbersome legislative process to nudge bureaucratic decisions.

Bureaucratic Layers

The bureaucracy, of course, is not an undifferentiated collection of administrators. There are important layers that affect its operations. Some come from the unusually deep penetration of political appointees into the American administrative system. Others come from layers that flow more naturally from the different functions of various individuals within the bureaucracy.

POLITICAL APPOINTEES

American bureaucracy is also distinctive for the sheer number of political appointees, who cascade deeper into the bureaucracy than in most other major democracies. The federal government has three thousand political positions in the executive branch; about fifteen hundred of those are at higher levels. Approximately one thousand are leadership positions, including the secretaries of cabinet agencies, the administrators of major agencies like the Environmental Protection Agency and NASA, regulators at agencies like the Federal Trade Commission and the Federal Housing Finance Board, as well as ambassadors to foreign governments. As Paul Light has shown (see Figure 2.3), the number has grown dramatically over time, far more rapidly than the increase in the number of cabinet departments.

Figure 2.3   Number of Federal Departmental Executives

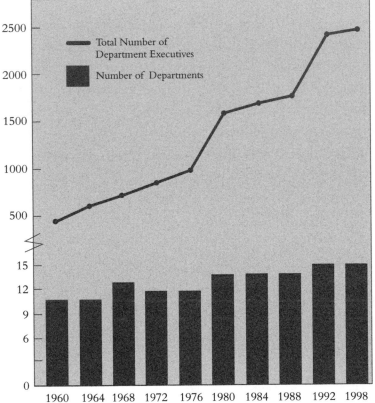

SOURCE: Paul C. Light, "The Changing Shape of Government," *Brookings Policy Brief #45* (Washington, D.C.: Brookings Institution, February 1999), at www.brookings.edu/comm/policybriefs/pb45.htm.

Much of the increase in political appointments has come with the addition of more layers at the top. New positions like "principal assistant deputy under secretary," "associate principal deputy assistant secretary," "assistant chief of staff to the administrator," and "chief of staff to the assistant administrator" have emerged.[7] This stands in sharp contrast with many parliamentary governments, where only the top officials' positions change hands when a new government takes power. In the government of Denmark, there is but a single political appointee—the minister—atop the career service. In the United Kingdom, there are a larger number of appointments, for both cabinet secretaries and confidential assistants. But career civil servants rise to very high levels of the government bureaucracy and face the constant challenge of balancing their professional judgment about how best to do their jobs with their constitutional obligation to follow the minister's direction. That tension spilled over into the very funny BBC series *Yes Minister*, in which exasperated careerists constantly worked to keep government from (in their view) going off the rails. Given the tremendous number of political appointees in the federal civil service, it would be impossible to imagine doing that show about American government.

Americans' distaste for bureaucracy has long led to large numbers of political appointees. They provide a new president with opportunities to reach deep inside every corner of the government and to put loyalists in charge. They provide a large number of positions with which to reward key campaign supporters. Some positions are even unflatteringly known as "turkey farms," where unproven or less-skilled administrators can be appointed with reduced chance of doing serious harm. The positions also provide Congress an opportunity to poke into administrative nooks and crannies. And when the president and key members of Congress—and the relevant committees—disagree, the appointments provide a battlefield in which to fight over their differences.

The large number of political appointees brings three serious problems. One is that some appointees lack detailed knowledge and long-term experience in the agencies they are charged with managing. The second is that, by dipping several layers into the bureaucracy, the risk of conflicts with career administrators multiplies. Finally, many of these political appointees serve for relatively short periods of time—often just eighteen months or a little more. That creates a revolving door at the top, with new officials stepping in just as the outgoing officials are beginning to master their jobs. This sometimes has created recurring problems of competence and continuity in key positions. Critics have suggested that one of the causes of the Federal Emergency Management Agency's grave difficulties in managing the response to Hurricane Katrina's 2005 assault on the Gulf Coast was that agency administrator Michael Brown did not have the background for the job and had served a relatively short time before having to face the crisis.

The managerial case for shrinking the number of political appointees is powerful. But despite repeated campaigns to do so, there has been no progress. No president has been willing to ask political friends to leave their posts or to reduce the opportunity to reward allies. Congressional committees have jealously guarded the leverage the appointments process gives them. With the political stars lined up against reform, there is little prospect of it happening. Indeed, the very large number of political appointees is a symbol of the political crosscurrents in which American bureaucracy has always found itself.

OPERATIONAL LAYERS

Beyond the layers of political appointees, a different set of vertical layers tends to affect American bureaucracy. James Q. Wilson has pointed out that different officials at different levels tend to play very different roles.[8] Bottom-level *operators* do the organization's front-line work. Top-level *executives* direct the organization's relationships with the environment, including with important political constituencies. In between, *managers* provide the crucial linkage between those responsible for the organization's external relations and its internal operations. This analysis provides an important explanation of the performance problems that sometimes plague bureaucracies. After the space shuttle *Challenger* exploded in 1986, investigators found that superhot gases had penetrated the rubber seals on the rocket boosters and created a blowtorch on the side of the thin walls of the shuttle's fuel supply, creating an enormous explosion. Worries from some of the shuttle's contractors about the seals never reached top NASA officials. The reason, investigators found, is that NASA's internal culture—and the choke points created by very different approaches of the agency's operators, managers, and executives—hindered the flow of information. Critical facts that executives needed to make their decisions never reached them, because managers filtered out the warnings.[9]

These two sets of layers—political and operational—provide an important perspective to important forces shaping bureaucratic actions. They also afford keen insights into the performance problems that sometimes plague bureaucratic action. Together, they yield important clues into the operating realities of American bureaucracy.

Bureaucracy, Regulation, and the Courts

American bureaucracy differs from that in other countries in another important respect. The courts play a significantly larger role in overseeing and sometimes in shaping bureaucratic action. In large part, this is because the judiciary is the check on the behavior of the other two branches. Since the bureaucracy sits at the intersection of cross-pressures from the presidency and Congress, disputes about which way to nudge the bureaucracy often end up in the courts. Moreover, since America's separation-of-powers approach creates multiple venues for influencing policy, interests that fail to win their points with the president or Congress sometimes take their battles to the courts instead, with the hope of winning arguments there that they have lost elsewhere. The federal courts have ruled that President George W. Bush acted illegally in conducting military tribunals for suspected terrorists held in Cuba at the navy's Guantanamo base. They have overseen desegregation efforts in several local school systems and have supervised treatment at prisons that have been ruled substandard. Compared to most other nations, the courts in the United States play an unusually strong role in shaping administrative action.

THE COURTS AND REGULATORY POLICY

The courts' role is most important in regulatory policy. Regulations are the central nervous system of most government bureaucracies. They shape what the bureaucracies do and how they do it. They transmit signals about desired action and shape the way that administrators exercise their discretion. Administrative discretion, after all, is a foundation of bureaucratic power. The posted speed limit on a road might be fifty-five miles per hour, but will a police officer pull over everyone driving above that speed? Will the officer provide drivers with a cushion of extra speed before making an arrest—and how large should that cushion be? What standard of treatment is acceptable within a prison? Just how "clean" does the water and air need to be? How much effort does an unemployed job seeker need to make to be eligible for continuing government support? In these and untold thousands of other daily decisions, government administrators exercise their discretion. In exercising their discretion, they are unquestionably exercising power. And in doing so, they inevitably create quarrels with those who disagree with their decisions.

The American system provides an unusually large number of avenues of complaint. Aggrieved parties can complain to the president and seek a change in law, but the president's agenda is so crowded that it is hard to attract attention or sustained action on any but a tiny handful of issues. It is far easier to get attention in

Congress, but Congress is so fragmented that it is difficult to get the institution to act on specific concerns. The courts, by contrast, offer the opportunity for pinpoint action, for judges (especially at the federal level) can issue opinions on individual decisions by individual bureaucrats. Moreover, since the 1960s, the courts have broadened the rules of standing, and that has made it easier for more people to seek judicial relief. The basic rule is that only an aggrieved party can bring suit. But the courts have allowed more individuals to claim injury on a wider array of claims. They have allowed a small number of individuals to sue on behalf of large numbers of individuals who share their circumstances. Called "class-action suits," these actions have significantly increased the leverage of special interests over administrative decisions.

These forces combined have made it possible for more people to contest more issues in the courts. The courts have been more willing to grant broader relief in these issues. The result has been a significant expansion of the role of the courts in administration. Many conservatives have harshly criticized this trend and have tried to push it back, but the basic trend toward the courts' expanding role seems irreversible.

The judicial role in administration is subtle. The courts rule only on individual cases, on particular matters brought by individuals with a stake in the issue. They decide only on basis of process, not on substance. That is, they cannot overrule an administrator for making a wrong decision, only for deciding it in the wrong way. Of course, clever attorneys long ago determined how to translate any important substantive issue into a procedural question. And that has further opened the door to the courts' growing role in administration. For example, experts in the environmental policy arena presume that interest groups will contest any significant new regulation. The issue is not whether but how the regulation will be contested in court. That means that Environmental Protection Agency regulators draft every new regulation, whether on clean air standards or steps for cleaning up toxic waste dumps, not only with policy outcomes but also with near-certain litigation in mind.

PARTICIPATION IN REGULATORY AND JUDICIAL POLICY

Most people do not typically think about the regulatory or judicial processes as opportunities for public participation or for shaping policy. But to an unusual degree in the United States, that is precisely the case.

In the regulatory arena, the process creates numerous opportunities for the public to join in the debate. Most legislation requires administrators to perform certain actions, whether cleaning up the water supply, building new jet fighters, or distributing social insurance checks. Even though legislation can often be very specific, it frequently leaves large gaps in prescribing precisely what government bureaucrats need to do to manage the program. To fill in those gaps, agency officials write rules to prescribe bureaucratic action: to define when discretion is allowed, when it is not, and how the program must work. In writing these rules, the regulatory process spelled out in the Administrative Procedure Act provides multiple opportunities for input. Regulators publish draft regulations in the *Federal Register,* the government's official daily source for rules and notices.[10] The process usually allows interested individuals a month or two to submit written comments, and regulators are obliged to review the comments before issuing final regulations. Any individual can submit facts or opinions on pending rules.

Of course, this is a very complex process. To participate requires knowing that a particular issue is in play, following the *Federal Register* closely to read the draft regulations, and the ability to write persuasive comments. This is a highly specialized and very complex business. Effective participation requires policy and technical knowledge and, especially, the ability (and often the contacts) to get the right information to the right people at the right time. That makes it hard for ordinary citizens to participate in most regulatory issues. Most citizens, for example, do not know about the *Federal Register*, let alone read it regularly. On the other hand, it increases the influence of members of the issue networks, who have established relationships with each other—relationships that help ensure that interests know which issues are emerging, how they will take shape, whom to try to persuade, and what forms of persuasion are most likely to be effective. Influencing the regulatory process thus is largely an insiders' game. It advantages those with the resources and ability to play it and those who are lucky enough to have cultivated the best relationships with the bureaucratic officials who will be making the decisions. That is one reason why former government officials, from both the executive and legislative branches, are in such demand as lobbyists. They know who to call and, when they telephone, their calls are more likely to be answered.

Of course, not everyone has that kind of influence, either because they lack the resources to play or because they do not have the right contacts. But the many doors of the American political system provide other opportunities for those without friends in power to nudge the bureaucratic process. Environmentalists unhappy with the policies of the George W. Bush administration successfully challenged clean air rules in court. Others sought relief at the state level, where they found officials who wanted to challenge the administration's position. Ultimately, the regulatory process offers many opportunities to shape the administrative process. The nation's intergovernmental system offers multiple regulatory arenas for action. Interest groups that lose at one level can often find another venue in which to influence the bureaucracy.

These multiple venues also provide additional points of access to the judiciary branch. In the mid-1990s, several state attorneys general began a series of lawsuits against major cigarette manufacturers. Their products, the attorneys general charged, were dangerous and were imposing substantial financial costs on state governments for the care of their citizens. This process of "adversarial legalism," as

Martha Derthick describes it, produced dramatic change in national policy, including a $250 billion settlement to state governments and new restrictions on cigarette advertising. Derthick argues that this process produced an unusual means of reshaping policy. Instead of working through the typical course of lawmaking, with proposals debated and passed by legislatures and signed by executives, individual attorneys general (some of whom were appointed, not elected) turned the administrative process inside out through the judicial branch.[11]

The regulatory and judicial arenas are especially important in American politics. They provide important but subtle avenues for shaping policy. The Constitution provides for lawmaking through a process that centers on the executive and legislature. The inevitability of administrative discretion creates the need for regulation, and regulations create opportunities for judicial scrutiny. But because the process is highly technical and relatively invisible, it creates a game that advantages those with the resources and connections to play it well. That, in turn, multiplies the points of access into the system. Together, these forces increase the importance of issue networks in American politics.

Government by Proxy

Compounding these complex relationships is the growing role of intergovernmental and non-governmental relationships in shaping public policy. Most of the discussion about American bureaucracy is *vertical*. That is, it focuses on relationships from elected officials to top administrators and then from the top to the bottom of the bureaucracy. This is for two reasons. First, it captures administrative orthodoxy, which has long focused on how best to maximize efficiency. Analysts have sought the "one best way," just as knights of old sought the Holy Grail.[12] The quest for bureaucratic performance has typically turned on how to structure public organizations to produce the best results, streamline rules, create the best budget and personnel systems, and find the right balance between managerial control and operating flexibility. Indeed, the foundation of much of the "reinventing government" movement that swept the public sector in the 1990s was about how best to realign these relationships to flatten government—that is, to reduce the distance from bureaucracy's top to its bottom—and to give bureaucrats more operating flexibility.[13]

Second, these vertical relationships have long defined the process of administrative accountability. In the American constitutional system, voters and elected officials have been able to trust the delegation of substantial power to bureaucrats (at least to the degree they trust them at all) only because the bureaucrats are held accountable for their actions. By law and constitutional practice, that accountability works through hierarchical authority: policymakers delegate responsibility and power to top bureaucratic officials; they, in turn, break down the administrative task into progressively smaller, manageable tasks; they assign responsibility for those tasks down the chain of command to specific members of the bureaucracy; and individual bureaucrats are responsible up the chain of command for the performance of their work.

In both operational and theoretical terms, it is a neat and clear notion. Vertical relationships, through hierarchy and authority, provide a straightforward way of answering the most important operating and political question of bureaucratic power: how to make bureaucracy strong enough to be effective but not so strong as to threaten democratic control. However, the operating realities of American bureaucracy have increasingly confounded this approach. Especially since World War II, American government has relied on a series of new administrative tools, which do not operate hierarchically or through authority. Many of them involve complex horizontal as well as vertical relationships. These tools therefore pose profound problems both for the effectiveness of government and for the eternal challenge of holding bureaucratic power politically accountable.

The Rise of Mixed
Administrative Tools

American government has always relied on a mixed administrative toolbox. With World War II, however, the government began relying increasingly on indirect tools—governmental mechanisms in which non-governmental partners became more responsible for the production of governmental goods and services.[14] The government increasingly depended on contracts with private companies for weapons and munitions. When the war ended, the federal government used the same strategy for building the capacity to fight the cold war and create the space program. That helped create the "military-industrial complex," about which President Dwight Eisenhower warned in his farewell address.

The same strategy spilled over to efforts to rid cities of blight and to reduce poverty. The federal government significantly expanded grants to state and local governments to pursue national policy. A combination of regulations, grants, and contracts shaped the environmental programs of the 1970s. A new generation of social regulations sought to make food and automobiles safer. Meanwhile, the federal government expanded the availability and reduced the cost of credit by subsidizing loans for college students, homeowners, and farmers. A "government by proxy" movement has spread, with more of government's administrative responsibilities shared with private companies and among the various levels of government.

Two important forces lay behind this movement. One was the ambition to increase the size and reach of government. Given the historic American nervousness about bureaucratic power, it was far easier to create new programs if their management did not require a substantial increase in the government bureaucracy. The United States did not create the substantial public health system of many European governments. It did, however, promise to provide health care for citizens over the age of sixty-five (through Medicare) and to poor citizens (through Medicaid). The government did these things with programs that by 2005 grew to 21 percent of the budget ($515 billion), in a peculiarly American strategy: the agency funds the programs but does not deliver it. The federal agency responsible for the program, the Centers for Medicare and Medicaid Services, employs just over four thousand persons, or less than 0.3 percent of all federal workers. That is because a vast and complex network of state governments, private and non-profit health care workers, and for-profit financial accounting firms are actually responsible for providing the goods and services. In fact, most persons receiving Medicare and Medicaid services do not meet government employees as they receive care. Instead, they work with private (and sometimes non-profit) doctors, hospitals, and clinics, who are paid through a network of for-profit financial intermediaries who collect the bills and process the payments. In the nation's space program, 90 percent of the space shuttle budget is spent through contractors, who also dominate the production of military weapons and supplies.

It is very difficult to measure the size of this indirect service system, compared with the more traditional system that relies fundamentally on hierarchical authority. The government does not keep its books in a way that allows good comparisons among these tools. In fact, the government does not even provide reliable statistics on the number of contracts and the amount of government spending through contractors. But, as the Medicare and Medicaid programs make clear, these strategies are important and their significance is growing.

The other important force is the belief that the private sector works better than the government: that it is more responsive and, especially, more efficient. The growth of public programs and government bureaucracies in the 1960s sparked a backlash in the 1980s, when the Reagan administration led a major campaign to shrink government by turning as many programs over to private companies as possible. Similar movements were occurring throughout the world, starting in New Zealand and the United Kingdom. But these were very different movements because the public sectors in these nations, as in many other countries, were substantially larger than in the United States. The British and New Zealand governments shrank by selling off state-owned airlines and utilities, which the American government never owned to begin with. These governments earned a global reputation as reformers, but even after their burst of reform, their public sector was actually larger than in the United States: in 2004, government spending was 44 percent of the gross domestic product in the United Kingdom and 37 percent in New Zealand, compared with 36.5 percent in the United States.[15]

Perhaps paradoxically, other nations sought reform by trying to shrink their governments closer in size to the American government, where citizens have never much liked their government to begin with. In the United States, privatization—turning important government functions over to the private sector—became an ideological movement embraced by conservatives. They believed that smaller government was better and that the private sector could do anything the government did far more effectively. Therefore, they argued, the nation should turn over as many functions as possible to the private sector. For those functions that remained within government, the government should administer the programs through the private sector, especially through contracts. For one leading champion of the approach, E. S. Savas, privatization was "the key to better government."[16]

Implications for American Bureaucracy

Debate about American bureaucracy is challenging because it is always—as it always has been—part instrumental (how best to do government's work) and part ideological (how to control and limit bureaucratic power). The government-by-proxy movement that began in earnest during World War II reached maturity by the end of the twentieth century. It is hard to find any significant government good or service that is produced within the confines of a single government bureaucracy, and the government manages a growing number of important programs through highly complex public/private/non-profit networks. From health care and welfare programs to national defense and space, from emergency services and housing programs to transportation and sanitation, there is virtually no nook or cranny of American government that is not intricately interwoven in complex partnerships.

The reasons for this complexity are varied. It has been easier to expand government's reach than its bureaucracy. Ideological pressures make it easier to expand government through partnerships with the private sector than through direct service delivery. The inherent complexity of many programs, like launching the space shuttle or building planes nearly invisible to radar, demand sophisticated private sector expertise. The pressures for self-government leave several programs in the hands of federal, state, and local governments that share responsibility for many programs. All of these issues have framed some very interesting normative debates, including whether the design of the system produces efficient, responsive services.[17]

Though there is a debate about whether the spread of government by proxy is a good or a bad thing, it has become a large, widespread movement that is unlikely to retreat. That movement, moreover, creates important challenges for democratic control of bureaucracy. The traditional American strategy for empowering bureaucracy enough to be effective without creating power that threatens democracy is the collection of vertical relationships, through hierarchy and authority, that define and limit power. The spread of government by proxy, however, undermines those vertical relationships. In some cases, it substitutes for vertical relationships new, horizontal ties among multiple organizations that share responsibility for producing public programs.

In all cases, this movement is creating important challenges to American bureaucracy. On the operational side, the more organizational units that are involved in the service delivery system, the more daunting it is to marshal the right collection of organizations and focus their energy on getting the job done. At the extreme are cases like the government's failed response to Hurricane Katrina, in which the Senate Committee on Homeland Security found a "failure of government at all levels to plan, prepare for and respond aggressively to the storm." (The committee might have added that Congress was also to blame.) The challenges were so substantial that, even a year later, the committee concluded that the United States remained "a nation still unprepared."[18] Complex interorganizational partnerships are harder to structure, to focus on a shared goal, and to manage in a way that consistently produces high levels of service.

On the political side, these partnerships are hard to control and hold accountable. When the production of public services involves partnerships, it is inevitable that multiple and potentially conflicting incentives distort the focus of the programs. No government contract with a private supplier can fully substitute for the democratic controls within a government bureaucracy. No intergovernmental grant or agreement can enforce a uniform interpretation of the public interest across multiple federal, state, and local governments.

Conclusion

This does not mean that democratically accountable, high-performing systems are impossible in the emerging constellation of American bureaucracy. It does mean, however, that the systems are inherently more problematic than straightforward administrative systems shaped by vertical governance arrangements. Given the scale and scope of America's service system, a retreat to these earlier systems is impossible. And given the complexity of these systems, it is impossible to layer the old vertical governance system, based on hierarchical authority, atop a system that is increasingly horizontal and based on market-based or politically driven bargaining. That, in turn, means that the greatest challenge for American bureaucracy is devising an approach to the special governance challenges of government by proxy: building a system that is competent in delivering ambitious services; pursuing effective coordination among related but sometimes only loosely connected organizations; and ensuring democratic accountability in a system fraught with centrifugal forces.

The situation, of course, is full of irony. In many ways, the dilemma is the result of the collision of the growing ambitions of Americans for a more expansive menu of services with the continuing struggle to limit the power of the nation's "most dangerous branch." In this quest, the United States is not alone. Many governments around the globe, even in Scandinavian nations where support for government programs and the bureaucracies that run them is very strong, are increasingly building partnerships with non-profit organizations to assist in the delivery of public services. The United States, however, is perhaps the world's leader in pioneering interorganizational, intergovernmental relationships of such complexity. As the world's nations struggle to deal with ever-larger issues and to satisfy citizens whose appetite for taxes is not keeping pace, American bureaucracy might become an international model: not so much one to be copied, but one that charts the land mines of a complex, interconnected service network.

As the United States works to master these challenges, it can draw on the great reservoir of pragmatism and inventiveness that has helped shape not only American government in general but also American bureaucracy in particular. It is a system that has insisted on competence but often prioritized accountability. It is a system that insists on tight command but which nevertheless provides multiple points of access to the administrative system. It is a system where multiple voices and multiple players make it difficult to judge results and define the public interest. But it is also a system that has proven remarkably robust in creating a bureaucracy that, despite the frequent complaints of citizens and the recurring investigations of reporters, works remarkably well much of the time.

The Founders dealt with the issue of bureaucracy largely by writing around it. It has long been the great residual of American politics, the repository of power (and conflict) that has defined much of the nation's growth and direction. Ensuring bureaucracy's effectiveness in an increasingly complex system, while controlling its power, is perhaps the most important challenge to American government for the twenty-first century. How the nation resolves this issue will define much of the behavior and performance of the nation's other institutions.

CHAPTER 3

The Legal System

Lawrence M. Friedman

All legal systems are distinctive in some ways, and America's is no exception. Lawrence Friedman shows that American law, although owing much to its English common law heritage, has been constantly shaped and reshaped by the special conditions of a remarkably diverse, dynamic, and market-oriented nation. In recent decades, the legal system has been driven by individualistic demands for "plural equality" overcoming the legacy of slavery and extending new rights to many different groups. It has also experienced an explosion of law and litigation into all areas of American life led by a rapidly growing legal profession that plays a powerful political as well as professional role.

Historical Background

LEGAL SYSTEMS, LIKE LANGUAGES, CAN BE GROUPED INTO FAMILIES traceable to a common ancestor. The American legal system is part of the *common law* tradition. Essentially, America's legal system, like its language, was an inheritance from Great Britain. The early settlers in the seventeenth century were mostly English, and though few, if any, were lawyers by trade, they still brought their habits, customs, ideas, and ways of thinking about law and law enforcement with them to the New World. In contrast, most legal systems in Europe and Latin America are *civil law* systems. These systems also have a common heritage; and that heritage is different in many ways from the common law heritage. The civil law systems, in modern times, are organized around carefully crafted *codes* that set out fundamental principles of law. Much of the common law, on the other hand, has never been codified; the judges themselves developed the essential rules and principles in the course of deciding actual cases. Historically, common law and civil law trials have followed rather different procedures; the common law was basically fixated on the spoken word: testimony, cross-examination, and the like. The civil law preferred the written word: documents and files. Additionally, the jury is a common law institution; most civil law systems have no jury.

The common law systems originated in England; all common law countries were once colonies of Great Britain, or colonies of colonies—examples include Canada, Australia, Jamaica, and Barbados. But the various common law systems have been going their own way for quite some time. They are now in many ways quite different from each other, despite their common origin. On the other hand, common law systems and civil law systems have been becoming more similar under the pressure of similar problems and conditions in a highly technological world.

Even before the American Revolution, the laws of the various American colonies veered significantly away from the law of England and, as a matter of fact, from each other. The differences were exacerbated by independence in the years that followed. The institutional differences were most glaring. While England had a unitary legal system, the American system was federal, a quarrelsome collection of small sovereignties, jealous of their individual privileges and resistant to English authority. The United States had a written constitution; Great Britain did not. In the United States, a powerful tradition of *judicial review* evolved: the right to declare acts of Congress, the states, and other organs of government illegal or unconstitutional. England, on the other hand, evolved a doctrine of *parliamentary supremacy*: no judge had power to question or overrule a solemn enactment of Parliament. Another peculiarity of the American system is how judges are chosen. While British judges, American federal judges, and the judges in a handful of states (Massachusetts, for example) are appointed, in the rest of the states, citizens are asked to vote for their judges—from municipal court judges all the way up to justices of the state Supreme Court. This practice dates from the first half of the nineteenth century. It developed as a response to a sober realization: though judges insisted they were neutral and objective, they were in fact powerful men whose decisions shaped public policy. The best way to control that power, people thought, was to subject these judges to the will of the people, just like other power-holders in government.

These institutional differences between England and the United States were and are important, but not as important, perhaps, as the *social* differences between the two societies. British society was highly stratified in the nineteenth century. The government was a monarchy, and a small group of elites, the landed gentry, owned virtually all the land and held virtually all power in the kingdom. Even in the colonial period, no nobility or landed gentry dominated life on this side of the Atlantic. On the contrary, land was abundant, especially after the settlers succeeded in dispossessing the native tribes.[1] In the northern colonies, people lived in small farm villages; the ordinary family owned a farm outright and paid no rent or tribute to some overlord. This social fact, more than anything else, molded the social system, and the legal system as well, as it evolved to meet the needs and demands of colonial society. Thus, in England, when a landowner died without a will, the eldest son inherited. This system—*primogeniture*—had an important social function: it preserved the great landed estates intact as much as possible. But primogeniture was pointless in the northern colonies, where there was land to burn, no great landowners, and no vast estates; primogeniture died out or never existed in these colonies.

Primogeniture lingered longer in the southern colonies, and this too is understandable. Here, in a milder climate, a system of large plantations developed. The lives of men like Washington and Jefferson were more like the lives of the English landed gentry than the lives of New England farmers. Unlike England, however, it was gangs of black slaves, not tenant farmers, who worked their land. Slavery, and the body of law regulating it,[2] became a vital aspect of economy and society in Virginia and the other southern colonies. The American law of slavery was developed from scratch in the colonies; there were no slaves in Great Britain. Some of the basic rules of the law of slavery would have a long-term impact on American society: for example, the rule that children of a slave woman would themselves be slaves, regardless of who the father was. This rule had an obvious economic advantage for slave owners; it also fostered the attitude that *any* admixture of black blood outweighed, socially and legally, a person's white ancestry and blood. Light-skinned or dark, all children of slaves were legally slaves, as were most blacks, of whatever shade.

Essentially, then, American circumstances molded American law. Of course, the English background was significant—it provided the framework, the basic plan, and the basic institutions—but social conditions were also and always decisive. Ideology was also meaningful. The law of Massachusetts Bay cannot be understood without reference to the intense religious zeal of the settlers, or at least that of their leaders and magistrates. Religion played and continues to play a key role in American history, and in the history of American law.

The Nineteenth Century

At the beginning of the nineteenth century, the United States was a small country, a string of settlements hugging the seacoast; by the end of the nineteenth century, it was an urban, industrial continent and an important player in world politics. As a mature capitalist society developed, it created mature capitalist law—on corporations, commercial transactions, patents, copyright, banking, and antitrust. Legal scholars tend to focus on great constitutional cases; but probably no single Supreme Court decision had as much impact on economy and society as the invention of conditional sales and chattel mortgages, humble devices that allowed farmers to buy tractors on time and city folks to get sewing machines and pianos. The bulk of the work of the courts reflected society's business—debt collection, land title disputes, and affairs of corporations and partnerships.

Family law and criminal law were also transformed in the nineteenth century. Under the common law, married women had no rights to own, buy, sell, or control their property; husband and wife were one flesh, but the husband owned and controlled their worldly goods. From the middle of the nineteenth century on, the states got rid of this ancient doctrine of coverture. Much earlier than England, too, states allowed spouses to sue in court for divorce. And, beginning with Massachusetts in 1851, couples were able to adopt children formally and legally (in England, legal adoption of children was not available until 1926). Family life was changing dramatically; yet the key issue here, perhaps, was inheritance of property. In America, ordinary families owned a farm, or a lot in town. Thousands of children were orphans, raised by family members or friends; in a restless, mobile society, many marriages collapsed; and people (mostly men) formed new attachments and started new families. Divorce was the gateway to remarriage, clarifying rights of inheritance and property rights; and adoption laws had a similar impact.[3]

The criminal justice system, too, was transformed in the nineteenth century.[4] The changes reflected deep structural changes in society. Punishment in the small communities of early New England relied heavily on stigma and shame. Everybody has heard of *The Scarlet Letter*; tourists to colonial Williamsburg pose for pictures with their heads in the stocks. Indeed, colonial punishment was always a public spectacle. Whipping took place in the town square; there too was where the condemned were hanged for their crimes, often after a speech confessing their sins and begging God's mercy in the shadow of the gallows. The system was rooted in community life and depended on the power of community opinion. The growth of big, raucous, brawling, riotous cities, crowded with immigrants, taverns, brothels, and slums, seemed to render this system obsolete.

From England, American cities borrowed the idea of a paramilitary force, the urban police, to patrol the cities and keep rioting under control. To replace community punishment—and to replace the gallows, which was used for fewer and fewer crimes—states began to build huge walled structures, which they called penitentiaries. Now for the first time, locking men and women up for years became the basic form of punishing those who committed serious crimes.

In the first half of the nineteenth century, slavery dominated public debate. Before the Revolution, every colony had slaves; but after the Revolution, the northern states abolished slavery, sharpening the division between slave states and free states. In the North, apprenticeship and indentured servitude (a form of temporary slavery) died out along with slavery. Workers in the North, on farms or in factories, were wage earners; in the South, slavery was vital to the economy, and even more crucial to the culture and social system. Consequently, it was crucial to the legal business of the South. The federal system was a house divided against itself; as the country expanded, new states were admitted to the union, threatening the delicate balance between slave states and free states.

Fugitive slave laws were another source of friction between North and South. Slavery's legal entanglements culminated in the infamous *Dred Scott* decision (1857).[5] The chief justice, Roger Brooke Taney, a slaveholder from Maryland, held that blacks could never become citizens, whether slave or free, and that Congress had no power to exclude slavery from any territory of the United States. The case set off a storm of protest in the North. If Taney thought the case would settle issues of slavery within the federal union, he was completely wrong.

Nor did the Civil War put an end to conflict over race. After the war, three new amendments to the Constitution abolished slavery, guaranteed the right to vote (on paper, at least), and barred the states from denying to any person due process and "equal protection of the laws." In the long run, these two phrases served as texts that underpinned some of the Supreme Court's boldest decisions. For years, however, they did nothing for racial minorities.

Shortly after the Civil War, Congress did pass strong civil rights laws. But within a decade or so, northern ardor for racial equality (such as it was) flagged, federal troops left the South, and the courts emasculated the civil rights laws. The country, in general, left the white South alone to deal with the race problem. The states of the old Confederacy proceeded to strip blacks of almost all of their rights—legally, if possible; by force, if necessary. The people of the North disliked slavery as an institution, but they by no means believed in racial equality. Northern indifference to the southern race problem allowed the white South to impose a kind of caste system on American blacks.

In the late nineteenth century, labor unrest convulsed the cities of the North. As usual, courts were in the thick of the battle. The right of courts to strike down laws that were (in their view) unconstitutional had been recognized from the very beginning of the republic; in the well-known case of *Marbury v. Madison,* decided in 1803, the Supreme Court even struck down an act of Congress. But judicial review of legislation was rare until the late nineteenth century, in federal and state courts alike. A number of famous (or notorious) decisions, state and federal, voided welfare and regulatory laws. One of the most prominent cases was *Lochner v. New York* (1905). Here the U.S. Supreme Court nullified a New York law that regulated hours of work (and sanitary conditions) in New York's bakeries. Moreover, from the 1880s on, courts developed and used the labor injunction, a powerful legal tool for breaking strikes. This only reinforced the image of courts as bastions of reaction.

The Twentieth Century

In the nineteenth century, the federal government, for the most part, was relatively feeble—a tiny central system inside a huge body, like the brain of a dinosaur. Washington was an insignificant village.

Most legal activity took place in the states. The twentieth century, however, brought a slow, dramatic flow of power out of the states and into Washington. The legal system as a whole grew by leaps and bounds, with explosive growth in statutes, rules and regulations, ordinances, and decided cases. The United States, like all Western democracies, became a massive welfare and regulatory state. The process started long before the New Deal and continued long afterwards; still, the New Deal spawned many new programs and federal agencies. The Securities and Exchange Commission (SEC) was meant to be a watchdog for Wall Street. Federal insurance guaranteed bank accounts. The National Labor Relations Board regulated union elections and collective bargaining. The Social Security Act established a system of old-age pensions, among other programs. All these were popular and durable innovations.

Underlying this explosion of federal power and authority was the revolution in transport and communication. The country could now function as a single unit in ways that were impossible in the nineteenth century. Despite all the talk about "multiculturalism" and America's huge diversity of races, religions, and national origins, in fact the country is currently much more of a single culture area than was ever true in the past. Commerce is national, entertainment is national, culture is national. People talk about their "roots," but one's long-ago "roots" in Italy, Africa, or China seldom count for much in day-to-day life. Politics, too, has transcended local institutions. The imperial presidency would not be possible without television and the other mass media. The president and his wife, his children, even his dog, are familiar celebrities; he is on television literally every day. National politics eclipses local politics to an astounding degree.

The states, despite the drift of power to the center and the nationalization of culture, are still in some ways the workhorses of ordinary American law. Commercial and criminal law are state law, and the states essentially run the education system. They make up the rules of traffic law. Family law, contract law, personal injury litigation, property law, land use and zoning—all of these are matters for the states, not the federal government. Probably 90 percent or more of all litigation is state litigation. To be sure, the federal government now has *some* role in every field, no matter how local. There is a cabinet-level Department of Education. Presidents have campaigned on issues of law and order and on tort reform. Federal money is pumped into law enforcement. Congress has added to the list of federal crimes. Still, in all of these fields, the federal government is secondary; mostly, it shovels out grants of money and regulates on the margins.

States have built up their own welfare and regulatory apparatus. Neither Wyoming nor New York has an atom bomb, or an ambassador in Paris; nor do they make the most important rules about air and water pollution; but all of the states have big bureaucracies, enormous statute books, and masses of rules about health, safety, and economic development. Cities adopt elaborate zoning ordinances. States regulate their public utilities. They license doctors, lawyers, architects, nurses, and dozens of other occupations. They have, in short, expanded enormously during the twentieth century, though the federal government has expanded even more.

Plural Equality

Perhaps the most far-reaching development in American law during the twentieth century (especially the last half of it) was the dismantling of a racial caste system that the law had maintained for more than three centuries. Litigation and legislation driven by the civil rights movement eventually extended equal legal rights not only to blacks and other ethno-racial minorities but also to women, the disabled, the elderly, illegitimate children, students, prisoners, sexual minorities, and (to a lesser extent) immigrants.

These developments, whose social effects are detailed in chapter 13, produced a huge change in the very concept of legal *equality;* it makes sense, today, to speak of *plural* equality. Nineteenth-century "equality" was in many ways not equality at all, certainly not for blacks; and for whites, an equality only within members of the dominant groups (Christians, for example; or English speakers), with "tolerance" for others. So, for example, there was genuine religious freedom; but only Christians could invoke laws against blasphemy. There are, today, no blasphemy laws. *Plural equality* means *acceptance,* not mere toleration. It weakens, and redefines, a majority's power to influence, dominate, and control minorities—on the legal, moral, social, and symbolic planes.

Social and legal changes of this magnitude always have deep roots and complex causes. Plural equality reflects the social and normative structure of a mature capitalist system. Plural equality rests on a mass middle-class culture that glorifies the *individual,* one in which individuals believe they have an inherent, inalienable right to choose their unique path through life, to realize their personal potential. Advertising, a consumer culture, leisure, and money to spend on entertainment and self-improvement profoundly affect social norms. People watch television, travel, are influenced by advertising, and observe how other people live—which in turn affects how people think, behave, and vote, as well as the legal system itself. And it encourages the demand of all the minorities for a truly level playing field in which each person is judged as an *individual,* not as a member of a group assigned to some second-class berth.

Controversy over Supreme Court decisions continued into the 1930s. The Court struck down key elements of Roosevelt's New Deal. The president, exasperated, hatched a plan to pack the Court with new members to dilute the power of the "nine old men." This scheme, a product of hubris and irritation, was one of Roosevelt's rare political blunders. The president lost this battle, but he won the war. He was elected four times; this was long enough for him to pack the Court in the usual, and legitimate, way—by appointing judges after his own heart and mind. The Court virtually abdicated any role in monitoring economic legislation. It conceded to Congress, in essence, full power to regulate the economy. The Constitution, for example, gave Congress authority over interstate commerce. The Court now read this as authority over any activity which had an *effect* on commerce—an almost limitless power. The Court turned its attention elsewhere. *Brown v. Board of Education* (1954)—the school desegregation case—was symptomatic of a new form of activism. In the 1950s, 1960s, and later, the Court intervened, not on behalf of big business, but on behalf of the underdogs—criminal defendants, aliens, sexual minorities, women, and African-Americans and other minority races.

Crime and Punishment

Notions of crime and criminal justice and methods of dealing with persons accused of crime have evolved over the years (see chapter 16 for a detailed analysis of America's criminal justice system). The penal codes of the nineteenth century reflected traditional morality. Adultery and fornication were crimes (at least when they were open and notorious). Vice and sexual deviance were, on paper at any rate, serious crimes. The enforcement picture was rather different. Gambling and prostitution thrived in the red-light districts of the cities. The police ignored vice or were bribed to ignore it. Laws against adultery and fornication were basically dead letters. Very few men or women were arrested for morals offenses. Drunks and prostitutes, vagrants and brawlers, marched in and out of the system, were jailed, fined, and let go. A kind of dual system prevailed, one we might call the Victorian compromise—a system where the law in action differed radically from the law on the books.

But the situation changed dramatically, beginning in the late nineteenth century. Laws against vice and sexual misconduct tightened. In 1910, Congress passed the Mann Act, making it a crime to transport a woman across state lines for purposes of prostitution, "debauchery and other immoral purposes." In this same period, a strong movement, the red-light abatement movement, aimed to drive brothels out of business and close down the red-light districts. The high (or low) point of the war on vice was national Prohibition. The Eighteenth Amendment to the Constitution, banning the manufacture and sale of liquor, was ratified in 1919 and went into effect in 1920. The United States was officially bone dry. The long war against the saloon had ended; and the forces of virtue and abstention had won.

Behind all these legal and social upheavals was a kind of cultural crisis. Old American values seemed to be in danger. Hordes of immigrants were swarming into the country, many with values different from the values of Protestant northern Europe. Farm girls and boys streamed by the thousands into the wicked cities, exposed to temptation, sin, and irreligion. The war on vice was a backlash against modernity, a rearguard attempt to restore a lost (and imaginary) Eden.

But in the end, the war on vice was a failure. Prohibition was one of the earliest victims. It became extremely unpopular, especially in the big cities. Evasion and corruption became epidemic, and Prohibition lost most of its political support. The Twenty-first Amendment undid the Eighteenth Amendment, and by 1933, Prohibition had ended its brief and inglorious life. In the last half of the twentieth century, the legal structure that sustained the war against vice crumbled into dust. One by one, adultery, fornication, and other crimes against morality were stripped from the penal codes, at least for consenting adults. After *Roe v. Wade* (1973), no state could simply outlaw abortions. The battle for gay rights was more intense and more difficult; still, most states repealed their sodomy laws by the end of the twentieth century. The surviving laws were chiefly in the Bible Belt, and the U.S. Supreme Court consigned them to oblivion in 2003. Censorship and regulation of pornography had all but disappeared. Nevada, a barren desert state without much of an economic base, pioneered in making casino gambling legal (and

profitable). By the early twenty-first century, the states were hawk-
ing lottery tickets to one and all, and casino gambling was now
available in Atlantic City, New Jersey, on riverboats plying the Mississippi River, on Indian reservations, and in many other places.

Drug laws were the one big exception to this decriminalization
trend.[6] Drug laws were essentially a product of the first third of the
twentieth century. Over time they grew harsher and harsher. Tens
of thousands of men and women sit in prison for drug offenses. The
intensity of the war on drugs may owe something to the image
of pushers who seduce middle-class children and turn them into
helpless addicts. Chapter 19 details the current state of this war and
its consequences.

The triumph of vice would have shocked the earnest citizens
who applauded Prohibition, and who dreamed of an end to prostitution, gambling, and public immorality. These men and women
earnestly believed that civilization, as it advanced, would reject immoral and debauched behavior—behavior they considered primitive and barbaric. Yet immorality as they defined it ended up on top.
This shift in morals and mores, like the earlier ones, surely had complex roots; but at the base of it, no doubt, was something profound
about modern culture: its deep *individualism,* its emphasis on doing
one's own thing, on self-realization, on personal liberty. The revolution spilled over into family law and transformed it, too. Cohabitation, once a crime, became a way of life. Bastardy lost much of its
stigma and almost all of its legal disadvantages. In the 1970s, no-fault
divorce swept away strict divorce laws, first in California, then in
most of the other states.[7] In no-fault jurisdictions, divorce became
almost as easy as marriage. Anybody who felt dissatisfied, or unful-
filled in marriage, was simply free to leave. It was no longer necessary to allege grounds. Property questions, and custody of children,
remained knotty issues—perhaps more than ever—but divorce itself
was legally unproblematic.

The Legal System Today

Perhaps the most striking aspect of American law today is how much there is of it, and how much it touches everything we do. Any activity in public, small or large, will somehow involve, depend on, or show the influence of law, laws, and the legal system. If we enter a supermarket to buy milk and a can of chicken soup, we enter a world regulated by health laws, labor laws, and dozens of other rules and regulations. A web of laws, page after page of statutes, covers the public schools our children go to. In April, most of us file a tax return. Some time in our life we may apply for a marriage license, a dog license, a hunting license. And so it goes. Law is all around us, whether we are aware of it or not.

Modern government, at whatever level, is a regulatory government; its story is a story of inexorable growth. This is not just an American story; it is true of all the developed nations. The growth may have crested somewhat in the late twentieth century; a wave of disillusionment and ideology has curbed the public's appetite for government ownership and management of public functions; the watchword today is privatization. But though many cities farm out garbage collection to private carters, that does not imply a public passion for raw, naked capitalism. All businesses of any size are still subject to health, safety, and environmental regulation, not to mention laws against discrimination and mistreatment of workers, or rules about fair competition and tax laws. No public company can float stock without the approval of the SEC, or merge with a rival that controls a big share of the market, without the approval of the Justice Department. The company's smokestacks have to satisfy clean air laws; its waste cannot be freely discharged into rivers; and so on. Particular kinds of businesses, from coal mines to banks to drug companies, have their own particular forms of regulation. At the federal level, the Federal Register is at least a crude measure of the sheer volume of government. This huge, cumbersome, and tedious work lists all proposed and final rules and regulations of administrative agencies, and all executive orders; in some years, it has run to as many as seventy-five thousand pages. And this does not take into account the laws of the fifty states, the local ordinances, or the thousands of reported and unreported decisions and cases that the courts churn out every year.

Why did this explosion of law take place? The sheer complexity of modern society is a major cause. In advanced societies, each of us is heavily dependent on utter strangers—people we do not know, and have no way of controlling. The pilot of our airliner is a stranger; yet our lives are in his or her hands. It is in the hands, too, of the elevator inspector, the meat inspector, the inspector of bridges and highways. In simple, face-to-face societies, social norms may be strong enough to govern the community. Our world relies on laws, rules, and regulations to keep us safe. We rely on law, too, where *somebody* has to allocate scarce resources, and the market is not up to the job for one reason or another. So, in the streets of big cities, jammed with cars, busses, and taxis, only traffic rules and traffic police can avoid total gridlock; in the crowded radio spectrum, a government agency allocates channels and acts to prevent a jumble of voices, none of them audible above the din.

Another factor that leads to more law is heterogeneity. A society of many races, religions, cultures, and, in general, many views and opinions cannot regulate itself by way of consensus. If some people think abortion is murder and some people think it is a woman's absolute right, the law will have to choose, perhaps finding an intermediate alternative. Sometimes societies resolve issues by tossing a coin, sometimes by majority vote, but sometimes also by rules or by litigation. Somebody has to decide whether mother or father gets custody of children after a divorce. Somebody has to decide if a broken leg was somebody's fault, and if so, whose, and how much should be paid to the victim.

There has also been tremendous growth in the social safety net: not only the social security system, but also Medicare and Medicaid, food stamps, bank deposit insurance, FEMA, unemployment compensation, soft loans for college students, and so on. The welfare state is both cause and effect of a major shift in culture. Modern medicine, the widespread use of insurance, the expansion of tort liability, and the welfare state itself have brought about a profound *cultural* transformation. People have come to *expect* compensation when calamity strikes; they expect doctors to cure them; they expect the social safety net to catch them when they fall; in short, they expect what I have called total justice.[8] This expectation produces big government and pervasive law. Another factor is America's status as a superpower, with a huge defense establishment, a large standing army, a gigantic navy, carriers, nuclear submarines, fancy new aircraft, and the infrastructure to make all this possible.

Defense and welfare cost money, and governments at all levels need to come up with billions and billions of dollars every year to pay for these programs, not to mention highways, national and state parks, public education, the national institutes of health, and hundreds of other matters. Taxes, and tax law, pay the bills. The federal income tax more or less dates from the second decade of the twentieth century. As the tax appetite grew, so did the text of the internal revenue code. No branch of law is as complex as tax law—a maze of exemptions, deductions, and other detours, imposed on the code by political pressures and pressure groups. In part, the complexity reflects a kind of arms race between the government, on the one hand, and businesses and rich individuals, on the other, who hope to find clever ways to evade and avoid paying taxes. Each new and ingenious loophole, dreamt up by tax lawyers or accountants, leads to another paragraph or page of contorted prose, or a new batch of regulations, drafted in an often vain attempt to close up the loophole.

The Legal Profession

Tax law, like business law in general, puts bread on the table of hosts of lawyers. Nonetheless, the legal system works for the most part without the need for lawyers. The police enforce traffic rules. Civil servants implement most regulations. Ordinary people file tax returns and follow the rules, most of the time without outside counsel. Still, there seems to be plenty left for lawyers to do. The United States has the largest legal profession in the world: more than 1.1 million men and women were practicing law in 2006. The numbers have been growing far faster than the overall population.

Exactly what do all these lawyers do? If you judged by movies and television, the answer would be: defending and prosecuting criminals. In fact, most lawyers never touch a criminal case. The newspapers suggest that lawyers work on hot-button issues— whether it is gay marriage, affirmative action, teaching or not teaching evolution in the schools, the death penalty, the war on terror, drilling or not drilling for oil in Alaska, and so on. But these absorb the talents of a tiny percentage of lawyers. By and large the business of American lawyers—and American law—is business. In an elaborate study of the Chicago bar, John Heinz and Edward Lauman divided the legal world into two hemispheres. Lawyers in one hemisphere worked for corporate clients; in the other, they worked for individuals, on divorce, personal injuries, or criminal matters. In 1976, the business hemisphere was bigger than the personal service hemisphere, and twenty years later, it was *much* bigger: 61 percent of lawyer efforts went to this hemisphere; and if you added in services to *small* businesses, the disparity between the two hemispheres would be even greater.[9]

Business lawyering is a growing business. Between 1967 and 2002, the total receipts of the legal services industry went from $22 billion (in 2000 dollars) to $166 billion. Individuals increased their spending on legal services by 463 percent; businesses by 821 percent. This high increase in business spending, moreover, does not include money paid to in-house lawyers, a growing category.[10] More and more, businesses feel the need to have lawyers on their payroll besides their outside law firm. And what is true of businesses is true of other organizations: universities and hospitals, for example. Organizational life has been legalized, and this means more work for the lawyers. Most of this work is not litigation; rather, it is advice on how to navigate a safe course through modern government.

Litigation, in fact, despite all the talk about a litigation explosion, is in decline—if by litigation we mean actual trials. In 1962, 11.5 percent of the civil cases filed in federal court ended up as actual trials. This was already low; by 2002, there were actual trials in only 1.8 percent of the cases. And a similar trend seems under way in the state courts. Litigation lawyers tend to do most of their work *before* trial. The lawyers negotiate, depose witnesses, and attempt to obtain documents and papers from the other side that might constitute or contain evidence. Most of the time, too, the trial does not even take place.

Going to trial, after all, is expensive and time-consuming. Businesses and lawyers consider it a last resort. It is also official policy to discourage litigation in favor of mediation, settlement, or alternative dispute resolution (ADR). Under the Civil Justice Reform Act of 1990 and the Administrative Dispute Resolution Act of 1996, Congress asked all federal courts and all federal agencies to adopt policies that encourage ADR. Parallel developments have taken place in the states.

But even though *litigation* may be in decline, lawyering, as we pointed out, is not. There is a literature of economic analysis, mixed with invective (the two are not always carefully separated), deploring the swarms of lawyers in America and their nefarious activities. Japan is often held out as a kind of model at the other extreme. The Japanese have a tiny legal profession. Only about 2 percent of the takers pass the bar exam. These numbers are slated to rise; but not very much by American standards. Since Japan is rich and successful, it seems to follow that lawyers may be unnecessary to economic success. They may even be parasitic, or dysfunctional. Yet the United States, with its flourishing law profession, is also rich and successful.

Lawyers perform certain functions essential in any advanced society, including Japan. And they *are* carried out in Japan, though not necessarily by lawyers (members of the bar). This is not to deny the significant differences between Japan and the United States. The enormous numbers of American lawyers, and their hustle and bustle, make law, legal process, and litigation much more salient in the United States than in Japan.

The American legal profession has been expanding for almost two hundred years. A society in which the average family might own a farm, a house, a bit of money, was a society that needed legal help from time to time—more than, say, English tenant farmers did. Lawyers have always been prominent in government and politics. But demographically, the profession is changing rapidly. It is no longer a white male club. Women first fought their way into the bar against determined resistance in the 1870s. But they remained a tiny minority for almost a century. In 1955, there were about five thousand women lawyers in the country, 1.3 percent of the total. There were exactly four women lawyers in New Mexico and three in Delaware. Today, almost half of all law students are women. Women make up about a quarter of the profession, and their ranks are growing. Many women are prosecutors, law professors, deans, and judges. There have been two women on the U.S. Supreme Court. Less dramatic, but real, has been the increase in African-American and Hispanic lawyers and judges. About 4.2 percent of all lawyers are black, about 3.4 percent Hispanic; while still seriously underrepresented, their numbers are definitely rising. Whether the feminization of the profession or the entry of minority lawyers makes a difference in the organization or practice of law is a vexed question, with no clear answer as yet.

The rise of the large law firm has also been dramatic. In the late 1950s, fewer than 40 firms in the United States had more than 50 lawyers. In 1988, the country's largest law firm had 169 lawyers. In 1995, there were over 700 firms with more than 50 lawyers. By

2005, Baker and McKenzie, the largest law firm, had grown to over 3,300 lawyers, and 19 law firms had more than 1,000 lawyers on the staff. At one time, too, all law firms were local, but by the beginning of the twenty-first century, the big firms had gone global, extending their tentacles into many cities at home and abroad. Baker and McKenzie lists 72 locations for its offices—only 9 are in the United States, while others are in cities as far-flung as Beijing, Kuala Lumpur, Barcelona, Kiev, Buenos Aires, and Calgary. Heller Ehrman, a San Francisco firm, which ranked forty-first in size (a mere 700 lawyers), had 11 offices, 8 in the United States, plus Hong Kong, Beijing, and Singapore.

Most lawyers practicing today are in private practice, either as partners or associates in law firms, or in smaller, specialized firms (boutique firms), or as solo practitioners. Despite the huge growth in law firms, almost half of all lawyers in private practice (48 percent, to be exact) still work for and by themselves, without partners. Only 20 percent work in firms with fifty or more lawyers. About 8 percent of the active lawyers work for government—federal, state, or local. Another 8 percent are in-house counsel—employees of private corporations. A small but important cluster of attorneys work as public interest lawyers; they represent the Sierra Club, or the NAACP, or other non-profit organizations. The work of these lawyers has sometimes achieved a good deal of success. Indeed, the civil rights movement owes a lot to the lawyers of the NAACP and their litigation strategies. Most public interest lawyers, historically, have been liberal to left in politics. But the right wing knows a good thing when it sees it; conservative public interest groups have flourished, too, in the last generation.

Convergence and Divergence

In many respects, developments in American law have parallels in other developed societies. Everywhere, law has expanded enormously.

An American lawyer could talk comfortably with a Japanese lawyer or French lawyer about antitrust law, bankruptcy, income taxation, pension law, land use controls, copyright protection for software, and many other shared problems, in branches of law that did not exist in the past, but which today are common to all developed societies. Each country, too, has moved toward plural equality among people of all races and ethnicities. All of them, to some degree, have responded to feminism. All have changed family law in the direction of more individual choice. Even Catholic countries like Italy, Ireland, Spain, and Chile now have divorce laws. In important senses, then, all modern legal systems are converging.

The differences that remain may be details, but they can be important details. The American social safety net is more limited than the net in most European countries. American companies can hire and fire workers more easily than firms in other systems. American law is far more fragmented and decentralized than British or French law. Not only are there fifty states, but many programs are even further decentralized—consider, for example, the thousands of local school boards. The police, too, are exceedingly local. They are not the president's men (and women), or even the governor's. They constitute thousands of little law-enforcement fiefs. Also, American law puts more emphasis on rights, lawyers, and litigation than do other countries. Adversarial legalism, to use Robert Kagan's phrase, is an American specialty, marked by a tendency to heavy use of lawyers, lawsuits, and litigators, in tort actions, and in actions against administrative agencies.[11] Other countries may have as much law as the United States, if we define law broadly enough. But they have much less lawyering. They are also less rights-conscious. They give more power and discretion to administrative agencies, and they make it harder to challenge these agencies in court. The vast proliferation of jokes about American lawyers, a genre which simply does not exist elsewhere, ironically suggests the greater salience of lawyers in the United States.[12]

Only the United States feels it is in the grips of a litigation crisis. The liability explosion of the twentieth century is beyond question. Many classic rules of tort law, developed in the nineteenth century, in the railroad age, strongly favored business. The infamous fellow servant rule closed the courtroom door to factory and railroad workers injured on the job. In the twentieth century, the tables were turned. Workers' compensation systems ended the fellow servant rule. Old, restrictive doctrines of tort law were relaxed or abolished. Medical malpractice and products liability cases became more common.[13] In no other country is it so easy to sue for personal injury, or to blame a drug or a defective product or a careless doctor for your suffering; in no other country can damages run so high— in some cases, into millions of dollars. A small but significant group of personal injury cases have enormous economic significance: cases with masses of alleged victims threaten whole industries with ruin. Lawsuits put an end to the asbestos business, for example; the Agent Orange case was another example of lawsuits arising out of mass toxic torts.[14]

Businesses and insurance companies, feeling the sting of tort law, have orchestrated a national campaign to curb what they consider the excesses of litigation, litigants, and lawyers. They joined forces with doctors scared out of their wits by malpractice lawsuits and municipalities in a panic over liability for accidents on roads or in playgrounds. The campaign has had some solid successes; most states have restricted tort recoveries in one way or another. In truth, the big recoveries, the megamillion verdicts, the huge awards of punitive damages, are on the whole quite rare. Huge tort actions frighten businesses and cost them dearly for legal defense, but most injured people in fact get little or nothing for their pains. And, in fairness, a young man or woman paralyzed by (alleged) malpractice *will* cost millions for lifetime care. The weaknesses of the American welfare system must bear some blame for any increases in the tort system. Other countries do not allow tort actions so freely, and never produce huge recoveries. But their social safety nets are much more likely to cover the costs of health care, disability, and wage loss.

What Lies Ahead?

If adversarial legalism is a fact, is it also a serious social problem? The American way of law (which may be spreading to Europe)[15] makes building a new airport, dredging a harbor, or drilling for oil offshore a slow and expensive process. But if adversarial legalism stands in the way of any drilling off the coast of California, or holds up a major highway because a handful of farmers object, the results are good or bad, depending on your values and goals. There are, of course, wider claims: claims (as we mentioned) that litigation is harming the economy, or that good government needs to be supple and flexible, and the emphasis on courts and rights stiffens the joints. Some also complain that activist courts ignore the will of the people and exercise dictatorial power. The Massachusetts high court legalized gay marriage. The Supreme Court wiped out sodomy laws. These were counter-majoritarian acts. Every aspect of these arguments, however, whether facts, values, or judgments, is hotly disputed. Indeed, some argue that the real problem is not too much litigation, but the opposite: the poor and the middle class are shut out of the courts. Justice is a luxury only the rich can afford. What all sides would concede is that courts, law, and litigation occupy a central role in American *political* life; and will continue to do so.

The Constitution and the formal legal system seem to create a system of thoroughgoing fairness; a system of checks and balances; a system of limited government. Official norms are exquisitely sensitive to problems of power, or rather, the lack of power. Criminal procedure tilts toward the defendant, at least on paper. He is presumed innocent. He can only be convicted if the evidence is "beyond a reasonable doubt." He has the right to remain silent. Of course, no system ever lives up to its ideals; and probably none ever will. American justice may come closer than most; but any complete history of criminal justice would also tell a story of race prejudice, vigilante justice, lynch law, police brutality, corrupt and inhuman prison conditions, the third degree, official neglect and abuse, and countless other instances of rampant unfairness.

Times of crisis and danger, real or imagined, put a special strain on civil rights and civil liberties. During and after World War I, an orgy of xenophobia erupted. During this first red scare, the government deported hundreds of aliens who were considered radical. Sedition laws, passed during this period, produced the first significant Supreme Court cases on freedom of speech. McCarthyism followed World War II, but Senator Joseph McCarthy was only the most blatant and outrageous political figure in the savage witch-hunt against reds, pinks, and fellow travelers. This was also a period of loyalty oaths and purges, and a handful of sensational trials. The Supreme Court responded feebly, and late, in defense of civil liberties and the rights of free speech and free association.[16]

Communism collapsed as a reality and as a bogeyman in the 1990s. A new enemy arose: terrorism, especially the threat posed by radical Islam. Congress, after the attack on the World Trade Center in 2001, swiftly enacted the sweeping USA Patriot Act. This law gave the government new and broad powers to conduct the global war on terror, powers that tended to target Muslims. The government launched actual wars in Afghanistan and Iraq and opened up a brutal camp in Guantanamo Bay, where men were held incommunicado for indefinite periods without the slightest shred of due process. Back home, people got used to taking off shoes, belts, and bracelets as they waited in long lines at airports; metal detectors sprouted everywhere like mushrooms after rain. Lawyers for the prisoners in Guantanamo, and for other prisoners caught up in the government's web, fought back slowly, trying to persuade the courts that the government had gone too far. The Supreme Court said yes to some of their claims, but not in a very loud voice; and not, perhaps, with much effect. The war on terror, like the war on Communism, which in many ways it replaces, has no obvious end point; and there is no sign of an armistice in the struggle between this war and American civil liberties.

Democracy is a fragile thing; and so is the rule of law. Modern technology can be intensely liberating. Satellite dishes and the Internet are deadly enemies of dictatorship. On the other hand, technology puts powers in the hands of government and large institutions that a Genghis Khan or even a Hitler could only have dreamt of. In a computerized society, large institutions and the state can gather huge amounts of data about everyone, almost at will; can store the data, costlessly and essentially forever; and can manipulate and deploy the data with astonishing ease. The very crudity of past technology helped, in a way, to safeguard personal privacy and individual liberty. Your home is a castle when you can bolt the door and keep everybody out. If there are devices that can look through the walls, or hear a pin drop in your bedroom, then the castle is not much of a castle anymore. Sustaining freedom and the rule of law in turbulent times, and in the teeth of the computer age, will be a daunting challenge to law and society in years to come.

CHAPTER 4

The Economic System

Benjamin M. Friedman

There are many countries with abundant natural resources and other phys-
ical advantages, but among large nations, only in America have they been
used to produce such a consistently high level of income, and with consis-
tent economic growth over time. The reasons, economist Benjamin Fried-
man argues, include institutions and attitudes that foster more work effort
from a more highly educated population and better choices in allocating
scarce productive capital. The role of government is important, too, both for
the lightness of government direction of private economic activity, compared
to many other countries, and for effective supervision and regulation that
buttress financial stability. Significant problems remain, however, especially
America's reliance on foreign supplies of energy and on the willingness of
foreign investors to lend to American borrowers, as well as the current stag-
nation of incomes for most families despite continuing increases in the econ-
omy's production.

THE ESSENTIAL ROLE OF ANY ECONOMIC SYSTEM IS TO ENABLE A
society to marshal its potentially productive resources—human,
material, and intangible—both to generate the goods and services
its citizens want and to distribute those goods and services to who-
ever is going to use them. The economic system of the United
States has succeeded more in this regard than any in world history.

I am grateful to Robert Gordon, Dale Jorgenson, Lawrence Katz, Gregory Mankiw, Michael
Pomerleano, James Poterba, and Robert Solow for helpful discussions, and to the editors for their
detailed comments on an earlier draft.

Apart from a few anomalous entities such as Luxembourg that are technically countries but are more like large suburbs in size (Luxembourg has a population of 450,000 about the same as Long Beach, CA), America currently enjoys the world's highest per capita income. This success is not a recent or short-lived phenomenon. Americans' standard of living has ranked at or near the world's highest for decades, far outranking all other countries of major size and geopolitical importance.

The American economy has been successful in other ways as well. The sustained increase in income per person has persisted over centuries now, in the face of (or perhaps in part because of) sustained population growth, including the country's continual absorption of large numbers of new immigrants. Moreover, within the last two decades the economy has proved remarkably stable by historical standards, both in the United States and abroad. The severe one-day stock market crash in October 1987, the collapse of a good portion of the nation's thrift deposit industry in the late 1980s, the protracted stock market decline of 2000–2003, and the tripling of world oil prices after 2002 all led to little if any visible impact on aggregate non-financial economic activity. During the last quarter-century, the American economy has experienced only two overall business downturns, neither lasting longer than eight months and neither leading to a decline in total production as great as 1.5 percent.

What accounts for this remarkable record? While a host of diverse underpinnings of America's economic condition have been important historically—such as ample natural resources, lengthy coastlines and navigable rivers, the large internal market that spans an entire continent, and the nation's unified and stable political structure—two related elements have been especially important in enabling the United States in recent decades to achieve continuing economic growth despite what was already a very high level.

First, more so than any other large nation, America has maintained a flexibility and fluidity in its economic arrangements that has

facilitated the continual reallocation of both labor and capital resources and has fostered economic initiative, entrepreneurship, and
creativity. The absence of many of the restrictive labor practices
and laws found in many other advanced industrialized economies,
together with Americans' willingness not just to change their workplace but to relocate their home, often over great distances, has
allowed human resources to move to where they can be most productive. The education system, mostly emphasizing general education (including some college years, albeit not necessarily a four-year
degree) for most citizens rather than specific vocational training
along separate tracks assigned at early ages, has also helped. Broad,
deep, and highly decentralized capital markets, with many kinds of
intermediary institutions and extensive public participation, have
likewise facilitated saving and investment, and more importantly in
America's case, the allocation of this investment to productive uses.
Not only is it easier to raise the necessary financing to start a new
business initiative than in other large industrial and postindustrial
economies, but the administrative and legal hurdles are typically
lower as well.

Second, public policy in America has played a positive role in
creating a setting in which private initiative can flourish. Part of that
story is what American government typically does *not* do (or at least
does to a lesser extent than elsewhere). For example, American laws
generally impose fewer burdensome regulations that discourage
firms from hiring workers and prevent them from either reassigning
or discharging existing workers. But regulation, too, is a vital part of
the government's economic role. One reason American financial
markets are so well developed, and attract such broad public participation, is that government regulation and supervision preserve the
soundness and integrity of the vast majority of private-sector financial institutions, while legally required disclosure renders these features transparent to the investing public. Similarly, the willingness to
intervene as needed in financial markets has helped to stabilize these

markets as well as the non-financial economy in the face of potentially disruptive aggregate-level shocks (like stock market crashes) or firm-level failures (like the collapse of Long Term Capital Management in September 1998). Flexible and adaptive macroeconomic policy, especially monetary policy, has also been important in this regard. Primary and secondary education is also very largely a public-sector responsibility in America, as is nearly two-thirds of higher education, and so the governing philosophy that produces a more generally educated labor force than in most other countries is likewise a matter of public policy.[1]

Neither fluid markets nor the public policies that support them, of course, emerged on their own. These characteristics, too, have origins. Although tracing the cultural and historical roots of these proximate causes of America's economic success lies beyond the scope of this essay, some aspects of America's past seem clearly relevant. At the very least, American attitudes and patterns of personal behavior that Alexis de Tocqueville already found noteworthy a century and three-quarters ago strongly presaged not only the country's subsequent economic success, but even some of the specifics of what has enabled that success over such a long period.

None of this is to suggest that the American economy is free of problems, either large-scale or small, or that the United States will automatically meet the economic challenges of coming decades with the overall success of the recent and more distant past. In the last three decades, Americans have questioned whether our prosperity can survive reliance on foreign energy and whether we can meet the competition of Japan, Germany, and other key European countries. In each case the answer has been yes; reliance on foreign energy persists but has not (yet?) defeated American economic success, and today both Japan and Germany are valued trading partners but neither presents a serious threat to America's economic well-being. At the beginning of the twenty-first century, new economic challenges come from China and, even more recently, from India.

Whether, and how, the United States will overcome these newer challenges of course remains to be seen.

Significant economic problems also persist at home. America today depends on importing more goods than U.S. producers export—and, in parallel, relies on saving borrowed from foreign sources—to a much greater extent than ever before in modern experience, indeed to an extent that in most other countries would be regarded as irresponsibly dangerous. Direct and indirect government subsidies distort the allocation of both production (through direct farm subsidies, for example) and consumption (through tax subsidies to housing). Most importantly, within just the last decade, the link between productivity gains and improvement in wages and living standards has been severed for the great majority of America's working population. Despite a welcome acceleration of productivity in recent years, the median family's income is falling after allowing for rising prices; only a relatively few at the top of the income scale have been enjoying any increase. These developments challenge not just the nation's economic success but also the deeper cultural roots that underlie American economic attitudes and institutions. The combination of market flexibility and adaptive public policy that has served America well in the past will be especially important as the nation moves to address these and other new challenges.

Basic Parameters of a Productive Economy

Almost 300 million people now live in the United States, of whom 188 million are of conventional working age (18–64). Not counting the uniformed military, 144 million Americans work at paying jobs in the formal economy. Another 7 million are seeking employment but unable to find a job. Among men (now including 16- and 17-year-olds as well as those over 64), 73.5 percent are in the labor force; among women, 59.4 percent are.[2]

Most economic production, not just in manufacturing, but likewise in agriculture and even the service sector, requires not just labor, but capital. American businesses, in total, use $13 trillion of plant and equipment of all kinds—factories, office buildings, research laboratories, power generators and transmission lines, machinery large and small, telephones, airplanes and trucks, computers, and much else besides—to produce what they make. With 112 million employees, business on average has $117,000 of capital deployed for each worker.[3]

Like most other advanced economies, the United States has followed a historical path beginning primarily in agricultural production, continuing through a major emphasis on manufacturing, and on to largely service-oriented production. As Table 4.1 shows,

Table 4.1   Composition of U.S. Employment and Output

Industry	Number Employed (millions)	% of Employment	% of Output
Agriculture	1.5	1.0	0.8
Mining	0.6	0.4	1.5
Construction	7.6	5.4	5.5
Manufacturing	14.3	10.1	12.5
Private-Sector Services	93.2	66.0	67.6
Utilities	0.6	0.4	1.6
Wholesale and Retail Trade	21.6	15.3	13.9
Transportation	4.4	3.1	2.8
Finance	8.3	5.9	16.8
Professional & Business Services	17.4	12.3	13.9
Education & Health Care	17.9	12.7	8.6
Other Services	23.0	16.3	9.9
Government	24.1	17.1	12.0
Total	141.2	100.0	100.0

today the private service-producing sector accounts for roughly two-thirds of both employment and output, and with government included, the service sector represents about four-fifths of the economy.[4] Manufacturing accounts for barely one-eighth of total output, and agriculture (even broadly defined) not even 1 percent.

Because industries differ in how productively they use labor, the share of a country's workers employed in any given industry need not match the share of output that that industry produces. These disparities are apparent in Table 4.1 as well. Most strikingly, the financial industry, broadly defined, employs fewer than 6 percent of the workforce, but produces nearly 17 percent of the output; in the other direction, the private-sector education and health care industries (especially health care) account for a distinctly greater share of employment than of output.[5] Moreover, over time, productivity differentials between one industry and another change. When an industry experiences more rapid gains than average, either its share of the economy's total output increases, or its share of employment falls, or both.

Within the business sector, where more than three-quarters of the American economy's total production takes place, the size of firms ranges from extremely large corporations—the largest is Wal-Mart, with more than 1 million employees and annual sales of $245 billion—to one-person proprietorships. The vast majority of today's more than 24 million separate firms are small; nearly 19 million are simply self-employed individuals. Among the 5.8 million that do have non-owner employees, nearly two-thirds have fewer than 10, and 85 percent have fewer than 100. By contrast, the large firms figure far more prominently in Americans' overall work experience, and they similarly account for much of the nation's economic output. Only 8,500 firms in the United States have over 1,000 employees, but together they employ 50 million people and account for more than half of the sales of all American businesses combined. And although there are fewer than 900 firms with more than 10,000 employees, they employ 30 million people and account for more than one-third of total business sales.[6]

In addition, a significant share of America's economic output—almost entirely consisting of services—is produced outside the for-profit market economy.[7] Within the private sector, non-profit institutions such as private colleges and universities, art museums, symphony orchestras, churches and synagogues, and charities like the Red Cross and the Salvation Army represent nearly 5 percent of the economy. Even the country's largest manager of mutual funds (Vanguard) is a non-profit organization. State and local governments, which bear the major responsibility for education, police and fire protection, sanitation, and many other similar services, employ 19 million people (nearly 10 million of them working in education). The federal government's payroll includes more than 2 million military personnel plus nearly 3 million civilian employees engaged in law enforcement, border security, space research, and the vast array of other activities that the government undertakes, including the operation of numerous independent but government-owned enterprises such as the postal service.

Finally, by trading with buyers and sellers in other countries, Americans have ready access to a rich array of goods and services that they do not produce themselves. Today just over 16 percent of what Americans buy—mostly goods such as cars, clothing, electronic equipment, cameras, and other consumer items, but also industrial equipment, petroleum and natural gas, minerals such as chromium, and services such as transportation and tourism—comes from abroad. In exchange, American firms on average sell more than 10 percent of what they make to foreigners—again, goods of all kinds, for both consumers and business, as well as services in areas like education, health care, finance, and tourism. (The resulting imbalance, equal to nearly 6 percent of the American economy's total output, is a recent development and, as the discussion below elaborates, a potentially dangerous one. The comparable deficit in relation to output is less than 3 percent for the United Kingdom and less than 1 percent for the countries in the Euro currency area combined; Canada and Japan both have sizeable surpluses.)

All this activity adds up to a total economic output of $42,000 for every person in the entire country, including both those who work and those who do not—to repeat, a higher average output and therefore income than in all but a few other independent political entities, and significantly higher than in any other sizeable country.[8] After allowance for differences in the cost of living, per capita income in the large continental European countries (France, Germany, and Italy) ranges from $28,800 to $30,500. In the United Kingdom it is $32,700, in Canada $32,200, and in Japan $31,400. All other sizeable countries around the world (population over 100 million) have even lower per capita incomes, in some cases far lower: Russia $10,600, Mexico $10,000, Brazil $8,200, China $6,600, Indonesia $3,700, India $3,500, Pakistan $2,400, Bangladesh $2,100, and Nigeria just $1,000. The only countries that come within even 15 percent of the American level are Luxembourg, Switzerland (with population 7.4 million, about the same as Virginia), and Norway (population 4.6 million, identical to Alabama).

With not only high per capita income but also the world's third-largest population, behind only China and India (and the European Union, if it were considered a single country for this purpose), the United States is also by some distance the world's largest economy, with total output in 2005 of $13 trillion.[9] When the economic output of other countries is simply valued in dollars at prevailing market exchange rates, the closest competitor to America in size is Japan, with $5 trillion in total output, followed by Germany with $2.9 trillion, and China with $2.3 trillion.[10] After allowing for differences in purchasing power from one country to another, however, China ranks second with output of $8.6 trillion, Japan third with $4.0 trillion, and India fourth with $3.8 trillion.

As is the case among the other advanced economies, however, America's rate of economic growth, in either per capita or absolute terms, is significantly below that of the more successful developing economies, and notably China and India. While the world's poor countries in general are not catching up with the rich ones, poor countries with successful economic development programs are doing just that. Between 1985 and 2005, American real output per capita increased by 2.0 percent per annum, compared to an 8.4 percent increase in China and 4.1 percent in India. (Between 1995 and 2005, the growth advantage was slightly narrower for China but wider for India: a 2.2 percent per annum increase in America versus 8.0 percent in China and 4.6 percent in India.) Moreover, these countries also have faster rates of population growth. While it will take them many years to catch up to American levels of output *per capita,* therefore, their economies will overtake America's in terms of sheer size of production within the foreseeable future. If each of the three countries' rates of population growth and per capita output growth continue along their respective trends of the last twenty years, then after allowing for differences in the cost of living China will become the world's largest economy by 2011, and India will achieve second place before midcentury.

Understanding America's Economic Prosperity

An economy can produce more than other economies because it employs more resources or because it uses them more efficiently. America's lead in per capita output results from both.

Understanding why America and today's other highly developed economies differ from newly developing ones is fairly straightforward. The most obvious differences include smaller shares of economic activity devoted to agriculture (typically just a few percent versus half or more in many poor countries) and correspondingly greater shares devoted to manufacturing and especially services; more highly educated populations; larger accumulations of plant and equipment; better infrastructure, such as roads and airport facilities; higher-level technology; more efficiently organized markets; and more effective government as well as more effective governance of private businesses, including in particular less corruption in both spheres.

The comparisons of greatest interest, therefore, are between the United States and other highly developed industrial and postindustrial economies: What features of America's economy enable it to produce so much more per person than France's, or Germany's, or Japan's? And why does America's economy exhibit these features more than others?

The answers differ from one country to another; there is enormous heterogeneity even among the handful of highest-income countries. One fairly consistent part of the story, however, is simply that Americans work more. Table 4.2 summarizes several key differences between work in the United States and work in the other six members of the traditional "G-7" group of countries. To begin, one potential advantage that America does *not* enjoy in this regard is demographic; the share of the American population that is of ordinary working age is about the same as it is on average in these six countries.[11] (By contrast, the share of the population age sixty-five and older is significantly smaller: just 12.3 percent in the United States versus 17.4 percent on average in the other G-7 countries.) But Americans nonetheless work more in two senses. Of those who are of normal working age, more are employed in paying jobs than is true on average in the other G-7 countries, and those who hold jobs put in more time working.

Three-fourths of all Americans ages fifteen to sixty-four are either employed or seeking work, modestly more than the average for the other G-7 countries.[12] Overall participation in the formal labor force in the United States has increased in recent decades, as the number of women choosing to work outside their homes has risen (and, in

Table 4.2   Relationship Between Output and Labor Input

	Output per Capita ($, PPP basis)	Share of Population Age 15-64 (percent)	Labor Force Participation (percent)	Unemployment (percent)	Hours Worked (per year)	Years of Education (years)	Output per Hour of Labor Input ($, EKS basis)
Canada	32,220	69.3	79.2	6.8	1,768	11.6	39.68
France	30,540	65.2	69.3	9.9	1,529	7.9	52.35
Germany	29,210	66.9	78.2	9.1	1,437	10.2	45.44
Italy	31,410	66.3	78.0	4.4	1,775	9.5	36.08
Japan	28,840	66.0	62.6	7.8	1,592	7.2	45.67
United Kingdom	32,690	66.1	76.0	4.8	1,624	9.4	45.09
Six-Country Average	30,818	66.6	73.9	7.1	1,621	9.3	44.05
United States	41,950	66.9	75.1	5.1	1,791	12.1	49.60

parallel, more career opportunities have become open to women) by more than enough to offset the tendency among men toward earlier retirement and therefore reduced labor force participation. These changes have been gradual, but over a period of decades the cumulative effect has been major. Compared to 75 percent today, the U.S. labor force participation rate averaged just under 72 percent in the mid-1990s and less than 68 percent in the mid-1980s. Before then, the overall participation rate rose even more rapidly.

In addition, Americans who want to work are actually doing so to a greater extent than on average in the other highly developed economies. Indeed, a striking characteristic of the American economy is how stable unemployment has been, as a share of the labor force, throughout the post–World War II era (and even well before, except for temporary fluctuations associated with the sometimes severe prewar business downturns). Apart from years during or immediately following recessions, the U.S. unemployment rate averaged 3.5 percent in the 1950s, 4.6 in the 1960s, 6.2 in the 1970s, 6.5 in the 1980s, and 5.2 in the 1990s. Since the 2001 recession ended, it has averaged 5.5 percent. Much of this gradual rise and subsequent fall has merely reflected the influence of demographic changes, as the effect of the postwar baby boom was first to increase and then to reduce the share of the overall labor force consisting of teenagers and other young, new entrants to the labor force (who are more likely than other workers to experience unemployment). By contrast, up until thirty or so years ago most western European countries enjoyed unemployment rates well below American levels—often as low as 1 to 2 percent—while today many countries in western Europe have unemployment rates at or near double digits. Even in Japan unemployment has evolved from always far below American levels (under 3 percent as recently as 1994) to a rate more comparable to America's in recent years.[13]

The combination, on average, of somewhat greater participation in the labor force and greater likelihood of having a job for those who do participate means that a significantly higher percentage of Americans age 15–64 are normally at work than is the case elsewhere: more than 71 percent among Americans versus less than 69 percent on average in the other G-7 countries. In addition, most American workers have shorter vacations (typically one or two weeks in the United States versus four in Germany and five in France, for example), take fewer paid holidays (typically twelve each year versus sixteen in both France and Germany), and work more days per week and longer hours during each working day, than do their counterparts abroad. As a result, the average American who has a job puts in 170 more hours each year, or over 10 percent more labor, than the average worker elsewhere in the G-7—the equivalent of an extra 5.5 weeks in each year.[14] The combination of a greater likelihood of having a job in the formal economy and the greater number of hours per person means that the amount of work Americans do in the formal economy, per person age 15–64, exceeds the average for the rest of the G-7 by 15 percent—nearly half the average 36 percent differential in per capita output.[15]

The *productivity* of American workers—how much each one produces in an hour's time on the job—is therefore also greater than that of workers in the other advanced economies, although less so than the simple difference in output would imply.[16] One influence that helps make American workers more productive, even compared to those in western Europe, is that they receive more schooling. On average Americans have nearly three more years of education than citizens of the other six G-7 countries.[17] In recent years, more than 90 percent of all young people in America, including resident non-Americans, have either graduated from high school or received a General Educational Development certificate, and nearly two-thirds of these go on to receive at least some college education by the age of twenty-five.[18] (Because many do so at two-year community colleges, however, and many of those who start at four-year institutions never finish, only 28 percent of Americans ever receive a bachelor's degree.) At the same time, the generalist nature of American education—in contrast to the vocational training emphasized in many European countries, often with students channeled into one educational track or another from very early ages—is also an advantage in an era when ever more economic activity, even in industries like manufacturing, requires adaptive cognitive skills.[19] (At the margin of new job creation today, one position in two involves using a computer keyboard.)

American workers also have the advantage of more capital with which to do their jobs. The $117,000 in plant and equipment that stands behind each worker in American private business well exceeds what workers in any of the other G-7 economies have. Table 4.3 summarizes how these differences join with the systematic

Table 4.3   Outputs, Inputs, and Total Factor Productivity

	United States (Index, U.S. = 100)	Average of Six Other G-7 Countries (Index, U.S. = 100)
Output per Capita	100.0	72.4
Input per Capita	100.0	73.8
Labor	100.0	80.2
Hours Worked	100.0	86.3
Labor Force Quality	100.0	92.5
Capital	100.0	67.9
Capital Stock	100.0	70.7
Capital Quality	100.0	105.8
IT Capital	100.0	43.8
Total Factor Productivity	100.0	98.3

differences in labor input to account for America's greater per capita output. Americans work more, in the sense of greater labor force participation and more hours on the job, as already shown in Table 4.2; and America also enjoys higher "labor force quality" as a result of more years of education. The combination of these three differences gives the United States a 25 percent advantage, on average, over the other six G-7 countries in effective labor input per person in the entire country.[20] But in addition, the United States enjoys an even greater average advantage—47 percent—in effective capital input per person.[21]

In most applications, especially in a modern economy, having the right capital is just as important as having enough capital. As Table 4.3 shows, America's capital stock is of modestly lower productive "quality" overall than on average in the other G-7 economies. (This is mostly because so much of the total stock of invested capital in the United States consists of residential housing.) But importantly, in light of how new developments in information technology during the last decade have helped foster productivity advances in many industries, IT investment has bulked much larger in American capital formation than in most other countries. More than one-third of total business investment in the United States now goes into information processing equipment and software. As a result, America has accumulated more than twice as much IT capital per person as in the average of other G-7 economies. This difference is consistent across all of the other six countries. Even Italy, which comes closest to the U.S. level in this regard, has just 52 percent as much IT capital per person.

Finally, some differences in what economies produce do not stem from either the quantity or the quality of their respective labor and capital inputs, but instead reflect their total factor productivity, or how productively an economy organizes and uses the total of all factors of production that it employs. Among the world's highly developed industrial and postindustrial economies, differences in total factor productivity are mostly small. Although these differences are notoriously difficult to measure, one careful attempt to do so (see again Table 4.3) concluded that America enjoys not even a 2 percent advantage, on average, over the other G-7 countries. Indeed, three of the six—Canada, France, and Italy—are modestly ahead of the United States in this regard. (In the case of France and Italy, however, the higher total factor productivity level may be mostly a consequence of labor market restrictions that keep many people, who would have low productivity if they were working, either unemployed or out of the labor force altogether.)[22]

Explaining Americans' Greater Work Effort

It is useful to know that the U.S. economy delivers a higher level of income per capita than in other countries mostly because Americans work more and have more and better capital behind them— and further, that these two sources of America's greater output per person are about equally important in explaining the resulting gap in per capita output. But these findings raise as many questions as they answer. Why do Americans work more than citizens of other countries? And what enables them not only to accumulate so much productive capital but also, leaving the housing stock aside, to allocate so well the plant and equipment that they accumulate?

A variety of institutional aspects of the American economy, many set by public policy, clearly contribute to these differences. First, the American workplace operates under far fewer restrictive requirements of the kind that make companies in Europe in particular reluctant to hire new workers. Rules governing what tasks which workers perform, what hours they may work, and under what circumstances their employers can reassign them or dismiss them altogether, are much less stringent in the United States. One effort to quantify how onerous such restrictions are, using a 1-to-20 scale for the restrictiveness of employment protection laws, puts

America at 1, Canada at 3, the United Kingdom at 7, Japan at 8, France at 14, Germany at 15, and Italy at 20.[23] In addition, labor unions are a far less influential force in the United States than in other countries. Today fewer than 13 percent of American workers belong to unions, and among private-sector workers the union share is less than 8 percent. On average in the other G-7 economies, the unionized share is 25 percent. The difference is even greater for the share of workers covered by collective bargaining arrangements: just 14 percent in America, versus more than half on average in the other G-7 countries (including more than 80 percent in Italy and more than 90 percent in France).[24]

Second, the income and other economic support that non-working citizens receive from their government is both less available and less generous in the United States than in most other advanced economies.[25] As a result, losing one's job is normally less financially burdensome elsewhere. American unemployment benefits typically replace 50 percent of a discharged worker's wage and last for six months after he or she loses a job. In France the replacement rate is 57 percent, and benefits last for three years; in Germany the replacement rate is 63 percent, and benefits last four years. (Italy is the only other G-7 country in which unemployment benefits have neither a higher replacement rate nor longer duration than in America.) The American welfare system, on which jobless citizens can fall back after unemployment benefits run out, is likewise less generous than in other advanced economies. Staying out of the labor force altogether for long periods of time, if not indefinitely, is therefore also much more difficult in the United States.

Third, income earned from working is typically taxed at lower rates in America than in most other advanced economies. More than three-fourths of all Americans who file tax returns face marginal income tax rates at the federal level of 15 percent or below, and for 95 percent the marginal rate is 25 percent or below.[26] In addition, most American workers pay a 6.2 percent payroll tax to the

Social Security old-age retirement system, and a further 1.45 percent to the Medicare old-age medical insurance system, in each case
matched by the employer. Residents of most states pay a further tax
on their incomes to their state government, and in some places also
to a city government. Even so—and despite the fact that most other
countries rely less on taxing incomes and more on taxing spending—
these successive layers of tax on labor income add up to a smaller
tax wedge between the cost of labor to the employer and what the
worker receives on a net basis than in any other G-7 country except
Japan. (The underlying reason is that a smaller share of economic
activity, including transfer payments, flows through government at
all levels in the United States.)

Economists and others disagree about how important these
lower tax rates are in encouraging Americans' work effort. Most estimates of the responsiveness of labor supply to tax rates in the
United States are small for "prime age" men because the only way
in which tax rates would matter for labor supply decisions of those
who are already employed, and are very likely to remain employed,
is for the choice of how many hours to work. Moreover, many
workers either do not have this choice at all, or get to exercise it
only within narrow limits. By contrast, married women, and both
men and women who are near the usual retirement age, exhibit
substantially greater sensitivity to tax rates in deciding whether to
take a job, or how early to retire.

An even broader question, likewise the subject of much disagreement, is whether Americans' greater work effort in the formal
labor force reflects an ordinary behavioral response to any or all of
these elements of the nation's work environment—more flexible
work rules, less generous government assistance, lower tax rates, and
the like—or instead stems from differences in people's underlying
preferences. Perhaps Americans simply place less value on leisure
time than do citizens of other countries. Or perhaps they prefer
meals at restaurants, which are part of measured national economic

output and are prepared and served by workers whose effort is part of the paid labor force, to meals at home. (On some estimates, as much as half of the measured difference in per capita income between America and the typical western European country would disappear if output were redefined to include meal preparation and similar work done at home.)

The distinction is not a mere matter of verbal classification. If underlying preferences are largely the same across advanced economies, so that what drives the observed differences in work effort and income levels among them is a behavioral response to identifiable elements of the environment, then a country that seeks a higher income level can achieve it by changing its work rules, or its welfare system, or its tax rates, or whatever the evidence identifies as the greatest existing impediment to higher per capita output. Much of the movement today for "structural reform" in Europe, for example, reflects just this line of thinking. But if the root of the observed differences is simply different preferences toward leisure versus consumption, or toward consumption of purchased goods and services versus those produced at home, then changing the relevant institutional arrangements is unlikely to affect outcomes significantly.

Even this way of thinking about the issue, however, implicitly assumes that institutions like work rules and welfare benefits and tax rates are simply imposed on an economy irrespective of the preferences of those who live and work in it. Especially in a democracy, these and other relevant aspects of a nation's economic institutions are themselves likely to reflect the preferences—not just the basic this-or-that choices, but the broadest aspirations and anxieties—of its citizens. And in this respect, the features that set America's economy apart from those of most of the other relatively high-income countries today are fully consistent with attitudes and patterns of behavior that Americans have exhibited virtually from the beginning. Visiting the United States in the early 1830s, long before institutions like work rules or welfare programs or income taxes even existed, Tocqueville commented at length on the "restlessness of temper" with which ordinary Americans went about their business. "It is strange," he remarked, "to see with what feverish ardor the Americans pursue their own welfare. . . . Everyone wants either to increase his own resources or to provide fresh ones for his progeny."[27]

Tocqueville attributed this phenomenon in turn to what he regarded as the most salient single characteristic of American society: the absence of defined political, social, and economic classes based on birth (his term was "equality of condition"). With limited opportunities for advanced education, or for scientific or other intellectual endeavor, and few leadership positions to be had in government or the military, economic success was the only route by which most people could achieve personal distinction. Further, since the earliest colonial time of Puritan influence, many Americans had attached religious significance to whatever activity enhanced the national wealth and contributed to the project of building a new nation, intended to be a "beacon" to all others, out of an untamed continent. The result was to transform the sense of opportunity that a classless society offered into a sense of obligation: in principle *any*one could get ahead economically, and so in practice *every*one felt obligated to strive toward that end. The same ethos continued to pervade American social writings for at least a century thereafter. In many respects, it still does. But whether Tocqueville's observation provides the explanation or not, it is clear that both Americans' greater effort in the paid workforce and the set of institutional arrangements that support and encourage it are coherent parts of an economic orientation that has characterized American society for a very long time.

Further Aspects of American Economic Advantage

Greater work effort is only part—on the current evidence, perhaps half—of the reason the American economy delivers greater per

capita output than those of other countries. Most prominently (see
again Table 4.3), America also has a large advantage in the accumulation of capital, especially IT capital, which in recent years has been
responsible for a sizeable part of the growth differential that has enabled America to pull even further ahead of most other advanced
economies. Between 1995 and 2005, output per hour of labor input
grew 0.8 percent per annum faster in America than on average in
the other G-7 countries, widening the productivity gap by a cumulative 9 percent over these ten years. One careful estimate attributes
0.4 percent per annum, half of this differential, to America's superior
capital accumulation during this period, and nearly three-fourths of
that to accumulation of IT capital alone.[28]

An economy could obviously accumulate more capital if people
saved more of their incomes. In fact, however, America's saving rate
is not only far below that of most developing countries but lower
than in any other country in the G-7. Even including saving that
merely finances the investment needed to replace physical capital
that wears out or becomes obsolete, the saving done by all American
families and American business firms combined, less the saving that
the government deficit absorbs, amounts to 13 percent of the nation's total income. Elsewhere among the G-7, the gross national
saving rate is 15 percent in the United Kingdom, 18 percent in France,
20 percent in Italy, 21 percent in Germany, 24 percent in Canada,
and 26 percent in Japan.[29]

In recent years, the United States has supplemented the country's domestic saving by borrowing heavily from abroad. Because
foreign producers expect to be paid for the goods and services that
they sell to American purchasers, the counterpart of the large imbalance between U.S. imports and U.S. exports is the accumulation of
either foreign-owned assets in the United States (over and above assets that Americans own abroad) or debts owed to foreigners by
American borrowers (over and above the debts that foreigners owe
to American lenders). But even this historically unprecedented net

borrowing from abroad leaves America's total domestic-plus-foreign saving, in relation to the size of American economic output, no larger than national saving in most other advanced economies. In 2006, U.S. net foreign borrowing amounted to a record 6.2 percent of U.S. national income—barely enough to boost domestic-plus-foreign saving to about the level of the national saving rate in most continental European countries. On average during the past ten years, U.S. net foreign borrowing has been 4.4 percent of the national income, a dangerously high level but still one that left the total amount of saving smaller in proportion to the economy's size than is typically true in other high-income countries.

The more significant advantage that America enjoys in support of investment in the economy is a set of richly developed institutions for gathering funds from either households or business firms that have income in excess of their current spending needs, and then allocating it among other households and firms (and government at all levels, too) that need funds in order to spend in excess of their current income. Financial markets in the United States have at least three related advantages compared to those in other countries. First, while banks play a significant role in America as well as elsewhere, the U.S. financial system is oriented around non-bank capital markets to a far greater extent than in any other large economy except in some respects the United Kingdom. As Table 4.4 shows, banking activity in America is distinctly smaller in relation to the nation's non-financial economy than elsewhere, and what stands out instead is the much greater role played by the markets for debt and equity securities issued by the private sector.[30] (Many other countries have large markets for government debt, but these typically have little to do with channeling funds to private-sector uses.) In both the bond market and the equity market, the volume of outstanding securities is larger compared to the size of the economy in America, and so is the volume of new funds raised each year.

Table 4.4   Banking System and Capital Markets

	Banking System		Equity Market			Bond Market		
	Bank Assets (% of GDP)	Total Deposits (% of GDP)	Equity Market Capitalization (% of GDP)	Annual Equity Trading Volume (% of GDP)	Equity Trans-action Costs (percent)	Value of Private Bonds Outstanding (% of GDP)	Annual New Bond Issues (% of GDP)	Bond Bid-Ask spread (basis points)
Canada	79.3	74.6	120.2	66.7	5.3	20.3	9.8	70
France	106.2	67.0	92.7	65.5	3.9	44.3	9.4	30
Germany	139.7	96.2	44.0	51.8	5.3	38.9	15.7	20
Italy	101.1	52.6	47.2	48.1	1.5	47.9	8.1	30
Japan	138.5	120.8	79.6	74.2	3.2	43.3	3.5	50
United Kingdom	147.8	115.3	131.5	171.2	6.3	16.0	11.6	40
Six-Country Average	118.8	87.8	85.9	79.6	4.3	35.1	9.7	40
United States	46.3	59.2	139.9	165.9	1.3	111.8	11.0	less than 10

Along with the much larger size of the U.S. economy, these proportionally greater roles for the bond and equity markets also make American capital markets far larger, and therefore more efficient, than those of other countries. Initial public offerings (IPOs), for example—shares issued by companies that are coming to the publicly traded equity market for the first time—are especially important in providing funds for new, innovative companies capable of pushing out the frontier of economic technology. In recent years, the information technology industry has been the source of much of America's advantage in productivity gains (see again Table 4.3), and it has benefited particularly from access to equity financing via IPOs. In 2004, the American IPO market provided a total of $45 billion in net financing to new firms, more than in the six other G-7 countries combined. As Table 4.4 further shows, transaction costs are also distinctly smaller in America, in both the bond and the equity markets.

Second, along with the greater relative role of capital markets as opposed to reliance on banks, American financial markets are widely diversified in terms of the different kinds of participating financial institutions, as well as highly decentralized in their decision making. Individual investors, mutual funds, both life and casualty insurance companies, pension funds sponsored by either corporations or state and local governments, venture capital firms, bank trust departments, private equity firms, endowments held by universities and private charitable foundations, and countless other institutions as well all bring different investment objectives and different sets of interests and skills to the marketplace. This vast heterogeneity of investment ideas and possibilities for allocating capital to different kinds of business applications is significantly greater than in other countries' markets. And, again in part as a result of the economy's size, so is the sheer number of investing institutions. American markets are also more decentralized, with less concentration of investment decisions among just the few largest firms in any given category. (This pattern is true within the banking system, too; despite the wave of bank consolidation over the last decade and a half, there are still more than 7,300 commercial banks in the United States.)

Third, along with this greater diversification, American financial markets also attract far wider public participation than do comparable markets elsewhere. Today 49 percent of all American families own common stocks, either directly or via mutual funds or individual retirement accounts, with a median family holding of more than $24,000 at market value.[31] Apart from mutual fund holdings, these investments are typically not very diversified. More than a third of the families that own stocks directly own only one company's stock, and nearly three-fifths own stock in three companies or fewer.[32] This profusion of individual investors not only furthers the market's decentralization of decision making—anyone who thinks he spots a good business prospect can readily invest in it—but also contributes to the sense of the market as a generator of wealth in which a broad cross section of the public has an interest (despite the fact that ownership is sufficiently concentrated that just 1 percent of the shareholders own half of the market value in individual hands).[33]

While these characteristics of America's financial markets may be in part the product of cultural traditions—the United Kingdom and other countries of British colonial origin are clearly the most similar in this respect—here, too, various elements of public policy have also been important in creating an environment in which widely decentralized capital markets with broad public participation can flourish. Since the 1930s, the Securities and Exchange Commission (SEC) has established and enforced regulations governing the public issuance and trading of securities in the United States. Further, under the authority of the SEC, privately held securities exchanges (most prominently the New York Stock Exchange, but others as well) serve as self-regulatory bodies for many of these purposes. Likewise, the accounting profession operates under a combination of government-imposed and self-regulation, as does the legal profession. The result is to give investors confidence that firms' financial statements and other claims made by either firms issuing new securities or underwriters acting in their behalf, as well as claims made by brokers dealing in securities in the secondary market, are seldom fraudulent, and that the market prices of shares are not regularly manipulated. Similar laws and regulations govern the conduct of mutual funds, insurance companies, pension funds, and other institutions that serve as conduits for investing individuals' assets on a collective basis. Since 1970, the Securities Investors Protection Corporation (SIPC), a private entity created and sponsored by the federal government, has also insured most brokerage accounts against losses due to fraud or other malfeasance at brokerage firms, or to the business failure of a brokerage firm itself. Under the SIPC, 99 percent of all eligible investors have been reimbursed in full for any losses under these circumstances.

The U.S. government has also encouraged participation in the securities markets by establishing tax-advantaged vehicles at both the institutional and individual levels. The pension industry, for example, is in part the product of arrangements that give both employees and employers an incentive to channel part of workers' total compensation into these funds rather than into current take-home pay. At the individual level, the greatest boost to financial market participation in recent decades has been the establishment, in 1978, of tax-advantaged 401(k) plans (named for the section of the federal revenue code under which they operate) into which individual employees can direct some percentage of their pay, typically with the further advantage of matching funds from the employer. Fifty percent of all American families now have one or more qualified retirement accounts, either a 401(k) plan or in some other form, with a median value of $35,000 (including not only stocks, as described above, but bonds, money market funds, and other assets).[34] Further, any 401(k) plan must offer participating employees a variety of investment options, typically including at least one money market fund, several bond mutual funds with differing maturities (and perhaps different average credit risk), and several equity mutual funds with differing investment strategies.

The role of government in requiring disclosure, providing prudential supervision and regulation, and insuring the assets of individual participants in the capital markets also extends to the banking system. Commercial banks in the United States, as well as other depository institutions like mutual savings banks and savings and loan associations, do business under charters issued by either the federal government or the respective states, and the prevailing system of supervision and regulation is implemented at both levels (and, at the federal level, by several different agencies). Banks face accounting and disclosure requirements and restrictions on the investment risks they may take, just as capital market firms do. U.S. law also imposes a separation of banking and commerce, as well as a separation of deposit-taking and capital market investments, so as to protect depositors from exposure to business risk. In addition, the Federal Deposit Insurance Corporation insures each depositor's assets, in each institution, up to the amount of $100,000. In large part because of this network of supervision, regulation, and insurance, bank runs of the kind that historically have often disrupted financial markets to the extent of imposing serious costs on many countries' economies (including the United States in episodes such as 1873, 1895, 1907, 1913, and especially the Great Depression of 1929–1933) have become virtually non-existent in America.

Further, at times when the failure of a large institution, or a sharp decline in prices, threatens to disrupt the functioning of financial markets more broadly, government authorities in the United States often intervene to stabilize them. Recent examples of such occasions for intervention include the failure of virtually all major banks in Texas when world oil prices declined in 1986; the stock market crash on October 19, 1987; the cumulative collapse of the savings and loan industry, and parts of the banking industry, in the northeast and California in the latter years of that decade; the collapse of the Mexican peso and subsequent bailout of that country's government in 1994–1995; the spillover from the Asian financial crisis of 1997; the collapse of Long Term Capital Management (a firm operating outside the reach of the ordinary prudential regulation) in 1998; and the terrorist attacks of September 11, 2001. All led to prompt but irregular intervention by the U.S. Treasury, the SEC, and above all the nation's central bank, the Federal Reserve System.

Especially for the Federal Reserve, this flexible approach to dealing with necessities as they arise in order to prevent potentially destabilizing shocks from carrying the day is of a piece with the American central bank's broader mission. Established in 1914 in response to the banking crises and consequent business downturns of 1907 and 1913, the Federal Reserve was initially charged to "provide an elastic currency"—that is, to meet the demand for liquidity, however large it became in times of trouble, in order to keep the banking system in operation. Over the years, as central banks around the world (and economists and others who studied them) became aware of the potential influence of central bank actions not just within the financial system but more broadly in the economy, the Federal Reserve, too, came to see "monetary policy" as a key tool for steering aggregate economic activity, importantly including prices. Unlike many other central banks today, however, which either have adopted a formal inflation-targeting regime (for example, in the United Kingdom, Canada, Sweden, and many other countries) or pursue a policy that clearly establishes low inflation as the primary monetary policy objective (for example, the European Central Bank), America's central bank continues to pursue *both* price stability *and* full employment as equal objectives: the prevailing legislation charges the Federal Reserve "to promote effectively the goals of maximum employment" and "stable prices."

It is impossible to know just how great a role the central bank's sense of responsibility for maintaining non-financial economic activity has played in bringing about the American economy's recent impressive stability—to recall, only two recessions during the last quarter-century, both brief in duration and mild in magnitude—and growth performance, compared to the influence of other factors (including plain good luck). But to the extent that both the central bank and other relevant agencies of American government have this orientation, and to the extent that investors in the financial markets and business managers evaluating new investments or expansion of their companies' operations have confidence that these agencies will act on it, the result is also an investment and business environment that encourages making greater use of an economy's existing resources and undertaking the initiative necessary to create new ones for future growth.

Challenges

To sketch the successes and relative advantages of the American economic system is not to overlook its failures, nor to claim that the nation's economic future will be without pitfalls. Americans have suffered economic misfortunes in the past, and no doubt will again, although some mistakes, like the passive and even perverse response of monetary and other economic policies to the cataclysm of the 1930s, are unlikely to be repeated. Like any other human enterprise, a national economy inevitably faces challenges. In America's case many of these are small in scale and likely to be transient. A few, however, are more fundamental and likely to loom large in the economy's future development.

One significant challenge is demographic. Although America enjoys a greater natural rate of population growth than in most other high-income economies, as well as the advantage of a significantly more open stance toward immigration, the aftermath of the post–World War II baby boom will nonetheless be problematic. At the turn of the new century, one American in eight was sixty-five or older. By 2025, one in six will be. Today, Social Security, the government pension program for the retired elderly, has one beneficiary for every 3.3 workers contributing to the system via payroll taxes. Under current legislation, by 2030 there will be one beneficiary for every 2.2 workers. The same adverse demographics will likewise affect Medicare, the government health insurance program for the elderly population, even as industry-specific economic factors and changing medical technology continue to boost the cost of care on a per-person basis. Without either fundamental changes to these programs or large amounts of additional financing, the result will almost surely be an increase in federal government borrowing sufficient to impair America's ability to invest in productive new capital formation.

A potentially more acute problem in the short term is the current trade deficit—and, correspondingly, the large annual net accumulation of debt owed to foreign lenders. From the perspective of non-financial economic activity, eliminating the gap between imports and exports will require either increasing what the American economy produces or reducing what Americans consume and invest by an amount equal to approximately 6 percent of the national income. With the economy's labor and capital resources already relatively fully employed, making this large adjustment any time soon would mean doing so primarily by reducing consumption, and especially investment. But extending the time over which the adjustment takes place would prolong the rapid buildup of America's foreign indebtedness (both in absolute dollar terms and relative to the size of the American economy). Meanwhile, the continuing imbalance renders the American financial markets vulnerable to disruption in the event that the foreign investors who are currently absorbing ever larger amounts of dollar assets (currently more than $2 billion per day) choose to allocate their portfolios differently.

The greatest economic challenge America now faces is to restore the relationship between productivity gains and improvement in incomes and living standards for the broad majority of the American people. After all, an economy is not an independent activity in which a nation engages for its own sake, but rather the means by which its citizens satisfy one key aspect of their most fundamental needs and desires. Historically, America's economy has succeeded in this dimension to a greater extent than just about anywhere else. More recently, however, the impressive advances in the economy's productivity, and hence in output growth, have not accrued to the advantage of the majority of American workers and families—not even those in the top quintile of the income distribution.

Since 2000, the median income among American families has consistently lagged behind rising prices, and only those who are already at the top of the income scale have experienced any improvement. Although output per hour of labor input in the economy's non-farm business sector rose on average by 3.1 per annum between 2000 and 2005, and total economic output expanded by 2.4 percent per annum after allowing for rising prices, the income of the median American family was only $56,200 in 2005, versus $57,500 (in 2005 dollars) five years earlier. For families in the bottom quintile, the average income fell from $16,000 to $14,800. Even in the top quintile, average income declined from $177,900 to $176,300.[35]

The resulting problem is not so much increasing inequality per se—although inequality is clearly increasing—but rather the fact that although the American economy is moving forward, most Americans are not. If aggregate income were increasing much more rapidly, so that most citizens were getting ahead but those at the top were getting ahead faster, as is the case today in China, for example, the matter would be less problematic. But an already highly advanced economy like America's is unlikely to achieve a growth rate comparable to China's.

This situation differs sharply from what America has experienced throughout most of the nation's past. At times when productivity gains were strong, and the economy as a whole moved forward rapidly—the middle of the nineteenth century, for example, or the early decades of the twentieth, or the quarter-century immediately following World War II, or most recently the mid to latter years of the 1990s—the bulk of the population likewise enjoyed rising incomes and improving living standards. Conversely, when productivity gains slowed, or the economy faltered for other reasons—in the late nineteenth century, during much of the period between the two World Wars, and for roughly two decades running from the early 1970s to the early 1990s—the public at large naturally saw little increase. What is different today is that both aggregate economic activity and productivity are increasing at a rate that is certainly acceptable for a mature postindustrial economy (although improvements here, too, would of course be welcome), while the living standard of the majority of the country's citizens is stagnating.

The reasons for the widening gap in incomes are many and varied: rapidly evolving new technology that places a premium on the skills some workers bring to the labor market while significantly reducing the demand for others, competition from the world's newly industrializing countries together with further technological developments that are opening an ever broader array of goods and services to international trade, corporate governance practices that increasingly reserve historically extraordinary rewards for managers as distinct from either owners or the workforce at large, and the disproportionate share of low-skilled workers in America's immigration inflow (especially among illegal immigrants), to name just a few. Unraveling the relative importance of each of these diverse influences, and others besides, is a daunting task. Devising effective responses, both within the realm of private-sector action and by public policy, is perhaps even more so.[36]

The chief lesson of history, however, at least in this regard, is that the American economic system rises to the challenges it faces.

CHAPTER 5

Federalism

Martha Derthick

With a federal system founded on separate sovereignties, the United States has a long history of decentralized government. Since the 1930s much centralization has occurred, but fifty state governments and thousands of their local subdivisions retain large responsibilities for education, law enforcement, land-use regulation, transportation, and much of health care. Political scientist Martha Derthick explains why the states don't die.

THE FEDERAL SYSTEM OF THE UNITED STATES WAS CONSTRUCTED in the eighteenth century from the bottom up, on a foundation of thirteen British colonies. Today, contrary to historical tradition, officeholders in the national government increasingly attempt to direct it from the top down. It has become common in the United States to refer to "the government" as if there were only one—the national government—but this ignores the fact that the U.S. Census Bureau counts 87,000 units of government, of which 50, relatively a very large number, are states—the constitutionally protected, decentralized members of the federal system—and 39,000 are general-purpose local governments.[1]

Students of American federalism typically remark on the chaos of this scene. Despite many decades of centralizing change, the thousands of state and local governments retain large responsibilities

The author thanks Timothy Conlan, John Dinan, and Richard P. Nathan, as well as editors Schuck and Wilson, for helpful comments.

for domestic functions, including education, law enforcement, regulation of land use, health care and social services, pollution control, and transportation. Decentralization in the United States thus contrasts both with unitary governments and with the federal states of continental Europe, which, with the exception of Switzerland, tend to treat federalism as a form of decentralized unitary government rather than as a product of formerly separate sovereigns.[2]

The United States resembles federal Australia in having a historically decentralized system that has become more centralized over time. It is less centralized than its federal neighbor to the south, Mexico; but more centralized than its federal neighbor to the north, Canada, whose strong provincial governments are better able to counterbalance Ottawa than states of the United States are able to stand up to Washington. Today's United States has no counterpart to Canada's francophone Quebec, which periodically threatens dissolution of the Canadian federation.

Origins: Building from the Bottom Up

Following their declaration of independence from Great Britain, the former colonists first attempted to govern themselves through the Articles of Confederation, under which the several members came together in a Continental Congress but retained sovereignty. The statesmen of the fledgling nation concluded that this form of government could not provide defense against foreign enemies, raise revenue, maintain domestic order, or promote commerce. Alexander Hamilton, an impassioned young genius from New York, denounced the "degeneracy" of the Congress and pushed for something better.[3]

Assembling in Philadelphia in 1787 to improve on the Articles, the Framers of the U.S. Constitution invented a new form of government that was neither unitary nor purely federal. James Madison, who joined Hamilton in forming this government, called it "compound" because it combined characteristics of both.[4] The Framers created a national government, endowed with only specified powers, whose laws would be supreme, but they did not abolish the states. They created a bicameral national legislature consisting of the House of Representatives, in which the people are represented directly, proportionate to their number in each state, and an upper house, the Senate, in which each state has two members. Initially, senators were chosen by the state legislatures. Since 1913 they have been popularly elected, but the fact that states of widely varying populations—ranging from Wyoming's 499,000 to California's 35 million in 2000—are equally represented, is a potent reminder that a federal principle is embodied in the U.S. Constitution. And unlike most upper houses in federal systems, the Senate is a potent legislative body.

The compromise of 1787 was indispensable to a successful outcome. The states were unwilling to give up their independence altogether, and the great diversity among them, above all the difference between the slaveholding South and the free labor North, made a complete consolidation impossible. The new form elicited admiration and emulation in other countries, especially the fledgling South American republics, as they secured independence from Spain in the nineteenth century.[5] In the United States the form has proved highly adaptable, not to say protean, and there is no disposition to discard it. It is, however, a very confusing form of government, with authority widely diffused and obscurely allocated. And it requires much tending. Issues of intergovernmental relations consume a great deal of official attention, including that of the Supreme Court. That the Court has been the umpire of the federal system is one of the sources of its preeminence in American government.

The Experiment with Dual Federalism

In *The Federalist,* Hamilton and Madison advocated adoption of the new government and claimed that it could not be deemed national "since its jurisdiction extends to certain enumerated objects only, and leaves to the several States a residuary and inviolable sovereignty over all other objects."[6] This core principle was embodied in the Tenth Amendment to the Constitution: "The powers not delegated to the United States by the Constitution, nor prohibited by it to the States, are reserved to the States respectively, or to the people." For much of its history the United States struggled to honor this principle. Doing so, however, was never easy because the powers granted to the national government were expressed in elastic terms, and the early Supreme Court under Chief Justice John Marshall (1801–1835) interpreted them expansively.

Later courts would labor to draw a line between powers of the national government and of the states in order to sustain what scholars came to call "dual federalism."[7] This doctrine held that within their respective spheres, the national and state governments were separate and sovereign. It also presumed that conflict between them was normal, and that the function of the Supreme Court as arbiter was to forestall or resolve the conflict with line drawing. Particularly in commerce clause cases, this line drawing was often tortured, entailing strained distinctions between the production of goods and their movement in commerce, as well as between "direct" and "indirect" effects on commerce.

The doctrine could be found in vivid form in such decisions as *Collector v. Day,* in which the Supreme Court ruled in 1871 that the federal government could not tax the salary of a local judge because he was a state officer; the *Civil Rights Cases* in 1883, which struck down congressional enactments regulating private conduct because they invaded the domain of local jurisprudence; and *Hammer v. Dagenhart,* which ruled in 1918 that Congress could not forbid the shipment in interstate commerce of the products of child labor because to do so encroached upon state authority.[8]

More consequential than the abstract struggles of the justices in establishing the decentralization of American government was the early shaping of domestic institutions. Although states were the core polities in constitutional theory, it was their local subdivisions—counties, municipalities, townships—that in the nineteenth century performed the bedrock public functions of road-building, poor relief, criminal justice, and schooling. They did so within a framework of law created by the states, whose legal creatures they are, but state governments at first did not supervise them closely. "Our local areas are not *governed,*" Woodrow Wilson wrote as a political scientist in 1898. "They act for themselves. . . . The large freedom of action and broad scope of function given to local authorities is the distinguishing characteristic of the American system of government."[9]

At the turn of the twentieth century, local governments were raising more revenue, doing more spending, and had more debt than the federal and state governments combined. In 1902, the debt of local governments, at $1.8 billion, was eight times that of state governments and $700 million greater than that of the federal government.[10] This situation was slow to change, even as state governments assumed more financial and supervisory functions in the twentieth century. As late as 1960, public social welfare in the United States was financed more by state and local governments (52.3 percent) than by the federal government (47.7 percent).[11] State spending for elementary and secondary education did not pass local spending until the 1970s, and as of 2002–2003, federal government spending was still less than 9 percent of the total.

Decentralization endured for a number of reasons. The social and economic differences among states and regions that underlay federalism at the founding persisted. The Civil War established that states do not have a right to secede, but rather than bringing the South into the union socially, it left the defeated states deeply damaged both physically and psychologically. Though freed from slavery, blacks remained oppressed and segregated, and much of the southern population was impoverished. The South was, for decades, an underdeveloped, third-world country within the larger, more prosperous whole.

Neither of the major political parties became an integrative force. The Democratic Party, dominant in the South, became the party of states' rights, while the Republican Party, the party of Lincoln and the Union, failed in its post–Civil War attempt to form a biracial coalition in the South and maintain a presence there. The populace retained a strong attachment to local government, creating a presumption against centralization. Within Congress centralizers bore a heavy burden of proof. A Senate staff member, working to achieve federal aid to elementary and secondary education in the 1960s, incredulously described the opposition that he was encountering:

> [T]hey clung on to some mythical constitutional principle: the last thing that could happen in the United States was for the federal hand to be laid on local education, which belongs to the hands of the school boards and local council of education or whatever they're called—which, of course, are all controlled by the Chamber of Commerce. . . . Now what all this was supposed to prevent or forestall I could never figure out, but it was a religious faith. They'd get white and scream and wave their hands in the air about the *horrible* prospects of this vicious, cold hand of federal bureaucracy being laid upon these pristine, splendid local schools that knew better than anyone what needed to be done, and so forth and so forth. . . . I don't know, it's a real mythology, but it was real and senators and congressmen had to deal with it.[12]

In world politics, the isolation of the United States until World War II and then the cold war with the Soviet Union limited external pressure for centralization of government. The tradition of local government was a luxury that could be indulged through many decades of relative peace and security. The country's only total war until World War II was the Civil War, whose potential centralizing effects, even though embodied in amendments to the Constitution, were compromised by the ensuing failure of reconstruction in the South. The Fourteenth Amendment, adopted in 1868, provided that "no State shall . . . deprive any person of life, liberty, or property, without due process of law; nor deny to any person within its jurisdiction the equal protection of the laws." The Fifteenth Amendment, approved two years later, prohibited denial of the right to vote on grounds of race. In the twentieth century these amendments would become the instruments for a recasting of federal-state relations, but in the short run, because none of the defeated southern states was abolished, the war's outcome could be interpreted as a confirmation of American federalism. In an 1869 case that raised the issue of whether Texas, which had seceded and had not yet been readmitted to the union, could bring a suit in federal courts, the Supreme Court asserted that the Constitution created "an indestructible Union, composed of indestructible States."[13]

The Fall of Dual Federalism and the Rise of Mandates

In the half century spanning from the start of Franklin Roosevelt's presidency in 1933 to that of Ronald Reagan in 1981, the federal system was drastically transformed. A presumption that the domestic sphere of government belonged primarily to the states—and that even in the regulation of commerce, an exclusive state sphere should be preserved—died. And as barriers to the scope of federal government activity fell, so did corresponding barriers to the federal government's regulation of state and local government conduct.

For much of American history, the state governments enjoyed immunity, as putative sovereigns, from affirmative federal government commands. As late as 1954, Henry M. Hart, a professor of constitutional law at Harvard, could write that, although federal law often imposed prohibitions on the states, it rarely went beyond that to say what they must do. Hart claimed that *Kentucky v. Dennison,* a Supreme Court decision of 1861 holding "that the Federal Government, under the Constitution, has no power to impose on a State officer, as such, any duty whatsoever, and compel him to perform it," was still good law.[14] The Supreme Court formally overruled *Kentucky v. Dennison* in 1987, but long before then the precept enunciated by the Court and by Hart had collapsed in a wave of statutory and judicial commands to the state governments.

The first of these two transformations dates from the Great Depression and the New Deal. In response to a catastrophic economic collapse, the Roosevelt presidency advanced and Congress enacted radical new laws to regulate production, prices, and wages in manufacturing, mining, and agriculture. At first the Supreme Court struck several of these laws down, but then it executed a famous reversal and began deferring to the political branches. A new constitutional law emerged after 1937 that swept away previous limits on Congress's power to regulate commerce and solidified its power to tax and spend for any purpose associated with the general welfare. In *U.S. v. Darby,* which in 1941 upheld a law that regulated the wages and hours of private employees, the Court overruled *Hammer v. Dagenhart* and dismissed claims of state prerogative by saying that the Tenth Amendment was "but a truism."[15]

From the states' standpoint, the most portentous of the New Deal laws was the Social Security Act of 1935, the charter of the American welfare state, which in its various titles created old-age insurance, an exclusively national program; grants to state governments for assistance to several categories of the poor (the aged, the blind, and dependent children); and a complex program of unemployment compensation that imposed a tax on employers but allowed it to be offset by state taxes for a comparable purpose. This gave state governments an incentive to create unemployment programs, which they did after the Supreme Court in 1937 upheld this title.

The constitutional revolution of the New Deal was not entirely disadvantageous to the state governments. Some of the economic regulation that the Court now permitted was regulation that they enacted. The Court's famous switch first became manifest in *West Coast Hotel Company v. Parrish* (1937), in which it upheld the constitutionality of a Washington State minimum wage law for women. The Social Security Act had ambiguous implications. On one hand, along with other New Deal statutes, it demonstrated that the states could no longer lay claim to an exclusive, sovereign sphere. Poor relief had previously been a function exclusively of state and local governments and private charities. Now it would be shared. But the sharing was testimony to the durability of federalism, and much would henceforth depend on the sharing's terms, which initially were not onerous. Congress dropped an administration proposal from the public assistance titles that would have required the states to pay "a reasonable subsistence compatible with decency and health." This could have opened the door to federal determination of the size of payments. Instead, the public assistance titles were framed so as to leave discretion with the states: "for the purpose of enabling each State to furnish financial assistance, as far as practicable under the conditions in each State."[16]

Federal grants–in–aid to the states, an important instrument of intergovernmental relations, were not a New Deal invention. Large grants of land had been made to the states in the nineteenth century, and they took a more modern form in 1862 with the Morrill Act, which gave land on condition that states use the proceeds to create colleges of agriculture and the mechanic arts. Morrill was a Republican senator from Vermont, elected in the very first election in which Republican candidates ran, and a merchant-turned-farmer who believed that agriculture could be improved by scientific education. His bill passed Congress in 1859 but was vetoed by President James Buchanan largely on federalism grounds. Buchanan said that instead of the financial operations of the federal governments being kept distinct, as good statesmanship required, they would be "confusedly" mixed. The law would also set a bad precedent: once the states got into the habit of receiving federal aid, they would continually ask for it. Moreover, the federal government had no constitutional power to enforce application of the grant to its intended purpose. Buchanan, as a sympathizer with the slaveholding South on the eve of the Civil War, is one of the least respected of American presidents, but to read his veto message in a modern light is to conclude that, as an analyst of federalism, he was not a fool.[17]

President Lincoln signed Morrill's bill, and in 1923 a unanimous Supreme Court turned aside a challenge from Massachusetts to a law that gave conditional grants to the states for maternal and child health. Massachusetts claimed that the law induced states to yield sovereign rights reserved to them. The Court held that the states' choice to accept the grants was voluntary and that there was no deprivation of a right that fell within judicial cognizance. Thus, the use of grants-in-aid in the Social Security Act of 1935 was not constitutionally problematic.

The second transformation of American federalism took place in the 1960s and 1970s, in connection with a civil rights revolution and Great Society legislation advanced by President Lyndon B. Johnson. It was more profound and sweeping than the New Deal revolution. After the New Deal, it was no longer possible to view the state governments as separate and sovereign. After the 1960s, they would be subordinate and inferior.

Courts were instrumental in this change. The Supreme Court's part in the revolution of the 1930s had been to retreat from legislative review. In the second federalism revolution it emerged as a reformer, and the institutions it chose to change were those of state governments. The peak of the Court's activism occurred under Chief Justice Earl Warren (1953–1969).[18]

Religious practices had been common in American public schools. Seeking to enforce separation between church and state, the

Warren Court struck down non-denominational prayer readings in a case from New York (1962), reading from the Bible in a case from Pennsylvania (1963), and required recitation of the Lord's Prayer in a case from Maryland (1963).

With respect to criminal procedure, the Court virtually rewrote the laws of the states to make them conform to its understanding of the Bill of Rights of the U.S. Constitution. Among leading cases were those that applied Fourth Amendment protections against searches and seizures to state trials, eliminated coerced statements of incrimination from state trials, and required a series of warnings that police must give to persons whom they had taken into custody.

Historically reluctant to enter the "political thicket" of defining representative districts for Congress and the state legislatures, which was a prerogative of state legislatures, the Court now rendered a series of major decisions announcing a strict rule of proportionality—one person, one vote. This had sweeping effects on the design of districts for the House of Representatives and both the upper and lower houses of state legislatures, though none on the Senate, wherein equal representation for each state is prescribed by the Constitution. State legislatures, in which rural areas had historically been overrepresented, had often emulated the U.S. Constitution by basing representation in one house on counties, which are units of government. The Court said that was impermissible.

Also of utmost consequence for federalism were the Court's decisions commanding an end to racial segregation of southern schools, followed by affirmative commands to achieve racial integration in the North as well as the South. As the Court struggled to overcome resistance, its decrees became steadily more detailed and prescriptive. They included mandatory busing of pupils in major metropolitan areas. Desegregation by judicial decree, the constitutional scholar Archibald Cox observed in 1975, required courts to formulate "controversial programs of affirmative action requiring detailed administration for protracted periods under constant judicial supervision."[19]

The federal courts' pursuit of school desegregation had consequences beyond the schools. The techniques of judicial policymaking that were developed in these cases soon spread across a range of state and local government functions, in lawsuits that are variously called "structural reform," "institutional" litigation, or "public law" litigation. Such litigation is not mere dispute resolution in individual cases, but seeks systematic remedies that affect large-scale organizations. Typically a court issues an injunction that requires affirmative steps to prevent constitutional violations from occurring. There is often judicial monitoring of agency conduct over a long period of time.[20]

The bureaucracies typically subjected to such "monitoring"—in truth, such judicial rule making—are the prisons and mental hospitals as well as the schools run by state and local governments. Federal judicial decrees have ruled prisons in 41 states and local jails in 50 states.[21] As of 2004, 358 school districts were still operating under desegregation decrees.

The federalism revolution of the 1960s was not the work of the federal judiciary alone. Congress similarly devised bold new techniques of supervision and command.

Historically, Congress had drawn a sharp distinction between state governments and private entities, refraining from regulation of the former in recognition of their status as sovereigns. For example, starting in 1938 Congress had regulated wages and hours in much of the private economy, but did not initially cover state and local government workers. It began to do so selectively in 1966 and finished the job by covering them all in 1974. In 1972 it prohibited job discrimination by state and local government on the basis of race, color, religion, sex, and national origin, extending prohibitions that it had imposed on private employers in 1964. A law of 1974 prohibited age discrimination in state and local government employment, which means, for example, that the public universities of the states cannot require tenured professors to retire at a stipulated age.

Congress also began to use grant-in-aid programs more aggressively, multiplying their number and elaborating the conditions that were attached. Traditionally, grants had been proffered on permissive terms, to induce states to undertake activities that members of Congress such as Morrill wished to promote. Typically states had to prepare plans for carrying out the aided function, and a federal agency had to approve the plans. In its grant programs, the federal government paid particular attention to the professional qualifications of state and local personnel, seeking to substitute merit system requirements for the use of political patronage. To enforce such standards, federal administrative agencies relied on threats to withhold funds, which had limited credibility because withholding was both inherently self-defeating and controversial in Congress, whose members came to the defense of threatened constituencies.

Congress in the 1960s and 1970s began to reach more deeply into the conduct of state and local government with the purpose of reordering local social and political structures. A leading instance was Title VI of the Civil Rights Act of 1964, which denied aid to states that engaged in racial discrimination. When combined with enactment of federal aid to elementary and secondary schools in 1965, this law was instrumental in ending southern school desegregation. Title VI became a precedent-setter. Having barred racial discrimination in federal grant programs, Congress proceeded similarly to protect the disabled, the elderly, and, in education programs, women.

As grant-in-aid conditions became more intrusive, they also gained effectiveness as federal courts joined administrative agencies in enforcing them. As part of the judicial revolution in federalism, courts became open to appeals from individuals who claimed that their constitutional or statutory rights had been violated by state or local governments. In doing this, courts sometimes rendered highly expansive interpretations of grant-in-aid statutes, as in a series of cases that the Supreme Court decided between 1968 and 1972 liberalizing eligibility in welfare programs, historically a matter that had been left to the states' discretion.

Another institutional innovation at this time was a technique called "partial preemption." With this instrument, Congress claims authority to regulate in a particular domain and sets federal standards. States then are encouraged or required to adopt the standards as their own and to be responsible for enforcement. Partial preemption has been used extensively in environmental protection, meat and poultry inspection, occupational safety and health, and energy regulation. If the states decline to accept national standards or fall short in implementation, at least in theory the federal government will take over the function, thereby displacing them.[22] The Supreme Court upheld the technique of partial preemption in 1981 in a case dealing with regulation of surface mining.

The advances in federal control of state and local governments that took place in the 1960s and 1970s often occurred synergistically, with Congress, the federal courts, and sometimes also the executive interacting to construct new terms of command, techniques of oversight, and policy results. A leading example of legislative-judicial interaction was the Education for All Handicapped Children Act of 1975, which required school systems to provide a "free appropriate public education" to all handicapped children and an "individualized educational program" for each such child, following an annual conference with the child's parents. This radical intervention in a traditionally local function rested on a foundation of federal district court decisions, and it was expanded upon in more such decisions that followed the act—all without federal financial assistance that either matched the promises that Congress had made earlier or constituted a reasonable proportion of the eventual costs to local districts, which were enormous.

The Counterrevolution

Changes as great as those just described can be expected to elicit a reaction, and one eventually arrived in the work of the Supreme

Court under William H. Rehnquist as chief justice (1986–2005). After the appointment of Clarence Thomas to the Court in 1991, there emerged a narrow majority, the "Federalist Five" (out of nine), that explicitly sought to honor federalism as a constitutional principle and to narrow the reach of federal power over the states. It tried to limit Congress's power under the commerce clause and the Fourteenth Amendment, to reduce the state governments' exposure to lawsuits, and to limit the federal government's authority to "commandeer" them as administrators. Whether this line of jurisprudence will survive Rehnquist's death and the departure of his ally Sandra Day O'Connor is uncertain in 2007. In any case, the efficacy of the Court's project is debatable.

To be influential, the Court needs political support, and not much was forthcoming for its federalism decisions. The Democratic Party, which in the 1960s came increasingly under control of its northern liberal wing, had buttressed the Warren Court revolution with major congressional enactments, the Civil Rights Act of 1964 above all. As the Democratic Party moved away from its traditional embrace of states' rights and lost power in the South, the Republican Party took up a defense of federalism, but nothing it did combined with what the Rehnquist Court did to produce a true counterrevolution.[23]

Republican presidents beginning with Eisenhower in the 1950s and continuing through the first George Bush (1989–1992) made symbolic and rhetorical gestures toward federalism and sponsored statutory proposals that purported to return programs to the states or give them grants on more permissive terms. Such measures had limited success, and even the presidents who seemed to have the deepest commitment to preserving a federal-state balance perforce made major contributions to the advance of national power.

It was under Eisenhower that the nationwide interstate highway system was begun, built by state governments with 90 percent federal matching funds and engineered to federal standards. This was a public works program of vast scope, and deeply nationalizing both in its impact on public works budgets and on the social, economic, and aesthetic fabric of the country. Reagan, who entered political life as governor of California and thought more highly of state governments than the national one, presided over an administration that often preempted state laws in pursuit of economic deregulation and issued *A Nation at Risk,* an alarming report on the nation's schools that added impetus to a gathering move for more federal intervention.

By the end of the 1990s, as the Rehnquist Court's counterrevolution was gathering steam, the interest of Republican political leaders in federalism was waning. The *Contract with America,* with which Representative Newt Gingrich successfully led the party to victory in the midterm election of 1994—giving it control of the House of Representatives for the first time since 1953—did not include decentralization as one of its main planks. Gingrich himself, who represented a Georgia district in Congress, was not deeply rooted in an American local place; he grew up as an army brat. He attacked big government, bureaucracy, redistributionist economics, and the country's deteriorating morality without proclaiming the advantages of decentralization within the federal system. Nevertheless, the *Contract* did contain two provisions that potentially were of benefit to the states. One of these promised to give them greater control over Aid to Families with Dependent Children, a controversial welfare program, while the other promised to ban unfunded mandates. Both yielded congressional legislation. Welfare reform, enacted in 1996, sought above all to substitute work for welfare. To that end, it mixed greater freedom for the states with new constraints. The Unfunded Mandates Reform Act, passed in 1995, posed procedural obstacles to new mandates but contained so many loopholes as to be of limited practical significance.

When President George W. Bush took office in 2001, he paid no honor to federalism, in contrast to a line of predecessors in the Republican Party. In his campaign he led the party in abandoning commitment to local control of the schools. The No Child Left Behind Act, which he advocated, rests on a bipartisan consensus in Washington that local schools are to blame for gaps in achievement between whites and Asians on one hand and blacks and Hispanics on the other, and threatens a variety of sanctions against schools that do not raise children's performance and close the gap. It is a coercive, punitive law that would brand schools as "failing" and teachers as "unqualified" in the hope that this threat would make schools do better. More than thirty state legislatures passed resolutions critical of the law after it was enacted, and Utah's legislature seriously considered withdrawing from the program. The federal Department of Education has modified some of its regulations in an effort to keep the states from rebelling.[24]

A second major accomplishment of the Bush presidency, a law adding a prescription drug benefit to Medicare, the nation's program of health insurance for the elderly and disabled, requires state governments to pay much of the cost even though they lack jurisdiction. States initially expected the new program to relieve them of their expense for prescription drugs for the elderly and disabled poor under their Medicaid programs, but Congress elected to finance the new program partly by withholding most of those savings. State officials angrily call this unusual measure the "clawback." When the Bush administration's war on terror got under way following the shock of 9/11 in 2001, the states were drafted for the war with the Real ID act, in which Congress imposed many requirements, effective in 2008, on the states' issuance of driver's licenses, a function that historically had been theirs exclusively. The Bush administration and Congress in effect turned the state driver's license into a national ID card, designed to meet the requirements of national security. Like No Child Left Behind, this act elicited strenuous protests from the states.

This history illustrates how enfeebled the barriers to centralization have become. Congress does not pause, as it once did, for fear of public reaction to radically intrusive measures that impose large costs on state and local governments. Historically, danger has driven centralization, and today the country does not feel safe. The Reagan era report on the schools declared ominously that "the educational foundations of our society are presently being eroded by a rising tide of mediocrity that threatens our very future as a Nation and a people." Federally regulated driver's licenses are a predictable response to the new threat of terror. Neither major party defends federalism. The contemporary Republican Party claims to favor limited government, but pursues privatization—the contracting of government functions to private organizations—more assiduously than decentralization to the states.

Is Federalism Dead?

Is one to conclude, then, that states once claiming to be sovereign have been reduced to ciphers? Far from it. They retain much power to act in a broad array of public functions. Holders of public office often find them more exciting places to work than the federal government. Former Senator George Allen of Virginia remarked to a reporter in 2006 that, "I made more decisions in half a day as governor [the executive head of his state government] than you can make in a whole week in the Senate."[25] This seeming paradox has several explanations.

Although the federal government has gone far to use state and local governments for its own ends, it has not displaced them. They survive with all the features of governments. They have their own constitutions, whose contents are the subject of deliberation and litigation. Litigants who fail to vindicate what they believe to be their rights under the U.S. Constitution can look to state constitutions instead—as they have done, for example, in trying to secure equalization of spending among local school districts and enlargement of school spending in all districts.[26]

State governments have executives, legislatures, and judges—the triad of American governing institutions—and these officials, often including judges, are elected by the constituency of their jurisdiction. They are not appointed from Washington, nor are they ordinarily recruited by the national parties to run for office. The office of attorney general, which in most states is elective, has emerged as a highly visible locus of power and entrepreneurship. Incumbents use it, often in nationwide collaboration with one another, to conduct campaigns against corporations that they accuse of misconduct.

Although the federal government contains some law enforcement agencies—the Federal Bureau of Investigation, the Drug Enforcement Administration, and the Federal Marshals Service, whose members ride incognito on airplanes since the terrorist attacks of 2001—most policemen in the United States are employees of state and local governments. An American motorist who breaks the law will be stopped, if at all, by a state highway patrolman or by a local policeman. If the latter, the motorist will be quick to suspect, often with reason, that the policeman is acting in response to the local jurisdiction's need to supplement its locally generated tax revenues with traffic fines that can easily be imposed on persons from outside the locality or, better yet, outside the state. An American motorist traveling for the first time south of the border, in Mexico, will likely be surprised to find that, in addition to the presence of local police, *federales* patrol major highways.

State and local governments employ many more people than the federal government: 18.6 million versus 2.7 million in the federal civilian workforce in 2003, counting part-time as well as full-time employees. They raise revenue independently—a total of $1.45 trillion in 2002, or $5,025 per capita, mostly from taxes levied on income, sales, and property, but also from license and user fees and sales of utility services and liquor. California's government, which raised $151.2 billion in 2002—in addition to the $174 billion raised by the state's local governments—is bigger than that of most nations.

State and local governments have 1,600 state and local prisons, which are overflowing with prisoners. (The federal government runs prisons, too, but has fewer than 90. Of the nation's 1.38 million prisoners in 2002, 1.24 million were under the jurisdiction of state governments.) Some states impose a death penalty for extreme violations of law. Between 1977 and 2004, Texas sentenced to death or executed 336 people. State governments own the nation's highways, including the interstate highways, and for the purpose of increasing revenue are engaged in selling or leasing toll roads to private parties, foreign consortia among them—a move made possible when Congress removed some of the restrictions on charging tolls on the interstate system.

State governments are usually first to act in response to new problems or issues, of which many arise in a time of rapid technological and cultural change. It is very rare in the United States for the federal government to be the first mover on a domestic question. Rather, it builds on the states' experience, seeking when it finally acts to make more uniform what would be inconsistent if left to state discretion.

State governments often respond to opportunities created by the paralysis of the national government. Vacuums occur when Washington succumbs to political gridlock. The United States is unusual among developed nations in lacking universal health insurance, with the result that gap-filling efforts proliferate at the state level, such as experiments in mandating health insurance or providing care through free clinics. Another example of gap-filling in the presence of federal gridlock is global warming. Many states have acted to reduce emission of greenhouse gases while Washington fights internally and with other countries over what to do.[27] States likewise have acted to curb illegal immigration while the national government has stalled.[28]

Federal commands, though numerous, are not all-embracing or immune from rebuttal. Areas of discretion, often quite large, remain to the states. Arguably the most controversial of all intrusions, with reverberations that have roiled the country's politics for more than thirty years, was the Supreme Court's decision of 1973 in *Roe v. Wade,* which struck down nearly all state laws regulating abortion at a time when state courts and legislatures were making progress toward reform. The Court produced a complex trimester regulatory scheme, which is a permissive law of abortion for all Americans. State legislatures did not take this lying down, but have sought to legislate in the interstices of the decision and even to goad the Court into reversing itself with overt acts of defiance.[29]

The country is so big, and its thousands of state and local jurisdictions so varied by population size and density, internal laws, governing structures, natural resources, socioeconomic conditions, and distinctive cultures, that uniform national regulations are often very difficult to apply on the ground. What fits Port Tobacco, Maryland (population 18), is not likely to be equally suited to New York City (population 8 million). Federal regional administrators, confronting a world of poor fits, may turn a blind eye to some of them, while federal officials in Washington get pleas from state officials for relief through waivers or rules changes.

Waivers of federal regulations have become a common technique in intergovernmental relations, available by law and at the discretion of federal administrators in numerous programs and policy arenas. They were introduced in the 1970s and 1980s when a search was under way in the federal government, think tanks, and private foundations for ways to change welfare policies through experiments in the states. They have since spread to other policy areas.

In grant-in-aid programs and in regulatory programs that use partial preemptions, state and local governments can in principle drop out. In constitutional theory, their participation is voluntary. Though extremely rare, dropouts do occur. For a long time Arizona did not participate in Medicaid, a hugely expensive nationwide program through which the federal government and the states collaborate to provide health care to the poor. Arizona left such care to its county subunits. The Kit Carson School District in Colorado has elected not to participate in the No Child Left Behind Act, concluding that the benefits in added federal aid are not worth the burden.

Far more often than they drop out of federal programs, state governments work to exploit them, maximizing the return in aid. Victimization can run in either direction in the very complicated world of American intergovernmental relations. In particular, the history of Medicaid is replete with instances of the states finding ways to manipulate federal law in order to get more money.

Finally, states that don't like what the federal government is doing can do what aggrieved Americans generally do—they can sue. State lawsuits brought against the federal government with the aim of getting more money, compelling changes in policy, or eliciting a ruling of unconstitutionality from the Supreme Court are increasingly common.

Is Federalism Beneficial?

Though federalism produced a union in the eighteenth century, it did not prevent a civil war. Even a federal United States could not endure half-slave and half-free. Using federalism to that end tainted the form in the eyes of many Americans and ultimately required radically centralizing changes.

Alexis de Tocqueville judged America's federalism very favorably, concluding that it was the decentralized practice of government that taught the citizenry to be self-governing. But if Tocqueville were to return, he would likely be dismayed. The town meetings he celebrated, though still extant in their New England home, are an archaic remnant of early American governance, no longer the country's or even one region's archetype. Nationwide opinion polls and statewide popular referenda, such as are common in California, would seem a poor substitute for making public decisions in democracies of a small scale.

The classic argument for federalism, which appears in *The Federalist* and in generations of textbooks, is that it is an essential component of the constitutional system of checks and balances whereby power is pitted against power. Thus, citizens can use the general government to fight tyranny in the states, and vice versa. In fact, the national government was the instrument for ending the tyranny of slavery and then state-sanctioned racial segregation in the South, but today it strains credulity to suppose that state governments, so pervasively entwined with the national one, are also an effective check on it. For that purpose, Americans depend on electoral competition between the two major parties, judicial review of the political branches by the Supreme Court, and media that since Watergate have moved beyond vigilance into habitual opposition.

Still another historical argument for federalism, which never quite dies, is that it facilitates a logical sorting out of functions such that each level of government does what it can do most effectively. The Founders purported to honor this principle by giving the national government enumerated powers only, but today nothing is too trivial for its attention if publicity or politics invites attention. Nor do local governments hesitate to take positions in foreign affairs. Many a local place has proclaimed itself to be a "nuclear-free zone."

Another argument in support of federalism is a watered-down version of Tocqueville. State and local governments can be both training grounds for officeholders and testing places for policies. Almost all political careers in the United States start at the state and local level. In 1992 the United States had 511,039 popularly elected officials, of whom only 542 were federal officials. About 19,000 were elected at the state level, and the rest locally. Taking advantage of experience, city councilors become state legislators, and state legislators become members of Congress. Governors become presidents, as with Carter, Reagan, Clinton, and the second George Bush, in recent years. There is solid truth to the claim that states are laboratories of experiment; of course, some states are much more active in policy experimentation than others, and the phrase certainly implies more of science than is ordinarily to be found in public policymaking. The "experiments" should be understood to be political as well as scientific in nature. States learn from one another, and the federal government learns from them as well. Examples abound in welfare, health care, transportation, and education.

The most ardent advocates of federalism today are libertarians and professional economists. Drawing an analogy to the private market in goods and services, they argue that competition among the states serves the public welfare. They say that government is more efficient and citizen preferences are better served if states compete with one another, offering different mixes of taxes and services. Such competition is readily visible, for instance, in the states' offering tax incentives or reforming their tort laws so as to become more hospitable to industries. Liberals, by contrast, deplore the idea of such competition, claiming that it results in a "race to the bottom" in social policy as states try to attract industry and wealthy citizens but repel the dependent poor by limiting welfare benefits.

It is not clear where the preponderance of truth lies in this continuing argument. The advocates of competition have noticed that state governments can collude as well as compete. They colluded in the late 1990s when their attorneys general took on the cigarette industry, successfully suing for billions in revenue. And it becomes hard to claim that states necessarily race to the bottom when their spending on health programs and education steadily grows, many extend greater protections to both legal and illegal immigrants than the federal government does, and some take aggressive action to control air pollution and to provide welfare-to-work services for low-income people. State governments appear to have concluded that business, even if liking tax breaks for industrial development, also values a healthy workforce that can read and write. At least one scholar has detected a "ratcheting upward of regulatory standards in competing political jurisdictions."[30] Thus, the casual assumption that federalism inhibits regulation of business and limits the growth of the welfare state, which was conventional wisdom for a long time, is subject to an increasingly skeptical reexamination from both scholars and officeholders.

Statesmen, political parties, and other holders of power have not defended federalism consistently and on principle. It has lacked steadfast friends, and because of its historic association with racial segregation, it has had passionate critics. On the other hand, it has had many and varied users, by no means confined to slaveholders and their racist heirs in the unreconstructed South. Expediency sooner or later teaches political actors that having access to many governments—and also to the many tools and tactics of influence that characterize intergovernmental relations in the United States—makes for a more richly representative array of institutions and a more flexible, responsive politics than would likely be had with a unitary form. It takes a very large leap to imagine the United States with a unitary government, run from Washington with the help only of wholly subordinate units, and a still larger leap to suppose that such a country—it would of course need a different name—would be a better place to live.

CHAPTER 6
Political Culture
Jack Citrin

Political culture is a patterned way of thinking about political life that is widely shared, spans the generations, and excludes other values and customs. Political scientist Jack Citrin explains defining aspects of America's political culture: identity, suspicion of authority, individualism, conceptions of equality, the political role of religion and morality, political participation, and institutional fragmentation. This culture, he argues, imposes constraints on what government can do and the way it can do it.

WHO ARE WE AMERICANS? WHERE HAVE WE COME FROM? WHERE should we be going? How can we get there? These fundamental questions about collective identity, collective purposes, and collective authority lie at the core of descriptions of a community's political culture, a concept that refers to a distinctive set of assumptions, beliefs, and practices. A political culture is a patterned way of thinking about political life that is shared by a number of people, spans the generations, and excludes other values and customs. It identifies the "correct" ways of behaving politically, indicating what actions are legitimate and what projects are feasible. Those who act on these assumptions widely shared in their collectivity "belong," while those who follow a different set of values and beliefs about proper modes of conduct will be viewed as outsiders or deviant.

Fifty years ago, Louis Hartz's *The Liberal Tradition in America,* building on de Tocqueville's century-old *Democracy in America,* provided the dominant interpretation of modern American political culture. Hartz portrayed America as an ideological nation, defining itself not ethnically but through the values of democracy, individualism, liberty, equality, and property rights. He argued that the overriding cultural belief in these values throughout American history defined rigid boundaries for state action. Accordingly, an important factor in the "exceptionalism" of its politics—the absence of a strong socialist party, the weakness of the labor movement, the acceptance of economic inequality, and the limited development of government programs in the area of welfare and health care—is the firm grip of its liberal tradition.

Today, the idea of cultural unity in American politics is under sustained attack. Looking backward, Rogers Smith holds that Hartz's characterization of a uniform American political culture is incomplete and that a rival inegalitarian tradition had widespread support, sustaining a racial hierarchy through Jim Crow laws and ethnocentric immigration and naturalization policies.[1] Looking forward, recent work from left, right, and center projects an image of America as a splintering society whose vaunted exceptionalism is a thing of the past. The country, in these views, is globalizing and fragmenting at the same time, making *e pluribus unum*—national solidarity based on a common culture—unsustainable.[2] Globalization, it is argued, has diminished the sovereignty of even the American superpower. Economic interdependence frays the connections between citizenship and personal welfare, and diffusion of global patterns of speech and communications erodes a nation's distinct culture, substituting a cosmopolitan commitment to universal human rights and international legal norms. At the same time, immigration-driven demographic diversity combines with identity politics to gnaw at the cultural consensus from within. Multiculturalism as an ideology celebrates the maintenance of cultural differences and regards the melting pot ideal as an oppressive symbol of cultural imperialism. This perspective suggests the creation of a deep new fault line in American political culture. Finally, modernization means the advance of an ethos of dissent, self-expression, and moral relativism at the expense of bourgeois values and manners. The result is one nation with two competing moral visions. One political consequence of this quasi-religious conflict of values is a party system in which, rather than seeking the political center, warring Red and Blue armies fight to the death over tradition and modernity, faith and science, nationalism and cosmopolitanism, equality of opportunity and equality of results. Of course, not everyone accepts this reasoning or agrees that America is breaking apart. In recent books, Alan Wolfe and Morris Fiorina emphasize the persistence of consensus and moderation.[3] Still, both sides in the debate about the contours of cultural division agree that something important has happened.

Thinking of American political culture as an "ideational code"— a set of plans or rules governing behavior—underscores that the focus is on collective norms rather than individual beliefs. Five conceptual issues can be distinguished. First, what are the boundaries of a political culture; that is, what types of assumptions and beliefs are included? Should it include general beliefs about the nature of causality, the trustworthiness of other people, and assumptions about economic activity, or should it be confined to beliefs about political identities and goals? Second, what degree of consensus must prevail for an abstracted composite of values and beliefs to be designated as a "culture"? Not every American shares or even knows all the dominant assumptions about politics that guide and constrain political action. Indeed, modern societies rarely display complete cultural homogeneity, and different ways of life make peaceful settlement of conflicts more difficult. Lockean liberalism, conventionally regarded as the core of American political culture, stresses both limits on political authority and broad religious toleration. Yet while few Americans publicly repudiate the liberal principle of tolerance, this seeming consensus on abstract values often breaks down over specific policies such as abortion or school prayer.

Third, since political culture is a property of a collectivity, which unit of analysis is being used? Most writing about American political culture focuses on the nation as a whole and contrasts the United States with other countries. However, one can analyze region, class, or ethnic group and compare these subnational entities to determine whether their way of thinking about politics is compatible with the dominant national culture. For example, can liberalism's insistence on equality and individual autonomy accommodate a subculture that rejects a woman's right to choose her own spouse or career?

Fourth, one must distinguish between the beliefs of political elites and those of ordinary citizens. Almost fifty years ago, Herbert McClosky showed that Democratic and Republican activists were ideologically far apart while their rank-and-file followers clustered in the middle of the liberal-conservative continuum. Soon after, Philip Converse demonstrated that while political leaders did organize their beliefs on the basis of abstract general principles, the vast majority of the American mass public was ideologically "innocent." Disputants about the existence of a culture war in America agree that competing moral and ideological visions pit activists and intellectuals against one another, but that the general population is less divided and more moderate.[4] The question that remains is how much less divided, and for how long. In a society rich with opportunities for political participation along with populist antagonism toward established authority, a large gap between elite and mass preferences is unlikely to endure, if only because such a gap emboldens opposition actors to mobilize the less vocal, if not necessarily silent majority.

A final conceptual issue is whether stated attitudes, beliefs, laws, and institutional practices truly reveal cultural preferences. A discrepancy between abstract ideals and prevailing practices, between rhetoric and reality, is commonplace. Gunnar Myrdal famously described race relations in the United States as "an American dilemma," because the commitment to equality of opportunity conflicted with institutionalized discrimination. Rogers Smith regards the inconsistency between liberalism's inclusionary conception of American citizenship and ethnocentric immigration and naturalization laws as evidence for the enduring potency of an inegalitarian ideology opposed to the liberal political tradition. Myrdal, though, believed that commitment to the liberal national creed was genuine and that America ultimately would resolve its "dilemma" through reforms providing full citizenship to African-Americans. Similarly, Samuel Huntington comments that "critics say that America is a lie because its reality falls so far short of its ideals. America is not a lie, it is a disappointment. And it can be a disappointment only because it is also a hope."[5] In the context of these dissenting views, it makes sense to define political culture in terms of values and beliefs and to leave its relationship to behavior as a matter for historical investigation.

American Identity

What does it mean to be an American? As a nation of immigrants, the United States has always faced the exacting task of balancing universality and diversity. At Independence, about 80 percent of the newly minted Americans were British in origin, so the problem of forging an identity separate from that of the mother country pushed toward a civic rather than ethnic definition of nationhood. America could be a universal nation founded on democratic political principles in part because, as John Jay wrote in *The Federalist* (no. 2), the country was "blessed" with a common language, values, and customs.

Early America was inclusive in principle, but not in practice. Blacks and Native Americans were excluded from citizenship. And each wave of immigration, whether from Germany, Ireland, Asia, Italy, or eastern Europe, raised fears about newcomers' capacity and willingness to adapt and live up to the democratic national creed. Nativism represented one ideological solution to the problem of a common national identity in a diverse nation. Immigration laws should favor people who already are familiar with the dominant national culture, and all newcomers should undergo a program of Americanization to speed cultural and linguistic assimilation. Theodore Roosevelt accepted immigration, but insisted that the new arrivals should feel, think, and talk "American." Conformity to an Anglo-Protestant culture was the goal.

The liberal conception of national identity associated with the Declaration of Independence is optimistic about American society's ability to absorb immigrants, whatever their origin. Zangwill's melting pot metaphor for the blending of cultures symbolizes this idea of nationhood. Yes, immigrants should adopt the national creed and learn to speak English, but this will happen without the need for a program of indoctrination that denigrates their original cultures. The political contest between the liberal and nativist conceptions of American identity was settled in the 1960s. The twinned passage of the 1964 Civil Rights Act and the 1965 Immigration and Nationality Act instituted a color-blind version of access to citizenship that steadily increased the Hispanic and Asian segments of the national community. And despite periodic outbursts of anti-immigrant sentiment, the legal foundations of this ethnic transformation of American society remain intact.

Ironically, though, liberalism's triumph quickly spawned multiculturalism as a new challenge to the dominant political culture. In the aftermath of the civil rights movement, disappointment about the failure to eliminate entrenched racial inequalities spawned cultural nationalism among blacks. The assertion of claims for equal rights and recognition on the basis of group membership spread to other ethnic minorities, women, homosexuals, and the disabled. Multiculturalism became the label for an ideological defense of redistribution on ethnic and gender lines. The fundamental tenet of this doctrine was that ethnicity imparts a distinct set of beliefs, values, habits, and observances, and that the freedom to live this way of life is essential to personal dignity and self-realization. Because no culture in a multi-ethnic society is privileged, the government should give official recognition and support to minority cultures that would otherwise disappear. Multiculturalism thus advocates group representation to govern the allocation of many political and economic benefits.

In its strong form, multiculturalism conceives of the nation-state as a confederation of equal cultural groups, an outlook that differs both from liberalism's insistence on equal individual rights and nativism's promotion of a cultural hierarchy. From this perspective, the answer to the question "Who are we?" is "Anyone who is here." The basis of American identity is simply subjective opinion, a willingness to identify oneself as an American and a commitment to the country's well-being.[6]

One sign that multiculturalist ideas have spread within elite intellectual opinion is the different reactions to David Fischer's *Albion's Seed* (1989) and, more recently, Samuel Huntington's *Who Are We? Challenges to American National Identity* (2004).[7] Both books state that Americans of all national origins share a political culture founded on British values and traditions. Fischer's book was received with general acclaim, whereas many reviewers accused Huntington of xenophobia and racism for proclaiming that English-speaking and Anglo-Protestant political values are the core of an increasingly fragile American identity.

Rather than embracing multiculturalism, most Americans still give priority to an overarching national identity. A 1994 national survey showed that 96 percent thought of themselves mainly as "just Americans" rather than as members of an ethnic, racial, or religious group. When given a chance to choose both labels, few white Americans do, suggesting that the various groups of European "ethnics" have indeed melted. Pluralities of black, Hispanic, and Asian respondents opt for the hyphenated ethnic-American option, although this tendency diminishes among naturalized citizens and those born in the United States. A 2006 national survey of Hispanics living in the United States confirms that a large majority feel strongly American, while retaining a sense of being Mexican, Puerto

Rican, and so on.[8] Both Hispanic and Asian immigrants over-whelmingly agree that it is crucial to learn English, and by the third generation most members of these ethnic groups are monolingual English speakers—just like the experience of earlier European im-migrant generations.

Probing mass beliefs about what makes someone an American also suggests continuing support for an inclusive egalitarian concep-tion of national identity. Several national and California surveys asked what respondents felt made someone a "true" American. Overwhelming majorities of all ethnic groups mentioned the creedal values of treating people equally, getting ahead on one's own, and participating in civic life as very important. Virtually everyone agrees on the importance of being able to speak English, something that one can learn whatever one's ancestry or place of birth. The more exclusionary or "ethnic" attributes of Americanism, religiosity and nativity, are least likely to be deemed important.[9] People who continue to believe that "America equals white and Christian" surely are a minority. Patriotism also remains the norm. Americans are much more likely to express love of their country and its institutions than other people. The vast majority of Ameri-cans also say that they would rather live in the United States than anywhere else. Ethnic differences on survey questions measuring pride in America are relatively small, and immigrants acquire this attitude relatively quickly.

Whether this positive outlook will persist is more difficult to say. Among non-Hispanic whites, the young and the college-educated are relatively less patriotic and more sympathetic to multicultur-alism and the emotional claims of ethnicity. And government policies can affect the future balance of national and ethnic identifi-cation. What schools teach often shapes attitudes toward the value of cultural assimilation, the meaning of American history, and the virtue of patriotism. Affirmative action programs create incentives for beneficiary groups to retain a strong sense of ethnic identity. Making dual citizenship legal may diminish the intensity of nationalist sentiment.

Today, however, there is broad agreement about what it means to be an American. Most Americans continue to support the ideal of an overarching common identity without denying the legitimacy of ethnic pride and diverse traditions. They believe that cultural assimilation and cultural pluralism are compatible, but also that the *unum* should have emotional precedence over the *plures*. For example, the pervasive desire that English remain the country's common language means that bilingual education programs win support only if framed as a transition to linguistic assimilation.

The liberal tradition's staying power even constrains the tactics of its nativist and multiculturalist challengers. Historically, supporters of restricting immigration argued that this was necessary to American democracy. Today, advocates of multiculturalism, with some success, appropriate egalitarian rhetoric to promote representation for minorities and women, arguing that equality entails diversity. Academic, business, and political elites mostly have signed on, and Justice Sandra Day O'Connor ultimately accepted this rationale as a valid justification for affirmative action in higher education. In the public realm, any hint of a racial slur or ethnic joke by a political candidate or entertainer generates first criticism and then an apology. And "festival" multiculturalism has gone beyond St. Patrick's and Columbus Days to give us various ethnic history months, Cinco de Mayo parades, karaoke, Kwanzaa holiday cards, Celebrate Diversity bumper stickers, and fusion cuisine. American political culture recognizes multiple identities and accepts ethnic differences more than it did fifty years ago. Yet this changed orientation leaves unchallenged the belief of most Americans that when push comes to shove, their national rather than their ethnic identity should be paramount.

Trust in Authority

Suspicion of political power is a distinctive feature of American political culture, making people reluctant to grant the state broad responsibilities. This entrenched antigovernment ethos coexists with patriotism, reverence for the Constitution, and pride in American democracy. But while strong public allegiance to the fundamental values and symbols of the American political system remains intact, trust in the motives and competence of government and other leading social institutions has sharply declined over the past fifty years.

Beginning in the 1960s, pollsters have asked the American public how often they trust the government in Washington "to do what is right" and how much confidence they have in "the people running" the main branches of government and other social institutions. Figure 6.1 tracks the trend in the proportion of respondents who say they trust the government "just about always" or "most" of the time" in the University of Michigan's biennial National Election Studies (NES). It shows a sharp drop between 1964, when 77 percent expressed trust in government, and 1980, when only 26 percent did. There was a rebound during the economic recovery under Reagan, another slide in trust to the nadir of 24 percent in 1994, and then another upward bounce during the economic good times in Clinton's second term. Although 9/11 was a national tragedy, a CBS poll conducted about a month later showed another large jump in political trust, with fully 55 percent saying they trusted the government "always" or "most of the time." This apparent resurgence of trust actually represented a temporary fusion of "government" and the "nation" in people's minds. An external attack on the country's economic and political institutions produced a bipartisan surge of patriotism, a rallying around the flag. However, the intense partisanship in domestic politics and renewed division over the war in Iraq engendered a new decline in political trust, particularly among Democrats, recorded in the 2004 NES data.

Figure 6.1   Trust in Government 1964–2004

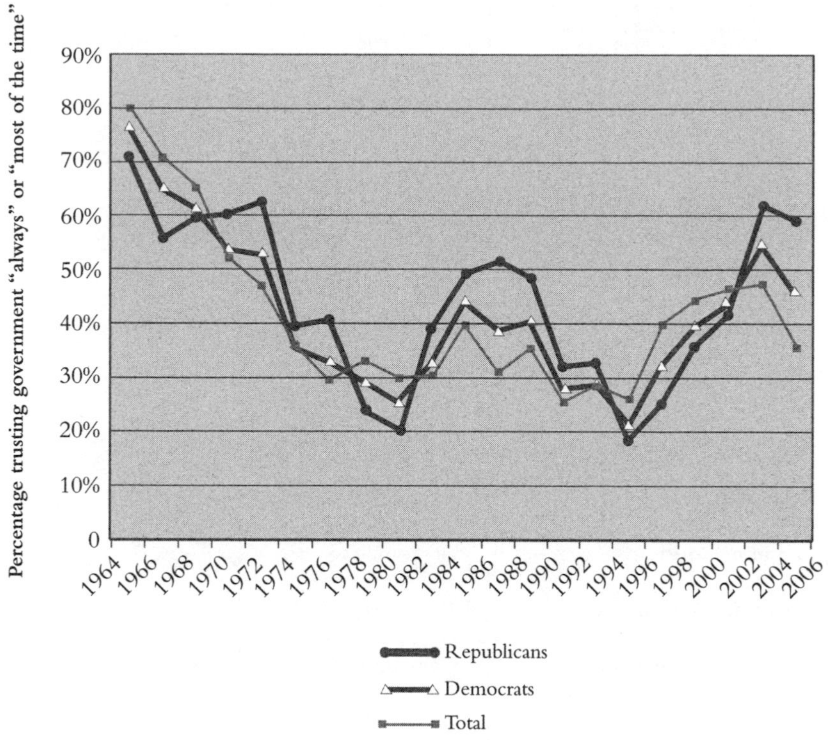

SOURCE: National Elections Studies (CPS, University of Michigan).

A major cause of these fluctuations is a change in how the public evaluates the performance of the incumbent presidential administration. Vietnam, urban riots, Watergate, stagflation, and the Iranian hostage crisis reduced trust in government, while the improved state of the economy under Reagan and Clinton helped reverse the trend. Nevertheless, declining confidence represents more than a short-term judgment about the competence of current leadership. Table 6.1 compares the proportion of respondents who indicate they had a "great deal" of confidence in the "people running" twelve political and social institutions in 1973 and again in 2004, according to National Opinion Research Center surveys. Except for the army and

Table 6.1   Declining Confidence in Institutions

	1973	2004
Business	31.4%	17.0%
Clergy	36.1	24.1
Education System	37.5	27.5
Executive Branch	29.9	20.8
Labor Movement	16.2	12.4
Press	23.4	9.2
Medicine	54.6	36.5
Television	18.8	10.3
Supreme Court	32.6	31.0
Scientific Community	40.1	42.5
Legislative Branch	24.1	13.3
Army	32.6	56.8

NOTE: Column figures indicate percent of survey respondents expressing a "great deal" of confidence for the people running a given institution.

SOURCE: National Opinion Research Center.

the scientific community, every institution experienced a drop in public confidence. In part, poor performance, scandal, and the rise of an adversarial mass media have fueled this broad loss of confidence. Beyond this, skepticism toward authority is a feature of modernity, as reason and science are elevated above habit and tradition. Finally, some expressions of political cynicism are merely ritualistic, an echo of the familiar cliché that "politics is a dirty business." In this regard, declining trust in government is not a uniquely American phenomenon. Critical citizens have increased in most European countries as well, suggesting a more general cultural shift in modern democracies.

A lack of trust draws attention to the question of "who guards the guardians." Pervasive political cynicism in the United States prepared the ground for ethics committees in Congress, special prosecutors, conflict of interest laws, campaign finance reform, open meetings rules, and term limits. But whatever their merit, these reforms have failed to boost public confidence in authority. Like a lost religious faith, trust in government is hard to regain completely.

Individualism

Liberty conceived as freedom from government implies individual responsibility. American individualism refers to belief in the value of human independence and self-reliance. Individualists oppose external interference with "the pursuit of happiness" and downplay collective obligation for economic welfare. A majority of all ethnic groups believe that getting ahead on one's own is important for making one "a true American," say they believe in "the American Dream," and agree that people who work hard can get ahead in this country. Blacks and Hispanic Americans, who, despite "faring poorly in the individualist social order, still support its basic premises are more like white Americans than Europeans in their optimism about the possibility of economic achievement and the need for personal responsibility."[10]

Americans are less likely than people elsewhere to expect the government to provide economic security. In 1994, less than a quarter of Americans completely agreed that "It is the responsibility of the government to take care of very poor people who can't take care of themselves," far less than the proportion of Germans, French, British, or Italians who completely agreed with this opinion. Only a minority of Americans agree that government should guarantee everyone a basic income, provide a "decent" standard of living, and reduce differences in income between the rich and poor. In contrast, the majority of Europeans supported this role for government.[11] The World Values Survey, conducted in 2001, compared American attitudes to those in fourteen other wealthy democracies and found among Americans more support for private ownership of business, more belief that poverty was due to laziness and a lack of individual motivation than unfair treatment by society, and less support for increased government assistance for the poor than elsewhere. These individualist values were widely shared in the United States: the modal viewpoints of men and women, black and white, rich and poor, and young and old were the same.

Consistent with these attitudes, Americans pay lower taxes than most Europeans. America also spends less on transfer payments such as pensions, unemployment insurance benefits, family allowances, and child care than other countries and is virtually the only wealthy democracy without a government-supported universal health care system. Moreover, the financing of Social Security and health care programs reflects the commitment to personal responsibility: individuals and their employers contribute to insurance funds. And unlike many European countries, America restricts the access of even legal immigrants to social services such as Medicare, with widespread public support. This, too, fits the idea that people should contribute before they receive public benefits.

It is striking that the American belief in individual achievement remains so strong despite evidence that upward mobility is slowing and income inequality has grown. For many years after the Great Depression, there was mass upward economic mobility in the sense that incomes were rising rapidly throughout the population. A blue-collar worker in the 1960s earned more than a manager had made in the late 1940s, even though his relative position within the income distribution had not changed. Starting in the 1970s, real wages have grown much more slowly and that kind of mobility has stalled. Yet optimism about getting ahead in America through hard work remains pervasive, possibly because in all circles there are vivid examples of "rags to riches" success stories. In the abstract, suspicion of political authority and individualist values yield a preference for "small" government. In practice, organized groups are quick to demand public protection and largesse.

Moreover, a "something for nothing" mentality governs public opinion. Majorities say they want more spending on a wide range of specific programs while they oppose higher taxes and "big" government. Similarly, the public decries bureaucracy while favoring more environmental regulation and consumer protection. Harold Wilensky argues that Americans embrace contradictory values when it comes to the role of government.[12] They are simultaneously individualistic and collectivistic, wanting to be rewarded to the maximum for economic success as well as protected from hardship by pensions and health insurance. Wilensky concludes that American individualism mainly explains the country's slowness in initiating welfare state programs, an emphasis on limiting access to welfare and income maintenance programs to those below a certain income level, and the private sector's relatively large role in providing pensions and health insurance. However, American public opinion is not an immovable barrier to the welfare state's growth. Indeed, despite differences in national political cultures, the common economic regimen imposed by global competition and the graying of populations are forces for convergence in social policies in rich democracies, with America expanding health care and job training programs while European countries reduce some benefits and impose more rules on access.

America's distinctive individualist outlook has endured despite waves of immigration creating new patterns of ethnic diversity. Recent immigrants currently are no different from native-born Americans in their beliefs about personal responsibility and individual economic opportunity. In fact, one can argue that those who choose to immigrate are carriers of American individualism. Immigrants are a self-selected group who leave family and home to start a new life as strangers in an alien culture, often enduring great hardships to get to America. Once arrived, they demand little from government, focusing mainly on the opportunity for economic success through hard work. And this is as true for black immigrants from the Caribbean and Africa as for Mexican and Asian newcomers.

Equality

If liberty is the most basic American political value, equality is a close second. However, equality is a more elusive concept than liberty in American thinking. People answer the questions "Equality for whom?" and "Equality in what respects?" in different ways. Most Americans distinguish between political and legal equality on the one hand and economic equality on the other. Originally, America restricted voting to propertied white men, but today there is virtually universal agreement that the ideal of political equality should be extended to all, with conflict confined to more restricted issues such as the fairness of registration laws and voting machines, felon disenfranchisement, racial gerrymandering, and the like. Discrimination on the basis of race or religion is widely considered un-American, and in the domain of criminal justice policy this has affected the rules for jury selection and sentencing. Finally, equality of respect is widely endorsed. Jim Rome, the iconic host of a nationally syndicated sports radio show, has laid down the law to his listeners: "In this day and age we are beyond mocking someone's ethnicity or sexual preference. So don't go there." There is a lot of grumbling about how political correctness amounts to a form of linguistic martial law, but the spread of this code for public discourse indicates pervasive agreement on an inclusive conception of the political community.

Though political equality and equality of respect are now integral features of American political culture, economic equality is not. More than people in other countries, Americans continue to tolerate great inequalities of income and do not call for changing the foundations of an economic system based on limiting government interference with the market. If one's earnings are based on ability, most Americans believe, there should be no limit. A comparative study of elite attitudes confirmed this cultural difference in the idea of equality.[13] For example, Swedish political party and union leaders are more likely than their American counterparts to favor limits on income and equality of results. And this matters; there is more inequality in the United States than in Sweden and most other Western democracies.

A distinction between equality of opportunity and equality of results resolves this apparent collision between the values of individualism and opportunity. Equality of opportunity means that everyone should have a fair chance to get ahead and go as far as possible. Liberty means the freedom to do well, not a guarantee that one will succeed. There is no right to an equal share of material goods. The value of personal responsibility implies that economic differences are the result of individual choices, effort, and abilities. As a result, inequalities in income are largely accepted as fair, despite numerous warnings about a shrinking middle class and excessive compensation for top executives. American reactions to inequality tend to be populist, not socialist. Voters periodically support attacks on concentrated corporate power but continue to espouse the benefits of capitalism and free enterprise. The fact that Americans are more likely than Europeans to attribute poverty to a lack of motivation and hard work than to luck is reflected in how America and Europe fight poverty.[14]

The strength of the individualist commitment to equality of opportunity is clear in the data about public attitudes toward affirmative action, a policy designed to increase the representation of women and minorities in employment and education. Like "equality," the term "affirmative action" is notoriously ambiguous. Does it only mean assuring fairness in recruitment and selection, or does it mean something more, for example, the use of explicit preferences in the allocation of scarce, desirable positions? "Soft" affirmative action aims at increasing equality of opportunity, "hard" affirmative action at moving toward equality of condition. Affirmative action policies force a collision between individualistic and egalitarian values, and most Americans believe strongly in both. Virtually everyone opposes discrimination on the basis of race or gender and agrees that society should do "whatever is necessary" to make sure there is equality of opportunity. And the great majority of the public believes that, due to past discrimination, a special effort should be made to improve opportunities for minorities and women. At the same time, Americans draw the line at any program that gives an absolute preference to blacks or women. Channeling resources in the form of special training programs or extra effort in recruiting is acceptable, but quotas, reserved places, and different admissions standards are not. This opinion is, generally speaking, the position reached after twenty-five years of wrestling with the constitutionality of affirmative action programs in employment and education.

Despite years of proselytizing by academic and, more recently, business elites, surveys reveal a remarkable continuity in the public's outlook. The more clearly a question is framed as preferential treatment, the more it is opposed. A 2001 national poll found that 92 percent of respondents agreed that hiring and college admissions should be based on merit and other qualifications besides race or ethnicity. Need-targeted programs—so-called economic affirmative action—are more widely accepted than those based on ascriptive criteria.[15] The overwhelming opposition to preferences in hiring and college admissions is unaffected when survey questions refer to the need to compensate for past discrimination or inequalities. Peter Schuck notes that differences in phraseology, question order, and other contextual factors influence the distribution of opinion toward affirmative action but concludes, "No researcher doubts that the public's opinion remains decidedly and intensely negative."[16]

There is a racial and ethnic gap in attitudes with blacks and, to a far lesser extent, Hispanics more favorable than whites to harder forms of affirmative action. Even so, polls show that more than one-third of blacks and two-thirds of Hispanics oppose preferences in hiring and college admissions. In part, the difference in white and black attitudes represents a response to their distinct historical experiences. For whites, the individualistic and egalitarian elements in American political culture tended to be complementary; for blacks, individualism, even after the success of the civil rights movement, failed to meet expectations for economic and social progress. And while most blacks endorse the principle of merit-based achievement in the abstract, they understandably are less likely than whites to attribute lack of economic success to individual failings rather than systemic flaws. By a significant margin, blacks are more likely than whites to favor government actions to improve the economic and social circumstances of minorities.

Some liberal scholars regard opposition to affirmative action and other policies to benefit blacks as evidence of racial prejudice. Others point to the role of self-interest. White males are the main losers under affirmative action, so it makes sense for them to be most antagonistic. Similarly, self-interest should spur blacks to favor affirmative action. Clearly, values and interests interact, but the fact that some whites may be disadvantaged by affirmative action does not mean that most opposition is selfish and unprincipled. The fact that opinions about affirmative action are usually race-neutral, with the level of opposition roughly the same whether blacks, women, or European immigrants are named as the beneficiaries, testifies to the important causal role of fundamental cultural norms.

In the court of public opinion, individualism trumps the desire for social equality. Quotas and numerical goals for diversity violate traditional conceptions of the meaning of equality of opportunity and thus are rejected. Even strong supporters of affirmative action accept that the equal treatment of individuals is the ultimate goal for a just society. They argue that preferential treatment is required for a limited period because the effects of institutional racism make the end of legal discrimination insufficient for achieving genuine equality of opportunity. A hobbled competitor cannot be expected to win a race, however fair the rules and judges.

Blacks aside, the strongest support for affirmative action comes from the intelligentsia, particularly in universities, big business, and liberal political elites. In the wake of recent Supreme Court decisions, the academy, in particular, has settled on the supposed educational benefits of ethnic diversity as its main justification for affirmative action. Institutionalizing diversity thus makes race and ethnicity legitimate, even preferred qualities, rather than suspect categories in policymaking. It is a way around individualism, but one that diverts affirmative action from its original purpose of improving the conditions of blacks and has little to do with reducing economic inequalities in the foreseeable future.

If there is a culture war about the meaning of equality, it is a war between elites allied with most blacks versus most other Americans. The affirmative action case illustrates that the causal influences of political culture and public opinion are limited. Race-based preferences have survived despite four decades of opposition. Invisible bureaucratic decisions initiated group-conscious employment and education programs and expanded them incrementally. Once in place, they provided benefits to a concentrated, well-organized constituency, and this clientele prevailed over the dispersed and unorganized majority for whom the issue was less salient. In this regard, affirmative action resembles farm subsidies. The American political system favors the status quo, and affirmative action received powerful support from a wide range of elites and opinion leaders. But when direct democracy moved affirmative action to the electoral battleground in California, Washington, and Michigan, voters in these Blue states rejected the preferential programs defended by the elites as indispensable for justice and progress. For the public, equality continues to mean equality of opportunity.

Although race and income influence political values and policy positions, no one seriously talks about a race or class war in America. From the nineteenth century on, scholars have agreed that working-class consciousness was stronger in Europe than in the more industrially advanced United States. In their recent book, *It Didn't Happen Here,* Seymour Martin Lipset and Gary Marks explain why the trade union movement and socialist political parties have been so weak in America.[17] Political culture is one important factor. Lipset and Marks, like Hartz, stress the pervasiveness and durability of bourgeois values in a nation without a feudal past, aristocratic tradition, church establishment, or great economic inequalities. The power of the liberal tradition is such that even American radicals have tended to espouse individualism, decentralization, and antistatism rather than the socialist solutions of public ownership and state power.

Electoral institutions are another reason for the failure to develop a successful socialist party. The plurality electoral system weakens the chances of all third parties to win legislative seats. The presidential system combines the plurality system with the need for a national majority in the Electoral College, a further disadvantage for the small working-class and socialist parties. In addition, American trade unions did not support an independent working-class political party, partly because of the dominance of more conservative craft unions in the decentralized union movement and partly because of the quintessentially American suspicion of the state among important union leaders such as Samuel Gompers, the longtime head of the American Federation of Labor.

The cultural, religious, and ethnic diversity of American workers also made it difficult for class identities to attain paramount importance. The strength and durability of religious and ethnic affiliations made cross-class electoral appeals more effective than calls for working-class solidarity. Waves of immigration from different countries periodically created new ethnic divisions among the working class, allowing employers to combat unions by exploiting conflicts between immigrant and native workers. Among immigrants, ethnicity was a stronger basis for political attachment than class. Finally, unrelenting racial prejudice excluded black workers from many trades, isolating them from the socialist political projects of whites.

During the Great Depression, the politics of the United States did shift in the European direction with the emergence of a more activist role for the state and pro-labor policies that boosted membership in trade unions. Because of Franklin Roosevelt's popularity among workers, immigrants, and blacks, however, the union movement generally allied itself with the Democrats rather than the Socialists, choosing political effectiveness over ideological purity. FDR, reviled as a traitor to his class, helped save capitalism.

After World War II, the depression era's tilt toward social democracy in America ended. The gap in social spending between America and Europe emerged in the decades immediately after the war. In Europe, Labor and Socialist parties held office and constructed a generous welfare state. In the United States, class tensions diminished as a result of sustained prosperity, the left wing of the Democrats lost ground, and individualist and antistatist values reasserted themselves.

Economic and political trends after the 1970s have pushed European politics in the American direction. Neoliberal economic policies presently hold sway worldwide, and even where there are socialist parties, there seems to be less and less socialism. The intriguing question for American political culture today is how the economic consequences of globalization will influence traditional conceptions of equality and the role of the state.

Religion and Morality

If there is a culture war in America today, it is not about segregation or free enterprise but about questions of personal and public morality. The major battles are over abortion, drug use, gay marriage, the death penalty, assisted suicide, school prayer, and pornography. Because these issues engage deep-seated beliefs about what is right and wrong, good and evil, they arouse strong emotions and make compromise more difficult. Underlying these policy debates is a conflict between moral traditionalism and moral individualism, between belief in unchanging standards of conduct derived from a transcendent authority on the one side and devotion to self-expression and personal freedom on the other. To the defenders of orthodox morality, "anything goes" means that nothing matters, while to those in the more permissive camp, it means live and let live; pornography, sexual activity, abortion, and family structure are private matters and the law should recognize this.

Individualism, however, is context-bound. Proponents of laissez-faire in economic life often want the government to enforce strict rules for drug use and sexual behavior, whereas advocates of government spending and business regulation demand that politics stay out of the bedroom. In other words, people align themselves differently on various issues, making for some fluidity in political coalitions. Fanatics exist on both sides of the moral divide; the extreme antiabortion activists bomb clinics; the animal rights zealots bomb research laboratories.

To some extent, religiosity underlies one's choice of moral vision. Religion has always been important in American politics. As Robert Wuthnow notes in his essay in this volume (see chapter 10), the original European settlers in America were "pilgrims" seeking the freedom to practice their own religion; observers such as de Tocqueville remarked that Americans were more religious than citizens of European countries. Americans are still more likely to belong to a church or religious organization and more likely to say they believe in God and that prayer is important in their daily life. Most Americans also agree that there are clear guidelines for good and evil, and this helps explain the unusually moralistic quality of American politics.[18]

American political culture celebrates freedom of religion, not freedom from religion. Religious leaders were important in the antislavery, temperance, and civil rights movements. In addition to taking stands on more clearly religious questions like abortion, school prayer, and stem cell research, many churches call for an end to American military involvement in Iraq, divestment from Israel and the Sudan, and sanctuary for illegal immigrants fleeing political persecution or domestic violence.

America has no religious oath for taking office, but all candidates for important elected positions proclaim their faith in God and praise the virtues of religion. Invocations and benedictions are a staple of political and organizational life. Congress has chaplains; college football teams at public universities routinely "take a knee" in prayer before taking the field. The Supreme Court has struggled to define how high and wide the wall separating church and state should be. Many legal scholars (and some of the justices themselves) criticize the Supreme Court for its muddled Establishment Clause decisions— for example, on the constitutionality of school prayer, the display of nativity scenes and other religious symbols on public property, the use of vouchers for tuition at religious schools, and the inclusion of the words "under God" in the Pledge of Allegiance—but public opinion clearly opposes the principle of complete separation.

No religious institution receives direct government support, but a diverse array of religious groups are active in civic life, providing food, clothing, health care services, job training, help in navigating government bureaucracies, and training in political participation. Most Americans favor allowing religious organizations to receive government funding to do this civic work, just as they favor school prayer, official recognition of Christmas (and Hanukkah), and the traditional Pledge of Allegiance. Religiosity remains a potent political force, in part because it has become more ecumenical in response to the proliferation of new religious choices and greater tolerance. Imams are joining ministers, priests, and rabbis on the podium for public ceremonies, and voters increasingly say they could be willing to vote for a Catholic or Jew for president.

The continuing importance of religion and traditional morality in American political culture is something of a puzzle. The "Protestant ethic," with its emphasis on faith and hard work, does fit with the American values of economic achievement and personal responsibility. But belief in a transcendent authority, deference to the church's leaders, and taking on communal responsibilities seem to conflict with the culture's emphasis on personal autonomy and mistrust of pronouncements from on high. Furthermore, many who write about economic modernization believe that it is associated with secularization, scientific rationality, and self-expression at the expense of religious authority, strict moral codes, and corporate identities. From this perspective, which some might challenge, the persistence of traditional values and religious orthodoxy in the United States, an affluent, technologically advanced democracy, is striking.

Conclusions about the distribution of "traditionalists" and "permissivists" in America vary with the measures of values and policy preferences used. James Davison Hunter places roughly 15 percent of the population in each camp, leaving about 70 percent of the public occupying a middle range of diverse and more nuanced moral perspectives.[19] On the abortion issue, only about one-third of the public takes the most extreme positions. As the results of many state ballot measures show, a large majority of the public insists on defining marriage in traditional terms. Yet there is substantial and growing support for the concept of civil unions and benefits for domestic partners of the same sex, a development that reflects the popular commitment to the idea of equality of opportunity. Moreover, the moral "traditionalists" and "permissivists" are not divided by religious denomination. There are Protestants, Catholics, and Jews in both camps, although the growing number who say they have no religion generally reject the orthodox moral vision. Among Protestants, the fundamentalist and evangelical sects are most prominent among the traditionalists, while liberal (and more upper-class) denominations such as Presbyterians, Episcopalians, and Unitarians tend to favor the permissive position on most of the current moral issues. Orthodox Jews are more likely to adopt the traditionalist viewpoint while reform Jews, who tend to be better off, support the permissive one.

Wayne Baker's exhaustive analysis of the cross-national World Value Survey concludes that America is unique among modern nations for the continuing hold that traditional values have upon it.[20] At the same time, permissiveness with respect to self-expression and self-realization has grown. America has a mixed value system, and many individuals hold seemingly contradictory traditional and modern values. What makes America exceptional among economically advanced democracies is the failure of secular rationality to become dominant, a failure that testifies to the central place of religion in the nation's cultural heritage. Baker rejects the portrayal of America as divided into two cohesive moral camps, arguing that the "traditionalists" and "permissivists" have similar attitudes toward national identity, the performance of political institutions, and the trustworthiness of other people. He does agree, however, that a broad range of moral perspectives leads to significant differences on issues relating to family, work, and the separation of church and state.

Given these and other data about ambivalence, moderation, and inconsistency in public attitudes, why is the claim that there is a cultural war in America plausible? The moral issues now debated involve vital personal choices, spanning the life cycle literally from cradle to grave. Fifty years ago, abortion, school prayer, and gay rights were non-issues. Today they are salient enough to dominate debate over Supreme Court nominations and generate initiatives and referenda at the state and local level. With cherished values at stake, political conflict resembles a holy war with total victory the goal of both sides. Partisan polarization and ideological consistency across economic, moral, and foreign policy issues have increased among the politically engaged. This activist minority chooses the battlegrounds and mobilizes grassroots troops to help do the fighting. Passionate rhetoric in Congress and campaign speeches, angry confrontations between rival protest groups, and the determination to carry on the battle in new political venues make warfare an appropriate metaphor for conflicts over partial birth abortion, the fate of Terry Schiavo, and stem cell research.

A number of developments combined to produce a rebirth of moral conflict in American politics. The onward march of modernization—bringing with it affluence, higher levels of education, scientific progress, and skepticism of authority—increased the ranks of the morally permissive and diminished belief in religious orthodoxy if not religious participation. The explosions of the 1960s decisively changed what was acceptable in speech, art, and personal conduct. The egalitarian impulse embodied by the civil rights movement also mobilized disabled, feminist, and gay and lesbian activists to challenge the prevailing norms about "reasonable accommodation," sexuality, the role of women, and child-rearing arrangements. Important decisions of the Warren Court expanded the domain of "inalienable rights" beyond established boundaries, spawning a political backlash.

Important changes in the structures of interest groups, party organizations, and media institutions help keep moral issues on the political agenda. New recruitment technologies such as direct mail, the availability of political entrepreneurs and organizers, and the sponsorship of government agencies and philanthropic foundations have produced a proliferation of interest groups across the political spectrum. These organizations carefully monitor political decisions that affect school curricula, the availability of antipregnancy measures, the separation of church and state, and other hot-button issues. Changes in the rules for nominating presidential candidates and financing election campaigns have enhanced the influence of advocacy groups and hugely wealthy individuals committed to diverse moral causes. Office seekers need more money and campaign workers than party organizations can supply. No Democrat can get ahead in national politics without supporting abortion rights and affirmative action. Republicans are increasingly beholden to fundamentalist churches and other morally conservative groups to mobilize their voters.

The political realignment that began in the late 1960s is now virtually complete. There is a two-party South with the Republicans now dominant. In a highly polarized Congress, ideologically homogeneous blocs of Democrats and Republicans diverge sharply when voting on cultural issues. Furthermore, the lack of competition in so many congressional races means that incumbents are as worried about being outflanked by ideologues in the party primary as much as they are winning the general election. The virtual extinction of conservative Democrats and liberal Republicans reduces incentives for bipartisanship and compromise, and the visible lack of comity among political leaders fortifies the public's negative image of party politics as selfish and aggressive.

The intense partisan polarization among elites has trickled down to the rank-and-file. The University of Michigan National Election Studies show a rise in the number of people calling themselves Independents with no partisan leaning between 1952 and 1980. On the eve of Reagan's election, 14 percent of voters surveyed classified themselves as "pure" Independents; in 2004 the proportion was just 8 percent. Furthermore, the relationship between party affiliation and presidential voting has become stronger in recent elections. Increased loyalty among "weak" identifiers and Independent "leaners" in both parties, together with the decline in the number of Independents, gave rise to Karl Rove's 2004 strategy of mobilizing the base rather than appealing to the median voter. The connection between party identification and issue beliefs also is growing at the mass level, partly because voters choose the party that represents their values and partly because partisans learn the positions that fit their inherited party affiliation.[21]

The rise of new media outlets makes it easier to wage a large-scale campaign on moral issues. Cable television and satellite radio, Internet Web sites, political bloggers, targeted mail, and political advertising are important conduits of communication. There are electronic churches whose preachers reach a vast audience. Radio talk show hosts mobilize listeners to bombard Congress with emails or join demonstrations. The relatively detached tone of network news is passé. People can and do choose news channels by their politics: conservatives gravitate to Fox, liberals to CNN. More and more, the talking heads who review politics and the news are deliberately strident and partisan. Listening to the passionate like-minded further reinforces existing opinions and devalues the ideas of the other side.

The new media environment contributed to the polarizing effects of the last two presidencies. The president is critical in defining the nation's agenda and focusing the attention of other political actors, the media, and ordinary citizens. The moral lapses of Bill Clinton, ultimately forgiven by the electorate, galvanized the morally orthodox. The faith-based politics of George W. Bush similarly enraged secular liberals. More generally, elite messages filter down to the public, creating opinions and solidifying preferences. The size and influence of the political center gradually shrinks when elites are deeply divided and competing messages reach millions of people who can choose whom to tune in or out.

Political Participation

Americans have more opportunities to vote than citizens of any other democracy. Staggered elections at set times; primary elections for nominating candidates; elections for judges, local administrators, and boards; and direct democracy at the state and local levels make for frequent trips to the polls to fill out truly long ballots. Despite their commitment to the importance of popular control, Americans vote at lower rates than the citizens of virtually every other democracy. Data from the International Institute for Democracy and Electronic Assistance show that between 1945 and 2005, the average turnout in elections to the House of Representatives (in presidential years) averaged 55 percent. In the same period, the average turnout to the lower house of the legislature was 90 percent in Italy, 85 percent in Sweden, 75 percent in Britain and France, and 74 percent in Canada and Spain. The main reasons for this large difference in electoral participation between the United States and other democracies are institutional, not cultural. Technical differences in how official turnout rates are calculated lower American turnout figures relative to those in other countries. The denominator for calculating the turnout rate in the United States is the voting age population, and this includes people ineligible to vote such as felons, people confined to mental institutions, and the growing number of non-citizens.

In contrast, other countries use the number of registered voters as their denominator. This practice is sensible, since voting is automatic in most of the world. In the United States, however, registration is the responsibility of the individual. The ease of registration varies from state to state and the rules matter. States with no registration and those allowing registration on Election Day have turnout levels well above the national norm; American turnout expressed as the proportion of those registered who vote hovers above 70 percent, a figure comparable to turnout in a number of European democracies. Recent reforms have made it easier to register and cast absentee ballots, but there are other factors that make the personal cost of voting higher in the United States than elsewhere. For example, in America most elections are held on a Tuesday, an ordinary workday, rather than on Sunday or a specially designated official holiday.

The British political scientist Anthony King suggests that turnout in America may be low because people are called on to vote so often and on so many things. The frequency of elections lowers the incentive to vote in any particular one. The number and complexity of items on the typical American ballot adds to the information costs; the fact that there always is another election just around the corner makes it easier to rationalize not doing one's civic duty.

By making the votes of third-party supporters more meaningful, proportional representation, a feature of many European electoral systems, also boosts turnout. In addition, political parties, the main instrument for mobilizing voters in modern democracies, are weaker in the United States. To summarize, Americans turn out to vote less not because they are more alienated from politics or less committed to democratic institutions than citizens of other countries, but because rules and regulations make it more costly for them to vote.

Despite rising levels of education, the single strongest predictor of turnout, and the steady easing of registration requirement, voting in American elections actually declined during the past generation. In the 1964 presidential election, 61.9 percent of the voting age population cast ballots; turnout sank to 48.9 percent in 1996, before climbing to 56 percent in 2004. Among the reasons for the downward trend in participation are changes in the composition of the electorate, the growth of immigration, and a decline in social and communal ties that motivate voting and other forms of civic engagement. Decreases in marriage rates, length of residence in a community, job stability, and church attendance contribute to the decline in American turnout.

The younger generation of fifty years ago learned to vote and became accustomed to doing so. A large segment of those under thirty today seem to feel that politics and voting simply is not for them. A recent study by Martin Wattenberg reported that people under thirty today are less likely than they were fifty years ago to read books or newspapers, watch the news on television, or have interest in and factual knowledge about politics.[22] They also are less likely to think that politics and voting have an impact on their lives. Moreover, the correlation between age and the most common forms of political involvement is much stronger today than fifty years ago, meaning that the gap between the young and older citizens has grown. The disengagement of the young is more pronounced in the United States than elsewhere but it also exists in most established democracies. To the extent that the ideology of the young and old diverges, the participatory gap between them may diminish the representative quality of government policies.

Voting aside, however, Americans are *more* likely than Europeans to be politically active. Surveys conducted by the European Social Survey in 2002 and Georgetown University in 2004 asked respondents whether they had done any of ten different political activities in the past year. The activities included contacting public officials, working in a political party organization, signing a petition, boycotting products, and participating in protest activities. The average level of participation was significantly higher in the United States than in Europe, both among those under thirty-five years old and those older. In the United States, the younger generation still was less politically active than those thirty-five and older. When asked whether they were active in a voluntary organization rather than merely belonging in the sense of formal membership, Americans were, again, more likely to be involved than Europeans, but this time young people were as likely as the older generation to be active.[23]

In 1835, de Tocqueville remarked on the American propensity to form associations of all types. In *Bowling Alone* (2000), Robert Putnam worried that civic engagement had declined since the 1950s with unfortunate implications for the vitality of democratic institutions. The empirical status of Putnam's claims about the United States remains unsettled, but in comparative perspective, at least, Americans remain a "nation of joiners" using a variety of tactics other than voting to advance political interests.

Culture, Institutions, and Policy

Peace *and* war are both features of American political culture. A strong consensus remains on the fundamental values that shaped the country's politics from its origins. The continued durability of these values is important for preserving a conception of America in which *e pluribus unum* is an attainable ideal and existing institutions enjoy broad legitimacy. Because the consensual values of patriotism, liberty, and equality are so abstract, however, they can be used to justify competing political positions. The Patriot Act, so named to symbolize action to thwart America's foreign enemies, has been called unpatriotic for undermining the constitutional rights to privacy and freedom of speech. The idea of equality is used equally to attack and defend affirmative action. Political conflict tends to be most intense and threatening to peaceful resolution when the issues involve collective ideals or a group's way of life. The debate between the advocates of competing moral visions for American society has this all-or-nothing quality.

Political culture is simultaneously a cause, constraining and guiding policy, and an effect, reshaped by institutional choices and patterns of political socialization produced by education, civic participation, and media consumption. In the United States, the liberal tradition created a political system design to limit power, protect individual rights, and prevent the tyranny of the majority. The Constitution created a fragmented and decentralized government with the intention of making rapid positive action difficult. In this the Framers largely succeeded. The separation of powers, federalism, the Bill of Rights, and an independent judiciary are buttressed by legislative procedures that benefit intense organized minorities, by plebiscitary opportunities in many states, by weak party organizations, and by a proliferation of interest groups with close ties to elected officials and bureaucrats. The result is great difficulty in linking national policies together or making major reforms except during a national crisis. Political fragmentation limits the power to achieve universal health care or gun control regardless of popular opinion. Institutional arrangements as well as political culture have created what scholars call path dependency, a circumstance in which initial

choices establish a trajectory that is very difficult to reverse. The
American distrust of authority produced institutions that effectively
limited government. These institutions reinforced dominant cultural
values through policies accommodating local control, creating access to political decision makers, and giving private organizations an
important role in social programs.

The institutional order that has governed America for more
than two hundred years is unlikely to change even if cultural values
move slowly in the European direction. Path dependency applies to
policy in the moral as well as the economic or social domains. No
matter how much people might welcome an *entente cordiale* in the
culture war, the American emphasis on individual rights, combined
with mistrust of authority and an adversarial media, make prolonged conflict without radical change likely. Because of regional
variation in the distribution of moral perspectives, the culture war
in America often begins with local skirmishes. Media attention then
mobilizes ambitious politicians along with the usual suspects in the
interest group world, moving the argument to a larger stage. In this
context, federalism creates intriguing possibilities. The Rehnquist
Court's resurrection of the framework of dual sovereignty grounded
in the Tenth Amendment of the Constitution opens the door for
states to chart their own moral path on assisted suicide and gay marriage, just as they can in promoting stem cell research or banning affirmative action. Overturning *Roe v. Wade* would mean a return to
state discretion over abortion policy. Not surprisingly, conservatives
call for the nationalization of law in domains such as tort reform or
drug use when permissive forces win at the state level, whereas liberals insist that rights guaranteed under the federal Constitution
trump local preferences regarding school prayer, adoption rights,
and abortion. The dual sovereignty scenario would allow more people to opt out of the culture war by relocating to a more congenial
cultural environment, thus posing a serious challenge to the traditional conception of One America with a common identity.

CHAPTER 7

The Media

S. Robert Lichter

*In democratic nations, the press is free, but in the United States it is also
(among newspapers) decentralized and locally owned and (among radio and
television stations) crowded, competitive, and opinionated. S. Robert Lichter,
who directs a non-partisan media watch group, points out that the American
press lost any ties to political parties in the nineteenth century, while in much
of Europe those ties were maintained. Today, with newspapers losing readers
and broadcasters fighting over viewers, the press has developed an adversarial
relationship to politics, and public confidence in it has declined.*

WHEN A. J. LIEBLING WROTE THAT FREEDOM OF THE PRESS BELONGS
to those who own one, he didn't intend it as a compliment. Liebling
meant this figuratively, as a way of saying that final decisions on the
news belonged to newspaper owners rather than working journalists. But it was literally true at the beginning of the American experiment, when any printer who owned a press could become editor,
publisher, and distributor of his own newspaper, with enormous
consequences for a nation in the making. Today it is becoming true
once again, as bloggers, podcasters, and online video sharers stretch
the definition of "journalism" to the breaking point, with unfore-
seeable consequences for a nation at the height of its powers.

   For all the excitement being expressed about the Internet, however, it is only the most recent of several technological innovations
that were predicted to make life more egalitarian or democratic by
revolutionizing communications. Among them were the telegraph,

the telephone, radio, and television in its various delivery systems—broadcast, cable, and satellite. Yet the result of innovation has always been evolution rather than revolution, expanding the media's role in American society without fundamentally altering its unique model of a free press.

The United States created the model of constitutionally recognized, lightly regulated, and privately owned communications media that deliver the news to a mass audience. Even today it remains close to the ideal type of a press that is free from government intrusion by intention rather than inattention. Within this broad framework, however, there have been dramatic changes in the ways the media has developed and influenced American society and, especially, politics. To understand the news media as the social institution at the meeting point of all other institutions, we must begin at the beginning.

A Distinctive American Media

An independent press began to develop in both America and Europe during the eighteenth century. But there were major differences from the outset, which set the two forms moving along separate routes. Political power in Europe was being centralized in the governments of great nation-states, while mistrust of centralized authority was so strong in America that it almost prevented the United States from coming into being. American newspapers were calling for revolution while the French court was still using censors and "book police" to suppress public discourse, and the English parliament was treating criticism as seditious libel and limiting newspaper readership through heavy taxation.

As a result, the press developed quite differently on the two continents. In Europe, most newspapers and magazines began as organs of ideologically aligned groups such as political parties and churches, with which they retained connections into recent times.

In the United States, most publishers had shed their partisan ties by the mid-nineteenth century. They were much more concerned with profit margins than group attachments.

This difference reflects America's heritage as the quintessential bourgeois liberal democracy, which operates within a widely shared ideological framework drawn from classical liberalism. America lacked Europe's feudal heritage, with the traditions and conflicts generated by the existence of a peasantry and landed aristocracy. Thus, American politics did not reflect the deep class consciousness that structured political parties abroad. The relative absence of sharp class prejudices and divisions made it easier to envisage a mass press and, later, electronic media that catered to popular tastes.

There is also a powerful populist strain in classical liberalism, which helps explain American journalism's propensity for exposing and denouncing political leaders. Americans feel a strong attachment to their political system, but they are wary of those to whom they delegate political power. Observers as early as Alexis de Tocqueville noted that Americans were more willing to criticize and expose political malefactors than were Europeans, but less likely to develop fundamental criticisms of their political system. This propensity gave impetus to the American press's role as a watchdog over those in power rather than an instrument of broader social change.

Thus, in America the press became the handmaiden of freedom from state oppression; in Europe it was either the object or the instrument of state control. Consequently, the European press operated under severe legal and economic strictures, and when electronic media came upon the scene, they developed as state-owned or controlled enterprises. By contrast, the mass media in the United States have primarily been privately owned businesses. Newspaper and magazine publishers have enjoyed unequalled freedom and government support, and electronic media have been regulated relatively lightly.

These different traditions have shaped American and European media down to the present day. Consider England, where the leading newspapers have easily identifiable ideological slants; e.g., *The Guardian* and *The Independent* lean to the left of center and *The Sunday Times* and *Daily Telegraph* lean to the right. But they are equally constrained in their investigative reporting. Not only does England's Official Secrets Act mandate jail terms for anyone who leaks or publishes classified material, it explicitly rejects the defense that disclosure may be in the national interest. It is difficult to imagine the Pentagon Papers being published under such circumstances.

Moreover, the burden of proof in British libel law has always rested on defendants. This is in striking contrast to U.S. law, which requires public figures to demonstrate that a reporter showed "actual malice" by publishing false information while knowing or not caring that it was untrue. Not until 2006 did British courts allow journalists to offer the defense that publication was in the public interest. In fact, plaintiffs who believe themselves libeled by a book that is printed in several countries routinely bring suit in England, where their chances of success are greatest.

The differences are even sharper regarding electronic media. The most important news organization in the United Kingdom is the British Broadcasting Corporation (BBC). The BBC was for many years state-owned and is still funded primarily by taxpayers. Today it is a quasi-public corporation with a government-appointed board of directors, a situation somewhat akin to that of PBS and NPR. But the BBC wields the kind of influence that commercial television has in the United States, particularly in the area of news. The government licensed only one commercial competitor (ITV) until the late 1990s. BBC television currently airs several channels of informational programming, including a 24-hour news channel that competes with CNN.

But the BBC's government connection is a double-edged sword. Although it is officially insulated from political influence, the government reviews (and may alter) the BBC's charter every ten years. Meanwhile, charges of bias or inaccuracy may lead to formal government inquiries. In 2004, after a judicial inquiry rebutted a BBC story that had criticized the Blair government, not only the reporter but the CEO and the board chairman resigned under pressure. This is the rough equivalent of Dan Rather, the president of CBS News, and the CEO of CBS all being forced to resign over the controversial 2004 *60 Minutes* story claiming that President George W. Bush received favorable treatment during his National Guard service.

On the continent governments have played an even more central role in directing the media. Most of them quickly turned the broadcast media into an arm of the state. Their role in disseminating propaganda during World War II produced widespread fears that the future belonged to Big Brother, George Orwell's personification of an all-seeing and all-knowing totalitarian state. Such fears accelerated a general loosening of government controls after the war, with some historically based variations. For example, U.S. influence over West Germany's new constitution facilitated a vibrant independent news industry there. Nonetheless, it remains illegal in Germany to express sympathy for Nazism or display Nazi symbols such as the swastika.

Since the 1980s, privatization has diminished government control of electronic media throughout Europe, resulting in some awkward hybrid systems. For example, the business holdings of former Italian prime minister Silvio Berlusconi included three national TV channels, which constituted nearly half the Italian market. While in office Berlusconi feuded frequently with RAI, the government broadcast service, whose three TV channels had most of the other half. Depending on one's perspective, Italy's prime minister was either trying to take sole control of the country's broadcast news, or the government news service was battling a chief of state who was also its chief business competitor. For all the interplay of media interests and government regulation in the United States, it is difficult to imagine, say, President Rupert Murdoch mounting a hostile takeover of PBS.

The Growth of an Independent Press

Why did the American media develop so differently from their European counterparts? The short answer is the First Amendment. However, constitutional protection was the legacy of a free press as well as its guarantor. A free press was something the Founders had fought for and were determined to preserve. The tradition of an independent watchdog press was established almost as soon as the first newspapers began appearing in the British colonies. Newspapers that dealt with public affairs were organs of opinion that expressed the views of their publishers and presented events in that light. The crucial event that politicized the press was the Stamp Act of 1765. This act is remembered for producing the rallying cry, "No taxation without representation." But its target was also crucial. The Stamp Act sharply increased the tax on printed material, threatening many printers with financial ruin. Newspapers throughout the colonies furiously denounced the tax as an immoral attempt to rescind the rights and freedoms of their countrymen.

The response of the newspapers not only emboldened the protesting colonists, it encouraged them to identify their interests with those of the printers and to regard a free press as an ally against abusive authority. On its side, the press had taken a step toward political involvement from which there was no going back. Publishers were increasingly forced to take sides, and most newspapers became vehicles for expressing grievances against England and then for supporting the Revolution.

Once a new nation came into being, however, partisan fervor quickly engulfed the press. More precisely, the united partisan support for the Revolution gave way to competing partisan supporters of the political interests that quickly emerged. Many newspapers became adjuncts to political factions and individual politicians. They derived much of their income from government printing contracts and even direct payments from politicians. For example, the *National Gazette* was paid for by Thomas Jefferson while he was secretary of state, and the *Gazette of the United States* was supported by Alexander Hamilton.

This gave an acrimonious tone to public discourse, since newspapers had no incentive to temper the language they used to criticize opponents. The Founders despaired at the negative effects on the fledgling republic and fumed over the personal attacks they endured. Even Jefferson, who famously preferred newspapers without government to government without newspapers, later complained that newspapers made their readers *less* well informed, because "he who knows nothing is nearer to truth than he whose mind is filled with falsehoods and errors."[1]

However, President John Adams went too far when he pushed the Sedition Act through Congress, making it illegal to "write, print, utter, or publish" anything that would bring into disrepute the president or Congress. Adams and his Federalist allies were voted out of office in the next election. It turned out that the country's sentiments were closer to those of Jefferson's earlier views. When presented with the prospect of government without (independent) newspapers, the citizens threw out the government.

The extent of public support for a free press seems remarkable in light of how inaccurate, biased, and rowdy the press was in those days. Eric Burns has noted the "remarkable contrast between the accomplishments of eighteenth century Americans and the vulgarity of their journalism."[2] But the American press was saved from further decline into vituperative partisanship by an unlikely deus ex machina—the invention of news as we now know it.

Beginning in the 1830s, a new type of newspaper showed that it was more profitable to provide useful information and entertaining stories to a large readership than to depend upon the caprices of political patrons and government subsidies. The penny press made money by targeting the commercial middle class and even working-men, instead of the lettered elites. Accordingly, the new product was both livelier and less lettered than its predecessors. For the first time, the activities of ordinary people were reported, including the titil-lating products of the gossip mills and police courts.

However, one aspect of life was conspicuously absent from the new wave of news. Most of the penny papers disdained partisan af-filiations, and many abstained from writing about politics altogether. This made economic sense; political stories would only bore some members of the new target audience and drive others away. But publishers presented this shift as evidence that they now represented the common good rather than partisan interests. Having previously identified its interests with those of the public through political en-gagement, the press now discovered that it best served the public in-terest by withdrawing from politics.

Thus, by the mid-nineteenth century, the commercial press had permanently replaced the partisan press as the dominant mode of American journalism. Henceforth the reader would typically be viewed as a consumer rather than a partisan, and the nostrums of private enterprise would replace those of political ideology in pay-ing the bills. Most newspapermen would identify both their social mission and their livelihoods with reporting the most important and interesting facts of the events of the day in a manner that would ap-peal to ordinary readers.

During the latter half of the century, rapid industrialization brought population growth to urban centers that vastly enlarged the potential newspaper audience. It also created new concentrations of wealth and power, along with their attendant corruption and social ills. It didn't take long for a new kind of newspaper entrepreneur to take advantage of this combination with a new brand of populist sensationalism. In New York City, Joseph Pulitzer's *World* and William Randolph Hearst's *Journal* perfected a highly profitable formula that critics called "yellow journalism." They fed the public a rich diet of crime, gossip, sex, and scandal, served up on a platter of big and bold headlines, colorful graphics, and unabashed self-promotion.

An important piece of the tabloid package was its exposés of crooked politicians and unsavory financial practices among the rich and powerful. This populist element reinforced the press's watchdog role in protecting the public against the misdeeds of the high and mighty. However, the daily press's concentration on political and financial corruption implicitly produced an agenda of change at the top, rather than systemic change from the bottom up. This was quite different from the more ideological social criticism favored by European journalists. Their style of criticism was better reflected in the magazine articles and books of muckrakers and political activists like Upton Sinclair and Lincoln Steffens.

Meanwhile, a quite different culture of journalism had developed, based on information rather than entertainment. The advent of railroads and the telegraph produced a market for something that was heretofore unthinkable—the immediate delivery of information to cities thousands of miles apart. This market was soon served by wire services such as the Associated Press, which could maximize their subscriber lists by producing reports that were brief, accurate, and politically neutral.

A new model of journalism soon fused the wire services' emphasis on factual accuracy with an upscale sensibility that set it apart from the populist yellow press. In 1896 Adolph Ochs purchased the *New York Times* and announced his intention to produce "a high-standard newspaper, clean, dignified and trustworthy" that would "give the news impartially, without fear or favor, regardless of any party, sect, or interest involved."[3] The *Times* provided the upper social classes with a high-minded newspaper that matched their own sense of respectability and propriety ("all the news that's fit to print"). Its modest circulation posed no threat to the tabloids, but advertisers paid more to reach the upscale readership, and the paper began to carve out a role for itself as the voice of the establishment.

The standards of respectable and objective reporting championed by the *New York Times* gave new prominence to reporters, both by placing a premium on their skills and by attracting attention to their procedures. This was particularly true after World War I, when the issue of journalistic objectivity first attracted scrutiny. Most journalists treated the facts they reported as something akin to grapes waiting to be plucked from a vine. They were there for the taking; it was up to the enterprising reporter to find them. Thus, the goal of objectivity was to get the facts accurately and without prejudice. These were skills that could be taught. It was just a matter of adding up the facts and subtracting your own opinions.

Soon after the turn of the century, journalism schools began to proliferate, with the mandate of upgrading professional training and standards. In 1923 the American Society of Newspaper Editors endorsed news coverage that was "free from opinion or bias of any kind." This goal received more than lip service. One study found that the proportion of "objective" newspaper and wire service stories (those not containing the author's overt opinions) doubled from 1874 to 1914.[4] Having previously served the common good by standing aside from the world of politics, the press would now do so by standing above it.

Another factor in reducing opinionated journalism was radio, which burst onto the scene in the 1920s. By 1930 nearly half of all households owned a radio set; by 1940 four out of five did. Broadcasters had a financial incentive to eliminate partisanship, which could limit a larger and more diverse potential audience than most newspapers could muster. Newspaper readers were paying customers, while anyone might tune into a radio broadcast. But tuning out was just as easy, making advertisers nervous about material that might give offense.

Unlike the print media, radio's political neutrality was also mandated by the government. The courts allowed far more government regulation of radio than of print, because they treated the airwaves as a scarce public resource that needed to be managed in the public interest. Many station owners found it safer not to air any potentially controversial speech than to risk having their license revoked by running afoul of the Federal Communications Commission, which Congress created in 1934. Meanwhile, President Franklin Roosevelt's "fireside chats" over the radio pioneered the use of broadcast media by politicians who sought to forge an emotional link with their constituents.

Although less free than the press, radio had far more latitude in the United States than in Europe, where governments quickly assumed direct control over the new medium, as noted above. Further, political advocacy still flourished. The most successful columnists and radio commentators, from Walter Lippmann to "radio priest" Father Charles Coughlin, became public figures who exercised considerable political influence. The point of the new professional ethic was to cordon off this kind of opinion from the realm of news. Professionalism demanded mastery of emotional commitment by detachment and expertise.

Of course, working journalists operated within certain limits. We know from a pioneering 1936 survey of the Washington press corps that reporters were already well to the left of the owners politically, and more liberal than the general public as well.[5] If a dispute arose over a politically tinged story, however, the owner decided what got printed or broadcast. As William L Rivers noted, "The publishers . . . hated [the New Deal]. And the reporters, who liked it, had to write as though they hated it, too."[6] Nonetheless, despite commercial and political constraints, the American press was unique in its avowed mission to provide an account of the world based on impartial observation rather than ideological principles and in its independence from government and interest groups in pursuing this goal.

Moreover, after World War II a momentous change began to occur in journalism's internal balance of power. The 1936 survey found that a majority of the press corps reported having stories "played down, cut or killed for 'policy' reasons."[7] A follow-up survey in 1961 found that only 7 percent recounted such ideologically based tampering with their work. In fact, the study's author concluded that the most significant change in journalism in the intervening twenty-five years was "a new sense of freedom from the prejudices of the home office."[8]

This change did not result from lobbying by reporters or readers. It occurred primarily because owners, pressured by new competition, realized that they could make more money by letting the professionals run the paper than by using it as their personal megaphone. In order to maximize profits, they were willing to accept the separation of "church and state"—boardroom and newsroom. Thus, decades of emphasizing professionalism and objectivity had created better-trained journalists who wrote for a more educated public. A few big-city tabloids remained profitable, but the mainstream press that survived the onslaught of television in the 1950s did so mainly by catering to a growing market for the dispassionate, fact-based daily journalism championed by the *New York Times*.

The Rise of Television

The most profound change in the media's structure since the mid-nineteenth century was the sudden centralization of influence that took place in the 1960s. And the most important factor in creating a centralized media system was television. Notwithstanding the rise of newspaper chains and radio networks, the American press had always been more localized than its counterparts abroad. And for all the prominence of the New York press, there was no American equivalent to the monopoly of nationally influential media outlets in European capitals like London and Paris.

This was partly due to the sheer size of the United States and the westward expansion that created new population centers served by locally based and regionally influential news organizations. The media's decentralized nature also stemmed from government policies that encouraged local ownership of electronic media and local decision making on programming. These policies in turn reflected a political culture whose long-standing suspicion of strong centralized authority dated back to the Articles of Confederation. It is easy to take such policies for granted, precisely because they reflect long-term assumptions about government's proper role. It is only in contrast to other countries, which have tried to hobble the independence of every new medium since the printing press, that we may fully appreciate the significance of our own preference for decentralized control over communications media.

Television challenged America's tradition of localism and, in the long run, weakened it. Suddenly the residents of Manhattan, Kansas, were getting the same news, at the same time, as the residents of Manhattan Island. Events and personalities that once seemed distant and unreal were brought close to hand with the flick of a switch. Political elites lost much of the advantage of their firsthand connections to leaders whose success now depended on their ability to establish a bond of pseudo-intimacy with people watching them from millions of living rooms. The town meeting had symbolized America's tradition of local government; now television news created a national town meeting in which we all became members of the same polity, connected by virtue of our shared experience of the day's events.

The first primitive newscasts functioned like wire services with pictures. But this changed dramatically during the 1960s, a decade that seemed made for television. Technological advances such as communications satellites and videotape expanded television's capacity to tell compelling stories, just as the play of history provided a series of dramatic events and riveting images everywhere from urban ghettos and college campuses to the jungles of Vietnam and the surface of the moon. By 1963 television had become the medium that the public relied on and trusted the most for news. But the novelty of seeing history unfold in their living rooms led many to overstate television's independent influence. To a considerable degree, the network news departments relied on the wire services and a few major newspapers to help set their daily news agenda. Network producers read the morning papers and wire copy to provide a framework for their decisions about which stories they should cover. Then they set about updating and translating these stories into visual formats for the evening newscast.

Television's backhanded compliment to newspapers' news gathering expertise increased the public influence and professional stature of major papers like the *New York Times, Washington Post,* and *Wall Street Journal,* which became known as the "prestige press." Together with leading newsweeklies and television news, these outlets became a de facto national news network centered in New York and Washington. For the first time, a handful of people in America's political and financial capitals provided the entire country with its news.

Despite television's reliance on the press, it remained a powerful new competitor with the newspaper industry in the battle for the public's attention. Evening papers all over the country closed, as workers headed home to watch the evening news instead of reading the evening edition. The survivors responded to the challenge of television's immediacy and visual impact by expanding their interpretive coverage and news analyses, where print held a competitive advantage.

Mainstream journalism began to take on a sharper point of view, just as the news agenda shifted toward divisive social conflicts that, to many journalists, seemed to call for taking a stand. For the next decade, reporters were thrown onto the front lines of political battlegrounds that ranged from the civil rights movement to campus protests, the Vietnam War, and the Watergate scandal. By the mid–1970s the media were widely credited or blamed for ending a war and unseating a president.

Although journalism played an important role in all these developments, the truth is a little more complicated. For example, Bob Woodward and Carl Bernstein eventually forced Watergate onto the public agenda with their intrepid investigative reporting. But just as important were the disaffected political insiders willing to leak information and the stubborn judge who threatened the burglars with long prison sentences unless they implicated the higher-ups who planned the break-in.

Similarly, television was credited with building opposition to the Vietnam War by showing pictures of carnage night after night on the evening news, but the influence of TV's "living room war" was not always what it seemed. One study found that during the Korean War domestic opposition actually rose more quickly—relative to the number of American casualties—despite the absence of televised images.[9] Recent scholarship suggests that the key factor in public support for foreign wars is not casualties suffered or observed, but the belief that they are not in vain, that progress is being made.[10]

This accords with the best-documented case of media influence on the Vietnam War, which few journalists are eager to claim. It occurred during the Viet Cong's Tet Offensive in 1968. This armed uprising throughout South Vietnam was a military disaster for the Viet Cong, but journalists mistakenly reported it as a military success that exposed the failure of American intervention. This self-fulfilling prophecy became a tipping point that turned significant numbers of the public permanently against the war in a matter of weeks.[11] It was not the pictures but the reporting that made the difference, by telling viewers what the pictures meant.

The New Journalism

Whatever the nuances of the actual events, the popular image arose of a powerful media that was both a major player in the political arena and a referee who kept the other players honest. For a tumultuous decade, journalists took sides in the major conflicts of the day on civil rights, war, and political corruption. Each time they ended up on the winning side. Not surprisingly, socially committed young people flocked to journalism as an avenue of social reform and personal influence, as the "wretched scribblers" of yore suddenly became well-paid professionals and even popular celebrities.

These new recruits came from more affluent backgrounds and were better educated and more culturally sophisticated than their elders.[12] They looked at themselves as the social and intellectual equals of the politicians and other leaders they were covering, and they were less predisposed to defer to them. The gratification associated with merely being an "eyewitness to history" seemed less appealing. Why shouldn't journalists help make history themselves?[13] Thus, beginning in the late 1960s and 1970s, many reporters seized the opportunity to act as the nation's teacher as well as its conscience.

Professionally, this development dealt a heavy blow to the old ideals of detachment and neutrality. News analysis, context, and interpretation gained a new cachet. The new breed viewed "objectivity" as problematic at best, and a dangerous illusion at worst. It was gradually superseded by the ideal of "fairness," an inherently more subjective standard. This went hand in hand with a revised version of the "watchdog" mentality. A newly adversarial temper led journalists to suspect all claims to represent the public good as masks for self-interest—*except* for their own. They were the public's tribunes, and their job was to serve as society's guardians against the rich and powerful, who tried to delude the public with their own self-serving claims. Having previously operated either within or "above" politics, journalism now proposed to serve the public interest by doing both simultaneously.

This self-made mandate, and the extraordinary power of television, helped fuel a massive expansion of media influence in every major sector of political life—the electoral process, the business of governing and making policy, and the mechanisms of public opinion that form the backdrop for political activity. Indeed, the national media became the single most influential factor in transforming political life into what it is today. This influence stemmed not only from political reporting, but from the sheer pervasiveness of the media's presence in politics.

Media influence is most visibly displayed during presidential election campaigns. Taking over the role once played by the political parties, journalists have become an alternative electorate whose responses are crucial to candidates' chances. Campaign organizations now plan their strategies—from fund-raising to policy decisions—around media considerations. As a campaign staff member explained Democratic dark horse Jimmy Carter's winning strategy in 1976, "We had planned only for the short haul. After that, it was all NBC, CBS, and the *New York Times*."[14]

Journalists' judgments not only help select the candidates who survive and the issues that emerge; they shape the perceptual environment in which the campaign takes place. Their role is strongest early in a race, when their perceptions of candidate support and potential can become self-fulfilling prophecies. Candidates soon discover that their goal is not so much to win primaries as to exceed journalists' expectations, reaping a bonanza of national publicity that improves their prospects in future primaries. Candidates from Eugene McCarthy in 1968 and Gary Hart in 1984 to "comeback kid" Bill Clinton in 1992 and Bill Bradley in 2000 all "won" early contests by losing less badly than pollsters had predicted.

The media's impact is as great on how candidates campaign as on where and when they campaign. Elections are fought in thirty-second commercials and catchphrases tailored to make the evening news. Voters serve as props in the never-ending search for symbols that can convey stock messages via visual stereotypes. This drudgery is punctuated by periodic flare-ups when a verbal or behavioral gaffe draws the media moths to a candidate going down in flames. From Gary Hart's tabloid trysts in 1987 to the (Howard) "Dean scream" in 2004, the media have shown they can break campaigns as quickly as they make them.

Whether knowingly or not, voters have always depended on elites to structure their choices. But party elites have given way to media elites as molders of political images and shapers of campaign realities. A candidate's most crucial personnel choice is the media advisor, who engages the press in a campaign-long tug-of-war over the candidate's public image. In the process, candidates have learned to communicate in ever-briefer sound bites. (The average length of a presidential candidate's televised sound bite has dropped from forty-two seconds in 1968 to eight seconds in 2004.)[15] The nagging question is whether they are also learning to think in eight-second sound bites.

The rare presidential candidate who successfully negotiates the campaign gauntlet quickly discovers the Faustian bargain he must make with the media. On the one hand, journalists enhance the president's use of the "bully pulpit" by vastly increasing the speed and reach of his political sermons. Television in particular has developed an almost fetishistic fascination with the presidency. On a "normal" news day, absent other events of great magnitude, the lead story on any newscast usually flows from the president's activities or agenda.

However, all this attention inflates public expectations of any president and reduces the time and policy options available to fulfill them. And the media spotlight casts heat as well as light—the policies of the Reagan, George W. Bush, and Clinton administrations all suffered about twice as much criticism as praise in the news.[16] George H. W. Bush's 1989 declaration of "war on drugs" produced a sharp jump in media coverage of this issue, but the coverage also became far more critical of his antidrug initiatives. The same pattern hampered Bill Clinton's health reform program in 1993. In an age of mediated politics, the president proposes and the media opposes.

This is not to say that relations between the media and government are purely adversarial. Rather, the media have become something of a political institution in their own right, engaging in constant interplay with the three formal branches of government in ways that are often mutually beneficial. Indeed, when today's politicians climb Disraeli's "greasy pole" of political advancement, journalists supply much of the grease.

Members of Congress and executive branch officials frequently advance or undermine policies and personnel changes by leaking information to reporters as trial balloons. Journalists discreetly trade favorable coverage for access to information. Government whistleblowers may win awards for reporters, but over the long haul it takes a stable of anonymous insiders to keep reporters' editors happy. Thus, journalists and politicians criticize each other so much partly because they need each other so much. Of course, all bets are off during moments of political theater such as reports of special prosecutors, campaign debates, or congressional hearings. In such instances the usual scripted scenarios of political journalism may be disrupted by sudden and unpredictable turns of events—as reporters put it, when news actually breaks out.

The new power of the media (especially television) at such moments was vividly demonstrated by two highly publicized sets of hearings in 1987. That summer, Lt. Col. Oliver North testified in the Iran-Contra hearings. North was implicated in a scheme to divert money from the illegal sale of arms to Iran into support for pro-American forces in Nicaragua's civil war. But in hearings that became must-see TV, North's stage presence and mastery of visual imagery (such as his military bearing and medal-bedecked Marine uniform) won him broad popular support that intimidated his interrogators. Within weeks his approval ratings in the polls surpassed those of both the president and Congress.

That fall witnessed the debacle of Judge Robert Bork's Supreme Court nomination. Bork's opponents conducted a full-scale media campaign, including negative television ads, to pressure senators to vote against him. The confirmation proceedings became a national referendum on Bork's decisions that led to his defeat. They also added the verb "to bork" to the political vocabulary, as a term for the politics of personal destruction. Ever since then, it has been taken for granted that controversial candidates for any major public office will have to run a media gauntlet in order to be confirmed.

The implications of these events were clear to Washington's media and political class—televised political conflict is theater and must be approached as such if you want to win. Both North's and Bork's opponents gained a critical political advantage by tailoring their messages to the audience in the living room rather than the hearing room. In both cases, the losers complained that image had triumphed over substance. In televised political debate, however, image trumps substance.

These hearings also illustrate how the leaders of social movements learned to bypass the political establishment with direct appeals to the public. Following a trail blazed by civil rights and anti–Vietnam War protesters, movements for social change on issues as diverse as environmentalism, women's rights, and gay rights relied heavily on media coverage. Marches, sit-ins, and other visible protests were staged as "pseudo-events" whose success was measured by the number of television cameras in attendance.

On the elite level, an entire new sector of influence arose with the proliferation of think tanks and self-described public interest groups, whose influence depends partly on their ability to generate news stories that are read by public officials and other opinion leaders. Some established organizations of this type, like the center-left Brookings Institution and the center-right American Enterprise Institute, had long produced scholarly studies that were respected by policymakers. But a new breed of public intellectuals began to release studies whose shocking (if suspicious) discoveries of outsized social problems were designed to force officials to act. And like politicians, they regularly tested proposals and mobilized support through an elaborate web of leaks and background discussions with journalists.

For example, a kind of "science by press release" has repeatedly produced public panics and inflated reports of health risks. It is *not* true that one out of eight children in America is hungry, that one out of nine women contracts breast cancer, that one out of four women is raped, or that teenagers are drinking, taking drugs, and having sex more than ever before.[17] Yet all these assertions have attracted heavy media coverage and widespread public acceptance. Other media-driven pseudo-crises have included "epidemics" of abducted children (mostly custody disputes), violent crime (at a time when crime rates were dropping), and infectious diseases (spurred by tie-ins to apocalyptic novels and movies).

Many people still accept such spurious statistics as valid, even though they have been repeatedly refuted. Of course, accusations are big news; refutations aren't. But they also stay in circulation because they are put forward by groups that aim to promote the public interest by making all Americans aware of the problems that they perceive. For "public interest groups" on the left and (less frequently) the right, making news is the first step toward creating conventional wisdom. Along the way, the publicity brings new members, supporters, and funders who help carry on the cause. This is not to question their sincerity, only their belief in their own propaganda. As Cynthia Crossen writes, "In the information business truth [belongs] to those who commission it."[18]

Paradoxically, despite the medium's "participatory bias," the era of media politics has also been one of reduced voter turnout and declining confidence in social institutions. This loss of confidence cuts across institutions and is independent of people's assessments of their own lives. For example, people tend to think more highly of their own congressperson than of Congress as an institution, just as they express optimism about their personal lives while worrying that the country as a whole is deteriorating. Pollsters first came across this phenomenon in the 1980s, about the same time scholars began to decry media negativism.

In general, media effects are most powerful on subjects that are divorced from people's everyday personal experiences. The closer to home a news story hits, the more people are inclined to trust their own knowledge of the situation, and vice versa. Political scientists Seymour Martin Lipset and William Schneider concluded that people's more critical judgments of government and other institutions reflected "negative information in the media," an increase in "the sheer quantity of bad news . . . presented in the context of implicit or explicit criticism of the country's leaders and institutions."[19]

Misreporting Crime and the Economy

The perverse effects of mediated judgments can be illustrated by media reporting on two perennial news topics—crime and the economy. Studies have long shown that economic news stresses the downside, to the extent that regularly released economic indicators (such as the inflation and unemployment rates) consistently get more media coverage when they are seen as bad rather than good news. This kind of skew can have a direct political impact, because perceptions of the national economy are more important than personal experience in voting decisions.

For example, an economic recession ended in 1991, when government statistics showed that the economy began to grow again. Yet reporters on network television stated that the economy was in recession more frequently in 1992 than they had in 1991, and over four out of every five reports on the economy's condition were negative in tone during a period of economic recovery.[20] This false image of unending economic distress caused serious problems for the reelection campaign of President George H. W. Bush by reinforcing the message of his Democratic opponent, Bill Clinton: "It's the economy, stupid." Although Republicans charged the media with partisan bias in that election, the bias that most hurt Bush was the media's economic negativism.

Perhaps the best-documented case of false mediation was the great "television crime wave" of the 1990s, when the television broadcast networks adopted the audience-building formula of local TV news: "If it bleeds it leads." This produced an inverse relationship between the growing network news coverage of crime and the simultaneous decline in actual crime rates. Between 1990 and 1999, for example, network news coverage of crime doubled and coverage of murders quadrupled, even as real-life crime declined and homicide rates dropped by over 40 percent.[21] This steep increase in coverage resulted partly from a genuine surge in youth crime linked to illegal drugs. But the networks also gave saturation coverage to sensational crimes such as school shootings, the murders of children such as Polly Klaas and JonBenét Ramsay, and homicides involving celebrities, such as Gianni Versace's murder by a serial killer and the notorious O. J. Simpson case.

Thus, crime became the most heavily covered topic on network news throughout the 1990s. Meanwhile crime remained the leading story on local TV news shows around the country, which focused heavily on inner-city violence and drug use. As a result, crime became the foremost concern of the American public, not only because of what happened in their neighborhoods, but also because of what they watched in their living rooms.[22]

The effects of crime and economic reporting are prominent examples of a more general phenomenon—the media's growing ability to set the national agenda and frame public issues. For example, experimental studies have shown that people who see a newscast containing a story about a particular social issue later consider that issue more important than do people who see the same newscast without the story.[23] And a large-scale study of the effects of TV news stories on policy issues during the 1970s and 1980s found that nearly half of the changes in public opinion on policy issues could be predicted from the way the different positions on each issue were represented on the evening news.[24]

Thus, the most pervasive impact of the news media lies in the effects of its style and content on the broader political culture. For many years media researchers argued that the news tells us not what to think, but what to think *about*—the attention it gives to some topics and issues rather than others tells the public which ones should concern them. The evidence now suggests that media reports also tell us *how* to think about public issues and institutions—the context within which we debate them. For example, the media frames high school shootings (such as the high-profile 1999 shootings in Littleton, Colorado) primarily in terms of the need for gun control. As a result, public debate focuses on this issue rather than such factors as parenting styles, school counseling, or teenage mental health.[25]

In fairness, public concerns about media influence often arise from the audience's preconceptions. When a story appears that a reader disagrees with, she tends to assume (falsely, in many cases) that it will have undue influence over others, even though people consider themselves immune to this effect. Indeed, the very fact that so many people complain about media bias is evidence of their resistance to messages that don't conform to their prior understanding or expectations. It is also a sign of public resistance to the increased visibility and influence of journalists.

Media Bias and Public Credibility

The story of the media's rising influence is also a story of the audience's growing dissatisfaction. Journalists justified their new role in terms of the public interest despite polling evidence consistently showing that the public felt otherwise. Beginning in the mid-1980s a series of surveys dismayed journalists by showing widespread public hostility toward their profession and its practices. For example, in 1937 two-thirds of the public agreed that the press was "fair." In 1984 only 38 percent said newspapers were "usually fair," and only 29 percent said this of television.[26]

Many journalists reacted with the surprise of politicians who are unexpectedly voted out of office. They saw themselves as acting for the public as its surrogate, defending the little guy against the rich and powerful. So it came as an unpleasant shock to find that they were widely perceived as just another cog in a distant establishment, an elite group of wealthy and influential snobs who had forgotten their roots.

These would-be public tribunes initially treated public criticism as a failure of communication. They assumed that people were re-acting this way only because they didn't understand that the media were just fulfilling their proper role in American society. As famed CBS *60 Minutes* producer Don Hewitt put it, "We are America's ombudsman."[27] However, it gradually became clear that the public did understand the media's new self-image as the country's political arbiter and social conscience. They just didn't buy it. It was journal-ists, having convinced themselves that they were acting in the public interest, who didn't understand. The public was still wedded to the older ideals of dispassionate observation and "objectivity" that jour-nalists were discarding. The apostles of professionalism had done their work too well; the public continued to hold on to its tenets, even when the journalists tried to move on.

The criticism that the media provides opinion in the guise of news had long been expressed by conservatives. At least since the Nixon administration, conservative politicians have run against the bo-geyman of an out-of-control activist media that sought political change by attacking traditional values and institutions. Rejecting this critique as a political stratagem, journalists reacted defensively to a series of surveys released in the 1980s, which consistently found them to be well to the left of the general public in their voting habits and their attitudes toward a host of controversial social issues such as abortion, affirmative action, and gay rights. The evidence was strongest among journalists at national media outlets, such as the television networks and the "prestige press." (More recent survey data have generally replicated these findings. But they also show journalists to be more conservative than the public on some economic issues, such as expanding free trade and reforming government entitlement programs.)[28]

Previously, most academic media criticism came from the left, faulting journalism for not being aggressive enough in supporting social reforms. Now some social scientists began to argue that news coverage reflected journalists' predominantly liberal or Democratic viewpoints on presidential elections and a host of public policy issues including race, religion, environmental protection, health risks, and homelessness. Some studies combined surveys with content analysis to argue that news coverage reflected the perspectives favored by journalists even when this contradicted expert opinion. For example, surveys showed that journalists were far more antinuclear than energy scientists, but the sources they trusted most were antinuclear scientists. A content analysis then showed that news stories mainly cited scientific "experts" who agreed with the journalists rather than representing the actual views of the scientific community.[29] Other studies found similar disconnects on such diverse news topics as AIDS, environmental cancer, and intelligence testing.[30]

Not surprisingly, the events most heavily scrutinized for bias are presidential elections. Large-scale scholarly content analyses of network news have been conducted for every general election since 1980. Many tallied the tone of every individual comment about the candidates, although some categorized stories as a whole. Some examined additional broadcast and print outlets, and a few looked at visual as well as verbal material.

The results are suggestive if not conclusive: Coverage of the 1984, 1992, 1996, and 2004 elections favored the Democratic nominee, while coverage of the 1980, 1988, and 2000 elections produced about equally negative portraits of both major party candidates. For example, a study of the 1996 general election found that half of all on-air evaluations of President Clinton were favorable, while two out of three evaluations of Senator Bob Dole were unfavorable. Four years later, however, the same researchers found that only 40 percent of Vice President Gore's evaluations were favorable, as were 37 percent of George W Bush's evaluations, a statistical wash.[31]

In sum, the mainstream media do not always favor one presidential candidate over another, but the candidates they do favor are usually Democrats.[32] It is also notable that in 2004 the broadcast networks gave John Kerry the best press ever recorded in these studies, while Fox News Channel gave Kerry some of the worst press ever recorded. Since Fox is widely regarded as more conservative than the other networks, this suggests that the deeper issue is not "liberal media bias" per se, but a general tendency for the news product to be influenced by the perspectives of those who produce it.[33]

The most consistent source of media "bias," however, was not ideology but negativism. It was rare for any candidate in a general election to receive a majority of good press, and the combined evaluations for all candidates were always predominantly negative. This is a reminder that the media's "bad news bias" is not only a matter of focusing on negative events but also a tendency to allot more blame than praise. As mentioned, news coverage of the presidency has been highly negative toward Republican and Democratic administrations alike. Similarly, some studies have found that Republicans in Congress have gotten worse press than their Democratic colleagues; others found their coverage to be about equally negative.[34] In this context any partisan bias is probably less pro-Democratic than anti-Republican. To paraphrase George Orwell, journalists see all politicians as evil, but some as more evil than others.

In addition to the gradual buildup of evidence through case studies, a widely debated recent study by a political scientist and an economist recently adopted a more systematic approach.[35] Based on advocacy group ratings, they arrayed members of Congress along a right-to-left spectrum. Then they tabulated each member's favorable references in speeches to various think tanks and advocacy groups. By comparing the groups cited in congressional speeches with those cited in news stories, they were able to locate the ideological "position" of news outlets relative to members of Congress. The result? Every major news outlet apart from Fox and the *Washington Times* was positioned to the left of the average congressperson.

Thus, evidence has been accumulating that, however unintentionally, journalists often present the news from their own point of view. Ironically, the more they fought against their depiction as a liberal elite, the less willing journalists became to admit that their perspectives might shape their work either consciously or unconsciously. The problem was that their defense was built on the very intellectual foundation they were abandoning—that journalists were trained professionals who didn't allow their personal views to influence the accuracy and fairness of their work. Of course, the more they asserted their right to greater interpretive freedom, the more their stories were subject to the partiality that all interpretation contains.

Thus, it was not by coincidence that the 1980s witnessed the large-scale entrance of political punditry into public discourse. If journalists were experts on public affairs, why shouldn't they go on television talk shows to discuss the issues they covered, then return to their day jobs in the newsroom? They could express their opinions in prime time and discuss the same topics objectively in the morning edition. Similarly, why shouldn't a career track move back and forth between journalism and politics, allowing talented people to express their values in one career while holding them in check in the other? Yet this increasingly popular "revolving door" also attracted attention from watchdogs who regarded it as a political form of double-entry bookkeeping.

For that matter, what was the difference between a journalist and a pundit? Both transmitted their knowledge of current affairs, which came from their proximity to the political world. At this point it became difficult to differentiate clearly between journalists and commentators. Not surprisingly, the general public tended to lump together the talking heads on their television screens, whatever the latter might call themselves.

Public Hostility
Toward the Media

More than ideological differences led to the growing public dissatisfaction with the media. If conservatives considered journalists to be politically biased, cross sections of the public were more irritated by their perceived arrogance and elitism. Highly publicized controversies and misdeeds at some of journalism's most respected institutions led many people to suspect that journalists believed they could play by their own rules, even as they enforced their rules of accountability against other powerful social groups.

The most notorious of these misdeeds were acts of pure invention: reporters at the *Washington Post, New York Times, USA Today,* and *New Republic* were all caught making up news stories. Other sensational stories were retracted when they could not be verified. Among the most prominent were a CNN/*Time* magazine report that the United States had exposed its own troops to a nerve gas during the Vietnam War and a CBS *60 Minutes* report, aired in the heat of a presidential election campaign, that new documents proved President Bush had received preferential treatment during his National Guard service.

As important as these ethical lapses were, other questionable practices stemmed from the more activist and socially engaged role that journalists were claiming as their prerogative. One area that troubled many people was a new willingness to probe into the private lives of public figures, particularly their sexual relationships. This began in 1987, journalism's annus horribilus, with a newspaper's decision to stake out a residence of presidential candidate Gary Hart to catch him in an extramarital liaison. This led to Hart's withdrawal from the campaign after an embarrassing sequence of events, culminating in a *Washington Post* reporter asking him on the record whether he had ever committed adultery.

There were many reasons for this breach of a long-standing "gentlemen's agreement" that had led the press to cast a blind eye to the personal flaws of the politicians they covered. There have been reasons, frequently good ones, for every subsequent foray into this once forbidden territory, which included bad behavior by other senators, a House Speaker, cabinet members, and (most notoriously) a sitting president. But the upshot was to reawaken dormant public perceptions of the "gutter press" from nearly a century ago and to blur the distinction between the tabloids and the "respectable" press that Adolph Ochs worked so hard to establish. Suddenly it seemed that no news was unfit to print.

Another page taken from the tabloids was the "ambush" or "gotcha" journalism that became a staple of television newsmagazine shows, in which reporters went incognito or used hidden cameras and other questionable techniques to catch alleged wrongdoers in the act. Unfortunately, this ambush journalism began to produce more lawsuits than Pulitzers. Political scientist Larry Sabato popularized the term "feeding frenzy" to describe the phenomenon of a media pack swarming around the unfortunate perpetrator of some embarrassing or scandalous behavior with an excessive enthusiasm that feeds on itself.

Believing they had been manipulated by campaign consultants and media advisors during the 1988 presidential election, the national media—especially the television networks—went on a crusade to wrest the campaign news agenda away from the candidates next time around. (For example, the Radio-TV News Directors Association exhorted its members to "take control of the political agenda in 1992.")[36] During 1992, national media outlets introduced such novel features as "ad watches," "truth boxes," and "reality checks," all designed to expose the candidates' lies or misrepresentations, while presenting the media as truth-tellers. The idea was to make campaigns cleaner and more substantive by aggressively holding candidates accountable for their conduct. Of course this also made journalists much more central to the campaign itself, by increasing their role as arbiters.

Indeed, the fact that so many journalists believed that they, rather than the candidates, were best equipped to interpret the campaign for the public indicates the heights to which their professional self-esteem had risen. And journalists were pleased with the results. A Times Mirror post-election poll found that four out of five journalists surveyed rated their coverage as "good" or "excellent."[37] However, the public was not convinced. When Times Mirror asked voters to grade the media's performance in the campaign on a scale from A to F, the average grade was C-. That was lower than the grades voters gave the parties, candidates, campaign consultants, and even talk show hosts. It appears that the reformers' prescriptions were better suited to satisfying the complaints of journalists than those of the electorate in whose name they were enacted.[38]

Thus, journalists have alienated the public not only by their evildoing, but also by their do-gooding. Projects like taking over the campaign agenda or the "civic journalism" movement, which can involve news organizations directly in local politics, are all about what the media can do to improve society. But the public prefers less rather than more "mediation" in public affairs. For example, they consistently give high marks to talk shows and campaign debates. These venues allow them to hear the candidates discuss issues at greater than sound-bite length and, in some cases, to participate in the discussion themselves. Nonetheless, most of the 1992 reforms have remained a part of election news, despite the fact that voters' ratings of the media have not improved in subsequent post-election polls. After the 2004 elections, for example, the media's "grade point average" from the public remained at C-, while record numbers of *both* Democratic and Republican voters described the campaign coverage as biased.[39]

Further, studies of election news suggest that the public's criticisms have some merit. Content analyses of the 1992 general election coverage found that it was no more issue-oriented than in 1988. However, it was more opinionated and less balanced, and it gave journalists far more airtime than candidates. Studies of subsequent presidential elections have found a continuing emphasis on who is ahead rather than what the issues are, combined with negativism, lack of balance, and diminished candidate airtime.[40]

In retrospect, it appears that journalists have been spending down the capital of credibility that their predecessors accumulated when their professionalism succeeded in improving journalism's public image. In the face of widespread dissatisfaction that journalists' responses only magnified, the audience lacked only the means to vote with their eyeballs by turning to suppliers of news products more to their liking.

Journalism Meets the "New Media"

Starting in the 1980s, new conditions began providing the disaffected news audience with new alternatives, although some didn't take root until the following decade. The first factor was not technological but political—the deregulation of electronic media as part of the Reagan administration's broader deregulation agenda. This made it possible for electronic media to feature discussions of public affairs without concern for factors such as fairness and balance. The immediate practical effect was to revitalize AM radio as a medium for political talk. Suddenly this once-bland medium crackled with political debate, giving voice and reinforcement to previously marginalized opinions.

Led by Rush Limbaugh, conservative talk show hosts turned radio into an interactive alternative to the traditional media for like-minded listeners. Other groups who felt ignored by establishment opinion, such as urban blacks, also used the medium to air their grievances. The underlying dynamic of the new forum was populist; conservatives simply proved more effective than liberals at using this format as a platform for their political agenda. They even activated their audience as a political force on issues such as congressional pay raises, in a manner that presaged the Internet's ability to force new information and opinion into public discourse.

The other major development of the 1980s was the success of CNN as a twenty-four-hour all-news cable network. Limited resources initially prevented CNN from challenging the hegemony of the big three broadcast networks, who derided their smaller competitor as the "chicken noodle network." The possibilities represented by this new format became evident only during the first Gulf War, when CNN's continuous coverage and overseas presence made it the network of choice for Americans seeking the latest developments in the big story of 1991.

During the 1990s, pent-up alternate perspectives on the news finally burst open the gates manned by the traditional media's gatekeepers. After a quarter-century of relatively stable but limited choices, the media landscape suddenly included such alternatives as political talk radio, competitive cable news networks, and numerous applications of the Internet, along with the convergence of multiple media via the personal computer. This fragmentation of the media, and the twenty-four-hour news cycle that accompanied it, have brought about the most massive change in journalism since the arrival of television.

However, the explosion of choices brought new problems. The hypercompetition of an all-news-all-the-time environment has accelerated the erosion of standards once enforced by the national media. The new premium placed on scooping the opposition increases the potential for errors, unethical practices, and media manipulation. On the cable networks, hasty and premature reporting turns events of dubious news value into drawn-out soap operas. The vastly expanded airtime, once a precious commodity, gets filled not with additional news but with mindless chatter, speculation, and news gathering on the fly.

On the other hand, this new setting promises greater diversity in both the style and substance of political affairs coverage. For example, the audience for political magazines like the *New Republic* and *National Review* is growing, even as the readership of daily newspapers continues to tumble. Web sites such as Slate and Salon have established themselves as important sources of news and commentary, as have many individual bloggers. Most conspicuously, the Fox News Channel showed that a twenty-four-hour format of news and talk with a populist conservative edge could yield profits while it wields influence.

Fox's journalism has been attacked by many critics who charge it with partisanship, sensationalism, and shoddy news practices. There is certainly a tabloid spirit to Fox's personalized and sometimes pugnacious talk shows. Like Pulitzer and Hearst before him, owner Rupert Murdoch understands the appeal of a pugilistic populism that socks it to the big shots. And the targets are often conservative bugaboos like woolly-headed intellectuals, Hollywood political activists, and the "establishment" media.

In addition, Fox's freewheeling presentation style, with its breezy tone and jazzy graphics, provides a casual counterpoint to the solemn and omniscient air long cultivated by network journalists. In a political environment that often treats news as politics by other means, this reinforces the network's antielitist tone, a case of style meshing with substance. (Disclosure: I am a contributor to Fox News, where I appear occasionally to discuss media-related issues.)

The Internet in particular has undercut both local newspapers and network news as the undisputed leaders of American journalism. Suddenly their business plans were challenged on a new "virtual" multimedia playing field. Segments of the news audience turned to gossip-driven Web sites such as the Drudge Report for revelations of the Monica Lewinsky affair; they turned to Web sites of British newspapers and the BBC for a different perspective on the wars in Afghanistan and Iraq; and they turned to little-known American bloggers to fact-check political and media scandals during the 2004 election.

At minimal cost to either bloggers or readers, blogs with compelling content have turned into instant media and political watchdogs with growing power to expose scandals, break stories, and even drive the news agenda. In fact, criticism of the establishment media (from both ends of the political spectrum) is a leitmotif of the blogosphere. This power to hold the traditional news media accountable resides in the ability of bloggers to reach a critical mass, which occurs when brand-name blogs feed on more obscure ones and amplify material they see as important until the traditional media are forced to take notice. This is how conservative bloggers eventually forced CBS to retract its exposé of George W. Bush's military service, just as liberal bloggers forced Trent Lott's resignation as Senate majority leader following his racially insensitive remarks.

Yet even as the greatest range of news and information in history has become available to anyone with a computer and a modem, public dissatisfaction with the media's performance remains high. In the race for audience share or partisan gain, standards have clearly eroded in electronic journalism, particularly on cable news shows. Viewers can get the impression that all the information in today's cacophonous media environment is the product of spin or ulterior motives.

At this point we simply lack a commonly accepted manual for creating, identifying, and interpreting the swarm of information that swirls around us. This decline of the national media's gatekeeping and editorial functions also carries potentially profound consequences for future social and political discourse. Many young people either rely on the Internet as their sole news medium or obtain news indirectly through the popular culture. In this new arena of alternative news media, the likes of Jon Stewart, the Wonkette, and YouTube may become the successors of Rather, Jennings, and Brokaw.[41]

Thus, today's news environment is becoming more vibrant but less reliable. A fragmented news market produces greater diversity and accountability in public discourse at the cost of declining standards and quality. The broadcast networks in particular have been steadily abandoning substantive coverage in both domestic and international reporting. The trend toward soft news and lifestyle coverage, entertainment, and consumer-oriented reporting was one of the most significant developments in the 1990s. Not even the war on terror has significantly reversed it.

Conclusion:
Profiting from Change

News has always been a business in America, and the news audience has been treated primarily as consumers for almost two hundred years. The current economic shake-up precipitated by new technologies has revived the struggle for survival among competing businesses, just as it did after the introductions of television, radio, and the telegraph. In this increasingly fragmented and competitive world, it makes economic sense to own as many media outlets as possible, and so mergers have led to rapid horizontal and vertical integration within the news industry. Newspapers are increasingly seen as just one of many "platforms" that distribute information and entertainment, and corporate resources are allocated among them according to their profit potential.

The view of news as a public good underlies the reasoning that led many other governments to nationalize the electronic media. But it runs directly against the American experience, where even the revered concept of the "free marketplace of ideas" is drawn from commerce. Moreover, a comparison of media ownership in ninety-seven countries, sponsored by the World Bank in 2001, found government ownership of the media to be associated with less press freedom and fewer political and economic rights.[42]

In fact, the best testament to the continued dynamism of American journalism may be the frequent grumbling from European pundits about the "Americanization" of their political life. Between the privatization of electronic media and the globalization of media conglomerates, European news organizations are increasingly influenced by the American model of independent journalism that functions as a watchdog rather than an ideological mouthpiece. To paraphrase Churchill on democracy, the United States seems to have the worst system of media—except for all the others.

Many of the elite news organizations in this country, such as the *Washington Post* and the big three broadcast networks, have depended on near-monopoly conditions to devote greater resources to newsrooms than purely economic motives might dictate. The reassertion of economic logic at media conglomerates such as Times Mirror and Knight-Ridder has proved wrenching to watch. But the inheritors of these organizations are making big bets on their future as multi-platform information providers by pouring seed money into their Web sites. Thus, the disappearance of independent local newspapers into national chains has occurred at the same time that the range of information available to anyone with a computer has grown exponentially.

The American media are in a technological transition period, and the public response to new media platforms and standards is only beginning to take shape. As this is written in 2006, the World Wide Web is only fifteen years old. In 1995 there were barely 5 million Internet hosts; a decade later there were over 300 million.[43] Fox's audience exceeded CNN's only five years ago. The regulatory framework for telecommunications was overhauled only ten years ago, and some of it already seems outdated because of rapidly changing technologies.

Currently there is a mismatch between the traditional media's self-conception as an agent of social and political enlightenment and the audience's rejection of this movement from bystander to participant. But this is not the first time technological change has helped drive a wedge between journalistic norms and audience expectations. As Paul Starr has shown, it has happened repeatedly without fundamentally changing the American model of privately owned and relatively unfettered communications media.[44]

Thus, the news industry may simply be caught between business models. This is part of the process of "creative destruction" that periodically affects every industry. The restructuring of this industry at this moment seems particularly wrenching because the media have become so pervasive and so tightly integrated into American social and political life. But some of their old bad habits are being uprooted, even as new ones inevitably appear. At this point in the process the losses to society are more visible and may in fact exceed the gains.

However, American journalism has repeatedly gone downscale, shaken off its barnacles, and emerged revitalized. The penny press, the big-city tabloids, and broadcast television were all condemned for lowering standards and impoverishing public discourse with their lowest-common-denominator journalism. Each time there was much truth in the criticism. But each change also brought an expansion of the news audience, a circulation of media elites, and new conceptions of journalism and the news itself. And each time they retained a distinctively American character. Despite some unpleasant shocks to the system, the current upheaval is making the news media simultaneously more decentralized, diverse, competitive, and contentious. In short, however much they change, the media still hew to the American grain.

CHAPTER 8
Popular Culture
Martha Bayles

*American popular culture is frequently deplored by elites and widely con-
sumed by ordinary people. And while some of that culture is trashy, much of
it, such as jazz, achieves the level of distinctive art. As Martha Bayles points
out, popular culture here is not recent but old, with roots among the many
ethnic groups and nationalities that settled in North America. Not only
jazz, but minstrelsy, vaudeville, and motion pictures were ways of bringing
human concerns to a popular audience. And today, popular culture, once denounced by the artistic avant-garde, has absorbed some of the avant-garde's
least creative and most destructive clichés.*

EVERY CIVILIZATION WORTHY OF THE NAME HAS PRODUCED
artworks both popular and high. By "popular" I mean appealing to
ordinary people, by "high" I mean cherished by elites. There are
many examples of art that meets both tests. In western Europe, examples of art both high and popular include the plays of Shakespeare and Molière, the operas of Mozart and Puccini, and the
paintings of Monet and Van Gogh. In the United States, major
artists have been inspired by popular genres: Herman Melville by
the explorer's journal, Mark Twain by African-American folklore,
Robert Venturi by the casinos of Las Vegas. Many works have begun
life as low entertainment and then gained acceptance as high art: the
jazz of Louis Armstrong and Duke Ellington; the films of Charlie
Chaplin and John Ford; the songs of Jerome Kern and Cole Porter.

And, on occasion, a figure labeled "high" and a figure labeled "popular" have engaged in fruitful interaction: for example, the cubist painter Stuart Davis and the jazz pianist Earl Hines.

American popular culture is generally assumed to have emerged at the turn of the twentieth century, along with the electronic media. But its roots go back to the colonial period, when British and other European settlers in the New World began to jettison the aristocratic ways of the Old. This jettisoning occurred faster on the frontier, and in the ethnically and religiously diverse Mid-Atlantic, than in New England and the South. But to the extent that all free North Americans were devoted to commerce, opposed to state religion, and jealous of their liberties against the British Crown, there arose among them sparks of hostility to all forms of inherited privilege that the Revolution fanned into a patriotic flame. By the time Andrew Jackson ran against John Quincy Adams in the presidential election of 1824, "eastern aristocrat" was a common epithet.

Yet as historian Lawrence Levine notes, "Americans, long after they declared their political independence, retained a colonial mentality in matters of culture and intellect."[1] According to Alexis de Tocqueville, there were three reasons why "few of the civilized nations of our time have made less progress than the United States in the higher sciences or had so few great artists, distinguished poets, or celebrated writers." First was religion: the Puritanism of America's first settlers was "naturally unfavorable to the fine arts." Second was pursuit of gain: the "breathless cupidity" of a "people who have fallen on a new and unbounded country." And third was the link to the Old World: Americans "could gather the treasures of the mind without working to produce them themselves."[2]

This may explain why the first real departures from European models were in the so-called useful arts. In mechanical design, Americans soon produced a vernacular style notable for its economy, simplicity, and ease of reproduction. For example, the long-barreled rifle that helped George Washington's Pennsylvania irregulars defeat the British army in the War of Independence was "developed during the 1730s and 1740s by patient experiment among the gunsmiths around Lancaster [Pennsylvania], a hunting tool that could pick off a 'coon or a rabbit at long range in the lonely forests."[3] This description comes from the historian John A. Kouwenhoven, whose account of "vernacular" and "cultivated" art making in America sounds an important theme: Americans are at their most creative when working at a certain remove from traditional high culture; but their creativity falters when that remove becomes too great.[4]

After the Revolution, efforts were made to foster a "new Arcadia" of republican ideals and national culture. In published sheet music, English and French tunes were spurned in favor of homegrown fare: New England hymns written in the old-fashioned "shape-note" manner, patriotic poems, and drinking songs modeled on *Adams and Liberty,* written in 1798 by Robert Treat Paine, Jr. But this attempt at a unified American culture was soon riven by regional and class divisions. By the 1840s, popular songs were being written in two different categories: sentimental ballads for singing around the piano in the middle-class parlor; and humorous, often salacious numbers for variety theater, taverns, and other rude settings. The gifted Stephen Foster was master of both, but the two cultural milieus were gradually diverging.[5]

This divergence showed up most plainly in the public theater. For a while in the early nineteenth century, scenes from Shakespeare thrived alongside jugglers, acrobats, comedy skits, and blackface minstrel routines. But as Levine argues, this mixing did not last. By midcentury, New York City's "kid gloves and white vest" set were patronizing finer, more upscale theaters, such as the Astor Place Opera House, and the "mass of vulgarity" were crowding into rougher venues such as the Bowery Theater. In the few theaters still shared by both, tensions grew between the rich in their boxes, applauding anything they thought refined and European, and the working poor in the pit and gallery, hurling vegetables and other missiles at anything they thought pretentious and foreign. In 1849, open conflict broke out between hoity-toity admirers of the English actor William Mcready and hoi polloi fans of his American rival Edwin Forrest. In the ensuing Astor Place Riot, twenty-two people lost their lives.[6]

When the tale is told this way, nineteenth-century American theater seems a failed experiment in cultural democracy. But a closer look reveals a different story, one in which distinctive American modes of comedy, drama, music, and dance emerged from low-status settings and gradually developed into high art. The most salient example is, of course, jazz.

The roots of jazz are entwined, first of all, with minstrelsy. No one knows when the first white American (or Briton) got the idea of smearing burnt cork on his face and imitating blacks for the amusement of other whites. Black makeup and masks have a long history in Europe, dating back to medieval depictions of Satan, the Lords of Misrule, Harlequin, and English Morris Dance leaders with names like Lord Coffee, Old Sooty Face, and Dirty Bet.[7] But not until the nineteenth century did blackface become the chief form of entertainment for a nation. In the 1820s, solo white performers such as Charles Matthews and Thomas D. Rice were famous for their renditions of slave songs and dances; twenty years later, minstrelsy was big business, with troupes like the Edwin P. Christy Minstrels touring the United States and Europe with polished renditions of "Ethiopian melodies" and comedy skits featuring the hayseed Jim Crow and city slicker Zip Coon.

Prior to the Civil War, minstrelsy was performed almost entirely by whites and was clearly racially degrading. Yet some scholars maintain that degradation was not the whole point. For instance, the music historian Eileen Southern writes that "the practices of white minstrels in the nineteenth century established unfortunate stereotypes of black men—as shiftless, irresponsible, thieving, happy-go-lucky. . . . And yet, blackface minstrelsy was a tribute to the black man's music and dance." Indeed, Southern reports one chronicler of plantation life accusing a well-known white group, the Fellow's Minstrels, of "not 'bearing comparison' with the plantation slaves, chiefly because of the former's artificiality."[8]

After the Civil War, minstrelsy was dominated by blacks, because as Southern notes, it "gave the creative black man an opportunity to acquire experience in the theatrical arts that could scarcely have been obtained any other way during the period." What is more, performers such as James Bland, Billy Kersands, and Bert Williams soon shook off the trappings of minstrelsy and toured Europe and the northern and western United States as elegantly dressed singers, dancers, and musicians. In the 1890s, when blacks in the South were suffering the horrors of lynching and the Ku Klux Klan, the first all-black musicals were premiering on Broadway, many of them created by blacks, and none employing burnt cork.[9]

Another humble root of jazz was ragtime, the music played in the black saloons, gambling dens, and brothels that sprang up along the Mississippi River and elsewhere in the Southeast after the Civil War. These "gin joints" provided the cheapest music available: a lone piano player with a powerful left hand. Some of these "piano thumpers" became legendary among African-Americans, their virtuosity and endurance earning them the title of "professor." Among whites, ragtime was known chiefly through minstrelsy until the 1890s, when it became available as sheet music and as rolls for mechanical player pianos. By 1900, the gifted black composer Scott Joplin was known throughout the world as "the King of Ragtime."

Jazz also grew out of such genteel sources as the "syncopated orchestras" that played dance music for wealthy whites. These bands, many of which were black, not only "syncopated" the standard written repertory (by introducing a more complex, toe-tapping rhythm), they also introduced new instruments, such as banjos, guitars, and saxophones. In 1914, when the white ballroom dancers Vernon and Irene Castle popularized the turkey trot, one-step, and fox trot, their favorite band leader was an African-American, James Reese Europe. A similar pattern appears with the brass bands that in every town square provided lusty music for civic ceremonies, holiday celebrations, and Sunday-afternoon diversion. Here, too, the black influence was strong, as listeners came to prefer rhythms a bit livelier than the "oom-pah-pah" of the Prussian prototype. During World War I, the U.S. Army's 369th Band (led by the same James Reese Europe) so impressed the foremost military band of France that the French musicians surreptitiously disassembled its instruments to see if they had been specially adapted for the purpose of ragging John Philip Sousa.[10]

All of these influences converged in New Orleans, where according to legend, jazz was born of illicit congress between "downtown" syncopated orchestras dominated by classically trained black Creoles and "uptown" brass bands dominated by untutored African-Americans skilled in the blues.[11] It is true that the Creoles' classical training enabled them to play ragtime with greater speed and dexterity, thus creating the propulsive rhythm known as swing. Some of the finest early jazzmen—Sidney Bechet, Edward "Kid" Ory, and Jelly Roll Morton—were black Creoles. Yet it is also true that jazz benefited from the remarkable virtuosity of black musicians with no such training, from the trumpeter Charles "Buddy" Bolden to the great Louis Armstrong. In any case, jazz soon made its way by paddle steamer up the Mississippi to Chicago, and from there by gramophone to Europe and beyond. Ragtime, writes historian S. Frederick Starr, "hit London in the 1890s like a tornado," and by 1913 Germany, France, and Russia also succumbed (like the French, the military bands of Tsar Nicholas II were learning to syncopate). And by 1924, "the musical shock wave" of jazz had "penetrated every major city in western Europe, and then beyond to such far-flung centers as Istanbul and Shanghai."[12]

What did "serious" music lovers think of jazz? To one discerning listener, the Swiss composer Ernst-Alexandre Ensermet, Will Marion Cook's Southern Syncopated Orchestra was sufficiently worthy to "mark the passage . . . from popular art to learned art,"[13] and lead clarinetist Bechet was an "artist of genius."[14] To others, jazz was anathema. In 1928 the Russian communist Maxim Gorky leveled a tirade against jazz that could just as well have come from an aristocratic or haute-bourgeois guardian of high culture: "The monstrous bass belches out English words; a wild horn wails piercingly, calling to mind the cries of a raving camel; a drum pounds monotonously; a nasty little pipe tears at one's ears; a saxophone emits its quacking nasal sound. Fleshy hips sway, and thousands of heavy feet tread and shuffle."[15]

Gorky's side lost the argument, needless to say. By the turn of the twenty-first century, jazz had risen from the status of "lowbrow"[16] entertainment to that of "America's classical music."[17]

It is all the more remarkable, then, to see how jazz was treated in the midcentury debate over mass culture. Dwight MacDonald's 1960 essay "Masscult and Midcult" rejects all popular music on the ground that it is entertainment manufactured by the capitalist system to keep the masses quiescent; but then the author makes an exception for jazz. Because he likes it, he places jazz in a different and more acceptable ideological category:

> The only major form of Folk Art that still persists in this country is jazz, and the difference between Folk Art and Masscult may be most readily perceived by comparing the kind of thing heard at the annual Newport Jazz Festivals to Rock 'n' Roll. The former is musically interesting and emotionally real; the latter is—not. The amazing survival of jazz, despite the exploitative onslaughts of half a century of commercial entrepreneurs, is in my opinion, due to its folk

quality. And as the noble and the peasant understood each other better than either understood the bourgeois, so it seems significant that jazz is the only art form that appeals to both the intelligentsia and the common people. As for the others, let them listen to *South Pacific*.[18]

Better to ignore inconvenient facts, such as the celebrated appearance of rock and roller Chuck Berry at the 1958 Newport Jazz Festival, or the demonstrated fondness of jazz musicians for the songs of Richard Rodgers, composer of *South Pacific*.[19] The point is that when faced with a product of "Masscult" that does qualify as art, all MacDonald can do is reclassify it as folk music.[20]

But jazz is anything but folk music. The scholarly definition of folk music was worked out at the turn of the twentieth century by the English folklorist Cecil J. Sharp and the Hungarian composer Béla Bartók. Roughly, their criteria required the music to be: (1) rural and slow to change, not urban and dynamic; (2) continually varied, with no definitive version; (3) simple, straightforward, and plain; (4) transmitted orally, not through formal training or writing; and (5) focused more on group sharing than on individual expression. Even in the 1920s, it would have been a stretch to apply the second and fourth criteria to jazz, and the other three did not apply at all. And the notion that any of these criteria would apply to such eminent jazz figures as Duke Ellington, Coleman Hawkins, Charlie Parker, or Miles Davis is ludicrous.

So why call jazz folk music? It will not surprise anyone who recalls the folk revivals of the 1930s and 1950s to learn that the answer is bound up with politics. Folk music became politicized in the mid-nineteenth century, when Europeans began to use it as a vehicle of nationalist sentiment. In Germany in 1896, this practice led to the *Wandervogel* (migratory bird) movement, which sent young men tramping through the countryside, singing everything from peasant ballads to beer-hall shouts to cabaret torch songs. During the Third

Reich, some of these groups were hijacked by the Hitler Youth and their songs turned into Nazi propaganda.

The left made better—and longer—use of folk music. Indeed, folk songs and progressive politics have become so intertwined that most people are shocked to see the conservatism of the scholarly definition. But significantly, the American left has rarely been purist about what qualifies as folk music. From Joe Hill in the 1920s to Bob Dylan in the 1960s, folksingers in the United States have borrowed freely from what the *Daily Worker* once called "commercial music tied to the Capitalist economic machine."[21]

And if leftists were willing to blur the distinction between folk and commercial, capitalists were downright eager. One of the purest folk traditions in America, a deposit of Scots-English ballads handed down from the eighteenth century, was discovered a hundred years ago in the southern Appalachian Mountains. One of the discoverers, a folklorist named Olive Dame Campbell, invited Cecil Sharp to visit the area in 1916 and worked with him on his magnum opus, *English Folk Songs from the Southern Appalachians* (1917).[22] That collection sold briskly, as had Sharp's previous books. Yet at that point in the early twentieth century, printed collections of folk music were already giving way to recordings. And swiftly the vaunted purity of the Appalachian tradition was made to turn a tidy profit, as hot on the heels of the folklorists with their notebooks came the entrepreneurs with their sound equipment. As the musicologist Judith Tick observes, "The record labels were in the mountains at the same time as the collectors, and often they worked together."[23] By the 1920s, "mountain music" was a staple of the "hillbilly" market, just as blues was of the "race" market.

During the Great Depression, when the federal government funded a major effort to study and preserve American folk music, commercial recording was accepted even by such staunch leftists as Charles Seeger, the Harvard-educated composer who went from writing reviews for the *Daily Worker* to collecting folk songs for the

Works Progress Administration. Working with Seeger were his wife, the composer Ruth Crawford Seeger, and the father-and-son team John and Alan Lomax. From these two dynasties grew a tradition of using commerce to preserve—and popularize—America's folk music legacy. A living example would be Charles Seeger's son Pete, a son of privilege who nevertheless became a folk music icon in the vein of Woody Guthrie and Huddie "Leadbelly" Ledbetter. These icons, including Bob Dylan and his many successors in folk rock, happily violate all five scholarly criteria, adding political lyrics to old tunes, writing new material and selling it as a commercial product, and in general becoming celebrities.

Herewith, a complication: America has never had folk music in the scholarly sense. The population of the United States is not descended from peasants who have tilled the same soil, spoken the same language, and sung the same songs for countless generations. Rather it is forged from Indian, African, European, Latin American, and Asian tribes whose traditions have been drastically altered by their chaotic mutual encounter in the New World. A better term, coined by folklorist Gene Bluestein, is "poplore," defined by him as a system "in which creative individuals integrated sources similar to those appearing in older, more traditional cultures with popular or commercial elements. Their artistry expresses itself within the framework of a folk process that, instead of developing over long periods, changes very quickly."[24]

A man of the left, Bluestein never meant poplore to include outright commercial material with no political message. Yet consider: the most truly authentic folk songs do not deal with politics. Some do, but like the English folk songs collected by Sharp, the majority of blues and ballads recorded by the Seegers and Lomaxes are about perennial human themes: love and betrayal, home and exile, good times and bad, the blows of fate. Thus in America, and increasingly in the rest of the world, the line between "folk" and "commercial" is dissolved, and the only real basis for judgment is musical quality.

The same trajectory from low entertainment to high art can be traced in the other performing arts. The first step was the professionalization and nationalization of vaudeville, the form of popular theater that emerged after the Civil War and thrived until the 1930s. In French, *vaux de ville* means "worthy of the city's patronage." But as suggested by the historian Albert F. McLean, what Americans found appealing about the invented term "vaudeville" was "its vagueness, its faint, but harmless exoticism, and perhaps its connotation of gentility."[25] Gentility is key, because while vaudeville drew upon the rough-and-tumble amusements found in frontier saloons, traveling circuses, variety theaters, and burlesque halls, it also made them palatable to the new urban middle class, especially women and children.

The birth of vaudeville is usually dated around 1881, when a New York impresario named Tony Pastor opened a lavish new theater in Union Square, near several major department stores, with the idea of attracting female shoppers to "refined" entertainment. (As the saying went: "From 14th Street down, the men were earning it, and from 14th Street up, the women were spending it.")[26] In Boston, B. F. Keith and Edward F. Albee founded a chain of theaters decorated as grand palaces, in which patrons could expect "a fixed policy of cleanliness and order" and performances that avoided "vulgarity and suggestiveness in words, action, and costume."[27]

Clearly, these constraints reflected the Puritanism that, for Tocqueville, "gave no scope to the Muse of Comedy" in America.[28] But it would be a mistake to assume that vaudeville was humorless or pious. On the contrary, it traded in irreverent, often outrageous comedy about a complex and challenging social reality: immigration. Between 1840 and 1920, the United States absorbed approximately

33 million Germans, Irish, Italians, Slavs, Jews, Britons, Scandinavians, and Canadians, as well as two-hundred thousand Chinese. The latter were ill treated, then barred entry by the Chinese Exclusion Act of 1882. The others, especially the Irish, Slavs, and Jews, were subject to prejudice and discrimination—including heavy-handed stereotyping on the vaudeville stage. Writes the cultural historian Lawrence E. Mintz:

> The Irish characters are drunk, belligerent, and dumb [which meant both unintelligent and naive]. . . . The Italians are happy rascals, promiscuous, profligate, and irresponsible, comically hyperemotional—and dumb; the Germans, usually called "Dutch" in vaudeville from the same corruption of Deutsch which gave us the Pennsylvania Dutch, are lazy, stodgily conservative, and of course, also dumb. Blacks are lazy, dishonest, promiscuous, profligate, irresponsible and—guess what—dumb. Jews are usually "canny" . . . that is, they are smart in the sense of too clever, manipulative, dishonest—but they are also portrayed, perhaps surprisingly, as dumb, especially as lacking in "street smarts."[29]

But stereotyping was not the whole story. From minstrelsy, vaudeville borrowed the "two-act," or dialogue pitting "a dumb or culturally naive character" (Jim Crow) against one who is "smarter, more hip" (Zip Coon). It is important to note, however, that the dumb character was not always so dumb. Indeed, he occasionally morphed into a "commonsense philosopher" whose role it was to deflate the "sophisticated error" of his city-slicker counterpart. In this way, vaudeville put a new ethnic face on the old stock figure of the rustic but sharp-witted Yankee.[30]

So vaudeville is the mother lode of all insulting American ethnic jokes, such as: "What's the right career for the son of a Polish-Jewish marriage? Janitor in a medical school."[31] But it is also the source of much ethnic self-ridicule, as in the Irish joke about the immigrant from Galway who, hearing of an accident in which forty Italians and one Irishman were killed, sighs, "Ah, the poor man."[32] Moreover, the audience could never be sure whether the Irishman telling the joke was really Irish—or even a man. Long before the social construction of ethnic and gender identity became a staple of higher education in America, it was fodder for low comedy. It was in vaudeville, after all, that the eldest Marx Brother, Leonard, adopted a fake Italian accent as "Chico." And until World War I made German characters unpopular, younger brother Julius, also known as Groucho, spoke with a "Dutch" accent. The critic Edward Rothstein offers this appreciative assessment:

> Irish, German and Yiddish accents were part of the patois of vaudevillian comedy, the mangled sentences echoing the increasingly familiar immigrant sounds of cities like New York. Oddly, though, these exaggerations were not generally an occasion for bigotry or hostility. There was an element of celebration in the mockery, partly because the actors were often themselves from these groups. Even stranger, ethnic actors would adopt alien ethnic identities for the sake of the comedy, making the artifice even more apparent. Blacks appeared as Chinese, Jews as Irish. It was as if, by some unspoken agreement, marginal groups had joined forces in displaying, to each other, the comic absurdity of their position.[33]

Understandably, none of these entertainments was regarded as real art. But over time, gifted vaudevillians such as the Marx Brothers, Irving Berlin, Eubie Blake, W. C. Fields, Will Rogers, Sophie Tucker, and Bert Williams helped to forge new modes of music, comedy, and dance that would conquer popular audiences everywhere—and, at times, win the approval of cultural elites.

As vaudeville grew in popularity, the most successful local impresarios built major companies, based in New York, which booked and coordinated all the acts for the large numbers of theaters, called "chains," which they owned. And just as Pastor, Keith, and Albee had insisted on propriety and decorum in order to attract large audiences and avoid being shut down by local authorities, so did the large companies they founded do the same: all those involved, performers and patrons alike, were expected to "clean up their act" in order to stay in business. Thus did vaudeville set a pattern that would be followed by the American entertainment industry for the next sixty years: self-regulation, including self-censorship, for the double purpose of maximizing audience size and minimizing government interference.

Next to enter were the electronic media: film and sound recording at the turn of the century; radio in the 1920s and 1930s; television in the 1950s. Clearly, these did not make their entrance onto an empty stage, but rather one fully stocked with sophisticated styles of performance and equally sophisticated business practices. And the story of each new medium, while unfolding differently, contains the same essential elements: first, the discovery of the medium's commercial potential and a no-holds-barred rush to exploit that potential; second, an era of rapid growth marked by cutthroat competition and a general lowering of tone; third, an attempt by government to regulate both the competition and the tone; and fourth, self-imposed discipline on the part of the industry, in order to retain its autonomy and keep officialdom at bay.

The American motion picture industry was born in 1896, when, following upon the invention of the Kinetograph for recording moving images and the Kinetoscope for viewing them (through a peephole), an employee of Thomas Edison invented the first projector, the Vitascope. In 1903 this led to the commercial success of a short film called *The Great Train Robbery,* and in 1910 the leading production studios relocated to a suburb of Los Angeles called Hollywood. From there, the most successful studios—Paramount, Warner Broth-

ers, Metro-Goldwyn-Mayer, and Radio-Keith-Orpheum (RKO)—
set out to conquer the world. They succeeded in part because during two world wars they aided Washington by producing training
films, propaganda, and (during World War II) sophisticated features,
and Washington repaid the debt by helping them muscle aside the
war-damaged European film industries after both wars. Just to cite
one example, the Marshall Plan of the 1940s contained a number of
special provisions tying aid to the reduction or elimination of European import quotas on U.S. films.

This Hollywood-Washington cooperation has been in force
ever since. During the cold war, the Motion Picture Export Association (MPEA) played such an active role in public diplomacy that it
was dubbed "the little State Department." Beginning in the 1970s, the
United States has faced stiff opposition, in the form of cultural pro-
tectionism, by France and its various allies (the latest being Canada).
But the association continues to exert strong counterpressure. As reported on its Web site, the word "export" was removed in 1994 "to
more accurately reflect the global nature of audiovisual entertainment in today's International marketplace."[34] At last count, the MPA
had branches in Brussels, Sao Paulo, Singapore, Rome, New Delhi,
Rio de Janeiro, Mexico City, Toronto, and Jakarta.

Hollywood, backed by Washington, has long used aggressive tactics to establish dominance in many world markets. But what many
denounce as U.S. cultural imperialism would never have succeeded
if Hollywood films were not hugely popular in their own right. To
quote the impresario Sol Hurok, "When people don't want to come,
nothing will stop them." What has made American movies popular
abroad is the same thing that has made them popular at home: their
seemingly uncanny ability to communicate with large numbers of
people across the barriers of class and nationality. Of course, there is
nothing uncanny about this ability—it was honed for more than a
century amid the freewheeling, crowd-pleasing atmosphere of minstrelsy and vaudeville.

Radio was invented overseas, but like motion pictures, it became a lucrative entertainment medium in the United States. The first broadcasts were created in 1920 by Westinghouse, Radio Corporation of America (RCA), and American Telephone and Telegraph (AT&T) to sell the radios they manufactured. By 1922, so many stations were on the air that the secretary of Commerce, Herbert Hoover, called for legislation requiring all broadcasters to be licensed in order to promote fair utilization of the broadcast spectrum, understood to be a scarce resource.[35]

But herein lies a major difference between broadcasting in the United States and in most other countries. The Federal Radio Commission (FRC), established in 1927, was responsible for licensing stations and regulating their content. But the stations themselves were privately owned, as were the networks: the National Broadcasting Company (NBC, created by a merger between RCA and AT&T), Columbia Broadcasting (CBS), and American Broadcasting Company (ABC). By the 1930s, these networks were relaying programs across the nation, fueled by revenue coming not from taxpayers but from advertisers.

In most other countries, by contrast, broadcasting was seen as a natural monopoly of the government. The political left tended to see this as a bulwark against the rapacity of private enterprise; the center and the right tended to support it as a guarantee of national security. Only in recent decades has there been a global shift toward the American model, based on private ownership and the ideal (if not the reality) of the unregulated free market. And needless to say, this shift has not escaped criticism, both in Europe and in many other countries with a history of government control of the mass media.

With the advent of television in the early 1950s, the national networks in the United States shifted their attention decisively away from radio and toward the new medium. (In 1947, 90 percent of the nation's radio stations were affiliated with NBC, CBS, or ABC; in 1957, less than 50 percent were.)[36] Television grew with a swiftness that to many observers was alarming: between 1949 and 1962, the percentage of American homes with a set rose from 2.3 percent to 90 percent. But perhaps this will appear less alarming when we consider that, just as film and radio ran along a fast track laid down by vaudeville, so did television benefit from the accumulated experience of all three predecessors. For example, one of the most popular television programs of the 1950s was *The George Burns and Gracie Allen Show,* which premiered on CBS in 1950 and was still going strong eight years later, when Allen decided to retire. (Burns continued to perform until the age of ninety-eight.) Burns and Allen had been headliners in vaudeville in the 1920s, then film and radio stars in the 1930s and 1940s. What could be easier, or more logical, than to transfer their polished routines onto the small screen?

Significantly, each of the new electronic media replicated the history of vaudeville in another way—by "cleaning up its act" before "taking it on the road." In the early days of film, various state legislatures established censorship boards aimed at suppressing the perceived moral decay emanating from such films as Cecil B. DeMille's *Why Change Your Wife?* (1920). In 1922, when the studios were under investigation for antitrust violations, they formed a new trade group, the Motion Picture Producers and Distributors of America (MPPDA), dedicated to refurbishing Hollywood's image. Heading this group was a former postmaster general named Will H. Hays, whose name soon became synonymous with the production code that regulated the content of Hollywood movies between 1927 and the mid-1960s, when the MPAA (formerly the MPPDA) abandoned the so-called Hays Office in favor of the somewhat ineffective ratings system still in place today.

The public airwaves were subject to more direct oversight, as the Federal Communications Act of 1934 obligated broadcasters to operate under the watchful eye—and disapproving "raised eyebrow"—of the Federal Communications Commission (FCC). But for many years, the censorship powers of the FCC were rarely invoked, because like the film studios, the radio and television networks exerted a fair amount of self-censorship through their departments of standards and practices. The same was true of cable television in the beginning, not least because the FCC had tried mightily to block its development. But with the massive deregulation of telecommunications in the 1970s and 1980s, to say nothing of the rise of satellite broadcasting and the Internet in the 1990s, this tradition of self-restraint has broken down. Occasionally the FCC will fine a radio station for allowing profanity on the air, or a politician will seek to enliven a dull campaign by attacking broadcasters. But in general, neither the MPAA ratings nor the FCC's fines nor any of the other controls traditionally placed on American entertainment have much force nowadays. This lack of control is unprecedented— and in an age of globalized popular culture, potentially quite troublesome.

Why troublesome? Because accompanying the transformations in media outlined above have been equal or greater transformations in culture. In brief, the dominant spirit of the arts, both popular and elite, has become one of testing the limits of public propriety. These cultural changes are not nearly as well understood as the technological ones. But they are equally if not more important. The fact is that, despite its great richness, American popular culture may be losing its universal appeal and becoming a negative rather than positive reflection of the country's freedom and diversity.

To aristocratic-minded critics, the degradation of culture is inevitable in a democracy. Plato accused poets of catering to the "small minted coin" of public taste and banned them all, even Homer, from his republic. From this perspective, there is no mystery about the debasement of American popular culture—it is debased because it is popular. Yet as we have seen, popular culture has long resisted debasement and, indeed, often risen to the level of high

art. Contrary to the claims of both traditional humanists and professors of cultural studies, no radical discontinuity exists between
the older arts (literature, theater, music, painting, sculpture) and the
newer ones (film, popular music, TV drama and comedy). To the contrary, many of the ideas, practices, and values of the old still survive
in the new.

Unfortunately, some of these survivals have a negative impact.
What are the claimed vices of popular taste? Sentimentality, bom-
bast, vulgarity, violence, oversimplification. American culture has
never lacked for these, but its genius has always been to offset them
with commensurate virtues: humor, vitality, openness, diversity,
dynamism, self-criticism. If the vices dominate today, it is only partly
because of popular taste. The real change has been among elites.
Historically, our cultural elites sought to educate and uplift popular
taste. Now many elites seem intent upon debasing popular taste—by
rejecting artistry and defining art not as beauty but as shocking the
sensibilities of ordinary people.

The imperative to shock is not new. On the contrary, it can be
traced back to expressionism, futurism, and Dada—late nineteenth-
and early twentieth-century art movements that embraced the idea,
taken from political anarchism, that the right outrageous gesture
made at the right moment and magnified by the media will cause
the repressive social order to implode. This shock impulse is not the
sum total of modernism, by any means. But it is the easy part. Millions of people who could never grasp cubism or twelve-tone music
have no trouble understanding shock tactics aimed at generating
publicity. Shock art remained an elite phenomenon until the late
1960s, at which point it was adopted by an assortment of artists and
rock musicians, from Frank Zappa and the Velvet Underground to
Andy Warhol and Yoko Ono. Soon it went mainstream, and Baude-
laire's line— *"Il faut épater le bourgeois"* ("One must shock the middle
class")—became the motto of every would-be punk rocker, gangsta

rapper, indie filmmaker, and stand-up comedian. Only now the idea is not to shock the bourgeois but to scandalize an already jaded public, to the point where a major label or studio offers you a contract.

During the 1980s and 1990s many Americans expressed concern about the coarsening tone of popular culture. Conservatives led campaigns against offensive song lyrics and Internet porn; liberals lobbied for an FCC crackdown on violent movies and racist video games; parents struggled to protect their children from what they saw as a socially irresponsible entertainment industry. And to judge by a Pew Research Center survey released in April 2005, these worries persist: "Roughly six-in-ten [Americans] say they are very concerned over what children see or hear on TV (61%), in music lyrics (61%), video games (60%) and movies (56%)."[37] Yet here is another difference between the United States and the rest of the world. Despite their worries, Americans resist government censorship. Reports Pew, "Most Americans say parents are primarily to blame when children are exposed to explicit sex or graphic violence. Fully 79% say inadequate parental supervision—rather than inadequate laws—is mostly responsible for children being exposed to this sort of offensive material; there are no significant political or religious differences on this point."[38]

One can argue in favor of censorship, on the ground that liberal democracy requires good character on the part of its citizens: if they cannot govern themselves individually, they will not be able to govern themselves collectively. Therefore, the argument goes, liberal government has an overriding interest in curbing negative moral influences, even if this means curbing free speech.[39] On the other side, the defenders of free speech warn that all governments, even liberal governments, tend to trespass on the liberty of their citizens. So it is better to tolerate negative moral influences, even flagrant abuses, than to give government the power to censor.[40] Both of these arguments are well known to most Americans. Yet their applicability to our contemporary situation is far from clear, in part because when it comes to censorship, the United States has long been not one regime but two.

The first regime governs print media, literature, and the fine arts, all of which now enjoy something close to total liberty of expression. This was not always the case: in 1920 the American serialization of James Joyce's *Ulysses* was halted, and the novel was not legally available in this country until 1933. But by 1973, a succession of obscenity cases culminated in the Supreme Court decision *Miller v. California,* which contains the definition of obscenity still in place today: the depiction of "sexual conduct" in a "patently offensive way" that, "taken as a whole," lacks "serious literary, artistic, political, or scientific value." This standard would be reasonable in a society capable of drawing a line between art that deals with the erotic side of life and trash that pursues sexual thrills for their own sake. But in 1973 America, the height of the sexual revolution, many people, including many artists, were intent upon erasing that line.

The unprecedented liberty granted by *Miller* has proven to be both blessing and curse. The blessing, obviously, is that genuine artists may now include sexually explicit references in their work without being called pornographers. Were Joyce publishing *Ulysses* today, he would not have to battle censors. But the curse is that "pushing the envelope" isn't easy when the law provides no envelope. Would-be transgressive artists must carry offense to ever greater extremes, to get a rise out of an increasingly jaded public.

The second regime governs the electronic media and (until recently) popular culture. As mentioned above, the electronic media in the United States have never been owned by the government. But they have been subject to varying degrees of government oversight, ranging from the direct licensing power of the FCC to the indirect pressures that led to the Hays Office, the network departments of standards and practices, and more recently the MPAA ratings system, parental advisory labels on CDs, and the V-chip.

The V-chip, much discussed during the late 1990s, is a device built into every television set manufactured since January 2000 that enables viewers to block certain programs according to a ratings system akin to that used by the MPAA. In political terms, the V-chip seems an effective solution, because it gives parents, not government, the power to censor. But in practical terms, it is not effective. First, it succumbs to the technological generation gap: typically children figure out how to disarm it before their parents have deciphered the instructions. Second, there has emerged no reliable means of rating the million or so hours of programming broadcast annually on America's numerous network and cable channels. (By contrast, the MPAA rates roughly one thousand hours of film a year.)

And third, the V-chip has already been rendered obsolete, as young people turn away from television and toward more interactive media, like video games and, of course, the Internet. In recent years, moreover, the second regime has begun to look more like the first, with a series of court cases granting to electronic media something like the unfettered freedom enjoyed by print and the fine arts. One such was the early 1990s prosecution of the rap group 2 Live Crew for obscenity, which resulted in acquittal after a number of prominent scholars testified, *Miller* fashion, that the group's blatantly pornographic lyrics were a legitimate expression of African-American culture.[41]

Then there is the thorny legal status of the Internet. According to a *Washington Post* reporter covering the oral arguments in *Reno v. the ACLU,* the Supreme Court case that struck down the Communications Decency Act of 1996, "the real question [wasn't] what's on the Net, but rather what is the Net."[42] The problem can be summed up this way: How to define a pornographer who does business through the Internet? As a creep threatening children in a city playground, to be publicly shamed if not locked up? As an X-rated movie theater, to be zoned into a red-light district and required to keep out minors? As a broadcaster, to be placed under the raised eyebrow of the FCC? As a video store, to be subject to local ordinance and/or company policy when it comes to requiring proof of age before renting R- and X-rated videos? As an artist, exempt from prosecution under the existing obscenity law? Or as a citizen exercising his right to political speech in a public forum? The legal arguments suggested by each of these scenarios are different, and to make matters worse, the technology keeps changing. Suffice it to say that the issue of censorship on the Internet is not going to be resolved any time soon.

But even if the law were clear and the technology manageable, the cultural problem would remain. And unfortunately, it cannot be resolved by social science. When it comes to such hot-button issues as sexuality in popular music or violence in films, the most effective advocates of control, surprisingly, have been liberals calling for a regulatory crackdown. This is because instead of harping on "soft" subjects like public morality, they stick with the "hard" facts gathered by social science. The trouble, though, is that the impact of media on behavior is one of those areas where there are no "hard" facts. What James Q. Wilson wrote thirty years ago is still true: "It is unlikely that social science can either show harmful effects or prove that there are no harmful effects. . . . These are moral issues and ultimately all judgments about the acceptability of restrictions on various media will have to rest on political and philosophical considerations."[43]

An acceptable means of taming the excesses of today's popular culture might be possible within the United States, if the problem were contained within its borders. As we've seen, Americans have a pretty good record of sorting out the censorship issues raised by each new generation of media. But today, the most salient fact about American popular culture is its globalization. In recent decades the export of American films, music, television shows, and other entertainment products has skyrocketed. This is not surprising, given the opening of vast new markets in Eastern Europe, Russia, China, and beyond.

But the numbers are staggering. The U.S. Bureau of Economic Analysis reports that between 1986 and 2005 (the latest data available), "the sales of services to foreign persons by the motion picture and video industries" went from $1.91 billion to $10.4 billion, in constant 2005 dollars, a nearly fivefold increase.[44] As MPAA president Dan Glickman said recently, "Alone among all the sectors of the U.S. economy, our industry is the only one that generates a positive balance of trade in every country in which it does business."[45]

Ironically, Americans have long assumed that their popular culture was the country's best ambassador. During World War II, the swing and jazz broadcast to American soldiers and sailors over the Armed Forces Radio Network proved so popular with European listeners that the government decided in 1955 to broadcast similar fare over the Voice of America. By the end of the decade, the VOA's beloved *Music USA* was reaching a regular audience of 100 million worldwide, 30 million behind the iron curtain. According to the Russian novelist Vassily Aksyonov, this program was "America's secret weapon number one . . . a kind of golden glow over the horizon."[46] It is hard not to feel a golden glow when recalling the mellow voice of host Willis Conover introducing the Duke Ellington Orchestra.

But America's typical export these days is not jazz composer Billy Strayhorn's "Take the A Train." It is rapper Eminem's "Ass Like That." This situation is unprecedented: never before in history has such a large stream of unfettered entertainment flowed from one country to such a large number of others around the world. One could argue that this is good news, because as the shock-for-shock's-sake material becomes mainstream, it faces something it has never had to face before: a plebiscite. It is hard to place too much faith in the judgment of the millions of consumers who will cast the deciding votes. But better they than the elite "arts community," with its mindless reverence for whatever offends ordinary people. Historically, the philistine public could be counted on to weigh the claims of art against those of civility, decency, and morality.

But a global plebiscite may also be bad news, because the worst kind of culture war is between artists who hate morality and moralists who hate art. Push the envelope hard enough, and you invite popular revulsion, which can lead all too swiftly to backlash, censorship, and worse. Consider, for example, this observation from a 2003 congressional report on America's declining image: "Arabs and Muslims are also bombarded with American sitcoms, violent films, and other entertainment, much of which distorts the perceptions of viewers. . . . A Syrian teacher of English asked us plaintively for help in explaining American family life to her students. She asked, 'Does *Friends* show a typical family?'"[47] Another suggestive anecdote comes from the upscale African-American women's magazine *Essence,* which in April 2005 held an online forum about the demeaning images of black women in rap, inspired by a protest movement organized at Spelman College in Atlanta.[48] According to editor Diane Weathers, several postings came from African countries where "People are disgusted with what their African-American brothers and sisters are doing in entertainment. They wonder if we've lost our minds."[49] Many charitable and educational institutions have recently reported a new reluctance on the part of foreigners to visit the United States, which some attribute to impressions received through popular culture.[50]

It is difficult to measure the impact of exported popular culture on anti-American feeling around the world. The conventional wisdom is that people like "American culture and values" (the phrase used in most surveys) but dislike U.S. foreign policy. But according to a new forty-seven-nation survey released by the Pew Global Attitudes Project in June 2007, this pattern may be changing: "In most parts of the world, majorities report liking American music, movies and television. However, there is greater dissent with regard to these pop culture exports; majorities in several predominantly Muslim countries, including Bangladesh, Pakistan, Turkey, Jordan, and Egypt, say they dislike American music, movies and television. Indians and Russians also express negative views of U.S. cultural exports."[51]

At the same time, the Pew survey has uncovered a startling rise in the number of respondents agreeing with the statement, "It's bad that American ideas and customs are spreading here." As the report states, "The percentage expressing disapproval has increased in many countries since 2002—including Great Britain (by 17 percentage points), Germany (14 points) and Canada (13 points). *Israel, Ethiopia, Ivory Coast and Nigeria are the only countries (aside from the U.S.) in which majorities say they like the spread of American customs* [emphasis added]."[52]

The Pew researchers draw no inference from these two sets of responses, but it seems reasonable to ask whether negative views toward "the spread of American ideas and customs" might be based partly on depictions of American life found in our entertainment media—in particular, images of Americans routinely engaging in violent, sexually promiscuous, criminal, and antisocial behavior.[53] Is the impact of these images stronger among respondents who have not "reality tested" them by spending time in the United States? An answer is implied by Pew's finding that, "Consistently, those individuals who have traveled to the U.S. have more favorable views of the country than those who have not."[54] Visitors to the United States are a self-selected group, of course, but among those involved in international exchange programs, there is a wealth of anecdotal evidence suggesting that visitors are very often surprised to see how family-centered, civic-minded, socially conservative, and religious Americans actually are.

Given the prospect of a global backlash against American ideas and customs as perceived through the lens of our entertainment media, it is distressing to see the apparent failure of today's popular culture impresarios to understand what their predecessors understood: that in the long run, public outrage is bad for business. Too often, their reaction to the moral outcries of their domestic audience is to fan the flames rather than dampen them, on the theory that any publicity is better than none. (About foreign outrage, they long cultivated indifference.) The pattern is numbingly familiar: third-rate material is shot into orbit by a first-class media blitz, and everyone forgets about the actual object or performance itself (who recalls what song Janet Jackson was singing at the 2005 Super Bowl?).

A few years ago, Robert Wright, then-president of NBC, wrote a letter to his industry colleagues complaining about the unfair advantage that HBO series such as *The Sopranos* enjoy in the race for audiences and awards. To account for the success of these and other cable television programs, Wright did not point to their extraordinarily high level of writing and acting. No, he pointed to the regulatory environment that allows cable to exert less censorship than the networks. This is a typical mistake—to assume that a show like *The Sopranos* was a hit simply because it offered bigger doses of sex, violence, and profanity than network shows. If the formula were really so simple, then wouldn't every trashy program be a hit? This is the intellectual fallout from the cultural changes described above: a preoccupation with being "edgy" and "provocative" that excludes from consideration any other definition of what makes cultural products both aesthetically good and commercially successful.

Some people, mostly the producers, consumers, and journalistic critics of popular culture, judge the merits of individual films, songs, and television programs according to standards derived, more or less, from the fine and performing arts. The closer one gets to the production end, the more one hears the language of aesthetics and craft. Some of this language is new, as in cinematography, recording, editing, and more recently, digital processing. But some is old, with words such as *plot*, *character*, *dialogue*, and *dramaturgy*—to say nothing of *beautiful* and *good*—in constant use. For example, the veteran film editor Walter Murch offers this summary of "the underlying principle" of his work: "Always try to do the most with the least . . . suggestion is always more effective than exposition."[55] Horace said it more eloquently in *Ars Poetica*—but not all that differently.[56]

But other people, mostly in the academy, practice the hybrid discipline of cultural studies that combines linguistics, literary theory, history, anthropology, and sociology. Cultural studies has produced some striking insights into the bewildering ebb and flow of globalized popular culture.[57] But like all rapidly growing fields, it is also full of weeds. As stated in one survey, "Popular culture studies have embraced such a range of issues with such an array of methods that they have become bafflingly diffuse."[58] And cultural studies eschews the language of aesthetics. A researcher will study "mosh pit" behavior at a rock concert, but not comment on the quality of the music.[59] A scholar will track the construction of gender in a television sitcom, but not pronounce on the cleverness of the script. Yet these scholars hardly refrain making value judgments. They assert, correctly, that "value-free" social science is unattainable by mortals. But at the same time, many scholars in the field of cultural studies take an activist stance, based in Marxist theory, in favor of any group deemed to be oppressed and marginalized. Not surprisingly, this leads such scholars to make a great many value judgments—in favor of cultural productions seen as "peripheral" (as opposed to "central"), "emancipatory" (as opposed to "disciplinary"), and "counter-hegemonic" (as opposed to "hegemonic").

Thus we are left with a truly daunting task: to evaluate how much good, and ill, is being wrought by contemporary American popular culture. If elites refuse to apply traditional artistic standards to popular culture, what standards should be applied? Rare indeed is the observer who can survey this global spectacle without making some sort of value judgment—and that includes the vast, imponderable, democratic audience that helped to make American films, television shows, and popular music what they are today. Popular culture is simply not something one can contemplate with passionless neutrality. But that, of course, is only a tribute to its amazing vitality.

CHAPTER 9

The Military

Eliot Cohen

In quality and technology, the American military is the best in the world, and its personnel have recovered from the drugs and disorder that afflicted them in the 1970s. The military's recovery from Vietnam had much to do with the reinvigoration of an old paradigm of war—conventional combat. But it has struggled to adapt to the requirements of irregular warfare of the kind being fought in Iraq. It is a military at once representative of a broad slice of American society and isolated from it, adapting to new forms of warfare while constrained, still, by older technologies and organizational cultures.

Old Wine in New Bottles

IT IS A RARE THING FOR A FIELD MANUAL TO MAKE THE NEWS, BUT in December 2006 that is what happened. The U.S. Army and Marine Corps released a joint field manual, FM 23–4, on counterinsurgency (COIN in military jargon). The issuing authorities were the military's premier counterinsurgency generals, David Petraeus and James Mattis, and the document itself the product of more than a year's labors by soldiers and marines, academics, and even human rights activists. It had many unusual features (not least the active participation of the generals whose signatures graced the cover page, who did not merely sign off on the document but helped write it). But perhaps most interesting was the sheer fact of its issuance, and its forthright declaration that:

Counterinsurgency operations generally have been neglected in broader American military doctrine and national
security policies since the end of the Vietnam War over 30
years ago. This manual is designed to reverse that trend. It is
also designed to merge traditional approaches to COIN
with the realities of a new international arena shaped by
technological advances, globalization, and the spread of extremist ideologies—some of them claiming the authority of
a religious faith.

The COIN manual brought the U.S. military full circle to
where it had been in the 1960s, wrestling with the strangeness of irregular conflict in the jungles of Indochina. But in the intervening
forty years, much had changed with respect to the size and culture—
no less than the technology—with which it approached war.

Quantity and Quality

"What is more important, quality or quantity?" Michael Handel, a
distinguished scholar of strategic studies once asked. "Quality, but
only if you have a lot of it," he decided. From that, and the equally
well-known Soviet dictum that "quantity has a quality all its own,"
derives the first observation to make about today's American military: it is, in relative and often in absolute terms, both extremely
wealthy and extremely large.

Indeed, what distinguishes the American military first and foremost from any other on the planet is sheer size, or rather, wealth. With
roughly 1.5 million servicemen and servicewomen on active duty, it
is not the largest—at 2.25 million, the Chinese military is bigger,
although interestingly it is larger than that of India at about 1.3 million. But nothing compares to the American military budget. At
nearly $500 billion it amounts to roughly 4 percent of GDP; again,
hardly the greatest amount proportionate to the American economy, but a gargantuan sum in absolute terms (only Singapore and

Burundi spend more). To put it in perspective, compare the American defense budget with that of its North Atlantic Treaty Organization (NATO) allies. All together, America's European NATO allies spend a bit more than half of what the United States does. The British defense budget is perhaps a tenth of that of the United States, as is the French; the German budget is smaller still. The Department of Defense's research and development budget is much larger than any of these (about $70 billion), and indeed, larger than the Russian defense budget, too.[1]

Moreover—and this is a point often lost in comparisons of this kind—American defense spending has large cumulative effects. Having spent sums of this magnitude for decades, the United States has accumulated a vast defense capital stock. Airplanes, tanks, and ships can last, with appropriate modernization, for two, three, even four decades. Runways, docks, and depots last longer yet. And wealth counts, because in military affairs quantity has a real effect on quality.

If you have lots of money you can train differently and often better than other countries. The U.S. Army, for example, has a maneuver ground in California the size of a small state; the U.S. Air Force and Navy can practice air-to-air combat over vast reaches of space. American units can consume oil and gas, burn their way through ammunition and spare parts, and construct mock towns and villages for urban combat in ways that other armed forces can only dream of. If you are rich enough to afford something so humdrum as unlimited quantities of batteries for night vision devices, you can exercise your forces, and use them, in hours of darkness. Even if, say, a band of al Qaeda guerrillas have such devices (and they do), they are highly unlikely to have the stockpiles and supply systems that can keep them going all the time in combat.

Wealth also makes for unique military systems. Conceivably, other countries could assemble the technology to build a stealth bomber; after all, most militaries incorporate "signature reduction" (ways of reducing—by use of shaping, special coatings, or other means—the susceptibility of a piece of equipment to radar or electro-optical detection). But no country, not even rising China, could afford it. This is something new in military history. In the past, the first-rate powers, say, on the eve of World War I—Britain, Germany, France, Russia, and the United States—had roughly similar kinds of first-line battleships. To be sure, there were important differences with respect to aiming systems and the like, technical differences that could affect combat performance, but by and large they were similar enough. Today, however, there is only one country that has stealth bombers or 90,000-ton aircraft carriers.

The technological edge goes further yet. Look at pictures of an American soldier during World War II, the Vietnam War, and today. The first two will, roughly, resemble one another—green fatigues, a steel helmet, a relatively simple rifle, and a canteen are his main pieces of kit. Today's soldier wears armor that can turn a bullet, talks to his comrades on a miniaturized radio, and carries a weapon that, with electronic sights, is far more accurate than its predecessors. With a laser range finder and designator he can call down vast volumes of precision firepower from jets, helicopters, long-range artillery, and missiles; behind him is a medical and health care system that will keep him healthy (most casualties in past wars came from illness, not enemy fire) and often save his life if he is wounded. Again, other armies can afford bits and pieces of this same outfit, but either in very small numbers, or at lower levels of effectiveness; witness, for example, British soldiers in 2003 who advanced on Basra under the light of flares because they did not have enough night vision devices to go around.

Finally, sheer wealth translates into capabilities that are unique, even when the technologies involved are not. Lots of countries have landing ships and can deploy a battalion or two, maybe even a brigade or two abroad for extended periods of time. No other country in the world can project expeditionary forces of tens or hundreds of thousands of men and women halfway around the globe, keeping them fed, supplied, and healthy virtually indefinitely. And no other country could have projected military power into a battlefield as remote and difficult as Afghanistan in 2001.

Quantity, then, translates in a number of ways into quality. But that quality reflects as well the nature of institutions and experience. During the early 1970s, one would not have called the American military a particularly high-quality force. Plagued by high rates of drug abuse, racial tension, and an erosion of discipline fostered by the turmoil of American society at that time, it was probably inferior in important respects to the Red Army and the militaries of leading European allies. But in a remarkable and still not entirely well-explained revolution, it transformed itself. A wrenching adjustment to the introduction of an all-volunteer force—this well ahead of any of its allies other than Great Britain—meant that the military would consist of young men and women who wanted to be there. Substantial budget increases during the Reagan administration rebuilt the military's capital stock, but no less important were fundamental changes in the spirit and tone of the force. Those changes endure to the present day, albeit with occasional stresses brought about by increasingly demanding deployments in the Middle East and elsewhere.

The first of these changes was a commitment to quality personnel: all of the services began purging themselves of members with drug or criminal backgrounds.[2] They began emphasizing the recruitment of soldiers who had at least high school backgrounds, this being viewed as an indicator of the kind of self-discipline needed to succeed in military life; they also began to avoid enlistees from the lowest mental category (Category IV on the standard test used— roughly the lowest 10 to 30 percent of the population). From less than half of the enlisted force having high school degrees, the services moved to nearly all of it having that qualification (albeit with some 5 to 7 percent attaining high school equivalency degrees during service), while the recruitment of Category IV personnel went from roughly 20 percent to 2 or 3 percent.[3]

Although many of the rituals of military life remained, including the rites of passage of basic training, the formal hierarchies of rank, the ceremonies of change of command and the like, deeper changes were at work. Gradually, the barracks of a draft-based military designed for single young males gave way to college dormitory-like collections of apartments; enlisted personnel were increasingly married, often living off-post; the irksome chores of kitchen duty and sentry duty handed over to contractors. The essentials of military life—submariners sharing berths, or soldiers wriggling under trucks to pull maintenance—might remain the same, but the spirit was different. Soldiers were now expensive specialists, costly to recruit, costly to maintain, and costly to keep in service. The old concept of a mobilizable force of citizen soldiers gradually vanished: this was not merely an All Volunteer Force, as the Pentagon called it, but a professional force, which is not quite the same thing.

A no less important transformation shaped the training of this force. The army's National Training Center, mentioned above, provided not only what may have been the world's largest instrumented maneuver area but its most sophisticated—transponders on every vehicle and laser simulated hits allowed impartial scoring of tactical training; cameras and sensors on mountaintops allowing a near perfect reconstruction of the fight. The navy and air force conducted increasingly sophisticated training not only in air-to-air combat, but in complex attack operations involving scores of aircraft. A combination of new technologies and dedication to high professional standards made the armed forces the best trained that the United States had ever had—which is why the Gulf War of 1991, against an admittedly feeble opponent, was by any reasonable historical standard a remarkably painless victory.

Part of the reprofessionalization of the armed forces after Vietnam was, as well, a much greater focus on operational doctrine, meaning the concepts guiding large-scale military operations. This was particularly true with regard to the army, which rewrote its premier manual, FM 100–5, in 1982 and again in 1986 along radically new lines. Focused primarily on conventional conflict with the Soviet Union, the FM–105 doctrine shaped thinking at the higher levels of warfare and again helped pave the way for the successes of 1991. Not since the period shortly before World War II had the intellectual side of the military art been so well developed in the United States. There was a weakness here, however, although it was little noticed at the time: this was doctrine for conventional war, in support of conflicts of limited duration whose beginnings and conclusions could be easily defined. There was much that was professionally satisfying in the preparation for such wars, but as the end of the twentieth and beginning of the twenty-first centuries would reveal, these were not the kinds of wars the United States would actually find itself conducting.

For a quarter of a century from the fall of Saigon through the first Gulf War, the American military was busy, but rarely at war. Short operations like the occupation of Panama in 1989 were the exception: for the most part the late cold war was a period of building a solid professional force; training, acquiring, and absorbing new materiel; and developing the concepts to buttress deterrence in the main theaters of potential war with the Soviet Union. Thus, the forces that went to war in 1991 were largely untested. Ever since then, however, the American military, and in particular the army and the Marine Corps, has been constantly involved in conflict of one kind or another. Two large military interventions in Yugoslavia, constant skirmishing with Iraq and a large war there in 2003, and the invasion of Afghanistan and counterinsurgency campaigns there and in Iraq were only some of the activities that engaged American forces. They did not meet comparable forces in combat, but they were engaged in real missions with increasing frequency. This became a force not only of professionals but of veterans—albeit veterans in a kind of combat very different from that which would attend a contest with a peer opponent.

Global Reach

The American military is unique in a different respect as well: it has global reach. During the cold war the Soviet Union arguably had something of the kind, but by the 1990s it had dissolved, and its successor state, Russia, was in no position to maintain the kinds of forces that had once conducted massive airlifts to the Horn of Africa, aspired to contest the control of the shipping lanes of the North Atlantic with the U.S. Navy, or operated from bases in Southeast Asia. Even during the cold war, however, there was nothing quite like the American global posture, with its large ground forces deployed across the Atlantic and Pacific oceans in Germany and Korea, respectively; its network of air and naval bases around the globe; and its fleets that cruised every sea and continued to assert transit rights accordingly. Even in space, where other countries could operate, the American network of satellites used for purposes of intelligence gathering, navigation, and communication were, and remain, unparalleled. American weapon systems—from cruise missiles to stealth bombers to special forces teams—can go many places with, at first, little effective opposition.

American military power is magnified by a web of alliance relationships. At the core of these is NATO, which links the United States to Europe in a variety of ways. But non-NATO members also figure as American coalition partners, including rising powers like India and, of course, Australia, Japan, and a host of other Asian countries. Many of these allies worry openly about their ability to keep up with their much stronger partner—sometimes even about their ability to sustain electronic communication. This helps explain why

American fighter planes do so well on the international market. More importantly, as the American-led interventions in Yugoslavia and Afghanistan revealed, the United States learned during the cold war how to operate with a variety of partners in sharing intelligence and coordinating various military activities. It rarely makes the front pages, but when American aircraft can deliver close air support to a beleaguered Norwegian outpost in Afghanistan, or when Singaporean ships can support maritime patrols under American command in the Persian Gulf, they do so as the result of a prolonged working out of protocols and procedures. An invisible infrastructure of exchanges, educational institutions, and constant exercises sustain this cooperation.[4]

This matter of global reach, however, goes well beyond the ability of the United States to operate on every continent and with a wide range of allies. It is a matter of strategic perspective. The combatant commands of the United States (European Command, Pacific Command, Central Command, Southern Command, and so on) embrace virtually the entire planet. They include massive headquarters, substantial forces assigned in peace with others waiting to be dispatched to the theater in times of war. They are led by four-star admirals or generals who usually carry far more weight with host countries than do American ambassadors, because unlike the ambassadors they have large resources available to do things. The combatant commanders, moreover, are the only American officials in the field who have a regional perspective and responsibilities; their view is of necessity wider than their fellow officials abroad.

Some have argued that the upshot of this global positioning is, willy-nilly, a militarization of American foreign policy, and this may be so. If so, it is not a matter of design, but of the facts on the ground, as it were. It bespeaks, as well, a peculiar fact of American strategic culture, namely, its global point of view. One might argue that the British Empire before the United States had a similarly sweeping worldview; after all, the Royal Navy's bases locked up the sea lanes, and British soldiers stood guard over outposts as distant as Aden, Peshawar, Singapore, and Capetown. But the American global military presence is something considerably greater. It is, for one thing, relatively far more powerful: where the Royal Navy had to plan to concentrate the fleet in home waters to protect the British Isles, American fleets in the Pacific, the Mediterranean, and the Persian Gulf are forward deployed perpetually. Where the British army could provide no more than a minor increment to the strength of local forces and was a major force only after mobilization or if it could bring the Indian army to bear, the United States remains a dominant force.

Consider, for example, the international forces deployed in Afghanistan. As of 2007, of thrity-two thousand NATO troops in Afghanistan, some twelve thousand were American, with an additional force of some six to eight thousand operating independently. Half of the NATO force, and the majority of those empowered to engage in combat with Taliban guerrillas, were thus Americans, even though Afghanistan had been designated an area vital to European as well as to American interests. And the Afghanistan deployment, while not quite an afterthought from the point of view of American strategy, was a fairly minor commitment of military resources.

The ability of the U.S. military to exercise weight, sometimes decisive weight, globally stemmed from changes in warfare that empowered relatively small but well-trained and technologically advanced armed forces. In the days of the Raj, the difference between a British rifleman and his Pathan enemy were not too great: the British soldier, of course, was better disciplined, and from a formal point of view, better trained. The Pathan was likely to be hardier, and an equal or a better shot. The technological differences between them were relatively minor—accurate single-shot rifles that might, in fact, be of the same manufacture on either side.

In modern warfare, however, the differentials are much larger. The expensive soldier of the U.S. Army or Marine Corps has at his disposal, as we have seen, technologies that are generations ahead of those in the hands of his enemies. Moreover, and no less important, the U.S. military has the skill in systems integration that allows it to orchestrate very large operations better than any military system in history. All this comes at a huge cost, of course, most notably in salaries, training expenses, and hardware. But it means that American military leverage is enormous. The United States thus possesses not merely a global military perspective, but the potential to exercise tremendous power anywhere it likes. It has the command system that allows it to do so quickly; the logistics to put the forces where they are needed and to support them once deployed; and above all the well-trained and well-equipped personnel to inflict tremendous violence on its enemies. This global reach, however, produces its own not inconsiderable difficulties.

From a strategic point of view, it is difficult to wield wisely the power that is at America's disposal. It is broadly true that in most governments, at most times, only a handful of individuals make important decisions about the use of force—two or three in some cases, no more than a dozen in others. With a global set of interests and concerns, the American decision makers—the joint chiefs of staff, the secretary of defense, the national security adviser, and of course the president—lack adequate time to give any particular problem, even a war like that being fought in Iraq, the concentrated attention that, say, their Iranian or Syrian counterparts can. Decision makers' attention is episodic and often inconsistent, and in the absence of consistent guidance from above, bureaucracies are left to their own devices, following what Carl von Clausewitz once called "routine methods" to deal with problems that are anything but. Thus, in any strategic interaction, be it with local enemy or ally, there is an asymmetry in attention and focus that always favors the opposition.

To make matters worse, the necessarily global perspective means that important decisions may emerge not from the requirements to wage a particular war but from broader considerations. Thus, in the debate about force levels in Iraq, it seems that senior commanders may have made calculations about what kinds of forces would be required based on their understanding of what was required by the military for other purposes. A local opponent can be wholehearted in his determination to fight a war: awareness of a bigger picture is, in some ways, a weakness.

The second disadvantage that stems from such strength is, of course, the hubris that it naturally invites. This takes different forms. The advent of routinely precise long-range missiles and GPS-guided bombs delivered from a distance made the precision strike a favored weapon of the Clinton administration in the 1990s. A scattering of such attacks against Serbs in the former Yugoslavia, or against the al Qaeda network in Afghanistan, however, could not substitute for the threat or the reality of serious ground combat. The George W. Bush administration used its forces on the ground in both Afghanistan and Iraq and, perhaps intoxicated with initial successes, failed to plan for the follow-up of wiping out the remnants of Osama bin Laden's organization or establishing the administration of a conquered Iraq.

Thirdly, such overwhelming power elicits responses from America's opponents. Those responses take various forms. At the high end of the spectrum of violence, this includes the development of weapon systems designed to negate American ability to project power over long distances—"antiaccess" capabilities, as the jargon has it. This includes weapons like very fast torpedoes, long-range cruise missiles, and submarines, whose purpose is not so much to defeat American forces as to make it too costly for them to put large forces into contested areas.[5] At the lower end of the spectrum of violence, Americans face challenges that take the form of guerrilla warfare, mines and roadside bombs, sniping, and terror directed against American clients or allies. And quite outside the realm of force is the use of propaganda and political means of struggle to undermine or delegitimate American use of military power. Whether this takes place in the European Court of Justice, or in the United Nations, or simply on the Internet, America's opponents hope to constrain Gulliver with myriad threads.

Institutional Repertoires

From the broadest strategic point of view, America's military faces four large challenges that pull it in different directions. The first is a set of conflicts in the Middle East and beyond, loosely (and not very well) defined as "The Global War on Terror." It is, in fact, a set of struggles with violent Islamists of a number of backgrounds and persuasions. This struggle includes, at least in part, the Iraqi insurgency (which has other elements as well), but also the conflict in Afghanistan and a number of minor engagements (many of which usually escape the notice of the press and the American public) in places like the Horn of Africa. The second and most easily defined challenge is arraying forces to contain (or at least manage) the rise of China, and in particular to deter a Chinese attack on Taiwan. This is a more straightforward and traditional kind of task, involving the navy and air force with rather little participation (other than in the area of air defense) from the army and virtually none from the Marine Corps. It is accompanied by a geopolitics that is surprisingly favorable to the United States. First, anxiety about China from its smaller neighbors leads them to seek to use the United States to balance their great northern neighbor, and second, the United States retains support from the two other great powers of Asia, Japan and India.

The third strategic challenge for the American military is more potential than actual: preparation for preemptive attacks on enemies possessing weapons of mass destruction. The flawed detonation by North Korea of a small nuclear device in 2006 reinforced the urgency of this task, but it has other aspects as well—preparation to cripple the Iranian nuclear program, in particular.

The final mission of the American military is difficult to define precisely. It consists of engagement and reassurance, developing networks of allies and clients and assisting them to develop their own strength and to contribute to ours. Training exercises in countries as different as Poland and Oman serve this function; so too do ship visits and the enrollment of foreign officers in American military schools.

These four missions require different kinds of military activities, and to some extent, different kinds of military forces and even military leaders. Some—the Chinese and preemptive missions, most notably—fit well with the traditional American way of war and with conventional modes of military thought. Both can be construed largely in technical terms—maneuvering conventional forces against particular targets in a variety of ways easily understood in traditional terms. These missions place large demands on the U.S. Navy and Air Force, which operate extremely sophisticated platforms; these are the most technology-intensive services and the ones less touched by ongoing irregular wars than the army and the Marine Corps. Indeed, in the American military today, there is a growing gap between the two pairs of services—the first preparing for a large-scale, conventional conflict or a set of preemptive attacks on narrowly defined targets, and the second engaged in a continual, grinding conflict with guerrillas, insurgents, and terrorists. All can, and do, undertake the reassurance and engagement mission, and all have roles in the two different kinds of conflict—the navy protecting ships against terrorist attack, for example, or army special forces having a role in preemptive attack against a hostile nuclear weapons program. But broadly speaking, the two kinds of conflict remain— one hypothetical, conventional, and dominated by air, space, and sea; the other constant, irregular, and dominated by land.

The irregular warfare mission is particularly troublesome. As the only mission that has until now involved fighting and loss of life, it deserves the closest look, and not least because it reflects a large paradox. Irregular warfare has been part of the American military tradition since colonial times. Although the decisive engagements of early American military history were conventional (think, for example, of the Battle of the Plains of Abraham in 1759 or the siege of Yorktown in 1781), woodland irregular warfare pervaded the early centuries of the American military experience. During the nineteenth and early twentieth centuries, American forces fought guerrillas in Mexico, Central America, the Philippines, and indeed on our own continent in the form both of Indians and Confederate raiders against Union lines of supply. In the wake of World War II, Americans were involved in counterinsurgency in Europe (Greece, most notably), Central America, and Asia. And, of course, there was the Vietnam War, a mixed conflict with both conventional and unconventional dimensions.

And yet, following that last conflict, the U.S. military, and the army most notably, rejected irregular warfare as a core mission. "Superpowers don't do windows," was the saying, and even as the army reluctantly undertook advisory missions in El Salvador and peacekeeping missions in the former Yugoslavia, it fell back on a series of doctrines—most notably, the Weinberger Doctrine prescribing the use of force in the most limited of circumstances, and the Powell Doctrine calling everywhere and at all times for overwhelming force—that seemed virtually to preclude counterguerrilla warfare. The first Gulf War in 1991 seemed to ratify a conception of war in which the U.S. military prepared for purely conventional conflicts.

The politics of the post–cold war era, however, made a mockery of the wish never again to be engaged in a long, irregular fight. A humanitarian intervention in Somalia went awry; similar projections of power in Yugoslavia and Haiti were rather more successful. Then came the attacks of 9/11, and with them, the overpowering need for an American response. Even in Iraq it became clear that the seemingly textbook use of force conducted along the lines of Weinberger's and Powell's doctrines was a failure that not only left the fundamental challenge of an aggressive Iraqi state unsolved, but bred new sources of violence as a result of a set of sanctions, inspections, precautionary American deployments in Saudi Arabia, and repeated skirmishing from the air that brought misery to the people of Iraq and stimulated the anger of Arab populations.

In both Afghanistan and Iraq, then, the U.S. military had to do things that were outside the range of operations that its dominant culture considered sound and normal. In Afghanistan, it toppled the Taliban government with a handful of CIA agents and special forces soldiers who had behind them the attack aircraft of the U.S. Air Force, Navy, and Marine Corps. Working with militias that had long been on the losing end of Afghan's multi-decade civil war, U.S. forces made short work of the Taliban government. In Iraq in 2003 the U.S. Army swiftly dispatched the armed forces of the Ba'athist regime of Saddam Hussein. With a remarkably small armored force—a mechanized division and a Marine division operating in a pincer movement, with other units attacking subordinate targets— its forces lunged out of Kuwait at Baghdad, toppling the regime in intense but short fighting. This too was a remarkable achievement. Urban combat, even in cities as large as Baghdad (the sprawling home to several million people), did not noticeably slow down the American blitz.

But although both of these operations began well—indeed, astoundingly so—the follow-up phases were inept. In Afghanistan many of the al Qaeda operatives slipped away, some staging a surprisingly vicious rearguard action as they did so.[6] In Iraq, the Americans were surprised by the guerrilla resistance of the *fedayin Saddam,* an irregular force originally conceived by the regime as a militia to suppress Shia insurgents.[7] In both cases, plans and preparations for military government, the building of security institutions, and counterinsurgency were sorely lacking. And the record of adaptation to the tasks at hand was none too impressive. American forces stumbled badly in training the Afghan and Iraqi armies, first handing the task over to contractors, then to ill-prepared reservists, and only after several years, to American advisers and trainers who had themselves been prepared for the task. The U.S. government proved incapable of adequately equipping those client forces with such mundane items as bulletproof vests and radios. Three years after encountering roadside bombs, which became increasingly lethal over time, the best the U.S. Army could do was to slap armor on the sides of the Humvee, the successor to the jeep. The country that had built fleets of tanks and aircraft from scratch in World War II could not come up with a couple of thousand vehicles with V-shaped hulls and other protective measures—even though half a dozen such were on the market from American and foreign firms. Such basic tools of counterinsurgency as national identity cards or a well-administered detention system that simply removed terrorists from the streets did not exist.

These lapses, which by 2007 brought Iraq certainly, and Afghanistan possibly, to the margin of failure, stemmed from many sources—the quirks of particular leaders, the ineffectiveness of the National Security Council system, the unavoidable chaos of war. Undoubtedly, the lack of preparedness of the government as a whole to engage in effective reconstruction of shattered countries made a huge difference. Whereas the Agency for International Development had some sixteen thousand employees at the height of the Vietnam War, a quarter of whom might be in Indochina, its successor in 2006 had fewer than a tenth as many. The feebleness of the U.S. government at the tasks of development that lie at the heart of effective counterinsurgency was not the fault of the U.S. military.

But the military did bear its own set of responsibilities for what ensued in these wars, and its failures resulted from a more fundamental problem, which Robert W. Komer had identified a generation before in his classic study of the American military in Vietnam, *Bureaucracy Does Its Thing.*[8] Komer believed that the American failure there resulted largely from the playing out of bureaucratic repertoires, not from poor individual decision making. While that may have been too kind to General William Westmoreland, the American commander in Vietnam (and even more so to the general in charge of Central Command in 2001 and 2003, General Tommy Franks), there is something to that thesis, disheartening as it is.

The bureaucratic dysfunctions of Vietnam did not merely repeat themselves in Afghanistan and Iraq: they were exacerbated. Vietnam was the searing experience not only for the generation of officers who fought there, but for those who came after and were molded by the collective memory of the experience. A collective narrative of the Vietnam experience emerged that held that the U.S. military should attempt only major military operations and not counterinsurgency or nation building; that the chief reasons for failure in Vietnam had to do with the press, interference by civilian leaders, or the sheer impossibility of the task; and that the keys to waging war successfully consisted chiefly of simple and unambiguous objectives and overwhelming force.[9]

Military professionals often operate from a paradigm of war that shapes the most fundamental beliefs and attitudes of the officer corps, and the civilians whom they advise and inform about military affairs. One can see that paradigm most clearly by visiting staff colleges and other educational institutions. The portraits on the wall are those of great field commanders (the Pattons and Ridgways) and the curricula include staff rides to the scenes of great battles such as Chancellorsville. The wars that officers study last between six days and six years. All these do not prepare officers to take with equal seriousness the task of winning wars in which overwhelming force is often not the solution, because the damage it does to civilians may only breed more guerrillas; in which what lieutenant colonels do may matter a great deal more to the ultimate outcome than what a lieutenant general believes; in which there will be no severe combat, or in which one can win all the firefights and still lose the war; and in which combat may last decades, not years.

In some corners of the military—among the officers who waged counterinsurgent war in Central America during the 1980s in the special forces and among a few particularly well-educated soldiers—there were those who realized that the old attitudes about conventional warfare would unfit the American military for its tasks in future years. But between the small-scale interventions in Somalia, Yugoslavia, and Haiti and the much larger challenges of counterinsurgency in Afghanistan and Iraq, the mainstream of the army gradually began to realize that the wars it would fight would not, in fact, resemble those of either its great campaigns of the past or its imagined campaigns of the future. Three years after the invasion of Iraq, and five years after the invasion of Afghanistan, the right kinds of institutional adjustments began to appear—highly selective training programs for military advisers, and a new counterinsurgency manual to replace the thirty- or forty-year-old texts still in circulation. Commanders like Lieutenant Generals David Petraeus and Peter Chiarelli found their stars in the ascendant as it became clearer that the orthodox armor commanders of the late cold war were not, as the army often seemed to believe, interchangeable cogs in the counterguerrilla machine. But would it be too late? And could these changes compensate for the other features of American military life?

The American People and Their Military

To visit an American base overseas—even Victory Base Camp outside Baghdad—is to be struck by the elements of American middle-class life transplanted to utterly different circumstances. Cinnabon is there, as is Pizza Hut; the PX (the military equivalent of a Target or K-Mart) has the latest electronic gizmos, and soldiers will sometimes withdraw to their air-conditioned huts at night to play X-box or listen to their iPods. The chow halls run by contractors are not all that different from a well-run food court at a middling kind of mall in the States. Soldiers can fight a year in Iraq sustained on soft American bread, peanut butter, and hamburgers—pita, lamb kebabs, and hummus might never pass their lips. In their command posts, Fox News is on all day; and there may even be Starbucks coffee to keep the troops going as they watch the Super Bowl on a break from their seven-day weeks and fourteen-hour days. The troops are healthy because of good food, excellent medical care, the fitness centers that allow them to work out, and the kind of basic hygiene that a base camp can provide, including mandatory hand-washing facilities at the entrance to any mess hall. Families are closer, too, than ever before. Most soldiers have access to e-mail and to telephone cards that allow weekly or even more frequent conversations with those back home. Digital pictures fly back and forth across the Internet, and where there is broadband access and a laptop computer with a Web camera, it can even be possible to conduct a video teleconference with the folks back home.

While Victory Base Camp is a dusty, nasty place, it has more amenities than many lonely outposts elsewhere in Iraq, which are far more austere. There are soldiers who will live on prepackaged meals and go without showers for weeks, who have to burn the contents of primitive latrines, and who may go many days without contacting families at home. And even in the most comfortable camp in Iraq there is the intermittent thump of a mortar round landing, the tightened feeling in the stomach that accompanies a patrol or a convoy leaving the well-defended perimeter, the solemnity of a memorial service for a fallen comrade, and the ache of loneliness.

All that said, however, one face of modern warfare is, most definitely, life on the FOB, or forward operating base.[10] It is a middle-American kind of life, and although it helps account for the remarkable (by any historical standard) salubriousness of American life, it poses a problem for the kind of wars the United States will face in coming decades. It is a life generally isolated from the populations the military seeks to influence; a life that consumes enormous resources in sustaining and protecting itself abroad; and a life that does not lend itself to the broader intellectual and cultural experiences that make soldiers (or anyone else for that matter) wiser and better leaders.

The norms and paradoxes of life on the FOB reflect the broader characteristics of the American military in the early twenty-first century. It is, in many ways, a life that can seem at times the epitome of a wholesome middle-class existence, which is not surprising, because the American military is a middle-class enterprise. Soldiers, sailors, airmen, and marines are, by and large, rather better educated than their counterparts across society. Nearly 99 percent of the enlisted force, and 100 percent of the officer and warrant officers, have graduated from high school; officers are between 95 percent and 97 percent college graduates, and even the enlisted ranks contain up to 5 percent college graduates.[11] Among the overall American population, 79 percent have graduated high school and something like 25 percent have completed B.A. degrees.[12]

With some exceptions the American military—and above all, its officer corps—hails neither from the American underclass nor its privileged elites—there are ROTC programs at some Ivy League and other elite campuses, but they are thinly manned. Cornell has some fifty cadets, for example; Dartmouth fewer than a dozen; Brown, Columbia, Harvard, Yale, University of Chicago, and Stanford do not have ROTC programs, although some of their students either go through the program elsewhere or enlist after college. The service academies provide under a fifth of active duty officers and ROTC more than a third; the remaining come either from officer candidate schools (that is, directly from civilian life or from the enlisted ranks—20 percent in all) or by direct appointment (for specialties such as medical or legal professionals or chaplains—15 percent).[13] It is an ethnically representative force as well—75 percent white and 13 percent black, 87 percent non-Hispanic and

13 percent Hispanic. If anything, and contrary to what many believe, minorities are *under*represented in the military, including in the combat arms. Women, of course, are underrepresented as well, making up roughly 15 percent of the total force.

All of the paraphernalia of American life can be found on military bases, from Little League to the Christian Fellowship—but those bases are themselves often remote from America's big cities and becoming more so, as the closure and realignment of bases leads to more consolidation in remote areas. The military, always probably more conservative than the society from which its participants hailed, seems to be ever more so, its members identifying with the Republican Party and a moderately conservative political code. It is multi-ethnic but not multi-class, or even multi-ideological.

It is a popular military in the twenty-first century, perhaps more popular than it has ever been since the end of World War II, and certainly than before it. Troops overseas wade through boxes of chocolate chip cookies, soldiers in uniform find strangers picking up their bar and restaurant tabs; troops coming home on leave from overseas get bumped up to first class and applauded by passengers as they exit the airplanes. And even when the newspapers carry reports of soldiers abusing detained suspects, or when it is clear that there have been failures on the ground, it is very rare to find the armed forces, as opposed to its civilian masters, being blamed. Particularly in comparison with European militaries, this remains a popular force.

How it fights, however, and what it can accomplish, reflect these sociological facts—that the military, while made up of a central slice of American life, is also isolated from much of society. Although the military academies recruit from the same applicant pool as Ivy League universities, most of the officer corps comes from large state schools such as Texas A&M. Though some elite universities have small Reserve Officer Training Corps (ROTC) programs on campus or available to students, the hard fact remains that the products of elite universities are not well represented in the officer corps. The officer corps does not draw its share from the same pool that provides the dominant intellectual, business, and even political classes of the country. The decline in numbers of politicians who have military experience reflects this fact, which has been noted in popular books such as Kathy Roth-Douquet and Frank Schaeffer's *AWOL: The Unexcused Absence of America's Upper Classes from Military Service and How It Hurts Our Country*. And, of course, the rank and file of the military most definitely lacks the proportionate elite representation that it had in World War II, the 1950s, and the early 1960s.

What the underrepresentation in the military of many parts of America means in the long term is less clear. Clearly, it has something to do with the ability of the United States to tolerate casualties and the strains of prolonged expeditionary warfare abroad. The residents of the Upper East Side in Manhattan or the tonier suburbs of Boston, Chicago, or Los Angeles do not, by and large, send their sons and daughters off to Iraq or Afghanistan. Those who go are volunteers, and both they and their families, with few exceptions, have the kind of patriotic zeal, or at the very least stoicism, that gets them through such trials. Nor does the military draw, as some believe, from the deprived strata of society: it still recruits its enlisted personnel overwhelmingly from high school graduates of middling to high intelligence scores on the standard tests and recruits its officer corps from college graduates. But the tone, to include the intellectual tone, is still largely that of middle America. The profile is certainly socially and politically more conservative than American elites, more religious, and less academic. Again, it is not clear what difference this makes in the end: the American military is a diverse organization, and includes officers of many different backgrounds and interests. But since 9/11 it has faced a world in which its previous routines and conceptions of war, molded largely in the period between Vietnam and the first Gulf War, have proven inadequate for a very different set of conflicts.

One must draw comparisons with one of the few armies in the world comparable to that of the United States in sophistication and effectiveness, though not size: that of Great Britain. Its leaders in recent years have been officers of considerable fluency and intellectual reach. Indeed, one of the most important books on modern warfare is by a British general, Sir Rupert Smith, who fought in Yugoslavia and Iraq, "amongst the people," as he puts it.[14] The hard fact is that American military leaders have not, with some notable exceptions, been able to articulate strategic issues and priorities nearly as well as their civilian counterparts. The issue is not, to repeat, differences in raw intelligence and certainly not ability, but rather in the ability to move smoothly and effectively in the realm of debates that are, of their nature, often abstract and theoretical. It in some measure reflects the nature of the American military: a practical, workmanlike slice of American society; a good representation of a middle class that is intelligent, hardworking, and impatient with theory and theoreticians as well.

A middle-class military is an expensive military. It is also one that feels particularly keenly the loss of its members. At one level one could argue that American casualty sensitivity has been vastly overstated for some time. In three years of grinding conflict in Iraq, more than three thousand servicemen and servicewomen lost their lives, and another twenty thousand were wounded. In the twenty-odd years between the Vietnam and the second Iraq war, that number of casualties would have been viewed as an unacceptable rate of loss. More important, perhaps, is the emphasis placed on "force protection"—seen, in part, in the restriction of movement outside FOBs. Losses that would have been acceptable to American commanders in World War II or Vietnam no longer are.

Why this is so remains a matter of scholarly debate. Some attribute it to changed societal attitudes to losses, perhaps losses of any kind. In some sense the very notion of "accident" has been undermined in an American society that tends to believe that nothing goes wrong without someone being culpable. But a deeper reason may have to do with the very nature of modern military leadership, which prizes soldiers as individuals much more highly than has perhaps been the case since the days of feudal knights. This reflects in part the enormous resources that go into the training and equipping of the individual soldier, who is no longer cannon fodder but an expensive and increasingly powerful actor on the battlefield. It reflects even more, however, changed attitudes toward soldiers and motivation. The disappearance of informally administered corporal punishment, the banning of most forms of hazing, and the relentless emphasis on developing soldiers through civilian as well as military education reflect a very different approach to the individual than was characteristic of the draft-era military.

The traditional American way of war, as exemplified by the Civil War and the world wars, was one of mobilization, mass, and aggressive action, to include direct and violent attacks on enemies at a considerable disadvantage in materiel. That way of war was stumped by the challenges of Korea and Vietnam; it was revived, in some measure, during the Gulf War of 1991, but only partly so. It has been stymied once again in Iraq and Afghanistan. The reasons for this are beyond the scope of this article: some of it surely has to do with the limitations of other parts of government—an aid system, for example, that was simply not up to the developmental side of counterinsurgency. Some of it may have had to do with the sheer difficulty of stabilizing countries that had been brutalized by decades of war, dictatorship, and social chaos. But some of it may reflect the inadequacy of that way of war in coping with low-level, irregular conflict.

While some aspects of the American way of war remain intact— in particular its aggressiveness, self-confidence, and technological intensity—others have changed. Of these, the most noticeable is mobilization. More than in any other conflict in American history, after 9/11 the United States went to war with an army of champions and a population of spectators. There was no call to arms, no summoning of volunteers for the duration of the fight, and certainly no talk, much less consideration, of reimposition of conscription. The bureaucracies were staffed not by "dollar a day men" but by the same civil servants as in the past. And even the industrial machine has proven incapable of anything faintly resembling the Herculean efforts of previous wars. The United States continues to produce tanks designed twenty-five years ago, modified, to be sure, but the products of cold war conditions and geopolitics nonetheless. New electronic systems appeared on the battlefield, but were trundled around in platforms older than the men and women who drove them. To move an entirely new weapon system from concept to design is not a matter of years but decades.

The American military of the early twenty-first century is also a much smaller military than the United States had at the peak of the cold war or even in the early stages of the All Volunteer Force. In 1960, before Vietnam, the United States had just under 2.5 million personnel on active duty in the military. By 1980, the number was 2 million, and by the early 2000s the number fluctuated around 1.5 million. The reduction was felt in all services other than the Marine Corps, which, remarkably enough, actually grew slightly. There were many reasons for this decline in numbers—the expense of personnel, surely, but also technological change, which made it possible to shrink the size, say, of destroyer crews. Outsourcing of everything from guard posts to maintenance, and even in some measure training and professional education, also contributed. The result was a military that no longer even thought about the kind of large-scale mobilization typical of the first half of the twentieth century, that could not think of drill sergeants hammering scared draftees into shape, or factories churning out thousands of tanks, or shipyards that could build a useful merchant ship in a week.

This was not, of course, simply an American phenomenon. Almost all modern militaries and their supporting industrial systems have become dependent on a combination of sophisticated technologies, elaborate contractor organizations, and archaic development bureaucracies. The trend everywhere seems to be fewer platforms—whether they be tanks or fighter planes, destroyers or artillery tubes—made more effective by information technology, ever more lethal munitions, and highly trained personnel. Such military organizations are suited to middling warfare: conventional contests that don't go on for more than a few weeks, albeit at high levels of intensity. It is not clear that they can cope with sustained high-intensity combat, on the one hand, or large-scale insurgency on the other. The debate about American troop levels in Iraq between 2003 and 2006 turned, to a remarkable degree, on the question of what the army could stand without overstressing a professional force, not about what was needed.

There is a deeper point yet. Americans seem to believe that war constitutes but a small divergence from the norms of civilian life, and that the extraordinary activity required can be met by normal efforts. The government wages war, and citizens seem to think one exists, without any noticeable sacrifice, or indeed much more effort (other than the spending of a few hundreds of billions of dollars, financed by deficits rather than tax increases or compulsory savings) than peace. It has worked—so far. But there is no guarantee that it will work indefinitely. In the event of challenges that require much greater effort, the American military of 2007—highly proficient, small, well paid, and narrowly recruited—may seem as odd to its successors as the professional army of *From Here to Eternity* seems to us.

CHAPTER 10
Religion
Robert Wuthnow

America is by far the most religious of advanced democracies and also the most religiously diverse and decentralized. Sociologist of religion Robert Wuthnow, tracing the social importance of religion to the country's earliest days, shows that many of America's most striking cultural features—market competition, individualism, ethnic and racial diversity, privatism, ideological division, localism, evangelicism, and moralizing political movements—are reflected in the evolution and roles of American religions. The global reach and ambitions of many denominations are another distinctive element.

AT HOME AND ABROAD, THE UNITED STATES IS POPULARLY regarded as one of the most religious countries in the world. The "nation with the soul of a church," as G. K. Chesterton once described it, has managed to progress economically and scientifically without abandoning its houses of worship.[1] But this perception, like many other naïve impressions of American religion, is only partly true. Faith is always complex, and American faith is no exception. If we are to understand it, we must move beyond simple assertions about religious vitality and the supposed uniqueness of this vitality in the United States. This essay examines the claims that have been made about the strength of American religion; shows that these claims must be regarded cautiously; and then focuses on the prevailing contemporary characteristics of private and public faith, including spiritual seeking, the effects of increasing religious diversity, the role of religion in partisan politics, government funding of faith-based initiatives, and the increasing globalization of American religion. If America is still a nation with "the soul of a church," it is one in which the meanings of "church" and "soul" must be examined closely. Both terms are contested, and both deserve greater scrutiny than academics and journalists have typically given them.

The Question of Religious Vitality

Judging from polls, it appears that religious activity is more prevalent in the United States than in such western European countries as France, Germany, Great Britain, and Sweden. Yet researchers question whether religion in America is quite as strong as such comparisons might suggest. Indeed, research increasingly indicates that religious participation in America is probably lower even than these polls would have us believe. For instance, a General Social Survey poll showed that only 27 percent of Americans claimed to attend religious services on a weekly basis in 2004, while 51 percent said they had attended no more than several times in the past year.[2] Counts of vehicles in church parking lots, numbers provided by congregations, and time-diary studies all suggest that only a quarter of the public—not the 40 percent that pollsters sometimes report— may be present at religious services on any given weekend. In any case, using survey data and diaries to measure the religiousness of a country is at best limited. Consider the great cathedrals of Europe, which are a lasting tribute to the religious influences there; it can be argued that American religion has not produced anything of that scope or magnitude.

Still, Americans have always liked to think that we are a special people, and an important part of our national story is imagining ourselves to be exceptionally religious, even divinely blessed. John Winthrop's speech aboard the *Arbella* in 1630, in which he referred to the new American settlement as a "city on a hill" with a special mission from God, continues to be echoed in our national rhetoric. "We raised a banner of bold colors—no pale pastels," President

Ronald Reagan declared at the 1984 Republican National Convention. "We proclaimed a dream of an America that would be a shining city on a hill." Building on the same theme, President George W. Bush observed in a 2006 speech: "We're a nation founded by men and women who came to these shores seeking to worship the Almighty freely. From these prayerful beginnings, God has greatly blessed the American people."[3] Associating ourselves with God and God's purposes is central to our civil religion, as Robert N. Bellah has argued. Presidents of both political parties routinely invoke God's blessings in addressing the nation—something that rarely happens in other Western countries.

The Place of Religion in American Exceptionalism

Beneath the rhetoric lies the reality. America may not be the most religious country in the world, but religion has played a strong role in the nation's history and continues to be a vibrant aspect of national life today. Winthrop's speech in 1630 was a sermon to men and women fleeing persecution for their religious beliefs. Although the American colonies were by no means settled only for religious reasons, religion had far more influence in colonial life than some scholars of late, who focus only on sparse records of church membership, have assumed. Church leaders determined who could become a church member and who could not, who would be welcomed to a colony or town and who would not, how much profit a business owner could earn, how fornicators were punished, and how orphans would be fed.

In the decades prior to the War of Independence, the revivals led by Jonathan Edwards and George Whitefield forged social networks and a sense of conscience that historians credit with helping to mobilize the colonists' cause. Founding Fathers Thomas Jefferson, James Madison, Benjamin Franklin, and John Adams held diverse views of religion, conditioned as much by the Enlightenment as by their own religious upbringing, but all recognized that religion was a fact of American life and was likely to remain so. Free expression of religion became the national standard, encouraging tolerance and diversity rather than an establishment of religion. During the early nineteenth century, religious revivals continued, most notably in the open-air meetings led by Charles Grandison Finney on the emerging frontier, but also at large gatherings in Philadelphia and New York. Congregationalists opened schools in Indian Territory and sent missionaries to the far corners of the continent. Presbyterians spread through Pennsylvania and the Carolinas and into Kentucky and Tennessee. Baptists and Methodists were especially successful in following the westward movement of the frontier. Mormons, Adventists, spiritualists, and utopian societies also emerged. Most notably, religion became democratized, reaching ordinary people in hamlets and towns, and a commonsense view of morality developed that credited people of all backgrounds and rank with an innate sense of right and wrong.

The Civil War fractured American religion as deeply as it did American politics. Denominations—especially Baptists, Methodists, and Presbyterians—divided along regional and racial lines. Both sides in the war appealed to God to advance their cause, and church auxiliaries played important roles in sending clothing and medical supplies to their respective armies. The war cast a shadow over the denominations' structure and teachings that remained evident even at the end of the next century, especially in divisions between northern and southern denominations. Freedmen and former slaves formed their own churches and carried these churches with them during the great northward migration. The South became solidly Baptist, with a strong emphasis on personal piety, but also with a sense of having been misunderstood and marginalized by the war. The North remained more religiously diverse, but took moral pride in having been on the winning side. Lincoln became a mythic figure, larger than life, serving as a national martyr and redeemer in America's growing consciousness of itself.

In the half century after the Civil War, America experienced record levels of immigration, and religion was both altered and revitalized as a result. From small settlements of Swedish Baptists and Russian Jews to large populations of Germans and Irish, houses of worship in these communities provided space in which to speak the old languages and strengthen ties with fellow ethnics. "Struggling against heavy odds to save something of the old ways," Oscar Handlin wrote, "the immigrants directed into their faith the whole weight of their longing to be connected with the past."[4] By 1929, when H. Richard Niebuhr published his famous book about American denominationalism, ethnicity and national origins had become as important to the religious landscape as race, region, and social class.[5] Religion not only provided refuge, respect, and resources for new immigrants but also encouraged assimilation into wider communities and larger national stories. As Will Herberg observed in the 1950s, being Protestant, Catholic, or Jewish had become the most accepted ways of being "American."

With each successive faith-related development, commentators found ways of explaining American religion's vitality that fit well with prevailing understandings of the nation's place in the world. In the early federal period, with the struggle for liberty so fresh in mind, it was *freedom* that writers most often used to describe the distinctive character of American religion. "Our country has been the first to prove to the world two truths," Thomas Jefferson wrote in 1820, "that man can govern himself, and that religious freedom is the most effective anodyne against religious dissension."[6] By the end of the nineteenth century, the nation's enormous westward expansion offered a new framework for explaining the apparent vitality of its religion. In his famous thesis about the impact of the frontier, Frederick Jackson Turner observed, "The contest for power and the expansive tendency furnished to the various sects by the existence of a moving frontier must have had important results on the character of religious organization in the United States." It was the "multiplication of rival churches in the little frontier towns," Turner believed, that had shaped both the quality and quantity of religious life.[7] The central reason for America's apparent religious strength shifted again during the twentieth century. When Sydney Ahlstrom published his definitive history of American religion in 1972, the feature that interested him most was the "radical diversity of American religious movements," including "secular" movements and convictions.[8] For Ahlstrom, the *disestablishment* of earlier denominations by subsequent waves of awakenings, sectarian movements, and Catholic and Jewish immigrants was the key to the continuing vitality of American religion.

The common thread in these various arguments is that Americans were free to pursue different and often competing versions of religious truth. Thus, it is not surprising that scholars today emphasize this thread in discussing continuities in American religion. What is notable is only that recent writers have felt obliged to describe their arguments as new. Yet the novelty of recent arguments lies merely in the fact that a new metaphor is being used: the idea of a religious *market*. This metaphor is as much a product of its times as were the earlier emphases on liberty of conscience, the frontier, and disestablishment. In an era when the United States prides itself on its markets, interprets the end of the cold war as a vindication of capitalism, and promotes neoliberal theories of international trade, it is little wonder that scholars have begun to claim that markets are as beneficial to spiritual vitality as they are to the pocketbook.

To understand American religion, it is thus necessary to move past simplistic assertions about market competition being the secret of its success. As with all half-truths, the market metaphor helpfully illuminates some aspects of Americans' faith and badly distorts others. Where it is most helpful is in drawing attention to the fact that

Americans are so thoroughly socialized to shop, buy, sell, and otherwise behave as consumers that their religious behavior is influenced accordingly. In a national survey, 41 percent of adults aged twenty-one through forty-five said they had "shopped" for a place of worship. In personal interviews, Americans explain that they compare congregations to find the best preaching or the most well-staffed nursery. Their devotional practices are especially affected by the fact that spirituality, like other products, is for sale. One can consume stories of angels and miracles on television; the life of Christ on the big screen at the local cinemaplex; gospel music on the radio; and inspirational reading at Wal-Mart.

The market metaphor also serves usefully as a reminder that American religion is big business. In recent years, individual contributions to U.S. religious organizations have topped $80 billion annually. Much of this money pays for clergy salaries and building maintenance at the nation's three hundred thousand local congregations, many of which have small memberships and operate on tight budgets. It is increasingly common, though, for congregations of three hundred to four hundred members to generate contributions of $1 million or more annually and for very large congregations (sometimes called "megachurches") to have budgets in the tens of millions. Prestonwood Baptist Church in suburban Dallas, for instance, has a full-time staff of more than one hundred, operates a full-service school, and sponsors its own symphony orchestra. At large churches, fees, rents, and royalties significantly add to voluntary contributions. At Saddleback Church in Lake Forest, California, Pastor Rick Warren has earned an estimated $25 million in book royalties. For a few entrepreneurs, religious television has also been a source of vast good fortune. Televangelist Pat Robertson sold the family entertainment branch of his broadcasting empire in 1997 for $1.9 billion. In 2005, Robertson's Christian Broadcasting Network (CBN) reported total assets of $252 million, contributions of $457 million, and expenses of $424 million. Rival company Trinity

Broadcasting Network (TBN) reported assets of $669 million, revenue of $184 million, and expenses of $113 million.

The market metaphor falters, though, in providing credible explanations for the growth of particular religious organizations or for the strength of U.S. religion compared to that of other countries. Research purporting to explain why religious activity was stronger in some U.S. counties in the early 1900s than in others has been shown to be a statistical artifact. Generalizations about the role of markets in encouraging nineteenth-century church expansion turn out to have misinterpreted early church statistics. Market theories attribute religious vitality to competition among congregations, but in so doing they fail to see that *cooperation* has been a significant feature of American religious history. For instance, cooperation among Congregationalists and Presbyterians was effective in launching the U.S. foreign missionary movement, and cooperation among mainline Protestant denominations is currently pervasive in rural America. Market arguments also emphasize the supposed competitive advantages of fundamentalists and other groups with strict theological doctrines, arguing that strictness itself is somehow more appealing and more conducive to high levels of commitment. Yet denominations that grew during the 1970s because they were strict did not grow during the 1990s when they were still strict. Indeed, variations in denominational growth or decline are largely a function of high or low birthrates and whether parents are younger or older when they have children.

Regrettably, the recent overuse of market imagery among scholars has led to an obsession with understanding American religion in terms of numeric growth and decline. This focus is to a small degree understandable in view of earlier predictions from social scientists of the demise of religion in industrialized countries. In the face of arguments presented by theorists such as Max Weber, Emile Durkheim, and Karl Marx, the continuing vitality of religion in the United States offers strong counterevidence to the idea that religion will simply wither away with time. Yet it is not at all clear that these important theorists of the nineteenth century would have been impressed by the kind of evidence recent scholars have assembled, usually focusing only on church attendance trends. Indeed, a more careful reading of those earlier works, informed as they were by strong normative concerns about the direction of modern societies, indicates that scholarly emphasis should be placed primarily on changes in the *quality* of religion, rather than on statistical changes in attendance. Marx may have predicted that religion would wither in a truly classless society, but no classless society has emerged, and Marx's observations concerning the continuing functions of religion far surpass, in their predictive power, his forecasts of decline. Weber and Durkheim can be read more accurately as analysts of the effects of rationality and individuality, respectively, on modern religion than as prophets of secularism. More recent observers—among them, Will Herberg, Robert Bellah, and Peter Berger—have also examined religion less for its directionality and more for an understanding of its normative role.

The Spirituality of Personal Seeking

The principal feature of American religion that has been qualitatively influenced by recent societal changes is the way in which spirituality is understood and experienced. These influences are harder to assess with numeric measures than are attendance and membership rates, so remain subject to a greater divergence of opinion. Nevertheless, dozens of ethnographic studies and thousands of qualitative interviews have examined them. One way of describing spirituality—by which people commonly mean their personal relationship to God—is to say that it has become increasingly private. This assertion requires some clarification. It does not mean that Americans refrain from speaking about their faith in public, or that religion never influences politics and business. It means instead that the source of *authority* in matters of faith increasingly lies with the individual person, rather than with religious institutions.

This emphasis on personal authority can be traced historically to the Protestant Reformation's emphasis on individual salvation and to a Lockean understanding of the free exercise of conscience. In both, responsibility for one's spirituality lies with oneself. And yet, personal spirituality is guided by the norms of a religious community, just as a person's conscience is molded by a good home environment. As recently as the 1950s, spirituality was popularly associated with images of immersion within religious institutions. What I have described elsewhere as "a spirituality of dwelling" emphasized spatial metaphors of home, family, habit, and habitat and perceived God to be found most vividly within familiar houses of worship. Herberg notably described Americans' faith not as a quest for self-identity but as a desire for self-*location*. In subsequent decades, though, metaphors of dwelling have become less prominent than images of seeking. The ideal life of faith in America is increasingly understood as being mobile, uprooted, adaptable, and willing to experiment. Spirituality is less a matter of staying put than of embarking on a journey. It has become increasingly important to "find God" in one's own way and on one's own. In their famous example, the authors of *Habits of the Heart* describe Sheila Larson, a young woman who looks deep inside herself and finds a spirituality she calls "Sheilaism."[9] In their study of *The Jew Within,* Steven M. Cohen and Arnold M. Eisen find a similar pattern among American Jews. Spirituality, they argue, is concerned above all with finding personal meaning that adds significance to daily life.

Spiritual seeking does not imply, as some observers have suggested, that the majority of Americans are becoming "spiritual, but not religious." For the most part, individuals with serious interests in spiritual growth remain involved in religious organizations. They attend worship services, join small fellowship groups, and develop friendships within their congregations. Their relationships with these organizations nevertheless emphasize the priority of personal experience. A worship service is meaningful if it evokes a sense of being in touch with the sacred. A fellowship group is worth attending if it provides emotional support. A person knows that his or her faith is genuine less by accepting the wisdom embodied in religious teachings and practices and more from having had a validating experience of the holy—perhaps during a worship service, but in wider venues as well, including times of private meditation, hiking, listening to music, viewing a painting, or making love. Such experience is authoritative, both in the sense of providing a source of personal guidance and in being unassailable in a way that doctrines and creeds are not.

In form and content, spiritual experiences vary widely; yet a common aspect, whether of being born-again or having achieved meditative enlightenment, is the necessity to find that which is personally most meaningful. God becomes a friend, more than a righteous lawgiver. The mark of true faith is that it relieves stress and helps a person feel fulfilled. Amidst multiple creeds and doctrinal interpretations, divine truth is more intuitive. Even among conservative Christians, the view has gained popularity that God is a mystery, that divine experience requires emptying one's mind, and that the path to salvation differs from person to person. "Restless souls," in historian Leigh Schmidt's apt phrase, hold themselves responsible for exploring the most personally suitable spiritual paths. Seekers exercise choice, sometimes by switching religious traditions, but more often by experimenting, tinkering, and piecing together a highly personalized bricolage of faith.

The private authority on which faith commitments rest in the twenty-first century is both a strength and a weakness of American religion. Strength lies in the fact that every person feels a right to have an opinion about God. The one who believes in reincarnation is no less authentic than the one who expresses faith in eternal salvation through Jesus. Religion is strong, or at least pervasive, because the opportunities for expressing personal opinions are abundant. As long as all opinions can be entertained, religion is not a conversation stopper, as Richard Rorty has argued, but a conversation starter. The possibilities for discourse are endless. The options for religion to influence opinions and behavior are also abundant. A person who wishes inspiration for artistic work, as well as a person who seeks reassurance about how to be a good parent or spouse, can each find what they are looking for in spirituality. With religion having been so prominent a part of American culture from the start, people who currently seek solace, advice, and inspiration can still find it in religious venues, rather than searching for it in the secular institutions that might be more attractive in other societies.

The weakness in spirituality's residing in personal authority is that spirituality is indeed a matter of opinion. What a person feels intuitively is harder to assert as a standard for moral conduct in the public life of the community. Everything "is to be permitted," writes Stanley Fish, "but nothing is to be taken seriously." Conviction matters in the "personal spaces of the heart, the home and the house of worship." But in the public sphere, "religious views must be put forward with diffidence and circumspection." Religious beliefs are "equally and indifferently authorized as ideas people are perfectly free to believe, but they are equally and indifferently disallowed as ideas that might serve as a basis for action or public policy."[10]

The Fracture in American Public Religion

In one perspective, it might be argued that the privatization of American religion has gone a long way toward quelling the religious hostilities that worried Locke and Jefferson and that continue in many parts of the world. Religious opinions are harder to fight about than religious truths. Yet American religion cannot be described only as a polite gentlemanly agreement to leave differences at the civic door. If anything, the public face of American religion in recent decades has been acrimonious. The fault lines between Catholics and Protestants and between Christians and Jews that interested Herberg have been replaced by a fracture—sometimes described as a "culture war"—between religious conservatives and religious liberals or secularists.

Approximately 80 percent of Americans currently identify themselves as Christians. Several more percent are Jewish or affiliated with offshoots of Judaism or Christianity (such as Unitarianism) or other world religions (such as Islam or Buddhism), leaving approximately 14 percent who claim no religious affiliation. Catholics, with some 23 percent of the population, constitute the largest single religious tradition, followed by Southern Baptists (8 percent), United Methodists (5 percent), and as many as a thousand other organizations that range from relatively large national denominations (such as the Presbyterian Church USA, the Episcopal Church, and the United Church of Christ) to smaller coalitions of independent congregations. The organizations that represent these various traditions continue to be important both to their members and to the wider society. Clergy appointments and pension plans are typically administered by these umbrella organizations, and religious statements about public policy are routinely vetted and publicized through their advocacy networks. However, faith communities are often divided between self-styled conservatives or orthodox constituents and self-identified liberals or progressive adherents. Baptists and Pentecostals feel greater affinity with one another as fellow evangelicals or conservative Protestants than in the past, while Presbyterians and Episcopalians find far less to disagree about. The fault lines also cut through denominations and faith traditions. Liberal Southern Baptists are likely to feel closer to liberal Presbyterians than to fundamentalists in their own denomination, and liberal Catholics may work with liberal Lutherans more easily than with conservative Catholics.

The culture war in American religion is most evident in the statements and activities of religious special-purpose groups. These groups, which numbered about eight hundred by the early 1980s, sponsored campus ministries, counseling centers, community services, educational programs, clergy alliances, ecumenical cooperation, publishing, broadcasting, and numerous other activities. A growing number of these groups were concerned with public policies, ranging from constitutional questions to gender equality to peace advocacy. Some had originated in the civil rights movement (for example, the Southern Christian Leadership Conference) or had gained momentum during the Vietnam War (such as Pax Christi), while others were more recent and reflected concerns about federal regulation of religious broadcasting, abortion policy, and local issues involving school prayer or the teaching of evolution. With access through direct-mail solicitations or television to constituencies spanning denominational lines, these organizations could focus more on controversial issues than denominations and local congregations could. Studying special-purpose groups' leaders, James Davison Hunter found that a deep cultural divide was often evident, with each side struggling to gain the upper hand in publicizing its views. Conservative leaders framed arguments in terms of divine revelation about absolute moral rules, whereas liberal leaders were generally more relativistic. This divide, Hunter argued, influenced activists' responses to many social issues, including homosexuality, pornography, funding for art projects that might be deemed morally offensive, the death penalty, welfare spending, and Supreme Court appointments.

Among grassroots Americans, talk of a culture war fails to capture the complexity of views and even the lack of interest in controversial issues that characterizes much of the public. Few of the more highly publicized activist groups of the 1980s, such as the Moral Majority and the Christian Coalition, attracted commitment from more than a small percentage of the general public. There is, as Alan

Wolfe has observed, a striking tendency for the personalized faith that describes many Americans to encourage a wishy-washy acceptance of all views. Especially among educated Americans, who have been taught to entertain multiple viewpoints, the preferred option is often to believe that any issue can be resolved with a "both-and" attitude: of course we believe in the sanctity of all life *and* in a woman's right to choose, and we see no conflict between believing in evolution and viewing God as the creator. Each individual comes up with his or her own opinions. Yet, despite these inclinations to accept multiple views, a cultural fracture does appear to characterize the American population. About a quarter of individuals identify themselves as religious "conservatives," and about the same proportion does so as religious "liberals." Since the early 1980s, when these labels started to gain traction in public discourse, the proportions at the extremes have increased, while the percentages in the middle or of those uncomfortable with all such labels have decreased. Not surprisingly, self-defined religious conservatives and liberals take radically different views on a wide range of hot-button issues.

The reasons for the left-right divide in American religion are complex. Churches' efforts to be relevant to the lives of individuals and the nation, as opposed to encouraging withdrawal from worldly affairs, meant that religion was influenced by broader cultural developments. Religion's sheer institutional prominence in local communities also enabled it to respond to these developments. The civil rights movement mobilized clergy both in support of and in opposition to racial integration, as did the Vietnam War. The regional realignment of the two major political parties that became evident with Ronald Reagan's election in 1980 had important ramifications for religion. Whereas southern evangelicals and northern Catholics had been strongly Democratic, the Republican party increasingly captured the votes of southern and northern evangelicals alike, while Democrats remained most solidly represented among African-Americans, Catholics, theologically liberal members of mainline Protestant denominations, and those without religious affiliations. In recent years, Republicans have more actively courted religiously conservative voters, whereas Democrats have been less successful at articulating issues in ways that resonate strongly with any religious constituencies. At the same time, denominational loyalties themselves were weakening, opening new opportunities for alliances among conservatives in various faith traditions and among their liberal counterparts. The rapid expansion of American higher education during the 1960s and 1970s has also had a continuing impact on American religion. Although religious liberals tended to be better educated than religious conservatives, a new elite of educated and prosperous evangelicals emerged, yet they came from less advantaged backgrounds, were more likely to be trained at church-related colleges, and like other newly arrived groups, often felt marginalized and discriminated against.

The split between religious conservatives and religious liberals has made religion a more visible aspect of public discourse. Because the media love conflict, a denominational split over questions about ordaining gay clergy is often deemed more newsworthy than if people quietly go about their business, praying when they feel like it and worshipping the way they have for generations. Despite an arguably weak role in partisan politics, the religious right has also become of special interest to the media and has sometimes exploited this attention to its advantage. During the 1980s and 1990s, Pat Robertson and Jerry Falwell were routinely courted by the media to make statements presumably representative of the religious right, and in recent years the media has paid increasing attention to such conservative leaders as James Dobson of Focus on the Family, Gary Bauer of the Family Research Council, Richard Land of the Southern Baptist Convention, and megachurch pastors Rick Warren and Joel Osteen. The impression left by journalists is that these public figures are the movers and shakers of American politics, whereas in fact their influence is seldom as strong the media portray.

Increasing Diversity

Although the split between liberals and conservatives has profoundly affected American religion, the nation's religious identity is undergoing a quieter transformation that is likely to have even more significant implications. Between 1965 and 2005, an estimated 22 million new immigrants came to America, along with perhaps as many as 10 million undocumented immigrants who arrived and stayed. The impact of immigration on the young-adult population has been especially evident. Among females in their twenties, the proportion of noncitizens or naturalized citizens rose from 4 percent in 1970 to 14 percent in 2000; among males the same age, the proportion jumped from 4 percent to 18 percent.

Approximately two-thirds of post–1965 immigrants are from predominantly Christian countries, such as Mexico, the Philippines, and South Korea, making Protestant denominations and the Catholic Church more ethnically diverse than in the recent past. Estimates of the number of Korean American congregations, for instance, range as high as three thousand; the majority are Presbyterian, Methodist, or Baptist. As many as a quarter of U.S. Catholics are of Latino origin, accounting for most of the recent growth among Catholic churches, and between 8 and 9 million Latino immigrants belong to Protestant congregations or hold dual affiliations with Protestant and Catholic churches. Contrary to the popular view that immigrants are more religiously active than the native-born population, statistics show that attendance at worship services among foreign-born Americans is actually lower: 28 percent attend religious services every week, compared with 34 percent of the native-born population. However, research suggests that religious participation among many immigrant groups is higher than for residents in their countries of origin. Research also indicates that middle-class immigrants quickly exhibit the highly personalized style of spirituality that characterizes other Americans.

In addition to the increasing ethnic diversity among U.S. Christians, immigration has for the first time in American history substantially increased the presence of non-Western religions. In 2000, more than 1,200 mosques existed in the United States with total adherents of approximately 2 million Americans. Nearly a third of these had been established in the 1990s and another third dated only to the 1980s. Seventy-seven percent of the mosques studied reported an increase in participation since 1995; only 5 percent reported declining participation. In the mid–1990s, there were at least 200 Hindu temples or meditation centers, 100 Sikh temples, and 60 Jain temples. Most were heavily concentrated in several metropolitan areas, especially Southern California, but there were also congregations located in every state. By 2003, a more comprehensive study had located 680 Hindu temples and centers, 219 Sikh temples, and 89 Jain temples. Approximately 1.5 million Americans were thought to be participants at these various temples and centers. The number of Buddhists in the United States is estimated at between 2.5 and 4 million. A 1998 study of more than a thousand Buddhist meditation centers found that 70 percent had been established since 1985. The majority of participants at these mosques, temples, and meditation centers are immigrants or children of immigrants, but more than 25 percent are converts.[11]

Public sentiment toward new immigrants has been mixed, especially after 9/11 and with increasing concern expressed in the media about broken borders and lost jobs. In a 2003 study, 42 percent of the public said they would not welcome Muslims becoming a stronger presence in the United States; 33 percent said this about Hindus; 32 percent about Buddhists; 22 percent about Asian Americans; and 21 percent about Hispanics. Negative views about Muslims were also evident in responses to questions about the perceived characteristics of various religions. Fifty-seven percent of Americans said the Muslim religion is closed-minded, 47 percent said it was fanatical, 40 percent said it was violent, and 34 percent said it was backward. The public viewed Hinduism and Buddhism more positively; yet 35 percent said Hinduism was closed-minded, and 30 percent said this about Buddhism.[12]

The growing diversity of American religion raises questions about fair treatment, just as racial and ethnic diversity do, and about how much or how little government should be involved in regulating religious activities. The courts have heard cases in recent years, for instance, about religious holidays, religious dress in schools and the workplace, zoning restrictions preventing Muslims or Hindus from constructing mosques or temples, hate speech and acts of violence directed against religious minorities, and numerous other issues. In addition to these civic concerns, religious diversity also raises issues about religion itself and about the religious character of American culture. Historically, America's civil religion has emphasized Christian teachings and has often encouraged citizens to think of the United States as a Christian nation. The God who blessed America was a biblical God. The phrase, "one nation under God," in the Pledge of Allegiance could be said without considering its meaning to Hindus and Buddhists. The Ten Commandments and the Sermon on the Mount provided a foundation for the nation's common morality. A large majority of the population continues to think in these ways, agreeing in surveys that America is a Christian nation, that Christianity is the wellspring of American democracy, and that America was founded on Christian principles. Not surprisingly, these views are even more widely shared among the third of the public who believe that Christianity is the only true religion. To them, the increasing presence of Muslims, Buddhists, and Hindus is unwelcome.

Although a relatively small percentage of the U.S. population is Muslim, Buddhist, or Hindu, the increasing presence of these religions thus poses an important problem for America's historic identity as a Christian nation. Americans often take pride in being pluralistic, viewing it as one of the distinctive features of American religion, and associating it with the nation's remarkable degree of tolerance for diversity. Yet tolerance is often a silent pact to disregard the other, rather than engaging long enough to acquire a deeper understanding. When American Christians say to Muslims, we respect your faith, but believe deeply that Muslims are practicing a false religion, this level of respect is, at best, likely to seem shallow or, at worst, give way to the kind of disrespect that leads to violence.

Partisan Politics

Outsiders often say that religious beliefs and practices surely do not matter very much. In this view, people are driven by economic self-interest and follow a live-and-let-live philosophy where religion is concerned. There is some truth in this view. Relatively few Americans say that their career decisions and financial dealings have been influenced by religion, and, despite their misgivings about non–Western religions, relatively few acts of violence against Muslims, Hindus, or Buddhists have been committed. Yet, public policy discussions frequently involve religion. Elections are said to be decided by voters representing one religious constituency or another, and religious advocacy groups contest even major governmental decisions, such as whether to go to war and how trade agreements should be drafted.

The division between religious conservatives and liberals has sparked questions about the degree to which religious leaders should seek political advantage and whether policymakers should exploit these religious differences. Most Americans support the separation of church and state; they do not want preachers to endorse political candidates or for laws to be written that either endorse a particular faith or deny people the right to worship according to their own conscience. Nevertheless, a majority of Americans think religion should have a place in public affairs and support cooperation between religious and governmental organizations. In one national survey, 68 percent of Americans agreed that "it is important to me that a president has strong religious beliefs," and 53 percent *disagreed* that "organized religious groups of all kinds should stay out of politics." In another national survey, 77 percent said they favored religious congregations "making statements to public officials on topics of community concern," and 71 percent favored congregations "sponsoring meetings to which public officials are invited." In the same survey, 87 percent favored religious congregations "working with government agencies to provide better services for low-income families." The public is more divided, though, about *how* religion should be involved in public affairs. When asked if they would like to see religious leaders running for political office, 58 percent of evangelical Protestants said yes, and only 39 percent of mainline Protestants did. Forty-two percent of evangelical Protestants said they would like to see religious leaders form political movements; 28 percent of mainline Protestants did.

The differences in this study between the views of mainline and evangelical Protestants are reflected in how the two groups engage with policymakers. Mainline Protestants (and mainstream Catholics) generally work quietly and behind the scenes by cultivating personal ties in Washington. They staff small advocacy offices in the nation's capital, testify at hearings, and speak to representatives about legislation. In addition, they pass resolutions at the meetings of church governing boards that encourage members to reflect on issues of the day and to submit letters and petitions expressing their views on issues ranging from international debt relief to global warming to corporate responsibility. Although mainline members generally support environmental, egalitarian, and humanitarian efforts, they are seldom well informed about what exactly their denominations' leaders are doing and sometimes express opposition when they find out. In contrast, evangelical Protestants have been more aggressive about appearing on television and radio talk shows and issuing statements to the media. Evangelicals have also organized special-purpose groups, such as the Moral Majority and the Christian Coalition, and have worked with conservative political organizations, such as Focus on the Family and the Family Research Council.

The larger issue is whether political operatives should—and are—exploiting the left-right division in American religion for partisan purposes. Some political analysts suggest that Republican leaders have courted the religious right by proposing policies about limiting gay rights or abortion that were then given low priority after the election. Observers also suggest that Democrats, though less effectively, have searched for ways to overcome what has appeared to many as a secularizing trend within their party and to reconnect faith with politics in the hope of mobilizing religious voters. Instances of Democratic public officials appearing at religious meetings and including religious language in speeches are not hard to find.

The highly personalized character of American religion probably deters religious groups from becoming sufficiently mobilized to be a decisive factor in American politics. But while most Americans believe religious truth to be a matter of personal opinion, the few who claim access to absolute truth gain more power than might be expected. Their refusal to compromise their principles gives them the authority to act to uphold them. For instance, leaders of advocacy groups may send out mass mailings proclaiming that immigration is threatening the Christian fabric of our society or that the United Nations is doing so. They may raise money for themselves and their ministries by threatening believers that the truth will be trampled unless they send in checks. They inspire that segment of the public that worries about moral laxity and views relativism as a slippery slope. The potential power of such leaders is disproportionate to their numbers, even though this influence may not carry the day. Their voice may also have the unanticipated consequence of mobilizing others, such as secularists or religionists with different views, to engage more actively in the electoral process.

Apart from partisan politics, religion contributes positively to the functioning of American democracy by encouraging civic involvement. Participants in congregations are more likely than other Americans to support charities financially and to serve as volunteers in their communities. Indeed, the likelihood of volunteering to help the needy is about twice as high among frequent attendees of religious services as among infrequent attendees and increases further among members of committees and participants in small groups and in congregations with more volunteer programs. Through volunteering, members forge ties with clergy, social workers, community leaders, people in other congregations, and secular nonprofit organizations. Houses of worship serve a civic function as popular venues for community meetings, especially in lower-income neighborhoods. Sermons frequently encourage members to assist the poor and pray for public officials. In one study, approximately a third of U.S. adults claimed to be involved in small fellowship groups, and of these, 56 percent said they had become more interested in peace and social justice, 45 percent had become more interested in social and political issues, 40 percent had changed their attitudes toward social and political issues, and 12 percent had participated in a political rally as a result of being in their group.[13] Active attendees in congregations are not only more likely to care for their neighbors but also to vote, assist with community projects, and work for political candidates.

In view of more general concerns about declining social ties, low voter turnout, and diminishing civic participation, religious congregations are one of the few voluntary associations that have remained relatively stable in recent decades. Congregations are by no means the only venue through which people participate in their communities. The number of secular nonprofit associations with which congregations cooperate has grown, and many of them have adapted to Americans' increasingly complex schedules. Large congregations increasingly use short-term volunteering, email networks, and greater reliance on professional staff to draw newcomers, while small houses of worship continue to be attractive in more stable communities. Congregations in the United States play a role similar to that of labor unions, fraternal orders, and extended family ties in other liberal democracies. These "mediating structures" provide citizens opportunities for meeting one another, forming and articulating their views, and serving their communities.

Faith-Based Initiatives

Religion's role in American public policy was evident in the welfare reform legislation of the mid-1990s. Religious organizations such as Catholic Charities, Lutheran Social Services, and the Salvation Army had received money from the federal government ever since World War II. Lawmakers, long aware of the role of religious organizations in providing voluntary assistance to their communities, increasingly emphasized private nonprofit efforts as a way of curbing rising government spending. Charitable Choice, a provision included in the Personal Responsibility and Work Opportunity Reconciliation Act of 1996 (PRWOR), provided detailed rules about the conditions under which faith-based organizations could receive federal funding. States were given the option of excluding all nongovernmental entities from the use of funds they received through federal block grants for assisting the needy. But if states dispensed any of these funds through nonprofit organizations, then faith-based nonprofits could not be excluded categorically. Providers could apply religious tests (such as being a member of a particular denomination or vowing to abstain from alcohol) in hiring personnel, but could not discriminate on other grounds, such as race, gender, disability, or national origin. They could maintain the "religious environment" of their organization, rather than having to remove religious icons, art, or publications. They need not alter their administrative structure in order to comply with government standards provided this structure was derived from theological and ecclesiological considerations, and they could isolate the portion of funds received from government for reporting purposes rather than having to disclose all sources and distributions. Clients were given the right to choose among religious and nonreligious providers and could not be refused services on religious grounds. Congress left implementation to the states; some implemented it more aggressively than others. Having been passed by a Republican majority in the Senate and approved by a Democratic president, the measure stirred relatively little controversy.

That changed in January 2001 when George W. Bush, as one of his first acts as president, announced a major new program called the White House Office of Faith-Based and Community Initiatives. The Bush plan included giving the service activities of religious organizations a higher national profile, establishing offices in the major executive agencies to promote faith-based grants, and setting new goals for allocating federal funds to religious organizations. Prominent evangelical Protestant leaders, who claimed to have been instrumental in Bush's narrow electoral victory, praised the effort, while moderate and liberal religious groups saw it as patronage for the religious right and worried that the new program was linked to an overall reduction in government spending on social services. The terrorist attacks on New York and Washington that September put the administration's faith-based initiatives on the back burner, but the debate over it continued.

The service activities of faith-based organizations are more complex than this controversy indicated. A majority of local congregations help support community service activities, such as soup kitchens, homeless shelters, and tutoring programs, but they typically spend no more than 5 percent of their budget on such activities. Coalitions among congregations and nonreligious agencies are often required to maintain these programs. Congregations understand themselves as mutual aid societies or "caring communities" that serve the needs of members through informal networks more often than they serve the needs of the wider community through formal programs. As such, congregations forge long-term relationships of trust and personal friendship among members, which serve well when spiritual and emotional needs arise but seldom address serious financial or health needs. Not surprisingly, relatively few congregations receive government grants. Specialized faith-based agencies such as Catholic Charities, and numerous local organizations, such as food banks and homeless shelters, are organized as tax-exempt nonprofits and employ trained staff with professional knowledge about social services. These organizations more often receive funding from federal, state, or local governments in addition to private donations. Faith-based organizations often differ little in practice and effectiveness from nonsectarian agencies, but they do serve more serious needs and clients regard them as more effective and trustworthy than public welfare departments.

Relatively little litigation emerged over the faith-based initiatives. For the most part, Charitable Choice has simply leveled the playing field so that faith-based agencies can compete for government funding alongside nonsectarian organizations, but some of the exceptions happen to be among the most effective faith-based organizations. Prison Fellowship, which provides prison and postprison spiritual counseling, and Teen Challenge, which rehabilitates victims of substance abuse, are two prominent examples. Turning clients into faithful Christians is the heart of their programs and thus raises questions about whether they should receive public funds, no matter how effective they may be in their secular missions.

On the whole, faith-based initiatives have heightened religion's visibility in the media and in policy circles, even though a relatively small fraction (13 percent) of federal grants to service agencies has been channeled through religious organizations. A controversial aspect of faith-based initiatives involves proposals to provide welfare clients with vouchers that they could use at religious organizations that proselytize or promote born-again experiences. Proponents argue that vouchers would expand clients' freedom, while opponents view the idea as impractical, divisive, and a possible first step toward instituting voucher programs in public and private schools. Another controversial aspect of faith-based initiatives is their role in partisan politics, especially in Republicans' efforts to court black voters. In the 2000 election, black voters and white evangelical voters were the most prominent supporters of government funding for faith-based service organizations, and in 2004, the percentage of black voters for Bush increased significantly, and clergy of some of the nation's largest black churches avidly supported faith-based initiatives.

Global Involvement

Religion has also become an important consideration in U.S. foreign policy. American leaders often distinguish their nation from other liberal democracies, such as England, France, and Germany, by claiming that it was never an imperial power. Nevertheless, the long history of U.S. involvement in other countries has often included a role for American religion. The first U.S. foreign missionaries were sent out in 1813 by the American Board of Commissioners for Foreign Missions (ABCFM), an organization founded by New England Congregationalists. By 1835, the ABCFM had distributed 90 million pages of religious tracts, opened 63 overseas mission stations with 311 staff members, initiated 474 schools for upwards of 80,000 pupils, and was actively supported by more than 1,600 missionary auxiliaries in local congregations. During the remainder of the nineteenth century, nearly every other denomination organized overseas missionary programs. By 1900, more than 100 of these organizations were sponsoring more than 4,000 foreign missionaries.

Further expansion of missionary efforts followed, especially through the work of new, independent evangelical mission agencies recruiting missionaries from a broader cross section of the U.S. population through Bible institutes, greatly reducing the amount of training they received, and enlisting the missionaries themselves as fund-raisers for their own support. They opened new mission stations, churches, schools, and hospitals, especially in Africa, China, and Southeast Asia. Despite setbacks during the two world wars, the U.S. foreign missionary staff grew to more than twenty-four thousand by 1957. East Asia scholar John K. Fairbank, who knew the extensive work of U.S. missionary organizations firsthand, called them the "first large-scale transnational corporations."[14]

Many scholars have assumed that U.S. religious efforts abroad diminished after this high point in the late 1950s. Independence movements in many parts of the world made local conditions unsafe for foreign missionaries or led to their expulsion. Postcolonial perspectives questioned whether missionaries adequately respected cultural differences. It became fashionable to argue that any religious developments in other countries were happening entirely through the work of indigenous pastors. In reality, U.S. religious organizations are more actively involved in other countries than ever before. In 2001, nearly 43,000 U.S. citizens were working full-time as missionaries in other countries, almost double the number in 1957, and another 65,000 non-U.S. citizens and foreign nationals working in other countries were sponsored by U.S. religious organizations. Another 350,000 were spending up to a year abroad as short-term mission volunteers. Of U.S. church members in 2005, 74 percent were in congregations that supported at least one missionary working in another country in the past year.[15]

Missionaries are only one way U.S. religious organizations are involved abroad. Religious organizations are among the nation's largest international humanitarian relief and development agencies. In the aftermath of the 2004 tsunami in Southeast Asia, 36 percent of Americans donated money to their churches for relief. The Southern Baptist Convention collected $16 million; Catholic Relief Services collected $114 million. World Vision, an evangelical organization that began in 1947, provided $513 million in overseas aid in 2003, an increase of 326 percent since 1981. Catholic Relief Services' overseas aid budget was $479 million. Samaritan's Purse and Mercy Corps each spent more than $100 million abroad and Habitat for Humanity and the Adventist Development and Relief Agency each supplied more than $50 million in foreign aid. In the 2005 survey of church members, 76 percent said their congregation receives offerings for overseas hunger and relief.[16]

The global involvement of American religion has been controversial. In the 1980s, Moral Majority leader Jerry Falwell condemned the imposition of sanctions on South Africa as a means of ending apartheid, applauded South African President Botha, and encouraged his viewers to invest in Krugerrands. In the 1990s, Pat Robertson praised Zaire's President Mobutu on Zairian television as being a fine Christian, despite Mobutu's soldiers having recently killed a large number of pro-democracy citizens. At the time, Robertson was engaged in diamond mining operations in the country as part of a contract with Mobutu. Robertson signed another mining agreement with Liberia's President Taylor, who was also accused of widespread slaughter, and defended him as a fellow Christian. In 2004, George W. Bush defended the U.S. invasion of Iraq by asserting that "America is called to lead the cause of freedom in a new century," adding, "Freedom is not America's gift to the world, it is the Almighty God's gift to every man and woman in this world." A critic wrote that Bush had "happily ceded huge swaths of his domestic and international policy" to Christian fundamentalists, even using "his global AIDS initiative, his foreign aid policy, and his war on terror to please religious radicals."[17]

The diversity of American religion is as evident in its international activities, though, as in the beliefs and practices of its varied faith traditions. Even as critics were associating evangelicalism with U.S. militarism, a national poll found that rank-and-file evangelicals were quite divided about unilateral military action. Thirty-five percent thought the United States "should take the lead in maintaining world peace, using military force if necessary," while 65 percent said the United States should "primarily cooperate with international organizations to maintain world peace."[18] During the Clinton and

Bush administrations, when the North American Free Trade Agreement (NAFTA) was being promoted in the nation's capital, only a few evangelical leaders spoke in favor of it, while others, especially Catholic and Presbyterian advocacy networks, roundly criticized it. Jewish and Christian leaders alike were divided about U.S. policies toward Israel and Palestine.

Although evangelical leaders claimed to have special influence in Washington, they seldom won battles without building coalitions, and, even then, often lost. For instance, the International Religious Freedom Act (IRFA), passed in 1998 during the Clinton administration, resulted from a broad alliance of evangelicals, Jews, feminists, and secular human rights organizations. Efforts to give the IRFA a more central role in State Department negotiations, though, have met with limited success. Similarly, in domestic policy, evangelical leaders often express frustration about weak support for efforts to curb stem-cell research or ban gay marriage.

Conclusion

Emphasis on religion is hardly unique to the United States, but it is important in the lives of a large majority of American citizens and continues to affect public policy in ways that earlier generations of social scientists did not predict. Pundits and politicians show an almost inexhaustible interest in what preachers may be saying about public issues. They wonder whether one political party or another is better at mobilizing its religious base, and whether the personal conduct of public officials violates religious teachings. Although the media frequently sensationalize these stories, there is little question that religion is an important and visible part of American culture and that far more of the public gravitates to houses of worship than to any other voluntary association.

Yet academics and journalists rarely take religion's social importance seriously. In public universities, religious studies departments remain sparse because campus leaders interpret separation of church and state to mean that even learning *about* religion is taboo. At the better private universities, a long-term process of secularization has occurred, leaving institutions that were founded by leaders of various religious traditions hardly recognizable as places where religion can still be discussed. In the sciences, professors' personal beliefs about religion might pose barriers to understanding why so many people in the real world continue to make faith commitments. In sociology, the discipline that claims to be interested in understanding ordinary people, only a handful of the four hundred faculty at top-ranked departments specialize in the study of religion. In international studies, where 9/11 has served as a wake-up call to the importance of religion in world events, religion remains sorely neglected. The typical college student is likely to learn more about religion in the dorm room than in the classroom—which would be considered scandalous if the topic were science, history, or literature. Journalists seldom find it newsworthy to provide background information about the deeper contours of American religion. Local clergy who already work long hours handling the usual routine of worship services, committee meetings, weddings, funerals, and hospital visits cannot hope to educate the wider public about religion. The Framers of American government believed religion should not be an overbearing factor in the nation's life, but they did recognize that it would be a continuing influence. They also believed that democracy is stronger when people reflect on and communicate about their values, rather than letting opinion leaders do the talking for them.

Part Two
American Public Policies

CHAPTER 11
The Family
Linda J. Waite and Melissa J. K. Howe

America, almost alone among developed nations, has a birthrate that, due to large families among immigrants, is high enough to reproduce its own society, but it also has a very large number of children being raised by single parents. Linda Waite and Melissa Howe, two demographers and family specialists, describe the implications of a growing population (stimulated by immigration) coupled with a decline in marriage (fostered by intense individualism).

THE POPULATION OF THE UNITED STATES PASSED TWO MILESTONES recently: it reached 300 million, and married couple families fell to fewer than half of all households. In terms of population growth, the United States is unique among advanced industrial societies; all of Europe, as well as China, Japan, and Russia, have fertility rates below the level necessary for replacement. And people in some societies, like Spain, Italy, and Greece, are having so few children that the size of the population will fall by half within the next fifty years if nothing changes. Russia in particular seems to be in a negative population spiral that is driven by a demographic "perfect storm" of high mortality and low fertility, and experts express concern that a dramatic decline and even the disappearance of the Russian population are inevitable.

To explain why America is producing enough children to replace itself while the rest of the industrialized world is failing to do so, we need to look carefully at the American family and at the forces that affect people's choices to have children, when to have them, and how many to have.

Defining the Family

The family is "a social network, not necessarily localized, that is based on culturally recognized biological and marital relationships."[1] In most times and places, families were responsible for the production, distribution, and consumption of commodities; for reproduction and socialization of the next generation; and for co-residence and transmission of property. For the most part, this is still true. However, the rise of alternative family structures, including single parents, gay and lesbian partnerships, and cohabiting couples, sometimes including children, raises the question of whether a "family" must have a culturally recognized biological or marital relationship. In most cultures, a cohabiting couple living with their own child would constitute a family. But what of a woman, her child, and her cohabiting boyfriend? Does the "family" consist of the woman and the child, or does it include the boyfriend who has no marital, legal, or biological relationship to either one?

In the United States and many industrialized societies, the structure of the family looks quite different than it did a half century ago. Fewer people live in *families* as traditionally defined. Fewer people are married, and alternative family forms, such as single parenthood, cohabitation, and same-sex unions are on the rise. Changes in family structures affect family members, especially dependent children and elderly relatives. The departure from traditional marital unions seems also to coincide with the decline in fertility rates. And lower fertility rates, in turn, alter family structures, reducing family size and the number of relatives—from siblings to cousins to aunts and uncles and grandchildren—that people have.

MARRIAGE

Permanence, joint production, co-residence, and the social recognition of a sexual and child-rearing union are, perhaps, the most important characteristics of the institution of marriage. When two adults make a legally binding promise to live and work together for their joint well-being, and to do so, ideally, for the rest of their lives, they tend to *specialize,* dividing between them the labor required to maintain the family. This specialization allows married men and women to produce more than they would if they did not specialize. The co-residence and resource sharing of married couples create substantial economies of scale; at any standard of living, it costs much less for people to live together than it would if they lived separately. The economies of scale and the specialization of spouses both tend to increase the economic well-being of family members living together.

To put it another way, the sharing of economic and social resources through the institution of marriage acts as a sort of risk-spreader. Spouses act as a small insurance pool against life's uncertainties, reducing their need to protect themselves against unexpected events. Marriage also connects spouses and family members to a larger network of help, support, and obligation through their extended families, friends, and others. The insurance function of marriage increases the economic well-being of family members, and the support function of marriage improves their emotional well-being.

The institution of marriage also builds on and fosters *trust.* Since spouses share social and economic resources and expect to do so over the long term, both gain when the family unit gains. This reduces the need for family members to devote scarce resources to making sure that others in the family are acting in the family's best interests, thus increasing efficiency.

Marriage changes the behavior of spouses and thereby their well-being. The specialization, economies of scale, and insurance functions of marriage all increase the economic well-being of family members, and the increase is typically quite substantial. Generally, married people produce more of the goods and services consumed in the home and accumulate more assets than unmarried people.[2] Married people also tend to have better physical and emotional health than single people, at least in part because they are married.[3] The social support provided by a spouse, combined with the economic resources produced by the marriage, facilitate both the production and maintenance of health.

In most societies, marriage circumscribes a large majority of sexual relationships. Data from the United States show that almost all married men and women are sexually active and almost all have only one sex partner—their spouse. Unmarried men and women have much lower levels of sexual activity than the married, in part because a substantial minority have no sex partner at all (just under a quarter of the unmarried men and a third of the unmarried women who were not cohabiting had no sex partner in the previous year). Men and women who are cohabiting are at least as sexually active as those who are married, but are less likely to be sexually exclusive.

Married people have higher fertility rates than unmarried. Indeed, a key function of marriage is the bearing and raising of children. In addition, children of married couples are better off, on average, on many dimensions than other children. A plausible explanation is that the institution of marriage directs the resources of the spouses and their extended families toward the couple's children, increasing child well-being.

Finally, marriage differs from other, less formal relationships primarily in its legal status. As mentioned above, marriage is a legally binding contract. Spouses acquire rights and responsibilities with marriage, enforceable through both the legal systems and through social expectations and social pressure. As such, the treatment of marriage in the law shapes the institution and the extent to which it ensures family stability.

DIVORCE AND UNION DISSOLUTION

Recent changes in family law appear to have made marriage less stable. Historically, in the United States and many other countries, both secular and religious law generally viewed marriage vows as binding and permanent. The marriage contract could only be broken if one spouse violated the most basic obligations to the other and could be judged "at fault" in the breakdown of the marriage.

Beginning in the mid-1960s, however, U.S. states substantially liberalized and simplified their divorce laws. One of the key features of these changes was a shift from divorce based on fault or mutual consent to unilateral divorce, which required the willingness of only one spouse to end the marriage. Most states also adopted some form of "no-fault" divorce, which eliminated the need for one spouse to demonstrate a violation of the marriage contract by the other. The shift to unilateral or no-fault divorce laws was accompanied by a surge in divorce rates in the United States. At least some of the increase in divorce rates appears to have resulted directly from the shift in the legal environment in which couples marry and decide to remain married, or in which they divorce.[4] Because easy divorce laws lead to more divorces, some states have enacted a plan under which a couple about to be married undergoes counseling and agrees not to divorce unless it meets tougher standards than those imposed by no-fault divorce rules. These are called "covenant marriages" and are entirely voluntary.

The divorce rate, which reflects the number of divorces in a year relative to the number of married people, rose continuously for more than a century in the United States and many similar industrialized countries, then leveled off at a fairly high rate in about 1980. In the United States, the best estimates suggest that around one-half of all marriages will end in separation or divorce rather than in the death of one of the partners. Recent data for the United States show that after five years, 20 percent of all first marriages ended through separation or divorce. By ten years after the wedding, 32 percent of white women's first marriages, 34 percent of Hispanic women's first marriages, and 47 percent of black women's first marriages had dissolved. Asian women show the lowest levels of marital disruption; after ten years, only 20 percent had divorced or separated.[5]

Marriages that end in divorce or separation due to marital discord differ from those that remain intact. The marriages most likely to end include those with no children, those with children from a previous union, or those with older children;[6] marriages begun at a young age; and marriages between partners with relatively low levels of education.[7] Black women are more likely to experience the disruption of their first marriage and any subsequent remarriage than are white or Hispanic women. Women whose religion is not important to them are more likely to divorce than women for whom religion is somewhat or very important.[8] Couples who share the same religion at marriage show a substantially lower likelihood of disruption than couples with different religious faiths. The destabilizing effects of religious intermarriage decrease with the increasing similarity of the beliefs and practices of the two religions and when mutual tolerance is embodied in their doctrines.

The Increase in Age at Marriage

Both men and women in the United States and many European countries are now marrying later than at any other time in at least the last fifty years. In the United States between 1970 and 2000, the median age of first marriage for American women increased by almost five years, from 20.8 to 25.1, and for men the median age increased by almost four years, from 23.2 to 26.8. In this same time period, the proportion of women who had never been married increased from 36 percent to 73 percent among those 20 to 24 years old and from 6 percent to 22 percent among those 30 to 34 years old. Similar increases occurred for men.

For African-Americans, the delay in first marriage has been especially striking. The median age at first marriage increased to 28.6 for African-American men and 27.3 for African-American women. This represents a six-year delay for African-American men and a seven-year delay for African-American women since the 1960s. And, in 2000, among those 30 to 34 years old, 44 percent of

African-American women and 46 percent of African-American
men had never married.

Similar changes in marriage patterns have taken place in most
European countries; recent cohorts are marrying at older ages and
over a wider range of ages than in the past. Notably, European
countries differ substantially in marriage ages. The Nordic countries
of Sweden, Denmark, and Iceland show the highest average ages at
marriage for women (around age 29), and the Eastern European
countries of Bulgaria, the Czech Republic, Hungary, and Poland the
lowest (around age 22).[9]

THE DECLINE OF MARRIAGE

Age at marriage has risen substantially, divorce rates are high and
stable, and rates of remarriage have fallen, so that a larger proportion
of adults are unmarried now than in the past. In 1970, unmarried
people in the United States made up 28 percent of the adult population. In 2000, 46 percent of all adults were unmarried. In fact, the
shift away from marriage has been so dramatic for blacks that in
2000, only 39 percent of black men and 31 percent of black women
were married, compared to 59 percent of white men and 56 percent
of white women.[10] The decline of marriage has been largest among
women with little education and almost non-existent among college graduates, creating a divide in the family building experience
along lines of class as well as race.

Though marriage rates have declined in the United States and
other developed countries, the vast majority of adults do marry at
some time in their lives. According to data from the United Nations,
in the United States, more than 95 percent of men and women
marry by age fifty. And 75 percent of women who divorce remarry
within ten years. Relatively high proportions of men and women
have not married by their late forties in the Nordic countries where
cohabitation is common and also in Caribbean countries such as
Jamaica and Barbados, countries characterized by a long history of

visiting relationships, in which couples are sexually active but live separately. In Sweden, for example, 24 percent of men and 16 percent of women in their late forties had never married, whereas in Jamaica, 48 percent of men and 46 percent of women had never married by these ages. Delayed and foregone marriage appear to contribute to declining fertility trends, even as children (and childbearing) feature prominently in alternative family forms.

Alternative Family Forms

The married, two-parent family has historically been the most common family form in the United States and other industrialized countries for some centuries. However, as just discussed, the proportion of women who are married has declined substantially over the last half century in developed countries. At the same time, the proportion of U.S. families consisting of a married couple with children fell from 87 percent in 1970 to 49.7 percent in 2005. Even at the height of the married-couple family era, many people lived in other types of families, most often due to the death of one member of the couple before all the children were grown. When death ended many marriages relatively early in life, remarriage and stepfamilies were common, as were single-parent families caused by widowhood.

High rates of divorce combined with relatively low rates of remarriage, especially for women with children, have led to sizeable proportions of families headed by a divorced single mother. In addition, the rise of cohabitation and non-marital childbearing, discussed in more detail below, has meant that unmarried-couple families and never-married mother families are now common alternative family forms. "Non-family" households are also on the rise; these consist of a person living alone or with non-relatives only, such as roommates or an unmarried partner. In addition to delayed marriage, non-marriage, continued high rates of marital disruption, and lower rates of remarriage, the rise in non-family living can also be traced to earlier nest-leaving by young adults and to increases in independent living at older ages. In 2005, 32 percent of all households did not contain a family compared to 19 percent in 1970. And people living alone formed 27 percent of households in 2005, up from 17 percent in 1970.[11]

GAY AND LESBIAN FAMILIES

One alternative family form consists of two adults of the same sex, sometimes raising children. Historically and traditionally, a *family* consisted of people related by blood or marriage in a culturally recognized social network of biological and marital relationships. *Marriage* continues to be largely defined as a legal relationship between an adult man and an adult woman to form a new family. Gay and lesbian families, sometimes based on a socially recognized and sometimes on a legally recognized relationship, challenge these definitions. Attitudes toward sex between two adults of the same sex have become substantially more accepting in the United States over the past several decades.[12] At the same time, extension of the definition of "family" and "marriage" to same-sex couples has been hotly contested and fiercely debated. In the United States, many attempts to extend access to marriage and family rights to same-sex couples have been turned back by legislators or voters, with some notable exceptions. Several European countries have moved furthest on these issues. For example, France allows same-sex couples to register their partnerships as civil unions; Denmark has extended child custody rights to same-sex couples; and perhaps most definitively, the Netherlands became the first country to grant same-sex couples full and equal rights to marriage in 2000. Since then, Spain, Belgium, and Canada have legalized same-sex marriage as well. In the United States, same-sex marriage has become legal, though contested, in Massachusetts, and domestic partnerships are permitted in California, Connecticut, the District of Columbia, Hawaii, Maine, New Jersey, and Vermont.

About 2.4 percent of men and 1.3 percent of women in the United States identify themselves as homosexual or bisexual and have same-gender partners.[13] Although information on the number and characteristics of gay and lesbian couples has not generally been available, one U.S. estimate suggests that, in 1990, fewer than 1 percent of adult men lived with a male partner and about the same percentage of adult women lived with a female partner.[14] These estimates are based on responses to the "unmarried partner" question in the U.S. Census and are thus thought to be conservative estimates of the numbers of same-sex cohabiters. This is the case because some of those living in gay and lesbian couples do not identify as such in survey and other data. Legal and social recognition of these unions as "marriages" is generally not available in the United States.

COHABITING FAMILIES

Many contemporary heterosexual couples begin their lives together not in a marriage, but when they begin sharing a residence. They form intimate unions by *cohabiting*, with marriage usually following at some later point unless the relationship dissolves. In the United States, unmarried heterosexual cohabitation has become so common that most young adult Americans cohabit at some point in their lives. Rates of women cohabiting before age twenty-five have climbed from 7 percent of those born in the late 1940s to 55 percent among those born in the late 1960s. According to a recent estimate, 46.6 percent of American women between ages fifteen and forty-five will cohabit at some time in their lives.[15]

Yet cohabitations tend to be relatively short-lived in the United States, with most either transformed into marriages or dissolved within a few years. The most recent estimates for the United States suggest that about 55 percent of cohabiting couples marry and 40 percent end their relationship within five years of moving in together. Only about one-sixth of cohabiting couples remain together without marrying for at least three years, and only one in ten last for five years or more without either splitting up or marrying.[16] As a result, the proportion currently cohabiting is only about 10 percent among women ages twenty to twenty-nine, compared to 27 percent to 53 percent currently married at these ages, respectively. At older and younger ages, fewer than one woman in ten is currently cohabiting.

In the United States cohabitation has become an increasingly common step in the courtship process, preceding the majority of marriages and remarriages. The percentage of marriages preceded by cohabitation increased from about 10 percent for those marrying between 1965 and 1974 to more than 50 percent of those marrying between 1990 and 1994. And cohabitation is especially common for those whose first marriage dissolved.

Although a number of European countries have experienced similar increases in cohabitation, some have experienced much more and some much less. Cohabitation is strikingly common in the Nordic countries of Denmark, Sweden, and Finland; France also shows fairly high levels, with about 30 percent of the women ages twenty-five to twenty-nine in cohabiting unions. By contrast, a group of countries including the Netherlands, Belgium, Great Britain, Germany, and Austria shows moderate levels of cohabitation— 8 to 16 percent of women from ages twenty-five to twenty-nine are in this type of union. And in southern European countries and Ireland, cohabitation is rare, with less than 3 percent cohabiting among women in this same age group.[17]

In some countries, cohabitation is a socially recognized form of partnership that is quite stable and seems to function more as a permanent alternative to marriage rather than a substitute for it. Sweden, France, and Canada fall into this category. In other countries, such as Belgium, Austria, and Germany, cohabitation appears to be more like a prelude to marriage or a stage in the courtship process. By contrast, cohabitation appears to be relatively rare in Italy, Poland, and Spain.

Cohabiting couples share a residence and a sex life, but they need share little else. Cohabiting couples are much less likely than married couples to combine financial resources, less likely to be sexually exclusive, less likely to share leisure time and a social life, less likely to have children, and less likely to remain together. The requirements for establishing or ending a cohabiting union are minimal, with no legal or religious or community formalities involved. Thus, some scholars argue that cohabitation and marriage are distinct social institutions. According to some scholars, cohabitation is much less *institutionalized* than marriage, at least in the United States and other countries in which it has become common relatively recently, because it is not covered by clear expectations or norms, and the legal rights and responsibilities of cohabiting partners have not been established.

So while many people choose cohabitation over marriage, a number of conditions will need to be met before cohabitation becomes indistinguishable from marriage. Cohabitation will provide a comprehensive substitute for marriage only when couples tend to select either cohabitation or marriage at the beginning of their relationship and rarely make the transition from cohabitation to marriage; when cohabitations become about as stable as marriages; when cohabiting couples become socially recognized as permanent unions and treated as "married"; and when childbearing takes place in cohabiting relationships at about the same rate as in marriage.

Although not all of the above conditions apply, the gap between marriage and cohabitation is narrowing in some countries, such as in the Nordic countries, where cohabitation has much the same legal and social status as marriage, and among Puerto Ricans in the United States. But even in the Nordic countries, cohabiting relationships are less stable than marriages.

SINGLE ADULTS AND SINGLE PARENTS

Given that many couples in the United States and similar countries begin their intimate lives together by cohabiting rather than by marrying, it seems that the *form* of the union has changed more than its existence. But even when we consider both marriage and cohabitation, young adults are less likely to have formed a union now than in the past. Among young women born in the early 1950s, about one-quarter had not formed a union by age twenty-five, compared to one-third of those born in the late 1960s. More adults are remaining single longer.

In many European countries, women typically are in either cohabiting or marital unions by their mid- to late twenties. However, over 60 percent of Italian women and 50 percent of Spanish women are single—neither cohabiting nor married at these ages, compared to around one in three Portuguese and Greek women. In the Nordic countries and France, about one-third of women ages twenty-five to twenty-nine are single, one-third are cohabiting, and one-third are married. Union dissolution contributes to the numbers of single men and women, as does postponement of union formation, cohabitation, and marriage.

A number of large-scale social changes are implicated in the postponement and decline in marriage and the increase in cohabitation, divorce, and unmarried childbearing. These include the development of effective contraceptives, especially the birth control pill and legalization of abortion, both of which contributed to the sexual revolution. These changes lowered the costs of sex between unmarried partners at the same time that attitudes toward sex between unmarried people liberalized dramatically. The sexual revolution also lowered the costs of delaying marriage, since one could have an active sex life while single, and gave women and couples much more control over the occurrence and timing of births. This latter change dovetailed neatly with women's increasing labor force participation, which was, in turn, both facilitated by and a consequence of rises in women's investment in their own education.

Consequences for Children

As the number of single parents has increased, the number of children living with both parents has declined over the last twenty-five years. In 2003, 32 percent of children lived with one parent, most often their mother, or with neither parent; 68 percent of U.S. children lived with both their parents, down from 85 percent in 1970.[18] Over the last decade or so, one out of three children was born to an unmarried woman, who may be either cohabiting or not living with a partner.[19] Marital disruption contributes to the number of mothers, and to a lesser extent fathers, raising children alone.

Cohabitation and single parenthood have important implications for children's welfare. Single parenthood means that one person, rather than two, bears the burden of providing the child(ren) with day-to-day care and, often, with most of their economic and emotional support. Single-parent families are much more likely to be poor than families headed by married or cohabiting couples, and are less likely to receive financial and other transfers from their extended families. So while the majority of children raised in single-parent families do quite well, the chances that they will complete high school, obtain a college degree, or enter a prestigious occupation are lower than for children raised by two married parents.[20] They are also more likely to divorce later in life than children of married couples. Perhaps more surprising, children raised in stepfamilies do little better than children raised by single parents.[21]

The rise of cohabitation has meant, among other changes, that more children are spending some time in a cohabiting union, either because their parents cohabit or, more commonly, because their mother lives with a man who is not their biological father. The most recent estimates for the United States suggest that about 40 percent of children born to unmarried mothers are born into cohabiting unions, including over half of white and Hispanic births to unmarried mothers and a quarter of black births to unmarried mothers.[22] For children born into cohabiting unions, about a quarter of their childhood years will be spent in a cohabiting union, about one-half in a married-couple family, and about one-quarter with a single mother, according to one estimate.[23] In a separate study, Heuveline and his colleagues find that "children born to cohabiting parents are more likely both to see their parents separate and to see them separate sooner than children born to married parents."[24]

Thus, cohabitational unions can be an especially uncertain context for child rearing. One explanation is that cohabitation appears to appeal to individuals who are relatively approving of divorce as a solution to marital problems[25] and those who are not committed to the institution of marriage.[26] So children living in cohabiting couple families face life chances that are less rosy than those facing children of married couples. For example, among mainland Puerto Ricans, fathers in cohabiting couples with children are less likely to provide financial support to the family and are less involved in child care than fathers in married-parent families.

The mechanisms through which married parents advantage their children are complicated and not completely understood, but include financial well-being, the time and energy of two adults, the involvement of members of the extended families of both parents, and a better relationship with parents. The greater financial resources of two-parent families lead to residence in neighborhoods with better schools and other amenities for children, better medical care, less residential mobility, and lower levels of family stress, which itself facilitates good parenting.

Another factor that can affect children's well-being is the number of siblings they have. If parents with fewer children have more time and resources to spend directly on each child, then those children will be more likely to fare better. Indeed, this consideration motivates some people to have smaller families and helps to explain lower fertility rates (the average number of births per woman over her lifetime).

America's Exceptional Fertility Rate

All developed countries have experienced declining fertility since the post–World Ware II "Baby Boom." Rindfuss and colleagues report a decline in average rates across twenty-two "low fertility" countries from 2.89 in 1960 to 1.71 in 1997.[27] In the United States, the fertility rate in 1965 was 2.6. The exceptionalism of American fertility has emerged over the past few decades, as rates in other developed countries have continued to fall below the 2.1 children per woman level necessary for replacement of the population over the long run, while the U.S. rate increased from its decade-long low of 1.8, during the period between 1975 and 1985, to 2.04 births for the period between 2000 and 2005. This rate has remained rather stable over the past decade. By comparison, during the 2000–2005 period, France had the next-highest fertility rate at 1.9; followed by Australia at 1.8; China at 1.7; Sweden at 1.6; and Russia, Japan, Germany, Italy, Spain, and Greece all at 1.3, well below population replacement. (Population replacement exists where the number of births and deaths are equal, so that the total population neither shrinks nor grows.) In most developed countries, mortality below age fifty has become quite rare, and life expectancy has risen to over seventy years. With low mortality rates like these, fewer births per woman are necessary to sustain total population levels.

Out of all developed countries, the United States comes closest to replacement levels. It stands apart from other advanced industrialized countries, with the highest projected growth rate of −0.1; on the opposite end of the spectrum, critically low growth rates exist in Japan and Germany at −1.5; Russia, Italy, and Spain at −1.6; and Greece at −1.7. Even developing countries are experiencing decreases in fertility and related population decline. Three-quarters of developing countries are at or below replacement levels, although high fertility rates averaging four births or higher occur in regions of northern India, Pakistan, Afghanistan, the Arabian Peninsula, and sub-Saharan Africa.[28]

Explaining Low Fertility Rates in Developed Countries

Experts agree that there is no single explanation for fertility decline that perfectly fits one let alone all low-fertility nations. Low fertility stems from a combination of economic, political, cultural, ideological, technological, and other developments—and the way these interact with each other, human biology, and people's decisions to have children, how many, and when.

From a biological standpoint, "fertility delay can lead to fertility foregone."[29] The ability of women to bear children, and healthy children at that, declines with age so that the timing of a woman's first birth has a large impact on her total number of births over her life course. Thus, women who wait to have children until their thirties are likely to have fewer children over their lifetime than women who begin having children at younger ages. As long as postponement of childbearing becomes increasingly common in developed countries, fertility rates are likely to remain low.

Delayed childbearing has become common in developed countries due, in part, to delayed marriage. As discussed above, age at marriage has risen in developed countries. So for women for whom marriage is a precondition to childbearing, getting married at older ages means having kids at older ages and thus, having fewer kids overall.

A number of widespread social and economic changes that have swept the developed world have made having and raising children both more costly and less attractive. "Social liberalism" has been identified as one change at the root of low fertility.[30] The values that underlie individualism and social liberalism privilege the individual and his or her choices, accomplishments, and resources, assigning both the rewards and risks of outcomes to people themselves. In this ethos, having children becomes one of a number of acceptable "lifestyle choices" that individuals make for which they pay the costs and from which they reap the benefits.

A second profound change that has made having children less attractive is centered in the economy. Rewards for advanced education and high levels of skills have come at the same time as rapid declines in opportunities for those with little education and training. Those who are successful in the new economy are richly rewarded, but those who fall short are held accountable. Women have moved into college and advanced degree programs and then into the labor force at a remarkable rate, so that now most families have two earners. Thus, childbearing decisions have come to depend much more than in the past on the ease with which women—and men—can combine their careers with parenthood.

For women or couples who want children, postponing marriage and/or childbearing buys time for attaining education, establishing a career, and amassing enough capital to afford a family, whereas getting married or pregnant at a young age puts them at risk for losing such opportunities. These "opportunity costs" provide incentives for men as well as women to put off marriage and childbearing. In fact, in many European countries, concern that education underpins very low fertility has recently led to proposals to compress education into fewer years, allowing young adults, especially young women, to finish school and begin childbearing earlier.

In addition to opportunity costs, the direct costs of children are higher in developed nations due to their status as consumers and dependants rather than producers and caretakers (such as in agricultural societies). For middle-class Americans in 2002, the estimated cost of one child was between $9,000 and $10,000 per year.[31] And the premium that industrialized nations put on obtaining secondary and higher education contributes to the prolonged financial dependence of many children and young adults on their parents. So anticipation of direct and indirect costs of raising children supplies a powerful rationale for delaying childbearing.

THE GAP BETWEEN FERTILITY INTENTIONS AND FERTILITY RATES

The factors just discussed also help to explain why fertility intentions have lowered in developed countries. Fertility intentions (the number of children women say they intend to have) have declined over the past few decades in the United States from about 2.6 in the 1970s to about 2.4 over the past decade. According to opinion surveys, most American women aged 18–46 would like to have 2 children.[32] The proportion of women desiring 2 children increased from 37.8 percent during the period between 1970 and 1974 to 50.9 percent during the period between 2000 and 2002. After 2 children, the next most favored family size in the United States is 3 children, then 4 or more, and lastly 0.

In Europe, fertility intentions are similarly low. On average, women between the ages of 20 and 34 report they want at least 2 children, but the average varies from country to country. European countries with intentions most similar to the United States are Finland, France, Ireland, and the United Kingdom at 2.5 and Denmark and Sweden at 2.4. Fertility intentions in Greece (2.3), Belgium (2.2), Italy (2.1), and the Netherlands (2.1) are all lower than in the United States. Yet these countries report intentions of 2.1 or above, indicating that if actual fertility were to match the desired number of children, fertility rates would reach or exceed population replacement in these countries. In contrast, countries like Luxembourg, Portugal, and Spain report below replacement intentions at 2.0, while Austria and Germany stand out with particularly low ideal family sizes of 1.7 and 1.6, respectively. Even if the fertility intentions matched actual rates in these 5 countries, their fertility would remain below replacement.

The fact of the matter is that ideal fertility rates tend to be higher than actual fertility rates in developed countries. While most women in developed countries intend to provide their children with at least one sibling, the number of single children and childless adults is on the rise.

So why is there a gap between fertility intentions and actual fertility? When we think about how many children women say they would like to have and how many they actually have and when, it is important to consider factors that encourage fertility as well as factors that discourage it. For example, fertility intentions can and do change

for individuals over the life course. On the one hand, couples may decide to have more children than originally planned in order to
achieve the sex composition they would like. Parents of boys only or
girls only are more likely to have additional children than those
whose families already include both boys and girls.[33] On the other
hand, personal or national crisis—or simply the realization of how
much time, money, and energy children require—can cause parents to
have fewer children than initially intended. And finally, a powerful explanation for the decoupling of ideal and actual fertility comes down
to the point we began with: "fertility delay leads to fertility forgone."
Women and men who desire large families of four or more children
will have trouble reaching their target if they postpone childbearing
for whatever reason.

Men and women who desire to postpone or forego having children benefit from the improved availability, social acceptance, and
effectiveness of birth control methods. The birth control pill, in particular, significantly reduces the number of unplanned pregnancies
in developed countries. Abortion also reduces fertility rates by enabling women or couples to terminate unwanted pregnancies. On
the other hand, advances in fertility treatments, such as hormone
therapy, artificial insemination, and *in vitro* fertilization help women
and couples overcome infertility. Debates about birth control methods, particularly on the topic of abortion and the relatively recent
introduction of the "morning after pill," highlight the mediating
roles that cultural, political, and religious institutions play in how
deeply reproductive medical advances might impact fertility rates in
each country.

The Unique American Family

What then makes the American family unique? Why is the United
States producing just about enough children to replace itself, while
most other developed countries are falling behind?

ETHNIC AND IMMIGRANT GROUPS IN THE UNITED STATES

The relatively high fertility of the American family owes much to the contributions of Hispanics, who, as a group, stand out for the number of children they bear. While the total fertility rate for the American population in 2004 was 2.05, it fell below that level for American Indians (1.73), non-Hispanic whites (1.85), and Asian/Pacific Islanders (1.90) and was approximately equal for non-Hispanic blacks (2.02). The fertility rate for Hispanics (2.82) exceeded the national average, with Mexican Hispanics contributing the highest fertility rate (3.02), followed by "Other Hispanics" (2.65), Puerto Ricans (2.06), and Cubans (1.73).[34]

Immigration inflates U.S. fertility by increasing the number of people of childbearing age in the United States who come from countries such as Mexico, where fertility rates are higher. Immigration to the United States increased 57 percent between 1990 and 2000, from 19.8 million to 31.1 million. By far, Mexico was the leading country of origin. In 2000, 9.2 million, or 30 percent of the foreign-born population, reported Mexico as the country of birth. The next two largest sources of America's foreign-born population were China with 1.5 million (4.9 percent) and the Philippines with 1.4 million (4.4 percent).[35]

RELIGIOUS DIVERSITY IN THE UNITED STATES

Fertility rates appear to vary by religious affiliation in the United States. According to Mosher and his colleagues, there are no statistically significant religious differences between blacks' and Hispanics' fertility rates or expectations.[36] However, they do find notable differences between non-Hispanic whites by religion.

One popular misconception is that Catholics have higher fertility than Protestants. However, fertility rates for Protestant Americans (1.91) are higher than for Catholic (1.64), Jewish (1.54), and non-religious Americans (1.12).[37] And the fertility rate for Mormons (3.03) is the highest of all. One thing these non-Hispanic

white religious groups have in common is that their fertility expectations are higher than their actual rates, on average. This falls in line
with the gap between intended and achieved fertility observed in a
number of developed countries, as discussed above.

However, the gap between non-Hispanic white Americans' expected and actual fertility does vary by religion. While Mormons'
expected fertility is quite similar to achieved fertility (the difference
is 0.10), there are notable differences between Protestants (0.31),
Jews (0.48), non-religious Americans (0.69), and Catholics (0.76).

A somewhat counterintuitive finding is that Catholics expect to
have slightly more children (2.40) than Protestants (2.22), yet
Catholics actually have fewer children (1.64) than Protestants (1.91).
The relatively large difference between Catholics' expected and
achieved fertility has been attributed to the tendency for Catholics
to marry at later ages than Protestants and therefore have less time to
achieve their higher ideal family size.[38]

COMPATIBILITY OF WORK AND CHILD CARE

One factor encouraging fertility in the United States may be improved compatibility of employment with child rearing for women.
Institutional responses to changing work and marriage roles explain
some part of the differentials in fertility rates between countries.
Pro-natalist government and employer policies entail benefits to
parents that are not also offered to childless adults. In the United
States these include tax breaks, flex-time, part-time work, parental
leave, child care subsidies, and school vouchers. In 1993, the Family
and Medical Leave Act was enacted, requiring employers of fifty or
more workers to allow up to twelve weeks of unpaid leave to those
having or adopting a child, with a guarantee that their job would be
waiting for them when they returned.

In addition, child care for preschool children is both widely
available and socially acceptable, through a variety of organized for-
profit, not-for-profit, family, and informal arrangements. This has
made work and family more compatible, especially for women.

Women are much more likely to find it acceptable for young children to be cared for in a day care center or by another person while the mother works than was the case three decades ago. In 1970, 73 percent of married women of childbearing age in the United States agreed with the statement that preschool children suffer when their mother works. This proportion declined to 34 percent in 1990.[39]

WEAKENED LINK BETWEEN MARRIAGE AND FERTILITY

In part, the high fertility rate in the United States reflects the weakened link between marriage and fertility here. Evidence of the weakened link may be found in the number and proportion of births to unmarried women, which has increased quite substantially in some countries. For example, 46.7 percent of children are born to women out of wedlock in Sweden, 31.0 percent in New Zealand, 30.7 percent in Austria, and 24.1 percent in Canada.[40] The United States falls into this category with 26.9 percent of children born to unmarried women.

FERTILITY AMONG COHABITING COUPLES

In the United States, never-married cohabiting women show high levels of contraceptive usage and are much less likely than married women to expect a birth in the near future, whereas previously married cohabiters resemble married women in their contraceptive behavior and birth expectations. But cohabiting women are much more likely to have a birth than women who are unmarried and not living with a partner. In fact, several recent estimates suggest that about 40 percent of births to unmarried women took place to cohabiting couple families.[41]

SINGLE MOTHERHOOD

The remaining births to unmarried women in the United States take place among women who are neither married nor living with a partner. Single women are at risk of unmarried childbearing, so the most effective route to low rates of out-of-wedlock births is a high proportion of married couples. But some countries, such as Italy, Spain, and Greece, which have seen substantial declines in marriage among young adults, have also seen very low levels of childbearing outside marriage, whereas in others like the United States, Iceland, and Britain, a sizeable minority of all children are born to women who are not married.

In the United States, the proportion of family groups with children headed by a single mother rose from 12 percent in 1970 to 26 percent in 2005, and the proportion headed by single fathers increased from 1 percent to 5 percent during the same period. In a recent study of seventeen Western countries, the United States showed the highest percent of children born to an unmarried woman living without a partner: 16.2 percent.[42] At the other end of the spectrum, Belgium reported a rate of 1.5 percent.

A proportion of single mothers in the United States are women who choose to have children outside of a relationship. Hertz finds that these women tend to be older and already established in their careers.[43] Some desire to marry eventually, but for one reason or another (often because of age), women who choose to become single mothers attempt to compensate for the father's absence through coordinating "social parenting," which involves relatives and friends who provide additional role models. Some make extra effort to include male role models for their child(ren) to make up for the lack of a co-residential father.

Unintended Pregnancies

In the United States overall, 10 percent of births in 1990 resulted from unintended pregnancies.[44] Contraceptive failure and unprotected sex cause accidental pregnancies among single women as well as among women in marital and cohabiting relationships. The prevalence of accidental pregnancies to adolescents in the United States has drawn the most attention.

In 1991 the number of births to American teenage mothers peaked. That year, the rate for the youngest teenagers, those ages ten to fourteen, was 1.4 per 1,000; the rate for teenagers between fifteen and seventeen was 38.6; and the rate for those eighteen to nineteen was 94.0. Since then, birthrates to teenagers have gradually declined. In 2004, females ten to fourteen years old were responsible for 50 percent fewer births than in 1991, with a rate of 0.7; births to teenagers aged fifteen to seventeen declined 43 percent to 22.1; and the birthrate for mothers between ages eighteen and nineteen fell 26 percent to 70.0.

This substantial decline has affected all races, with the greatest decline across all three age categories occurring among non-Hispanic blacks. For females ages fifteen to nineteen, the national average is 42 per 1,000. Asian or Pacific Islanders have the lowest rate (17), followed by non-Hispanic whites (27), American Indians and Alaskan Natives (53), black/African-Americans (64), and Hispanic/Latinos (82). Non-Hispanic blacks had the highest birthrate (1.6 per 1,000) for girls aged ten to fourteen, while Hispanics had the highest birthrate (49.7) for girls aged fifteen to seventeen and for females aged eighteen to nineteen (133.5).

Despite the decrease in teenage births in the United States, American rates remain higher than in most other developed nations. Given that childbearing at younger ages is associated with higher fertility rates, the high rate of births to adolescents may explain part of America's exceptionally high fertility rate. In addition, more than 80 percent of American teen mothers are unmarried, reflecting the weakened link between marriage and fertility. But teen mothers are not the only contributors to single motherhood in America today. Motherhood among unmarried American women who are well into their thirties has increased as well. Between 1970 and 1993, the birthrate doubled for unmarried women ages thirty and older, increasing from 8 percent in 1970 to 16 percent in 1993. Since then, this rate has declined to 12 percent.[45]

SINGLE-BY-CHOICE MOTHERS

The proportion of single-by-choice mothers to unintended single mothers is shifting as more American women elect to get pregnant before marrying or even cohabiting. Many of the single-by-choice mothers interviewed by Hertz have established careers and financial independence but have not found a suitable mate by the time they are ready to become mothers. Aware that chances of becoming pregnant decline rapidly at older ages, single-mothers-to-be put the socially endorsed ideal of a two-parent family on hold, or even permanently aside.[46]

GAY AND LESBIAN FAMILIES WITH CHILDREN

Many gay and lesbian families opt to have children, either through birth to one or both members of a lesbian couple or through adoption. Black and his colleagues estimate that 22 percent of partnered lesbians and 5 percent of partnered gays currently have children present in the home, about three-quarters of whom are under age eighteen. Some gays and lesbians are single parents and some are in heterosexual marriages. Including these families in the estimates suggests that over 14 percent of gays and over 28 percent of lesbians have children in the household. About 25 percent of gay men and 40 percent of lesbian women are, or were, married.[47]

Implications of Low Fertility for Aging Populations and the Elderly

Evolving family forms and their accompanying fertility rates play a key role in the age of a country's population. When fertility is high, a large share of the population is young; when fertility falls, the population "ages" because there are fewer children relative to the number of adults. If fertility falls quickly, as in China, then a country will age quickly.

Mortality rates are the other key determinant of a population's age structure. Fertility levels and change are especially important in countries where mortality has been low and stable for a long time.

As a result of the fertility decline over the last fifty years, the United States and much of the rest of the world is aging rapidly. Both the number and proportion of people who are age sixty-five or older is increasing, although at different rates in different countries. The number of older adults has risen more than threefold since 1950, from approximately 130 million in 1950 to 419 million in 2000. During this period, the elderly share of the population increased from 4 percent to 7 percent. In the United States, those aged sixty-five and older now make up about 13 percent of the population, but by 2030 this figure will exceed 20 percent.

Europe has the highest proportion of elderly and will probably remain the "oldest" region for decades. More than 18 percent of Italians and almost as many Swedes, Belgians, Greeks, and Japanese are sixty-five or older. The rapid decline in fertility in Asia, Latin America, the Caribbean, the Near East, and North Africa, combined with increases in life expectancy, mean that the elderly proportions in these regions will more than triple by 2050.

Throughout the world, oldest-old members (those aged eighty-five and older) are increasing at a much faster rate than any other age group. This means that both the *numbers* of very old people and their *proportion* of the population will rise. The U.S. Census (2004) projects that the U.S. population aged eighty-five and older will double from about 4.3 million today to about 7.3 million in 2020, then double again to 15 million by 2040, as members of the very large baby boom cohorts born after World War II reach these ages. If the Census Bureau is correct, by 2050, one American in twenty will be eighty-five years old or older, compared to one in one hundred today.

It has become clear that over the next fifty years the United States will undergo a profound transformation, becoming a mature nation in which one citizen in five is sixty-five or older, compared with one in eight today. These dramatic increases will exert powerful pressures on health care delivery systems and programs such as Social Security, Medicare, Medicaid, and Supplemental Security Income (SSI) that provide financial support to the elderly, poor, and disabled.

These changes will also have profound implications for social institutions, such as the family, that provide instrumental, financial, and emotional support for the elderly. Most older adults receive whatever help they need from relatives. Married older couples almost always live alone and almost always count on each other for help. Husbands care for wives with Alzheimer's disease; wives care for husbands who need help bathing and getting dressed. The situation faced by older men is substantially better on this dimension than that faced by older women, because most men are married until they die, but most women experience the death of their husbands and end their lives as widows. Three-quarters of older men but only 41 percent of older women are married and live with their spouse.

The family experience of black and Hispanic elderly people differs in important ways from that of white elderly people. Older black men and women are much less likely than either whites or Hispanics to be married; only a quarter of black women aged sixty-five and older are married, compared to 42 percent of whites and 37 percent of Hispanics. For men, the differences are even more striking; 57 percent of older black men are married, compared to 77 percent of whites and 67 percent of Hispanics. And dramatic declines in the proportion of black adults who are married suggest that future generations of black elderly will have substantially fewer family ties to draw on for support than the black aged of today.[48]

Conclusion

The United States is in the distinctive position among developed societies of producing just about enough children each year to replace the population in the long run. No other country in Europe or East Asia is so lucky, and some have levels of fertility so low that they threaten the health of their society if not increased soon.

Why has the United States succeeded, at least on this dimension, where others have not? Clearly, the answer is *not* that Americans want to have more children than women in these other countries, since fertility intentions are generally similar. The answer is *not* that Americans have given up marriage for cohabitation and extended singlehood, since rates of cohabitation are higher in the Nordic countries where fertility rates, while relatively healthy, are lower than in the United States. The answer is *not* that the link between marriage and childbearing has weakened more in the United States than in other countries, allowing women unable or unwilling to marry to contribute to fertility; a number of countries in Europe show higher levels of childbearing by women in informal unions or outside any union than the United States but have lower fertility rates overall.

The answer in large part is immigration: Hispanics, especially Mexican-Americans, keep our fertility rate up. In fact, if the parents of today are raising the workers and caregivers of the future, then one could argue that other racial and ethnic groups are free-riding on the fertility of Hispanics, particularly those of Mexican origin.

Further, immigration can offset declines in the total population and the working-age population, both of which result from low fertility rates. A United Nations report released in 2000 estimated how many immigrants each country would need in order to sustain its total population size and its working-age population size, given each country's fertility rates. Compared with other developed countries, the United States is unique in that its 1990s immigration rates are more than sufficient to ensure replacement of *both* the total population and the working-age population. Immigration rates in France and the United Kingdom, by contrast, could sustain population size but would need to double in order to replace the working-age population. At the other end of the spectrum, Italy would need three times its 1990s immigration rates to sustain population size and more than five times that rate to maintain the size of the working-age population.[49]

With regard to lower fertility among all developed countries, we discussed how widespread economic and ideological changes

(namely, toward individualism) have made having and raising children less attractive in developed countries. The time that parents
spend raising children could be invested in a career or leisure pursuits,
and the money could be invested in, well, investments, or consumer
goods, or travel or entertainment; in modern societies the list is endless. Consequently, in many societies, the "choice" to have children
has fared badly in the marketplace of consumer products.

The flaw in this accounting system lies in the *societal* benefits
that healthy, well-educated children raised to young adulthood
bring to the country in which they live. These children constitute
arguably the most important asset of a developed society, and the
benefits from these children accrue to all members of the society,
not just those who raised them. So parents pay the tremendous time
and money costs of having and raising children and all benefit from
these investments.

Low fertility, especially persistent and very low fertility, threatens
the very future of the society in which it occurs. The seriousness
of the threat suggests that we should take steps to make it easier and
more attractive for women and men to become parents and to raise
children. This might include financial support for those with young
children. It might include services and facilities to help parents
combine employment and child rearing. It might include increased
social recognition of the service that parents provide to the society
at large by having and raising children. And it might include policies
and programs to encourage women to have children at somewhat
younger ages. This reduction in childbearing age would increase period fertility and rejuvenate the age structure of the population.

Government policies can make a difference in national fertility
rates. Pro-natalist policies, such as tax breaks and enforced maternity
and paternity leave for parents, alleviate some of the costs of having
children. Norwegian parents, for example, benefit from state interventions providing maternity and paternity leave, as well as greater
availability, accessibility, and quality of child care.[50] Antinatalist

policies, such as China's one-child policy, discourage large families through taxation, thereby increasing the expense of having additional children. In general, those societies that provide social and economic support for working parents have seen higher fertility as a result, whereas those, like Japan and Germany, which have maintained a fairly rigid and traditional division of labor, have witnessed dramatic declines.[51]

Many of the countries facing the specter of a population made up predominantly of old people, with few children and young adults, a population facing decline and extinction, have long viewed decisions about whether and when to have children and how many to have as personal and private. And these decisions *are* made by individuals and couples, weighing the costs and benefits to themselves. But the *consequences* of these individual choices are felt by us all. So collective responsibility for supporting those who make choices beneficial to the society seems only prudent and only fair.

CHAPTER 12

Immigration

Peter H. Schuck

From American's very beginnings, large-scale immigration has transformed every aspect of society. The long history of immigration, argues legal scholar Peter Schuck, reveals certain recurrent features. Immigrants' astonishing ethno-racial diversity has periodically aroused illiberal attitudes, restrictionist movements, and anxieties about assimilation, yet immigration has expanded dramatically since 1980. Americans continue to feel ambivalently and even inconsistently about immigration. Current policy debates focus on illegal migration, the effects of immigrants on low-income American workers, the number and kinds of immigrants who should be admitted, and how to incorporate them into American society.

OF ALL THE FEATURES OF AMERICAN SOCIETY THAT DISTINGUISH the United States from other liberal democracies, immigration is perhaps the most far-reaching. It drives the demography, infuses religiosity, populates cities, expands the economy, affects schools and other public services, influences foreign policies, and constructs the future of our constitutional community by constantly altering the composition of "We, the People." Indeed, it is hard to think of an aspect of American life that immigration has not transformed. Along with individualism and suspicion of governmental power, immigration constitutes a core element of America's national identity.

A Thumbnail History of Immigration to the United States

DIVERSITY

When the first Dutch and English settlers arrived in what is now America, they found an indigenous population of some 500,000 natives divided into three decentralized cultural groups occupying the eastern seaboard. As early as 1643, a Jesuit visitor to New Amsterdam could remark that eighteen languages were spoken on its streets. By 1770, Britons composed only a third of the colonies' residents; Germans, the largest other immigrant group, were viewed as being most different from the English, Scots, Irish, and other whites. No other Old or New World society, Jon Butler observes, knew such remarkable mixtures of peoples.

Pre-Revolutionary ethnic relations were hardly harmonious. All ethnic groups were divided on the issue of independence. The Scots notably favored the Crown, many loyalists returned to England, and many more fled to Canada where their presence would later attract English migrants who might otherwise have gone to America. According to scholarly analyses of the first U.S. Census in 1790, English-stock Americans accounted for only 49.2 percent of the 4 million total and 60.9 percent of the white total, with the composition varying among the different states. Blacks constituted 19.3 percent nationally and constituted over 40 percent in Virginia and South Carolina. The other major ethnic groups were Germans (7 percent), Scots (6.6 percent), Scotch-Irish (4.8 percent), Irish (3 percent), Dutch (2.6 percent), French (1.4 percent), and Swedes (0.5 percent).

Between 1790 and 1815, the migration flow was modest in size and familiar in composition. After 1815, when peace was restored in Europe and the United States, migration increased briefly until the Panic of 1819, which led to economic dislocation, reduced it. This situation continued until 1830, leading many Irish, Scots, and Welsh to go instead to

England or Canada. During the 1830s, especially before the Panic of 1837, four times as many immigrants came to the United States than in the 1820s. The number almost tripled again in the 1840s, especially with the Irish potato famine, overpopulation, and deteriorating economic conditions throughout Europe. A much smaller factor was the 1848 revolution in Germany, with German-speakers constituting the first sizeable influx of a non-British group since the colonial era. This large 1840s immigrant cohort doubled again in the 1850s, only to fall back in the 1860s during the U.S. Civil War. From the Civil War to the 1880s, Irish and German immigrants continued to dominate the flow, followed by the English-Scots-Welsh group, Scandinavians, and both English- and French-speakers from Canada. By 1890, 32.7 percent of the almost 63 million residents (37.4 percent of the whites) were either immigrants or the children of at least one immigrant parent; for each ethnic group, moreover, immigrants exceeded the native-born by a considerable margin. And by 1890, Catholicism, which hardly threatened Protestant hegemony in 1790 when Catholics constituted less than 1 percent of the population, was the largest Christian denomination in the country, constituting approximately 7.5 percent of the population and much higher concentrations in the great cities, with a national diocesan infrastructure.

More than 18.2 million newcomers entered the United States between 1890 and 1920, almost double the number in the 1860 to 1890 period. Most came from southern and eastern Europe, regions that previously had sent relatively few to the United States, and some came from the Pacific and Caribbean islands conquered in the Spanish-American War. The old source countries in northern and western Europe, moreover, continued to send large numbers of migrants. Many immigrants, especially those from Russia, the Balkans, Spain, the Austro-Hungarian Empire, and Italy, later returned home in large numbers.

Immigration fell sharply during World War I. After the war, new immigrants increased despite a new literacy test, an economic slump, and a demand for organized labor for the suspension of all immigration. Congress, employing blatantly racist rhetoric and overriding the veto of the lame-duck President Wilson, enacted the Immigration Act of 1921. Later extended for two more years, it imposed an annual overall ceiling with additional per-country limits of 3 percent of the number of its foreign-born U.S. residents counted in the 1910 census. When restrictionists found that the favored countries in northern and western Europe did not fill their immigrant quotas but the less-favored ones from the south and east did send new immigrants, they pressed for tighter limits. The Johnson-Reed (or National Origins) Act of 1924 passed by overwhelming margins, with most opposition coming from north-eastern cities where so many of the new immigrants had settled. The new law set an annual limit of 150,000 Europeans, a complete prohibition on Japanese immigration, a system of visa screening abroad rather than on arrival, and quotas based on the contribution of each nationality to the overall U.S. population in 1890, thereby preserving the racial and ethnic status quo. A reluctant President Hoover put the new system into effect in 1929. During the entire Depression-plagued decade of the 1930s, only 500,000 immigrants came to the United States, representing just over 10 percent of those who came in the 1920s. Many of these did not remain, and in 1932 almost three times as many immigrants left the United States as entered it.

The urgent political and economic needs generated by World War II affected immigration policy in several respects. The United States negotiated a large-scale program with Mexico for temporary farm workers, known as *braceros,* in order to fill labor needs in the South and Southwest, a program that continued until 1964. The wartime alliance with China led Congress in 1943 to repeal the legislation dating back to the 1880s that barred most Chinese immigration. In the postwar years, the United States admitted hundreds of thousands of refugees under cold war legislation aimed largely at

Communist regimes. Migration from Puerto Rico, whose inhabitants had been statutory U.S. citizens since 1917, brought most of them to the New York City region, where they settled. This migration was facilitated by declining air fares, the ease of returning to the island, and the much higher U.S. standard of living.

In 1952, Congress enacted the McCarran-Walter Act, which preserved the national origins quotas over President Truman's veto denouncing them. The statute also repealed Japanese exclusion and established a small quota for the Asia–Pacific region. In the wake of President Kennedy's assassination, Lyndon Johnson's landslide victory in 1964, and the more enlightened attitudes toward minorities that led to the passage of the Civil Rights Act of 1964, Congress finally abolished the national origins quotas in 1965, establishing a system whose basic structure of family and skills preference categories, a refugee quota, and overall and per-country numerical limits remains largely intact today.

A vast expansion in legal and illegal immigration from Latin America, the Caribbean, and Asia followed, with stunning effects on America's demographic diversity. Today, more than 35 million foreign-born individuals live in the United States, with well over a million added each year. In 2006, Europe's share of U.S. immigrants was only 13 percent, the share of Latin America and the Caribbean was about 29 percent, Asia's was 33 percent, Africa's was 9 percent, and Canada's was 1.4 percent. Even these numbers understate substantially the magnitude and regional diversity of the flow. First, they do not include non-immigrants (175 million admitted in 2006), who enter the United States on temporary and restricted visas for a variety of business, diplomatic, and tourist purposes. Many of these non-immigrants overstay their visas and join the large undocumented population. Second, almost a third of the foreign-born are undocumented; each year, an estimated 250,000 to 300,000 of them settle more or less permanently in the United States, the vast majority from Mexico.

ILLIBERALISM, RESTRICTIONISM, AND ANXIETIES

As Rogers Smith has shown, the long history of U.S. immigration and citizenship policies exhibits liberal, republican, and racist-patriarchal strands, with the emphasis on the latter until 1965. As he puts it, "For over 80% of U.S. history, American laws declared most people in the world legally ineligible to become full U.S. citizens solely because of their race, original nationality, or gender. For at least two-thirds of American history, the majority of the domestic adult population was also ineligible for full citizenship for the same reasons. Those racial, ethnic, and gender restrictions were blatant, not latent."[1]

During the nineteenth century, bitter political struggles occurred over the Sabbatarian, temperance, and common school reform movements, as well as over the issues of naturalization reform and public funds for parochial schools. An important battleground in the war against Catholics was slavery. Most immigrants, whether Catholic or not, opposed abolition for a number of reasons, including the fact that many leading abolitionists were ardent nativists, anti-Catholics, and Whigs. A nativist party, often called Know-Nothings because of their secret practices, won a large national following during the mid–1850s, sending seventy-five members to Congress, taking control of several state governments in the Northeast, and also doing well in other regions. For a number of reasons, including the sharp decline in immigration after 1854 due to the end of the Irish famine and the Panic of 1857 in the United States, the party quickly faded. Although both the Union and Confederate armies fielded a disproportionate number of immigrant soldiers, the Civil War was stridently opposed by many immigrants who protested against it and rioted in many cities against conscription for a cause that was not theirs. Especially violent was New York's Draft Riot just after the Battle of Gettysburg in July 1863, which was led by Irish immigrants, claimed well over one hundred lives, and gained infamy as the bloodiest episode in American urban history. By the 1870s and 1880s, however, the groups that had naturalized in large numbers prior to the Civil War began to emerge as formidable voting blocs, with the Irish increasingly taking control in New York, Boston, and other cities where they were concentrated. By 1886, one-third of the police force of Chicago was foreign-born, largely Irish, and the remainder contained many second-generation Americans.

In 1875, Congress enacted the first substantive federal limit on immigration. This law was expanded in 1882 and 1891 to bar criminals, prostitutes, idiots, lunatics, and persons suffering from loathsome or contagious diseases or those likely to become a public charge. Federal restrictions supplanted others that the states had imposed much earlier,[2] and although these restrictions only barred 1 percent of the immigrants who sought entry, they succeeded in establishing exclusive federal control over immigrant admissions, exclusion, and deportation. Anti-Chinese fervor in California led Congress to enact a series of laws that excluded Chinese workers, and those stranded in the United States were denied the most basic elements of due process. The U.S. Supreme Court, however, upheld these enactments and enforced others making Asians and other non-whites ineligible for naturalization.

The immigration restriction movement during these years was by no means confined to California or the Chinese influx, nor was racism its only motive—or perhaps even its main one. Businessmen, politicians, and others identified labor unrest, particularly in economic sectors manned mainly by foreign workers, with the radical ideologies of socialism, communism, syndicalism, and anarchism that they thought immigrants had brought with them. The American Protective Association (APA), organized in Iowa in 1887 to demonize Catholic immigrants, spread to other states, appealing to many earlier immigrant Protestant groups and reaching its zenith in the Panic of 1893 when it helped to secure victories for Republican candidates. When the APA passed from the scene, other nativist groups arose that feared the demographic changes spawned by the newcomers—for example, the Immigration Restriction League

founded in 1894 by elite academics, bluebloods, and scientists prop-
agating the new eugenics orthodoxy. In 1903, the list of excludable
aliens was again expanded to include, among other groups, anar-
chists and advocates of political violence.

In 1907–1908, President Theodore Roosevelt responded to
anti-Japanese pressure in California by negotiating a Gentlemen's
Agreement that limited Japanese migration to the United States and
its territories. An English literacy requirement for admission was
finally enacted over President Wilson's veto in 1917—though it
required only literacy in a language of the applicant's choice for
those sixteen or older. This law also banned immigration from the
Asia-Pacific triangle, a blatantly racist exclusion that would not be
fully rectified until 1965. Hostility to German-Americans during
World War I grew so virulent, historian Thomas Archdeacon writes,
that they "were finished as a culturally vital element in the United
States. They could no longer pursue the illusion that success and acceptance in America did not demand complete Anglicization. After
the war German-Americans did not dare to speak against the harsh
terms imposed on the fatherland at the Versailles peace conference,
and the disintegration of their separate identity . . . accelerated."[3]

During the postwar period, a number of developments—labor
strife, urban unrest, abhorrence at the Bolshevik Revolution in Russia, and a Red Scare campaign against suspected alien radicals—fed
the popular opposition to immigration. Also aiding the restrictionist
cause was a resurgence of Protestant fundamentalism, the Ku Klux
Klan, and support for prohibition, all of which were aimed in large
part at the supposedly baleful influence on American values of immigrants, particularly urban Catholics and Jews. These pressures led to
the national origins quotas, discussed earlier. The McCarran-Walter
Act, enacted in the early years of the cold war, preserved the quotas
and also adopted new political and ideological restrictions.

The 1965 immigration reform decisively repudiated this illiberal tradition. But this repudiation—complete and permanent as I

think it is—does not mean that Americans are wholly enthusiastic about immigration. Quite the contrary; they are not—and never have been. Anxiety about immigration has always been aroused by the newer immigrant groups, a bias that a 1982 Gallup poll places in a revealing historical light. When asked about its views on the contributions of particular immigrant groups, the public gave the highest scores to precisely the groups that had been widely reviled in the nineteenth and early twentieth centuries; the lowest-scoring groups were the newer arrivals (in 1982, Cubans and Haitians). Professor Rita Simon has captured this ambivalence in an arresting metaphor: We view immigrants "with rose-colored glasses turned backwards."[4]

Economic Forces

The most powerful spurs to immigration have always been economic. The vast majority of immigrants, in classic migration theory terms, have been pushed by the straitened economic conditions in their countries of origin and pulled by the economic opportunities—agricultural and industrial jobs, entrepreneurship, investment, higher education, and technology—presented by American society. But many Americans have also always had a vested interest in promoting immigration, quite apart from family unification. Significantly, the Declaration of Independence's list of "abuses and usurpations" included the British Crown's interference with much-desired "migrations hither." Until the closing of the frontier at the end of the nineteenth century, the United States contained vast tracts of land to be settled, improved, fortified, and marketed—and a vast industry of sellers, builders, speculators, brokers, lenders, insurers, service providers, and of course politicians who stood to profit from immigration and the rapid population growth and land development that it would propel. The shipping, railroad, and other transportation companies that brought immigrants to America and thence to the interior were, as Aristide Zolberg has shown, pivotal forces in encouraging immigration through their marketing efforts in Europe.

Even more important, they organized to defeat the periodic political efforts to restrict immigration.

Today, the economic interests in the United States favoring immigration are even more varied and powerful. Large sectors of the economy—agriculture, tourism, restaurants, information technology, construction, clothing, and many other businesses—depend on the labor, skills, and cultural patterns of immigrants. Other large sectors, including government and many non-profit agencies, provide them with goods and services. They have revitalized many struggling metropolitan areas and, increasingly, rural ones. In recent years, they have accounted for approximately 40 percent of America's population growth—and thus of its future economic and taxpaying base.

If the economic interests that benefit from immigration are immense, those arrayed against it are few, consisting largely of local governments that must provide costly public services to immigrants while most (though not all) of the tax revenues generated by immigrants' activities, particularly their payroll taxes, flow to Washington— a serious fiscal mismatch that Congress has failed to rectify. The main restrictionist group, the Federation for American Immigration Reform (FAIR), draws from environmental and population control activists, labor union professionals, demographers, and some politicians who in other areas generally subscribe to liberal public policy positions. But even labor unions, which traditionally spearheaded the economic opposition to immigration, now see new organizing opportunities among immigrants as well as the economic benefits that they create, even as they compete with low-skill native workers. Unions have used this latter threat to buttress demands for stronger enforcement of fair labor standards for *all* workers, thus reducing the incentive to hire undocumented workers.

Indeed, the large and diverse economic interests favoring immigration have helped to produce a political mismatch as well as a fiscal one. That is, these interests have pressed—with considerable success, as we shall now see—to expand immigration, even as the general public favors less of it.

PUBLIC ATTITUDES

Over the last fifty years, Americans who were asked (in slightly different formulations) whether immigration levels should be increased, reduced, or kept the same have responded, generally speaking, in remarkably consistent ways, with majorities or substantial minorities favoring a decrease. The trend in attitudes has been toward greater negativity. In fact, Americans like immigrants more than they like immigration, favor past immigration more than recent immigration, prefer legal immigrants to illegal ones, prefer refugees to other immigrants, support immigrants' access to educational and health benefits but not to welfare or Social Security, and feel that immigrants' distinctive cultures have contributed positively to American life and that diversity continues to strengthen American society today. At the same time, they overwhelmingly resist any conception of multiculturalism that discourages immigrants from learning and using the English language.

Today, the resistance to immigration proceeds largely from pragmatic concerns rather than nativist or xenophobic attitudes. Americans do not oppose immigration in principle, in general, or unalterably, but they do want less of it (or at least no higher). Even here, they are open to argument and evidence about what the levels and mix should be and about what the actual effects of immigration are. Thus their views about the wisdom and level of restriction are capable of being changed. Finally, as the next section explains, immigration policy driven by pro-immigration elites has been far more expansionist than these attitudes alone would suggest.[5]

POST–1980 EXPANSION

During the 1970s, almost 4.5 million legal immigrants were admitted to the United States as permanent residents. This increased to

7.3 million in the 1980s, 9 million in the 1990s, and 6.9 million in just the first seven years of the present decade. Together with the estimated 11–12 million illegal aliens now residing in the United States more or less permanently—perhaps twice the number in the mid-1980s—the foreign-born now make up 12 percent or more of the population, the highest share since the first decade of the twentieth century. Their total number is higher than ever before.

Changes in immigration law since 1980 have facilitated this expansion.[6] In the Refugee Act of 1980, Congress established for the first time a systematic legal structure for controlling refugee admissions and adjudicating refugee and asylum claims. Six years later, in the Immigration Reform and Control Act of 1986 (IRCA), Congress tried to make sweeping changes in immigration enforcement and in admissions. On the enforcement side, it enacted an employer sanctions program intended to prohibit employers from hiring undocumented workers, but these sanctions are weak and not well enforced. The Immigration Marriage Fraud Amendments of 1986, passed just before IRCA, sought to prevent aliens from using sham marriages to gain admission. In the years that immediately followed, Congress also adopted a number of criminal enforcement provisions relating to drug trafficking and other criminal conduct by aliens.

On the admissions side, IRCA established several amnesty programs (for agricultural workers, other workers, and Cubans and Haitians), which invited aliens in the United States illegally since early 1982 to apply for temporary legal status, which could eventually lead to permanent legal status and citizenship. Of the 2.76 million who applied under these programs, 2.67 million were granted legal status. IRCA also created a supposedly temporary program designed to favor European (especially Irish) immigrants who would not otherwise qualify for visas. These diversity provisions used a lottery to select the lucky winners. Finally, IRCA adopted a new anti-discrimination program that was intended to protect legal workers (especially Hispanics) against the discrimination that might result from the threat of sanctions against employers hiring aliens.

Only four years later, the Immigration Act of 1990 was enacted. The most far-reaching reform of immigration and naturalization policy since 1965, the 1990 act raised legal admissions to 50 percent above the pre-IRCA level, eased controls on temporary workers, made the diversity visas program permanent, and limited the government's power to deport for ideological reasons. The 1990 act remains the centerpiece of legal immigration policy today. In 1995, the Clinton administration negotiated with Cuba a limited but regularized quota for the admission of up to twenty thousand Cubans each year.

In 1996, reacting to national outrage over the Oklahoma City bombing, a bipartisan Congress quickly enacted two statutes—the Anti-Terrorism and Effective Death Penalty Act (AEDPA), and months later, the Illegal Immigration Reform and Immigrant Responsibility Act (IIRIRA)—that completely revamped the enforcement process as applied to immigrants convicted of crimes in the United States, reducing their procedural rights and making their deportation both faster and easier. In an effort to streamline deportation further and to prevent immigrants' lawyers and the federal courts from protracting the process, IIRIRA extended AEDPA in certain ways that even many immigration officials find arbitrary, unfair, and in some cases unworkable. For example, the new law required immigration officials to exclude aliens at the border summarily and without judicial review if they seem to lack proper documentation. It made asylum claiming more difficult and barred the agency from granting discretionary relief from deportation to many aliens even for compelling humanitarian reasons, as pre-IIRIRA law permitted. It mandated the detention of many deportable aliens, perhaps indefinitely if their countries would not take them back, and equated the rights of aliens who entered illegally and live in the United States with those of aliens with no ties to the country. It limited the rights of illegal aliens to reenter legally, further expanded the already broad category of aggravated felon aliens, who can be deported summarily even if they have been long-term residents, and barred judicial review of many deportation decisions. The courts have upheld most of these provisions while interpreting others narrowly in light of constitutional concerns.

But even IIRIRA's harshness should not obscure a fundamental fact about contemporary immigration policy: challenges to the high levels of legal immigration set in the 1990 law, such as the Jordan Commission's proposal to reduce inflows by more than one-third, have all failed. Tough on undocumented and criminal aliens, and arbitrary toward asylum seekers and deportation hardship cases, IIRIRA had only one important provision directed at law-abiding immigrants; it raised their sponsors' income requirements. Perhaps the best evidence of the strength of the pro-immigration consensus lies in Congress's treatment of *illegal* aliens. In 1997 and 1998, Congress enacted new amnesties for an estimated 155,000 Nicaraguans and Cubans, a large number of Haitians, and approximately 240,000 Guatemalans and Salvadorans who were in the United States illegally. In December 2000, Congress revived a lapsed provision of the immigration statute to enable about 400,000 illegal aliens who had been ruled ineligible for earlier amnesties going back to 1986 to obtain green cards nonetheless. The newly elected George W. Bush administration twice mobilized Republicans in Congress to support extending the application deadline, rendering eligible hundreds of thousands more. In March 2001, the administration also gave temporary legal status to as many as 150,000 undocumented Salvadorans. President Bush then launched a campaign for another large amnesty, this time for Mexican agricultural workers employed by American growers. At the same time, Congress continued its vast expansion of the number of temporary H1B visas available to technical workers, mostly in computer services. Many of them, it was anticipated, would later adjust to LPR (legal permanent resident) status. Finally, LPR admissions continued to increase substantially after IIRIRA.

This largely expansive immigration policy was convulsed by the destruction of the World Trade Center and other homeland sites on September 11, 2001, by foreign terrorists. In the aftermath of 9/11, the administrative processing of LPR visas and naturalizations slowed considerably, albeit even then remaining well above 1980s levels. Recent proposals for comprehensive immigration reform, which died in Congress in the summer of 2007, would vastly increase the paperwork burdens that are already overwhelming immigration administration and enforcement. Significantly, both the president's proposal and the Senate-passed bill would have expanded legal immigration far beyond the levels authorized in the 1990 law,[7] while even the avowedly restrictionist House bills would not significantly cut back on those levels. Immigration policy appears to be a one-way ratchet upward.

The Current Immigration System

ADMINISTRATIVE STRUCTURE

In the aftermath of 9/11, responsibility for the administration of the immigration laws was moved from the Department of Justice, where it had been lodged since 1940, to the new Department of Homeland Security (DHS), which took over these responsibilities on March 1, 2003. Heeding the recommendations of decades of reformers, Congress separated the immigration enforcement and immigration services into different entities within DHS. Several other departments also play important administrative roles. Formal adjudication of immigration cases continues to be the responsibility of the Department of Justice, through several hundred immigration judges and the Board of Immigration Appeals (BIA). The State Department continues to process visa applications through its embassies and consulates abroad. Reacting to the visa administration failures that contributed to 9/11, however, Congress authorized DHS to administer and oversee visa processing in conjunction with the State Department. The Department of Labor processes petitions for employment-based visas, and the Department of Health and Human Services cares for unaccompanied children and reviews exclusions of non-citizens on health-related grounds.

ADMISSIONS

Broadly speaking, three categories of aliens are admitted to the United States. First, immigrants are admitted as permanent residents (LPRs)—1.26 million in 2006.[8] Second, "non-immigrants" receive temporary visas that impose restrictions as to the purposes and duration of their visit (e.g., as tourists, students, workers, diplomats, and many other specifically regulated categories). Two important categories are the H1B program for highly skilled specialty workers, and the H2A program for agricultural workers. On any given day, an estimated 3.8 million non-immigrants are in the country. Third, parolees are admitted for special humanitarian or other administrative reasons; they hold a revocable legal status that treats them as if they stood at the border seeking initial entry.

The law establishes an overall cap on LPR admissions of 675,000 per year, but this cap can be (and invariably is) breached if the number of immediate relatives (spouses, minor children, and parents of U.S. citizens), who are exempt from this numerical cap, exceed a certain level. In 2006 581,000 immediate relatives were admitted as LPRs. The number of overseas refugees allowed entrance is determined annually after negotiations between the president and Congress (only 41,000 in 2006), whereas there is no cap on the number of asylum seekers who may be admitted. After a year, refugees and asylum seekers are eligible to petition for adjustment to LPR status; 216,000 of them became LPRs in 2006. Also exempt from the 675,000 cap are Amerasians (Asians of American parentage, usually the children of U.S. soldiers fighting in Vietnam), the 50,000 visas authorized under the diversity lottery, those legalized under various amnesties, parolees, and some other groups.

The 675,000 annual cap for LPRs is divided into three major categories of immigrants, each governed by its own intricate eligibility rules. These categories are: family-sponsored (480,000, further divided into four subcategories with ceilings); employment-based (140,000, further divided into five subcategories with ceilings); and diversity visa winners (50,000). Although this system places somewhat greater emphasis than the pre–1990 law did on employment-based admissions (and especially those with higher-level skills), the family-sponsored admissions (including the unlimited immediate relatives and family members accompanying the main visa recipient) still accounted for more than 63 percent of the total in 2006. Almost two-thirds of those admitted as LPRs that year were already resident in the United States, many illegally, and adjusted their status without having to return to their country of origin. The leading countries of origin in 2006 were Mexico (14 percent), China (7 percent), the Philippines (6 percent), and India (5 percent).

Within these overall preference ceilings, every country is subject to a further annual ceiling of at least 25,620 with respect to family-sponsored and employment-based admissions. Diversity admissions are subject to a per-country annual ceiling of 3,850. Chargeability against these ceilings depends on the immigrant's country of birth, not the country of nationality. These per-country ceilings mean very long waiting times for those born in countries with many recent and current applicants; their actual waiting times depend on the particular subcategory under which they applied. In an extreme case, the State Department in December 2007 was processing visa petitions for Philippine-born siblings and married children of U.S. citizens filed back in 1985.

ENFORCEMENT

As noted earlier, an estimated 11–12 million aliens resided in the United States without valid documents in 2007—roughly double the number twenty years earlier when IRCA was enacted. Almost half of the illegal alien population entered legally but overstayed or otherwise violated their visa conditions; the remainder crossed the border illegally (entered without inspection). Most aliens who seek to cross the Mexican-U.S. border illegally eventually succeed in doing so, often after multiple attempts. In 2006, the DHS reported 1.3 million arrests, the vast majority made by the Border Patrol (a politically popular unit, temporarily augmented by the National Guard), almost all on the southern border; 87 percent of them were of Mexicans. The Border Patrol returns the vast majority of illegal entrants across the border informally and has experimented with sending them back to places far distant from the border in order to make subsequent crossing efforts more costly. In a small fraction of the cases (208,000 in 2005), the aliens are placed in formal removal proceedings before an immigration judge; most of these cases involve aliens convicted of crimes. Because aliens in this situation seldom have valid legal or factual defenses, almost all such proceedings result in removal orders, which the alien may appeal to the BIA and then to the federal courts. Certain aliens, notably those in the frequently broadened category of "aggravated felons," may be removed summarily under procedures providing for administrative review but little or no court review. In 2005, 35 percent of all formal removals were summary. DHS administers one of the largest detention operations in the federal government, expected to rise to 27,500 beds in 2007.[9] The need for detentions largely reflects the very high absconding rates of aliens released pending their removal hearings and actual expulsion. Only by detaining them can removal be effectuated.

CITIZENSHIP

American law makes citizenship comparatively easy to acquire and almost impossible to lose. Regardless of the parents' legal status, a child born on American soil becomes an American citizen at the moment of birth under the rule of *jus soli* (law of the soil). The American version of this rule, which dates back to the sixteenth-century English common law, is probably the world's most liberal.[10] One can also become a U.S. citizen through a citizen parent under the rule of *jus sanguinis* (law of blood or descent). For immigrants, citizenship through naturalization is readily available after five years as an LPR (subject to certain rules concerning absences). The English language and literacy tests are notoriously easy to pass—the statute mandates a simple literacy test and exempts many disabled individuals and older immigrants who are illiterate in English from having to take it—and the American history and government test requires only rote responses. Indeed, making these requirements a bit more rigorous might actually strengthen the argument for more immigration, just as the 1996 welfare reform statute limiting immigrants' access to welfare benefits may have undermined a traditional argument for immigration restriction. Although the naturalization statute disqualifies those individuals and members of groups deemed subversive or not attached to the principles of the Constitution, this bar has been considerably narrowed by statute and judicial interpretation since the 1960s, as has the good moral character requirement with respect to non-criminals, although it does flatly ban aggravated felons. Finally, the Supreme Court has narrowly interpreted the law's provisions for rescinding the citizenship of those who procured their naturalization through fraud or misrepresentation, while denationalization due to the commission of expatriating acts is not possible unless the citizen specifically intends thereby to renounce his U.S. citizenship.

More than 702,000 LPRs were naturalized in 2006, with a larger surge in naturalizations expected for 2007 in the wake of LPRs' anxieties surrounding the immigration reform struggle in Congress. The processing backlog is very large, but DHS is committed to reducing it. The median elapsed time between gaining LPR status and naturalization is eight years, but nationality groups naturalize at different rates and after remaining in LPR status for different periods of time. Mexicans and Canadians, for example, are less likely to naturalize, and take longer to do so, than many Asian groups. This reflects, among other things, their greater proximity and hence their more enduring ties to their homelands.

Dual citizenship is increasingly common, the result of more international marriages, legal changes in other countries, and a softening of traditional opposition to dual citizenship by the United States and other governments. Americans can acquire the nationality of two or more states in a number of ways—by birth in the United States to immigrant parents; by birth abroad to a U.S. citizen parent and a foreign parent, both of whom can transmit their nationality to the child; by marriage to a foreigner who transmits his or her nationality to the spouse; and by naturalizing in another state after having acquired U.S. citizenship. In addition, the renunciation oath required of all naturalizing citizens in the United States may be legally ineffective in the state of origin; even if effective, the naturalized U.S. citizen may be able to reacquire nationality in that state. Nearly 90 percent of legal immigrants to the United States today come from states that allow dual citizenship; under a recent legal change, Mexico even promotes it for the U.S.-born children of its nationals. Such laws are encouraging naturalization in the United States by Latin American immigrants who previously resisted it; they also encourage foreign politicians to seek votes and campaign funds from their compatriots in the United States who are dual citizens.

Immigration Policy Debates

Immigration is perhaps the most atavistic of our public policies: it bespeaks where we imagine we came from, who we think we are as a nation, and what we want our collective future to be. Constitutionally and politically, it defines who "We the People" are. But for most Americans, its importance is more mundane, directly affecting their daily lives, the people with whom they interact, the schools their children attend, the taxes they pay, the neighborhoods where they live, the public services they receive, the stores they shop in, and much more.

Much of U.S. immigration policy is path-dependent: fundamental choices in the past charted a well-defined course that is changeable only at the margins. For example, the United States long ago came to think of itself as a country of immigration and of ethnically (if not always racially) diverse immigration at that. It gave the states almost no role in immigration policy, unlike in Canada, Germany, Switzerland, and other federal systems. The courts have long been highly deferential to the elected branches in immigration matters, usually on the ground that such matters are intimately linked to foreign policy, national security, and sovereignty. Despite these embedded political structures, important policy issues are very much on the current political agenda.

THE EFFECTS OF IMMIGRATION

Most Americans think that immigration has been very beneficial to the United States and that earlier waves of immigrants have assimilated fairly well into the American mainstream. Almost all analyses confirm that from a purely economic perspective, immigration increases economic growth, although a comprehensive review of the subject commissioned by the National Academy of Sciences and published in 1997 concluded that the net benefit was modest relative to the economy as a whole (i.e., on the order of no more than $10 billion).[11] Nevertheless, Americans worry about how immigrants (especially the undocumented) affect local budgets for schools, hospitals, and other public services, as well as crime rates, low-income Americans (especially blacks), and the primacy of the English language (the concern about English-language fluency is discussed below in the "Immigration Integration" section).

Local Governments.   Precise estimates of the effects of immigration on local budgets and public services are impossible for many reasons. Expenditures are offset to some degree by immigrant-generated tax revenues, some of which (e.g., local property and income taxes paid by their landlords) are indirect. More generally, the flow of immigration-related tax revenues and public expenditures between different levels of government is very complex and opaque. Aggregating legal and illegal immigrants in the analysis is misleading because they present such different cost and benefit profiles. Finally, many of the costs and benefits of immigration are diffuse, extending far beyond the localities in which immigrants live and work and in which their effects are usually measured.

Despite these methodological difficulties, it seems clear that immigrants often impose large fiscal burdens on local communities, particularly on those near the southern border. These burdens are most noticeable in public hospitals, schools, prisons, and social service agencies. Congress, in recognition of the fiscal mismatch discussed earlier and perhaps of federal failures in enforcing the immigration laws, has authorized funds to reimburse localities for some of these costs. Actual appropriations for this purpose, however, have been far from adequate.

Crime.   Crimes committed by aliens drive much public hostility to immigration. Government Accountability Office (GAO) reports in 2005 suggest the magnitude of the problem.[12] The number of aliens incarcerated in federal facilities increased from about 42,000 in 2001 to about 49,000 in 2004, a 15 percent increase. Aliens are about 27 percent of all federal prisoners, accounting for approximately $1.2 billion in federal costs in 2004. In a study of more than 55,000 illegal aliens in federal prisons, the GAO found that the average one had about eight arrests (for thirteen offenses); 26 percent of them had eleven or more arrests. About 45 percent of the offenses committed by this population were for drug or immigration crimes, but 12 percent were for violent crimes such as murder, robbery, assault, and sex-related crimes, and 15 percent were for property-related crimes. These statistics, of course, do not include the very large number of aliens in state prisons and local jails. In California, more than 20 percent of the inmates during the mid-1990s were thought to be foreign-born, with roughly the same share in Los Angeles County jails.[13]

These statistics reflect the high levels of immigration in recent years, but they do *not* mean that immigrants are more prone to crime. In fact, incarceration rates for foreign-born men aged eighteen to thirty-nine are much lower than for native-born men (in 2000, 0.7 percent versus 3.5 percent); moreover, this difference has increased substantially since 1990. Indeed, if we exclude island-born Puerto Ricans, who have far higher crime rates but are citizens, the foreign-born rate is even lower and the difference correspondingly greater. The crime problem arises chiefly in the second generation; the incarceration rates of the U.S.–born children of immigrants are higher than those of both their parents and of non-Hispanic white citizens, and their incarceration rates generally increase the longer they are in the country.[14] Strikingly, these patterns hold even controlling for age, education, race or ethnicity, and citizenship.[15]

Low-Income Americans.   Labor economists disagree about the magnitude, and even the direction, of immigrants' effects on those Americans living in or near poverty. George Borjas, for example, claims that the infusion of millions of low-skill immigrants has inevitably reduced wages for American workers, particularly high school dropouts; he finds a wage loss of 5 percent during the 1980s and 1990s, some $1,200 a year. In contrast, David Card argues that this downward pressure on wages is mitigated, if not eliminated, by the market's complex adaptations to new workers, and by a growing demand for unskilled workers fueled in part by the declining high school dropout rate among U.S. workers. Card finds that cities with large immigrant influxes like Miami have absorbed immigrants rapidly, with no apparent harm (and possibly some gain) to low-wage American workers there.[16] This largely technical debate will not be resolved soon.

What does seem clear is that immigration, particularly by the undocumented, has contributed to the increased inequality in the United States over the last few decades, although the size of this effect is difficult to determine. A recent summary of the literature notes the declining wages of each succeeding wave of immigrants, comprised increasingly of low-skill Mexican and Latino workers, relative to their American counterparts.[17] But economist Robert Lerman finds that because such low-skill workers greatly improve their wages by entering the United States—a 2006 study estimates that Mexican workers with a high school degree earn seven times as much in the United States as they would in Mexico—including their gains from migration would reduce the growth of income inequality in the United States by two-thirds.[18] As Lerman has explained, trying to understand inequality in the United States without taking account of recent immigration trends is like trying to understand inequality in today's Germany without taking account of its recent absorption of East Germany.

NUMBERS AND CATEGORIES

As noted earlier, current legal (and illegal) immigration levels are high by historical standards, and the American public seems to prefer less of it. In its 1997 report to Congress, the Jordan Commission recommended annual admissions of only 550,000, about half the levels of recent years. But putting these public preferences aside (which Congress has done for decades by adopting expansive immigration policies), a strong case can be made for admitting more, rather than fewer, immigrants—so long as the newcomers are well adapted to the needs of American society. Even today, the United States remains a country with a comparatively low population density.

Even its largest and densest cities are thinly populated relative to other cities in the world, including the most famously attractive ones. Indeed, the population density of New York City is about half what it was a century ago; other major cities are also less densely populated than they were. The Senate debates over comprehensive immigration reform in 2007 revealed much support for increasing family-based quotas for a number of years until the large backlog of petitions by siblings of citizens and LPRs could be eliminated or reduced.

From a policy perspective, then, the critical question about immigrants is not so much how many should be admitted but in which categories. There is almost universal agreement that within whatever numerical quotas are established (and setting refugee admissions to one side), the United States should admit those immigrants who add the most social value to the existing population. Hotly disputed, however, is whether and to what extent that value should be defined by family ties or by job, language, and other skills. Under the current system, only 13 percent of permanent visas were allocated on the basis of skills in 2006, and only one-third of these visas went to the jobholders; two-thirds went to their accompanying spouse and children. Indeed, between 2000 and 2007, more than 180,000 authorized job-based visas were not given out because of the agency's processing delays,[19] and Congress felt obliged to enact special legislation to allocate the unused ones for 2005 and 2006.

As the United States increasingly competes with other countries for skilled workers, its admissions policy will need renovation, and finding the appropriate balance between family-based and skills-based admissions is essential. A larger total quota, of course, would make the political and policy tradeoffs entailed by this rebalancing somewhat easier. One model for reform is the Canadian point system, which rewards skills, language proficiency, ties to Canadian society, and other aspects conducive to rapid assimilation. The 2007 Senate debates revealed growing interest in a point system that would give somewhat greater weight than the current system does to skills and less to family ties. Another more controversial model would auction off visas, which presumably would go largely to those whose bright economic prospects in the United States helped finance their successful bids. Their productivity would benefit not only American society and their families but also their source countries, through remittances and technological and cultural transfer.

ILLEGAL IMMIGRATION

So long as the great American jobs machine attracts workers from nearby countries who are desperate to improve their incomes and cannot or will not wait for many years for a permanent visa, illegal migration will continue. Congress has already tried every reform strategy that seemed politically feasible. Some have produced modest improvements, others have made the problem worse. More border enforcement can help deter new illegal entrants, but it also encourages those who are already in the United States to remain rather than risk returning home and then being unable to reenter. Moreover, a few thousand National Guardsmen acting as advisers (the Bush administration's most recent tactic) will not succeed where more than twelve thousand Border Patrol agents have failed. The congressional immigration debates that climaxed in 2007 indicated widespread support for further expansion of the Border Patrol, further construction of a fence along portions of the southern border, improved surveillance and database technology, and other enforcement enhancements. Controlling visa abuse by lawful entrants, which accounts for almost half the illegal population, requires more effective screening by consular officials abroad, yet they operate under severe time and information constraints that are only growing worse. Indeed, Congress passed a bill in July 2007 that expands the visa waiver program, which enables more visitors from designated countries to enter without visas.

The legislation that the Senate debated and killed in June 2007 failed largely because of lack of agreement on a new program for giving legal status to the undocumented. Indeed, the senators bitterly disagreed over what to call it: "earned legalization" (proponents) or "amnesty for lawbreakers" (opponents). Nor could consensus be reached on the many other elements of such a program: trigger date, duration, eligibility criteria, employer sanctions, documentation, other antifraud safeguards, fees, a "touch-back" requirement to avoid queue-jumping, a path to citizenship, and so forth. Similar disagreements also defeated proposals for a new agricultural guest worker program. The debaters seemed to recognize both that mass deportation of undocumented workers was not a realistic prospect, and that every new hurdle to legal status simply meant that fewer of them would apply for it, defeating the whole purpose of the reform.

Some of the obstacles to meaningful reform are more cultural and bureaucratic than political. Americans will never view employers who hire willing workers as serious criminals; tough sanctions will rarely be imposed (2005 saw a grand total of three notices of intent to fine). Until the law requires everyone to carry a tamper-proof identity card (a measure common in Europe but opposed in the United States by civil liberties groups), and until the government's far-flung databases are better integrated and more reliable, resourceful and desperate foreign workers will continue to take their chances against the law—and will often win the bet. The REAL ID Act of 2005 was intended to help deal with the secure and fraud-resistant identification problem, but the states have strongly protested the costs associated with it, and Congress has postponed its implementation until 2009.

The battle against illegal immigration and the political rhetoric that it inspires lend themselves to a comforting illusion. Illegal immigration, after all, confers significant benefits on almost all concerned, while the costs of eliminating it (in terms of enforcement resources, opportunity costs, civil liberties, foreign policy interests, and so on) would be manifestly prohibitive. This means that the socially optimal level of illegal migration—the policy that balances its social benefits and costs—is far above zero. Indeed, in a nation of 300 million people, the optimal level may even exceed today's actual level. If so, the failure of immigration enforcement serves an important latent function by sustaining the attractive, reassuring, ennobling myth that the rule of law is a paramount, priceless ideal that we relentlessly pursue.

Despite the failure of comprehensive reform legislation in 2007, there is widespread agreement that the problems the reformers sought to address remain: a huge undocumented population, high demand for temporary agricultural workers, the need to compete for higher-skill immigrants, the porosity of the southern border, the pitifully inadequate database for effective enforcement of employer sanctions, and others. Some items on the reform agenda are more politically palatable than others, and it seems likely that certain pieces will be taken up separately and perhaps enacted, even before President Bush leaves office.

Immigrant Integration

The goal of immigrant integration (a less contentious term than "assimilation") is almost universally accepted by citizens and immigrants alike. This goal, however, raises a host of difficult questions. What does integration mean? Why is it a good thing? What is the national culture and identity into which immigrants are integrating? And how successful is the integration project? Many scholars (including me) have analyzed these crucial questions at length elsewhere.[20] Here, I address only the last: how well immigrants are being incorporated into American society today, briefly comparing the situation in the United States with that in Europe.

By almost any definition, the integration of immigrants into American life is proceeding rapidly, though at rates that differ from group to group (and indeed subgroup to subgroup). The dynamic U.S. economy, both formal and informal, produces a very low immigrant unemployment rate, in contrast to European economies. (In 2006, the unemployment rate for young French people was well over 20 percent, and it was higher for immigrant families.) Market pressures also magnify immigrants' intense desire to learn English. Most studies find that the immigrant generation acquires fluency at roughly the same rate as earlier waves did, that the one-and-a-half generation who arrived as children and second generation (American-born children of immigrants) learn it at school and strongly prefer it to their parents' native language, that virtually all of the second generation speak it proficiently by the end of high school, and that the third generation is largely monolingual in English and likes it that way. But this optimistic picture is marred by the estimated 3 million or more U.S.-born students with limited English proficiency (LEP) despite (or perhaps because of) bilingual education programs. Indeed, 10 percent of LEP students are third-generation Americans, and the 1990 U.S. Census found that almost 8 million households (8.3 percent of the U.S. total) were linguistically isolated, meaning that no person fourteen or older spoke English well.[21]

The rates of interethnic marriage (a strong sign, as well as a contributing cause, of integration) are very high, particularly marriages between Asian women and Hispanics and whites, and the residential integration of those groups into white-majority urban and suburban communities is growing rapidly.[22] Also important to the integration of immigrants are the allure and ethnic diversity of a powerful mass media and popular culture (including minority-dominated sports teams) and the receptiveness of America's religious communities to newcomers who are reinvigorating and often transforming these communities.

Although this swift pace of assimilation is generally desirable, one aspect of it has a darker side. In a process that sociologists of immigration call downward or segmented assimilation, very young immigrants and the young children of immigrants often adopt norms and conduct—gang membership and violence, rejection of parental and other authority, scorn for academic achievement, "gangsta" talk, and the like—all too common and dysfunctional in the United States, that may impede their future mobility and integration. Although immigrant parents try to use the cultures of origin to inoculate their children against these dangerous aspects of American life and to provide a cultural shelter and breathing space in which their youngsters can flourish, this is a daunting task, and some groups are more successful at it than others. Among at least some immigrant groups (e.g., Vietnamese), the best academic achievers are usually those who assimilate more *slowly* to American culture, while the delinquent youngsters are quicker to abandon their ethnic heritage. The earlier discussion of immigrant criminal activity suggests one important aspect of this problem.

Because Mexicans are the largest immigrant group by far, the pace of their integration is of special interest. A recent analysis of Mexican economic assimilation reveals a mixed picture: second-generation Mexican men and women are upwardly mobile but remain far behind whites.[23] Other groups exhibit equally intricate and multi-factored patterns.[24]

Multiculturalism, a perennial *casus belli* in the culture wars, affects the nature and process of immigrant integration into an ethnically diverse society.[25] Canada is officially, indeed constitutionally, committed to multiculturalism, and other states like Australia affirm it at a subconstitutional level. Although the United States has no explicit constitutional provision of that kind, the U.S. Supreme Court broadly interprets other principles to protect cultural diversity in religion, dress, language, and other areas. In addition, federal and state laws have established (and sometimes disestablished) specific multicultural policies like bilingual education. Indeed, so widespread are these policies in the United States that Nathan Glazer, an early skeptic concerning many of them, was able to write a book entitled *We Are All Multiculturalists Now,* though Glazer recognizes that this thin consensus ends as soon as a discussion of specific policies begins. Finally, increases in dual nationality, particularly among Mexicans and others from Latin America, may (views differ on this) slow immigrants' political integration into American society, a possibility that seems likely to arouse public concerns at some point, as it has begun to do in Canada.

If past is prologue, immigrants to the United States will shed some aspects of their ethnic identities as they live here, particularly in the second and third generations. The melting pot metaphor, then, is not obviously inapt, even when many immigration advocates and scholars now deride it or prefer other images like a mosaic or salad bowl. The kind of identity-stifling assimilation demanded by some in the Americanization movement, which arose early in the twentieth century and thrived amid the nationalist passions stoked by World War I, was often paternalistic, bigoted, and coercive. Despite these abuses (or perhaps *because* of them), it was quite effective at a time when the stakes in rapid integration were very high. More nuanced, well-designed, sensitively implemented, and diversity-friendly versions of Americanization would be welcome today.[26]

Even without such a program, however, immigrant incorporation in the United States has generally been far more successful than that in European countries. This is most obviously true in the case of Muslim immigrants to those countries, who express far more alienation than those in the United States.[27] In part, this reflects demographic differences between the groups. The roughly 2.5 million Muslims in the United States are highly diverse in terms of countries and regions of origin (Mideast, Africa, continental Asia, Indonesia, and other Pacific archipelagos); languages (Arabic, Farsi, Kurdish, Urdu, Hindi, and English); Islamic sect (Sunni, Shia, Ismaili, Druze, and Alawite); and even race (half of native-born Muslims, 20 percent of the total, are black). American Muslims are also more prosperous, well educated, politically active, and integrated into the larger society (including possessing American citizenship) than their European counterparts; indeed, American Muslims equal or exceed the income and education levels of the general population. Many Muslim families have been in the United States for three or more generations, while the Muslim migration to Europe largely began with the guest worker programs in the 1950s and has only recently reached significant levels. The greater religiosity of Americans makes for a more congenial environment for devout Muslims (and other immigrants) than in the far more secular societies of Europe. The lower barriers in the United States to family-based immigration, entrepreneurship, and employment growth also play their part, as does the traditional celebration of ethnic diversity in America.

None of this is to deny the existence of anti-Muslim sentiment and activity in the United States, particularly after 9/11. As political scientist Peter Skerry has emphasized, the targeting of Muslims as a group for special registration and questioning may be producing a degree of solidarity among Muslims that their pronounced diversity (in the many ways just mentioned) had previously denied them.[28] And while the vast majority of American Muslims are already plunging into the mainstream of broader community life, a significant minority of them (especially among young Muslims) harbor views about U.S. foreign policy, Jews, those responsible for the 9/11 attacks, and the value of Islamic jihadism and even of suicide bombing that resemble the extremist views that are all too common among Muslims in Europe, where they are arousing great fear and hostility in the general population.[29]

It would be churlish and misleading, however, to end an essay on immigration to America on so negative a note. The United States continues to be the world's strongest magnet for the talented, the ambitious, the dispossessed, and the desperate. It remains a country with immense assimilative capacity, which however strained never seems fully exhausted. Not only are immigrants essential to

America's soft and hard power in the world; perhaps more important, most Americans appreciate this fact, and recurrent political efforts to limit immigration almost invariably fail. If legal immigration
focuses on those with needed job skills and family ties to the United
States, undocumented migration (with its periodic amnesties) disproportionately favors those who come with little but a steely determination to make a better life. Together, they sustain a mythos of
rebirth and revitalization in America that never ceases to astonish.

CHAPTER 13

Black Americans

Orlando Patterson

As sociologist Orlando Patterson explains, the history of American race relations is filled with paradox: a Declaration of Independence that proclaimed equality, a Constitution that condoned slavery, a Civil War waged to end it, a long period of legally and socially enforced segregation, and a civil rights movement that repudiated this segregation and extended the equality principle to many groups other than blacks. Patterson brings an immense body of data and analysis to bear in chronicling the enormous progress that has been made by blacks in almost every area of American life as well as the difficult challenges—in terms of family breakdown, dysfunctional attitudes among many inner-city youths, social isolation, and educational deficits—that remain if they are to take advantage of the expanded opportunities available for the upwardly mobile.

No area of American society and culture is more easily misunderstood than the condition of blacks, and more generally, the nation's ethno-racial relations and policies. American history is a record of extreme oppression and near extermination of non-white peoples, yet also one of extraordinary effort and sacrifice on behalf of blacks, including a civil war in which thousands of non-blacks died. The American Declaration of Independence extolled the virtues of equality, yet its Constitution condoned slavery.

These paradoxes persist today. The civil rights movement and subsequent policies aimed at socioeconomic reform have resulted in

My thanks to Jessica S. Welburn for research assistance in preparing this chapter.

the largest group of middle-class and elite blacks in the world, several of them leading some of the most powerful corporations in the nation and the world; yet the bottom fifth of the black population is among the poorest in the nation and, as Hurricane Katrina exposed, often live in abysmal third world conditions. Politically, blacks are a powerful presence and the most loyal members of one of the nation's two leading parties; yet, "race" still remains a central component of American politics and sustains its most fundamental regional and ideological alignments. Blacks have a disproportionate impact on the nation's culture—both popular and elite—yet continue to face major problems in the educational system and are badly underrepresented in its scientific and high-end technology. And although legalized segregation has long been abolished and antiexclusionary laws strictly enforced, the great majority of blacks still live in highly segregated communities. It is a record of remarkable successes, mixed achievements, and major failures. Trying to make sense of them is a formidable challenge to American social scientists and other analysts.

Defining Ethno-Racial America

Who are black Americans, how many of them are there, and where do they live? Answering these seemingly simple questions illustrates the perplexities and contradictions of ethno-racial relations in America. Ethno-racial classification and counts is the joint product of the U.S. Census Bureau's disturbingly named "Department of Racial Statistics" and of the policy analysts and activist groups who wish to challenge the department's prevailing classification. The government lists numerous ethnic groups that are supposed to belong to five "races": White or Caucasian; Black or African-American; American Indian or Alaska Native; Asian; and Native Hawaiian and other Pacific Islander. In addition, the officially designated pan-ethnic category of Hispanic Americans or Latinos adds that "Hispanics can be of any racial group."

There is no sociological, anthropological, or logical foundation whatsoever for this classification, which David Hollinger has dubbed the "ethno-racial pentagon." Asian Americans and Hispanics are both clearly pan-ethnic groups embracing a vast array of distinct ancestry groups. Ethnically, the Japanese have nothing in common with South Asian Tamils, Laotian Hmong hill people, or the Ifugao people from the Philippines, but once they land in America they all become members of the Asian American "race." Similarly, American-born Puerto Ricans in New York, Mexican farm workers in Texas and California, and professionals from Argentina and Chile share little, except that their ancestors were once part of the Spanish empire and spoke a common imperial language, but the same is true of English, Irish, Barbadian, Jamaican, and Ghanaian immigrants who do not thereby constitute a "race." Stranger still is the department's insistence that although Asian Americans are a "race," Hispanics "can be of any racial group." Why does Asian regional origin constitute a "race," but Latin American does not, given that the former exhibits, if anything, greater somatic and cultural variation? One may speculate that the presence of blacks in Latin America, and their absence from the Asian mix, partly explains the difference in treatment.

To complicate matters further, the department, under pressure from "mixed race" Americans, a small but growing and vocal group, recently discarded centuries of official views on racial purity in allowing Americans not only to self-identify their "race" but to choose as many races as they pleased. The second of these innovations created a nightmare for demographers and sociologists. For, as Table 13.1 indicates, there are now six different ways of identifying and counting blacks, as well as the four other "racial" populations in America, yielding a total of thirty racial categories! Thus, one may refer to the "Black or African-American alone," population, of whom there are 37.5 million. There is the "Black or African-American in combination" population, meaning people who listed themselves as black as well as one or more other "races," which results in the largest population count and is strongly favored by black leaders. Third, there is the category of blacks who are not Hispanic or Latino. The "Not Hispanic" category exists mainly to distinguish traditional, mainstream whites of European ancestry from people designating themselves white who come from Latin America. Just why this distinction is needed is not entirely clear, unless some notion of the "truly white" still lingers from the nineteenth and early twentieth century, when the poverty and low status occupations of groups such as the Irish and southern Europeans made their claim to whiteness suspect.

The 2000 Census aroused much commentary on two apparent developments: that blacks had been displaced as the nation's largest

Table 13.1 Census Bureau's "Racial" Classification of the U.S. Population, 2004

Characteristics	Number (1,000)	% Total	% Change 2000–2004
TOTAL POPULATION	299,655	100	4.3
ONE RACE	299,217	99. 85	4.2
White alone	236,058	78. 8	2.5
Black or African American alone	37,502	12. 5	5.0
American Indian or Alaska native	2,825	.94	6.0
Asian alone	12,826	4. 3	16.0
Native Hawaiian and Pacific Islander	506	.17	9.3
TWO OR MORE RACES	4,439	1. 48	19.9
Race Alone or in Combination			
White	239,880	80 0	2.6
Black or African American	39,232	13. 1	5.7
American Indian or Alaska native	4,409	1. 49	4.4
Asian	13,957	4. 65	16.2
Native Hawaiian and Pacific Islander	976	.325	7.7
Race, Not Hispanic or Latino	252,898	84. 4	2.5
ONE RACE	249,478	83. 25	2.4
White alone	197,841	65. 02	1.2
Black or African American alone	35,964	12. 0	4.9
American Indian or Alaska native	2,207	.73	5.2
Asian alone	12,069	4. 02	16.5
Native Hawaiian and Pacific Islander	398	.13	8.5

Table 13.1 Continued

Characteristics	Number (1,000)	% Total	% Change 2000–2004
Two or More Races *Race Alone or in Combination*	3,855	1.3	13.2
White	201,148	67. 12	1.3
Black or African American	37,428	12. 5	5.4
American Indian or Alaska native	3,574	1. 2	3.4
Asian	13,580	4. 53	16.3
Native Hawaiian and Pacific Island	808	.27	6.8
Race, Hispanic or Latino	41,322	13. 78	17.0
One Race	40,739	13. 6	17.0
White alone	38,217	12. 75	17.5
Black or African American alone	1,539	.51	10.6
American Indian or Alaska native	618	.14	9.1
Asian alone	258		10.9
Native Hawaiian and Pacific Islander	107		12.8
Two or More Races *Race Alone or in Combination*	583	.19	18.7
White	38,732	12. 9	17.5
Black or African American	1,806	.60	12.5
American Indian or Alaska native	835	.27	8.6
Asian	427	.14	13.8
Native Hawaiian and Pacific Island	174	.05	12.0

SOURCE: Adapted from U.S. Census Bureau. *Statistical Abstract of the United States,* 2006. Table 13.

minority group by so-called Hispanics, and that the non-Hispanic white population was in sharp decline, with America well on the way to becoming a "majority-minority" nation. Thus, the Census Bureau recently announced that Texas had just joined California, Hawaii, and New Mexico as "majority-minority" states and that five other states, including Georgia and New York, were "next in line."[1]

These claims are sociologically suspect and politically mischievous. Blacks and Hispanics are not comparable. Hispanics, as just noted, constitute a cluster of very varied peoples whom certain ethnic leaders, for political and economic reasons, are trying hard to construct as a single ethnic group. Mexican Americans, Puerto Ricans, Cubans, and Guatemalans are distinct ethnic groups with very

different identities, socioeconomic statuses, and priorities. Blacks remain by far the nation's largest genuinely ethnic group.

The view that America is fast becoming a nation of ethno-racial
minorities only makes sense if we insist on considering current
non-Hispanic whites as the only mainstream whites of the future. In
fact, as Figure 13.1 shows, the population that considers itself white
is growing in absolute terms due to the massive infusion of white-
identified people from the Hispanic cluster and is declining very
slowly as a percent of the total population. In 2050, over 74 percent
of the total population will still be white-identified. Given the high
intermarriage rate of whites of the Hispanic cluster with non-
Hispanic whites, and the strong tendency of the progeny of such
unions to shed any Hispanic identity that leaders of their parents'
generation attempt to impose on them, the native white population

Figure 13.1   Projected U.S. Population by Ethnicity: 2000–2050

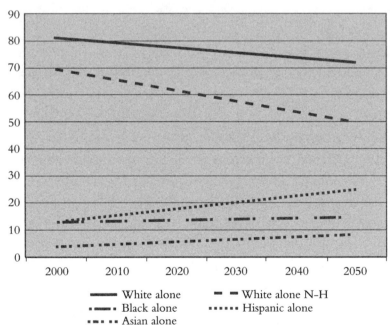

SOURCE: U.S. Census Bureau, 2004. "U.S Interim Projections by Age, Sex,
Race, and Hispanic Origin," Internet release date: March 18, 2004.

is very unlikely to dip below 70 percent at any time during this century, and its share may well begin to rise again after 2050.

Second, the different groups are geographically dispersed. The current wave of immigrants and their children is concentrated in only a few gateway metropolitan areas of certain regions, and the black population has a distinctive regional distribution. Figure 13.2 shows that the great majority of Hispanic and Asian ethnic groups are located in the West and South of the country. While blacks are still disproportionately located in the South, the proportion that does has declined dramatically since the start of the twentieth century when 90 percent of blacks were still living in the South.

The northern migration entailed more than a south-to-north transition; it was also largely a change from rural sharecropping or impoverished own-account farming to urban proletariat life. Indeed, the urbanization of the black population and its concentration into urban ghettos—which also occurred in the South—was as important as the regional change. As late as 1940, over a half of the black population was still rural (52.4 percent); within a decade, 62 percent was urban, and by 1960 nearly three in every four. The 1960s, however, marked the end of the migration out of the South,

Figure 13.2 Region of Residence by Ethnicity and Hispanic
Cluster, 2000

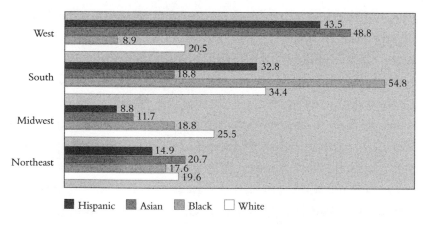

SOURCE: U.S. Census Bureau, "Demographic Profiles, Census 2000."

followed by a reversal of the flow as blacks began to move back to the South. This "new great migration," as it has been called, has accelerated; between 1995 and 2000, a net flow of 346,546 blacks went south. The South—especially the newly industrialized and expanding metropolitan areas of southern states such as Georgia, North Carolina, Florida, Texas, and Virginia—gained blacks from all other regions of the country but especially from the northeastern metropolitan regions. College-educated blacks led this reverse migration, the direct opposite of the earlier migration north, when the migrants were typically less educated than blacks already in the North. The present southern flow has expanded the black middle class, who now find greater economic opportunities and a more congenial cultural and social climate in the growth centers of the South and Southwest. And because this reverse flow is urban to urban, the highly urbanized location of the black population persists.

We should view the projected leveling off of the black population at between 14 and 15 percent of the total American population within this demographic context. It means that blacks will remain by far America's largest meaningful minority ethnic group for the foreseeable future.

The Historical Background

Between the late fifteenth and late nineteenth centuries, some 9.9 million Africans and their descendants were enslaved in the Americas, of whom less than 10 percent went to what became the United States. Comparing enslavement in Latin America, the West European systems of the Caribbean, and the United States, the latter had the most distinctive system.

First, the United States had a large resident Euro-American population, which, with the exception of the Carolinas up to the end of the eighteenth century, greatly outnumbered the slave population. Second, American slavery's greatest period of expansion— prompted by the cotton-based system of the deep South—came after external sources of slave supply were cut off in 1808. Relatedly, it was one of the few large-scale slave societies in world history in which the slave population reproduced itself. From the first half of the eighteenth century, native blacks outnumbered African new-comers, and blacks are among the earliest post-Columbian popu-lations of the United States. Finally, the United States is distinctive in the severity of its restriction of manumission and its hostility toward those few slaves who managed to gain their freedom.

The most important common consequence of slavery was the experience of racism: the deeply held prejudice that people of African and slave ancestry were genetically inferior and could be justifiably discriminated against in economic and social life. A sec-ond major feature of slavery was the natal alienation of the slave, the view that they were deracinated persons with no civic existence. This engendered among non-blacks the ingrained view of blacks as people who did not belong to the society at large, only to individu-als and private estates. That view was to persist, with devastating consequences, long after the formal abolition of slavery.

Another deleterious consequence of slavery is often overlooked: the fact that slaves could not own property—were themselves property owned by others—meant that the vast majority of them could never accumulate and pass on property to their descendants. Closely linked to the absence of material capital was the lack of ac-cumulated mainstream cultural, including technical, resources. Slaves were very carefully screened off from all the advanced cultural re-sources of Western culture, the most important being the capacity to read and write. In several of the slave states, slaves were taught some of the more basic technical skills, but even this was not allowed to be passed on: one of the cruelest developments in postemancipation America was the often violent exclusion of skilled ex-slaves by working-class whites, many of them recent immigrants, and their as-sociations. By the closing years of the nineteenth century, there were fewer skilled blacks than existed during the days of slavery.

Slavery also had certain devastating internal social consequences. The most important of these was the way it violated and distorted familial and gender relations throughout the Americas. The slave master encouraged the development of reproductive units and these have misled a whole generation of revisionist historians in America to the view that stable families existed under slavery. This is a historiographic travesty.[2] More recent scholarship has reemphasized the continuities between slavery and the fraught gender relations and fragile familial ties that have plagued black life to this day.

Finally, there was the tragic level of personal distrust that slavery created. It takes little imagination to understand how a slave population would come to view the slaveholding racial group with deep suspicion. Sadly, however, this distrust was directed also at fellow blacks and especially in male-female relationships. This lingers today in the fact that, by any measure, blacks express the lowest levels of trust in other persons and institutions of all ethnic groups.

The exclusion of blacks from the advanced and more public institutions of white society did have one major unintended effect that must surely rank as one of the great ironies of American civilization. This is the fact that blacks, drawing on their own invented resources, on those African cultural traditions that survived the middle passage and plantation life, and on those expressive and intimate areas of white cultures that they were exposed to, ended up creating one of the greatest, and perhaps the most distinctively American cultural traditions on the continent. Indeed, to the degree that America has a folk culture, it is that created by blacks, since all the other competing folk traditions—Appalachian, Cajun, Tejano, Chicano, Mountain, Okie, whatever—are either too local, too recent, or still too infused with their provenance to make such a claim.

Between Farm and City

Unlike other slave systems in the Americas, U.S. slavery only ended after a savage civil war which engendered deep bitterness in the Caucasian population that was taken out on the ex-slaves. Indeed, what emerged in the United States was a neo-doulotic system in which the personal ownership of the master was ended but the culture of slavery persisted. The withdrawal of northern military presence after Reconstruction resulted in a seventy-five-year disaster: a vicious system of terror during which some five thousand African-Americans were slaughtered, many of them ritually burnt alive.[3]

As was untrue for Latin America, there emerged in the United States a binary conception of "race" more commonly known as the one-drop rule: the classification of all persons either as "white" or "black," including in the latter category all persons with any known African ancestry, however somatically light-skinned they may be. Although originally motivated by notions of racial purity, both blacks and whites came to accept this binary system, which, ironically, later worked to the benefit of blacks since it has forced successful blacks who looked Caucasian, and who in Latin America would have been defined out of the group, to identify with blacks and provide them with leadership. In Latin America, which recognizes a continuum between white and black, poverty integrates, while in North America it segregates. Above the middle classes of Latin America, however, there is a sharply demarcated ceiling, and elites are now far more exclusively white and racist than those of the United States, propagandistic talk of racial democracy notwithstanding.

The period between the end of Reconstruction and World War II witnessed important developments in black life, in spite of the unrelenting tyranny of the Jim Crow system and the hostility of northern labor and political elites. In the South, communities consolidated and various kinds of proto-political activities developed, ranging from the shrewd accommodationism of Booker T. Washington that shrouded a subversive cultivation of black pride and self-help, to the emigrationist or separatist nationalism of those who had given up on America. In the North, the emergence and growth of the NAACP laid the foundation of the biracial coalition that was to transform national politics later in the century. And the separatist Universal Negro Improvement Association, led by the Jamaican back-to-Africa nationalist, Marcus Garvey, initiated the first mass movement of urban blacks, with surprising links to the rural South. In New York, more conservative West Indians—the generation that nurtured Colin Powell—paved the way in urban coalition politics. It is, nonetheless, an exaggeration to rebrand the subaltern and highly localized coalitions, solidarities, rumors, church meetings, and kin-based networks of the rural South as elements of a major political process that "decisively shaped the South and the nation," as some revisionist historians have attempted.[4]

Politically thwarted by the violent white majority and a compliant judicial system, blacks turned their creative energies instead toward the cultural and spiritual arenas, with truly remarkable results. Within a half century, they had generated major cultural genres in music, folk arts, and dance and, as a growing body of cultural research indicates, had inaugurated a vibrant literary movement that reached its first high point in the Harlem Renaissance of the 1920s. And while the black church was in large part pacific in relation to the white world, it quietly fashioned the institutional foundation as well as the rhetorical strategies upon which Martin Luther King and other leaders of the Southern Christian Leadership Conference would later build.

From the Civil Rights Era to the Present: Achievements and Failures

The civil rights movement was transformative, setting in motion radical changes in the political, social, cultural, and economic life of blacks. Using 1964 as a base—the year of the passage of the Civil Rights Act and the high point of the movement—let us examine the degree to which the condition of blacks has changed and the problems that still beset the group. In absolute terms, there has been striking progress, but when compared to changes in the white population, the record is decidedly mixed, and in a few areas quite disappointing.

Most remarkable for a group that spent most of its history in brutal slavery is its integration into the nation's social, cultural, and moral fabric. In less than half a human generation, America not only dismantled the entire infrastructure of Jim Crow but included black Americans as an integral part of any moral and political vision of what is American.

The black cultural and political presence in contemporary America is, if anything, out of all proportion to the size of the black population, leading many Americans, black and white, to wildly erroneous views about its actual size. As one of the base constituencies of the Democratic Party, blacks are now fully represented in the nation's political offices at all levels. Many of the nation's major cities have been led by black mayors. The Congressional Black Caucus is an important, if not always effective, force in national politics. With supreme historic irony, the first black to be elected governor held office in Richmond, the capital of the Confederate states; another was recently elected governor of Massachusetts. In the mid-1990s a black general, Colin Powell, stood a strong chance of becoming the Republican presidential candidate until he voluntarily withdrew from the primaries. Today, one of the nation's most popular senators, Barack Obama of Illinois, is a major contender for the Democratic Party's presidential nomination. Many of these blacks were elected by constituencies which were or are predominantly white. In addition to elected officials, blacks have been appointed to some of the highest appointed offices in the nation, including the head of the military and the secretary of state.

Paralleling this political transformation has been a cultural revolution. In all aspects of its high and popular cultures—music, art, literature, dance, fashion, education, sports, cinema, and television—the black presence is not only pronounced but in many areas dominant. American popular culture, in sharp contrast with the nation's political repute, is now globally hegemonic, thanks in good part to black artists and athletes.

Behind these developments are undeniable changes in the racial attitudes of white Americans. Most competent students of public opinion now agree that the great majority of whites reject traditional supremacist views and, in principle, favor integration and increased opportunities for blacks and other disadvantaged groups. Numerous polls also indicate that a majority of whites are tolerant about interracial unions. All surveys find an inverse relationship between age and liberality of racial views, with young people now favoring racial equality and interracial dating by wide margins. However, while favoring racial equality in principle, the views of whites are more complex and less uniformly interventionist in regard to the policies and practices, discussed below, that are aimed at greater equalization. For now, the point to note is that there has been a genuine sea shift in the attitude of the white majority regarding the civic inclusion of blacks and the provision of equal access to public institutions. Racism itself has not vanished; my own estimate, based on polling and voting behavior, is that about 20 percent of the white population still remains racist in the traditional sense. Furthermore, some negative stereotyping persists even among those who may reject traditional, supremacist racism. For example, a little over a half of all whites believe that blacks are more likely to prefer living off welfare, and police profiling remained a serious problem up to a decade ago.

What accounts for the striking changes in white attitudes? It is certainly true that economic, demographic, and other structural factors encouraged attitudinal and cultural changes, but I reject the priority given to materialist or structuralist factors by many sociologists. The most cursory examination of the comparative data on ethno-racial prejudice provides numerous instances of group progress independent of prejudicial attitudes toward them, as in the case of European Jews.

Among the factors leading to a change in attitudes toward racism was the Nazi holocaust, World War II, and America's emergence as a superpower. Nazism brought racial prejudice into tremendous disrepute. Closely related also was the fact that America's emergence as one of the two great superpowers in the postwar era and its promotion of itself as the leader of the free world were greatly compromised by the existence of Jim Crow and the general condition of blacks throughout the nation, as Gunnar Myrdal's now classic report, *An American Dilemma,* made clear to the world. Of equal importance were the changes in the attitudes of blacks themselves. The wartime experiences of blacks, both in the military and in the greatly expanded job opportunities of the war economy, were powerful catalysts. But of equal importance were the previously noted reforms in black Christian doctrine and practice. The Ghandi-influenced non-violent doctrine of Martin Luther King, Jr., and his associates was no doubt influential in shifting white attitudes toward a national consensus that racism and the institutional constraints on blacks were morally indefensible and had to go.

Material Progress

Changes in the material condition of blacks have been facilitated most by the greatly improved opportunities for education. However, these impressive improvements should be considered in relation to the greater changes in white attainment.

As Figure 13.3 shows, blacks have made striking progress in high school completion rates, especially between 1960 and 1980, substantially reducing the gap between blacks and whites. Nonetheless, the official statistics may fudge the true rates, in part because of political and economic pressure to show good results. For example, completion rates are given only for students who become seniors, not for all students who ever enrolled. The true rate, according to some studies, is more like 78 percent for whites and 56 percent for blacks, twice the gap indicated by the official figures.[5]

The substantial gap between the groups in college graduation rates may be widening. Of special concern is the gender gap among blacks that is now growing wider each year. Nonetheless, the quintupling of college graduation rates from 3.5 percent of the twenty-five to twenty-nine age group to almost 18 percent has propelled what may be the most significant socioeconomic development over

Figure 13.3   Educational Attainment by Ethnicity, Persons Age 25
               and Older, 1940–2005

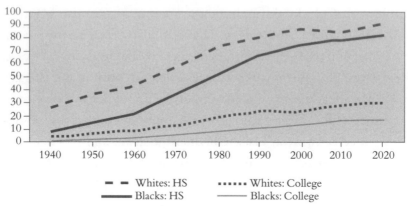

SOURCE: National Center for Education Statistics, *Digest of Education Statistics*,
2006.

the past forty years: the growth of a substantial black middle class.
Evaluating middle-class status is a complex matter, too often treated
superficially in simple income terms. Being middle class entails a
mix of income, wealth, education, occupational status, and, to some
degree, lifestyle.

The American median household income in 2003 (expressed in
2005 dollars) was approximately $46,000. If we take $50,000 as the
bottom end of middle-class family incomes, 34 percent of blacks,
compared with 59 percent of whites, earned income at or above this
figure. Many analysts would place the middle-class income bar for
households somewhat higher, more in the $75,000 or more range.
Only 17.4 percent of blacks fall into this income category, compared with 37.7 percent of whites.[6] A realistic estimate would fall
somewhere between these two—roughly a quarter to 30 percent
of the black population. This is well above the 12 to 14 percent of
black households that qualified in 1972 using similar measures, but
in relative terms the situation has improved only slightly and in the
last few years the gap has widened. In constant dollars, the white
median household income inched up only slightly (by $130) be-

Figure 13.4   Income Quintiles and Black Mean Quintile Income
as a Percent of White

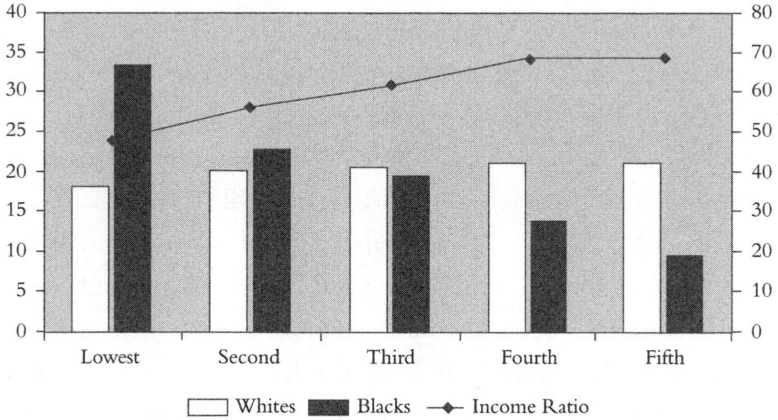

SOURCE: Composed from U.S. Census Bureau, *Annual Demographic Survey*, March Supplement, 2006, Table HING–05.

tween 2003 and 2005 to $49,554, while that of blacks declined significantly by $552, down to $30,954 annually.

Another, perhaps more accurate, way of assessing the relative income status of blacks is to look at household income quintiles (see Figure 13.4). By most measures, the third and fourth quintiles would constitute the broad range of middle-income families. A third of black households fall into this category, compared with 41 percent of whites. Note that there are over twice as many whites in the fifth quintile as blacks. This figure indicates another important feature of black income distribution: it is more unevenly distributed than that of any of the other major groups. Over a third of all black households are in the lowest quintile. But the relative quintile distribution tells only a part of the story. In each quintile the mean income of whites is substantially more than that of blacks. The mean income of the bottom quintile for whites is $16,440, compared with the lowest black mean of $7,869. For the other quintiles the white means are $37,036, $57,867, $84,155, and $169,871. The line graph shows the black mean for each quintile as a percentage of these white means. It indicates that better-off blacks earn a somewhat higher ratio of the mean white income, but this rises only to 68.5 percent for the top quintile. Furthermore, the historical trend in these ratios (not shown) is discouraging. The mean income of the top quintile has remained the same percent (68) of its white counterpart between 1967 and the present. The third and fourth quintiles showed modest improvements, moving up between 8 and 10 percentage points. However, the bottom quintile's ratio has gotten much worse. It is now 48 percent of what the bottom fifth of whites earn, compared with 54 percent in 1967. Thus, in both relative and absolute terms, the black poor have lost out badly in relation to the white poor as well as in relation to the black middle and upper classes. Given the growth of income inequality in America, this situation is likely to get much worse in coming years. A recent study shows that 54 percent of African-American children of parents in the lowest quintile remain in the bottom, in contrast with 31 percent of the poorest white children.[7]

The relative fragility of the black middle class's base becomes apparent when we shift from income to net worth, a more complete picture of economic status. In 2000 the median net worth of non-Hispanic whites was $79,400, which was 10.5 times that of black householders, estimated at $7,500. This enormous gap is growing. Since 1996 the median wealth of blacks has been declining while that of non-Hispanic whites and people in the Hispanic cluster have been increasing, a gap widened by the economic downturn that began in late 2000. As of 2002, the median net worth of non-Hispanic whites was $88,000, which was 14.5 times greater than that of black householders, which went down to $6,000.[8]

What accounts for this enormous gap? Differences in education and other forms of human and social capital only partly explain it because a substantial gap remains even after controlling for these factors. Asset difference matters most, capturing "the historical legacy of low wages, personal and organizational discrimination, and institutionalized racism."[9] Home ownership is the single most important source of wealth for most Americans, and many middle-class whites acquired homes either through inheritance or with the help of their parents. Until as late as the 1960s, U.S. government housing policies actively discriminated against blacks and favored whites in mortgage and other housing policies. The suburbs in the postwar era also discriminated against blacks who were either deliberately kept out as a result of naked racism or disqualified on other terms that Oliver and Shapiro refer to as the "sedimentation of racial inequality."[10] Housing in segregated neighborhoods is worth substantially less than similar units in white or non-segregated neighborhoods.

But differences in wealth accumulation over a single generation for blacks and whites with similar incomes and education may partly reflect different lifestyle choices. International comparisons indicate, for example, striking variations across Europe in homeownership. In Bulgaria, Ireland, and the United Kingdom, 80, 74, and 68 percent, respectively, of homes are owner-occupied, whereas Switzerland, perhaps the world's most prosperous country, had a rate of only 34.6 percent in 2000. Parisians, with a rate of only 29.6 percent, make blacks, with a rate of 48 percent, seem like conservative burghers. The Swedish economist Mikael Atterhog observes that "different people may attach different importance to these [homeownership] values and these value orientations may differ between populations (nations) and between groups within a population."[11] He also notes disadvantages to homeownership that may influence different groups in different ways: it restricts residential mobility, and it may trap people in poorly maintained buildings or neighborhoods and impose substantial opportunity costs and debt risks. Sadly, his analysis has proven prescient in light of the sub-prime mortgage crisis of 2007 in America. African-Americans were between 6 and 34 percent more likely to receive a higher-rate sub-prime loan with a prepayment penalty than similarly financially situated white borrowers.[12] Largely as a result of this, there was a projected net loss to foreclosures of 9 percent of all homes purchased or refinanced by African-Americans in 2005.[13]

In a recent study of interactions between different black communities,[14] Mary Pattillo-McCoy disputes the view, made popular by William Julius Wilson, that the black middle class has withdrawn from the lower classes into their own suburban enclaves, thereby denuding the other group of leadership and role models. She found just the opposite: that these enclaves are themselves highly segregated and either adjoin or overlap with lower-class ghetto areas and become a kind of buffer between the black poor and the white middle class. They share many neighborhood facilities with the black poor and only partly succeed in limiting the encroachment of the black lower class and its problems. Even in very stable communities, networks promote access both to positive role models and to the "criminal temptations" and other pathologies of lower-class black life. Middle-class black youth are especially vulnerable to these temptations. Pattillo-McCoy's work highlights a tragic irony: the major source of black culture's outsized influence in the nation's popular culture and sports is the problem-ridden urban lower class. Successful entertainers and athletes from the ghetto are heavily promoted by the national media, providing middle-class black youth "a fashion and behavioral manual for deviance" while scoffing at "the ordinariness of middle-classdom."

The black middle class, limited in the pre–civil rights era, always had to deal with a socially deviant but culturally creative lower class. But earlier generations of middle-class parents managed to better protect their children from the problematic aspects of lower-class black life. They had strong help from the black church, which then embraced all middle-class youth, and they did not have to compete with a powerful mass media that relentlessly undermined their authority by celebrating the most deviant expressions of "gangsta" culture. This problem, combined with persistent (albeit greatly lessened) labor market discrimination, the black middle class' fragile wealth base, social and residential isolation from the dominant white majority, lower quality education and children's segregation, and the strain of coping with real and imagined racial slights and prejudice, may account for startling recent findings concerning inter-generational mobility from black middle class status. A joint Pew Foundation/Brookings Institution study reports that "a majority of black children of middle-income parents fall below their parents in income and economic status" and, more alarmingly, that about a half of the children of middle class African-Americans "end up falling to the bottom of the income distribution, compared to only 16 percent of white children."[15] These findings are consistent with those of other recent studies.[16]

All of which bring us to the less successful and failed aspects of post–civil rights America. Persistent residential segregation ranks among the most important failures. In their frequently cited work, *American Apartheid*, Massey and Denton described segregation in the 1970s and 1980s as a form of apartheid caused by deliberate racial practices and policies by the private sector and government. America today remains highly segregated residentially.

Table 13.2 indicates a black-white dissimilarity index of 58.7— meaning that almost 60 percent of blacks would have to move to realize a distribution across neighborhoods that reflected their actual proportion of the population—for all metropolitan areas, compared with 42.9 for Asians and 42.2 for ethnics of the Hispanic cluster. Both the level of segregation and the extent to which it is changing vary considerably by region. The highest segregation rates in metropolitan areas are, surprisingly, in the "liberal" regions of the Northeast and Midwest: Gary, Indiana; Detroit; New York; Newark; Milwaukee; and Chicago. Southern metropolitan areas have significantly lower dissimilarity rates than the Northeast. The lowest rates are found mainly in the Western states.

Recent trends, however, are modestly encouraging. Segregation between blacks and whites throughout the nation is clearly declining. The same is true of white-Asian segregation, which had been increasing up to 1980. White-Hispanic segregation has increased a bit, due largely to the massive growth of the Hispanic immigrant population. Declines in segregation are greatest in the newer, smaller,

Table 13.2   Mean Indices of Dissimilarity with Whites, 2000, and Changes for Blacks, Asians, and Hispanics (Metropolitan Areas)

Metro Category	Indices of Dissimilarity versus Whites*								
	BLACKS VS. WHITES			ASIANS VS. WHITES			HISPANICS VS. WHITES		
Mean Index N**	2000	Change 1990– 2000	Percent with declines	2000	Change 1990– 2000	Percent with declines	2000	Change 1990– 2000	Percent with declines
All Metropolitan Areas									
Mean Index	58.7	-4.7	93%	42.9	-3.8	83%	44.2	1.7	43%
N	287			236			281		
Region									
Northeast	66.0	-3.3	93%	46.4	-1.4	69%	54.0	0.0	48%
N	44			36			42		
Midwest	63.2	-5.1	95%	46.6	-5.6	93%	42.9	1.0	52%
N	65			57			66		
South	58.8	-4.6	91%	42.6	-3.9	86%	42.9	2.7	38%
N	125			88			109		
West	46.7	-5.8	94%	37.6	-3.2	80%	41.1	1.7	36%
N	53			55			64		
Size									
1,000,000 and over	65.9	-4.1	97%	44.5	-0.8	61%	51.0	4.5	18%
N	61			61			61		
250,000– 9,999,000	58.8	-4.9	93%	42.6	-4.3	94%	44.7	1.5	41%
N	112			111			116		
Under 250,000	54.7	-4.7	91%	42.1	-5.6	89%	39.6	0.2	58%
N	114			64			104		

* Whites, blacks, and Asians pertain to non-Hispanic members of these groups; non-Hispanic persons who identified as more than one race in 2000 were proportionately allocated to these groups (see text).

** Metropolitan areas with at least one thousand members of race-ethnic group in 1990 and 2000.

SOURCE: William H. Frey and Dowell Myers, "Racial Segregation in U.S. Metropolitan Areas and Cities, 1990–2000: Patterns, Trends, and Explanations" (Population Studies Center, University of Michigan, Report 05–573, April 2005), Table A1, 38.

faster-growing metropolitan areas of the South and West with small but growing black populations and considerable housing construction. Areas with declining segregation are also multi-ethnic: diversity seems to increase white tolerance for a higher proportion of black neighbors.[17] In addition, the higher the ratio of black household income to that of whites, the lower the predicted level of segregation, which strongly suggests that class explains much segregation.[18]

Why, then, does the black middle class remain so segregated? Sociologists maintain that white racism remains the main culprit, but this ignores the preferences of black middle-class householders. Surveys show that while blacks would prefer integrated neighborhoods, they do not wish to live in areas where their proportion is under 40 percent, which is more than triple their proportion of the nation's population, whereas most whites say they are comfortable with a black share of about 30 percent, more than twice the black population share.

A famous model of residential segregation, developed by economist Thomas Schelling, holds that even a very small difference between the size of whites' preferences for living with fellow whites and the size of blacks' preferences for living with fellow blacks will trigger a tipping point leading to total segregation. However, there is no empirical foundation for this model. Recently, the economist William Easterly has shown that, contrary to the model's predictions, more white flight occurred from neighborhoods with large initial white population shares than from mixed neighborhoods and that the demographic history of neighborhoods that did change or tip did not accord with Schelling's tipping point theory.[19] In the vast majority of neighborhoods studied, Easterly found no pattern of acceleration of white decline, no evidence of a sudden, extreme exodus at the fabled tipping point but instead a steady, almost constant decline in the proportion of whites from one decade to the next since the 1970s. Moreover, the typical neighborhood that did change from being more white to more black in this period still had a significant proportion of whites living in it, in sharp contradiction to Schelling's model.

If there are signs of progress in desegregation, the same cannot be said of the seemingly intractable problems of poverty; relatively high unemployment; extraordinarily high incarceration rates for black men; extremely high levels of criminal victimization; high levels of impoverished female-headed households and paternal abandonment, and extremely fraught gender relations resulting in low rates of marriage and high rates of marital disruption; and a growing AIDS epidemic, itself reflective of poor health and low life expectancy.

In 2005 nearly 23 percent (22.8) of all black families and 25.6 percent of all black individuals were in poverty; the general national rate was 12.6 percent, with individual whites having a rate of 10.4 percent and households 7.5 percent. As Figure 13.5 shows, between the late 1950s and mid–1970s, the black rate declined dramatically, from 55 to 30 percent, but the trend since then has been disappointing. Unemployment and underemployment are the main culprits. The overall rate has remained twice that of whites from the early 1970s, even while falling to historic lows of under 10 percent in the late 1990s and again in 2006 when it stood at 8.8 percent, compared with the white rate of 3.8 percent. But an increasing proportion of the impoverished are working people who, because of inadequate skills and education, cannot earn enough to rise above the poverty line. And general unemployment rates conceal the exceedingly high youth unemployment rate of 37 percent among young black men. The true rate, however, is even higher because it neglects the substantially lower labor force participation rate among young black men and the astonishingly high proportion of young black men in prison or jail, who are not included in the unemployment figures.[20]

As of June 2005, approximately 25 percent of the 2.2 million persons incarcerated in U.S. prisons and jails were black men between twenty and thirty-nine years of age. Twelve percent of all black men between twenty-five and twenty-nine were incarcerated, compared with 3.9 percent of Hispanics and 1.7 percent of white

Figure 13.5   Black and White Poverty Rates, 1959–2005

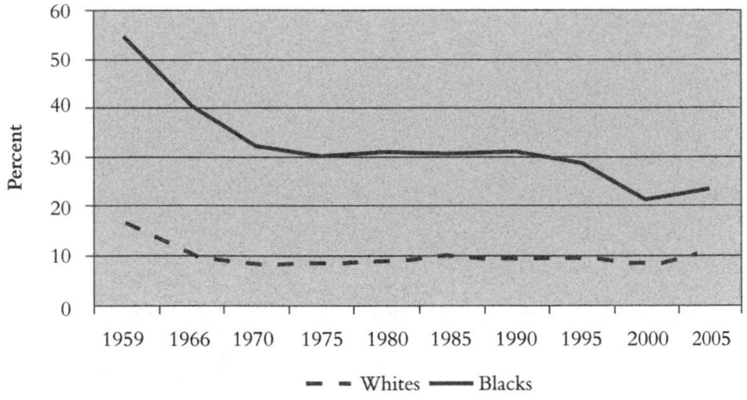

SOURCE: U.S. Census Bureau, "Historical Poverty Tables," www.census.gov/
hhes/www/poverty/histpov/hstpov2.html.

males of that age group.[21] Figure 13.6 shows the grimness of this
explosive growth since 1990 when the black rate was 6.3 times that
of whites. The only news that is not utterly bleak is the fact that the
black rate has gone down from 6.3 times the white rate to 4.8
times—but this is because the white rate nearly doubled. This high
rate is correlated with poor educational attainment. Western observes that six of every ten male high school dropouts in their thirties have an average prison record of approximately twenty-eight
months.[22] It is not clear, however, how much the *growing* incarceration rate is explained by education. Dropout rates have remained
fairly constant over the past thirty years at a time when the crime
and incarceration rates have oscillated wildly. More tellingly, the
black dropout rate of 13.1 percent (calculated as the proportion of
people ages sixteen to twenty-four out of school without a high
school certificate) is less than half that of the Hispanic rate of 27.8
percent, not to mention the horrendous dropout rate of 44 percent
for immigrants from Latin America. Yet, as we have seen, people in
the Hispanic cluster are substantially less likely to be incarcerated
than blacks.

Figure 13.6   Incarcerated Male Population per 100,000 Residents by Age and Ethnicity

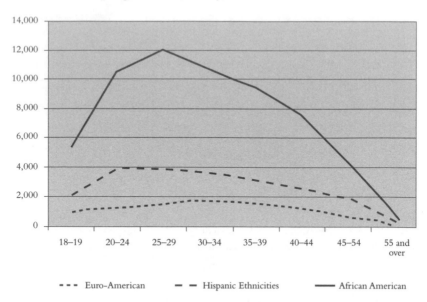

SOURCE: Based on data from U.S. Bureau of Justice Statistics, "Prison and Jail Inmates at Midyear 2005," Table 13, U.S. Department of Justice, 2006.

A better explanation is the epidemic of drug use and sale in the ghettos since the 1970s and the draconian laws passed in the so-called war on drugs. These laws disproportionately affect black youths by meting out far more severe punishment for the kinds of drugs that they are more likely to use. But the war on drugs can explain only a part of the extremely high crime and incarceration of blacks. As the liberal criminologist Michael Tolnay concludes, the evidence points to a simple explanation: young, poor black men are incarcerated at far higher rates because they commit far more imprisonable crimes.[23] The statistic for homicide is immune from the charge of racism. Figure 13.7 shows the tragic facts, and one need only add that almost all the victims of this carnage are fellow blacks, and that the black female homicide rate is actually higher than the white male rate.

Figure 13.7   Homicide Rates by Ethnicity and Gender,
1980–2002

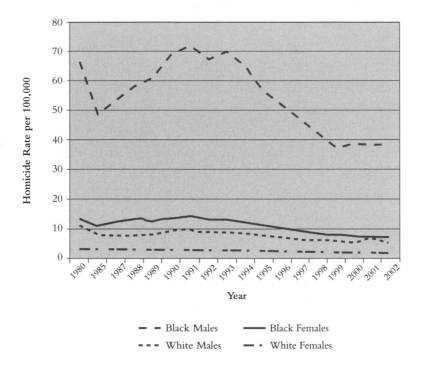

SOURCE: Erika Harrell, *Black Victims of Violent Crime* (Washington, DC:
Bureau of Justice Statistics, 2007).

We get closer to a genuine causal explanation by considering
household composition, especially within the wider framework of
gender relations and marital status. Blacks marry at far lower rates
than any other ethnic group. In 2004 only 28.4 percent of black
women over fifteen were married and living with their spouse,
while 42 percent had never married, compared with 54 and 21.5
percent of white women, respectively. When blacks do marry, their
divorce rates are substantially higher than other groups: after ten
years, 47 percent of first marriages among blacks are dissolved, compared with 32 percent of whites and 34 percent of Hispanics. And
after first divorce, a much lower proportion of black women remarry: ten years later, there is only a 50 percent probability of

remarriage; the probability is nearly 80 percent among white women and 68 percent among Hispanics.[24] Consequently, black adults, especially women, are far more likely to live without adult company: 72 percent of black women are on their own, including even many of those who are formally married but whose husbands are away, compared with 46 percent of white women and a half of all Hispanic women.

These figures, seldom mentioned, underscore the fact that blacks are among the most isolated of Americans—isolated collectively in their segregation from other groups but also isolated from basic human companionship in their lack of stable, durable adult relationships. They are also the loneliest. The common notion that they have wide friendship patterns and enriching communities that compensate for their absence of dyadic bonds is a complete myth: network data on the group indicate that they have the fewest friends and relatives to turn to for material and emotional help.[25]

The other major consequence of blacks' low rate of stable unions is more often commented on: the high proportion of households headed by a single woman and its deleterious consequences. An almost equal number of black families are headed by a single female (44.7) as a married couple (46.5 percent), compared with white families, 82 percent of which are headed by a married couple and only 13 percent by a single woman, or Hispanics, among whom the rates are 71 and 20 percent, respectively. The much higher risk of poverty in female-headed households thus partly accounts for the higher poverty rates of blacks. As Figure 13.8 shows, the risks of poverty are substantial for all groups, but there is an important additional difference between blacks and other groups that the figure masks: a much larger proportion of blacks, and especially their children, live in these households with consequences that go well beyond the already harsh realities of income poverty. Figure 13.9 demonstrates what I mean.

Figure 13.8   Poverty Rate by Family Type and Ethnicity, 2005

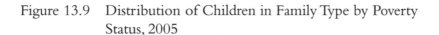

SOURCE: U.S. Census Bureau, Current Population Survey, *Annual Social and Economic Supplement*, 2006.

Figure 13.9   Distribution of Children in Family Type by Poverty
Status, 2005

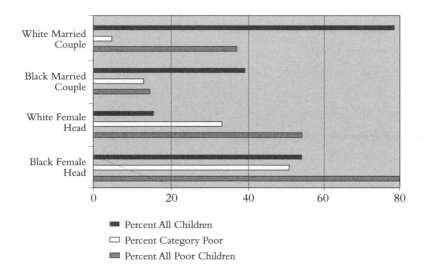

SOURCE: U.S. Census Bureau, Current Population Survey, *Annual Social and Economic Supplement*, 2006.

Note first that over half of all black children are poor, compared with 12.5 percent of whites. Second, most black children are being raised in households headed by a single woman—54.4 percent compared with 39.4 percent of white kids. Now while poverty per se undoubtedly has many disadvantages for children, a growing body of research suggests that its effects are surprisingly modest.[26] Of equal concern is the fact that 80 percent of all poor children are being brought up by single mothers, compared with 54 percent of poor white children. This distribution is important. The disadvantages of being brought up by a single mother go beyond the risk of being poor: being raised by a single mother also increases the risk of lower educational attainment, higher delinquency, poorer health, and becoming an unwed parent.[27] Thus, children who are poor but are being brought up in stable families headed by a couple have substantially better life prospects than those being brought up by a single parent. The single most important contrast between whites and blacks, then, is the fact that there are three and a half times as many children being brought up by single mothers among blacks (54 percent) than among whites (15.5 percent). Furthermore, black female-headed families differ from their white counterparts in that the vast majority of the former originate in unwed pregnancies, while the majority of the latter originate in divorce. Thus, the white child growing up with a single mother is less likely to have been exposed to poverty in early childhood before the parents divorced, when the effects are likely to be most harmful, especially for cognitive development.

Further complicating the situation of the black poor is the large influx of immigrants that began to pour into America from the mid-1960s. There were 35.7 million foreign-born persons in America in 2005, to which should be added at least another 10 million unauthorized persons, substantially above the 38 million black (alone) population that year. Economists are deeply divided about the impact of this inflow on the native population and especially on blacks.[28] Most immigrants are located in areas of the country with a smaller proportion of blacks. However, there are major overlaps in several of the gateway metropolitan areas such as New York, Chicago, and Miami, and here the weight of evidence does suggest a modest depression of income for unskilled natives and even greater employment consequences. Even so, immigrants seem not to be competing directly with most blacks in these areas. Middle-class and secure working-class blacks occupy occupational niches in the public sector that are largely closed to immigrants.[29] And, by increasing the size of these metropolitan populations, immigrants enhance the demand for public services, thereby benefiting the black middle class. On the other hand, immigrants increasingly dominate the low-end service jobs and a surprising number of better-paid service occupations in these areas, just the kind of jobs the unskilled black poor need. There is some evidence that some blacks may have been pushed out of these jobs by immigrants, who are often preferred by employers.[30] There is evidence, too, that immigration is changing the nature of employment for unskilled labor, creating an off-the-books, contractor-dominated informal labor market that has a disproportionately adverse effect on the black working poor.[31]

Another serious problem of the black population is its disproportionate and growing health risks. The Centers for Disease Control and Prevention documents this crisis:

[T]he infant death rate among blacks is still more than double that of whites, heart disease death rates are more than 40 percent higher, and the death rate for all cancers is 30 percent higher and for prostate cancer more than double that for whites. Black women have a higher death rate from breast cancer despite a mammography screening rate that is nearly the same as for white women. The death rate from HIV/AIDS for Blacks is more than seven times that for whites; the rate of homicide is six times higher.

Life expectancy at birth is the best index of a group's overall health and physical life prospects. For blacks, it is 72.7 years—69 for men and 76.1 years for women—compared with 78 and 80.5 years for white men and women, respectively. Remarkably, the black rates are lower than those of the Third World countries of Jamaica (75 years) and Barbados (74 years), even though the three populations have nearly identical regional provenance in Africa and thus are subject to the same kinds of genetically determined diseases such as sickle cell anemia and high rates of prostate cancer.

What, then, can explain the lower life expectancy? The answers are found partly in differences in access to, and willingness to use, health care at all levels of income; partly in cultural and behavioral practices; and partly in the psychological stress of living as a racial minority. Blacks have poorer access to adequate health care, but the reasons for this are still not clear. Racial bias in the health care profession is generally not considered a major factor.[32] The disparity remains when income is held constant; indeed, differences persist even when controlling for insurance coverage. Cultural and behavioral factors are obviously implicated.

This is particularly true with the extremely high incidence of AIDS among black men and women. Half of all new AIDS cases in the nation are among blacks, and in 2004 the disease was diagnosed ten times more often in blacks than in whites. Black women were diagnosed at twenty-three times the rate for white women. The disease ranked among the top three killers of black men aged twenty-five to fifty-four, among the top four causes of death among women in this age group, and as the main cause of death among black women between twenty-five and thirty-four. A major reason for the high rate of the disease among black women is the "down low" behavior of bisexual gay black men who conceal their sexual orientation from their wives and female lovers and are often themselves unaware of the fact that they are infected, thereby becoming an infectious "bridge" between gay men and heterosexual women. An increasing number of young black women live in fear of catching the disease in this way.

Policies and Prospects

The positive changes we have identified are the combined result of blacks' individual and collective agency as well as bitterly contested and hard-won public policy and legal transformations aimed at creating a more favorable environment for them. The two programs that have generated most controversy were mandatory busing to achieve school integration and affirmative action.

Busing failed to achieve its goal of integrating the nation's public schools. Indeed, the typical black and Latino child now goes to a school that is more segregated today than in the late sixties.[33] The failure was largely a reflection of the persisting spatial segregation of blacks from whites, now reinforced by growing economic inequality and ethnic preferences. But it was not entirely in vain. To the degree that the struggle resulted in improved school quality for blacks, it very likely had significant payoffs for them measured in terms of increased earnings after leaving school, regardless of changes in achievement levels, as David Card and Alan Krueger have shown.[34] (See also chapter 14 in this volume.)

If busing and school integration are now largely spent controversies, the same cannot be said of affirmative action. It is one of the most ethnically divisive policies in America, pitting white and black elites against each other and dividing the liberal establishment that so strongly supported other civil rights measures. Ironies abound in the history of affirmative action, as John Skrentny has shown.[35] Affirmative action came about in the late 1960s without any lobbying, debate, or controversy. Elite bureaucrats—largely conservative, establishment white men—instituted it simply and quietly. Initially, black civil rights leaders viewed the policy with some skepticism; at one point, the White House had to lobby them to support it. The person most responsible for it was none other than President

Richard Nixon, who anticipated—and welcomed—the strong reaction and resentment from white males. He used affirmative action as a Republican wedge policy that would help to destroy the Democratic Party's century-long hold on working-class white males and the South and to create a historic realignment leading to the Republican ascendancy. It also guaranteed that race would remain a central element in American politics, even as blacks made strong gains as participants, legislators, and officeholders in the system.[36] Although improvements began from the 1960s, affirmative action was critical for black entry into the elite professions and classes, especially via increased enrollment in elite colleges and professional schools[37] and recruitment by the nation's top firms.[38] For demographic, historical, racial, and ethno-cultural reasons, color-blind recruitment to elite jobs will nearly always result in an all-white executive suite and this is true even for high-achieving Asian Americans, who remain grossly underrepresented in the elite jobs of firms other than those they founded themselves.[39] Affirmative action and the broader diversity management programs of companies effectively leveled the corporate and educational playing field for qualified blacks and women as well as Asian Americans.

Nonetheless, the program may have begun to run its course, in good part because it has succeeded in its goal of seeding the nation's elites and middle classes with individuals of black ancestry. Chief Justice Sandra Day O'Connor's proposal of another fifteen years of legal life for affirmative action is not off the mark. Costs—measured in terms of white male hostility and an understandable sense of grievance about affirmative action's fairness and in terms of the political support it provides for forces arrayed more broadly against positions advocated by black leaders—are now simply too high and may well erode white support for other policies. Maintaining the program too long may harm blacks themselves by encouraging them to take preferential treatment for granted in recruitment and promotion and to relax their efforts. Reflexive support for affirmative action has become, in some quarters, the measure of middle-class black solidarity, exposing black critics to charges of racial treachery. Like other government preferential programs, and like affirmative action programs in other countries, the program could evolve into a permanent ethnic entitlement.

Black leaders' decision to shift the program's rationale from compensation for centuries of black deprivation to the promotion of diversity was misguided. Properly conceived, diversity is a worthy goal, but it embraces all Americans and inevitably expands the number of groups claiming preferences, many of them immigrants and their children who could claim no history of persecution or discrimination in America. This understandably alarmed white males, the one group unambiguously excluded from such preferences.

Nor has diversity lived up to its nobler expectations. Too often it has promoted ethnic distinctiveness and pride in one's difference. For blacks, this has been a two-edged sword. At a certain period in their struggle for inclusion, it was vital that blacks develop a positive self-image. Collective ethnic pride was also a powerful mobilization tool in the civil rights movement. Studies of collective self-esteem all indicate that blacks have successfully rid themselves of what used to be called the "marks of oppression" and now have a healthy view of themselves as black people.[40] And as already noted, the great majority of whites have embraced the inclusion of blacks in their vision of America. Yet, blacks remain socially isolated, cut off from the vital social networks and cultural capital that account for success in America's hypercompetitive economic environment. Their celebration of difference, to the degree that it reinforces this separation, works strongly against their best long-term interests.

Conclusion

The color line, which W. E. B. DuBois presciently espoused as the problem of the twentieth century, had a dual character. One part was the near complete exclusion of blacks and other non-white minorities from the upper echelons and leadership of American society and from its public life and national identity. The other was the segregation of blacks from the intimate, social, communal, and cultural life of white Americans. In the second half of the century, America struggled mightily with, and largely resolved, the first part of its ethno-racial problem and is today a model for all other advanced multi-ethnic nations in the sophistication and effectiveness of its civil rights and antidiscrimination laws, the diversity of its elite, the participation of blacks and other minorities in the direction of its polity, its great corporations, its public cultural life, and in the embrace of the black presence as an integral part of the nation and what it means to be an American. But, paradoxically, this triumph of public integration was correlated with, and may even have worsened, the private isolation of blacks who today are nearly as segregated from whites as at the start of the twentieth century. Compounding this paradox is the simultaneous growth of a thriving black middle and upper class with an impoverished lower class in the ghettoes of the inner cities whose crippling sociocultural problems have defied most public remedies.

While public policy still has an important role, the major problem of the new century will be the reformation, by all parties, of those ethnic preferences, intimate networks, cultural practices, and other ingrained habits of the heart that separate blacks, Hispanic groups, and whites and largely sustain persisting gaps in achievement. The main question today, then—especially for blacks who have most to lose from inertia in this area—is, assuming continued complementary changes in white attitudes, whether they are prepared to meet the challenges of internal lifestyle and interethnic changes and to do the cultural and interpersonal work required for integration into the private sphere of the "beloved community" for which Martin Luther King, Jr., so often yearned.

CHAPTER 14

Education

Paul E. Peterson

The American elementary and secondary education system, the envy of the world as recently as 1960, has become mediocre compared to those of other advanced societies. This deterioration, political scientist and education researcher Paul Peterson points out, has occurred despite parents' higher educational attainment and increased per capita expenditures on students. The strains placed on the system by broad cultural changes, desegregation, legal challenges to the authority of teachers and school administrators, immigration, disability rights, litigation over funding, and collective bargaining have all played their part. The burgeoning "excellence movement" emphasizes accountability and transparency, incentives to attract better teachers, and increased parental choice to force performance-based competition among schools. But it is by no means clear that these reforms will succeed.

IN 1960, THE AMERICAN EDUCATIONAL SYSTEM WAS THE ENVY OF the world. Though it had many warts—southern schools were racially segregated, disabled students were excluded from schooling, and facilities varied widely from one part of the country to another—a larger proportion of the next generation was attending school for a more extended period of time than in any other major industrial country. That system, which had evolved over the preceding century and a half, had helped propel the United States from a developing country to one of the world's superpowers.

As Figure 14.1 shows, Americans were moving toward a universal system of education in the period immediately following World

War II. Rates of attendance in secondary school had exploded in
the 1930s so that already, by 1940, some 72 percent of all those in the
relevant age cohort were in school, a percentage that grew to 90
percent by 1960. Graduation rates were over 50 percent in 1950,
then climbed to over 70 percent over the next twenty years. College
enrollment rates more than doubled between 1940 and 1970.

Today, the lower tiers of America's educational system, the focus
of this essay, no longer appear exceptional. While U.S. colleges and
universities still attract students from abroad, the elementary and
secondary pillars on which the higher educational system stands
rank, at best, near the average of all industrialized nations. As can be

Figure 14.1   Trends in High School and College Participation and
Completion, 1940–2005

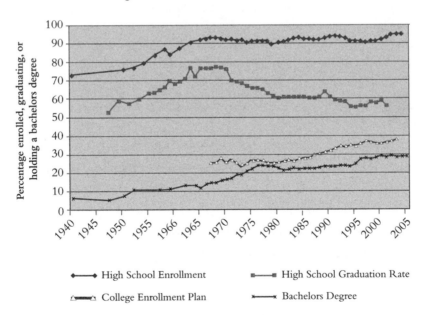

SOURCES: National Center for Education Statistics, "120 Years of American
Education: A Statistical Portrait," January 1993; National Center for Education Statistics, "Digest of Education Statistics, 2005."

Figure 14.2   Secondary School and College Completion, 2004

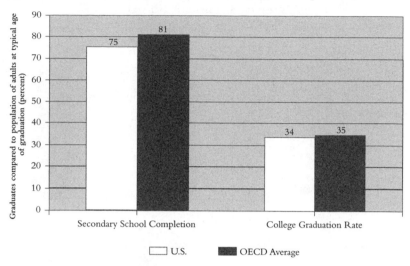

SOURCE: Organisation for Economic Co-operation and Development, "Education at a Glance, 2006."

seen in Figure 14.2, high school graduation rates, which once led the world, now fall short of the average for all industrialized countries, and college graduation rates are just at the industrial international average.[1] According to various international measures of high school student performance in science, math, and reading, America's schools range from just average to well below that level (see Figure 14.3). If anything, school quality seems to have deteriorated since 1960. This, despite the following facts: America's parents are better educated, earn more, and have more time to devote to their children's instruction; U.S. schools have far more fiscal resources per pupil—in real dollar terms—than ever before, and the number of professionals per pupil within the school building has grown steadily over the decades so that classes in the twenty-first century have, on average, nine fewer students than they did in 1960 (see Figure 14.4).

Why has a once-dynamic educational system turned stagnant? Were resources, though expanding, still inadequate? Was it the racial

Figure 14.3   Performance on the 2003 Programme for International Student Assessment (PISA)

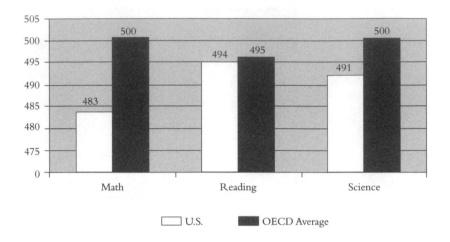

SOURCE: Organisation for Economic Co-operation and Development, "PISA 2003."

turmoil that accompanied the efforts to desegregate the schools? Was it the rise of stronger teacher unions and collective bargaining practices? Was it a change in pedagogical practice? Had school systems become overly professionalized, legalized, and bureaucratized? Answering these questions requires an examination of some of the key turning points in the development of the country's schools.

Reforming a Voluntary, Local, and Decentralized System

At the time of the nation's founding and during the early decades of the nineteenth century, schools in the United States were modeled on English and Scottish arrangements marked by voluntary enrollments, fee-based education, religious instruction, and local control. But over the next two centuries, through a process of self-conscious reform, U.S. schools gradually became compulsory, secularized, cen-

Figure 14.4   Trends in Expenditures and Class Size

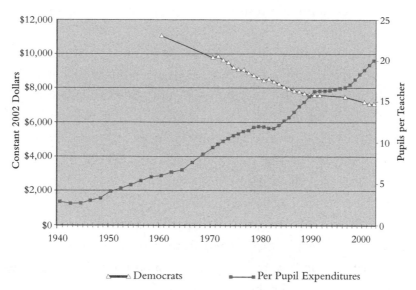

--△ Democrats   ■——■ Per Pupil Expenditures

SOURCE: National Center for Education Statistics, "Digest of Education Statistics, 2005."

tralized, professionalized, and highly regulated and bureaucratized. Those changes came in four distinct waves, led by four distinct types of school reformers.

The initial group of reformers, working in the 1830s and 1840s, were nation-builders who wanted to use the school as a tool that would construct a people suitable to a burgeoning democracy. To achieve that purpose, schooling needed to be compulsory and brought more tightly under government control. The progressive reformers, whose work began in the latter part of the nineteenth century and extends through much of the first half of the twentieth century, sought to take schools out of the hands of politicians and place them safely in the hands of professional educators familiar with the latest educational pedagogy. The rights reformers, particularly active in the 1960s and 1970s, sought to democratize the educational system, extending liberties, equality, and access to previously disadvantaged groups and individuals. The turmoil surrounding many of their innovations spawned a fourth wave, led by the those concerned that schools had sacrificed excellence in education to a misguided application of the egalitarian ideal. The excellence reform was sparked by a 1982 government commission report, "A Nation at Risk," which had found a "rising tide of mediocrity" in American education.

Each wave of reform had consequences unanticipated by its strongest advocates. The culturally sophisticated nation-builders who constructed the public school system did not expect that it would be captured by the immigrant groups whose values differed from their own. The progressives edged the politicians from power but then left the schools isolated from bases of power at a time when new demands were being placed upon them. The rights reformers democratized public schools, but the benefits for the disadvantaged have remained inconsistent and uncertain. The current excellence movement in education is still in its early stages, but it has thus far been frustrated by the political obstacles it has encountered. This essay explains the structure and character of American education today by examining how one reform wave—together with its unanticipated consequences—set the stage for subsequent ones.

Schools in the Early Republic

The U.S. Constitution makes no mention of education, but the Continental Congress, meeting in 1785, set aside in the new territories west of the Appalachians one section of land out of sixteen, the proceeds from which were to be used for the "maintenance of public schools within the said township." That did not mean secular public schools as we think of them today, because only two years later the same Congress affirmed that "religion, morality and knowledge, being necessary to good government and the happiness of mankind, schools and the means of education shall forever be encouraged." Even the most advanced thinkers did not envision anything like the compulsory, secular, state-run system that would evolve decades later during the 1790s. Benjamin Rush, a physician who was very much a part of the founding political elite, wrote that "free, public schools" should be supported by letting each "scholar pay the schoolmasters." Note that the words "free" and "public" meant only that the school was freely open to all who were willing to pay at least a minimum amount for their child's education. Thomas Jefferson favored a state-run university for his beloved Virginia, but for elementary education favored something along the lines of what today would be called minimalist school vouchers: "Free" children, he said, should be "entitled to receive tuition gratis, for a term of three years, and as much longer, at their private expense, as their parents guardians or friends, shall think proper."

As haphazard, religiously directed, and unorganized as the postcolonial educational system was, many Americans were quite literate. Newspapers were the major forum for communication during the revolutionary period and they carried the debates that took place at the time of the ratification of the U.S. Constitution. During the Revolutionary War, Thomas Paine's *Common Sense* sold 100,000 copies, and it is thought that 25 percent of the white adult population read the book.

The Nation-Builders of the Early Nineteenth Century

That haphazard school system, relying as it did on fee-collecting schoolmasters, churches, and local school boards, was overwhelmed by the massive in-migration of Catholic peasants from Ireland and Germany during the 1830s and 1840s, many of whom fled only when the Irish potato blight reached an intensity that made it cheaper for a landlord to pay for passages to America than for minimal food supplies. Enlightened Protestant reformers, such as Horace Mann, the first secretary to the state board of education in Massachusetts, created systems of state-directed, compulsory education expected to lead children from the rum–filled darkness into the Protestant light. No less concerned, the Catholic Church responded by building parochial schools of its own.

Despite its proselytizing, divisive character, the first wave of reform succeeded, perhaps because its most sectarian objectives were thwarted. In New York City, for example, a Protestant-dominated charity society had tried to become the sole, public-funded provider of schooling, despite the fact that most students were Catholic immigrants. But power was sufficiently distributed that the immigrants were able to block that move and secure instead a system of public schools under secular, not overtly Protestant, control. However, the Catholics were unable to get public aid for their own parish schools.

On this compromise, a rapidly expanding system of elementary education was constructed in the decades before and after the Civil War. The power of cultural elites was checked by democratic institutions and machine-style politics that gave ordinary citizens some say about the new schools. Schools became a key component of the democratic experiment. As Alexis de Tocqueville wrote admiringly, "In no country in the world do the citizens make such exertions for the common weal. I know of no people who have established schools so numerous and efficacious."[2]

The Late Nineteenth-Century School

As the nineteenth century ended, America's schools were governed by local school boards, whose members were typically elected in partisan elections. Administrators were at least as gifted at the art of patronage dispensation as at the articulation of fine philosophies of teaching and learning. School principals had tight connections with ward bosses, schools were beholden to city councils for their financing, and school superintendents were recruited from within the community and could be easily removed from office. School districts were small and numerous, numbering over 120,000 in 1890.

Schools themselves averaged only about forty students per school. In rural areas, the "little red schoolhouse" dotted the landscape, governed by local leaders committed more or less equally to community progress and personal advantage.

This might all smack of politics and provincialism, but it provided a robust, democratic base for a rapidly expanding system that commanded broad support throughout the political community. Both rural Americans and immigrants from abroad saw the schools as vehicles for social mobility. Urban schools were often under the control of Irish board members, administrators, and teachers, who exploited the fact that their native tongue was English, giving them an edge over other immigrant groups both in politics and education. In Chicago and San Francisco, for example, they were well represented among public school administrators and teachers. In New York City, the Jews, with their passion for education, were similarly prominent.

With widespread support from across the political spectrum, elementary schooling became universal by the late nineteenth century, and secondary education took off at a rapid pace in the early decades of the twentieth century. Leading the charge were small-town leaders who wanted a new high school that could rival those in competing towns nearby. Politics, competition, decentralization, democratic control: all combined to generate a dynamic, expanding system that gradually acquired an international reputation.

Progressive Pursuit of Professionalized Political Power

Still, there was much to criticize. And by the end of the nineteenth century, a group known as progressives had acquired the wherewithal to articulate potent objections. The progressives were gathering strength in politics, journalism, the universities, and the professions. Many were themselves educators, building their own professional careers as psychologists, economists, political scientists, sociologists, or experts in pedagogy. It was only a matter of time before schools would capture their attention.

No one person better exemplified the spirit of the day—or had more influence on the direction schooling would take over the next half century and more—than John Dewey, who arrived at the University of Chicago in 1894 and opened the Laboratory School the following year. Influenced by Rousseauian idealism, Hegelian logic, and Prussian practice, Dewey found a way to transform continental thought into an American idiom that seemed to address the curricular and structural elements in American education that progressives found disquieting.

Consider, for example, the heavy-handedness of the traditional curriculum. Young people were expected to memorize passages from English classics (Shakespeare's *Julius Caesar*, Eliot's *Silas Marner*, Dickens's *Tale of Two Cities*) or patriotic American poems (Longfellow's "Revere's Ride" and "The Village Blacksmith"), to read character-building homilies put together in the best-selling McGuffey's readers, and to learn to read and calculate by rote methods later characterized as "drill and kill." Sitting stiffly in hard-back chairs at fixed desks or long tables, children were asked to sing, to the tune of "Yankee Doodle," such nonsense as "five times five is twenty-five and five times six is thirty." Phonics, penmanship, spelling bees, punctuation practice, sentence deconstruction, and other boring routines were part and parcel of school life.

Influenced by the great French philosopher Jean-Jacques Rousseau, Dewey and his followers sought to change those practices. The best education, Rousseau thought, was one that the child discerned for himself. The tutor was to "do nothing and let nothing be done" so that the child would learn whatever he needed to know without instruction, keeping "the mind inactive as long as possible." While Dewey rejected Rousseau's stricture that "reading is the greatest plague of childhood," he and his followers readily agreed that no pupil should ever learn anything "by heart." Like Rousseau, Dewey thought that "if nothing is to be exacted from children by way of obedience, it follows that they will only learn what they feel to be of actual and present advantage," which he thought to be the route to a lifelong passion for learning.

After first trying out his ideas at Chicago's Laboratory School, Dewey and his followers pushed implementation nationwide. Phonics was deemphasized in favor of the "whole word method," which required no specific instruction but simply the opportunity to see words time and again. "Run, Spot, run," said Dick to his dog in one of the most widely used of the new texts that had come to replace the McGuffey reader. In math, students were no longer required to memorize multiplication tables or learn long division, but asked instead to learn their fractions by carrying out such exercises as cutting pieces of construction paper into quarters. In literature, students no longer memorized Lincoln's "Gettysburg Address" but instead explored the world about them in "projects" about themselves or their immediate surroundings. Instead of sterile book learning, students were invited to participate in the world of manual training, vocational education, and life-experience courses. Girls learned to cook and sew, while boys did woodworking, metalworking, agricultural studies, and, later on, automobile mechanics. The fixed desks gave way to moveable furniture, rugs, and open space.

This progressive celebration of the natural had a reactionary twist, however. Influenced by Herbert Spencer's Social Darwinism, many progressives believed that some children were born to learn more, others less. Along with moveable desks and school projects came I.Q. and aptitude testing. Used in World War I to identify men fit to be drafted, the testing movement solidified during the 1920s on evidence that one's aptitude had remarkable stability over the course of one's life. Soon, most educators concluded that about one-quarter to one-third of the population was capable of academic learning, while the remaining two-thirds were better suited to vocational education and life-experience courses. As schools expanded to include a larger proportion of the population, these allegedly "scientific facts" were increasingly taken into account. The testing movement would reach its apotheosis in the remarkable SAT, a pencil-and-paper test that could predict students' college readiness regardless of their high school curriculum. With a high enough SAT score, Rousseau's "Emile" could matriculate in college without any education at all.

Not every progressive project managed to make it into the mainstream of American education. Many ordinary Americans— and some contrarian scholars as well—wondered whether learning could be made as much fun as Rousseau, Dewey, and the progressives imagined, so the pedagogical ideas that were being expounded encountered more than a little resistance. And American schools were too diverse and decentralized for any curricular reform to gain swift, much less universal, acceptance. To carry out their curricular objectives, the progressives also needed to reorganize the political structures that governed American education.

To allow greater professional control over America's schools, the progressives sought to remove distracting political influences and weaken provincial bases of power. School board elections were shifted from the November Tuesday on which presidents and Congress were chosen to almost any other month and day. That reduced the size of the electorate, allowing those with a strong interest in education to have an especially large voice. Party labels were stripped from the ballot, so that party politicians would lose a key electoral advantage. School boards were asked to remove themselves from the selection of personnel, so that a professional administrator trained at one of the country's leading schools of education could choose those who would help run day-to-day affairs. School finance was shifted from the local property-tax payer to those who paid the state sales and, later, the income tax. Whereas the local taxpayer was paying 80 percent of the cost of education in 1920; by 1980, that percentage had dropped to about 40 percent.

The rule book followed the dollar, as state departments of education began limiting the discretion of local boards. State officials campaigned for a more efficient system with fewer school districts and school boards to oversee. The number of school boards dropped precipitously, from over 120,000 at the beginning of the century to around 15,000 by its end. The larger school systems, running bigger schools, undermined local bastions of power and gave professionals more opportunities to move upward and expand their domains of control.

To guard against favoritism and patronage, states also began to certify which individuals could teach in schools. A credential earned at a teachers college became the ticket to a career in education. To check cronyism, teachers were paid according to a standard salary schedule that varied only with the academic credential and the number of years the teacher had been employed. To ensure academic freedom, teachers were granted tenure after a few years of teaching. Similar rules were put into place for principals and other school administrators.

The machine politicians and the local notables did not accept defeat gracefully, fighting rearguard actions when and wherever they could. But the long-term trajectory favored education professionals, so that by the end of World War II success was at hand. When veterans returned to father the babyboom generation, the demand for education soared. With new construction came the opportunity to create newly designed classrooms and playgrounds reflecting the latest progressive thinking. Armies of new teachers, many with master's degrees, graduated from the rapidly expanding colleges of education. As high school enrollments exploded to include most of the adolescent population, new curricular ideas became fashionable. After battling machine politicians for generations, sophisticated administrators found themselves warmly accepted on all sides. Even Richard Daley, Chicago's powerful machine mayor, decided to leave educational matters to others.

Questions Posed by the Progressive Reforms

The progressives succeeded in shifting power from rural bumpkins and ward heelers to a new class of educational professionals, and their new pedagogical approaches gradually spread throughout much of the country's educational system. But were the professionals really as public-spirited, politically disinterested, and scientifically grounded as they claimed? Would the schools of education, now in control of the paths to teaching, counseling, and administration, be capable of turning out a talented workforce? Would the large, new schools, run by larger school districts, acquire capacities that greatly exceeded those of the "little red schoolhouse"? Would advanced pedagogical techniques be as effective in mainstream classrooms as in university laboratories? Would public employees, now given tenure, place their autonomy in the service of education or for narrower, more occupational interests? All of these questions were left hanging in the air when a new wave of reform of near tsunami proportions fundamentally rearranged the educational landscape.

The Rights Reformers

The new movement's origins can be dated quite precisely: May 19, 1954, the day the Supreme Court decided *Brown v. Board of Education*. The decision proved extraordinarily complex and controversial, opening the school door to political passions that proved more powerful than any expressed by the professional educators of the progressive era. *Brown's* desegregation order was anything but self-implementing; many schools remain racially distinctive to this very day. But the call for equal opportunity, regardless of race, creed, or national origin, sparked rights movements that spread from African-Americans to other ethnic groups, as well as to the disabled, the politically outspoken, and even to organizations of public school employees that demanded the right to bargain collectively. Each of these extensions of *Brown* affected America's schools differently. Together, they transformed the nation's schools so that by the 1980s they hardly resembled a once-entrenched professionalized system.

Schools nationwide—not just the defiant ones in the Deep South—were traumatized by the unforeseen bitterness that accompanied racial integration. Hardly a city was untouched by the fervor of civil rights demonstrators and of bitterly opposed whites who feared for their children, property, and community life.

So intense was white opposition to school desegregation that they often fled school districts to outlying areas whenever a desegregation order was put into place. When the Supreme Court, in *Milliken v. Bradley* (1974), decided that *Brown* required desegregation only within a school district, not across school districts within a metropolitan area, whites who wished to avoid schools where many blacks went could do so. The net effect was to leave the schools nearly as segregated in the first decade of the twenty-first century as they had been in 1970.

Within schools, classrooms remained racially distinctive (as academic distinctions overlapped racial ones), peer group relationships were defined along racial lines, and school officials found a growing need to institute a host of safety measures that could minimize crime and intimidation on playgrounds and even within school buildings. Locked doors, metal detectors, and police officers became as common in urban areas as books, pencils, and guidance counselors.

More than ever before, school leaders needed the respect and deference of those in their charge. But it was precisely at this great, democratizing moment in American education that authorities lost their moral advantage. Amid insistent demands for civil rights and equality of opportunity, countered by the protests of white families feeling under siege, the schools were caught in a cross fire. Yet there was more to come, much of it at the instigation of the federal government.

Before the passage of the Elementary and Secondary Education Act (ESEA) in 1965, the federal government had provided only a token role in American education, providing little more than 2 or 3 percent of all educational funding for isolated activities such as vocational programming or math and science innovations. But with the launch of President Lyndon Johnson's Great Society, the federal government for the first time provided a large-scale compensatory education program whose funds were to be directed to those local schools that had students with the greatest financial and educational needs. By 1980, federal funding grew to about 10 percent of total funding, the lion's share going for compensatory and special education.

The compensatory education program was nobler in its aspirations than it was sophisticated in its pedagogy. Just exactly what disadvantaged students needed that they were not receiving was never spelled out by federal programmers. Should the extra monies be used to hire non-professional aides to work with students within the classroom? Should the disadvantaged students be "pulled out" of class for special attention? Should the monies be used to improve the overall functioning of a local school? All these approaches were tried, but none was ever identified as particularly effective. In fact no study has ever documented clearly a positive, nationwide impact of ESEA programs. Yet much local time and energy was spent complying with the numerous regulations and guidelines that came down from Washington. In 2002, ESEA would be transformed into new legislation, which would give compensatory education an entirely new meaning.

The motives behind the Education of All Handicapped Children Act of 1974 (EAHC), the second major federal undertaking of this era, were no less praiseworthy. The act, still in effect in a revised form, mandates equal educational opportunity to all children, ages three to twenty-one, regardless of their disability. Before EAHC, many mentally retarded children were simply excluded from public schools as uneducable, while those with physical limitations, or who were blind or deaf, were placed in special schools. To integrate such students with peers not suffering from such disabilities, EAHC mandated the education of the disabled in the "least restrictive environment" feasible. The phrase has been generally interpreted as requiring that disabled students be "mainstreamed" along with other students in ordinary classrooms.

EAHC opened the school door to some 4 percent of the population that had previously been underserved, changed the architecture of schools—and public space more generally—and altered perceptions of disabled members of society. All those extraordinary benefits must be calculated in any weighting of the impact of a federal program that has sustained broad, bipartisan public support across several generations. But the benefits did not come without some notable costs. The percentage of students identified as disabled grew rapidly, as the law provided extra monies for every child so labeled. The numbers of students with relatively mild disabilities— attention deficit disorders, learning disorders, and behavioral problems—soon swamped the number of those with severe or profound disabilities (mental retardation, autism, and the multiply handicapped, for example). Program costs escalated well beyond original calculations. But, for teachers, the most critical questions had to do with day-to-day life in the classroom. Just where disability ends and bad behavior begins can be difficult for anyone to discern.[3]

Nor was the impact of the rights revolution limited to new federal programming. Every bit as important, perhaps more so, was the new interest in education taken by the nation's courts. Quite apart from *Brown,* judges uncovered rights for teachers, students, and advocates that had not previously been discerned.

In 1859, a Vermont court ruled that the schoolmaster acted *in loco parentis* not only in school but in the vicinity thereof, saying, "Most parents would expect and desire that teachers would take care that their children, in going to and returning from school, should not loiter, or seek evil company." That precept had not changed for more than one hundred years.

But in the midst of the Vietnam War, three high school students in Des Moines, Iowa, were suspended for protesting U.S. involvement by wearing black armbands. When the students claimed their freedom of speech had been violated, lower courts, applying long-standing precedent, rejected their claims. The Supreme Court, however, ruled in favor of the students: "It can hardly be argued that either students or teachers shed their constitutional rights to freedom of speech or expression at the schoolhouse gate. . . . In our system, state-operated schools may not be enclaves of totalitarianism. School officials do not possess absolute authority over their students."[4]

Especially noteworthy was the implication that, when it comes to free speech, the court treated "students" and "teachers" as having equal constitutional rights inside the schoolhouse. *In loco parentis* no longer.

The Court extended further rights to students in a 1975 decision, *Goss v. Lopez*. In this case, several students in Ohio were suspended from school for ten days, without being given a hearing, for carrying out demonstrations and other disruptive conduct. The Court objected, reasoning that students have a right to a public education, a right that cannot be withdrawn, "on grounds of misconduct, absent fundamentally fair procedures to determine whether the misconduct has occurred. Where a person's good name, reputation, honor or integrity is at stake, proper procedures must be followed." Since only ten-day suspensions had been imposed, the Court ruled that legal formalities were not required in this instance, but "longer suspensions or expulsions may require formal procedures." In response to this constitutional ruling, school systems elaborated complex procedures to protect themselves from liability. A former superintendent noted: "In Fairfax County [VA], not unlike any other place, a youngster who is suspended from school for one day can appeal from the school to the area office to the superintendent's office to a three member panel of the school committee or school board, and then to the full board."[5]

Legalization has not moved forward apace in all domains, to be sure. The Court has refused to extend to a student locker the same protection from searches as a private home, or ban random testing for drugs, or forbid paddling junior high students as an instance of "cruel and unusual punishment." But school boards have become increasingly sensitive to the potential for legal action, stifling the willingness of teachers and principals to impose discipline.

Not just passive targets of evolving court doctrine, educators themselves have contributed to the increasing legalization of American education by filing lawsuits asking for additional funding that will help ensure equitable, adequate education for all students.[6] Initially, lawsuits focused on inequities in educational financing, with plaintiffs charging that wealth-related disparities in per-pupil spending between school districts violated students' rights to equal protection under the law. That doctrine was first embraced in the celebrated California decision *Serrano v. Priest,* handed down by the state's supreme court in 1971. "Quality is money," the plaintiff's legal team had argued, and the court ultimately agreed that the state's school finance system would be constitutional if it were to produce approximately equal spending per pupil across the state's school districts.

Although the *Serrano* decision was a great breakthrough, the attempt to immediately nationalize the issue by making equity claims under the U.S. Constitution failed when a divided Supreme Court ruled in *San Antonio I.S.D. v. Rodriguez* (1973) that education was not a fundamental right requiring the highest level of judicial scrutiny. Rebuffed at the federal level, equity advocates turned their attention back to the states. If educational equity were not a fundamental federal right, they claimed, it was guaranteed by state constitutions that explicitly ordered the legislature to provide for the education of its citizenry. Success remained uneven. More than a few state judges proved unwilling to take this step. Even when plaintiffs in state-level equity litigation were successful—New Jersey's 1973 *Robinson v. Cahill* case being the most celebrated example— the implementation of court orders proved to be a political challenge. Remedies typically pitted the interests of high-spending districts against lower-spending ones, and the shifting of resources from one jurisdiction to another inevitably caused consternation among legislators asked to vote against their constituents' particular interests. In California and elsewhere, overall spending on education began to fall.

To counter such trends, advocates soon inserted another, more robust arrow into their legal quiver. Rather than simply asking for fiscal equity, they argued that spending on education must also be *adequate* to provide all students with an education of the quality guaranteed by their state's constitution. In a Kentucky case, *Rose v. Council for Better Education,* decided in 1989, Kentucky's highest court declared the state's entire public education system unconstitutional and ordered the legislature to provide "funding sufficient to provide every child in Kentucky with an adequate education." Later that same year courts found similar grounds for their decisions in favor of plaintiffs in Montana and Texas. By 2006, advocates for increased school spending had gone to court in thirty-nine states. Armed with photographs of run-down school buildings, data revealing large numbers of unqualified teachers, and evidence of abysmal and unequal student performance, teams of lawyers alleged that schools lacked sufficient funding to provide children with the quality of education guaranteed by the state's constitution. As a remedy, they asked courts to mandate large increases in state aid for public schools.

The proposed dollar amounts are often staggering. A 2006 ruling in New York, for example, ordered the state's elected officials to increase operating aid for schools in New York City alone by approximately $2 billion per year (roughly $2,500 per student) on top of an additional $9.2 billion over five years for capital improvements.

The path from courtroom to classroom is long and uncertain, however. Legislatures have opted not to comply with mandated spending increases, causing the lawsuits to fail on their own terms. Increases in state aid mandated by the court have been offset by property-tax cuts at the local level, leaving the total level of spending for the schools little higher than before the suit has been filed. Even where additional money reaches the schoolhouse door, there is little evidence that it has lifted student performances.

As much as federal programs and innovative court doctrines have shaped the modern school, neither has had as critical an impact on school operations as the extension of collective bargaining rights to public school employees. Until the 1960s, the law sharply distinguished between employees in the private and public sectors. Within the private sector, employees had the right to form unions, bargain collectively with employers, and withhold their labor in concerted actions. Public sector employees, however, were treated differently; they could not bargain collectively with executive branch officials and thus bind the legislature. Conservatives and liberals alike viewed strikes against the commonwealth as tantamount to civil disobedience. Even President Franklin D. Roosevelt, who expanded workers' collective bargaining rights through federal law, limited these rights to private sector workers.

All that changed, however, when President Kennedy, on January 17, 1962, issued Executive Order 10988 granting federal workers the right to bargain collectively. While any fiscal decisions were still reserved to Congress, representatives of employees could negotiate the terms of their work situation. Strikes remained unlawful, but decisions were subject to binding arbitration by neutral independent experts.

Kennedy's action was anticipated by similar developments at the local level, particularly in New York City, where Mayor Robert

Wagner, as part of his 1957 antimachine candidacy, promised teacher union leaders that he would sponsor an election to see whether teachers wanted to bargain collectively. When the newly elected Wagner was advised that such an election was illegal, he retreated from his promise. In retaliation, union leaders called a strike on November 7, 1960, one day before the presidential election. When approximately five thousand teachers (about 10 percent of the workforce) went on strike, Wagner agreed to set up collective bargaining procedures.

New York City's teacher union called another strike in 1962, this time for higher pay and other benefits under the bargaining agreement. As strikes spread to other large cities, collective bargaining became prevalent.

The collective bargaining movement was reinforced by the competition between the small but energetic American Federation of Teachers (AFT), a constituent member of the larger union movement, and the much larger National Education Association (NEA), which had nearly ten times the teacher membership of the AFT but had long been dominated by school administrators. Initially, the NEA condemned the striking teacher unionists as unprofessional, but, in the wake of Kennedy's order, the NEA, fearing a loss of members to the competition, changed policy direction and also became aggressive in the pursuit of collective bargaining privileges. In the end, both organizations prospered, NEA membership climbing from 700,000 in 1960 to 3.2 million in 2007, while the smaller AFT grew from under 60,000 to 1.3 million teachers over this same period of time. Collective bargaining, unknown in education before 1960, became pervasive in most states outside the South.

The fiscal impact of collective bargaining agreements has been mostly indirect. Contrary to expectations, in the years since collective bargaining began, teacher salaries have risen more slowly than that of other college-educated workers. The bigger impact of collective bargaining has been on employment rights, privileges, and working conditions. Teacher recruitment has become excessively regulated, teacher compensation overly standardized, and teacher dismissals subject to elaborate grievance procedures included in bargaining contracts.

Desegregation, legalization, disability rights, fiscal lawsuits, and collective bargaining all granted rights and privileges to individuals and groups who previously lacked them. Almost all have become an integral component of the American educational fabric. Yet the forward march of democracy left few satisfied with the educational system they had created. School doors were open to all, but what was happening inside the classroom? Money was more abundantly and equitably distributed, but had it made much of an impact? Teachers could bargain collectively, but was that power being used to yield greater educational benefits for children?

All these questions became particularly telling as it became increasingly evident that the rights revolution was no longer opening up new opportunities for minority students. Distressingly enough, the achievement of white seventeen-year-olds in reading and math remained essentially unchanged between 1970 and 2004 (see Figures 14.5 and 14.6). Of even greater concern, the gains made by African-American seventeen-year-olds peaked around 1988, with a significant decline in reading becoming quite apparent after that date. Hispanic trend lines were similarly disconcerting. Meanwhile, the position of the United States vis-à-vis other countries, continued to erode (see Figure 14.3). Such facts would drive still another wave of reform, one yet to reach its crest.

The Excellence Movement

Just as was the case with the rights reform movement, the beginnings of the excellence reform movement can be tied to a particular moment, April 26, 1983, the day the National Commission on Educational Excellence, appointed by Secretary of Education Terrence Bell, a Reagan administration appointee, issued its report "A

Figure 14.5   Performance of Seventeen-Year-Olds on
the NAEP Reading Assessment

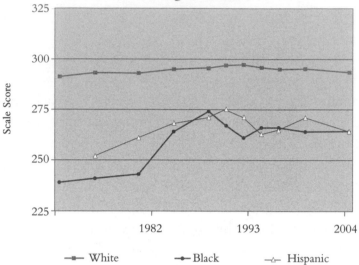

SOURCE: National Assessment of Educational Progress.

Figure 14.6   Performance of Seventeen-Year-Olds on
the NAEP Mathematics Assessment

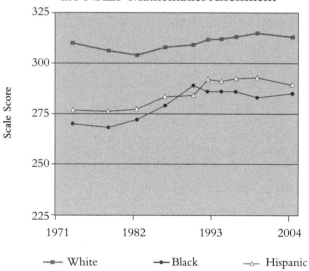

SOURCE: National Assessment of Educational Progress.

Nation at Risk." Its impact on the federal system would prove to be quite ironic, for President Reagan's educational vision, like that of the Framers, expected states and localities to run their schools with no help from the federal government. Indeed, Reagan had promised to eliminate the same Department of Education over which Secretary Bell presided and had refused Bell's request to appoint a presidential commission to consider educational questions. So Bell's group was only a "national" commission, with few prominent members and little chance of getting much attention.

Yet the report proved to be the match that lit the kindling that fueled the excellence movement, a triggering event that mobilized a national dissatisfaction with the state of the schools. "Our nation is at risk," it said. "The educational foundations of our society are presently being eroded by a rising tide of mediocrity that threatens our very future as a Nation and a people. What was unimaginable a generation ago has begun to occur—others are matching and surpassing our educational attainments."

The commission stressed that average SAT scores had fallen by over ninety points between 1963 and 1980. "Average achievement of high schools students on most standardized tests is now lower than 26 years ago when Sputnik was launched," it lamented, concluding that, "For the first time in the history of our country, the educational skills of one generation will not surpass, will not equal, will not even approach, those of their parents."

The commission's indictment was better defined than its solutions, which were little more than platitudes about the need for greater commitment and dedication. But so sweeping and credible was its critical assessment, the report set off a fourth wave of reform, consisting of three different thrusts: school accountability, reform of the teaching profession, and parental choice. In all three instances, the excellence movement has sought to use market-like arrangements to improve school quality. School accountability is expected to make schools more transparent to the consumer; teacher reform is expected to use market-like incentives to attract more effective teachers; and school choice is expected to place all schools in competition with one another.

The seeds that ripened into the accountability movement had been planted as early as 1969, when the government initiated a national, periodic survey of student performance in math and reading. Before long, the optimistically named National Assessment of Educational Progress (NAEP) became the yardstick by which both policymakers and the news media measured the country's educational performance. Indeed, the commission drew upon this very survey, now known as the nation's report card, when it concluded that the schools, far from making progress, were stagnant or declining. As the excellence movement drove forward, the fact that overall educational performance was being measured regularly drove innovation. As each new NAEP yielded dismal results, reform pressures intensified, especially after the release of "A Nation at Risk."

The accountability movement first swept through many states, then entered national politics, and finally culminated with the passage of No Child Left Behind (NCLB), a remarkable extension of federal power into what had traditionally been perhaps the most sacrosanct domain of local government. Governors, especially those in southern states, were the first to seize the opportunity created by the commission's report. Facing a newly enfranchised black electorate but hoping to retain the support of white voters as well, political candidates embraced education reform as something all could unite behind. More resources would be poured into the newly integrated educational system, but those resources must be used efficiently, which required holding schools accountable for the money they spent. Tennessee, North Carolina, Kentucky, Texas, Florida, and other states directed their schools to test their students and report the results publicly. Within three years of the commission report, the National Governors Association (NGA) agreed on the need for greater school accountability. "To sum it up," said Tennessee governor and NGA chairman Lamar Alexander, in 1986, "the Governors are ready for some old-fashioned horse-trading. We'll regulate less, if schools and school districts will produce better results." A few years later, Alexander would become the secretary of education under President George H. W. Bush, the first of many governors who would ride the education reform wave into national prominence. In 1989, Bush, together with the governors, proclaimed Goals 2000, specifying concrete objectives, including universal high school graduation, within only one decade.

The movement transcended partisan lines. Throughout the 1990s, many states made serious progress; in most cases, bipartisan coalitions remained intact and fairly sophisticated accountability systems were put in place. President Bill Clinton signed into law a 1995 ESEA revision that asked states to hold their schools accountable. Many states had already been doing so, and in those states, student math test performance on the NAEP improved at a higher rate than in the other states. As encouraging as these signs were, the 1995 law lacked a clear enforcement system, and many states dragged their heels. As high school graduation rates lagged behind other industrialized nations, and seventeen-year-olds continued to show few test-score gains on the NAEP, the stage was set for a new national initiative.

The charge was led by a Republican presidential candidate whose education policy seemed an almost complete reversal of that taken by the Reagan administration a generation earlier. Rather than abolishing the Department of Education, the younger Bush promised to institute the most sweeping expansions of federal power over the nation's schools ever attempted. Every school would be held accountable, with students at schools that failed three years running to be given the option to use a voucher to pay for attendance at a private school (a topic explored in greater detail below). Upon his election, Bush placed school reform alongside tax cuts at the top of his legislative agenda, and within a year of his inauguration, Congress passed and the president signed NCLB into law.

Although Congress forced a number of compromises on the president, the law did require every state receiving federal dollars to establish a testing system in reading and math for all students in grades 3 through 8, and again in grade 10. By 2014, all students were expected to reach a proficiency standard to be set by each state. In the intervening period, each school had to show that the percentage of its students deemed proficient was steadily increasing—at a pace that would bring it up to 100 percent proficiency by 2014. Key subgroups of students within the school—ethnic minorities, low-income students, and the disabled—also were expected to show comparable gains.

Traveling along the path toward full proficiency was not especially challenging for those schools whose students arrived at school with a strong educational endowment and solid parental backing. But inner-city schools, with large minority populations, had to achieve remarkable progress in a short period of time if they were to avoid sanctions. By 2007, many of them were identified as falling short. When that happened two years in a row, parents were given a choice of another public school within the same school district—as long as that school was not also failing. The choice Congress authorized was not the voucher program George W. Bush had envisioned when running for president. Nor would Congress assure inner-city students' access to public schools in neighboring districts, as opening up suburban public schools to minority students would have aroused fierce opposition. Many inner-city schools were ineligible to receive students because they had been identified as failing. Those that had passed were not eager to accept newcomers from failed schools. So limited were the choices, and so poorly were they promoted that, in 2006, five years after NCLB's enactment, fewer than 1 percent of all eligible students were participating in the choice program.

NCLB also gave students access to supplemental educational services offered by private providers, if their school failed three years running. In 2006, this option was exercised by about 10 percent of eligible students, most of whom attended after-school programs at which additional instruction was given in small classroom settings. The program seems to be growing in size, fairly popular among disadvantaged families, and marginally successful.

Still, NCLB's main impact was expected to come not from choices or supplemental services but from the stigma schools would suffer if they were identified as failing, which, it was hoped, would stimulate more energetic engagement among teachers, students, and administrators alike. School boards would have their feet held to the fire by their constituents whenever testing results revealed serious deficiencies. In practice, these expectations have not been met. Initially, board members did encounter more political opposition when schools performed badly. But as time went by, voter and media attention drifted. Critics said the tests were a poor measure of school performance and questioned the accuracy of the NCLB measuring stick. The criticisms had a special bite whenever federal and state accountability systems yielded different results. In Florida, for example, a third of the schools that failed according to NCLB rules received an A under the state's own accountability system.

Politically, accountability remained a popular goal, but in practice NCLB had many flaws. Still to be determined is whether its imperfections turn out to be temporary glitches remediable as Congress renews NCLB, or whether accountability will be only the latest reform gone awry.

At school, the teacher is the single most important determinant of student performance. Thomas Kane and his colleagues at the Harvard School of Education have shown that students taught by highly proficient teachers (those in the top quartile) learn more than a year's additional material, compared with those taught by the least proficient teachers (those in the lowest quartile). In other words, those with a series of top teachers over a four-year stretch will outpace by four years those with low performing teachers. Achieving excellence in education thus requires a highly qualified teaching force.

To achieve this goal, excellence reformers are attempting to alter the processes by which teachers are recruited, the way in which their compensation is determined, and the policies that affect their retention. In all three cases, excellence reformers are seeking to institute practices similar to those conventionally used in the private sector.

During the second reform wave, professional reformers had removed politics from the recruitment of teachers and administrators by requiring that educators be state-certified. To obtain certification, teachers needed to take a set of substantive and pedagogical courses appropriate to the subject matter and the age of the child they were teaching. Similarly, principals and other administrators were expected to take advanced degree courses in educational administration. If all these state regulations curbed partisan patronage, they unfortunately did little to attract a qualified teaching force, a fact revealed by the numerous studies that show certified teachers are no more effective than those lacking certification. Nor are teachers with master's degrees more effective than the ones lacking such a credential. Those findings have not prevented certification practices from becoming increasingly byzantine, with ever more specific types of credentials for each teaching specialty. Missouri, for example, has over two hundred distinct certificates, many for different vocational specialties.

Unfortunately, the emphasis on certification has been intensified since NCLB's passage. The federal law requires a high-quality teacher in every classroom—and, as implemented in most states, has equated high quality with state certification (in the specific subject) rather than with actual classroom performance. In response, reformers have urged a deregulation of the teaching profession, opening the classroom door to any college graduate, regardless of the number of education courses he or she has taken, as long as local administrators deem the teacher qualified. An innovative program, Teach for America, has recruited students from highly selective colleges and universities into teaching by finding them positions in cities that are willing to ignore state certification requirements, at least temporarily. Many states are allowing alternative certification, weighted more heavily toward actual teaching experience, to substitute for traditional certification practices.

Excellence reformers are also seeking to alter the standardized salary schedule that was put into place at a time when professional reformers were trying to quell special arrangements for the politically well connected. That standard salary schedule, a staple of American education, pays teachers strictly according to the number of years they have taught and the academic degrees they have earned. Since collective bargaining was introduced, unions have fought hard to sustain that standardized schedule. Unions have also demanded higher benefit packages (health insurance, pensions, and so forth), so that today the share of teacher compensation that comes in the form of benefit packages exceeds by about 20 percent the compensation packages received in the private sector.

Excellence reformers argue that standardized salary schedules and high benefit packages do not fit well with modern economic practice. As the demand for skilled workers has increased rapidly, the salaries of the college-educated worker have risen rapidly. Teacher salaries, although higher than those of average workers, have grown more slowly than those of their college-educated peers. The emphasis on benefit packages, which disproportionately reward senior teachers, makes it harder to recruit talented young newcomers.

The impact on the teaching profession has been particularly great in recent decades as other job opportunities have opened up for women, who still constitute over 70 percent of the teaching force. As talented women entered business, law, medicine, higher education, and many other professions, the quality of women teachers, as measured by their SAT scores and the selectivity of the college they attended, dropped noticeably.

To recruit talented women—and men—back into teaching, excellence reformers call for a more differentiated pay schedule, with a smaller proportion of total compensation allocated to benefits. Higher levels of compensation can help address shortages in math, science, special education, and other critical areas. To keep experienced, effective teachers in schools serving the disadvantaged, the reformers propose extra "battle" or "hazard" pay. They also recommend that teachers be compensated according to how much the children in their classroom are learning, not simply according to the number of years they have been teaching or the credentials they have earned.

Union opposition to any changes in the traditional pay standards has stymied these efforts in all but a few places, such as Denver and Florida. Unions have been even more aggressive in maintaining grievance procedures that make it extremely difficult for principals to dismiss ineffective teachers unless moral turpitude can be identified. To help rectify the situation, some have suggested that teacher tenure be delayed for up to five years so that actual classroom effectiveness can be determined before job protection is granted.

If market incentives are being proposed as a way of enhancing the quality of the teaching profession, those proposals are not as sweeping as the ones designed to expose all schools to market competition by giving parents a choice in the school their children attend. The intellectual roots of the choice movement were planted by John Stuart Mill. But in its modern incarnation, the choice idea first appeared in 1955 (one year after the *Brown* decision), when Milton Friedman, a Nobel Prize–winning University of Chicago economist, proposed school vouchers as a solution to monopoly control of public education. Within any geographic area, all public schools are run by a single entity—usually a school board and the administrative staff it appoints. Given their monopoly over the production of schooling, and their access to tax dollars, school boards and administrators lack market incentives to provide the best education at the lowest price. As a remedy, Friedman proposed publicly funded vouchers that paid for the tuition at the families' school of choice. The ensuing competition ensures that students receive the services the family desires and, in the long run, generates higher levels of educational productivity.

Friedman's idea was perverted when southern states seized upon the voucher idea as a way of preserving racial segregation. They passed voucher laws that redirected children to private schools, which unlike public schools could remain racially segregated. Although federal courts struck down such racist laws, the voucher concept remained tainted for years. Even today, some civil rights groups regard vouchers as a prescription for segregated schools.

But the concept of choice was used to help achieve more positive objectives as well. When school busing and other forms of compulsory school desegregation encountered stiff opposition in the North as well as the South, many educators turned to school choice as a way of promoting school integration. "Magnet schools" were created in the hopes that they would attract students from across a school district, so that school boards could choose among the applicants a sustainable balance of students from various ethnic backgrounds. After federal funding for the idea was secured in 1972, the idea spread across the country so that, by 2002, over 3,200 magnet schools had been created. Similarly, some suburban school districts agreed to accept, voluntarily, a limited number of students from central-city school districts, thereby giving some parents greater school choice.

As interesting as these early choice experiments proved to be, they did not introduce competition along the lines that Friedman had envisioned. That did not occur until 1990 when the State of Wisconsin enacted legislation that gave 1,500 low-income families in Milwaukee a choice of the private, secular school of their choice.

The experiment proved successful enough that it was expanded in 1996 to include religiously affiliated private schools as well, and the maximum number of participating students was enlarged to 15,000. In 2006, the program was further enlarged to a maximum of 22,000 students.

Teacher unions and other groups filed a lawsuit challenging the program's constitutionality on the grounds that the inclusion of religious schools violated the First Amendment's ban on the "establishment of religion," but the Wisconsin Supreme Court ruled that no "establishment" occurred if parents were given a choice of school, secular or sectarian. The issue continued to boil, however, when a lower federal court ruled unconstitutional a similar voucher program in Cleveland, Ohio. But in 2002, the U.S. Supreme Court overturned the lower court decision on grounds similar to the ones set forth by the Wisconsin court.

Though school vouchers passed the First Amendment test, opposition to their expansion continued. When voucher programs were passed by state legislatures in Colorado and Florida, teacher unions and the People for the American Way, a group committed to the strictest separation of government and religion, again filed lawsuits. This time, state courts found clauses in state constitutions that were interpreted as prohibiting voucher-like arrangements.

Because of intense opposition, both inside and outside the courtroom, publicly funded school voucher programs have not been given a substantial test outside of Milwaukee. However, my colleagues and I have evaluated by means of randomized field trials the impact of several privately funded voucher programs on students from low-income families.[7] We found high levels of parental satisfaction with the voucher option and positive impacts on the test performance of African-American students, though not on the performance of students from other ethnic backgrounds. In Milwaukee, support for the voucher initiative has steadily grown among the low-income families for whom this option is available, and graduation rates of voucher students exceed those in Milwaukee's magnet schools, while the impact on the performance of students in the public schools in Milwaukee seems to have been positive. The short-lived program in Florida also had a positive impact on the public schools challenged by the voucher option.

If school vouchers have been both the most interesting and most controversial of the excellence reforms, voucher programs remain few and far between, largely because of the intensity of the opposition from public schools, teacher unions, and various state judges.

Charter schools, an alternative form of school choice, have gained broader political support, in part by avoiding some of the religious issues that surround school voucher proposals. As in the case of school vouchers, parents are given a choice between a charter school and a traditional public school. And, as in the case of vouchers, most charter schools are managed by a private concern, either for-profit or non-profit. However, a charter school cannot operate unless it is granted a charter from an authorizing authority established under state law, though it is exempt from many state regulations. However, unlike voucher schools, all charter schools must be secular (in order to comply with the establishment clause of the First Amendment).

First established in Minnesota in the early 1990s, charter schools have spread to over forty states. As of 2006, over two thousand charter schools had been established, serving approximately 1 million students, or 2 percent of the public school population.

The schools have tended to concentrate in urban areas and disproportionately serve minority, low-income students. After Hurricane Katrina in New Orleans, charter schools became the dominant type of public school in the city. Charter schools are also enrolling a large percentage of students in the District of Columbia, Milwaukee, various cities in Ohio, Arizona, and in other parts of the country. While some charter schools have been badly managed and forced to close, overall charter enrollments have grown steadily, and many schools are oversubscribed. A wide variety of studies of charter school effectiveness have been undertaken, but few studies are of a quality that allows independent observers to draw definite conclusions. One conclusion is clear, however: charter schools are the most diverse, dynamic, and rapidly changing element in American education.

Whether or not the charter schools will continue to capture an increasing share of the public school market is an entirely open question. While there is strong parental demand, there is intense political opposition, and no charter school can open its doors without securing a charter from a public agency. Whether charter schools will become more than a small experiment on the edges of American education or the defining institution of the future remains an open question.

Conclusions

If charter schools, coupled with voucher programs, continue to expand and become the dominant form of school organization in the twenty-first century—a real though perhaps still unlikely possibility—it would constitute a curious revival of the way in which schools were organized during the very earliest period of the American republic. Recall that those schools were small, locally controlled, fee-based institutions that reflected the values of the local community. Today's charter schools are much smaller than traditional public schools. Many are run by local entrepreneurs. A good deal of private financing helps to sustain their operations. Parents participating in some school voucher programs can—or even must—supplement school funding with their own contributions. Most charter and voucher schools are exempt from many state regulations. Collective bargaining agreements are notable for their absence. Students may be removed from the school if they do not conform to school policies. Instructional climates are highly specific to particular schools. If carried to its logical conclusion, the fourth reform wave may return the country's educational system back to one that, with all of its modern appurtenances, would resemble the one Tocqueville celebrated in the 1830s.

But one should not necessarily expect that outcome, however much it might be celebrated by many of today's excellence reformers. Every school reform wave has yielded consequences unanticipated by its enthusiasts. The nation-builders, active during the antebellum period, wanted schools controlled by cultural elites, but public schools were instead captured by machine politicians and village provincials. The progressives sought to shift control of education from lay elites and partisan politicos into the hands of professional educators. They proved more effective at isolating schools from politics but at the cost of creating highly bureaucratic, overregulated systems that were ill equipped to meet the post-*Brown* demands to open school doors to minorities and the disabled. The rights reformers pursued equity but the changes they introduced failed to close the achievement gap between ethnic groups.

The excellence reformers remain on the advance, but there are plenty of reasons to think their hopes may be dashed. The accountability movement has yet to find a measuring stick that accurately identifies good schools and sound methods to motivate higher teacher and student performance. Reform of the teaching profession has encountered intense union opposition. School vouchers remain a marginal element of American education, while charter schools continue to grow but have not yet shown the capacity to transform the system. Clearly, democracies can build schools of a certain sort. But once built, can they be altered? Can they create dynamic systems capable of sustained improvement, with ever-increasing levels of productivity? Markets have done that in many other sectors of society. But using the market to reform a state-run public education monopoly is a daunting task.

CHAPTER 15

Health Care

David Cutler and Patricia Keenan

The American health care system is unique in many respects, as health care scholars David Cutler and Patricia Keenan show, but perhaps its most striking aspect is that medical spending in the United States is far greater than elsewhere, while the public sector's share of that spending is much lower. This higher spending, however, leaves life expectancy in the United States lagging behind that of many other countries. Whether the spending produces higher quality of life is a separate question. Medical insurance, provider reimbursement, and access to care rules in the United States also differ greatly from those in other countries. Three challenges to the American system are particularly salient: expanding coverage, increasing the value that health care produces, and reducing group disparities in health outcomes.

DECENTRALIZATION IS THE HALLMARK OF MANY ASPECTS OF THE United States, and health care is a prime example. Most developed countries have a single health care system, with a common philosophy about coverage, access, and costs. The United States does not. Here, the multiple aspects of health care access, delivery, and performance make the job of describing health care in the United States particularly onerous. While countries differ in health care system approaches, unhappiness with medical care is more universal. In the United States, the unhappiness is because people fear the high cost of medical care. Elsewhere, cost is less of an issue, but people fear they will not have access to services when needed. No country has discovered the formula for medical care happiness.

We start with the set of issues that *any* health care system must confront, and then describe how the United States and other countries go about addressing them. The basis for our analysis is the medical care triad. There are three participants in the medical care system: patients, providers, and insurers. Patients pay money to insurers (either directly or indirectly, as we discuss below) and pay for some care directly. Insurers reimburse providers for care and set rules under which the care can be provided. Providers diagnose and treat patients.

Corresponding to these three participants are three sets of interactions. The first is a set of rules about who is insured and how that insurance is financed (the coverage rules). Second is a set of rules about how physicians are paid for care (the reimbursement rules). Third is a set of decisions about when people can use care and what types of services they have access to (the access rules). We discuss how each of these rules operates in practice in the United States, and to a limited extent elsewhere.

Before we embark on our tour, some limitations are in order. We primarily limit our analysis to medical care. Health care is broader than just medicine. Restrictions on smoking, for example, are an example of health care outside of the medical system. (The United States is notably schizophrenic here: we preach about the evils of smoking but subsidize tobacco farmers.) Public health infrastructure is important, too. But medical care is where most of the debate has occurred, and so we focus on that area. For the most part, we focus on how medical care systems operate and their effects, rather than on their origins.

Medical Care System Performance in Developed Countries

The performance of medical care systems differs enormously across countries. We assess system performance on two dimensions most relevant for economists: how much the system costs, and how healthy people are, perhaps as a result of the medical system.

The average American spends nearly $6,000 annually on medical care, including what is paid by insurance and out of pocket. That works out to about 15 percent of GDP—roughly one in every seven dollars. The next highest-spending country, Switzerland, allots only 11.5 percent of GDP to medical care, about $3,800 per person in U.S. dollars. The United Kingdom is at the low end of the spectrum; until very recently, it spent only half what the United States did as a share of GDP, even lower in dollar terms. The United Kingdom has recently concluded that it was spending too little on health care and is increasing its spending to the average of other member nations of the Organization for Economic Cooperation and Development (OECD). Across the developed countries as a whole, OECD data show that average per person spending is about $2,300, roughly 9 percent of GDP.

While medical spending as a whole is higher in the United States than elsewhere, the public sector share of medical spending is much lower. Government accounts for about three-quarters of medical spending in the average OECD country; in the United States, government spending is only 44 percent of total spending. Ironically, the high rate of total spending offsets the low public share, so that government spending on medical care is roughly the same in the United States as elsewhere.

What does additional spending in the United States go for? Three factors are important. The first is prices. Physicians in the United States are paid more than their counterparts elsewhere, and pharmaceuticals cost more as well. To some extent, the high prices are a result of decentralization. In many other countries, the government is the only payer, and it drives down the prices of physicians and pharmaceuticals. High prices for physicians are also a reflection of the fact that the wage distribution as a whole is wider in the United States than elsewhere. Top earners in the United States—managers and professionals, CEOs, lawyers, and the like—all earn more in the United States than in other countries. To keep up with this higher external market, physicians in the United States must be paid more.

Another factor in higher U.S. spending is administrative expense. Again, decentralization is costly. Having multiple insurance companies means that hospitals and physicians' offices need extra administrative help. The average private insurance company in the United States charges 15 percent overhead; without marketing costs or the need to earn a return on capital, public insurers charge four to five times less. A focus on administrative costs leads one toward a single-payer system. Why not have one insurance company, save money, and use the savings to cover everyone? We are not particular fans of single-payer systems. For one thing, prior efforts to enact this approach have failed politically. In addition, some administrative expense can be valuable (an electronic medical record, should we ever have one, would be an "administrative expense"). More generally, there is more to health care than just administration. The real key in medical care is whether people receive the right services—neither too many nor too few. There is no obvious relation between low administrative expense and appropriate care received.

This leads to the third difference between countries: the care received when sick. People in the United States receive far more intensive care when they are sick than do people in other countries. At least half of people having a heart attack in the United States will receive a major surgical procedure—coronary bypass surgery (to create a new blood flow to the heart) or angioplasty (to clean out clogged arteries). The share in Canada is less than half as high. More people with mental illness are treated in the United States than Canada (the severely ill are treated in both countries; the less severely ill are also treated in the United States). Cancer care is more intensive as well.

The natural question is whether people are healthier as a result. The most common summary measure of health is life expectancy at birth. On this metric, the United States does not do particularly well. The mean across developed countries is seventy-eight years. The United States, with a life expectancy of seventy-seven years, ranks twenty-third of the thirty countries. Japan is the clear high-end outlier, with life expectancy of eighty-two years. The United States is, and has for some time, been a laggard.

Of course, life expectancy is influenced by many factors. Lifestyles (smoking, diet), environmental conditions (air pollution), and other economic conditions are all important. For example, the United States is the most obese country in the OECD, though U.S. smoking rates are far below those of most other developed countries. One cannot take the lower life expectancy at birth in the United States as being definitive about the value of more care. Reporting differences may also affect international comparisons. For infant mortality, where the U.S. rate is also higher than other countries, some research suggests that the United States reports more preterm and very low birth weight outcomes as live births than other countries, potentially contributing to the higher U.S. infant mortality rate.[1] Still, there is precious little evidence that the United States does better than other countries in any material outcome.

One common view is that U.S. use rates (for example rates of physician visits, hospital stays, and services provided) are excessive, and this explains why we get little for the additional care received. Even though heart attack patients in the United States receive more care than do heart attack patients in other countries, survival one year after a heart attack is no greater in the United States than elsewhere. This possibly reflects the low value of additional care—though it might also reflect factors such as the quality of the surgeons or hospitals providing the additional care. The fear of malpractice can justify such excessive use, though studies suggest that the cost of malpractice—direct, and through defensive medical practice—is no more than 5 percent of total spending. Payment issues are perhaps more important; the United States has a system that rewards high-tech provision. We come back to payment issues below.

Perhaps the most obvious area of waste is care at the end of life. About one-quarter of Medicare spending occurs in the last six months of life. This share has been constant over time; care at the end of life has been increasing at the same rate as care in other settings. While some care at the end of life is appropriate—one never knows exactly who will die—some care is clearly not necessary. People die in hospitals when they would prefer to die at home, and most families experiencing a recent death wish that less care had been provided.[2] Exact comparisons are difficult to make, but end-of-life care is almost certainly less plentiful in other countries.

The issue of end-of-life care brings up the broader issue of quality of life. Even if people in the United States do not live longer than people in other countries, perhaps they live healthier. Quality of life comparisons across countries are very difficult, since there is no single measure of quality that is widely accepted as definitive. Some studies have found that quality of life is higher in the United States than in other countries. Not all authors agree, however. And the improvement in quality of life has not been compared to the additional spending in the United States. The overall evaluation of where one would most like to be sick is thus difficult to make definitively.

The United States is widely regarded as having a health care cost problem—the high level of medical spending is believed to have a deleterious impact on the economy. As the previous discussion shows, this conclusion is premature. High costs are a problem if they are not matched by commensurate benefits. Full evaluation of those benefits has not been conducted. Rather than focus on "problems" such as costs, access, or quality, we focus on the fundamentals that affect how medical care is provided and who pays for it.

Insurance Coverage

The first job of a medical system is coverage—getting people insurance so that they can use care. There are a number of variations in rules about coverage. In some countries (the United Kingdom and Canada, for example), insurance is provided by the government. In other countries, such as Switzerland and the Netherlands, insurance is private. In private systems like the U.S. employment system, the contribution for insurance is often termed a "premium." Everyone pays the premium, and subsidies are provided to the poor. In public systems, the contribution is generally termed a "tax" and is paid for by the rich more than the poor. The difference between these is less than the words suggest. In *any* universal coverage system, everyone gets care from some insurer, and the rich pay a good part of the costs for the poor.

SOURCES OF COVERAGE

As in everything else, the United States combines some of everything. Table 15.1 summarizes the sources of insurance coverage in the United States. The source of care and nature of coverage are in the first two columns. The third column reports the share of the population with that coverage. To the extent that the United States has a national health system, it is the Medicare program. Medicare became law in 1965, with the wave of universal coverage enactments occurring in other countries around the same time. Universal coverage was (and still is) too much of a stretch for the United States. A more limited goal was coverage for the very needy—the elderly and very poor non-elderly (see the discussion of Medicaid below).

Medicare provides coverage to virtually everyone over age sixty-five, as well as people under sixty-five who are blind, disabled, or suffering from end-stage kidney disease (about 10 percent of the Medicare program is non-elderly). Eligibility for Medicare is (virtually) automatic at age sixty-five, and the program is heavily subsidized. Very few elderly drop out of it. Medicare-for-all is the mantra for some health care reformers and the fear of others.

Medicaid, enacted at the same time as Medicare but as an afterthought in the legislation, provides insurance on a means-tested

Table 15.1   Sources of Health Insurance Coverage

Source	Groups	Services Covered	Share of People
Public			
Medicare	Elderly; disabled ESRD	Hospital; physician Rx Drugs	12
Medicaid	Poor; Elderly; Blind and disabled	Hospital; physician; Rx drugs durables; long-term care	8
Private			
Employer Non–group	Workers and deps Families	Hospital; physician; Rx drugs	56
Uninsured			
		Catastrophic care	16

SOURCE: Based on data from U.S. Bureau of the Census, Current Population Survey.

basis for poor women and children under sixty-five and the blind and disabled; it also provides long-term care for persons age sixty-five and older. Sixteen percent of the non-elderly population is covered by public insurance. Where Medicare is entirely a federal program, Medicaid is run by states (and some localities), with the federal government providing broad rules and a good share of the money. Medicaid coverage has expanded over time. In the 1960s, coverage was limited to single mothers and their children; the typical income eligibility threshold was about half of the poverty line. Since then, Medicaid has been expanded to families higher up in the income level, particularly children, and with fewer restrictions on family composition. Medicaid is the dominant insurer for children below the poverty line, providing two-thirds of their coverage.

The majority of the non-elderly, nearly three-quarters, are covered by private insurance. Most of this is provided through employment, but a small share comes from individual purchase as well. The comprehensiveness of this coverage varies by employer, ranging from very complete coverage to relatively limited coverage.

Sixteen percent of the population, in total 46 million people, is without health insurance, almost all of them non-elderly. The uninsured are a heterogeneous group. Some are young and perhaps feel that health insurance is not a pressing need. Others are near poor—above the poverty line but working in jobs that rarely provide health insurance. Many are unemployed or employed by small firms that don't provide insurance, and still others have chronic diseases that prevent them from buying insurance. Some of the uninsured are eligible for Medicaid, but don't use the insurance.[3]

The uninsured do not go entirely without care. Typically, they receive care through hospital emergency rooms. Much of this care is for serious illness or accidents, providing a sort of partial catastrophic insurance paid for by insured patients, who pay more than the price of their care. The quality is low, however; the health of the uninsured suffers because they are uninsured. The Institute of Medicine estimates that eighteen thousand adults ages twenty-five to sixty-four die each year because they are uninsured.[4] And even as a financing mechanism, the catastrophic coverage route is inefficient.

As noted above, the public sector pays for about 45 percent of medical care. Medicare and Medicaid are most of this, but there are other programs through the Department of Defense, the Department of Veterans Affairs, and state and local governments. The rest comes from private insurers and out-of-pocket payments. Three-quarters of private payments are made by insurers; one-quarter—13 percent of total medical spending—is paid out of pocket. A relatively large proportion of out-of-pocket payments are for outpatient prescription drugs, though that is changing with the new Medicare drug benefit recently brought online. In addition, much long-term care spending is out of pocket. As a result, people worry about these costs more than they do other costs.

PAYMENTS FOR INSURANCE

Corresponding to the different methods of insurance coverage are different financing sources. Medicare and Medicaid are public, and thus funded largely through the tax system. A payroll tax funds part of the cost of Medicare, with general taxes (largely income taxes) supporting most of the remainder and all of Medicaid. There is an enrollee premium for parts of Medicare, currently equal to about 13 percent of the program cost. The predominance of taxes on the working population to pay for medical care receipt by the elderly is an enormous intergenerational transfer, the magnitude of which is on the order of the entire Social Security system. It is also increasing more rapidly. The financing challenge to support an aging population is thus severe.

Private insurance is financed largely through premiums. For the typical person with private health insurance, the insurance is arranged for and bought by the employer. On average, the employer pays for about 75 to 80 percent of the cost, and the employee pays the remainder. But employers do not really bear the cost of health insurance. Substantial evidence shows that employers respond to rising costs of health insurance by increasing wages less rapidly.[5] In the end, health insurance is paid for by workers.

The government has no direct role in paying for private health insurance, but it has an indirect one. Employer payments for health insurance are not taxed as income, while wage and salary payments are. As a result, there is an enormous tax benefit—perhaps 30 percent of total premiums—to be realized by running insurance through employment. This is why employers provide the coverage in the first place. One might imagine this tax subsidy being part of a foresighted government unable to commit to universal coverage. Alas, that is not the case. Employers started to provide health insurance when wages were controlled in World War II and benefits were not. The IRS ruled in the early 1950s that it would not tax such benefits as income, and the policy has stuck since then.

Economic transactions can happen smoothly or with rough edges. This one is as rough as it gets. Employers writing checks to health insurance companies fear that they will be made to bear the cost; workers are afraid to leave their jobs because health insurance is tied to work; and everyone is a pink slip away from losing coverage. A raging debate in policy circles concerns the extent to which the United States would be better off or worse off without employer-based insurance. Some favor retaining employer coverage because the obstacles to dismantling the system appear too great. Others believe that the frictions are too rough and employers will ultimately stop providing such insurance, but disagree on alternatives to the existing system. Some prefer market-oriented insurance purchased by individuals to replace employer coverage and criticize the inefficiencies of employer or government health programs. Others favor replacing the employer-based system with expanded government insurance programs and fear an unregulated individual market—sick people priced higher or denied coverage; poor people without a place to get insurance. Our own research has highlighted the rapid deterioration in private coverage, especially for the less healthy and poor.[6] We find it hard to imagine keeping afloat a system with so many leaks.

COMPARISON WITH OTHER COUNTRIES

It is useful to contrast the United States with another typical developed country—to the extent that any country is typical. Most countries would have a simpler version of Table 15.1. There would be one row, and it would indicate that everyone was on a single health insurance plan. That plan would pay for about three-quarters of care, without about one-quarter of the costs coming from direct individual payments. The public component would be financed by a tax—income, payroll, or value-added.

The biggest difference across countries is the nature of the insurance plan—what services are covered? At what price? And what

do people do if they don't like the public program? We first address
the issue of physician payment, and then turn to these issues next.

Reimbursing Providers

Given the many different ways that people can obtain health insurance, it is not surprising that there is a wide range of reimbursement
systems in use. The reimbursement systems differ enormously in the
incentives they provide.

Perhaps the most critical feature of reimbursement systems is
the degree to which payments are related to costs. Some reimbursement systems pay more when more care is provided, and others pay
less. Consider the relation between medical payments and two types
of costs: practice costs (office expenses, non-physician administrative
personnel, malpractice insurance, and supplies) and time costs. The
time costs represent the opportunity costs of the physician devoting
additional hours to care.

Historically, medical care in the United States and many other
countries (Canada, Japan, and France for example) was paid for on
a *fee-for-service* basis. In this system, reimbursement is equal to
the average cost of care provided (with some division between
insurer and enrollee payments). In the United States, the reason for
taking this approach was practical. When private insurers started to
cover medical care, they did not know how to pay for care; medical
care was separate from insurance. Doctors had list prices, however,
and so insurers paid those prices. This ultimately turned into the
fee-for-service system.

There is a distinction between marginal and average cost that is
important in understanding the incentives of fee-for-service systems. Medical care has very high fixed costs, but the marginal cost of
additional production is often low. For example, it costs about $800
million to develop a new drug, but the cost of producing additional
pills once the drug is developed is only pennies. Similarly, many of the
costs for a physician are sunk costs—the opportunity cost of med-

ical education most particularly. Other costs are fixed costs, depending only on the decision to practice medicine. Examples of these costs include malpractice insurance, office rent, and equipment overhead. True marginal cost is low.

Traditional fee-for-service payment systems pay on the basis of average costs. This reimburses physicians for sunk and fixed costs as well as marginal costs. In practice, this creates large profits for providing additional care, because payment far exceeds costs at the margin. Thus, fee-for-service payment systems strongly encourage provision of medical care in almost all circumstances.

A somewhat less generous set of incentives is provided by a *salary* system. In many Health Maintenance Organizations (HMOs) in the United States and in some European countries, physicians are paid a salary for providing care. The physician earns a fixed amount of money and does not have to pay for any practice expenses, but is not reimbursed more for additional time costs.

The salary system provides fewer incentives for care provision than does the fee-for-service system. In a salary system, additional care provided is not reimbursed at the margin, so there is no financial incentive to do more. In particular, because the doctor's time cost is not reimbursed at the margin, the doctor has an incentive to cut back on time inputs. A doctor on a salary earns the same amount if he shows up for a full day or half day of work (assuming his salary is not docked). Thus, doctors will attempt to arrive late and leave early, and to substitute tests and devices for additional time.

The ability of physicians to do this varies by setting. In some countries, such as Italy, monitoring of physicians is poor, and doctors routinely violate the guidelines as to hours that must be worked.[7] In many HMOs, in contrast, monitoring is stronger, and physicians are not able to shirk.

The third type of payment system is *capitation*. In the extreme version of this system, physicians are paid a fixed amount per patient and must pay for all care provided out of the capitation amount.

This type of system is most common with primary care physicians. If a patient of a doctor paid this way uses medications that the doctor prescribes or is admitted to the hospital, the costs of the medications or hospitalization are paid for out of the capitation amount.

With earnings falling as additional care is provided, the capitated system provides the least incentives to do more. A purely profit-maximizing doctor paid a capitation rate would not provide any care. Of course, HMOs monitor physician behavior, and patients will find other doctors if no care is provided, so that future income will decline. The example is grossly exaggerated, but it shows the nature of the incentives.

Over time, both Medicare and the private sector have moved away from pure fee-for-service payment with some elements of capitated payment. Medicare currently pays physicians on a fee schedule, based loosely on the estimated cost of services provided. In a number of detailed studies, the government attempted to determine the cost of different services and now reimburses physicians on that basis. The payment is still per service performed, but is somewhat less generous than it once was.

Bigger changes have occurred in the payment system for hospitals. Since the early 1980s, payment for Medicare patients admitted to hospitals has been under a partially capitated system termed the Prospective Payment System, or PPS. When a Medicare patient is admitted to a hospital, the hospital reports the diagnosis the patient received and whether a surgical procedure was performed or not. These two attributes are used to classify patients into one of about 470 Diagnosis Related Groups, or DRGs. The payment received for the patient depends only on the DRG and on a few hospital-specific factors such as the region of the country and whether the hospital is a teaching hospital, not the specific services provided (other than how the surgical/non-surgical distinction affects DRG coding). Thus, additional days in the hospital, tests, and the like are no longer reimbursed.

In the private sector, reimbursement is more variable, depending on the specific payer. Some physicians are paid on a fee-for-service basis, although usually one where the payments are substantially less generous than they were formerly.[8] More common is for physicians to be paid on a salary basis or by full or partial capitation. Hospital payments are generally along the lines of Medicare, with a payment per admission (using the DRG system) or per day of care received (a per diem system). In the latter methodology, the payment does not vary with the services provided in each day. Thus, intensive care in the stay is discouraged, while marginal days of care are not so heavily penalized. With payment rates falling in recent years (see below), the incentives for limited service provision are even stronger.

How much do these incentives matter? A large literature has examined how physician behavior responds to payment incentives.[9] The issue is complicated because the incentives of patients may be different from those of physicians, and one does not know which views will prevail. But the bottom line is clear: when more is paid, more is done.[10] Thus, paying doctors on a fee-for-service basis gets the most care provided. Less is done in a salary system, and less still occurs when physicians are capitated.

Whether fee-for-service or capitated payment is superior depends on health outcomes as well as costs. Most evidence suggests that quality of care is relatively similar in capitated and fee-for-service arrangements.[11] Thus, with lower costs and equivalent quality, recent payment reforms can be seen as quite valuable. Despite this economic analysis, patients and providers have deep antipathy toward payment systems that bring cost into the medical care decision process. HMOs—the groups that use capitated payments most frequently—are not seen as good innovations in medical care. We return to "managed care" and the issues it raises below.

A limitation of both capitated and fee-for-service payment systems is that in some instances, physicians may be punished, rather than rewarded, for providing high-quality care. Under fee-for-service incentives, a physician group that invests time to develop a diabetes management program that reduces the need for office visits will lose money. Under a capitated system, a physician known to provide good care to patients with multiple conditions may lose money if payments do not reflect patients' greater sickness level.

"Paying for performance" is a relatively new approach that aims to reorient incentives to reward quality improvement with higher payments. The basic idea is simple: provider payments should reward care that improves health.[12] Linking payment to quality would provide higher reimbursement to providers with improved care or outcomes. Under this approach, providers have incentives to devise ways to deliver care that results in better health outcomes. For example, a hospital might invest in a computerized order entry system and bar coding to reduce medication errors. A large physician group might hire a nurse to help diabetic or hypertensive patients monitor blood glucose levels or blood pressure.

There is no single type of pay for performance. These programs are increasingly common in the private sector, with insurers taking different approaches in choosing what to reward and types of rewards. The Medicare program is adopting pay for performance slowly, soliciting input from provider and beneficiary groups. While the approach attracts many supporters, critics claim that paying for performance may create incentives for providers to avoid patients who are sicker or perceived to be less likely to adhere to a treatment regimen.

COMPARISON WITH OTHER COUNTRIES

Medical care reimbursement systems differ enormously across countries.[13] Indeed, some countries use multiple types of payments. In Canada, for example, physicians are paid on a fee-for-service basis, but hospitals are paid a "global budget" (a single negotiated amount for the year, somewhat akin to a capitation payment). Both physicians and hospitals in Japan are paid on a fee-for-service basis. In the United Kingdom, primary care physicians are capitated—sort of—while hospitals are capitated to a stronger extent. Recently, the United Kingdom adopted a general practitioner contract that includes rewards for delivering high-quality care.

The generosity of the payment also varies greatly. In Canada, payments are relatively generous, so most physicians work happily under Medicare. In the United Kingdom, payments in the public system are lower. Many physicians supplement their income by seeing patients privately, and charging them more than the National Health Service will pay. In Japan, the payment system for routine visits is so low that physicians could not make a living off of that amount. Physicians supplement their income by providing excessive medications (for which they make a profit) and performing well-reimbursed diagnostic scanning.

With few exceptions, the payment side of most systems does not work well. Costs are rarely low enough to keep spending at desired levels while still ensuring adequate supply. Rather than rely exclusively on payments to control utilization, countries rely on overall limits to constrain what is done—e.g., setting hospital capacity to ensure that too many people are not operated on. The United States has fewer overall limits than other countries, but higher spending. These rules about access are what we turn to next.

Access Rules

Access rules are among the most complex areas of medical care. Many varieties of medical services can be provided, with different rules for each. For example, patients may have different access to primary care, mental health specialists, and orthopedists. We synthesize the access rules in three parts. The first element is the set of services insurance covers. The second element is the financial payments that individuals have to make when they use care (termed "cost sharing"). Finally, there are sometimes non-financial barriers to the use of services such as preauthorization requirements or limits on what services can be accessed.

COVERED SERVICES

In the United States, there are enormous differences in what is covered by different types of policies. Private insurance policies generally cover hospital care, physician services, outpatient tests, and prescription drugs, though there is variation in coverage across policies. Long-term care is usually not covered, but those services are used infrequently by the non-elderly population, so the omission is not as major as omitting care for other services such as mental illness would be.

Medicare is significantly less generous than the typical private insurance policy. Medicare covers hospital services, physician expenses, and laboratory tests. Some long-term care is covered, but not an enormous amount. In 2006, Medicare began to cover outpatient prescription medications, although not as generously as in private insurance. After having up-front coverage for medications, there is a "donut hole" where Medicare coverage stops, before resuming again a few thousand dollars later. The donut was to save money; it has unwittingly become a symbol of how bad government policy can get made.

Medicare benefits are largely oriented toward acute, often costly services to diagnose and treat illnesses. Preventive services historically were not included in Medicare benefits. It requires an act of Congress to add a preventive service to Medicare; many preventive services have limited coverage although they may be cost-effective. For example, Medicare now covers smoking cessation services after a person develops a smoking-related illness (when it is considered a treatment), but not before (when it would be preventive). Medicare's policies on incorporating new treatments into benefits also further the emphasis on technological, acute benefits. Unlike many countries, Medicare does not explicitly consider information on cost-effectiveness when deciding whether to cover new treatments.

Medicaid covers essentially all acute and long-term care services. On paper, Medicaid is among the most generous insurance plans available. In practice, though, Medicaid payments are so tightly constrained that access to care for Medicaid beneficiaries is a significant concern. Only about half of primary care doctors (60 percent of all physicians) will accept new patients insured by Medicaid.

The Medicaid experience raises the broader point that access is not just about covered services but also about how much access the policy allows. A major issue in the United States, discussed below, is whether the receipt of medical care is "managed" or not. Private insurance and Medicaid are largely managed; Medicare is not.

Cost Sharing in Insurance

Almost all insurance policies require patients to pay something when they access care. Cost sharing evolved as a way to limit moral hazard—excessive use of medical services because people are insured. Since its beginnings, cost sharing has become much more elaborate.

Traditionally, private insurance policies have had a varying schedule of patient payments. A typical "indemnity" insurance policy has a deductible of about $500. After the deductible, costs are split between the insurer and the enrollee. The share of enrollee payments is termed the "coinsurance rate"; a standard coinsurance rate is 20 percent. Coinsurance continues until the patient reaches a specified maximum, termed the "stop-loss." Past this point, the insurer pays all the costs of medical care. A common stop-loss is about $1,500.

The optimal insurance policy considers both risk sharing and moral hazard. Greater individual payments reduce excessive use but also increase financial risk. Insurance policies must trade off these two components. In practice, the tax system subsidized generous insurance and thus tilted policies toward being overly generous. Employer payments for health insurance are not counted as income for tax purposes, while individual payments are. It was noted above that this provides incentives for people to have insurance through work. In addition, it encourages very generous insurance, since insured services are paid for with pretax dollars rather than posttax dollars. This leads to a welfare loss—too much moral hazard, and not enough risk borne by individuals.

A substantial literature has examined the impact of this tax subsidy on overall medical spending and the losses to the economy. A consensus estimate is that total medical spending is perhaps 5 to 10 percent higher as a result of the tax subsidy.

The traditional Medicare program has the opposite problem. Cost sharing in the Medicare system is very high, particularly for catastrophic expenses. An analysis done a few years back showed that, on cost-sharing grounds, Medicare was less generous than 95 percent of private insurance policies. That will change somewhat with the new drug coverage, but Medicare's cost sharing will never be the envy of those with private insurance. Even for hospital and physician care, Medicare cost sharing can be high—far higher than economic calculations suggest is optimal. By this reasoning, the donut hole in the new Medicare drug benefit is similarly misguided.

In response to this high degree of risk bearing, almost all Medicare beneficiaries have more coverage than Medicare provides. For the low-income population, Medicaid provides this additional insurance, paying for the cost sharing required by the Medicare reimbursement schedule. Others enroll in Medicare HMOs to obtain lower cost sharing. Many large employers pay for wraparound services to cover Medicare cost sharing for their retired employees. And some purchase insurance solely to cover Medicare cost sharing. These supplemental policies reduce risk, but also drive up medical spending. Rationalizing cost sharing in Medicare would be a welcome change: covering more of the very expensive bills, but leaving more of the routine costs to the individual.

SUPPLY-SIDE CONSTRAINTS

All insurance plans impose some non-financial barriers to access medical care. People need physician approval before they can receive prescription medications or be admitted to a hospital, for example. But some plans have additional barriers to the use of care. This is particularly true of private insurance in the United States. The Medicare program covers patients to see whatever doctor they want (assuming the doctor will see them; almost all do) at whatever time they want (subject only to the usual office wait, smaller for specialists than in other countries). Private insurance restricts what services can be provided and by whom.

Non-financial barriers to care are a fundamental aspect of managed care. At the broadest level, managed care is a system of insurance that seeks to integrate payment and service provision, which were traditionally separated. In managed care, insurers take an active role in influencing what care can be provided and who provides it. Managed care comes in many varieties, but the structural elements are similar. Utilization review—monitoring of providers to restrict the services that are performed and deny or reduce payment—is a central element. Utilization review can be conducted on an individual basis, as in tissue review committees; or on a statistical basis, by monitoring a physician or hospital's overall utilization. Many managed care plans also form a network of providers who can be seen for a lower out-of-pocket payment. To get into the network, providers agree to discounted fees. The quid pro quo is the additional patients that network providers will receive. In some cases, the network is exclusive. Group/staff model HMOs—as with Kaiser Permanente—contract exclusively with physicians and pay them a salary for working in the plan. The utilization incentives in these plans are that much stronger.

In exchange for tight access restrictions, most managed care plans have low patient cost sharing. A person might face a $10 co-payment for seeing a network physician, compared to full price for the first dollar of care in some indemnity insurance plans. In some HMOs, patients can go outside of the network and still receive some reimbursement, but reimbursement out of network is not as generous as reimbursement within.

Obtaining lower prices from providers was a clear strategy of managed care. Studies suggest that hospital and physician prices were about 20 to 30 percent lower in managed care than outside of managed care.[14] There were also some quantity changes. Patients with mental health problems, for example, were much more likely to receive medications than psychotherapy in managed care plans.[15] By and large, these changes did not seem to harm patient outcomes. It is difficult to find systematic evidence that managed care results in lower-quality care compared to fee-for-service insurance.[16]

Managed care swept the medical system in the United States. In 1980, managed care was less than 10 percent of private insurance. Today, it is over 90 percent. But the heyday of managed care has passed. By the late 1990s, many Americans were sick of the restraints that managed care, particularly HMOs, imposed on them. Cost sharing was low, but physicians had to see so many patients that they rarely had adequate time with each one. Managed care might have eliminated overused care, but how was one to tell which care was overused? By early in the 2000s, managed care insurers had to relax their strong limits or risk losing enrollees. The overall degree of management in American medicine has declined significantly in the past half decade.

COMPARISONS WITH OTHER COUNTRIES

There are two ways to restrict what is done in medical care. The first is the demand-side approach: impose high cost sharing and rely on patients (guided by their physicians) to decide what care is needed and not. The second is the supply-side approach: impose limits on what a physician can do in a particular setting or on the availability of services as a whole. Care is then provided within those overall limits. The United States has a hybrid system, perhaps the worst of both worlds. Cost sharing can be high, but is not uniformly high enough to provide an effective constraint on spending. Care is managed, but not systematically enough to make people feel comfortable with the results.

Around the world, supply-side limits are far more common than are demand-side limits. Canada, for example, imposes very tight controls on the number of hospitals that can acquire expensive new technologies. There is less technology than physicians would use by choice, so some rationing must occur. In practice, the rationing is done by physicians, who decide which patients most need access to the technologies. The same is true for hospital care in the United Kingdom and France.

Supply-side constraints save money, but they impose costs in other ways. The most noticeable cost is waiting lines. In the United Kingdom, waits for non-emergency surgery can be as long as eighteen months. Perceiving this to be too much, the British government is increasing spending by 20 to 25 percent, with the hope of greater service provision. In countries that spend more, waiting lines are shorter, but they are still prevalent. Supply-side limitations also lead to some inefficiencies. When care is rationed by supply, the available care may go to the wrong patients, allocated on bases other than need, like politics or the whim of providers.

The net result is that unhappiness with medical care is common across countries. Surveys in several developed countries (the United States, the United Kingdom, Canada, Australia, and New Zealand) have asked people their view about their own country's medical system.[17] In all of these countries, no more than 25 percent of people are very happy with the health system.

Conclusions

Forecasting is hazardous, and we are not good at guessing the future. But it is worthwhile discussing some of the challenges that the United States will face. We emphasize three challenges. The first issue is expanding coverage. Many people want the United States to enact universal insurance coverage, but no consensus has been reached on the best approach. Some favor private market approaches that provide subsidies to workers or employers to purchase employment-based health insurance. Subsidies have the advantage of building on the existing employment-based system but can leave gaps for people who are unemployed and can be costly to implement. Another approach would extend coverage for high-cost, catastrophic medical care while subsidizing costs for the poor. Proponents of this approach often favor expanding coverage using Health Savings Accounts (HSAs), which are available to people who enroll in a high-deductible health plan. HSAs may be most advantageous for healthier people, while sicker individuals will use more funds to pay for care. Others support government program expansions, such as a Medicare-for-all approach, because they favor the broad risk pooling and government-created cost controls in traditional Medicare. Yet others raise concerns about increasing the government's role in financing and organizing U.S. health care. Medicaid expansions more directly target the lower-income individuals who are more likely to be uninsured, yet would not reach the higher income uninsured.

Many prior health reform efforts have failed over inability to reach political compromise on the balance between public- and private-sector roles in providing health insurance. Today, compromise proposals are increasingly being discussed that would combine public coverage expansions for lower-income individuals with private insurance subsidies for higher-income individuals, but the financing for expanded health insurance coverage remains a challenge without a clear solution.

The importance of financing mechanisms points to a second challenge, the need to increase the value gained from health care. Some approaches, like pay for performance, redesign payment systems to create incentives for hospitals and physicians to provide better care, instead of more care. Other approaches, like the high-deductible health plans noted above, aim to lower costs by making patients more cost-conscious consumers of health care. There are advocates for each approach, and no clear way to know what approaches will take hold.

The need to improve value raises a final challenge—disparities in health. In the United States and internationally, lower-income people have less access to care and worse health outcomes than people with higher incomes. In the United States, lack of health insurance is part of the reason, but the relationship between higher economic status and better health is found even in countries with universal coverage, such as the United Kingdom. Understanding and ameliorating the sources of these disparities is an active area of research and policy.

The three challenges are interrelated. Achieving expansions in health insurance, either to cover the uninsured or enhance the generosity of coverage, may require effective approaches to increase the value of health care spending. Efforts to increase value, in turn, have the potential to reduce health disparities if they result in improved health for the most vulnerable groups. Since many nations face these challenges, innovations in the United States and internationally may create opportunities for cross-national learning that could lead to improved health within and across borders.

CHAPTER 16

Criminal Justice

James Q. Wilson

America's decentralized political system profoundly affects how the criminal justice system operates. As political scientist James Q. Wilson points out, it makes crime control responsive to public opinion in ways that are quite different from what one finds in Europe. That responsiveness helps explain why America imprisons so many people and thus why its property crime rates are lower than in many other democratic nations. Not only does punishment differ by locality, so also do opportunities for acquiring drugs and carrying firearms.

A DISTINCTIVE FEATURE OF THE AMERICAN CRIMINAL JUSTICE system is its decentralization; the most salient aspects of American crime rates are their high level of homicide and moderate level of property crimes. To comprehend criminal justice policy here, we must first understand its localism; to appreciate our crime rates, we must recognize that they have moved in directions quite different from what one finds in much of Europe.

In Europe, the criminal justice system tends to be centralized, with national police forces and government ministries that oversee law enforcement. Though Great Britain has fifty-two police departments, America has at least seventeen thousand and maybe more. In Britain there is a national police college that trains almost all of the high-level officials, a lord chancellor who selects and oversees most British judges, and a Home Office that supplies to Parliament proposals designed to guide criminal justice policy for the country as a whole. None of these agencies exists at the national level here.

In America, every city, county, and state has its own police department; every county and many cities have their own elected district or city attorney; and every state has its own correctional system. There are national law enforcement agencies such as the FBI and the DEA, but they have a modest number of employees, investigate only a small fraction of all crimes, and arrest only a minor part of all suspects. One might imagine that this decentralized system would produce conflict, in ways that might be familiar to anyone who has watched fictional rivalries between the FBI and local police departments on television. But local police departments work well together, and the FBI and local authorities share information quite readily.

Criminal Justice and Public Opinion

The main consequence of America's decentralized system is that public opinion closely watches and deeply influences law enforcement. Police chiefs are selected by mayors who must run for reelection. District attorneys are elected by the voters. State prison systems must be designed and paid for by elected governors. In many states the voters can set criminal justice policy directly by voting for initiative and referenda measures.

Public opinion makes American criminal justice policy highly sensitive to popular worries about the crime rate, even when that rate is falling, and to some dramatic cases that capture the headlines.

Many people in Europe think that America's close link between politics and policy is a serious problem. Some British officials frequently complain that this connection leads America to have policies they oppose, such as the death penalty, three strikes laws, and statutes that allow people to own or (even worse) to carry guns.

Doubtless the intensely democratic nature of American criminal justice policymaking can err. When voters demand longer maximum sentences for a crime that has recently made the headlines, they sometimes ignore the fact that many people who commit that crime do not go to prison at all and those that do may often be kept in prison long after there is any chance of their repeating the crime. A longer mandatory sentence is meaningless for an offender who is not convicted of the crime, and it may be useless for an inmate who dies in prison.

But the democratic link has an offsetting virtue: When the crime rate goes up, the public demands that elected officials do something about it. And they do.

In 1976, the crime rates in America and England were both rising sharply. At that time, England was more likely to send a robber to prison than was California.[1] In the midst of this crime wave, American politicians, prodded by public opinion, decided to get tough, but British ones, stimulated not by public opinion but by the therapeutic sentiments of political elites, decided to become soft. The Criminal Justice Act, passed by Parliament in 1991, discouraged judges from sending offenders to prison unless the crime was very serious. And in deciding if the offense was very serious, judges were supposed to ignore any prior convictions the offender had acquired.[2]

The American prison population started to rise while in England it started to decline. Between 1980 and 1985, the American prison population increased by more than half; between 1985 and 1990, it increased by another half. But between 1987 and 1992, the British prison population dropped by almost five thousand inmates. By 1996, America and England had changed places with respect to property crime: England now had a higher property crime rate than did the United States.

There are two ways to measure crime rates; one is by offenses reported to the police, the other by surveys of people to find out how many have been victims of crime. Police reports may not be reliable, and in England they have become quite suspect. If we use victim surveys and compare England to the United States, we learn that the British robbery rate is one-quarter higher, the auto theft rate one-third higher, and the burglary and assault rates twice as large.[3]

The English responded to these problems in the mid-1990s by passing, under the leadership of Home Secretary Michael Howard, some new criminal justice laws that urged judges to be tougher. In 1997 the law allowed life sentences for some second-offender adults and required burglars who had committed three offenses to spend at least three years in prison. But these changes, while helpful, did not make a fundamental difference: the risk of going to prison remained higher in America than in England for burglary and robbery, and by 2003 the lord chief justice was once again asking judges to send fewer first-time offenders to prison.[4]

Does Prison Work?

It is possible that tougher American sentencing practices did not make our crime rate go down or that more lenient ones in England did not make theirs go up. We have no direct comparison of American and British sentencing practices, but in this country the weight of scholarly opinion is that prison sentences do deter crime. Steven Levitt, Daniel Nagin, and other scholars have produced studies that convincingly show that, even after controlling statistically for other factors, a higher risk of going to prison in states is associated with lower crime rates in those states.[5] One study by William Spelman and another by Thomas B. Marvell and Carlisle E. Moody, Jr., suggest that about one-quarter of the crime drop in America in the 1980s was due to imprisonment. Stated another way, an increase in the prison population by 1 percent led to a 0.16 percent drop in the crime rate.[6]

Imprisonment explains much but not all of the American crime drop. There is a lively scholarly debate about what other factors may be at work. One possibility is that crime rates drop when there are fewer young males in the population, but the evidence for that is not entirely clear.[7] Another is that crime rates are affected by the frequency with which new drug users are recruited: the new users

often steal to pay for their drugs and dealers often shoot one another to maintain control of their territories. A third possibility is
that as crime rates rise, ordinary citizens make greater efforts to resist crime by locking their homes and cars, installing alarms, and
avoiding tough neighborhoods. And a fourth is that (at least in this
country) people have armed themselves so as to discourage crime
by brandishing (and sometimes using) a weapon.

But whatever the reasons, what is striking is that "criminal"
America has lower rates of most property crimes than do many
democratic nations. According to international surveys of victims,
America has a lower burglary rate than does Australia, Canada, Denmark, England, and Finland; a lower robbery rate than does Australia, Canada, England, the Netherlands, Poland, Portugal, Scotland,
and Spain; and a lower auto theft rate than does Australia, Canada,
Denmark, England, France, and Italy.[8]

Murder

However, America has a much higher murder rate than many European nations. It is tempting to explain that by looking at some contemporary features of American society, such as violent motion
pictures, the private possession of guns, and a large drug culture. But
our homicide rate has been high for a very long time before there
was violent media, heavy public gun possession, or the invention of
heroin or cocaine. For the last two hundred years the murder rate in
New York City was between ten and fifteen times higher than that
in London.[9] Today, the rate at which Americans kill each other *without* using guns but relying instead on fists, knives, and blows to the
head is three times higher than the non-gun homicide rate in England. Even when the motive for crime is a robbery and no gun is
used, the fatality rate from New York City robberies is three times
higher than it is for those in London.[10]

To put it bluntly, Americans are a more violent people than are
the British, though the latter have been trying hard to catch up. If

you wish to explain why we are more violent, make a list of all the leading features of American history and assume that in some combination they tell the story. This country was built along a gradually expanding frontier where human settlement often occurred before any local government that could control violence was in place. We never had a landed aristocracy that monopolized the control of firearms. We kept millions of blacks in slavery, denying them the right to own property and exposing them to the weakly checked arrogance of slave owners. When the slaves were emancipated, many police forces ignored black-on-black crime but took very seriously black-on-white crime, real or imagined. We are a nation of immigrants where ethnic groups have often bumped rudely into one another. And we have celebrated personal liberty, empowering people to do not only great and noble things but mean and wicked ones as well.

Scholars have studied the relationship between income inequality and crime, especially homicide. Many have concluded that places with high rates of income inequality will have higher rates of crime, especially homicide, than will nations or states with low levels of income inequality.[11] Since incomes in the United States are much more unequal than those in, say, Sweden, and since incomes in North Dakota and Vermont are much less unequal than those in California or New York, this argument might explain why murder rates are higher in the United States than in Sweden and in California and New York rather than in North Dakota or Vermont.

These studies, of course, show statistical correlations but they do not necessarily demonstrate social causes. However, the findings are so uniform that one must take the correlations seriously. There are several possible explanations for the linkage.

One is that the connection between inequality and homicide is misleading because so many factors are associated with inequality that it is hard to be certain that the cause is inequality itself or instead something correlated with inequality, such as education, family structure, or the presence or absence of gangs that makes the difference. Consider race: black Americans have a murder rate that is six to eight times higher than the white murder rate. In fact, in Chicago, the black homicide rate is more than three times higher than the white rate even in neighborhoods where blacks earn the highest incomes.[12] If blacks killed people at the same rate as whites, the nation's murder rate would fall without any change in income inequality, but it would still be about twice as high as that rate in most European nations.[13] Were blacks to have the same homicide rate as whites, America would still be an aggressive nation.

But suppose inequality itself, and not something else, explains murder rates. Perhaps inequality produces social strain or a sense of despair or anger among the poor, who respond by stealing and assaulting. Where income levels are more equal, by contrast, the poor feel less estranged and so commit fewer crimes. Another reason is that as people become richer they become more attractive targets for theft, including robberies that may result in injury or death. The more the number of rich people, the more opportunities there are for crime and hence more crime. A third reason is that more affluent people have a larger store of social capital that moderates conflict and provides mutual aid. Sorting out these possible connections statistically is very difficult because too many hard-to-measure factors are associated with both inequality and crime.

What is remarkable today is not that we have a higher homicide rate than can be found in other industrial democracies but that it has come down so sharply in the last two decades. That fall has not been steady and it is unlikely that it will continue indefinitely. In the early 1990s, youthful homicide rates went up dramatically, probably because young drug dealers were beginning to exploit the new market for crack cocaine, and they used murder as a way of controlling territories, frightening off competitors, and managing difficult customers. But when new recruits to crack began to lessen because so many of them died, got sick, or went to prison, the market stabilized and youthful rates of violence declined.[14] Moreover, we know from history that murder rates go up and down; there is no reason to think they will not go up again.

Whatever explains changes in crime rates, the central question for both public opinion and policymakers is how to make crime rates low. There are several ways to do this, among them deterring crime by punishment, rehabilitating offenders through treatment, preventing crime by interventions, reducing threats by gun control, and lessening criminal motives by altering drug control policies and keeping unemployment down.

Controlling Crime: Deterrence

For many years, there was a lively scholarly debate over whether imprisonment reduced crime by persuading would-be offenders not to misbehave. The controversy involved complicated statistical problems that are well summarized in a report by a National Academy of Sciences panel.[15] But imaginative scholars have overcome those problems and have shown that deterrence works. If one compares the crime rates of states and controls for all factors that may contribute to crime, those states with higher rates of imprisonment have lower rates of property crime.

Moreover, people in prison cannot directly harm people on the outside (though some prison-based gangs can order assaults on civilians). No clever statistical tests are needed to show that taking offenders off the street (incapacitation) works. The median number of offenses prison inmates commit when they were free on the street is somewhere between twelve and sixteen.[16] By not imprisoning them, the median inmate would add that many crimes per year to the nation's total.

The death penalty, in the eyes of some people, is a deterrent to murder, but proving this statement is extremely difficult. We have no national count of how many homicides are first-degree murders that qualify the criminal for the death penalty. And when that penalty is imposed, it typically occurs some eleven or twelve years after the offense. When a rare and delayed penalty is imposed on people who have committed an unknown fraction of an uncounted number of murders, it is very hard to figure out if death deters would-be murderers.

The claim that it does was examined by a National Academy of Sciences panel in 1978 and found unpersuasive. Recently, however, a spate of new studies suggests that the death penalty does deter homicide, but the statistical difficulties already mentioned leave us uncertain whether executions deter murders.[17] Indeed, we may never know.

The best arguments for and against the death penalty are moral ones: either the sanction is what the offender deserves, or the execution is a morally objectionable action. In America, a large majority of Americans support the death penalty, probably for moral reasons.

Controlling Crime: Rehabilitation

For a century or more, we have tried to change criminals into law-abiding persons, or failing that at least to reduce significantly their crime rate. Accordingly, we called prisons "correctional institutions" and sent juvenile offenders to "reformatories."[18] But when crime rates rose sharply in the 1960s and 1970s, government leaders began to dismiss rehabilitation measures as "coddling criminals." Then when crime rates dropped in the 1990s, we again read renewed defenses of rehabilitation.

Beneath these changing views is a difficult intellectual question: what evidence do we have that rehabilitation works? Gathering that evidence would require scientific experimentation, not just moral enthusiasm. It is much easier to start a rehabilitation program than to evaluate one. Evaluation means randomly assigning offenders either to the rehabilitation program or to ordinary prison care, making certain that the rehabilitative efforts have actually been delivered, and following up on offenders' behavior for a long time

after they leave the program. Random assignment is important because it minimizes the chances that something other than the treatment made a difference. Insuring that rehabilitative efforts were
made is vital because some programs promise to make an effort but
then do not. Following up is important because lots of programs
will change people while they are in it but the effect may not last
after they leave it. Moreover, a follow-up is hard: one can measure
convictions, but that ignores valid arrests that did not result in a
conviction; one can measure arrests, but that ignores crimes that did
not lead to arrests; and one can interview ex-offenders to see if they
were committing crimes, but this creates a chance for the ex-inmates
to lie.

In the 1950s and 1960s, scholars believed that rehabilitation
worked, but studies published in the 1970s suggested that most carefully studied rehabilitative efforts did not work.[19] Indeed, a National
Academy of Sciences panel reported that it could find few examples
of rehabilitation making a significant difference.[20] But more rigorous studies in the 1980s and 1990s, including meta-analysis, which
combines the results of many studies into an overall estimate, produced some signs of hope.

Many such meta-analyses have been done. Taken as a whole
they suggest a batting average of about 0.10. That means that, on average, people in the rehabilitation programs committed 10 percent
fewer crimes than did similar people not in the programs.[21] This is a
gain, but a small one. About two-thirds of all released prisoners
commit a new crime within three years. A 10 percent cut would reduce the recidivism rate a bit, but still leave well over half of all
ex-inmates breaking the law again.

But some larger reductions (up to 30 percent) can be achieved
by offender-tailored programs. Deciding just what is an "appropriate" intervention is difficult, of course, but the better programs seem
to address those factors that both contribute to criminality and are
changeable, such as pro-criminal attitudes and low self-control.

Unfortunately, public enthusiasm often endorses programs that we know do not work, such as "scared straight" and boot camps. Studies of these efforts suggest that they have had no useful effect and may, indeed, have had harmful ones.[22]

Controlling Crime: Prevention

Preventing people from becoming offenders in the first place would make more sense. After all, it must be easier to work with young minds still unaffected by criminal associates than with experienced offenders who have never finished high school, held a paying job, or been free of a gang's influences. But two problems dog prevention: First, we would not know whether the prevention program worked until the young participants had grown much older. The second problem is targeting. These programs would have to be made available to millions of young people, many of whom would never commit crimes anyway.[23]

Testing prevention programs entails all of the difficulties of testing rehabilitative ones, and in addition the follow-up would have to be much longer. If we teach a ten-year-old how to avoid delinquency, we must wait many years to see if we have succeeded. Happily, a few prevention programs have been rigorously tested, and a research center at the University of Colorado has published a series of booklets that describe those that have met several tests: they have been carefully evaluated (using random assignment and careful analysis) in more than one location (two or more cities or counties) with a follow-up of participants for at least one year after the program ended.[24]

Among programs found to reduce delinquent behavior are nurse home visitations for unmarried pregnant women, Big Brothers/ Big Sisters mentoring, a bullying prevention program, and various efforts to provide extra educational benefits in school. Some of the effects of these programs lasted one or two years, others continued into the teen years.

The challenge is to make these programs available to many at-risk children. No program has yet been adopted by an entire state, much less by the whole country, even though some, such as Big Brothers/Big Sisters, are available on a voluntary basis throughout the nation.

Persuading the public to fund what works is as difficult with prevention as with rehabilitation programs. And funding is not cheap: many of the most successful programs, such as home visits by nurses, may cost over $7,000 per subject; a special kind of preschool program can cost twice that. Since good evaluations are costly and time-consuming, communities adopt many "crime prevention" programs without any real evidence that they work.

Controlling Crime: Guns

Americans own something like a quarter of a billion guns, about one-fourth of which are handguns. The media is filled with stories about shootings, especially efforts by teenage boys to shoot up their own schools. Guns clearly affect the death rate. We do not have drive-by knifings or drive-by poisonings, but we do have drive-by shootings.

If all of these privately owned guns were suddenly to disappear, the murder rate would go down. But that will not happen. The Second Amendment to the Constitution restricts the government's authority to confiscate weapons, and few sane politicians would suggest that we try. But there are other problems as well. First, we kill each other *without* using guns at a higher rate than do the English. Second, so many other factors contribute to fatal encounters that there is no correlation among states between gun ownership and murder. If such a connection existed, North Dakota would have a very high homicide rate and Washington, D.C., a very low one. But in fact North Dakota has just about the lowest homicide rate and Washington one of the highest.

Moreover, guns can be used for self-defense. The number of such uses is not known exactly, but it is not a small number. The victim surveys taken by the American government, which allow the respondent to volunteer statements about self-defense, found that guns were used for self-protection about one hundred thousand times a year. Private opinion surveys that directly ask people about gun use assert that there were over two million cases of gun-involved self-defense a year.[25]

These surveys are not clear about what "use" means. In some cases, persons may brandish guns to fend off someone who is attempting to burgle their homes. In other cases, two people may angrily confront each other with guns drawn; each may later say that the gun was for "defensive" purposes when in fact it was displayed to intimidate an opponent. But because many people actually defend themselves from robbers and burglars by displaying (or using) a gun, this ambiguity in the survey results should not lead us to downplay the reality of defensive gun use.

Many American states allow law-abiding people to readily obtain a police permit to carry concealed weapons. A lively scholarly debate has ensued over whether states with these "shall-carry" laws have lower rates of homicide than do states that sharply restrict private gun carrying. One group, led by John Lott, has argued that if one compares county homicide rates across all states, controlling statistically for every factor that might affect the murder rate, states with shall-carry laws have lower homicide rates than do states without such laws.[26] Another group of scholars, notably Ian Ayres, John Donohue, Daniel Black, and Daniel Nagin, argues that the data do not support this conclusion.[27] A panel of the National Academy of Sciences/National Research Council issued a report that said that Lott's findings were "fragile." I was a member of the panel and disagreed with that conclusion. To me, the panel's testing of the Lott findings still showed that homicide rates were lower a few years after states adopted shall-carry laws.[28]

But what is perhaps most striking is that, according to most studies, these shall-carry laws did not lead to higher murder rates.

America may be more violent than Europe, but letting law-abiding people carry concealed guns does not make us more so.

Given the high rate of gun ownership in this country, the key problem is how we can reduce the extent to which guns are used for criminal purposes. Federal law already prohibits convicted felons, illegal aliens, drug addicts, mental patients, and people guilty of domestic violence from owning guns. No one may purchase automatic weapons or guns that the law proclaims to be "assault weapons." A federally licensed gun dealer (and almost all dealers are so licensed) may not sell handguns to people under the age of twenty-one or rifles to people under the age of eighteen and must obtain from every purchaser personal identification that can be checked against criminal records.

Additional rules exist among the states. You cannot buy a handgun at all in Chicago or Washington, D.C., unless you are involved in law enforcement. In states such as California, you may only buy one handgun a month, you must take a course in gun use (unless you are a military veteran), and to get a permit to carry a concealed weapon you must satisfy some very tough police rules. In other states, such as Vermont, there are scarcely any limits at all on who may carry a gun.

In order to restrict access to guns even further, one must control the illegal market in which criminals trade. Guns in this market are either stolen, borrowed from friends, or bought from people ("straw purchasers") who have purchased them legally but sell them illegally. Government investigations of licensed dealers who traffic in guns illegally only reach a fraction of the guns in improper hands. The illegal gun market is much more decentralized and small-scale than the illegal drug market, and so it will be very expensive to round up many weapons this way.

A demand reduction strategy is more promising than a supply reduction one. Demand can be reduced in several ways. States can increase criminal penalties imposed on people who, while committing a crime, display or use a weapon. This has been done in several states, and there is some evidence that this policy reduces the homicide rate.[29] One can take guns out of the hands of people not authorized to own them by conducting more intensive street searches of people who are on parole, probation, or otherwise meet legal tests that determine who may or may not be searched. And one can invest in technology (which now exists) that will enable the police to determine from a distance who is carrying a concealed weapon, thus equipping the officers with the grounds for stopping and questioning such persons. Finally, the police can monitor homes and bars where violence has been reported in order to make carrying weapons in and out of these places more risky.

Controlling Crime: Dangerous Drugs

There is no doubt that people under the influence of alcohol, cocaine, heroin, and certain other drugs are more likely to commit crimes than either these people when they are sober or similar people who do not abuse these products.[30] Moreover, obtaining money to buy cocaine and heroin can induce people to steal, and managing the distribution of illegal products gives people an incentive to rely on violence. These facts have led many observers to suggest that if we were to legalize the sale of certain drugs the crime rate would go down.

As Jonathan P. Caulkins and Mark A. R. Kleiman point out in chapter 19 in this book, it is not clear what "legalization" means: Wholly free markets? Government-regulated and taxed sales? Private prescription by physicians? A wholly free market would cause prices to drop dramatically and thus usage to increase. A government-controlled and taxed market might lead to the persistence of a black market that undersells government-determined prices.

We do not know by how much crime rates would drop if drug sales were somehow legalized. No doubt much violent crime would be reduced since no one would use force to accomplish what contracts can achieve. But it is quite possible that property crimes would increase. If, as is likely, legalization made crack, cocaine, and heroin cheaper and safer, demand for them would increase. Some new users would not become dependent on these drugs but some would. These addicted users would be unable to hold jobs and thus would either have to steal money to buy drugs or receive subsidies from the government. Because Congress would never approve welfare for addicts, theft would remain as the only source of income for deeply dependent users and so theft might well increase.

We do not know whether drug legalization would reduce, increase, or leave unchanged the crime rate. But the question cannot be answered by uttering slogans such as "taking the profits out of drug dealing." And legalizing drug sales in some states would not teach us much because those states would experience a rush of users entering their territory and find it hard to control their borders to prevent easy distribution across state lines. When pressed, advocates of drug legalization tend to rely on libertarian arguments: "People should be free to swallow whatever they want." But no society has ever embraced that view; all act as if maintaining some degree of character among the citizens is an important public goal.

If we are uncertain about the effects of legalization on crime, then we must try to manage better the current system of illegal drugs. Our heavy emphasis on supply reduction has had little success. The reason is clear: the huge markup in the price of cocaine or heroin from when it is a raw material produced overseas to when it is sold on American streets. Even if law enforcement managed to double the import price, the street price would rise by only 10 to 20 percent.[31]

Forcing governments abroad to curtail drug production and interdicting supplies entering this country have had little effect on drug availability; indeed, the black market prices for cocaine and heroin have fallen, not increased. We have also placed immense burdens on other nations by pressing them to do very difficult things that often lead to corruption and civil war.

There are two ways to manage America's demand for drugs. One is to make the lives of drug users safer by supplying them with clean needles and protected places in which to ingest drugs; the other is to reduce demand by some combination of education and sanctions. Reducing the health risks of drug use would help the lives of some addicts, notably heroin users who rely on syringes, but it would not do much for crack users who inhale the product or methamphetamine users who swallow it.

Reducing demand would require the government to become stern with people who are at high risk for drug use. Although we do not know who all of these people are, and cannot easily find out, people seeking jobs with employers who conduct drug tests is one group. Perhaps these private tests discourage drug use among would-be employees. Another important group consists of people who have been arrested for a crime. Studies in American jails and prisons suggest that half or more of the arrestees have been using illegal drugs within seventy-two hours before their arrest.[32] Most of these people are put on probation or, after serving a sentence, on parole.

Cutting drug demand among this population requires not only drug treatment programs in prisons but, just as important, continued treatment once they are back on the streets. Drug treatment programs are helpful provided people remain in them. To do this, Kleiman has suggested that probationers and parolees be frequently tested for drug use and, if they fail the test, be required, by administrative order of the probation or parole officer, to spend some time in jail. These sanctions would start small (perhaps just a weekend in jail) but steadily increase in magnitude with each successive failed test. This strategy is not designed to punish users but motivate them to stay in a treatment program. This policy would require more than one drug test a week and quick administrative imposition of sanctions (rather than a time-consuming referral to a judge).

Kleiman's demand-reduction idea has begun to be tested. In Hawaii, one judge began a program called Hawaii's Opportunity

Probation with Enforcement, or HOPE. Under it, probation officers referred to the judge offenders who had failed a (frequent) drug
test. A prosecutor and public defender were available to hear these
cases quickly. After a warning, each violator was given a short jail
sentence. Quickly, drug offenses among these declined sharply.[33]

Controlling Crime: Unemployment

People are tempted to explain changes in the crime rate by looking
at the unemployment rate, but in America and probably in most advanced industrial nations there is only a weak and probably insignificant correlation between property crime and unemployment. One
study, but one that is deeply flawed and that no independent investi-
gator has been able to reproduce, argues that the homicide rate rises
with unemployment.[34]

Several studies have suggested that for every 1 percent change in
the unemployment rate there is a 2 percent change in property
crime rates. Quickly read, this sounds like a big effect. But in practical terms it is quite small. Suppose the unemployment rate rises
from 4 to 8 percent. This would be a huge change, one that would
imperil whichever political party was in power. Never since 1942
has the unemployment rate reached 8 percent. But if it occurs, the
property crime rate will rise by 8 percent, a small fraction that could
easily be lost in our imperfect crime measurement data.[35]

This weak link may explain why, during the 1960s when there
was a very high level of employment, the American crime rate nevertheless rose sharply, and why in the 1930s, in the midst of the Great
Depression, crime rates (based on data from several cities) fell.

But the absence of a strong link between crime and unemployment does not mean that the labor market has no effect. Unemployment, after all, is the ratio of people out of work but looking for
jobs to the total labor force. But some adults may not be in the labor
force because they not only have no jobs, they are not looking for
them. They may have found crime more interesting or drug dealing more profitable. Or they may have been raised by a single

mother and have known no employed father. Boys in this group are much more likely to be idle—out of school and out of work—even after controlling for race, ethnicity, and income. These problems are especially bad in neighborhoods where there are very few resident fathers.[36]

Improving participation in the labor force is a much more difficult task than simply finding jobs for people. A careful review of many programs designed to help disadvantaged youth to find and hold jobs showed, at best, mixed results. As the authors put it, "The problems are no longer just economic, but social, and therefore require solutions that deal with problems such as alcoholism, lack of family cohesion, welfare dependency . . . [and] social capital."[37]

Crime and Justice

The principal goal of any criminal justice system is not to deter crime, rehabilitate offenders, or remove the causes of crime, but to do justice. Though crime reduction and crime prevention are important, they are secondary to a fair system for distinguishing between guilty and innocent persons and for imposing a philosophically defensible pattern of penalties that are proportionate to the magnitude of the crime and the prior record of the offenders.

This is a difficult task. Some critics allege that the American system unfairly punishes people on the basis of their race. This has certainly happened in the past and, sadly, will occur again to some extent, but the most rigorous studies find that, for most offenders, race does not determine the outcome of an arrest or trial. Victimization surveys taken among ordinary citizens reveal something about the race of people who attempt to rob or assault victims. The proportion of these offenders whom the victims describe as black closely matches the proportion of arrested and convicted persons who are black.[38] For these offenses, the racial composition of people in prison corresponds closely to that of the people who have broken the law. The death penalty is imposed equally on black and white offenders who have committed similar crimes and have comparable criminal backgrounds. But there remains the question of whether a black who murders a white victim is treated more harshly than a black who kills a black victim. There is evidence both for and against this proposition.[39]

There has also been a concern about racial profiling: that is, the tendency of the police to arrest people who are black for non-existent or minor offenses, especially traffic violations. The claim that the police arrest people for "driving while black" is a familiar argument in the American press. It is very difficult to test this assertion; one has to find a way of checking whether officers know in advance the race of a motorist before making a stop and then choose to stop them for behavior that would be ignored if the driver were white.

One fascinating evaluation was conducted in Oakland, California, by scholars from RAND. Oakland has a sizeable black population as well as many whites. The scholars studied over seven thousand traffic stops that occurred both during day and night hours. With the skies dark, the police could not tell in advance whether the driver was white or black. The proportion of stopped people who were black was essentially the same in both day and night hours. And of those stopped, black drivers were slightly *less* likely to receive a traffic ticket than white ones. However, for reasons that the RAND researchers are unclear about, blacks were stopped for longer periods of time.[40] At least in this large city, obvious forms of racial profiling are absent.

The decentralized American criminal justice system allows some variation in justice across jurisdictions, but in recent decades the differences between (for example) justice in northern and in southern states have narrowed dramatically. With respect to criminal justice standards, we are becoming one nation with one ideal: fairness. But decentralization still produces a criminal justice system that closely tracks public opinion. It is also one in which crime rates differ sharply across cities and counties and in which the level of public and government toleration of crime varies with local political and cultural arrangements.

CHAPTER 17

Inequality, Economic Mobility, and Social Policy

Gary Burtless and Ron Haskins

America, once widely viewed as the land of equal opportunity and upward mobility (except for most segregated blacks), is no longer distinctive in this regard among advanced democracies, and its levels of inequality are relatively high. Social policy experts Gary Burtless and Ron Haskins closely examine the changing patterns of income and wealth distribution and social mobility in America. The poor have gained in income, but the wealthy have gained even faster. The public safety net is not as broad or as deep as in western European systems, especially for children. Progress in reducing poverty among the non-elderly is limited by the rise of female-headed families, low and stagnant wages for the unskilled, and immigration. Recent economic gains have gone disproportionately to the wealthy. In all of this, strikingly different attitudes persist between Americans and Europeans concerning the causes of and remedies for poverty, which affect the size, shape, and legitimacy of the American welfare state.

THIS CHAPTER EXAMINES THREE QUESTIONS ABOUT INEQUALITY IN America: How is economic well-being distributed, and how has this distribution changed over time? Do Americans have good prospects to improve their economic status? How do U.S. government programs affect poverty, inequality, and economic mobility? Our answers to these questions can be summarized briefly. Inequality is greater in America than in other rich countries, and it has been increasing since the late 1970s. Economic and social mobility are alive and well in America, but for the U.S.–born population, upward mobility is

495

not especially high compared with mobility in other rich countries. On the other hand, America offers rich opportunities for upward mobility to immigrants, especially those who arrive from impoverished circumstances. The U.S. government spends large sums on public pensions and health care for the aged and disabled. It spends less on social programs that reduce destitution among the working-age poor and their children. Compared with similar programs in other rich countries, U.S. public pensions and social assistance programs have smaller budgets, are less generous, and have less impact on poverty and inequality. The main government programs designed to boost upward mobility are public education and legal prohibitions on discrimination based on gender, race, religion, age, or disability. Each of these generalizations necessarily represents an oversimplification, but a useful and generally accurate one.

Inequality and Poverty

Figure 17.1 provides an overview of changes in inequality since the end of World War II by comparing trends in the ratio of incomes at the 95th and 50th percentiles of family income (top line) and the ratio of incomes at the 50th and 20th percentiles. The 95/50 ratio shows the proportional difference in pretax incomes between well-to-do and middle-income American families. This income gap narrowed in the immediate aftermath of World War II but was then relatively flat from the early 1950s through the late 1960s. After 1969 the proportional gap widened steadily, indicating that very affluent Americans have been moving further away from Americans in the middle of the income distribution for more than three decades.

The lower line in the graph shows the ratio of pretax family incomes at the 50th and 20th percentiles. There was no clear trend from the late 1940s to the late 1960s, but the gap widened from 1969 to 1989, just as it did in the top half of the distribution. However, unlike the gap between the top and the middle, the income difference between middle- and lower-income Americans showed only a modest increase after 1990. Although the slight rise in the

Figure 17.1   Ratio of Incomes at Selected Points in U.S. Family
Income Distribution, 1947–2005

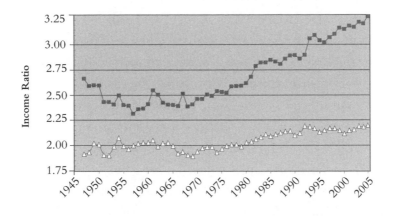

—■— 95th Percentile Income / Median Family Income
—△— Median Family Income / 20th Percentile Income

SOURCE: U.S. Census Bureau.

50/20 gap shows that there has been some recent increase in inequality between the middle and the bottom of the distribution, most of the overall rise in inequality since the mid–1990s has been due to a growing gap between high-income Americans and everyone else.

Recent work by Thomas Piketty and Emmanuel Saez[1] sheds more light on the income gains at the top of the distribution. Based on tax-return data between 1917 and 2004, they examined the share of income going to the top 1 percent, the next 4 percent, and the next 5 percent of the U.S. income distribution. Combining income for the entire top 10 percent of income recipients, the researchers found a U-shaped trend in the percentage of income received by the most affluent Americans. In 1940, near the end of the Great Depression, the top one-tenth of income recipients received about 45 percent of all income. This percentage dropped precipitously over a four-year period during World War II and then held more or less steady until the late 1970s. Starting in the early 1980s, however, relative income of the top 10 percent began a rise that has lasted for a quarter century. This rise brought the income share of the top tenth to well over 40 percent, very close to the high level of the Depression years. When Piketty and Saez break down the top 10 percent of income recipients into three subgroups, they find that the income trend among the top 1 percent of recipients differs significantly from trends among high-income Americans further down the distribution (see Figure 17.2). All three of the top income classes saw sharp declines in their income shares during and immediately after World War II. However, income recipients between the 90th and 95th income percentiles enjoyed a slow but steady gain in income share between 1950 and 1985, while income recipients between the 95th and 99th percentiles saw their income share begin to improve after 1960. These gains accelerated after the mid–1980s but ceased in the mid–1990s.

Most of the gain in income share enjoyed by the top 10 percent of income recipients since 1985—and all of the gain since 1995—

Figure 17.2   Income Shares Received by Top U.S. Income
Recipients, 1940–2004

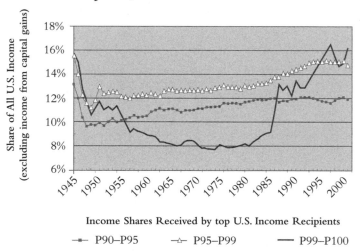

Income Shares Received by top U.S. Income Recipients
—■— P90–P95   —△— P95–P99   —— P99–P100

SOURCE: Picketty and Saez (2006),
http://emlab.berkeley.edu/users/saez/TabFig2004prel.xls.

has been due to gains enjoyed by recipients in the top 1 percent of the U.S. income distribution. When Picketty and Saez analyze income gains within the top 1 percent of income recipients, they find that a large fraction of the gains are concentrated among the top 0.1 percent and top 0.01 percent of income recipients. Almost all of the income gains in the top 1 or 2 percent of the U.S. income distribution are missed in standard U.S. Census Bureau tabulations of income inequality, because the incomes of top earners are poorly measured in census surveys. Nonetheless, both the census statistics and tax statistics compiled by Picketty and Saez suggest that the rapid increase in the incomes of the richest Americans accounts for much of the growth in economic inequality since 1980.

A major part of the inequality story is that very rich Americans are getting richer. But there is more to the story. Consider Figure 17.3, which summarizes changes in household income over the period 1980 to 2004—the period during which the rich got much richer—as measured by absolute thresholds. Using cutoffs of $15,000, $25,000, $35,000, $50,000, $75,000, and $100,000 in constant 2004 dollars, the figure shows the fraction of all households in each of seven income categories in 1980 and 2004. The percentage of American households in the bottom five categories of income shrank between 1980 and 2004, but the percentage in the two highest income categories increased. Over a quarter-century period in which U.S. inequality increased, households were flowing out of the income categories below $75,000 and into the categories above $75,000. Whereas only 16 percent of households had incomes above $75,000 in 1980, almost 27 percent of households had achieved this benchmark by 2004. The fraction of households receiving incomes above $100,000 more than doubled during the period. The rise in income produced by a growing U.S. economy has helped more than just the superrich. In spite of the rise in inequality, Americans in the middle and at the bottom of the economic ladder have also enjoyed some of the benefits flowing from economic growth.

Figure 17.3   Percent of Households in Seven Income Categories,
1980–2004

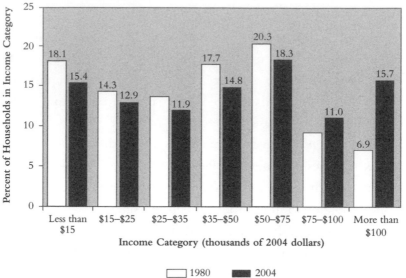

SOURCE: U.S. Census Bureau, *Statistical Abstract of the United States, 2006.*
http://www.census.gov/compendia/statab/tables/0750671.xls. Accessed
December 3, 2007.

It is possible to measure the trend in living standards at different
points in the income distribution. One way to do this is to calculate
the amount of goods and services that families can buy after they
have paid income and payroll taxes. The calculation should include
in-kind benefits, such as food stamp coupons and rent subsidies, as
well as cash income payments. Households that are given food
stamps or publicly subsidized housing can buy more goods and services than can be purchased with their cash incomes alone. (The
calculations in Figures 17.1–17.3 above are based on household cash
incomes before any adjustment for taxes, and they exclude in-kind
benefits.) Another useful adjustment takes account of differences in
spending needs that result from differences in household size. Since
larger households need more money than smaller households to
enjoy the same standard of living, it is useful to adjust households'
reported incomes to reflect this fact. A common adjustment is to assume that household spending needs go up in proportion to the

Figure 17.4   Trends in Size–Adjusted Household Incomes Before and After Taxes and Transfers at Selected Points in Distribution, 1979–2004

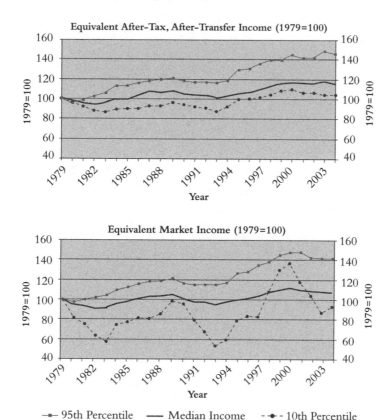

SOURCE: Authors' tabulations of U.S. Bureau of the Census, 1980–2005 March Current Population Survey files.

square root of the number of household members. Figure 17.4 shows trends in U.S. living standards after taking account of changes in household tax burdens, transfer payments (including food stamps and means-tested housing benefits), and shifts in household size. We have calculated the net, household-size-adjusted incomes of Americans in each year since 1979 and estimated the trend in personal living standards at three points in the distribution: the 10th percentile, the 50th percentile, and the 95th percentile.

The results of these tabulations are displayed in the top panel of Figure 17.4. Like Figure 17.1, Figure 17.4 shows that inequality grew after 1979. But whereas Figure 17.1 shows no change in the gap between the bottom and the middle during the 1990s, Figure 17.4 shows that, once we adjust for changes in household size, subtract taxes, and add non-cash benefits (other than medical care), the gap between the bottom and the middle narrowed significantly during the first half of the 1990s. The gap between those at the top and those in the middle of the distribution continued to widen after 1993, just as it did in Figure 17.1. Figures 17.1 and 17.4 both show that recent income gains have been much slower for low- and middle-income Americans than they have been for Americans at the top of the income distribution.

Even though the calculations in Figure 17.4 reflect a more comprehensive definition of income than the definition used in Figure 17.1, they do not include all the income sources that help pay for Americans' consumption. More than two-thirds of American families own the house or apartment they live in, and the rent savings from home ownership is not reflected in Figure 17.4. In addition, most of the cost of Americans' health care is financed by government or private employer health plans. Americans pay for only about one-eighth of their health care with direct payments to doctors, hospitals, and pharmacies. The other seven-eighths of the cost of care is paid through government insurance, private health insurance, or some other financing source. Many Americans must make premium contributions for their health insurance, of course, but an overwhelming share of the premium contributions for employer-sponsored health insurance is paid by employers, not by employees. Premium contributions for government-provided health insurance finance only a small percentage of the cost of government health insurance. If the value of employer-provided and government-provided health insurance were included in Americans' incomes, U.S. inequality would seem smaller. Poor Americans consume more health services than middle-income and rich Americans, mainly because they are in poorer health. At the same time, they pay for a smaller percentage of the health services they consume, because their government-provided health insurance is usually free and does not require them to make co-payments for doctor and hospital visits or prescription drugs. The rising importance of health care in consumption means that the omission of free and subsidized health insurance in the U.S. income statistics represents a growing problem for measuring the income distribution.

After-tax incomes are affected by trends in the private economy and by the changing distribution of tax burdens and government benefits. The lower panel of Figure 17.4 shows trends in Americans' private or market incomes, which we define as income before taxes are subtracted and government transfers are added. Market income includes income from self-employment, wages, interest, dividends, rents, and occupational pensions. It does not include income from public assistance or Social Security. Year-to-year movements in market income are much bigger than those for income after taxes and transfers, especially for Americans near the bottom of the distribution. Between 1979 and 1983, when unemployment reached its highest rate since the 1930s, market income at the 10th percentile fell 43 percent, whereas income after taxes and transfers fell only 13 percent.[2] Market income at the 10th percentile was no greater in 1989 than in 1979, but then rose during the 1990s, ending the decade almost 40 percent higher than it had been in 1989. Unfortunately, some of the income gain was lost following the recession of 2001.

In view of the statistics on income at the 10th percentile, it is not surprising that those at the bottom of the income distribution have at best made modest gains in recent years. U.S. poverty dropped substantially during the 1960s, more modestly during the 1970s, drifted up in an uneven pattern until the early 1990s, and then declined smartly until the recession of 2001. After 2000, the poverty rate increased every year until falling slightly in 2005, but remained below its 1993 level.

Most analysts agree that progress against poverty since the early 1970s has been disappointing. Some of the disappointment is traceable to problems with the standard census income definition mentioned above. Nick Eberstadt and other analysts have pointed out flaws in the official poverty measure used by the Census Bureau.[3] Among other problems, Eberstadt shows that a variety of measures of what low-income families actually consume—including housing, food, medical care, and overall consumption—have improved over the period since 1973 when the official poverty estimate failed to show any improvement. Similarly, Bruce Meyer and James Sullivan show that overall consumption in the bottom 10 percent of female-headed families fails to show the sharp drop that income shows over the period 1997–2000 as compared with 1993–1995.[4] The trend in poverty as measured by indicators of consumption is different and more hopeful than the trend as measured by official poverty indicators based on income. Even using official income measures, however, America's low-income elderly have fared rather well since the early 1970s (see Figure 17.5). Until 1970, the poorest group in America and in most other countries was the aged. In the late 1960s, for example, when the poverty rate among non-aged Americans was about 11 percent, the poverty rate of the population sixty-five and older was 25 percent. However, by the early 1980s, the elderly poverty rate had fallen to about 15 percent. By 1990 it was 12 percent and in 2005 it was less than 10 percent. In the latter year, the poverty rate among non-elderly adults was 11.1 percent and that among children was 17.6 percent. Social Security cash payments, which increased dramatically during the 1960s and 1970s, boosted the absolute and relative incomes of older Americans and sharply reduced their poverty rate. In 2002, for example, the poverty rate among the elderly before they received any transfer payments from government was 50 percent. Social Security payments cut this

Figure 17.5   Poverty Rate by Age Group under Official
U.S. Poverty Definition, 1959–2005

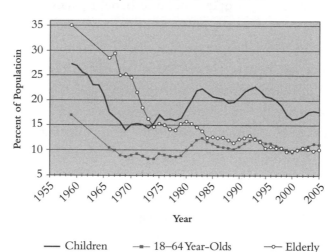

SOURCE: U.S. Census Bureau.

rate by nearly four-fifths to just 11 percent. Clearly, generous government payments can boost incomes and reduce poverty among
people who receive such payments.

The problem with this antipoverty strategy is that few Americans support giving no-strings-attached aid to able-bodied adults,
even those with children. Offering transfers to the aged and disabled
arouses much less controversy. American voters generally favor Social Security for two main reasons. Most voters do not expect the
elderly or disabled to work, so they have little concern that generous benefits will reduce recipients' employment or self-sufficiency.
In addition, the basic design of Social Security and the rhetoric surrounding it ensure that payments will be viewed differently from
benefits provided under typical government-aid programs. Workers
must contribute to Social Security for a number of years before
they or their dependents become eligible for benefits. The benefits
are not scaled in proportion to a claimant's "needs" but are calculated as a percentage of the contributor's earned income when she

paid taxes into the system. Social Security redistributes income in favor of low-earning workers, because benefit payments are larger in proportion to contributions for workers with low lifetime wages than for workers with above-average wages. Nonetheless, Social Security payments are widely regarded as benefits earned as a result of past premium contributions. It is harder to view means-tested benefit payments in the same way. For most American legislators, the "give them cash" solution to poverty for the young and able-bodied is not feasible because of voters' opposition to giving money to people who are expected to earn it for themselves. This preference is reflected in federal government spending. Federal programs providing benefits to the aged consumed $615 billion in 2000, or about $17,700 per person sixty-five and older. In the same year, federal programs giving benefits to children and their parents consumed a little less than $175 billion, or just $2,500 per person under age eighteen.[5]

If voter preferences sharply limit the amount of means-tested aid that can be provided to adults who are expected to work, what can be done to reduce poverty among non-elderly adults and their children? Many shelves have been filled with books devoted to interpreting and explaining the causes of American poverty. This research points to a complex web of causation that contributes to poverty among working-age adults. At least three factors are especially important in slowing U.S. progress against poverty: the rise of female-headed families, low and stagnant wages, and immigration. If a family contains only one adult rather than two, it is much harder for that adult to act as both child caregiver and family wage earner. Two demographic trends have pushed up the percentage of American families containing only one adult—higher divorce rates and higher rates of childbearing outside marriage. By 2000, around one-third of all children, and nearly 70 percent of black children and 45 percent of Hispanic children, were born outside marriage. The increased rates of divorce and non-marital childbearing have produced a sizeable decline in the percentage of American youngsters who live with two married parents. In 1960, 88 percent of children lived in a family with two married parents. By 2005, only 67 percent lived in a family containing two parents. Twenty-eight percent lived with a single parent, usually the mother, and 4 percent were in the care of another relative or a non-relative.[6]

The long-term rise in the percentage of children living with a single parent raises concern because so many of these children end up living in poverty. Further, researchers broadly agree that children in single-parent families have more developmental problems than children reared in married-couple families. Youngsters raised by a single parent have higher rates of school failure, more arrests, lower rates of high school graduation, higher incidence of mental health problems, and higher rates of teen pregnancy.[7] Until the mid-1990s, the poverty rate among children in female-headed families was four or five times greater than the poverty rate of children in married-couple families. The high prevalence of poverty among female-headed families has meant that the growth of this type of family has been a powerful factor boosting overall poverty.

A second key determinant of poverty is the state of the U.S. economy. President John Kennedy once observed that "a rising tide lifts all boats." This aphorism describes a plausible expectation about the relationship between the state of the economy and the incomes of American families. Statistics on U.S. poverty suggest that Kennedy was right about the effects of general prosperity in the 1960s, but his observation has been less accurate since that time. Consider the statistics on family poverty and income growth displayed in Table 17.1. The first column shows that average gross domestic product (GDP) growth was exceptionally strong in the 1960s, but growth was also reasonably robust in the 1970s, 1980s, and 1990s. GDP per person rose almost 35 percent in the 1960s. As shown in the last two columns, this growth was associated with a reduction in the family poverty rate of nearly 9 percentage points, or almost half. But GDP growth rates of over 20 percent in each of the

Table 17.1   Economic Growth and Poverty Since 1959

Years	Percent change in GDP per capita	Family poverty rate (%)		Change in poverty rate	
		Start	End	Percentage Points	Percent
1959–1969	34.8	18.5	9.7	–8.8	–47.6
1969–1979	23.7	9.7	9.2	–0.5	–5.2
1979–1989	22.8	9.2	10.3	1.1	12.0
1989–1999	20.1	10.3	9.3	–1.0	–9.7
1999–2004	7.4	9.3	10.2	0.9	9.7

SOURCE: R. Freeman, "The Rising Tide Lifts . . . ?" in S. Danziger and R.Haveman, eds., *Understanding Poverty* (Cambridge, MA: Harvard University Press, 2001), 101, and authors' recalculations using Bureau of Economic Analysis and U.S. Census Bureau data.

next three decades were associated with only modest reductions or actual increases in the poverty rate. After a brief recession in 2001, the American economy grew from 2002 through 2005, but poverty failed to decline. In fact, it rose modestly. General prosperity in recent decades has had a smaller impact on the incomes of families at the bottom end of the income distribution—and for good reason.

As we have seen in Figures 17.1 and 17.4, income gains from American prosperity have been concentrated on the well-to-do. The wage gains of workers who earn average or below-average pay have been small or non-existent for most of the past three decades. Figure 17.6 shows trends in real hourly wages at selected points in the hourly wage distribution. The chart shows real pay of workers who earn the 10th percentile hourly wage, the median hourly wage, and the 95th percentile wage between 1979 and 2005. These estimates show that inflation-adjusted pay of wage earners receiving median or below-median wages either declined or remained stagnant for much of the period between 1979 and the mid–1990s.

Only in the years after 1996 did wage rates begin to climb notice-ably. Of course, the estimates miss changes in employer-financed fringe benefits, which rose faster than money wages over the period. For example, between 1979 and 2005, the average money wage in-creased slightly more than 25 percent, but average employer contri-butions for employees' private health insurance coverage increased 163 percent. However, these fringe benefits are not counted when the Census Bureau calculates the official poverty statistics. For fami-lies who are supported by only one wage earner, the trend in real wages has meant that it is hard to achieve income gains without in-creasing weekly work hours.

Changes in American immigration patterns are a third factor that played a role in keeping U.S. poverty rates high. If immigrants are less skilled than natives, as has often been the case, the distribu-tion of income will change if the ratio of immigrants to natives

Figure 17.6   Trend in Real Hourly Wages at Selected Points in U.S. Wage Distribution, 1979–2005

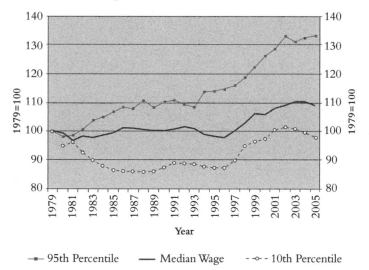

SOURCE: Economic Policy Institute, www.epinet.org/datazone/05/wagecuts_all.xls.

changes or if the skill gap between the two groups changes. Both these things have happened during the past generation. In 1970, less than 5 percent of the resident population was born abroad, and recent immigrants earned 17 percent less than natives on average. By the end of the 1990s, 11 percent of the resident population was born abroad, and recent immigrants earned 34 percent less than natives.[8] Many immigrants enter the United States with very little schooling. About one-third of immigrants who are at least twenty-five years old have not obtained a high school diploma or an equivalent degree. Among adults who were born in the United States, only 12 percent lack a high school diploma.

Not surprisingly, immigrants' poor educational credentials limit their access to jobs paying average or above-average wages. In spite of the impressive credentials brought by a minority of immigrants when they enter the United States or acquired after they arrive, the average job skills of immigrants have declined over time in comparison with those of native workers. In the 1970 census, male immigrant workers who entered the United States between five and ten years before the census interview earned wages that were 5 percent lower than those of native-born men. In the 2000 census, male immigrants who resided in the country between five and ten years before the interview earned 27 percent less than native-born men. This kind of wage deterioration suggests there has been a sizeable decline in the relative job skills of immigrants entering the United States since the late 1960s.[9] The poverty rate of first-generation immigrants reflects this deterioration. In 2003, foreign-born adults between eighteen and sixty-four had a poverty rate of 16 percent versus 10 percent among native-born adults in the same age group. Immigrant children had a 2003 poverty rate of 29 percent, and the children of immigrants had a poverty rate of 22 percent. In the same year, the children of native-born parents had a poverty rate of 16 percent.[10]

There is an irony in the high rates of poverty among immigrants in the United States. Most immigrants come from countries where wages are low and average family income is below the U.S. poverty line. The overwhelming majority of immigrants enjoy higher incomes in the United States than they did in their countries of origin. Economist Mark Rosenzweig recently estimated the wage gains that workers in Mexico could expect from moving to the United States in 1990. Workers with a high school diploma could expect to see their real wage rise by a factor of seven. Mexican college graduates could anticipate a ninefold rise in salaries. Many U.S. immigrants come from countries even poorer than Mexico, and they can expect bigger wage gains.[11] Even if immigrants' incomes place them near the bottom of the American distribution, they are almost always better off than they would have been in their country of birth. Slowing the flow of new immigrants or increasing the skill requirements for entry would reduce both inequality and poverty in the United States. However, the potential immigrants who are excluded by these policies would be much worse off—and so would the many Americans who benefit from the relatively cheap labor supplied by immigrants.

America's current immigration policy probably reduces global inequality at the same time it increases inequality within the United States. Indeed, the increase in inequality within the United States is to some extent a misleading byproduct of the fact that the Census Bureau tabulates incomes among people who are U.S. residents at a particular point in time. If census data on trends in inequality between 1970 and 2000 included the 1970 incomes of those who moved to the United States between 1970 and 2000, the 1970 distribution would look far more unequal. This change in perspective would not alter the fact that the income gap between the top and the middle has widened, but inequality for the population as a whole might well show a decline.[12]

In sum, the United States has made some progress against poverty since the late 1970s, especially among the elderly and, as we will see, among children in female-headed families. The mild recession of 2001 increased poverty modestly after a continuous and substantial decline between 1993 and 2000, but poverty fell again in 2005. Special analyses by the U.S. Census Bureau show that adding the value of government in-kind benefits and the Earned Income Tax Credit (EITC) reduces poverty a few percentage points below the official rate.[13] The trend in poverty looks more encouraging if we measure the consumption instead of the money incomes of the households at the bottom of the income distribution. Real consumption of low-income families has increased faster than real incomes, especially if we measure health care consumption at its cost to taxpayers and employers as well as its cost to final consumers. Nonetheless, the evidence for increased inequality since the 1970s is overwhelming. The top of the distribution is pulling away from average and below-average earners, and until the early 1990s there was evidence that the bottom was falling further behind the middle of the distribution. The most favorable interpretation of income distribution trends since 1979 is that the rising tide has lifted about one-quarter of boats into a comfortable harbor where annual incomes are above $75,000. Unfortunately, income gains since 1979 have had only a small impact on the official U.S. poverty rate.

How does American inequality compare with that in other countries? Comparisons among rich countries almost always show that the United States ranks at the top or near the top of the inequality league tables. Comparing income inequality across countries is not easy. Differences in national arrangements for financing health care, housing, and education mean that money income is more important in determining overall consumption in some countries than it is in others. Income differences are likely to produce wider differences in health care, housing, and education in places where families must finance these things out of their own pocket than in places where such costs are largely financed from taxes. In the United States, however, low-income families often receive subsidized health care, food, housing, and higher education, while the more affluent pay higher prices. As a result, it is hard to be sure whether inequality in disposable income overstates inequality in consumption more in the United States or in other rich countries.

Table 17.2 shows some measures of income poverty and inequality in nine rich countries. The data come from the Luxembourg Income Study (LIS), which is a cross-national project that assembles and tabulates income distribution statistics using consistent methods for all countries. The table shows the year of each country's income survey in the first column. Our income estimates are based on the same measure of after-tax, after-transfer "equivalent income" that we used in the top panel of Figure 17.4. Each person in the national population is ranked from lowest to highest in terms of income adjusted for family size. The second column in the table shows the percentage of each national population receiving a family size–adjusted net income below 40 percent of the national median income. The third column shows the percentage of people below 50 percent of the national median. These benchmarks are used to show the fraction of people who fall below a poverty threshold, in this case one that is measured as a percentage of the median income in a country. We have listed the countries in order of overall inequality, with the most equal society, Sweden, at the top and the most unequal society, the United States, on the bottom.

Almost 11 percent of Americans receive a net income below 40 percent of the U.S. median income. This is exactly twice the average percentage of people who receive incomes below that threshold in the other eight countries. Using a higher poverty threshold does not change the story very much. The U.S. poverty rate also looks high if the poverty threshold is expressed in terms of an absolute U.S. dollar amount and net incomes for each country are converted to dollars using purchasing-power-parity exchange rates. In a group of nine industrial countries, Timothy Smeeding[14] found that the United States ranked second highest in absolute poverty. The other eight countries had average incomes that were one-quarter below the

Table 17.2 Relative Poverty Rates and Income Inequality in Nine Industrial Countries

Country	Year	Percent of population with equivalent income below		Ratio of incomes	
		40% of median income	50% of median income	10th percentile/ median income	90th percentile/ median income
Sweden	2000	3.8	6.5	0.57	1.68
The Netherlands	1999	4.6	7.3	0.56	1.67
France	1994	3.4	8.0	0.54	1.91
Germany	2000	4.7	8.3	0.54	1.77
Canada	2000	6.5	11.4	0.48	1.88
Japan	1992	6.9	11.8	0.46	1.92
United Kingdom	1999	5.8	12.4	0.47	2.15
Italy	2000	7.3	12.7	0.44	1.99
United States	2000	10.8	17.0	0.39	2.10

SOURCE: Authors' tabulations of data from LIS Key Figures, www.lisproject. org/keyfigures.htm (downloaded August 24, 2006); T. M. Smeeding, "Public Policy and Economic Inequality: The United States in Comparative Perspective," LIS Working Paper 367 (Luxembourg: Luxembourg Income Study, 2004); and T. M. Smeeding, L. Rainwater, and G. Burtless, "United States Poverty in a Cross-National Context," in S. Danziger and R.Haveman, eds., *Understanding Poverty* (Cambridge, MA: Harvard University Press, 2001).

average U.S. income, but only one of these eight countries, the United Kingdom, had a higher fraction of people receiving incomes below the U.S. poverty threshold.

The last two columns in Table 17.2 offer a different perspective on inequality. They show the ratio of incomes received by people in different positions of the national income distribution. The first of these columns shows the ratio of the 10th percentile income to the median national income. Not surprisingly, this ratio is lowest in the United States and highest in Sweden. Whereas a Swede with the 10th percentile income receives 57 percent of Sweden's median income, an American with the 10th percentile income receives just 39 percent of the U.S. median income. The last column shows the ratio of the 90th percentile income to the median income in each country. Using this measure of inequality, the United States appears more similar to the other countries in the table. The United Kingdom has a higher 90–50 income ratio than the United States, and the Japanese and Italian 90–50 ratios are not far below the U.S. ratio. Measured in absolute U.S. dollars, America's low-income population receives smaller incomes than the poor in nearly all the other industrial countries, and America's rich receive much higher incomes than the rich anywhere else. At the lower end of the income scale, the main explanation for the difference is the relatively small size of the American welfare state. In comparison with some other countries, the United States also has a high proportion of youngsters in single-parent families, where they are more likely to be poor than would be the case if they lived with two parents.

Economic Mobility

Inequality is exceptionally high in the United States when it is measured using a single year's income.[15] Does rapid income mobility offset the impact of high inequality? There are two ways this might be true. Americans who have very low incomes in one year might enjoy big income gains in the next. By the same token, workers or families with high incomes in a given year may experience big declines later on. Over time the incomes of many families could be near the national average, even though they are far from the average in many years. Second, low- and middle-income parents might believe high inequality is offset by high mobility if they think their children have good opportunities to move up the income ladder.

When children are expected to earn very different incomes from their parents, parents may be willing to tolerate wide inequality and accept a poor position in the income distribution.

How does income mobility affect our interpretation of U.S. income inequality? Inequality measured over a many-year period is lower than when measured using a single year's income. Nonetheless, the best current evidence suggests that long-term income inequality has been rising more or less in line with the trend in one-year inequality. The year-to-year variability of American family income has risen, but permanent or long-term differences in income have risen, too. It should be stressed that few people are happy about the recent rise in income variability. Most Americans would prefer to face smaller income fluctuations rather than bigger ones, assuming the average income in the two situations is the same. Big changes in income make it hard for families to budget for housing and other fixed expenses, and they might make it impossible to pay for emergencies, like a child's illness or a hole in the roof.

Recent research has added tremendously to our knowledge about intergenerational mobility. Americans typically believe their society offers rich opportunity for upward advancement, even to people from poor circumstances, and their families' own immigration histories tend to fortify this belief. This view of U.S. social mobility is shared by many people in the rest of the world. Americans as well as many Europeans tend to think family background counts for less in America than in Europe. This assumption is rooted more in history and culture than in current experience, however. Recent studies of intergenerational mobility find the United States has below-average income mobility compared with other rich countries. However, a limitation of the studies is that they largely ignore the experience of immigrants, who obtain large income gains from moving to the United States. By focusing on people whose parents were U.S. residents, the studies miss much of the upward mobility that is so striking to American and foreign observers. Other rich countries, like Australia and Canada, also have a long tradition of accepting immigrants, and immigrants in those countries have also achieved impressive income gains. In most rich countries, however, immigration rates are lower and large-scale immigration is fairly recent, so the upward mobility associated with cross-border migration has probably been less important.

One way to measure intergenerational mobility is to calculate the correlation between parents' incomes and their children's incomes after the children establish households of their own. Economists usually favor an alternative measure of the association between a parent's and a child's position called the "intergenerational elasticity," which tries to cancel out the effects of other changes in inequality over time. The interpretation of this measure is similar to that of the correlation coefficient. If the intergenerational elasticity is high, children will assume positions that are similar to those of their parents; if low, children's positions as adults will be largely independent of their parents'.

Economists and sociologists have tried to measure intergenerational mobility using three variables: parent and child occupational status; wage income; and family income after adjustment for family size. The most informative of these is family income, but this variable is also the hardest to measure reliably for both parents and adult children. It is easier to collect information on the occupations of fathers and adult sons, so this is the correlation that social scientists examined in early studies. Such correlations tend to be highest when we rank both fathers and sons on the basis of their occupation's educational requirements and economic rewards. We have correlations of this kind for large samples in the United States, Britain, the Netherlands, Germany, and Ireland. The correlations for the United States and Britain are almost identical (0.34 and 0.35). The correlations for the Netherlands, Germany, and Ireland are all somewhat higher (0.40 to 0.49).[16] This evidence suggests occupational mobility is higher in the United States and Britain than it is in the other three countries. Robert Erikson and John Goldthorpe compared the United States, Britain, and Sweden using somewhat different measures and found little clear evidence of differences, suggesting occupational mobility is roughly the same in those three countries.[17] Thus, the data on occupational mobility show the United States may have moderate though not exceptionally high rates of intergenerational mobility.

The past decade has seen a rise in the number and quality of studies that examine the relationship between fathers' and sons' earnings in the United States. One result of the new evidence is a better estimate of the correlation between fathers' and sons' earnings. Another is a more pessimistic assessment of intergenerational earnings mobility in the United States compared with other rich countries. Early estimates of the intergenerational elasticity of father-son earnings suggested that it might be about 0.2 in the United States. This implies that any large earnings advantage or disadvantage of a father would be substantially eliminated in the generation of his grandsons. Recent estimates of the intergenerational elasticity suggest that it is in the range between 0.4 and 0.5, and it may be as high as 0.6.[18] If the highest estimate is correct, it would take up to six generations, or 150 years, before the descendants of a low-income father could expect to earn wages that are near the national average. Ominously, the highest estimates of the elasticity have been obtained in studies that use the most reliable measures of a father's long-term earnings.

Cross-national studies of earnings mobility have also improved over time. The better studies are based on data sets that are similar across countries and use identical statistical methods to measure each country's intergenerational mobility. Unfortunately, this technique can only be applied in the handful of countries that have high-quality data on parents' and children's earnings. The results usually show that earnings mobility is lower in the United States than in other rich countries. Markus Jäntti and several coauthors recently compared father-son and father-daughter earnings mobility in the United States, the United Kingdom, and four Scandinavian countries.[19] Although they did not find statistically significant differences across countries in father-daughter earnings mobility, they found that sons' earnings mobility was significantly lower in the United States than in Britain, and lower in Britain than in the four Scandinavian countries. Particularly disturbing is the finding that the biggest cross-country gap was at the bottom of the earnings distribution. American sons whose fathers earned low wages were unlikely to earn wages that brought them into the middle or the top part of the earnings distribution. In addition, both American and British sons of high-wage fathers were unlikely to earn wages near the bottom of the earnings distribution. Both at the high and low ends of the American earnings distribution, there is an unusually small amount of father-son earnings mobility. This evidence, which is probably the most reliable now available, suggests that high inequality in the United States is unlikely to be offset by high mobility. With respect to individual earnings, the effects of high U.S. inequality are likely to be compounded by the effects of unusually low earnings mobility.

This kind of analysis, however, ignores much of the income and earnings mobility experienced by families that move to the United States, especially from countries where incomes are far below those in this country. Few data sets contain good information on immigrants' incomes both before and after they immigrate. Even if such data were available, researchers would find it difficult to compare immigrants' positions in their home countries with the positions they occupy in the United States. College graduates from many poor countries can earn better wages cleaning houses and driving taxis in the United States than they can earn teaching school or managing offices in their country of origin. An immigrant with strong qualifications may give up a good position in a poor country's hierarchy in order to obtain a worse position in a much richer country's hierarchy. Immigrants' incomes rise as a result of moving to the United States, even if their relative position in the pecking order declines.

The income gains from international immigration are far from trivial. The United States remains one of the world's richest countries. Most Americans who receive middle-class incomes enjoy a standard of living that compares favorably to the one they would enjoy in other countries, even other rich countries. For Americans who are themselves immigrants or who are the children or grandchildren of immigrants, the gap in U.S. and foreign living standards may seem particularly vivid. More than one American in five is an immigrant or is the child of an immigrant; for young adults, the figure is about 25 percent. For the great majority of these Americans, the move to the United States is associated with a leap in family well-being, which many of them probably regard as upward mobility.

The fact remains, however, that people born in the United States do not enjoy exceptional opportunities for upward mobility compared with people born in other rich countries. The wages of American fathers and sons are more similar than wages earned by fathers and sons in other rich countries. This may imply that family background matters more in the United States than it does elsewhere. Particularly at the bottom end of the income distribution, American institutions are less successful than those in other rich countries in equalizing the opportunities available to children.

This fact should dismay American voters. Their country relies heavily on education to equalize the opportunities available to rich and poor, but the schools are not very successful in improving the earnings prospects of children reared in the poorest families. One reason may be that children from disadvantaged backgrounds are concentrated in ineffective and underperforming schools. Another is that, unlike students in other rich countries, Americans are not entitled to a free education after they obtain a high school diploma.

Public and private universities charge fees, and the best ones charge the highest fees. The U.S. government has tried to improve poor youngsters' access to college by providing financial aid and low-cost loans to the needy, and private donations significantly augment these resources. Both public and private colleges have offset some of the effect of this policy by boosting their tuition and fees. Poor adolescents may not be able to borrow enough money to go to college, or they may not be able to earn enough on a job to pay their college bills while still making progress toward a degree. In spite of the faith that Americans place in their education system as an institution for equalizing opportunity, children from poor backgrounds fare badly in school. Compared with middle-class children, low-income children are less likely to achieve basic competency in math or reading, graduate from high school, and attend or complete college. In addition, children from the most affluent one-quarter of U.S. families account for about three-quarters of the students in America's top-ranked colleges and universities. The United States clearly has a long way to go to equalize educational outcomes of rich and poor youth.

Government Programs

For many observers, America's growing inequality and its comparatively modest level of upward mobility offer powerful arguments for public intervention to reduce poverty, equalize incomes, and promote social mobility. By international standards, however, the U.S. government has established relatively small programs to promote these goals. Most programs are aimed at specific populations—the aged, the disabled, or indigent children—or at insuring Americans against specific risks, including short-term unemployment, large medical bills, or injury on a job. Some are designed to encourage able-bodied adults to work. Taken together, the scores of federal and state programs designed to help the poor do not constitute a coherent or rational system for alleviating poverty. Rather, they were developed at specific times for specific purposes over the past six decades, often in bursts of legislative activity. Many are duplicative and overlapping.

With the exception of public schools, which are mainly supported by state and local taxes, most social programs in the United States derive much or all of their financing from the federal government. Although there is no formal law outlining the relative responsibilities of local, state, and federal governments, over time a broad division of responsibilities has emerged. The federal government plays the leading role in providing Americans with cash insurance protection against the risks of old age, death, and disability and protecting them against high health care costs when they are old or disabled. The federal government began its campaign to improve Americans' economic security by creating means-tested benefit programs and public insurance for people who are not expected to work, not able to work, or temporarily out of work as a result of an involuntary layoff. Most benefits from the nation's social welfare system are showered on people who have a long record of previous employment but who cannot or do not work as a result of illness, injury, old age, or involuntary unemployment. The most important of these programs were created by the Social Security Act, passed by Congress in 1935. Signed into law by President Franklin Roosevelt, the act established the Old-Age and Survivors Insurance program, the state-federal unemployment insurance system, and the state-federal system of means-tested cash assistance for indigent parents and children, the indigent blind and disabled, and the low-income elderly. Later amendments to the Social Security Act created the Disability Insurance program in 1956, the main public programs providing health insurance to the aged and disabled (under Medicare) and to the indigent (under Medicaid) in 1965, and a controversial prescription drug benefit for the elderly in 2003.

The biggest and most costly programs created under the Social Security Act are based on insurance principles. Nearly all working Americans and their employers make regular payments into government-managed trust funds, and benefits are paid out of funds held in these trust accounts. In the case of Old-Age and Survivors Insurance, Disability Insurance, Unemployment Compensation, and the main part of Medicare, workers' contributions are calculated based on their earnings. As a result of their contributions, workers build up credits that determine future eligibility for benefits. In the case of cash insurance programs, the weekly or monthly benefit payment is also determined by the workers' past earnings credits. One part of Medicare health insurance is financed with beneficiaries' own monthly premiums as well as annual appropriations from the federal budget. The federal government has established separate trust fund accounts for the Old-Age and Survivors program, the Disability Insurance program, and the two parts of the Medicare health insurance program.

The Unemployment Compensation program has a federal trust account for every state as well as several federal accounts. In 2005, these four programs had a total of 99.3 million recipients and their benefits totaled $885 billion, or more than one-third of all federal government spending (see Table 17.3). These four programs are the main pillars of the American social welfare state.

Table 17.3   Number of Beneficiaries and Spending on Social Insurance Programs, 2005

Programs	Beneficiaries		Outlays	
	Millions	Percent of U.S. Population	Billions of Dollars	Percent of U.S. Federal Spending
Old Age and Survivors	40.1	13.6	$434.0	17.6
Disability	8.3	2.8	84.2	3.4
Unemployment Insurance	8.4	2.8	33.1	1.3
Medicare	42.5	14.4	333.8	13.5
Totals	99.3	33.6	$885.02	35.8

SOURCE: Congressional Research Service; U.S. Office of Management and Budget; and Bureau of Economic Analysis, U.S. Department of Commerce.

The social insurance programs just mentioned provide benefits that ordinarily go to people with zero or low current labor incomes— the retired, the temporarily or permanently disabled, dependents of deceased workers, and the temporarily unemployed. Unlike means-tested benefits, however, social insurance payments are received by middle- and high-income Americans as well as by the poor. If well-to-do workers reach age sixty-five, retire, and have made payroll contributions to the Social Security and Medicare programs for a minimum number of years, they can receive Social Security pensions and Medicare, regardless of the family's wealth and other sources of income. For most families with income under $32,000, the Social Security benefit is tax-free. In contrast with the insurance programs, means-tested programs distribute money and other resources directly to poor or near-poor families. Middle- and high-income families are not eligible for these benefits unless they have suffered serious economic reversals that reduce their incomes and wealth to very low levels. Certain kinds of means-tested benefits are restricted even more narrowly to particular classes of poor Americans—the aged, the disabled, and single parents and their children. Examples of means-tested programs include Temporary Assistance for Needy Families, food stamps, and Medicaid. These programs are typically referred to as "welfare." They suffer a worse public reputation than social insurance because benefits are offered solely to the indigent. American welfare programs serve two broad purposes: to provide both cash and services to the destitute who do not work and to supplement the earnings of low-income workers who support children. The design of welfare programs is powerfully affected by voters' concern over work incentives and the possibility of fraud among beneficiaries.

The Social Security Act created the first federal welfare programs in 1935. The most controversial program established under the act was Aid to Dependent Children (later called Aid to Families with Dependent Children or AFDC before being replaced by Temporary Assistance for Needy Families in 1996). This modest program, designed originally to provide support to poor widows with minor children, began a federal commitment to the poor that eventually grew into a complicated array of federal and federal-state social programs. The federal commitment to the poor grew dramatically during President Lyndon Johnson's War on Poverty, which began in the 1960s. The three most important programs established in the 1960s and early 1970s were the federal-state Medicaid program, which pays for health care for the poor and nursing home care for the indigent elderly; the federally financed food stamp program, which provides food vouchers to the poor; and Supplemental Security Income (SSI), which offers federal cash payments (with state-financed supplements) to the low-income blind, disabled, and elderly.

The programs just mentioned are entitlements, meaning that they provide benefits to all eligible individuals who apply. Government appropriations to pay for the programs depend on the number of people who apply and the benefit formulas that are specified by law, not on the annual appropriations process. Many other programs providing aid to the poor are discretionary, meaning that Congress must make an annual decision about how much money to spend on the programs. Some people who are technically eligible for benefits may not receive them because the budget is too small. The most expensive programs of this type are those providing rent subsidies and subsidized housing to the poor. Many more Americans are eligible to receive these subsidies than actually receive them. In contrast with the large insurance programs, which are financed and largely administered by the federal government, many smaller programs are run by state or local government agencies, usually with generous financing from the federal government. Sometimes the federal government provides fixed annual grants to states, and the states decide how to spend the money under broad federal guidelines. In other programs, the federal government offers to pay a fixed percentage of eligible costs, and states and local governments must finance the remainder.

It is possible to impose some conceptual order on U.S. social programs by conceiving of them as consisting of three tiers. In the top tier are the federal insurance programs providing universal benefits—Social Security Old-Age, Survivors, and Disability Insurance; Medicare; and Unemployment Compensation. In the second tier are the large entitlement programs for poor Americans—Temporary Assistance for Needy Families, Medicaid, food stamps, SSI, and a few others. Finally, the third tier consists of many scores of programs for poor and low-income individuals or families, most of them small and in competition with one another for annual congressional appropriations. The biggest and most important programs in the third tier are the housing programs.

Table 17.4 divides the programs in the second and third tiers into eight program categories based on the type of benefit provided: medical insurance or services, cash payments, food and nutrition assistance, housing subsidies, educational aid and instructional services targeted on low-income children, social services (including direct child care subsidies), job training and placement services, and energy assistance. The first data column shows state and local spending in each program area; the second data column shows federal spending. The budget totals make it clear that American government has accepted major responsibility for helping poor and low-income citizens. In 2004, public spending on programs for the poor amounted to 5 percent of U.S. national income. Most of the burden of paying for these programs falls on the federal government. Within each of the eight types of spending on the poor, federal spending predominates. Before 1965, there were relatively few federal programs that provided benefits for the poor. By 2004, nearly 75 percent of means-tested benefits were financed by the federal

Table 17.4   Spending on Major Means-Tested Programs, Fiscal
Year 2004

Type of Program	State Expenditure	Federal Expenditure	Total Expenditure
Medical	$127.8	$194.8	$322.6
Cash assistance	18.1	94.0	112.0
Food	2.7	45.5	48.1
Housing		38.9	38.9
Education	1.8	27.4	29.2
Services (including child care)	4.9	18.3	23.2
Jobs/Training	0.9	6.1	7.0
Energy assistance	0.1	2.1	2.3
Total	$156.2	$427.1	$583.3

SOURCE: Congressional Research Service, *Cash and Non-Cash Benefits for Persons with Limited Income: Eligibility Rules, Recipient and Expenditure Data, FY2002–FY2004* (RL33340). Washington, DC: Congressional Research Service, March 2006, 3.

government, and federal spending on these programs accounted for almost 19 percent of the federal budget.

Most public spending targeted on the poor pays for medical benefits and cash assistance. Spending on cash programs is more than twice as high as spending on any of the six categories below it, and spending on medical programs is more than twice as high as spending on cash programs. American social policy places a premium on ensuring that the poor have health care and on giving them cash so they can make their own decisions about how best to meet their needs. Spending on means-tested programs has grown rapidly over time. Between 1968 and 2004, state and federal spending on these programs increased from about $89 billion to $583 billion in inflation-adjusted 2004 dollars.[20] During this thirty-six-year period, spending increased in all but four years and rose almost twice as fast as U.S. national income. Much of the rise resulted from rapidly growing health care costs and the creation and rapid growth of several new programs, such as food stamps, child nutrition programs, and the EITC.

In addition to supporting direct spending programs for redistribution, the income tax system redistributes money from the well-to-do to the poor. Tax rates are progressive, so high-income families face higher average tax rates than low- and moderate-income families. In addition, the tax system contains a complex set of tax credits, income deductions and exemptions, preferential tax rates, and income deferrals. The Congressional Joint Tax Committee recently analyzed these benefits for tax year 2003 and identified thirty-seven provisions that provide tax benefits to further a social purpose such as encouraging retirement saving and health insurance coverage, providing benefits to the poor, rewarding employment, reducing taxes on the disabled, and improving the nation's housing stock, particularly its low-income housing stock.[21] The most important tax provision helping poor and low-income working families is the EITC, which functions as a wage supplement, primarily for workers with children.[22] In 2003, the credit provided $34 billion to over 19 million households with annual incomes below $34,000.[23] The EITC supplements the wage earnings of low-income breadwinners by providing them with a refundable income tax credit. Instead of shrinking as a recipient's earnings grow, the credit rises up to a specified limit. At low earnings levels, the credit increases by $0.34 or $0.40—depending on whether the worker has one or more than one dependent child—for each extra dollar earned by the breadwinner. In 2006 the maximum annual credit was $4,536 for a family with two children and $2,747 for a family with one child. When parents' incomes rise above $14,800 a year, the EITC begins to be phased out. Parents who have no wages are not eligible to receive the credit, so the credit provides a big incentive for unemployed parents to find work.

Other tax provisions to help the poor or promote employer benefit plans include tax preferences for employer-sponsored health insurance and company pension plans, a credit for child care expenses, credits for employers hiring former welfare recipients and other low-income workers, credits for education expenses, special exemptions for the elderly and disabled, and tax incentives for investors in residential rental property where a fraction of rental units are set aside for low- and moderate-income families. The Organization of Economic Cooperation and Development (OECD) refers to these tax provisions as "tax breaks for social purposes." It estimates that the United States spends much more on these kinds of tax preferences, in proportion to its national income, than other members of the OECD.[24] One result is that the United States depends much more on the private provision of welfare benefits than other OECD countries. Among the seven largest industrialized countries— Canada, France, Germany, Italy, Japan, the United Kingdom, and the United States—the U.S. spends by far the most on private and voluntary provision of social welfare benefits, especially for health insurance and occupational pensions (see the lower panel in Table 17.5). In many cases the tax preferences have relatively small impacts on low-income households. In spite of a substantial tax preference for providing health and pension benefits, for example, many companies that employ low-wage workers do not offer either health or retirement benefits to their workers. About 11 percent of American children under eighteen and 21 percent of adults between eighteen and sixty-four do not have any health insurance. People who are uninsured are not totally cut off from medical care. In emergencies most of them can obtain free or generously subsidized care in hospital emergency rooms, though this is not a good way to obtain high-quality care. For most employed Americans who lack insurance, the main reason is that their employers do not offer insurance or do not allow them to enroll in the company plan.[25] An even

larger percentage of working Americans is employed by firms that
offer no occupational pensions. Workers who earn higher wages are
more likely to be offered health and retirement benefits and to participate in their employer's plans. In comparison with a system of direct, government-provided benefits or of legally mandated private
provision, the system of tax-preferred, voluntary social welfare provision leaves many low- and moderate-income employees without
benefits.

By the standards of many industrialized countries, the publicly
financed social welfare system in the United States is modest.

Table 17.5   Public and Private Social Expenditures as a Percentage
of GDP, by Broad Social Policy Area in Seven Industrialized Countries, 2001

| Country | Cash benefits | | Services | | | |
	For working -age and children	For old-age and survivors	Medical care and health insurance	All social services except health	Other	Total social expendi- tures
Government Funded						
France	6.0	11.9	7.2	2.0	1.4	28.5
Germany	4.5	11.2	8.0	2.6	1.1	27.4
Italy	3.3	13.8	6.3	0.6	0.4	24.4
United Kingdom	5.9	8.3	6.1	1.2	0.3	21.8
Canada	2.8	5.3	6.7	2.7	0.3	17.8
Japan	1.5	7.6	6.3	1.3	0.2	16.9
United States	1.8	6.1	6.2	0.5	0.1	14.7
Privately Funded						
France	0.4	0.3	1.2	0.0	0.0	2.0
Germany	1.5	0.6	1.3	0.0	0.0	3.5
Italy	1.4	0.0	0.1	0.0	0.0	1.5
United Kingdom	0.7	3.4	0.3	0.0	0.0	4.4
Canada	0.0	3.4	1.1	0.0	0.0	4.5
Japan	0.2	3.3	0.0	0.0	0.0	3.5
United States	0.5	3.8	5.0	0.0	0.0	9.3

SOURCE: W. Adema and M. Ladaique, "Net Social Expenditure, 2005 Edition:
More Comprehensive Measures of Social Support" (Paris: OECD, 2005),
Chart 2.

Among the seven largest industrial countries, the United States spends the smallest percentage of its national income on direct government provision of social welfare benefits (see the top panel in Table 17.5). In 2001, U.S. social welfare spending represented a little less than 15 percent of U.S. national income. In the other six countries, it averaged almost 23 percent of national income. By spending less, the United States also accomplishes less. Tabulations of household market incomes in rich countries suggest that in the bottom 98 percent of the income distribution, U.S. market incomes are about as equally distributed as market incomes in the average country for which such tabulations are possible. After-tax, after-transfer incomes are more unequally distributed in the United States than they are in other rich countries, however, mainly because the U.S. tax and transfer system has a smaller impact on the final distribution of income.[26]

Why has the United States chosen a relatively small social welfare state? While almost two-thirds of Americans agree with the statement that "income differences in the United States are too large," policies aimed at reducing income differences command relatively little popular support.[27] On the whole, Americans are not particularly concerned about the income distribution and are less persuaded than citizens in other rich countries of the need for public policies to temper inequality. Only about a quarter of Americans strongly agree that the government should guarantee each citizen a minimum standard of living. In contrast, over half of the population in Japan and in each of five European countries strongly agrees that the government has such a responsibility.[28]

Americans' distinctive views about economic inequality may stem from two related beliefs about the way a just society ought to operate and the way they think their own society functions. A large majority of Americans believes that individuals should bear primary responsibility for supporting themselves, whereas voters in other rich countries are more inclined to believe that governments have an obligation to assure that everyone is provided for. Large majorities of Americans also believe their society offers an equal opportunity for people to get ahead and think that hard work will ordinarily translate into a better life. Residents of other rich countries are less likely to think their societies provide equal opportunity and are more inclined to believe that differences in individual success are due to luck or personal connections rather than individual effort.[29] As we have seen, comparative international statistics on upward mobility do not support Americans' relative optimism or Europeans' pessimism on this score.

Historians of the welfare state have long noted the distinctive values held by most Americans,[30] especially their distaste for means-tested assistance and their emphasis on self-reliance. Socialist and union-dominated parties have never been an important force in American politics. Although there is little question that Americans hold different views than Europeans on social protection, two episodes in U.S. policymaking highlight some of the differences. In 1969, President Richard Nixon proposed the Family Assistance Plan (FAP). This reform in means-tested assistance programs would have revolutionized American social policy by providing every working-age family containing children with a guaranteed minimum income. A moderately conservative president introduced the plan and fought hard for its acceptance. One reason the plan was defeated in Congress was the opposition of liberal legislators, who were dissatisfied with the meager benefits offered under the plan.[31] If enacted, Nixon's proposal would have copied a feature common to social assistance programs in other rich countries, namely, a guaranteed income floor for indigent citizens. After the plan was rejected in 1971, no other universal guaranteed benefit has come close to passage in either house of Congress. The near passage of President Nixon's guaranteed income plan is now seen as the high water mark of support for European-style social welfare in the United States.

When major reform in social assistance finally came in 1996, it moved the United States much further away from the European social welfare model. The main focus of reform was AFDC,[32] the principal cash assistance program providing aid to working-age parents and their children. The reform passed in 1996 was designed to reduce dependency on cash assistance by ending the automatic entitlement to benefits. AFDC was abolished and replaced with Temporary Assistance for Needy Families (TANF). The new law placed pressure on all states to adopt aggressive policies to restrict or eliminate cash benefits to poor parents who were capable of working but who did not work. Work requirements were stringent, and the new law imposed financial penalties on states that failed to require parents to meet them. The law also imposed time limits on the assistance payments families could receive. Most families could receive federally financed cash benefits for no longer than five years. The law permitted states to impose even shorter time limits, and more than half of them have done so. Although the 1996 reforms were the focus of a bitter congressional debate, in the end the bill passed with overwhelming bipartisan support and was signed by a Democratic president who had campaigned on a promise "to end welfare as we know it."

The welfare reform law reflects the value most Americans place on work and self-reliance. The law requires even mothers of young children to work. Both federal and state officials have shown willingness to impose severe penalties—including complete cessation of cash benefits—when mothers do not cooperate with program requirements. This willingness to use strong measures, imposing substantial risk on poor and low-income families, marks a sharp contrast with social policy in much of Europe. Although some European countries have moved toward the U.S. policy of pushing single mothers toward work, no European government has been willing to impose the tough measures that are now common in the

United States, such as time limits on benefit receipt or cessation of benefit payments for mothers who refuse to work.

There is another side of the American welfare state, however. Over a two-decade period beginning in the mid–1980s, Congress and successive administrations reformed a variety of tax laws and assistance programs to provide more generous benefits to working-age families that contain active workers. Programs that give cash or in-kind support to working families now constitute a loose safety net called the work support system. The most important and novel element in this system is the EITC, which subsidizes the wages earned by low-income parents. Congress also passed important changes in Medicaid to make that program more generous to low-income families containing a breadwinner. When first enacted in 1965 and for two decades thereafter, Medicaid provided coverage that was largely restricted to families collecting means-tested cash benefits. Cash assistance, in turn, was mostly restricted to families without an active breadwinner. If mothers collecting public assistance took a job, both they and their children would usually lose both their cash assistance and their coverage under Medicaid. A series of reforms beginning in the 1980s made it possible for children in low-income families to maintain their publicly provided health insurance, even if their parents held jobs and did not collect any public assistance. At the same time, Congress and state legislatures sharply increased funding for child care subsidies to low-income families.[33] A federal tax change provided partially refundable child tax credits in 1997. In 2002, Congress made changes in the food stamp program to make it easier for working families to collect benefits. Many states have mimicked federal policies by expanding state-financed benefits for low-income working families.

These reforms mark a major change in American social policy. Before the 1980s, most means-tested programs provided benefits to families without a working breadwinner. Since then U.S. welfare policy has been reoriented to limit benefits available to low-income parents who do not work while boosting benefits to low-income families where there is a working breadwinner. The Congressional Budget Office has estimated the value of benefits available to low-income working families under program rules in effect at two points in time, in the mid–1980s (before reform) and in 1999 (after reform).[34] The study showed that, without the work-support reforms enacted between 1985 and 1999, low-income families with working breadwinners would have received less than $6 billion in benefits in 1999. Under the work support system actually in place in 1999, these families received nearly $52 billion in benefits. More recent estimates by the Urban Institute show a similar pattern of rapid growth in earnings supplementation after 1985.

When the welfare reform law passed in 1996 and replaced AFDC with TANF, the U.S. economy was growing strongly. This expansion would ultimately produce a net increase of 23 million jobs.[35] The combined effects of a strong economy, tougher restrictions on public assistance for jobless adults, and more generous income supplements for the working poor were large and sustained. Many poor and low-income single mothers left the public assistance rolls and, in most cases, found jobs. The welfare rolls dropped 50 percent between 1994 and 2000, the first sustained decline since the creation of the cash assistance programs in 1935. The employment rate of low-income single mothers increased strongly, reaching its highest level ever. Single mothers' income from public assistance fell, but their wage earnings and EITC wage supplements increased, leaving them with a net income gain of 25 percent in inflation-adjusted dollars over the period. The U.S. child poverty rate saw its first sustained decline since the 1960s (see Figure 17.5). Both the African-American child poverty rate and the poverty rate of children in single-mother families reached their lowest levels ever. Even after a mild recession in 2001 and a modest rise in the child poverty rate, poverty among children in female-headed families remained one-fifth lower than it was in 1994. In spite of the major shock caused by welfare reform, national surveys showed that almost every measure of child well-being except obesity improved during the 1990s.[36] Notwithstanding the success of welfare reform, it has left some problems unresolved. Not all single mothers have been able to adapt to the rigorous work requirements of the new regime. Some have lower net incomes today than they did before reform. Former welfare recipients who have entered the workforce have generally not moved up to higher paying jobs. Poor men, who are the absent fathers of many poor youngsters, were given no additional assistance under the reforms. Nonetheless, reform has resulted in at least 1.5 million previously poor mothers entering the workforce and establishing their independence from cash welfare. Even more important, it has converted the nation's main welfare program into a work support system.

Conclusion

On the whole, U.S. social policy has become less generous to the non-working (but working-age) poor and much more generous to the working-age poor who take jobs and stay employed. For many low-wage breadwinners with children, the increased generosity of the EITC, enlarged child care subsidies, and improved access to public health insurance for their children have more than offset the loss of cash assistance payments and the long-term decline in poor breadwinners' hourly wages. Because of changes in the income tax schedule and successive expansions in family tax credits, the after-tax incomes of low-wage parents who remain steadily employed have increased significantly since the mid–1980s. The net income gains have occurred even though the hourly wages paid by employers to unskilled workers have stagnated or declined.

Recent American policy changes have had important economic effects in addition to offsetting the long-term decline in wages at the bottom. Poor single mothers with children have been induced to enter the workforce and stay there. The entry of never-married mothers and other disadvantaged new workers into the job market puts some downward pressure on wages of the least skilled (though real wages at the bottom have improved since the mid–1990s). In effect, public subsidies to the working poor and cutbacks in social assistance benefits to the non-working poor help keep employer costs low and encourage U.S. companies to create millions of poorly paid jobs.

More generous public programs have improved the circumstances of many low-income American workers, assuming they can find and keep jobs. But America's new policies have not been so generous that poor, working-age Americans have shared proportionately in recent U.S. prosperity. Compared with other rich countries, the United States continues to experience very high rates of poverty, particularly among working-age families and families that contain children (see Table 17.2). One reason is that U.S. policies offer Americans much less assurance they will enjoy comfortable or even minimal incomes should they become and remain unemployed.

A more generous welfare state would obviously produce different outcomes. Generous assistance programs, like those available in much of Europe, can greatly improve the circumstances of low-wage workers and the long-term unemployed. On the other hand, some side effects of such programs, including high joblessness and heavy taxpayer burdens, are not especially attractive. Many American voters, even those on the political left, might hesitate to adopt policies that boost joblessness and average tax burdens. Few U.S. voters favor giving undisguised cash transfers to people who are old enough and healthy enough to work, particularly in an expanding economy in which even unskilled immigrants manage to find jobs and support their families.

While acknowledging that the consequences of inequality can be unattractive, most defenders of American economic and political institutions point out that inequality plays a crucial role in creating incentives for people to improve their situations through saving, hard work, and investment in education and training. Many would also argue that income disparities must sometimes grow larger to send correct signals to people to save more, work harder, change jobs, or increase their investment in schooling. Without the powerful signals provided by increased inequality, the economy would operate less efficiently and average income levels might grow less rapidly. In the long run, poor people might enjoy higher income and consumption in a society where income disparities are permitted to widen compared with one where legal and social institutions keep income differentials small. According to this argument, the widening inequality we have seen in the United States may be in the long-term interest of the poor themselves.

For low-income Americans, however, the theoretical advantages of greater inequality are not easy to see in recent statistics. Their living standards have improved much more slowly than those of people further up the economic scale. At the bottom of the distribution, Americans' absolute incomes are almost certainly smaller than the incomes received by citizens in other rich countries who occupy a comparable position in their country's income distribution. Among fifteen countries providing information to the Luxembourg Income Study, only low-income residents in the United Kingdom are worse off than the poor in the United States. People at the 10th percentile of the income distribution in the thirteen other countries receive higher absolute incomes than a person at the same position of the income distribution in the United States. What makes this statistic remarkable is that average U.S. incomes are considerably higher than incomes in other rich countries.[37] Clearly, many of the efficiency advantages of wide and growing inequality have not trickled down to America's poor, at least so far. To the extent such advantages exist, they have been captured by Americans much further up the income scale, opening conspicuously wider gaps between rich, middle-class, and poor Americans.

CHAPTER 18

Philanthropy and the Non-Profit Sector

Arthur C. Brooks

Americans rely on non-profit organizations and contribute more to charity than do the citizens of any other developed nation. Arthur Brooks, a professor of public administration, shows that this stems from a long civic tradition of private initiatives to solve social problems and satisfy unmet needs. The roots of this tradition can be found in America's unique history, the deep religious involvement of so many Americans, and a popular skepticism about the government's role in redistributing resources to those in need. America may be a nation preoccupied with profit, but it is the non-profit sector and massive private voluntary support for it that truly sets the nation apart from the rest of the world.

WHAT MAKES AMERICA DIFFERENT FROM OTHER NATIONS? IS there an essential, uniquely "American" character trait? American historian Morris Berman claims that this characteristic is mass consumerism, which defines the American landscape (and lies behind international hostility toward the United States, as well).[1] Others have defined America in terms of money: one American author calls the United States "a Promised Land of profit, glory and unfettered growth."[2]

It might seem fairly intuitive that the emblem of America would involve money, given the nation's phenomenal wealth, compared to most of the rest of the world. So it is especially interesting that some foreign commentators on the United States have focused not on profit, but rather on non-profit. That is, some visitors to America have found that its true essence lies outside the realm of lucre—in voluntary activities and charitable acts. For example, as Alexis de Tocqueville famously noted in *Democracy in America,* the difference between Americans and Europeans was the tendency to join together for non-commercial purposes and to give of themselves.

> Americans of all ages, all conditions, and all dispositions constantly form associations. . . . The Americans make associations to give entertainments, to found seminaries, to build inns, to construct churches, to diffuse books, to send missionaries to the antipodes; in this manner they found hospitals, prisons, and schools. If it is proposed to inculcate some truth or to foster some feeling by the encouragement of a great example, they form a society. Wherever at the head of some new undertaking you see the government in France, or a man of rank in England, in the United States you will be sure to find an association.[3]

This chapter is devoted to understanding the giving, volunteering, and not-for-profit activity that seemed so peculiar—and uniquely "American"—to Tocqueville, and which still sums up America today.

The Dimensions of Non-Profit America

Most developed economies have something called a "non-profit" or "non-governmental" sector. What sets America apart from other countries is the importance non-profits have in providing key public services and the generous private support the non-profit sector receives.

The non-profit sector represents 13 percent of American gross domestic product (GDP).[4] This came to about $1.4 trillion in 2002, or approximately two-thirds the annual revenues of the U.S. federal government. This is a bit less than half as large as the total value of annual retail trade and is larger than the revenues of the American construction industry. The non-profit sector is more than three times as large as the industries in hospitality and food services, utilities, or transportation.

More than 11 million workers are currently employed by the American non-profit sector, or about 7 percent of the U.S. workforce. This makes the non-profit sector nearly half as large an employer as all types of manufacturing put together, and makes it three times larger than American agriculture.[5] Further, this only counts paid employees. If we count the full-time equivalent labor from volunteers in the non-profit sector, the non-profit workforce swells to about 17 million.

It is nearly impossible to avoid non-profits in America. If you get sick and go to the hospital, you are as likely as not to be in a non-profit institution. About half of American colleges and universities are non-profits as well. Four out of five social service agencies are non-profits, as are 90 percent of "high culture" groups, such as symphony orchestras and opera companies. Virtually all houses of worship possess *de facto* non-profit status. In short, practically everybody in America patronizes non-profit organizations on a fairly regular basis. Further, there is evidence that Americans have great confidence in non-profits to provide the services they need, especially compared with governments. For example, after Hurricane Katrina devastated the city of New Orleans in 2005, Louisiana residents were asked to rate the effectiveness of various relief agencies on a scale of 1 to 10, 10 being the best. Religious non-profits scored 8.1, on average, while secular non-profits were given a rating of 7.5. In comparison, the U.S. federal government's relief efforts were rated at 5.1, and state and local agencies were given a lowly 4.6.[6]

The growth in American non-profit activity has been nothing short of phenomenal. For example, from 1996 to 2004, the number of 501(c)(3) non-profits—so called "public charities" dedicated to activities from social welfare to education to the arts—grew by 53.5 percent, from 535,888 to 822,817. The number of small non-profits with gross receipts under \$25,000 and not incorporated as 501(c)(3)s exploded by more than 100 percent over this period. From 1987 to 1997, non-profit sector revenues grew from \$453 billion (in 1997 dollars) to \$665 billion. Growth was especially high in certain areas: for example, health non-profit activity grew by 51 percent in real terms over the decade; social welfare activity increased by 67 percent; and the arts and culture increased by 79 percent.

How different is America's non-profit sector from that in other countries? The most recent comparative data on non-profit activity come from the late 1990s. At that time, the largest non-profit sector in Europe—Great Britain's—was about 14 percent as large as America's non-profit sector. On a per capita basis, two small European countries (Belgium and the Netherlands) had greater non-profit revenues than the United States, although in both these cases the bulk of the revenues were government subsidies. All other countries saw lower per capita non-profit activity than in the United States. For reasons discussed later in this chapter, it is most likely that the difference between European and American non-profit activity has, if anything, grown over the past decade.

The size and importance of America's non-profit sector are impressive by international standards. But even more exceptional is the fact that so much of the support of the sector is purely voluntary. In fact, private charitable donations in the United States add up to about a quarter-trillion dollars per year—enough that the entire national income of any of the Scandinavian countries could be financed in its entirety through American donations. About three-quarters of this giving comes from living individuals; the rest comes from foundations, corporations, and bequests. Charitable contributions in the United States have remained fairly steady over the past fifty years, at about 1.5 percent of GDP. Americans have been consistent in sharing a meaningful portion of their growing prosperity with charities, churches, and other causes. This fact is at variance with much popular wisdom about giving, which we sometimes hear is declining.

A large majority of U.S. citizens give of their money and time. Most estimates place the percentage of American households that make money contributions each year at 70 to 80 percent, and the average American household contributes more than $1,000 each year. And it is not the case that American giving goes all—or even mostly—to religion. About a third of individual gifts go toward sacramental activities, primarily supporting houses of worship. The rest goes to secular activities, such as education, health, and social welfare.

Of the quarter-trillion dollars Americans give each year, more than three-quarters comes from private individuals. The second largest source—between 10 and 15 percent of all giving—comes from private foundations. Private foundations are tax-exempt institutions designed to pool the charitable funds of an individual, family, corporation, or community. The first American foundation was formed in 1907 by Margaret Olivia Sage—the widow of financier and railroad magnate Russell Sage—with a $10 million gift. Within a few years, several major foundations were formed by wealthy industrialists, including the Carnegie Foundation, Rockefeller Foundation, Kresge Foundation, and later, the Kellogg Foundation, Lilly Endowment, and the Ford Foundation.[7] In recent times, the number of foundations has exploded; from 1996 to 2004, the number of private foundations grew by 75 percent (from 58,774 to 102,881) and have combined assets approaching a half-trillion dollars. About 95 percent of foundations are private—not corporate or community foundations—and overwhelmingly are connected to family fortunes.

Most of the American non-profit sector relies critically on the various sources of donated support. For example, donations make up 16 percent of the revenues to non-profit education organizations (and far more to private universities), 20 percent to human service charities, 44 percent to the arts, and 84 percent to religious institutions.[8] Small, grassroots organizations rely even more heavily on donated support because government grants and earned revenues are frequently not available to them. The bottom line is that, without private charitable giving in America, many critical services would simply disappear, and many needs would go unmet. It is inconceivable that the American public sector could or would step in to provide all the funding that private citizens currently donate to charities and causes across the country.

Between 50 and 60 percent of American households formally volunteer their time each year, volunteering an average of almost fifty hours annually. About 40 percent of volunteer hours go to religious causes, followed by about 30 percent for youth-related activities, such as the PTA and children's sports. Poverty-related causes, health charities, and activist causes also receive significant amounts of volunteer time.

The Americans who give money, volunteer, or both, are the people most likely to behave charitably in informal ways as well. For example, formal money donors are nearly three times as likely to give money informally to friends and strangers as non-donors. People who give to charity at least once per year are twice as likely to donate blood as people who don't give money. They are also significantly more likely to give food or money to a homeless person on the street.

No developed country approaches American giving and volunteering levels. For example, in 1995, Americans gave, per capita, three and a half times as much to causes and charities as the French, seven times as much as the Germans, and fourteen times as much as the Italians. Similarly, in 1998, Americans were 15 percentage points more likely to volunteer than the Dutch, 21 points more likely than the Swiss, and 32 points more likely than the Germans. These differences are not attributable to demographic characteristics such education, income, age, sex, or marital status. On the contrary, if we look at two people who are identical in all these ways—but one is

European and the other American—the probability is far lower that the European will volunteer than the American. For example, an Austrian who is otherwise identical to an American will be 32 percentage points less likely to volunteer, a Spaniard will be 31 points less likely, and an Italian will be 29 points less likely.

In sum, it is indisputable that the non-profit sector is one of the dominant features of the American economic landscape, that voluntary support for the sector is abundant in the form of money and time, and that America is exceptional in both these ways, compared with other developed nations. The question we are left with, if our objective is to understand America, is *why* these things are so.

Why Does America Rely So Much on Its Non-Profit and Voluntary Sector?

Democratic countries can organize the provision of their public goods and services in many ways, depending on the will of the people. They can leave public services in the hands of private markets. They can rely on the government to meet most social needs. Or they can adopt a mixed model, wherein private markets, governments, and non-governmental organizations overlap to meet needs.

Europe over the past fifty years has trended steadily toward heavier and heavier state provision as its demands for social safety nets have risen. America has seen a similar increase in demand for services, but a more limited appetite for the state's role in providing these services. The result has been a large and growing non-profit sector. The American dependence on non-profits owes primarily to three related forces: a strong history of citizen participation in civil society, the fact that the American non-profit sector is more economically efficient than the government or commercial sectors in many cases, and a general uneasiness among Americans about the effects of government on society.

Tocqueville observed that America's leadership and governance in 1835 was largely non-governmental. Indeed, he noted that the ablest citizens tended to exclude themselves from positions in government, choosing to participate in civil society instead. The preference for civil society over governments—paired with a vast frontier, making formal governance that much more difficult—led to a tradition of reliance on voluntary associations not seen in European nations. This was reinforced across succeeding American generations and in a Constitution that placed sharp limits on the extent to which the government could provide many goods and services to the population. A notably religious population provided the organizational infrastructure to meet many needs voluntarily through charity. The results were an American welfare state that was both smaller and that came later than its European counterparts and an enduring tradition of non-profit organizations supported heavily by private contributions of time and money.

Economists have studied the non-profit sector in America under the assumption that it must exist because it has an efficiency advantage in some spheres and hence it is not displaced by other institutions (commercial or governmental) through the natural forces of markets or politics. For example, non-profits can be more efficient than commercial organizations in cases in which information to consumers is in short supply.[9] Certain types of public services, such as medical care or social welfare services, are often characterized by esoteric but important functions. If my appendix is infected, it has to come out, and I need a surgeon to do it. But if I am worried about the integrity of surgeons—because of a profit motive—I might be disinclined to seek services early enough. Removing the profit motive with legal non-profit status (which enjoins an organization from distributing profits to owners) can have the effect of reducing the incentive to exploit this kind of asymmetric information. In other words, why would a doctor take out a healthy appendix if he can't keep the money?

Asymmetric information can make non-profits more efficient than commercial firms. Non-profits can also be more efficient than

governments, as well.[10] There are two reasons for this: non-profits
have an incentive to behave economically, and they can operate at a
more appropriate scale than governments for certain services. First,
non-profits have a clear "bottom line" to their finances—they can
and do go out of business when costs exceed revenues over time.
In contrast, governments have a flexible budget. Within certain
limits, governments can cope with rising costs through deficit
spending or raising taxes. The absence of a budget constraint does
not enhance government's incentives to provide goods and services
in a cost-effective way, many economists argue. Second, many public
services are specific to relatively small communities. For example, it
may be of great benefit to a neighborhood to have a children's
baseball league, yet the government may not be able to provide services efficiently at such a small scale. While a local kids' baseball
league is completely normal in America, the idea of establishing a
state, county, or city agency to organize and oversee the league
would strike many people as unwise (perhaps even ridiculous) and
probably costly. It is also likely to displace private civic participation.

This last point is especially important. All the available evidence
suggests that there is a substantial negative relationship between
government activity and private, voluntary action. Scholars have
consistently found a substantial degree of "crowding out" of both
donated money and time when governments step in to provide or
pay for public services. Indeed, economists have estimated that a
dollar in public support for social welfare services displaces at least
25 cents in private giving, and defrays private voluntarism as well.[11]

Given the fact that government funding displaces private giving, it may seem odd that both types of funding have increased over
the years. Indeed, government funding to non-profits increased by
64 percent (in inflation-adjusted terms) from 1987 to 1997, while
donations increased over the same period by 27 percent.[12] It might
seem that if government funding increases, donations would have to
fall. However, crowding out simply says that government money

will cause private donations to grow *less* than they otherwise would. In fact, conservatively estimating crowding out at a rate of 30 cents for each dollar of government funds, we can predict that, if government funding to non-profits had not grown from 1987 to 1997, donations would have increased by more than 50 percent.

The growing level of government involvement in non-profits means that today many non-profits are effectively wards of the state. In 2002, 13 percent of human service charities got at least 80 percent of their income from the government—and these were generally the largest agencies, receiving an average of $3.7 million each per year from the state.[13] A quarter got more than 50 percent of their funding from the public sector. This has imposed a substantial amount of risk on American non-profits, because government funding is a much less stable funding source for non-profits than is private giving. Indeed, the data show that non-profits are more than twice as likely to lose government money as they are to lose private support over a two-year period. Tax revenues and thus state budgets are "pro-cyclical": they increase or decrease even more than changes in the economy. In contrast, charitable donations are "countercyclical," in that they fluctuate less than the economy as a whole.

The discussion here of "crowding out" assumes that it is a negative phenomenon: while state support might be useful or necessary, it is not costless in terms of the charity it displaces. Some Americans, particularly on the political left, would assert that this assumption is invalid—not that crowding out exists, but the assumption that private charity is a good thing at all. The author John Steinbeck sums up a certain view that private giving is actually a bad thing.

> Perhaps the most overrated virtue in our list of shoddy virtues is that of giving. Giving builds up the ego of the giver, makes him superior and higher and larger than the receiver. Nearly always, giving is a selfish pleasure, and in

many cases is a downright destructive and evil thing. One has only to remember some of the wolfish financiers who spent two thirds of their lives clawing a fortune out of the guts of society and the latter third pushing it back.[14]

This viewpoint is generally accompanied by the opinion that governments should provide basic goods and services to those in need. According to one scholar and critic of private charity, "By harnessing a wealth of volunteer effort and donations, [charities make] private programs appear cheaper and more cost effective than their public counterparts, thus reinforcing an ideology of voluntarism that obscures the fundamental destruction of rights."[15] From this vantage point, crowding out is a very good thing, and not any kind of cost.

This is surely a minority viewpoint, however. As evidenced by their exceptionally charitable behavior, most Americans value voluntary charity as an important virtue and reasonably see government as a force that can do violence to this virtue.

Some Americans, especially on the political right, believe that non-profits and other voluntary associations are an effective defense against social harms from bureaucracy. In 1977, Peter Berger and Richard John Neuhaus made the point in their famous book *To Empower People: From State to Civil Society* that non-profits are an important bulwark against the corrosive impact of governments on the ability of people to govern themselves effectively.[16] This work argued what many Americans find uncontroversial (but which is alien to many Europeans): that people, not governments, were best positioned to make decisions of social importance, and that citizen-empowering "mediating structures"—neighborhoods, families, churches, and voluntary associations—should be protected and incorporated into the policymaking process. Berger and Neuhaus warned, for example, "The danger today is not that churches or any one church will take over the state. The much more real danger is that the state will take over the functions of the church."[17] When they wrote this, protecting non-profit America was contrary to a decade of policy trends in which the American government was expanding and taking over greater and greater ranges of services. The ideas in *To Empower People,* however, evidently described the American public will better than the Europeanizing state. Since 1980, both main political parties in America have increasingly turned to non-profits—including religious non-profits—to provide critical public services.

The Forces of American Generosity

The support for American non-profits comes from governments and earned revenues, but also, as we have seen, from huge amounts of private charitable giving. How can we understand the American tendency to give so much, when other nations give relatively little?

THE UNDENIABLE ROLE OF
RELIGION IN AMERICAN CHARITY

Religious behavior is the single biggest predictor of American charity in general and the most compelling explanation for why Americans give so much more to charity than people in other countries.

Consider formal donations of money and time. In the year 2000, religious people (which I define as the 33 percent of the population who attend their houses of worship at least once per week) were 25 percentage points more likely to give than secularists (the 27 percent who attend less than a few times per year, or have no religion). They were also 23 points more likely to volunteer. When considering the average dollar amounts of money donated and time volunteered, the gap between the groups increases even further: Religious people gave nearly four times more dollars per year, on average, than secularists ($2,210 versus $642). They also volunteered more than twice as often (12 times per year, versus 5.8 times).

Naturally, these group differences could be due to religion itself, or rather to some other personal characteristics such as race, education, gender, or income. If we control for all these demographic differences, we still find an enormous charity gap between religious and secular people. For instance, imagine two people who are identical in income, education, age, race, and marital status. The only difference between them is that, while one goes to church every week, the other never does. Knowing this, we can predict that the churchgoer will still be 21 percentage points more likely to make a charitable gift of money during the year than the non-churchgoer, and will also be 26 points more likely to volunteer. Furthermore, he or she will tend to give about $1,400 more per year to charity, and volunteer on about six more occasions.

Of course, measuring religiosity in terms of attendance at a house of worship might be inadequate. So it is worth examining other kinds of religious and spiritual behaviors to see if the charity differences persist. Doing so does not change the story at all. For example, in 1999, people who prayed every day were 30 percentage points more likely to give money to charity than people who never prayed. Simply belonging to a congregation of any type made a person 32 points more likely to give. And people saying they devoted a "great deal of effort" to their spiritual lives were 42 points more likely to give than those devoting "no effort."

The enormous differences described here are not a simple artifact of religious people giving to their churches. Religious people are more charitable in every measurable non-religious way—including secular donations, informal giving, and even acts of kindness and generosity—than secularists. For example, in 2000, religious people were 10 points more likely than secularists to give money to explicitly non-religious charities and 21 points more likely to volunteer. The value of the average religious household gifts to non-religious charities was 14 percent higher than the average secular household's.

Religious people were also far more likely than secularists to give in informal, non-religious ways. For example, in 2000, people belonging to religious congregations gave 46 percent more money to family and friends than people who did not belong. In 2002, religious people were far more likely to donate blood than secularists, to give food or money to a homeless person, and even to return change mistakenly given them by a cashier.

As we all know, Americans are more religious than people in most other developed nations. With the exception of Ireland, the percentage of the population that practices no religion is higher in every European country than it is in the United States, and in most cases, the differences are dramatic. For example, a British citizen in 2002 was three times as likely to be completely secular as an American. In the Netherlands, 9 percent of the population attends church regularly; in Norway it is just 4 percent. European secularism is also more aggressive than American secularism. For example, in 1998, Swedes and Norwegians were five times as likely as Americans to agree with the statement, "Looking at the world, religions bring more conflict than peace."

Secularism has a clear association with low rates of charity in Europe, just as it does in the United States. For example, imagine two Europeans in 1998—one typical secularist and one churchgoer—who were identical with respect to education, income, age, marital status, and gender. The churchgoer would be 30 percentage points more likely than the secularist to volunteer each year, and 15 points more likely to volunteer for explicitly non-religious charities. And the impact of being both European *and* secular makes the difference explode. For example, take two people in 1998 who were identical except that one was a secular and French while the other was religious and American. The secularist Frenchman would be 56 percentage points less likely to volunteer than the religious American.

EARNING MONEY, AND GIVING IT AWAY

Religious or not, it is obvious that, in order for a person to give money away, he or she must have it in the first place. Not surprisingly, then, income and charitable giving in America are positively related. For example, in the year 2000, families earning $20,000 or less gave an average of $458 to charity, while families earning more than $100,000 gave away an average of $3,089. It is less obvious that people with higher incomes should be more likely to make a gift of any size, yet while 64 percent of the low-income families gave in 2000, 94 percent of the high-income families gave. The American rich are generous, on average.

Besides the dollars given and the likelihood of donating, another interesting measurement is donations as a percentage of income, reflecting the level of one's "sacrifice." Doing this reveals a surprising result: low-income families are the *most* generous group in America, giving away about 4.5 percent of their family income in 2000, on average. This compares to about 2.5 percent among the middle class, and 3 percent in the high-income families.

How is it possible that low-income families are less likely to give, but give away a higher percentage of their incomes? The answer is that the poor are far from a homogeneous group. On the contrary, when it comes to charitable behavior, one group of the poor is far more generous than the population as a whole, while the other is far less so. And the salient difference between these two groups is the source of their incomes—earned wages versus government transfers. For example, only considering the bottom fifth of earners in 2003, we find those who earned their income were more than twice as likely to give, and gave away three times as much money each year, as welfare recipients. They were also nearly twice as likely to volunteer their time, despite apparently having less time to spare. What this tells us is that the non-working poor are driving the statistic that the poor are less likely to give than other income groups, while the working poor are behind the finding that low-income families give away a large percentage of their incomes.

Note that the amount of disposable income is essentially the same between the working and non-working poor, so the explanation must lie in some other area. Many authors have asserted that there is a corrosive cultural element to welfare receipt, and this view is consistent with several economic studies that find a negative "welfare elasticity of giving" (the percentage change in giving that occurs when welfare income increases by a certain percentage).[18] Specifically, one study using nationwide income data from 2001 finds that, while a 10 percent increase in earned wages tends to push up charitable giving by 7 percent, a 10 percent increase in welfare income pushes giving down by 1.4 percent.[19] It would appear that charity is a pro-social behavior that is suppressed by welfare receipt (or at least welfare dependency). This is not a radical suggestion, but rather one that has a long tradition in American thinking. For example, Franklin D. Roosevelt warned that dependency on government support "induces a spiritual and moral disintegration fundamentally destructive to the national fiber. To dole out relief in this way is to administer a narcotic, a subtle destroyer of the human spirit."[20]

Besides charity, another difference between the working and non-working poor is income mobility: working people are far more likely than the non-working people with the same household incomes to rise economically. For example, a working family in the bottom half of the income distribution in 2001 was three times likelier than a welfare family to make it into the top half by 2003. The working poor—who tend to be exceptionally generous—give like rich people, because they believe they have a meaningful chance of becoming prosperous.

FAMILIES

Family life in America is connected with charity. First, in a purely arithmetic sense, families are good for charity, because, except in a few cases (such as single parenthood), people who have children are more generous than people who don't. Perhaps the act of having children stimulates giving, or givers are more likely to have children, but we find that, for example, a household with four members is more likely to give and volunteer each year than a household with only two members. If two married adults are identical in income, education, religion, race, age, and political views, but the first has one more child than the second—the odds are that the first parent will be more likely to give, and will give away more dollars each year.

A second fact about charity and families is that generous parents make for generous kids. In one large survey from the year 2000, a sample of Americans was asked about their parents' volunteering, as well as their own volunteering. People who said they saw their parents volunteer when they were children were 28 percentage points more likely to do the same when they grew up than people whose parents did not volunteer. This difference persists even when we correct for other demographics. For example, if two people had the same income, education level, gender, race, and marital status, but the first had volunteer parents while the second did not, the first person would be 12 points more likely to volunteer as an adult than the second.

The effects of giving and non-giving parents become especially large when combined with religion. For instance, 61 percent of adults who belonged to a house of worship in 2001 and whose parents had been volunteers were volunteers themselves. In contrast, only 30 percent volunteered whose parents were secularists and non-volunteers.

Researchers came to similar conclusions in a major 2001 study of American families.[21] The authors looked at similarities in the giving patterns of older Americans and their adult children. They found that people are much more likely to give to both religious and secular causes if their parents give. Even after controlling for income, education, age, race, and many other factors that might affect giving among families, they found that increases in parental giving were associated with higher giving by their adult children. The researchers interpreted this finding as evidence that some families have a culture of giving, while others do not.

As in America, there is evidence that Europeans without children are less likely to donate charitably than are those with children. For example, imagine two French couples who resemble each other in income, age, education, and even religious participation—the only difference is that the first couple has two children, while the other has none. The first couple will be 33 percent more likely to volunteer for charity than the second.

Fertility levels in Europe are far lower than they are in the Unites States. A replacement fertility level—meaning that a population stays constant because as many people are born as die each year—in the developed world is about 2.1 children born to each woman. In 2005, this was almost exactly the average number of children born to women in the United States. In stark contrast, the European Union has a birthrate of 1.5 children per woman. In France, the number is 1.8; in Britain, 1.7; in Spain, 1.3. In Germany, where the number of children per woman is currently 1.4, the most recent data tell us that 30 percent of German women will remain childless.[22] These low fertility levels contain some of the explanation for the European–American charity gap.

Charity, Left and Right

There is a persistent stereotype about charitable giving in politically progressive regions of America and other parts of the industrialized world: while people on the political right may be hardworking and family-oriented, they tend not to be very charitable toward the less fortunate. In contrast, those on the political left care about vulnerable members of society and are thus the charitable ones. Understanding "charity" in terms of voluntary gifts of time and money (instead of government income redistribution), this stereotype is wrong. Understanding this fact illuminates yet another dimension of America's non-profit nature.

The fact is that self-described "conservatives" in America are more likely to give—and give more money—than self-described "liberals." In the year 2000, households headed by a conservative gave, on average, 30 percent more dollars to charity than households headed by a liberal. (Both groups gave more than moderates, however.) And this discrepancy in money donations is not simply an artifact of income differences. On the contrary, liberal families in these particular data earned an average of 6 percent *more* per year than conservative families.[23]

These differences go beyond money. Take blood donations, for example. In 2002, conservative Americans were more likely to donate blood each year, and did so more often, than liberals. People who said they were "conservative" or "extremely conservative" made up less than one-fifth of the population but donated more than a quarter of the blood. To put this in perspective, if political liberals and moderates gave blood like conservatives do, the blood supply in the United States would surge by nearly half the current level.

The giving patterns that distinguish conservative individuals also distinguish conservative communities, which tend to be more charitable at the individual level than liberal communities. One way to show this is by comparing the results from the 2004 U.S. presidential election to the percentage of household income given away. State-by-state data from the Internal Revenue Service shows that the states won by Republican George W. Bush gave away a higher income proportion than the states won by Democrat John F. Kerry. In fact, of the twenty-five states that donated a portion of household income above the national average, twenty-four gave a majority of their popular votes to Bush for president, while only one gave the election to Kerry. Of the twenty-five states below the national giving average, seventeen went for Kerry, but just seven for Bush.[24]

One major explanation for the giving discrepancy between conservatives and liberals is surely religion—American conservatives are about twice as likely as liberals to attend a house of worship every week, and half as likely to say they have "no religion." A direct way that politics influences giving, however, is by way of attitudes about income redistribution. In 2004, 80 percent of American liberals said they thought the government should "do more" to reduce income inequality, versus just 27 percent of American conservatives. And people who favor forced redistribution are far less likely to give and volunteer for charity than those who oppose such policies. For example, in 1996, people who believed the government should *not* take greater measures than at present to reduce income inequality gave, on average, four times as much money to charity each year as those who believed the government should do more to equalize incomes. This result persists even after correcting for other demographics. It even holds for all sorts of non-money giving. For example, people who stated in 2002 that they thought the government was "spending too little money on welfare" were less likely than those saying the government is "spending too much money on welfare" to give food or money to a homeless person.

Taken together, this evidence suggests something that is, perhaps, obvious: Conservative Americans tend to favor private giving over government income redistribution and act in accordance with this view. The negative effects on charity from support for government income redistribution provide further explanation for the charity gap between America and Europe. Higher percentages of the population in every European country favor redistribution than do Americans. When Europeans and Americans were presented with the statement: "The government has a responsibility to reduce income inequality," 33 percent of Americans agreed—compared with 77 percent of Spaniards, 65 percent of Italians, and 49 percent of Germans. Considering 22 eastern and western European countries together, a 10 percent increase in the percentage of the population that believes the government has a responsibility to reduce income inequality is associated with a 6 percent decrease in the percentage volunteering for non-religious causes and a 5 percent decrease in religious volunteering.

Politics is an issue not just in individual giving; it involves foundation giving as well. Indeed, political ideology is a major fault line between different foundations today. While conservative individuals tend to be the biggest givers, in the foundation world it is liberal organizations that donate the most. The reason for this, however, has more to do with assets than any difference in giving spirit.

The early foundations in the United States initially focused on the advancement of learning, with John D. Rockefeller and Andrew Carnegie making large donations to set up schools and libraries. By the 1960s, the large, older foundations in America were virtually all run by boards and staffs with no firsthand memory of the founders or their philanthropic intent. These foundations began to direct their efforts at modern and politically progressive concepts of "social justice." This led to the perception that persists to this day that many of the largest foundations—despite their founding by conservative titans of industry—are tools of liberal public policy. It also created a backlash in philanthropy among a number of smaller foundations intent on protecting the intent of their conservative founders. Today, explicitly conservative foundations, despite having annual expenditures of barely $100 million—in contrast to the $1.5 billion in annual expenditures of the five largest liberal-leaning foundations in the United States—have significant influence on American public policy by funding think tanks and conservative advocacy organizations.[25]

Philanthropy and American Prosperity

There is a pervasive belief in America that philanthropy and prosperity are interrelated. And this is not just the obvious economic point that higher income can lead to higher giving. Rather, it is the religious or quasi-religious notion that giving itself drives prosperity.

In the words of John D. Rockefeller in 1905, "God gave me my money. I believe the power to make money is a gift from God . . . to be developed and used to the best of our ability for the good of mankind. Having been endowed with the gift I possess, I believe it is my duty to make money and still more money and to use the money I make for the good of my fellow man according to the dictates of my conscience."[26]

Despite the unscientific sound of Rockefeller's beliefs, they are generally supported by economic research. First, an emerging body of work on "social entrepreneurship"—entrepreneurship for the purpose of high social rewards instead of financial returns—has helped to legitimize the idea that many charitable activities create economic returns. For example, the value from an innovative program to protect poor kids from preventable diseases might create social and economic conditions congenial to economic development, if healthier kids grow up to be productive workers. It may also bring great joy to the giver and give him a healthier community in which to live.[27] Second, charitable giving can also generate "social capital"—the trust and social cohesion a community enjoys. Scholars have shown that such social networks provide employment possibilities, business opportunities, and access to capital.[28] Third, many economists have demonstrated that charity and related behaviors, such as religiosity, bring out industriousness in people. In the words of the famous early twentieth-century economist Thorstein Veblen, "[The] residue of the religious life—the sense of communion with the environment, or with the generic life process—as well as the impulse of charity or of sociability, act in a pervasive way to shape men's habits of thought for the economic purpose."[29]

Psychologists provide other reasons why voluntary charity might lead to prosperity. For example, one line of thinking suggests that charity creates a personal transformation in the giver, making him or her more self-efficacious and empowered, and thus industrious and successful. There is also evidence that givers are better liked, and thus more successful, than non-givers. For example, in 2006, British researchers conducted an experiment on human subjects in which participants were given money and asked if they wanted to share it voluntarily with a larger group. Some did, and some did not. Without announcing it beforehand, the researchers followed up the cooperation exercise by asking the participants to vote for a leader. Eighty percent of the time, the person who had contributed the most to the other members of the group was elected. The biggest givers were also the most often-chosen partners in follow-up tasks, while selfish participants were shunned.[30]

Empirical evidence provides support for the contention that giving stimulates economic prosperity. First of all, prosperity and charity are strongly and positively correlated, as we saw earlier. Emerging research has tried to move from this *association* between giving and income in America to an understanding of *causation*. Does income push giving, giving push income, neither, or both? At the level of the individual giver, it appears that the answer is *both:* charity pushes up income—and income increases charity as well. Survey data from 2000 indicate that, controlling for education, age, race, and all the other outside explanations for giving and income increases, a dollar donated to charity generated $3.75 in extra income. This is most likely evidence that givers have certain characteristics that make them more economically effective than non-givers for the reasons already discussed. It may also be an explanation for average material prosperity levels that are consistently higher in America than in Europe.[31]

The individual benefits of giving can be aggregated up to the level of the economy as a whole: American charity stimulates economic growth. Per capita charity and per capita GDP in the United States have moved together over the years, with the former increasing by 190 percent in real terms since 1954 and the latter rising by 150 percent over the same period. Evidence that the two forces cause each other comes from analysis of how past values of one variable affect future values of the other. This analysis shows that a 10 percent increase in GDP per American leads to a 1 percent rise in charitable giving. At the same time, a 10 percent increase in charity per person provokes a 3 percent increase in GDP. In dollar terms, this means that $1 given privately tends to increase GDP by about $19—an excellent rate of return by any standard.[32]

While the link between private giving and prosperity is far from settled and studies of this matter are still sparse, the early evidence is provocative and important for understanding American giving attitudes. More research in this area would be very useful.

The Future of Non-Profit America

In the country we often think of as a land of consumerism and profit, it is actually "non-profit life" that better captures the true essence of America and differentiates it from other developed countries. Non-profit organizations dominate the landscape of many American public services due to a long tradition of civic participation, a belief that non-profit and voluntary organizations are more efficient than governments at many tasks, and a commonly held suspicion of government. Most Americans give and volunteer generously to support these organizations.

Will non-profit life continue to characterize America in the future? This is not an idle question, given the insignificant role that voluntary and civic activities now appear to play in many other developed nations. Probably the most accurate view of the future of non-profit America comes from the forces that lie behind it: American civil society, views on government, religiosity, work patterns, family life, and political views. To the extent that America maintains a high level of religiosity, resists any radical political trends, continues to support traditional family structures, and refuses to accept state control of social and economic institutions, it will probably continue to be a uniquely "non-profit nation."

CHAPTER 19

Drug Policy

Jonathan P. Caulkins and Mark A. R. Kleiman

Like the citizens of almost every other developed nation, Americans consume a lot of dangerous drugs. But as drug researchers Jonathan P. Caulkins and Mark A. R. Kleiman show, for most drugs, Americans are not very different from Europeans and probably consume even less alcohol. But the consumption of one drug, cocaine, is much higher here than abroad, and that consumption, especially of crack, is associated with high levels of disorder and many violent deaths. The U.S. criminal justice system arrests and imprisons more drug dealers (and more offenders generally) than its European counterpart.

U.S. DRUG USE AND DRUG PROBLEMS ARE WIDELY THOUGHT TO BE far worse than those of any other country. This is sometimes taken as reflecting a general proclivity toward intoxication or self-gratification in the American population. In fact, with the exception of cocaine, the proportion of Americans who use illicit drugs is only modestly higher than in most other urbanized, affluent democracies. Since alcohol remains by far the most prevalent and most widely abused intoxicant, and since U.S. residents are somewhat less likely to drink or to drink heavily than are residents of most member countries of the Organization for Economic Cooperation and Development (OECD),[1] the aggregate number of intoxicated hours per person— could such a quantity be measured—might well turn out to be lower in the United States than it is elsewhere. Americans are also far less likely than other residents of high-consumption societies to use tobacco.

But while Americans are no more intoxication-prone than residents of other affluent democracies, the U.S. illicit drug problem is abnormally serious, primarily along four dimensions: drug-market-related violence, crime by users of illicit drugs, aggressive enforcement and incarceration, and HIV/AIDS among injection drug users. In these respects, the United States more closely resembles some developing nations with severe drug problems, such as Colombia or Nigeria, than it does other OECD member countries.

U.S. Drug Use in Comparative Context

For three of the four principal illicit drugs of abuse (marijuana, heroin, and amphetamine-type stimulants [ATS]), U.S. rates of use and abuse are fairly typical of those of urbanized, affluent nations more generally, but rates of dependent or problematic use of the fourth (cocaine, including crack) are much higher. Were it not for cocaine, drug use in the United States would not stand out as especially problematic. However, since cocaine (including crack) accounts for roughly two-thirds of the social costs associated with illicit drugs in the United States, it could still be true that damage done by drugs per capita is something like three times as high in the United States as it is in otherwise comparable nations.[2]

For example, a comparison of urinalysis results for arrestees in the United States and England found modestly higher positive drug test rates in England for marijuana, opiates, amphetamines, and methadone, but cocaine rates were vastly greater in the United States (over 40 percent in the United States versus roughly 10 percent in England), making the overall drug prevalence rate slightly higher in the United States than in the English cities.[3]

Illicit drug abuse tends to be more prevalent in urban and affluent countries than in poorer and more rural nations; U.S. residents, for example, are about twenty times as likely to have used any illicit drug in the previous year as are Mexicans (11.6 percent versus 0.6 percent). By contrast, rates of alcohol use were similar, with past-year heavy alcohol use actually being higher in Mexico (45.8 percent vs. 39.6 percent). Poor countries with high rates of illicit drug use are typically producers (e.g., *basuco* use in Colombia), near neighbors of producers (e.g., Thailand or Iran), or transshipment countries that sit astride the transit routes between producers and major markets (e.g., the Bahamas).[4]

A common benchmark of the prevalence of use is the proportion of people who used an illicit drug in the past year. Comparing the past-year prevalence of drug use in the U.S. young adult population (roughly ages fifteen to thirty-five) with those reported by European countries, rates in the United States are all about one to two standard deviations above the European average, but in no case does the United States report the highest prevalence (see Table 19.1).[5] Figure 19.1 displays the same data, adding information about alcohol and tobacco.

There is less systematic evidence concerning older age groups; it appears that U.S. and Dutch rates of cannabis use among those thirty-five to fifty years old are substantially higher than in Canada, Germany, or England and Wales. Prevalence rates among U.S. adolescents are unexceptional. They rank near the middle of the pack (see Table 19.2) except for cocaine, amphetamine, and inhalants.[6] When we look at dependence or problem use of illicit drugs other than cannabis (all ages, not just youth), the U.S. rate is about three times the average reported by the European Monitoring Centre for Drugs and Drug Addiction (EMCDDA), with all of the difference in the rate of cocaine abuse. Cocaine use has peaked and is generally falling in the United States while it is still rising in Europe, so there may be some partial convergence in those rates over time.[7]

Australia, like the United States, is an affluent democracy with criminal justice institutions grounded in English common law. Rates of heroin and marijuana use are roughly similar in the United States and Australia. Australians use a bit more of the amphetamines and more alcohol. Americans are much less likely than Australians to

Table 19.1 Last-Year Prevalence of Drug Use Among Young Adults (15 to 34 Years Old)

	Year	Age Range	Sample Size	Cannabis	Cocaine	Ampheta-mines	Ecstasy	LSD
Czech Republic	2002	18-34	1,002	22.1		2.3	5.9	2.5
Denmark	2000	16-34	4,141	13.1	2	3.1	1.2	0.3
Germany	2003	18-34	3,775	14.6	1.7	2.2	1.9	0.5
Estonia	2003	15-34	646	10.1	1.2	2.9	3.7	0.8
Greece★	2004	15-34	2,620	3.2	0.2	0.1	0.4	0.2
Spain	2001	15-34	6,915	17.3	4.6	2.3	3.8	
France	2000	15-34	4,749	17.0	0.5	0.4	0.5	0.5
Ireland	2002-03	15-34		8.7	2	0.8	2.2	0.2
Italy	2003	15-34	5,231	12.8	2.3	0.4	0.7	0.6
Cyprus	2003	15-34	580	18.6	1	0.3	3.1	
Latvia	2003	15-34		8.1	0.4	2.4	1.9	1
Hungary	2003	18-34	2,319	7.7	0.7	1.9	2.6	0.8
Netherlands	2001	15-34	6,687	11.8	2.1	1.2	3.2	0.1
Poland	2002	16-34		6.3	1.3	1.6	0.5	1
Slovakia	2002	18-34		7.7	1.4	0.4	1.9	
Finland	2002	15-34	1,240	7.1	0.7	1.3	1.3	0.2
Sweden	2004	18-34	2,985	5.3				
England and Wales	2003-04	16-34	8,590	19.5	4.9	3	4.1	.05
Norway	1999	15-34	794	8.1	1	1.5	1.2	
United States	2002	14-34	34,771	21.6	4.7	2.8	3.5	1.2
U.S. Rank				2	2	4	5	2
Out of				21	19	20	20	16
Non-U.S. Average				11.3	1.6	1.5	2.2	0.6
Non-U.S. Standard Dev				5.4	1.3	1.0	1.5	0.6
U.S. z-Score				1.93	2.37	1.28	0.90	0.96

SOURCE: http://stats05.emcdda.europa.eu/en/elements/gpstab05-en.html.

Figure 19.1 Legal and Illegal Drug Use in the General Population for Various Countries Relative to the Average for Those Countries

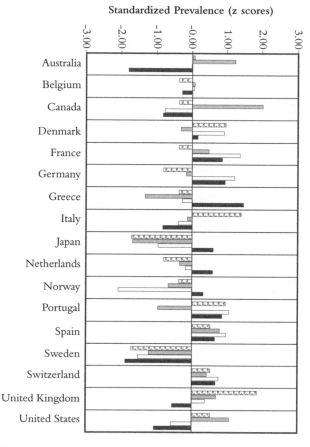

Standardized Prevalence (z scores)

☒ Opiate Abuse Annual Prevalence (Ages 15–64) circa 1997–2004
☐ Cannabis Abuse Annual Prevalence (Ages 15–64) circa 1999–2004
☐ Adult Alcohol Consumption (liters per person) 2000–2003
■ Adult Smoking Percent of Population

SOURCE: http://stats05.emcdda.europa.eu/en/elements/eyetab04-en.html.

abuse alcohol; the rates of problem drinking among drinkers are similar, but many more Americans abstain from alcohol entirely. They are also less likely than Australians to be dependent on illicit drugs.

The most striking differences concern cocaine and injection of drugs other than heroin. In the United States, cocaine (including crack) is by far the leading illicit drug problem; in Australia, it is seen

Table 19.2   Recent School Surveys: Lifetime Prevalence of Psychoactive Substance Use and Last Month Prevalence (LMP) of Cannabis (Percentages) Among Students 17 to 18 Years Old

Country	Year	Age range (years)/cohort	Cannabis	30-day prevalence Cannabis	Inhalants	Amphetamines	Ecstasy	LSD & other hallucinogens	Cocaine	Heroin
Belgium (Flemish)	2003	11 to 22	47.0		9.7	5.5	8.9	8.3	4.0	1.4
Czech Republic	2003	born in 1985	56.2	22.3	6.4	8.4	11.4	11.7	1.6	2.7
Greece	2003	11 to 18	10.3	3.7	12.9	0.9	1.7	1.6	1.5	0.6
France	2003	12 to 18	54.2	29.9	12.2	2.4	4.5	1.4	2.3	1.6
Italy	2003	15 to 19	39.0	21.9	7.4	3.1	3.6	3.5	6.3	1.5
Cyprus	2003	14 to 17	1.6	0.7	3.7	0.2	0.5	0.1	1.2	0.2
Latvia (Riga)	2003	13 to 20	30.1	6.9		6.4	5.2	2.7	2.2	1.0
Hungary	2003	14 to 22	36.8	16.5	4.1	12.1	12.4	7.5	3.6	2.7
Netherlands	2003	11 to 18	43.8	17.6		5.2	7.5	8.6	4.6	1.2
Austria	2003	17 to 18	36.9	18.0	14.6	4.7	6.9	5.0	5.3	2.1
Portugal	2003	13 to 18	25.9	10.7			4.3	3.7	1.4	
Slovakia	2003	15 to 19	35.6	11.9	9.5	3.4	6.0	6.6	1.5	0.8
Bulgaria	2003	15 to 18	30.6	9.3	3.6	3.0	3.3	1.1	3.3	2.0
U.S. MTF	2003	~13 to 18*	33.3	15.2	13.2	12.0	5.6	3.8	5.5	1.5
	2003	Seniors	46.1	21.2	11.2	14.4	8.3	5.9	7.7	1.5
	2003	Sophmores	36.4	17.0	12.7	13.1	5.4	3.5	5.1	1.5
	2003	8th graders	17.5	7.5	15.8	8.4	3.2	2.1	3.6	1.6
Notes on U.S. Figures								LSD only		
U.S. Rank (out of 14)			9	7	2	2	7	7	2	6
Average Non-U.S.			34.5	14.1	8.4	4.6	5.9	4.8	3.0	1.5
Std Dev Non-U.S.			15.6	8.5	4.0	3.3	3.5	3.5	1.7	0.8
U.S. z-score			0.7	0.8	0.7	3.0	0.7	0.3	2.8	0.0

SOURCE: http://stats05.emcdda.europa.eu/en/elements/eyetab04-en.html.

primarily as a "club drug" and poses a minor problem compared to heroin and amphetamines. Australians report extraordinarily high rates of injection drug use, including a surprisingly large number of recreational users who inject occasionally. That stands in marked contrast to the typical pattern in the United States where injection drug use is largely confined to heavily dependent "hard-core" users. The overall rate of non-medical injection drug use in the United States is no more than half the estimated rate for Australia. The United States has failed, while Australia has largely succeeded, in preventing needle sharing, and thus the transmission of HIV and other infectious diseases among injection drug users is higher in the United States.

To summarize, cross-national comparisons suggest that, except for cocaine, U.S. rates of drug abuse are high but not extraordinarily higher than are rates in other peer countries. The same is true of mental health problems generally, with more than a quarter of Americans having met diagnostic criteria for mental illness in the previous year, more than in any of the other thirteen countries studied by the World Health Organization Mental Health Survey Consortium. Since co-occurrence of drug dependence and other mental health disorders is common, with causal arrows pointing in both directions, higher prevalence of drug abuse may result from higher prevalence of mental illness or vice versa. Alternatively, it may simply be that the United States is better than average at measuring both sorts of problems.

Explaining the High Rates of Cocaine Use in the United States

The extraordinary cocaine problem in the United States is an accident of history. Due in part to its geographic and cultural proximity to Colombia, the United States was the first affluent country to experience an upsurge in cocaine availability and use in the late twentieth century. Cocaine was initially something of a stealth drug, whose risks manifested themselves only over time. So Americans embraced cocaine in large numbers before its dangers were well understood. Lack of early availability prevented residents of other countries from making the same mistake; they had the chance to see the havoc it wreaked in the United States before many had a chance to try the drug.

The baby boom—era wave of cocaine hit the United States about a decade earlier than it did elsewhere; so much is clear from arrest and seizure data. The most plausible—albeit conjectural—explanation for its early arrival in the United States is simply proximity. For this purpose, "proximity" is measured not so much in miles (though Miami is indeed much closer to Medellin than Amsterdam is) as in the licit flow of people and goods. Illegal drugs have to be moved covertly and sold to trusted confederates, and common ethnicity is a key source of trust. The United States, particularly Florida and New York, had large, established communities of Colombian immigrants, and there was substantial legal trade within which cocaine shipments could be hidden. Moreover, the United States imported substantial quantities of cannabis from Colombia, especially after strong efforts in the late 1960s and early 1970s to reduce cannabis imports from Mexico via border interdiction efforts (Operation Intercept) and eradication efforts using the defoliant Paraquat, which was believed to leave residues dangerous to smokers on the marijuana harvested from sprayed cannabis plants.

While the crack epidemic of the 1980s is sometimes seen as marking the beginning of America's modern cocaine wave, cocaine actually became popular in the 1970s, with initiation rates rising sharply from at least 1973 on and peaking in 1979. But cocaine emerged as a marked social problem only with the spread of crack and crack markets in the mid–1980s. The social and economic status of the typical cocaine user in the 1970s, and the discreet operation of drug markets that grew up around users, framed cocaine as a drug that did little social harm and so deserved little policy attention.

Normalization came through explicit mention in popular media (e.g., Eric Clapton's song "Cocaine"), association with successful performers (notably comics such as Richard Pryor, Robin Williams, and George Carlin), and articles in popular outlets that downplayed cocaine's risks (e.g., a 1982 *Scientific American* article). While a few academic students of drug abuse, looking at reports of the first cocaine epidemic in the late nineteenth and early twentieth centuries, warned that cocaine use was likely to spin out of control, and a few treatment providers began to encounter rising numbers of problem cocaine users, cocaine was widely regarded, even among experts who in retrospect should have known better, as largely benign. The rather subtle effects of the highly dilute cocaine powder snorted during the 1970s led to a widespread underestimation of the drug's potential to form a powerful bad habit. The absence of a physical withdrawal syndrome (then regarded as one of the defining characteristics of addiction) led to its being widely considered non-addictive.

During this period, cocaine remained expensive, and its use was identified with affluent, sophisticated young adults: "yuppies." Such users usually had the resources to deal with their own drug problems without relying on public assistance and without committing crimes to support their habits. They sought to purchase relatively large quantities of the drug in one transaction, both for convenience and to minimize their exposure to law enforcement. Drug deals for powder cocaine tended to be in bars or residences rather than on street corners or in dealing houses. This made drug sellers safer from both law enforcement and buyers who might rob them. Though high-level cocaine dealing created great illicit wealth and considerable violence in cities such as Miami, the word "cocaine" in those days summoned up images of youth, affluence, and sensual indulgence rather than of overdose, addiction, or crime. Mass opinion and political attention focused on rising rates of cannabis use among adolescents. Elite opinion (insofar as it paid attention to drugs at all) remained focused on heroin, the original drug menace, whose use had soared during the late 1960s and early 1970s and was strongly implicated in rapidly rising crime rates.

The crack epidemic of the 1980s presented a quite different face of cocaine. Crack is cocaine prepared for "smoking" as opposed to snorting. (Technically, crack is vaporized and inhaled, not literally smoked, because there is no combustion.) Any drug is far more potent and far more reinforcing when it is administered directly to the lung than it is when taken into the nasal mucosa by snorting, simply because smoking delivers the molecules to the brain very quickly and all at once, while snorting both delays and flattens the peak concentration of the drug. The minimum dose to get a pleasurable experience is lower for a drug taken in smoked form, but the duration of action is typically shorter. Crack is thus cheaper than powder cocaine per dose, though not per unit weight or per use session. Moreover, unlike powder, which is somewhat difficult to handle in very small quantities, crack can be divided into single-dose "rocks," easy to handle even by inexperienced dealers.

Crack is widely viewed as an unpredictable technological innovation whose effect was to open cocaine use to young, poor, low-income users. The actual history is more complex. "Freebasing"— converting cocaine powder into smokable form—was well known by the mid–1970s, but the chemical process involved highly inflammable chemicals. Cocaine remained expensive, and freebasing was the province of a relatively small and affluent subpopulation of cocaine users. This changed when dealers discovered that a stable form of base cocaine (later called "crack") could be made by methods as simple as heating cocaine with baking soda. Still, as long as a "rock" of crack cost $20, the product had little mass-market attraction. But in the 1980s cocaine prices collapsed, apparently because illicit entrepreneurs rushed in to serve the rapidly growing demand and wound up competing prices down. By the mid–1980s, dealers could sell rocks for $5 each. That brought a potent cocaine experience within easy financial reach of millions of people who had little in common with the young trendies snorting powder cocaine through rolled-up $100 bills at fashionable clubs typified by the notorious Studio 54.

Crack smokers are more likely than powder snorters to buy many times during a single binge. Crack dealing therefore involved more transactions, at lower prices per transaction, than powder dealing. Thus crack sellers must be conveniently available in places where they can quickly make many transactions with many different buyers, and so they congregated on street corners, in parks, or inside "crack houses." Frequent transactions meant a need for many retail dealers who, unlike power dealers with their smaller customer bases, had to serve many anonymous users. Instead of using relatively skilled and trusted adults who were embedded in the users' social milieux, crack distributors found that they could employ teenagers, who were not only more reckless than adults but also less vulnerable to criminal prosecution and thus less prone to implicate their employers in return for lesser sentences. Teenagers also had fewer life commitments, so they could stand around waiting for customers.

In its early days, the retail crack trade was relatively lucrative, though extraordinarily risky: dealers in Washington, D.C., in the late 1980s, earned $30 per hour, not counting the value of the drugs they consumed, while risking prison (about a third of a year in prison per year of full-time dealing), violent injury or death, and addiction. These financial rewards brought in large numbers of workers; of the black men born in the District of Columbia in 1966, almost a third had been charged with a crime by the time they reached the age of nineteen, and the most prevalent cause of arrest was selling crack.

By dealing in public locations to users who might resort to violence to get drugs, the sellers opened themselves to the risk of robbery either by users or by opportunistic criminals attracted by inventories of salable drugs and wads of cash in the hands of persons who were unlikely to call the police if robbed. That implied the need for protection. In the United States, unlike in many other industrialized countries, firearms are widely available. Given the high prevalence of crack dealing in some neighborhoods, often ones with a tradition of low social control, and drug sales revenue making the cost of weapons no longer a substantial barrier, the knife, the homemade "zip gun," and the cheap "Saturday Night Special" handgun were replaced by new and expensive high-caliber automatics.

The resulting crowd of armed, edgy, and socially marginal young men, some of them under the influence of cocaine (or cocaine and alcohol), created a "street culture" in which willingness to accept affront without violent retaliation is understood as weakness and in which weakness is seen as an invitation to attack. That culture is a breeding ground for deadly violence in which an actual or imagined slight, a disagreement over a woman or a debt, can lead to gunfire. Where the young men are members of street gangs, gunfire can lead to more gunfire, as the colleagues of the victim seek revenge on the perpetrator and his colleagues. Thus the tendency of police and journalists to attribute the violence to "drugs" was a half-truth; the drugs provided the money and the motivation for being armed, but they were not the sole or perhaps even the most proximate cause of violent incidents.

As the tide of violence rose, so too did the importance to young men in crack-dealing neighborhoods of having a firearm and being willing to use it. The spread of the crack market in the late 1980s coincided—not just nationally but city by city—with rising levels of urban minority youth homicides involving handguns. Murder, which had been very largely an adult affair, became more and more frequent among adolescents as young as fifteen. (Homicides by those over thirty, especially in domestic disputes, continued their long-term decline.) The "drive-by" shooting, last practiced by Al Capone's mobsters and their rivals in the 1920s, returned. The minority of the victims who were innocent bystanders—especially children—commanded public sympathy and the attention of the press, but most of the dead strongly resembled their killers and had criminal histories of comparable length and seriousness.

Over time, the violence tapered off (the juvenile homicide arrest rate fell by more than 70 percent from 1994 to 2004). This resulted in part from targeted police interventions and in larger part from markets shifting away from flagrant, place-based exchanges serving anonymous customers toward "beeper sales" made through discreet meetings arranged by pagers or cell phones. There is considerable debate as to whether that change came primarily because get-tough policing drove markets underground, because demand became heavily concentrated among a smaller number of heavy users who had a stable source of known suppliers and so relied less on public markets, because of the information revolution's effect on cell phone prices, or from other factors.

Social learning among adolescents about the high mortality rate associated with the armed-and-dangerous lifestyle, the death and incarceration of a large proportion of those most prone to kill, and changes in dealing patterns as the population of crack users shrank and aged also contributed to the decline in violence. Prices and wages in the crack trade fell, in part at least because the hundreds of thousands of men sent to prison for crack dealing and then released with very limited legitimate economic opportunities constituted an "industrial reserve army" that bid down the wages for retail crack sellers and crowded younger men out of the trade. It now appears that 2004 marked a trough in homicide rates, with a resurgence in killings among men in their twenties and thirties; whether or not that resurgence will prove to be temporary no one can forecast with confidence.

America learned about the dangers of cocaine the hard way; Europe and Australia were able to learn vicariously. That helps explain the gravity of the American problem. By the time the dangers of cocaine, and specifically of crack, were widely known, the United States had widespread cocaine markets with a large population of already-established users, and those markets and users continued, and continue, to wreak damage.

What remains to be explained is why problems peaked in the mid to late 1980s if initiation peaked in the 1970s and why the cocaine problem has ebbed so slowly after the drug's problems became manifest. The answer, in short, is that dependence takes time to develop—and even longer to shake. Most users of any drug never develop a pattern of problem use. (The principal exception is nicotine in cigarette form, where dependence is common but the damage from long-term use is primarily somatic rather than social or behavioral.) The modal "career" of drug use is very short. Most people who try any given drug either don't like it, find it only mildly interesting and use it at most a few times, or quickly discontinue it for other reasons. A smaller but not insubstantial number develop a stable pattern of use that does not interfere substantially with their other activities. Examples include those who drink, smoke, or take other drugs only when they go to clubs. A minority of users, however, fall into patterns of problematic use, persisting despite adverse consequences and not fully under volitional control: that is, they develop clinically diagnosable drug abuse or drug dependency.

Of that drug-abusing minority, most recover without ever entering formal treatment. But a minority of the minority of drug users who develop a substance abuse disorder do not recover spontaneously; they may quit or moderate their use repeatedly, but they fail to maintain abstinence or controlled use and repeatedly revert to problematic use. These addicts have a chronic, relapsing disorder; most will never succeed in using their problem drug stably and remain at risk of relapse to problem use even after years of abstinence. Addiction is atypical, not merely among drug users, but even among persons who develop substance abuse disorder. It is widely regarded as typical because it is addicts who fill the prisons and treatment centers and account for the great majority of all cocaine and heroin consumption in the United States.

Though dependency on cocaine, and especially smoked cocaine, typically develops more quickly than dependency on alcohol, on average there is still substantial latency—measured in months or years rather than weeks—between initiation and the development of problem use. Most problem users of cocaine, as of other drugs, recover within a similar period. But for the minority of the minority of cocaine users who develop cocaine addiction, that addiction persists for years. A twelve-year follow-up of cocaine-dependent veterans admitted to treatment found that almost 10 percent had died and about half had never been abstinent for any five-year period. Similar studies of heroin dependence are even more sobering.[8] As a result, the cocaine problem continued to grow long after the number of new cocaine users started to fall. Likewise, cocaine consumption has been ebbing only very gradually and remains high even though the number of past-year users is far below peak levels. The 2005 U.S. Household Survey estimated there were 5.4 million past-year cocaine users, likely an underestimate, but still down dramatically from its peak of 12 million in 1982. Annual consumption, however, which at its peak totaled some 300 metric tons, has fallen only to about 250 metric tons, or roughly 5 billion doses with a total retail value of about $25 billion.

Persistence in frequent use by a minority of a minority of users, together with the highly skewed distribution of offense rates is what, in short, explains why the United States continues to have so much drug-related crime. The (estimated) three-quarters of a million long-term dependent heroin users in the United States is an unusually large number mostly because the United States is the third most populous country in the world, not because the United States has a high per capita rate of opiate addiction. However, adding in another 2 million or so long-term dependent stimulant users (mostly cocaine, some methamphetamine) creates a pool of individuals who collectively are responsible for a great deal of property crime.

Dependent drug offenders are a quite modest share of all criminal offenders, but high-rate drug-using offenders commit a truly extraordinary number of offenses per year. Indeed, multiplying conventional estimates of numbers of drug offenders by typical assumptions of crime rates per user gives estimated numbers of crimes by drug users that approach the total number of crimes reported. Empirically, well more than half of arrestees for non-drug crimes test positive for one or more illicit drugs.

It is not clear whether U.S. drug addicts commit any more acquisitive crimes per year than do comparably dependent addicts in other countries. Obtaining good comparative data is very difficult because it is all but impossible to obtain random samples of dependent drug users in any country. It is possible that U.S. addicts commit more crimes per capita: that might be expected, given that they have less easy access to treatment and only very limited access to public income support payments. On the other hand, burglary rates, as measured by victim surveys, are higher in Australia, Canada, England, Scotland, and the Netherlands than they are in the United States.[9] Since the United States has substantially more dependent users and yet fewer property crimes per capita, it may be that offenses per dependent user are actually lower in the United States.

The overdose death in 1986 of basketball superstar Len Bias crystallized growing public, expert, and official concern about cocaine and especially about crack; up to that point, the drug was widely considered to be a relatively "soft" drug, certainly much less hazardous than heroin. The Bias event, the drastic enforcement policies it helped create, the association with violent crack markets in disadvantaged neighborhoods, and the accumulation of more people with more years of experience with cocaine accelerated the already-established downtrend in cocaine initiation, which had peaked as early as 1979. The decline was extremely sharp, especially in neighborhoods where potential users had vicarious experience with the toll that crack had taken on the lives of their friends, siblings, and neighbors. Among samples of young arrestees in Manhattan taken in the early 1990s, 78 percent of those born in 1968 (and who thus turned eighteen in 1986) tested positive for cocaine, while those born as little as seven years later had a positive-test rate of only 10 percent.[10]

However, the persistence of heavy cocaine use means that the problem continued to grow long after the initiation rate started to fall; as late as 2004, most of those in treatment for cocaine use had initiated before 1985. And the easy availability and low price of the drug due to the massive illicit market—by one estimate, about 1 million Americans engage in cocaine-selling over the course of any given year—guarantees that, even after the terribly expensive process of social learning the country has undergone, the initiation rate has not fallen to anywhere near zero. Americans are still trying cocaine at about one-quarter the rate they were during the peak initiation period, with about eight hundred thousand new users per year.[11]

Distinctive Characteristics of U.S. Drug Policy

As with the drug situation, so too with drug policy: the United States stands out from the rest of the developed world, but not precisely in the ways ordinarily imagined either by Americans or by others. What is certain is that the United States has a very high rate of incarceration for drug offenses. What is less certain is why.

Compared to other countries, the United States has more drug dealers in prison; more aggressive and militarized drug enforcement, especially against low-level retail dealers; more violent and socially disruptive drug markets; and a group of heavy users of expensive drugs that is more heavily drawn from otherwise disadvantaged ethnic minorities and from high-crime neighborhoods and which is also sicker, more socially dislocated, and more criminally active. It is also true that the United States has larger populations of disadvantaged ethnic minorities, a generally more punitive criminal justice system, a weaker "social safety net," and a more pronounced and politically relevant "culture war" still echoing the tensions stirred up by protest movements of the 1960s.

How that first group of differences relates to the second it is hard to say; very likely, there are causal arrows pointing in both directions. For example, the more marginalized, disadvantaged, and criminally active the typical "drug addict" is, the greater the tendency to meet drug use and drug dealing with punishment rather than social services. The weaker the social safety net, the greater the likely financial dependence of heavy users of expensive drugs on crime (as opposed to income-support payments) to pay for drugs and other living expenses. In the end, it may not make sense to ask in general whether America treats its addicts especially badly because they are especially socially obnoxious, or whether American drug addicts are especially socially obnoxious because they are treated so badly. Both are likely true. But America's exceptional incarceration rates and overall focus on supply control still require explanation.

While it is true that the United States incarcerates an extraordinary number of people for drug law violations, it also incarcerates an extraordinary number of people, period. Incarceration rates in the United States generally grew dramatically over the last thirty years. This stands in marked contrast to the previous fifty years, which saw remarkable stability in incarceration rates at much lower levels. Drug-related incarceration has been one important driver, but policies such as mandatory sentencing, "truth in sentencing," and "three strikes and you're out" also played prominent roles. Thus the mass incarceration of drug dealers may be as much a function of a generally heavy-handed criminal justice system as it is of a particular hostility to illicit drugs. Indeed, despite the high absolute rate of incarceration, it is estimated that cocaine sellers in the United States spend, on average, less than two hours incarcerated per drug sale, though the high transaction rate for a full-time seller makes that small expected penalty-per-sale amount to about 3.3 months incarcerated per year of active selling.[12]

Contrary to widespread belief both in the United States and elsewhere, American prisons are not filled with people whose only crime was using drugs (as opposed to helping to distribute them). There are more than 1 million arrests per year in the United States for drug possession (of which a very large proportion are for possession of cannabis), but few of them result in prison time, or even jail time following a conviction. That is especially true of cannabis possession, even in states where it is not formally "decriminalized." Possession of quantities suitable for personal consumption by itself is usually punished, if at all, with probation, fines, community service, or shorter jail terms, not prison sentences. The exceptional user sentenced to prison by a judge for possession alone is usually a courier carrying very large quantities, is already on probation or parole for another crime, or has a long record of non-drug crimes. Among prison inmates, those doing time for simple possession have more prior convictions for non-drug crimes than those doing time for property or violent crimes. Using the four major illicit drugs in the United States (cocaine, heroin, methamphetamine, and marijuana) leads to an average of one to six hours spent in prison per $1,000 worth of drugs consumed.[13]

Labels and official figures can be misleading in this regard: not infrequently, someone arrested for drug dealing (or the related offense of "possession with intent to distribute") is allowed to "plead down" to a charge of simple possession and may serve time on that count, but almost always the underlying offense was involvement in drug dealing.

However, drug users are subject to loss of parental rights, employment, and public benefits (including subsidized housing and even student loans) and face a massive private-sector effort that attempts through drug testing either to deter them from continued use or exclude them from employment. About three-quarters of the largest five hundred companies, and a smaller proportion of smaller employers, use preemployment drug testing, as does much of the public sector. Preemployment and on-the-job testing are legally mandated for safety-sensitive workers, including truck drivers.

In addition, offenders under "community supervision"— probation and parole—(including those convicted of simple possession and other public-order offenses, but overwhelmingly those convicted of dealing or of property or violent crimes) are subject to random drug testing and may be incarcerated or reincarcerated for testing positive or skipping the drug test, since drug use is a violation of the terms of their release. So while there are few users behind bars merely as users, there are substantial numbers of violators of other laws who would be free were it not for their continued illicit drug use.

Although roughly 80 percent of U.S. drug control expenditures are devoted to law enforcement, this country also does better than many others in maintaining treatment programs. The United States has 215 illicit-drug treatment admissions per 100,000 population, putting it behind only Italy, Portugal, and Malta; adding in alcohol treatment raises that figure to 470 per 100,000.[14]

Nor is it true, as is sometimes supposed in South America, that the dominant focus of U.S. drug policy is on source-country control. International drug control operations of all sorts accounted for just $1.3 billion in the FY 2006 budget, out of total drug control expenditures of perhaps $50 billion annually. Thus international operations account for less than 3 percent of U.S. drug control expenditure. It is not that U.S. source country control operations are small; $1.3 billion is not an insignificant sum. However, it is false to assert that the United States expects other nations to take care of its drug problem while failing to make serious efforts at home to disrupt domestic distribution and demand. The utility of some of those domestic efforts may be open to question, but the efforts are undeniable.

While efforts to control drug crops and processing activity in drug-exporting countries represent a quite modest share of U.S. drug-control activity, it is true that the United States puts far more energy into source-country control than does any other individual nation. However, that is what one would predict given U.S. consumption's large market share in certain well-defined places. In particular, the United States accounts for roughly 40 percent of global cocaine consumption, and historically its share was even larger; no other country accounts for more than 8 percent of consumption. Hence, for any country other than the United States, over 90 percent of any benefits flowing from investments in reducing cocaine production would accrue to other countries. So when it comes to disrupting cocaine production, every country except the United States faces a significant free-rider problem. Mexico, the other object of significant U.S. international pressures, is another special case inasmuch as Mexico does not export significant quantities of drugs to any country other than the United States. Hence, even though the United States accounts for a quite modest share of global cannabis and opiate consumption (perhaps on the order of 5 to 7 percent in each case), the vast majority of Mexican cannabis and opiate production is destined for U.S. markets. There are few if any other instances around the world in which one nation consumes such a large share of another nation's drug production; here again, unusual U.S. policies come in the context of an unusual set of relationships.

What might account for such widespread misperceptions concerning U.S. drug policy? An important one may be the United States' federal system of governance and, more generally, the extraordinary decentralization and complexity of the institutions that make drug policy. The federal government spends less on drug control than the states and local government do collectively, but pronouncements out of the White House Office of National Drug Control Policy (the "drug czar's" office) dominate perceptions of U.S. drug policy.

This distinction between state and local government on the one hand and the national government on the other hand is important. States retain a substantial degree of sovereignty. So for example, most drug law offenders are sentenced under state laws and most of those sent to prison serve their time in state prisons. The federal prison system does not even rank second in terms of numbers of inmates within the overall U.S. criminal justice system. There are actually two and half times as many drug offenders incarcerated in local jails (typically county-run facilities housing people for no more than a year) as in federal prisons. Hence, the commonly reported statistics on federal drug inmates reflect only a quite modest share of total U.S. drug law enforcement.

Individual states' drug policies can depart substantially from what the Office of National Drug Control Policy (ONDCP) advocates. In many states marijuana possession has been, in effect, decriminalized. Several states allow the distribution of marijuana for medical purposes. In California there is a large-scale prison diversion program. Similarly, syringe exchanges operate in many cities even though there is a ban on using federal dollars to support such programs.

There is federal policy on the one hand and the policy of fifty states, more than three thousand counties, and many, many more municipal jurisdictions on the other, with sometimes considerable differences in policy as one crosses state or local jurisdictional boundaries. For example, Michigan's mandatory minimum sentences are far more stringent than those in neighboring Wisconsin. Likewise, syringes can be legally purchased over the counter in some states but not in others. Policing presents the extreme example. As James Q. Wilson has noted in chapter 16 in this volume, the United States has more than seventeen thousand different local police agencies, each accountable only to the local municipal government. In contrast, Australia has essentially eight police agencies (one for each state plus the Northern Territory and Australian Federal

Police), and in some sense England has just one, inasmuch as all effectively report up through the Home Office.

In addition to local municipal police agencies, the United States has many other policing organizations with overlapping jurisdictions, including county police, state police, several different federal agencies, and in many larger cities various other agencies (transit system police, public housing agency police, and so on). When multiple agencies enforce drug laws in the same geographic location, it is very difficult for dealers to corrupt all those agencies simultaneously. Knowing that, there is a very strong disincentive for personnel in any one agency to become corrupt. So one side benefit of the seemingly chaotic decentralization of U.S. drug enforcement is that the United States enjoys relatively lower levels of systemic official corruption surrounding drug trafficking than do many other countries.

The U.S. "drug czar," that is the head of ONDCP, is a czar in nickname only, with a surprisingly small budget and relatively limited powers. If the ONDCP wants law enforcement to take marijuana more seriously, it has little capacity to make its will effective except through attempts to direct public attention to the dangers of marijuana use, in hopes that rising public concern will influence the diffuse collection of decision makers around the country.[15]

The United States is a major participant in international drug policy consultations, almost always from a hawkish perspective. The "certification" process, by which the United States presumes to evaluate every other country in the world in terms of its contribution to controlling actions in its territory that result in drug exports and to threaten sanctions for nations that fall short of a unilaterally set standard, is unique. The process is largely driven by tensions between the Congress and the executive branch, and is never actually allowed to lead to sanctions against any country to which the United States is not hostile on other grounds (so that when sanctions lead to a cutoff of aid, there is generally little if any aid to cut off). Even the government of Mexico, despite its familiarity with

U.S. politics, seems to take the threat of decertification with a seriousness all out of proportion to its probability. Nonetheless, it remains true that the United States tries to act as a brake on any "dovish" tendencies in drug policies elsewhere (for example, trials of heroin maintenance in Europe and Canada and cannabis decriminalization in Canada), sometimes with substantial impacts, especially in dealing with states such as Colombia and Afghanistan.

To a degree, there is a parallel reification of "non-U.S. drug policy." No discussion of comparative international drug policy is complete without reference to Dutch policy, particularly its system of quasi-legal retail cannabis distribution through coffee shops. However, Dutch policy generally, and the "commercialization" of marijuana distribution allowed under the coffee-shop system in particular, are not followed universally around the world outside the United States. Indeed, one could argue that Dutch policy is almost as atypical as U.S. policy, at least when one moves outside of Europe. Likewise, there are more countries around the world that, like the United States, have not embraced harm reduction than there are countries that do so, at least explicitly, and more than a few (Thailand, Iran, Singapore, much of the Arab world) that are at least as hawkish as the United States. Even within Europe, drug policy is not a monolith, and U.S. policy seems less dramatically distinctive in light of the full range of policy differences displayed among other countries.

Furthermore, it is often possible to explain important differences in various countries' drug policies by reference to their unique experiences or the institutional and organizational structures onto which drug policymaking was grafted. For example, it might be natural for countries with very strong social welfare systems to let those systems take the lead role in responding to the emergence of growing substance abuse. The United States has never had a social welfare system as comprehensive or as integrated as those typical in northern and western Europe. That vacuum may have contributed to the tendency in the United States to define drug abuse as predominantly a criminal-justice rather than a social-welfare problem. Likely even more important are the twin facts that the United States is plagued with deadly violence and beset with a stimulant problem, whereas almost every other affluent nation has far fewer killings and is wrestling mostly with opiate addiction (among illicit-drug problems). Both distinctions are crucial.

As noted, the rapid spread in the 1980s of violent crack markets was terrifying. Homicide rates soared. To some it seemed as if civil society was losing control of large swaths of many American cities, with devastating effects for local communities, businesses, and schools. When a crack house opens next door, horrified neighbors will get little relief by calling local treatment service providers; only the police can put the crack house out of business within a time frame relevant for protecting local residents' children and their ability to sit safely on their front porches. It would require an extraordinary degree of compassion to look at drug abusers primarily as victims of society when tucking children to bed in the bathtub in hopes of protecting them from stray bullets flying from the drug markets those drug abusers support.

Some ten to fifteen years past the peak of the crack epidemic, many flagrant street-corner markets have gone underground; selling within social networks rather than from designated turf engenders far less systemic market-related violence. One might, therefore, expect U.S. drug policy to soften, and in some respects it has. New York State's oft-criticized Rockefeller Drug Laws have been modified, and even such punishment-oriented states as California have instituted sweeping programs to divert drug offenders from prison into treatment. Still, there is considerable inertia in hawkish drug policy. There are far greater political rewards for ratcheting sentences up in the midst of a crisis than there are for moderating them when the problem has receded into the background. It would be rash to predict any swift reduction in the number of drug-law violators in American prisons.

The United States is often criticized for not pursuing a harm reduction policy. By that is meant a policy to create interventions such as syringe exchange programs or operate supervised injection facilities. But no matter how effective the most prominent harm reduction programs may be with respect to heroin injection, they are largely irrelevant to crack use or to drug-market violence. (Attempts to craft drug law enforcement to minimize violence and disorder might logically be considered "harm reduction" approaches, but neither proponents nor opponents of the "harm reduction" ideology think of them that way.) Likewise, a range of treatments have been clearly demonstrated to be effective for treating opiate dependence, including several successful pharmaco-therapies, but at present there is no similarly effective technology for treating stimulant dependence.

As was the case in Sweden, American policy has been lastingly shaped by what seems to have been a historical accident: a period of generally liberalizing drug policy (in the mid–1960s in Sweden, in the mid–1970s in the United States) was followed by what were perceived as disasters: the methamphetamine epidemic in Sweden and the rapid rise of juvenile cannabis use and then the crack epidemic in the United States. The "parents' movement"—largely a grassroots phenomenon, though subsidized by the federal Drug Enforcement Administration—was energized by the finding that, in 1979, more than 10 percent of U.S. high school seniors reported daily or near-daily use of cannabis (twenty times per month or more). The popular anger at this fact helped turn back what had been a tide of cannabis decriminalization (involving twelve of the fifty states) and forced the replacement of a "dovish" drug czar by a much more "hawkish" one. The Carter administration had at one point endorsed the decriminalization movement, but that effort quickly lost presidential support in the face of pressure from parents' groups. The violence surrounding high-level cocaine trafficking and the bloodshed and disorder in brazen street-corner markets for crack played a key role in cementing American perceptions that the drug problem was inextricably linked with crime, and that aggressive policing need play a central role in the national response.

During the 1980s, it was not only cocaine markets but also heroin and sometimes other drug distribution that was more flagrant and more violent in the United States than in Europe or elsewhere. That fact can be traced quite directly to crack. Before the cocaine epidemic, retail heroin distribution in the United States— with the exception of a few parts of New York City—was done stealthily, not brazenly. Once the police were overwhelmed by crack markets, heroin sellers could step out of the shadows. When they did so, and began sharing curb space with armed crack sellers and violent predators seeking to rob street dealers, the heroin sellers adopted at least some of the noxious practices of their crack-selling counterparts. Even the retail cannabis trade can be the focus of violence when it takes place in high-crime neighborhoods. So the culture of crack markets infected U.S. drug retailing more generally.

Cautious Projections of the Future

Predicting the future of drug use, drug problems, and drug policy should be done with great caution, if at all. In the United States, the last fifteen years have been characterized more by stability than by great change, and there is no compelling reason to rule out another decade of relative stasis. However, in other times and places, drug use, drug problems, and drug policies have all changed rapidly after long periods of inertia, and it is not hard to construct plausible scenarios involving considerable change. Continued stability, then, is far from certain and perhaps not even probable.

In terms of use, the greatest argument for stability is that the markets for three of the four major drugs (cocaine, heroin, and marijuana) have stabilized with high availability, moderate prices (compared to other times), and great capacity to replace individuals and organizations eliminated by enforcement, and the corresponding use patterns are fairly stable, not rapidly growing (i.e., more endemic than epidemic). The fourth, methamphetamine, reemerged more recently as a major drug and has still not penetrated the East Coast or the African-American population. In addition to the possible expansion of methamphetamine use, the threats to stability in drug use include the substitution of domestically produced synthetic opioids of the fentanyl family for imported heroin and the continued growth in non-medical use of prescription painkillers, tranquilizers, and stimulants among adolescents, now at prevalence levels rivaling cannabis.

With respect to drug problems and policy, it would require an exceptional, even Micawberish, capacity for groundless optimism to expect substantial change over the next several years. The unusual and unusually harmful aspects of the current American situation derive from deeply ingrained characteristics of the nation's social structure, political culture, and dominant worldview, notably the existence of large disadvantaged ethnic-minority populations, individualism leading to a comparatively weak welfare state, high levels of deadly violence both in general and in the drug markets, and a harshly punitive criminal justice system. The last is caused in turn by a combination of stable factors including unusually harsh public attitudes and a political system in which policy elites lack the capacity to resist strong and persistent trends in public opinion, especially on issues with great emotional salience.

Mentioning potential for policy change inevitably raises the question of legalization, although it is neither the most plausible nor the most appealing type of reform. Legalization's effects are hard to estimate in part because the term is attached to such a broad range of proposals. Legalization could mean either a scheme of commercial distribution subject to taxation and regulation, resembling the current alcohol control regime, or a tighter system based on a public-sector monopoly or a "medicalized" regime in which physicians were given authority to permit their patients to use otherwise forbidden drugs and the responsibility for confining that use within limits consistent with physical and mental health, as with opiate-maintenance therapies.

Legalizing drug use could be done on a drug-by-drug basis, and since cocaine does most of the current damage, the most important part of the legalization question concerns cocaine. Unless the taxes and regulations involved in a postprohibition control regime for cocaine were so high and so tight as to leave the current illicit market largely in place, the result would almost certainly be a very large increase in the number of heavy cocaine users, especially once cocaine and its users started to lose the bad reputation given in part by the drug's illegal status. Against that must be set the enormous reduction in violence and incarceration that would result from abolishing the illicit market in cocaine. (The net impact on property crime is unclear; presumably, users would steal less, but some dealers, deprived of their customers by legal competition, might switch to theft as a source of illicit income. On the other hand, legalization would free substantial police, prosecution, and prison resources for use against predatory crime.)

It's likely that the greatest damage done by cocaine legalization would be in the areas where cocaine is currently least available; by the same token, those areas would gain little from reduced violence and incarceration. Conversely, those neighborhoods where cocaine is already easy to obtain, and where the burden of violence, property crime, disorder, and incarceration is greatest, would suffer the least increase in heavy use and the greatest relief from the side effects of illicit dealing and enforcement. Since high-cocaine-availability areas are disproportionately poor, urban, and African-American and Latino, while low cocaine availability is characteristic of prosperous, white, English-speaking areas of lower population density, cocaine legalization could tend to help the minority urban poor at the expense of the white suburban and exurban middle class and wealthy. According to a plausible set of principles of policy evaluation, those distributional consequences make legalization a more attractive option than it would otherwise be, but they also make it utterly implausible as a political platform. Consequently, discussion of cocaine legalization likely will remain a question of largely speculative interest.

Lesser changes, by contrast, are more plausible. Public attitudes toward cannabis have been softening in recent years, despite quite vigorous efforts by both the federal government and some NGOs to keep them as rigid as possible. As the pre–Baby Boom population shrinks as a proportion of the voting population, and a falling proportion of the Baby Boomers themselves have adolescent children to worry about, the shift in opinion might be expected to accelerate, with some positive feedback if it became politically possible for federal policy and research agencies to express more differentiated views than the currently dominant "drug war" orthodoxy allows. The risks of an upsurge in cannabis use under legalization are notably smaller for cannabis than they would be with cocaine, both because prohibition is currently less effective and because cannabis is somewhat less likely to lead to a persistent bad habit (and the bad habit, even if it develops and persists, is less dangerous). By the same token, the potential gains in reduced violence, crime, and incarceration from cannabis legalization are also much smaller, because cannabis dealing and cannabis enforcement do far less social damage than cocaine dealing and cocaine enforcement.

There are also opportunities for doing much better while still operating within the current prohibition regime. For example, recent innovations in enforcement against illicit markets offer some hope for reduced harm from dealing. "Low-arrest crackdowns," in which enforcement agents identify all the retail dealers in a given market area, develop evidence against them, and then simultaneously threaten all of them with prosecution and incarceration unless the dealing stops, have shown dramatic success in reducing violence and disorder, though probably not the volume of drugs sold. Enforcement and sentencing focused on violence and violent dealers rather than on drug distribution generally could shift the incentives that now make being heavily armed seem a good business decision to drug-market participants. The use of frequent testing and immediate, predictable, but mild sanctions to deter continued illicit drug use by offenders under community supervision has the capacity, if widely adopted, to greatly shrink the size of the markets and thus the damage they inflict. Combined, these three innovations could reduce the costs of the current prohibition regime. However, all of them are operationally and managerially complicated and require enforcement agencies and the elected officials to whom they are accountable to tolerate a reduction in the number of drug dealers going to prison: a number that, much as it looks like a cost to the policy analyst, is treated as a figure of merit and a measure of accomplishment in law-enforcement and political discourse. It is therefore far from clear that these innovations will become routine practices. The CompStat process, in which police (and other agencies) offer to hold themselves and their component parts accountable for reductions in crime rather than increases in outputs such as arrests and incarceration, is perhaps the single strongest force now apparent that might push the current drug enforcement regime toward policies with greater benefits and fewer unwanted side effects.

Dramatic changes are certainly possible with respect to drug use and/or drug policy. However, looking forward a decade, or even two decades, it is likely that the United States will still have a substantially greater cocaine problem, substantially more crime and violence around drug markets, and substantially more drug dealers in prison per capita than the countries to which it is otherwise comparable.

Part Three
A Larger Perspective

CHAPTER 20

A Canvas, Not a Country: How Europe Sees America
Josef Joffe

Josef Joffe, a leading German journalist, a prolific writer on America, and a longtime observer considers how Europeans view the United States. He finds in those perceptions an exotic brew of admiration, revulsion, envy, fear, ignorance, wishful thinking, attraction, and incomprehension. Joffe explains that Europeans have always tended to see America as the "steamroller of modernity"—a model as well as a monster. To them, this means many things: the transcendent world that attracted many millions of their immigrant ancestors; the avatar of a particularly harsh form of market economics; the bearer of a new and powerful mass culture; the last bastion of the individualistic, liberal conception of citizen and state; and a superpower at once naïve, generous, and overbearing. For Europe, America has never been a normal country; it was always a canvas on which they could project their fondest dreams and fiercest nightmares.

America as Project and Projection

IT ALL STARTED WHEN COLUMBUS FOUND AMERICA AND thought it was India. In his mind, the "West Indies," where he made landfall, were populated by "Indians." Ever since, America has been an object of the imagination rather than a mere chunk of real estate "in the center of an immense continent," as Alexis de Tocqueville

Parts of this essay have been adapted from "The Rise of Americanism," chapter 4 of Josef Joffe, *Überpower: America's Imperial Temptation* (New York: W.W. Norton, 2006).

put it. Long before the thirteen colonies jelled into union, America was a construct more than a country—or more apropos, a canvas onto which Europe would endlessly project its fondest dreams and fiercest nightmares.

On the rosy side, take Turgot, the eighteenth-century *philosophe,* who saw America as a triumph of the Enlightenment's faith in Progress. America was the "hope of mankind," he exclaimed in an oft-quoted letter to Richard Price in 1778. And why? Because it "must show to the world by its example, that men can be free and tranquil, and can do without the chains that tyrants and cheats of all garb have tried to lay on them. . . . It must give the example of political, religious, commercial and industrial liberty. The shelter which it is going to offer to the oppressed of all nations will console the earth." That example "will oblige governments to open their eyes and to be just."[1]

Three years earlier, Edmund Burke had sounded the same theme—liberty—in his speech on "Conciliation with America": "In this character of the Americans, a love of freedom is the predominating feature which marks and distinguishes the whole." And like Tocqueville fifty years later, Burke called attention to the conspicuous fusion between faith and freedom that distinguished the not-yet Americans from all others: "Religion, always a principle of energy, in this new people is no way worn out or impaired; and their mode of professing it is also one main cause of this free spirit." In Europe, "religion" meant war or oppression; in America, it turned out to be the very source of freedom—what an early paeon to American exceptionalism![2]

The American "example" surely did *not* push "governments to be free and just," but it certainly exerted an irresistible pull on their subjects. It began with the Puritans, who landed on Plymouth Rock in 1620, followed by the Jews from Recife, who escaped from the Portuguese Inquisition to New Amsterdam in 1654. And so it continued through the ages—with Pietists from Germany, Catholics

from British-ruled Ireland, more Jews from Eastern Europe, Orthodox from (Ottoman) Greece, Christians of all stripes from Araby.
Somehow, "God's Own Country" could be owned by many gods,
which added to the business opportunities of them all and helps to
explain why religiosity, in spite of its decline in Europe, remains so
strong in America. Supply-side religion, like supply-side economics,
creates its own demand.

A magnet, haven, and example—this, of course, is how Americans saw themselves, ever since John Winthrop delivered his famous
sermon "A Model of Christian Charity" ten years after the Pilgrims
had landed on Plymouth Rock. This new settlement was a "cittie
uppon a hill," he orated, with "the eies of all people upon us"[3]—
on a community with a special mission and obligation. And so it
continues until this day in every inaugural address or State of the
Union Message: America as example, as beacon, as secular "light
unto the nations." No other Western nation, not even France, speaks
about itself in such a transcendental language.

Abroad, though, for every Turgot, there was a Talleyrand (or
Buffon, Stendhal and Maistre, or Hegel and Herder) who would
paint America in the bleakest of colors. Escaping to Philadelphia
from the *Terreur* of the Revolution, Talleyrand quipped: "Thirty-two
religions and only one dish to eat." This jibe foreshadowed a very
modern attack on America: too much faith and too little class.
Stendhal has one of his characters deliver this broadside against Turgot's "hope of mankind." That "model country" was "vulgar," a "triumph of stupid, egotistic mediocrity." As early as 1794, the Duke of
La Rochefoucauld-Liancourt, another escapee from the Jacobins,
summed up the opinions of his compatriots-in-exile thus: "They
depict [the Americans] as vain, greedy, grasping, and engaged in
cheating in all of their business activities." This, too, is a modern
trope: America not as a shiny "cittie upon a hill," but as citadel of
crass materialism. At the end of the eighteenth century, notes
Philippe Roger, a "universally negative image of America [was]

firmly anchored in cultivated people's minds."⁴ And "by the end of the 19th century," writes historian Simon Schama, "the stereotype of the ugly American—voracious, preachy, mercenary, and bombastically chauvinist—was firmly in place in Europe."⁵

A canvas, not a country, an object of longing and loathing—this is what America always has been and will be in the European mind. India and China, Araby and Africa also have offered plenty of Play-Doh for the imagination, as have Atlantis and Shangri-La, not to speak of the original "Land of Milk and Honey" whose promise sustained the Israelites in the wilderness for forty years. But in modern times, no country has exerted such a powerful grip on the European mind as has America—chalk up another one for "American exceptionalism." (The term "America" is used deliberately because Europe's fascination antedates the founding of the United States by almost three centuries.) America is truly in the eye of the beholder—the product of projection rather than observation. And no wonder. The United States is not a "normal" country.

First of all, America is literally the "New World," rupture incarnate. It did not emerge from the mist of history, as did the lands of Europe, which had been around in various shapes for ages before being pounded into distinct nation-states by dynastic power in the fifteenth century. Even when Europe was practically congruent with "Rome," it consisted of recognizable ethno-cultural entities—from Lusitania (Portugal) in the west to Dacia (Romania) and Macedonia (Greece) in the east. Yet America was practically *ex nihilo,* the original state of nature, as in Locke's imagination, when he famously proclaimed in the *Second Treatise:* "In the beginning all the world was America."⁶

The country was not *in* history, to use a Hegelianism; it was deployed *against* history. It was the first polity that made itself, so to speak; it was not the fruit of royal conquest, like England, Spain, and France, or of wars of national unification like Germany.⁷ It was of Europe, but it left Europe—the rebellious child of yet another Exodus. And it was to be the "Un-Europe," the very opposite of a miserable and oppressive order beyond redemption like Pharaoh's Egypt. Beyond the wilderness of the Ocean, America would overcome history, and it did—as the first "modern" and "universal" nation.

Modernity is programmatically enshrined in the "*novus ordo seclorum*" of the Great Seal, which graces every one-dollar bill. This "new order of the ages" is best defined by what the young republic wanted to leave behind: feudalism, despotism, state religion, inequality of birth and station. Against this past, Americans wanted to build a polity "deriving [its] just powers from the consent of the governed." That was quite a departure from "divine right" or just right by conquest. Universality, the other distinctive trait, is bound up with the peculiarly American notion of citizenship as an acquired (or willed) rather than inherited attribute; hence, the peopling of America by a myriad races and nationalities—and not to forget, religions. Whereas in Europe, full citizenship was tied to the proper faith all the way into the early twentieth century, "Congress [was to] make no law respecting an establishment of religion," as the First Amendment proclaimed in 1791.

No feudalism, no socialism; no established church, no religious wars (or *cuius regio, eius religio*[8]); no absolutism, no statism—that is the gist of the American story, which also explains why in the United States market and modernity keep trumping the providential state embedded between Iberia and Siberia.[9] Modernity and universality were the unique qualities that made the country so seductive: *anybody* could become an American, and even better, "make it" in that "land of unlimited opportunity, the *goldene medineh*— "land of gold"—as the Yiddish moniker has it. Thomas Paine, a miserable failure back in England, made it, and so did Louis B. Mayer, *né* Gelbfisz, who rose from glove salesman to MGM founder. Henry Kissinger, the son of a small-town teacher in Franconia, went from Washington Heights to Harvard and to the seventh floor of the

State Department. Madeleine Albright, a Czech refugee, would later follow in his footsteps.[10]

Add to opportunity and openness the growing wealth and power of the country ("where the streets are paved with gold"), and you have the mightiest of magnets—or one huge "demonstration effect," the term favored by sociologists when they want to avoid a normative concept like "model." There is an American Dream, but no French, Russian, or Italian Dream that would power the engine of desire. The downside of seduction is of course revulsion. We hate the seducer for beguiling us, or others, and we despise those, including ourselves, who succumb to temptation as something we want, but should not. So attraction went hand in glove with repellence from day one.

A haven of opportunity? No, America was a jungle of rampant materialism. Equality? No, it was the epitome of "vulgarity" and "mediocrity," as Stendhal fumed, a deformation caused by false equality: the "tyranny of public opinion." Liberty? Here the indictment ranges from anarchy to unbridled greed. Freedom of religion? Thundered Heinrich Heine, the liberal revolutionary and German-Jewish poet: "Worldly gain is their true religion, and Mammon is their God, their only all-powerful God."[11] Sigmund Freud, who scored his greatest triumphs in the United States, is said to have put it *tout court:* "America, is a mistake, a giant mistake." For every European who pined for the Promised Land, there was another who condemned and despised America as a cultural, social, and even racial aberration (Hitler called it a "half-Judaized and half-negrified society"[12]). A favorite biological trope of the seventeenth and eighteenth century, America-the-Degenerate, has disappeared from the ledger. But all these other themes have survived into the twenty-first century.

America as Steamroller of Modernity

The United States has always rumbled across the world as steamroller of modernity—that is the long and short of it. What does this metaphor imply? A steamroller is irresistible and crushes everything in its path. Even the detractors of America felt in their bones that the country was indeed something new under the sun—and subversive, to boot. Modernity *Made in U.S.A.,* they feared, might bring about on their own turf precisely what Turgot had predicted. This Un-Europe, this enemy of the past, was a threat to Europe's ancient power and status structures. A market economy, it menaced enshrined privilege. Free-holding and homesteading threatened the grip of the landed classes from three thousand miles away. Trading labor for money would fray the bond between lord and servant. Mobility, the prototypical American habit, would literally remove the great unwashed from the grasp of their betters. If you didn't like the Puritans, you went off to the Quaker State or to Maryland. Or later, if you were a victim of Jim Crow, you left the Carolinas for Chicago and Detroit.

And so it came to pass. Early industrialization, gathering steam after the War of 1812, battered agrarian wealth, which in Europe shored up the primacy of the nobility until World War I. Then, the Civil War (1861–1865) destroyed the political power of America's informal plantation aristocracy along with the Confederacy. Democracy, as it spread beyond the propertied classes, empowered ever larger masses. "Do-it-yourself" religion, as ridiculed by Talleyrand, did not sit well with the established churches of Europe. Listen to Hegel who bemoaned too many "sects which rise to the extreme of insanity, many of which conduct services in the grip of ecstasy and even the most sensual silliness."[13] So Turgot had it right when he celebrated the American example as enemy of Europe's *ancien régimes.* If everybody could "do his thing," then America was sheer poison for the continent's age-old public order.

Modernity (or the promise of transcendence) pulled millions and millions of Europeans across the ocean. And so "Americanism" bred anti-Americanism, as seduction breeds resentment. America was both model and monster, both "dream and nightmare," as

Hannah Arendt put it—what Europe either wanted or feared to become.[14] What she postulated in 1954 could have been penned at
any time in the history of the republic: "Today, the image of America is modernity." What Europeans reviled as "Americanization" was
in fact the "emergence of the modern world with all its perplexities
and implications."[15] And the American "canvas" was broad enough
to accommodate the aversion of both Left and Right, who used different terms, but meant the same thing.

When the Left targeted the "alienation" wrought by capitalism,
the Right bemoaned the loss of community, a classic complaint of
conservatism. What the Left called "consumerism," the Right called
"materialism"—with "rampant" attached to either. Together, both
sides scorned the idea of freedom—as license for the few (Left) or as
tyranny of the many (Right). But what were they painting on this
canvas—America or Europe? Since so many of America's harshest
European critics have never set foot on American soil, we might
surmise that the true object of fear and loathing was in fact their
own European world as it stumbled into modernity—urbanization,
capitalism, proletarization, alienation, and all.

The Europeans, it should be stressed, pretty much followed the
same path into modernity as their American cousins. But in the
process, they carried the baggage of two thousand years, which
Americans had dumped into the ocean, so to speak, as they sailed
for the New World. This "baggage"—a magnificent civilization with
a global sway—did not make for speedy locomotion. The revolu-
tions of 1789, 1830, 1848, and 1918 were convulsions that triggered
conservative, if not reactionary backlashes, but not a truly *novus ordo*,
which would sink roots only in the second half of the twentieth
century. Failed dreams turned into the nightmares of the early
twentieth century when continental Europe's answer to modernity
came in the guise of Stalinist and Hitlerian totalitarianism plus their
weaker brothers, fascism and authoritarianism, as ensconced between Portugal and Poland.

As Lenin famously put it, "Socialism is electrification plus So- viet power." Hitler could have put it similarly: "National Socialism is Fordism plus Der Fuhrer." In translation both read: "Community and equality is modernization plus dictatorship." The totalitarians promised to square an impossible circle: restoring the cozy order of a long-dead past, its sense of belonging and predictability, while whipping the *volk* or proletariat forward into frenzied industrializa- tion. In the Old World, that road led to the concentration camp and the Gulag; in the United States, the convulsions of modernity brought forth Franklin Roosevelt's welfare state. When Upton Sin- clair wrote *The Jungle,* his attack on ruthless capitalism in Chicago's meat-packing plants, he meant to speed the triumph of socialism; what he got was the Food and Drug Administration.

Naturally, figures like Stalin and Hitler hated the very guts of America because across the sea, modernity proceeded quite nicely without Fuhrers, Politburos, and Caudillos, churning out endless wealth without grinding down freedom. This is where Turgot, the Enlightenment optimist, erred when he surmised that the American example "will oblige governments to open their eyes and to be just." It just made them mad; hence the compulsion to wipe that shiny example of liberal capitalism off the face of the earth.

In the second half of the twentieth century, Europe's and Amer- ica's paths to modernity reconverged, and this time more briskly than ever—as in the 1920s, when American imports like the Charleston and Taylorism[16] became all the rage. After 1945, western Europe re- gained its freedom, embarking on one "economic miracle" after an- other. Rapid growth and liberal democracy evened out age-old inequalities in favor of unprecedented upward mobility. As the United States returned to the stage as Great Liberator and Benefactor, the Old World began to lap up all things American—from white-wall tires to rock and roll, from crew cuts to blue jeans. The West Ger- mans even looked to the U.S. Constitution for inspiration when they wrote their own in 1948. Americanization-as-modernization, to recall Hannah Arendt, was the dynamic that narrowed the psychological distance between Europe and the United States. Still, the twain never did meet when it came to "hard-wired" mindsets. And so in Europe, attraction and revulsion kept traveling in tandem. As "Americanization" accelerated, anti-Americanism[17] in its classic variations kept its grip on the European consciousness (and unconscious).

"Americanization" may be broken down into three parts. *Politically*, it implies the liberal, that is, limited state, plus the primacy of the individual and the expansion of political participation. *Economically*, Americanization means "free markets"—competition among producers, prices set by supply and demand rather than by regulation or custom, low barriers to market entry, and constraints on the power of corporations in the form of guilds, unions, and trade associations. *Cultural* Americanization, the most familiar use of the term, implies a many-hued set of traits. In no particular order: informality of dress and manners, work ethic (or workaholism), mobility (geographical and economic), acquired rather than prescriptive status, youth culture (since the 1960s), expansion of individual rights and entitlements, community participation, self-improvement, a "better life" for the next generation through wealth accumulation and education, consumerism, and the predominance of mass over elite culture as well as its mandarins.

Leaving aside such quintessentially American habits as football, flag waving, and the West's highest religiosity[18], we have a rough-and-ready description of modernity as it has traveled across the Western world and to its outriggers in Oceania and Asia. What sprouted first in America moved eastward across the Atlantic, where it was eventually absorbed or adapted.

More recently, this holds true even for postmodernity's repressive cultural habits, such as smoking bans, speech codes, or sanctions on "inappropriate" behavior. The irony is rather thick here. Traditionally, Europeans have derided the United States as a stronghold of yokels and Puritans who made up for their lack of *savoir vivre* with a surfeit of social or even legal controls on drinking, gambling, and extramarital sex. Now, even France, Ireland, and Italy—once proud believers in *laissez-faire*—have proscribed smoking in public places. "Gender" and "gender-mainstreaming" have entered European languages as English terms. German companies and public bureaucracies have *Frauenbeauftragte* (women's advocates) who watch out for inappropriate male behavior.

Perhaps the most profound cultural transformation in the West, also *Made in U.S.A.,* is the shift in the target of sexual repression from females to males. As depicted in nineteenth-century literature—from *The Scarlet Letter* to *Madame Bovary*—women traditionally have been the victims of society's sanctions on "indecency." Postmodernity has reversed these roles, starting in America. Though "date rape," "sexual harassment," and the "hostile workplace" are theoretically gender-neutral, these indictments fall most heavily on men (and, in truth, are so designed). As these offenses, as well as "hate crimes," enter into Europe's legal codes, they offer yet another poignant testimony to the power of America-as-trendsetter, whether its impact is liberating or proscriptive.

America as model or innovator—this is where the steamroller metaphor begins to run out of steam. For such engines push and crush, whereas "Americanization," which at bottom is but another word for modernization, pulls and beguiles. Put very simply, this is the way most people *want* to live in that happy locale that stretches from Berkeley to Berlin (and points east). People would rather elect than suffer their leaders. They prefer unalienable rights to privileges parceled out by the state. Western man and woman want to shop till they drop—and keep what is theirs out of the government's hands. They want to improve their social status, and not have it granted by the powers that be. They want careers, a.k.a. "self-realization," not occupations handed down by their parents. They want to move around freely instead of being tied to lords or corporations. In short, modernization is individuation, autonomy, and acquisition, and by leaving the Old World and dropping two thousand years of history into the Atlantic, Americans simply got there first.

Not that they came there empty-handed. They brought with them America-as-blueprint, that is, eighteenth-century British thought, especially that of the Scottish Enlightenment, with its revolutionary ideas about freedom. In religion, freedom meant dissident Protestantism, as opposed to theocratic Calvinism[19] or to Lutheranism, which soon turned into state or privileged religions in an arc between Switzerland and Scandinavia. In politics, freedom implied Hutchinson, Locke, and Hume, that is, property rights, the limited state, and Natural Law, which stood in stark contrast to divine right and absolutism. In economics, it was Adam Smith and the superiority of the market over the *dirigisme* of guilds, officials, and royals.

Classical liberalism has always remained a minority creed in continental Europe. Not so in America, the only full-blooded child of the English and Scottish Enlightenment.[20] Untethered from the past, the United States could set the pace and the model, presenting itself to the world as an example both subversive and enticing. With a bow to Karl Marx, we might put it thus: America created a "superstructure"—values, habits, and "stuff"—in synch with a rapidly changing "substructure"—the way we produce, accumulate, and exchange.

Unencumbered in ways the continental Europeans were not, this "universal nation" could create images, icons, products, and ways of life that matched modernity's progress. Presumably, this is why the world looks through Microsoft Windows and YouTube and listens through iPods, why it takes to fast food as mothers abscond to the workplace, why it bypasses libraries in favor of Google, why it prefers the egalitarian habits of American social life to the stern rules of tradition. "Hi" and "hello" are sweeping the West as universal greetings, as "OK" has done long ago as universal assent. Rome's and Habsburg's cultural power stopped exactly at their military borders, and so did Napoleon's. American cultural clout, however, needs no gun to travel. The world eats, drinks, watches, and dresses American—and speaks "Bad English," the world's most rapidly expanding language, usually with an American accent. No force is applied to drive the masses into a McDonald's or a multiplex screening half a dozen U.S. blockbusters at once.

The Malaise of Modernity

If there is a global culture, it is American. But if all the world is becoming America, to rephrase John Locke, all the world doesn't necessarily like it. Here are some numbers. "Is the spread of American ideas and customs a good thing?" pollsters asked in five countries. "No," answered 71 percent in France, 67 percent in Germany, 58 percent in Italy, 54 percent in Canada, and 50 percent in Great Britain.[21] Nor has the world ever liked America-the-Intruder because modernity keeps "revolutionizing the instruments of production [and] with them the whole relations of society" ever since Marx and Engels penned these famous lines of the *Communist Manifesto* in 1848. Those who lose out to this impersonal revolution naturally tend to turn the abstract into the personal, and the personal into the political. The pain inflicted by widening markets, accelerating technology and obsolescence, disappearing borders and collapsing traditions used to be blamed on capitalism and capitalists (with Jews in the forefront); today the *mot juste* is "globalization." In turn, "globalization" is conflated with "America," and no wonder, for the United States, that steamroller of modernity, *is* change incarnate.

To daub the American canvas in the darkest of colors serves two functions. One is the spinning of a cautionary tale: Lo, this is what we don't want to become. As you are lured to those shores by the promise of freedom and opportunity, or as you copy the seductive ways of America, you are signing a Faustian bargain, and the price will be the loss of your soul. The second function is projection: Let's externalize what ails *us;* let's call "Americanization" what is happening to *us. We* are not doing this; it is being *done* to us. Projection, to borrow from Freud, is a defense mechanism by which we attribute to others traits we loathe or fear in ourselves. Blaming others as agents of misery is a convenient shortcut to the relief of anxiety—in this case, about the strains and upheavals of ineluctable change.

Americanization is change, plain and simple, as unavoidable as it is unwanted—at least by those who have something to lose from it. Though only an anecdote, the following conversation this author had some twenty years ago with a father of three, a member of the Hamburg *haute bourgeoisie,* makes the point very nicely. He started out with a profession of disgust for McDonald's that triggered the following dialogue:

"Why do you hate McDonald's?"

"Because you never know what kind of *dreck* its hamburgers contain."

"But that is the least of McDonald's problems. We know exactly how they are made—with buns, beef, ketchup, mustard, pickles. What we really don't know is what goes into a German *wurst,* nor do we want to know."

"True, but I still hate McDonald's."

"Why?"

He burst out: "I hate it because my children don't come home for dinner anymore. They just go to the burger joint whenever they feel like it."

"So the real reason for your anger is that you hate your kids' freedom to choose between mother's and McDonald's. You resent the fact that they are no longer tied to the family table, that you have lost power over them."

"Yes, they no longer respect order and tradition."

In the mind of this irate father, a mere meat patty had become a tool of subversion wielded by America, and he was right. From childhood, we all remember the anxiety that attended our first unaccompanied trip to a traditional restaurant. We did not know how to order, tip, and behave. But today, a twelve-year-old need not conquer such fears. Ordering is done by picture; tipping as well as the proper use of utensils are unnecessary. The child can just sail in, pay, and eat—while his parents rightly bemoan the loss of yet another tradition (and source of family power) that is the price of modernity.

Another instructive example is the attack on *amerikanische Verhältnisse*—"American ways"—during the German electoral campaign of 2002. In 2005, the enemy was yet another American interloper—private equity and hedge funds, a.k.a. "locusts"—accused of gobbling up German companies and destroying jobs for the sake of a quick profit.[22] "I don't want *amerikanische Verhältnisse*," thundered Chancellor Gerhard Schröder as early as 2001.[23] This weapon was deployed not only by the chancellor, a Social Democrat, but also by his rival Edmund Stoiber, a Conservative, who lectured: "Of course, you could quickly produce more growth with maximally flexible labor markets. But we have a completely different history and mentality. For us, solidarity and social protection play a completely different role, as compared to America."[24] "American ways," a seemingly neutral term, was in fact a fighting word with the same import as French prime minister Lionel Jospin's warning against the "the unbridled laws of the market."[25]

"American ways" were pernicious to the better ways of Europe, or as Schröder put it: "We have no reason to hide the German, the European social model from the Americans. I have enough self-confidence to say that it is superior."[26] *Amerikanische Verhältnisse* were the foes of predictability, protection, and redistribution. They were a battering ram aimed at high wages, employment security, and the munificent state—against the social-democratic dispensation that is the core of Europe's unwritten social contract from Lisbon to Leipzig, from Narvik to Naples, no matter what the government's ideological coloration.

Like Turgot's "model," America as "un-model" is a historical fixture of the European perception. But why raise this flag on the threshold of the twenty-first century? Because the "European ways" that had ensured both private and public prosperity could no longer be sustained. The state that had typically taken around half of the gross domestic product in taxes and levies and disbursed about one-third of GDP as transfer payments like social supports and subsidies—almost twice as much as in midcentury—depended on sustained growth. With sustained growth, the expanding welfare state could give to Peter without taking from Paul, thus muting society's conflicts. Yet growth began to falter and then to stagnate in the mid–1990s.

And so, the blissful arrangement of the postwar period began to groan under its own weight. Full employment gave way to stubborn joblessness of around 10–12 percent (more if make-work and wage subsidy schemes were added). As tax revenues declined, social expenditures soared. Enter globalization, or more accurately, "Europeanization," that is, the admittance of ten low-wage East European states to the EU (and yet another two, Bulgaria and Romania, in 2007). "China" as the epitome of the low-wage competition, was suddenly right next door. Economic decline and EU enlargement began to gnaw away at the very foundation of the welfare state, which presupposes a closed economy. "Closed" does not mean "no trade," for a typical EU country exports about 30 percent of its GDP, three times more than the United States. "Closed" rather means a high degree of state control over the economy plus a tacit social contract that favors producers (including workers and farmers) over consumers, jobholders over job seekers, domestic suppliers over foreign ones, and consensus over competition.

When Germans disparage "*amerikanische Verhältnisse,*" or when a French premier denounces the "unbridled laws of the market," they respond not to the United States, but to the travails of societies that can no longer hold back pent-up change. Such statements, then, are not descriptions, but projections of the mind. For all continental leaders have been in the business of transformation since the late 1990s, as Britain had been in the 1980s. They have tried to chisel away at labor market rigidities, constraints on competition, and lavish welfare payments. All of them, especially those of France and Germany, were punished in and at the polls. In truth, the real culprit is not the United States, but the European Commission, which has been hammering away at fenced-in capital and labor markets, forcing privatization and deregulation on previously well-protected national favorites like telecoms, utilities, banks, and airlines. But it is *infra dig* to attack the European project. So scapegoating America confers a number of domestic advantages on parties—Left or Right—that must compete for the allegiance of electorates weaned on the comfortable "European ways" of yore.

To portray *amerikanische Verhältnisse* as justice denied is to delegitimize those rivals in the political arena—business and the neoliberal right—who praise America's flexible labor markets as a "model," as the German Federation of Industry has done. Summing up a survey of German business leaders, the monthly *Capital*[27] reports, Turgot-like: "80 percent say that the future belongs to the American system." This was a nice testimony to America's cultural clout, especially during the boom years of the 1990s, when U.S. unemployment was half that of Europe's, as it has remained in the first five years of the twenty-first century. The implicit prescription is: "We ought to become like America." But this does not sit well on leaders who can change course by only a few degrees when their clientele is wedded to maximal social protection.

But change they must, and so *amerikanische Verhältnisse* serve as a nice distraction from the evil that must be done. As the bitter medicine is dispensed in small doses, the soothing message is: "We will never be like America." Another part of the sugarcoating is: "We are better than America—and so we *need* not become like them." Hence the tone of superiority and deprecation that runs through the European discourse, as it has done throughout the ages. The subtext is that America, the home of "predatory capitalism," is to blame for the tribulations of modernity. Next to Turgot's "hope of mankind," this is the oldest motif Europe has painted onto the American canvas: turn the abstract into the political, and the political into the personal—into the "Other." Thus, misery is neatly explained and exorcized in the way of the biblical scapegoat who was loaded with the sins of Israel and dispatched into the desert.

This reflex—"who is to blame?"—is not a novel feature of European history. Go back to the height of the Great Depression in Germany. In November 1933, nine months after Hitler had become Reich chancellor, the German-Jewish author Lion Feuchtwanger published *Die Geschwister Oppermann,* a prescient account of early Nazism in the guise of a tragic family saga. Oppermann's is a furniture store chain that has recently shifted from handcrafted to mass production, whereas its "Aryan" competitor, Heinrich Wels, sticks to the traditional, but more expensive ways:

> Heinrich Wels regarded this development with bitterness . . . . He could not compete on price with Oppermann's standardized products. . . . Perhaps Wels's beds were more cozy, and his tables more sturdy. But people preferred to spend less, which Wels could not understand. Had the feel for quality gone dead in Germany . . . ? Wels's embitterment grew. . . . But in recent years, things had changed for the better. A movement had taken hold and spread the message that craftsmanship was better suited to the German character than standardized, internationalized production. This movement called itself national-socialist. It proclaimed what Wels had long felt: that Jewish department stores with their cunning sales pitches were responsible for Germany's decline. [28]

"Standardized, internationalized production" is an old-fashioned word for "globalization." In the Depression era, the new "conditions of production," as Marx had it, were identified with pernicious modernity, and, in Heinrich Wels's worldview, with the Jews as culprits. Today, capitalism/globalization is being equated with America—with relentless, brutal change that spells: "compete or collapse!" To recall the battle cry of *amerikanische Verhältnisse,* the injunction should actually read: "Hold on to what you have and blame the Other for the painful adaptation you cannot evade!"

The Curse of Power

Ever since John Winthrop's "cittie uppon a hill," Americans—and those Europeans who shared this shiny vision—have portrayed the land across the sea as a wondrously attractive "Un-Europe." Those who saw but darkness have resorted to mirror-imaging: Europe as "Un-America"—as a superior countermodel, whose features have proven remarkably resilient over the centuries: solidarity versus greed, community versus naked self-interest, social justice versus the rule of the strong, culture versus vulgarity, stability versus rootlessness, secular enlightenment versus religious bigotry.

Two contemporary statements illustrate the long-term point. One is by Hubert Védrine, when he was foreign minister of France. America is the "ultraliberal market economy," the "mistrust of the state," "non-republican individualism," the "reflexive pursuit of the universal and 'indispensable' role of the USA," flanked by "common law, the English language, [and] Protestant rather than Catholic values."[29] This is "Un-Europe" in a nutshell. The second comes from the German social theorist Jürgen Habermas and the French postmodernist Jacques Derrida in a joint "Appeal" to Europe written in the wake of the Second Iraq War."[30]

The shibboleths are: "a model-like European welfare system," "taming of capitalism," "pacification of class conflicts," "skepticism about markets," "trust in the steering capacities of the state," "limited optimism about technological progress," "preference for the protective guarantees of the welfare state and for solidaristic solutions," low "tolerance for force." All these European virtues ought to feed into a "common [European] identity." And against whom might this identity be affirmed? Against those who stand for an "individualistic ethos that accepts flagrant social inequalities" and who have refused to heed the moral lessons learned by postimperial Europe: no more war and, instead, the "mutual limitation of sovereignty." Though uttered in the twenty-first century, the message echoes innumerable assertions about Europe's civilizational superiority since the eighteenth century. The Old World has risen to a higher moral and social plane while America remains mired in its pre-postmodern state.

Although cast in a leftish language, this appeal sounds more like a latter-day conservative utopia. Psychologically, it owes less to Karl Marx and his Enlightenment faith in progress than to Joseph de Maistre (1753–1821), France's counterrevolutionary philosopher who loathed technology, empiricism, and liberalism—all those forces that in his mind were breeding the ravages of modernity. Naturally, he had no "confidence" in the American system of governance, abounding as it did with "weakness and decay."[31] So what is new?

Note the phrases in the Derrida-Habermas appeal that inveigh against "force" and praise the self-curtailment of the European nation-state. These words sketch a new chapter in an old tale. Traditionally, Europe has portrayed the United States as haven of either hope or horror, as land of promise or perversion. Now, after the self-destruction of the Soviet Union in 1991, the United States was the last superpower standing. An unchallenged No. 1, it would liberally use its clout first in Iraq in 1991, then in Afghanistan in 2001, and again in Iraq in 2003. By the time the United States prepared to inflict its awesome military on Saddam Hussein, the American canvas had become three-dimensional, so to speak. As the United

States began to bestride the world as unfettered, fearsome Gulliver, the new dimension was power contained versus power unleashed.

Gulliver mutated into a Cyclops, and the "beacon" was no longer just a distant source of inspiration; now, Turgot's "model" came on tank tracks and bomb racks. The world has never seen such a giant. Neither Rome nor Habsburg bestrode all four corners of the earth simultaneously. Rome was done in by a host of barbarian tribes, and during the four centuries of its ascendancy, Britain could not win without lots of allies. Yet the United States can fight any war anywhere without recourse to bases and partners (but not necessarily prevail against the "asymmetric warfare" unleashed by Islamist insurgents). Britain upheld free trade and the gold standard in a less-than-global part of the world economy, but Sarbanes-Oxley[32] demands fealty from every public company in the world doing business with or in the United States. In short, the pull of America-the-Beguiling was being overwhelmed by the push and shove of America-the-Intruder in the European perception.

In a French poll in 2002 that asked, "In this list of words, which ones fit the United States best?" the two most highly ranked responses were "power" (73 percent) and "violence" (53 percent); these are concepts charged with high negativity. In 2004, "power" was also ranked first, while "violence" had dropped to third place, and "imperialism" had moved up one notch. "Good" moral qualities like "freedom" and "generosity" remained at the bottom of the field.[33]

In a six-country poll in Europe, only 14 percent opined that the United States "should remain the only superpower." In France, that number shrunk to 3 percent.[34] Another survey report sums up the numbers as follows: "The problem is bigger than Bush . . . American policies and power fuel resentment for the U.S. throughout the world. The administration brought those resentments to the surface and intensified unhappiness with the U.S. . . . [While] these sentiments were evident well before the war in Iraq . . . *resentment of*

American power, as much as its policies or leadership, also drives anti-American sentiments. People around the world, and particularly in western Europe and the Middle East, *are suspicious of America's unrivaled power."*[35]

Confronted with Gulliver Unbound, Europe began to attack the canvas with a new brush—call it the vocabulary of multipolarity. "Any community with only one dominant power is always a dangerous one, and provokes reactions," lectured French president Jacques Chirac whenever given a chance. "That's why I favor a multipolar world, in which Europe obviously has its place. . . . And anyway; the world will not be unipolar." So the giant had to be tied down again, with Chirac exclaiming: "I am totally against unilateralism in the modern world. . . . If a military action is to be undertaken, it must be the responsibility of the international community, via a decision of the Security Council."[36] The message, *tout court,* was: The strong must submit to the veto of the weak.

In the midst of the Second Iraq War, German chancellor Gerhard Schröder sounded the same theme: "Our conception of world order is not a unipolar, but a multipolar one. This means that the settlement of conflicts must respect state sovereignty and international law, and it must proceed under the aegis of the United Nations."[37] French foreign minister Dominique de Villepin darkly threatened a worldwide coalition against the United States: If "a country [relies] solely on its own power," it "will draw together all the forces of opposition, frustration and resentment."[38] The "hope of mankind" was suddenly the "last remaining rogue power." According to Villepin, Europe's "conception of world order is being shared by a very large part of the international community. . . . No nation must arrogate unto itself the right to solve all conflicts on its own."[39]

Bind yourself or be bound, these messages read in translation. Fear of power unshackled suggests why 50 to 73 percent in key NATO countries prefer more independence from the United States, and why even larger majorities throughout the world (from

58 to 85 percent) don't want the United States to remain the one and only superpower.[40] Worse, in a poll taken in Europe in 2006, the United States leads all possible comers as "greatest threat to global stability." The United States was named by 30 percent of respondents, whereas Iran trailed with 23 percent and North Korea with 8 percent. China came in with 15, and Russia with a mere 2 percent.[41]

To borrow from Lord Acton: Power breeds resentment and angst, and unbridled power breeds them in multiples. This is why the canvas is now three-dimensional, so to speak, with sociocultural attraction/repellence as the old axis, and the acceptance/defiance of American power as a new one. Nor will this change as long as the United States remains in its solitary perch as the world's "last remaining superpower." This new twist has not simplified the reading of the American canvas.

The Stranger in Our Bed

"Imitation without intimacy" may be the best shorthand guide for the perplexed. How shall we count the ways in which Europe *continues* to appropriate all things American?[42] The gamut runs from "Deulish" to "Franglais," from Halloween to the garish Christmas decorations of American suburbia, from bagels to muffins, from PowerPoint to podcasts, from delis (a re-import of the German *Delikatessen*) to Starbucks and its European knockoffs, from skateboards to boy bands, from megabookstores to "arenas" (which are replacing low-slung, roofless "stadiums"), from running shoes as foot gear for kids and grannies alike to baseball bats as the weapon of choice among young neo-Nazis. Why would a Hamburg salon use "American-Style Nailcare" (in English) as a storefront sign? Why would an outdoor café on a canal running through Berlin's government district advertise itself with "Capital Beach?" Hubert Védrine, the French foreign minister, gave the best and most concise answer when attributing to America "this certain psychological power . . . this ability to shape the dreams and desires of others."[43] The universal nation has turned into the universal trendsetter.[44]

Nor is this just a matter of low culture—it is hip-hop *and* Harvard, Madonna *and* MoMA. It is "chilling out" for the kids (the German word is "chillen") and charity galas for the rich—straight from New York and L.A. It is jogging for the masses and *JAMA*, the *Journal of the American Medical Association,* for their doctors. When New York's Museum of Modern Art (MoMA) took two hundred of its *objets* to Berlin in 2004, more than a million visitors stood in line from February to September—for a cumulative total of 446 years, according to the city's *Tagesspiegel.* To replicate *The New Yorker* or *Vanity Fair* is the dream of every ambitious publisher, and so is a stint in a fancy American summer camp for the offspring of well-to-do parents. Better even Stanford or at least Georgetown.

America's great research universities offer the most poignant illustration of the mighty imitation effect the country casts over the twenty-first century. In the attempt to reverse their postwar decline, the continent's universities, once the model for the rest of the world, have taken to the American version as antidote of choice. Open admission (or nationwide allocation by a central bureaucracy) is giving way to selection-by-university. Ancient degrees are yielding to B.A.'s and M.A.'s. Previously a sacred pillar of the European welfare state, "no tuition" is crumbling. So is the right to an interminable sojourn on the campus, as time limits and performance checks spread across the continent.

Now, to the downside. It is attraction without affection. There is no power in this "soft power," to pick up the term coined by Joseph S. Nye, the Harvard political scientist,[45] if power is defined as the capacity to make others do what they would otherwise not. To the contrary, for America's rise to the pinnacle of "hard power" has sharpened the repellence effect. Europe takes from, but not to, America. In fact, its commentariat paints the canvas in the darkest colors. The dominant motif of yore was Vulgar America as Europe's cultural and moral inferior. To the classic indictment has been added a new one. It is Yahoo America—Rambo and Globocop rolled into one, a rogue among the nations, who refuses to live by those rules of good citizenship perfected by Europe.

Illustrating the point, there are some stark differences in legitimizing the use of preemptive force in international affairs. Only 30 percent of Americans (and 33 percent of Britons) think that preemptive force is rarely or never justified. In France, it is 56 percent, and in Italy almost six out of ten. In Germany, the proportion rises to two-thirds, and in Spain to 69 percent.[46]

America the Modern, Europe the Postmodern

In addition to the new three-dimensionality of the canvas, there is another twist. Traditionally, from Stendhal to Maistre, Europe has held up conservative utopias against the American engine of modernity. The themes were order and stability, solidarity and community, wisdom and refinement. The past was good, the future-qua-America an aberration—dystopia incarnate. Now, the classical critique coexists with a new, reversed one. Europe represents not only a better past, but also a worthier future. The contemporary reaction-formation might be labeled "postmodern utopia." It attaches itself to the European Union as a latter-day "cittie uppon a hill," an empire not by imposition, but by invitation. Its members must subscribe to the fusion of their sovereignties, to pacificity in domestic and international affairs, to the expansion of individual and social rights, and to the munificent state as generous provider of public goods.

Add to this a postmodern cultural agenda. It favors, or at least accepts, subnational over national identities. The ethos of diversity is successively enshrined in EU and national law. The trend is to define ethnic and religious identities as hard-shelled givens, while biological identities are viewed as malleable "constructs" and sexual ones as "preferences." This leads the state to enforce appropriate speech and conduct and to validate institutions like fatherless families or homosexual marriages considered deviant in pre-postmodern times.

The privileges of citizenship tend to loom larger than its obligations. Once the avant-garde of nationalism, the European intelligentsia has executed a U-turn. In the new dispensation, nationalism is the evil that poisoned the past while "Eurocentrism" is the driver of cultural imperialism. Force, once the trusty servant of the national interest, can be redeemed only in the service of humanitarian purpose. Europe's postmodernity is postnational and postheroic; its ethos that of a "civilian power." Shrinking steadily, European armies are no longer repositories of nationhood (and ladders of social advancement) but organizations with not much more prestige than the postal service. The European state does not go abroad in search of fame and riches.

In the postmodern state, "the individual has won," notes Robert Cooper, and "foreign policy is the continuation of domestic concerns beyond national borders. . . . Individual consumption replaces collective glory as the dominant theme of national life [and] war is to be avoided."[47] But let us not overdraw the Western divide, for all of these features are present in the United States as well. In fact, diversity, affirmative action, and speech codes were invented there while deconstructionism traveled from France to the rest of Europe via an invigorating detour to the United States, which is another telling illustration of America-as-demonstration-effect. Americans are just as consumerist and preoccupied with self and family as are Europeans. Nor do Americans exactly loathe the culture of entitlements that has spread through the West in the last half of the twentieth century.

Yet this is where the similarities end. Curiously, America remains both more modern and premodern than postmodern. America's premodernity comes in two guises. One relates to the different role of the state on either side of the Atlantic. Since the late nineteenth century, the European state has steadily expanded as it pushed into realms once considered private, such as charity, social work, and education. Now contrast this trend with an enduring antistatist bias in the United States, which has never sat well with the Europeans who look to the government as principal agent of distributive justice. The bias is nicely reflected in the $250 billion Americans give annually to philanthropy and nonprofit ventures, not to speak of billions of hours in unpaid work, or "volunteerism."[48] According to a study of the U.S. Bureau of Labor Statistics in 2001–2002, more than a quarter of American adult citizens—or around 60 million—donated their time during that period.[49] No other Western nation comes even close in the private production of public goods.

A second feature of America's premodernity is its extraordinary attachment to faith and organized religion, while Europe has been secularizing, indeed, "de-Christianizing" since the end of World War II. Hence the ridicule bestowed not only on George W. Bush, who supposedly listened to voices in his head like a latter-day Joan of Arc, but on all presidents who either were devout (Jimmy Carter) or acted thus (Richard Nixon). In America, 94 percent believe in God, whereas only 56 percent do so in France, and 50 percent in Germany.[50] The gap is as wide when it comes to church attendance. Naturally, enlightened Europe regards America-the-Religious as retrograde—as it has done since Talleyrand. Revivalist Protestantism remains a source of bewilderment, if not derision.

So much for America, the Pre-Modern. But America also is more modern than postmodern, when compared to Europe. The modern state, as it arose in the wake of the French Revolution, based its enormous power on nationalism, mass mobilization, and a sense of mission. What sets America apart is its enduring identification with flag and country. For all of its multi-ethnicity, America possesses a keen sense of self—and of what it should be. Patriotism scores high in any survey, much higher than in Europe, including France. There is a surfeit of national symbols throughout the land, whereas no gas station in Europe would fly an oversized national flag. Though invented in Europe, nationalism is a fire that has burnt itself out—and no wonder, considering the inferno it unleashed in twentieth-century Europe.

Its sense of nationhood intact, the United States naturally is loath to share sovereignty and reluctant to submit to international institutions where it is "one nation, one vote." Since 1945, Europe has done well by being good, and hence, just as naturally, it draws satisfaction from looking down at the Yahoo state that is America. America's armed forces can still draw on remnants of a warrior culture, especially in the South; they still offer minorities and newcomers one of the swiftest routes to inclusion and citizenship. America's military, unlike most of its counterparts in Europe, is a central tool of statecraft. No Western nation, with the exception of Israel, has used force more often in the post–World War II period than the United States.

But the divergent paths cannot be explained fully by historical memory and the culture it has shaped after World War II. The deepest divide between America and Europe comes from power and position in the global hierarchy. The United States is the country that dwarfs the rest. With its planetary clout, it is the universal intruder and hence in harm's way everywhere. Its very power is a provocation for the lesser players, but unlike Europe and Japan, the United States cannot huddle under the strategic umbrella of another nation. Nor can it live by the postmodern ways of Europe, protected as it was by American might during the cold war and facing no strategic challenge at the beginning of the twenty-first century. Neither would Europe be so postmodern if it had to worry about its own security; just compare Sweden's aggressive career in the seventeenth century, and Germany's in the twentieth, with their pacificity today. In contrast to Europe, the United States must endure in a Hobbesian world where self-reliance is the ultimate currency of the realm—and goodness is contingent on safety. The anatomy of the international system, to borrow once more from Sigmund Freud, is destiny. Where you sit is where you stand— postmodernism, postnationalism, and all. Power and position are the givens that shape incompatible worldviews above and beyond the impact of culture and self-conception.

America the Beguiling, the Intruder, the Depraved—these are, and will be, the key motifs on the canvas painted by Europe. What conclusion follows from this tale? America and Europe are "The West," but they are like Notre Dame in Paris: two spires towering over a common nave. Or to change the metaphor: if America is the "daughter of Europe," as Charles de Gaulle put it, it is an offspring who left home in the eighteenth century and never returned.

The British Enlightenment the young Americans brought with them was an extraordinary moment in the West; it was defined by historical optimism, faith in progress, the liberation of the individual from church and state, and the belief in the malleability of human affairs. But America was also lucky, as Europe was not, where the promise of transcendence was so often drowned in terror and war— from the French Revolution to the triumph of the totalitarians. "Luck" was surely rooted in geography. "Separated from the rest of the world by the ocean," Tocqueville noted, "[America] has no great wars to fear."[51] The point here is the link between serendipity and security. Spared the curse of existential threats, Europe's daughter could take the Scottish-English Enlightenment across the Atlantic and implant a truly "New World" in a soil both virginal and safe.

And today? Any "new world" is as tempting as it is threatening, but when it comes with untrammeled power, both cultural and strategic, it terrifies even more and shapes images accordingly. Whatever it does, America will remain model and monster because of what it *is*. Still, what it *does*—how it uses its awesome might—will affect the composition and coloration of the portrait. In order to build the "cittie uppon a hill," John Winthrop counseled his flock to "doe Justly, to love mercy, to walke humbly with our God [and] make others Condicions our owne rejoice." If not, "wee shall be made a story and a byword through the world, wee shall open the mouthes of enemies." That was in 1630, when vast patches of the canvas were still white. But the foresight was as uncanny as the counsel was wise.

CHAPTER 21

Looking Back

Peter H. Schuck and James Q. Wilson

IN 1835, ALEXIS DE TOCQUEVILLE WROTE THAT AMERICA WAS
"exceptional," by which he meant that it alone had produced a nation that was "eminently democratic" with a society based on a
"general equality of condition." Since then, the United States has
become genuinely democratic in ways scarcely imagined by Tocqueville, extending the formal and informal processes of full political participation to those who were then excluded: racial minorities,
women, young adults, those without property, and in some cases,
immigrants.

Many other nations have also become democratic as the principle of human dignity has expanded globally, although not universally. Indeed, some countries, by some measures, are even more
democratic, egalitarian, and prosperous than is the United States.
These developments lead many people to think that America today
is no longer exceptional. In this common view—widespread in Europe, as we learn from Josef Joffe's chapter—the United States stands
out as the sole superpower, the global hegemon, but is otherwise no
more distinctive than any other democratic polity that, like all nations, bears a singular history, culture, and identity.

The contributions to this book, however, strongly suggest that
this common view is mistaken. In fact, America is much more different from other modern democracies than those polities are from
each other. Obviously, no rigorous definition of exceptionality exists, much less an agreed-upon metric of it under which particular

nations' distinctiveness can be assessed. The approach to this question that we as editors of this volume have taken is to invite the nation's leading social scientists to describe and interpret the facts, and then to let those findings speak for themselves. So informed, our readers can draw their own conclusions.

Here are *our* own conclusions. Based on these chapters and on our long professional immersion in the scholarly literature on these subjects, America is indeed exceptional by any plausible definition of the term and actually has grown increasingly exceptional over time. Our book's principal goal is not to "prove" America's exceptionalism—although the cross-national comparisons presented in the chapters provide decidedly strong evidence of it—but rather to mobilize the best, most up-to-date social science in the service of a sophisticated, fact-based understanding of the most important institutions, cultural forms, and public policies that define America's national character.

This summary, which can only hint at the rich analyses contained in each of the chapters, can be organized into seven sections under which the main, cross-cutting themes of the chapters can be presented: culture; constitutionalism; economy; social diversity; civil society; welfare state; and demography.

Culture

We begin with America's distinctive culture for a very good reason. Before a Constitution and other political institutions were adopted, there was the culture that shaped them and would in time infuse them with an easily recognizable national spirit. This culture, which of course has evolved throughout the life of the Republic, has many features. Four of the principal aspects are patriotism; individualism; religiosity; and enterprise.

PATRIOTISM

When the Pew Research Center conducted polls among some 91,000 people in fifty nations, it found that 71 percent of Americans were "very proud" to be in America, while only 38 percent of the French and 21 percent of the Germans and Japanese said they were proud to live in their countries. The display of flags, national symbols, and patriotic bumper stickers, so common in American life, puzzles Europeans. Even more puzzling, and often troubling, to them is the sense of national mission and idealism that always plays some significant role in America's civic life and foreign policy.

The military, with its ethos of sacrifice and devotion to the nation, has been a traditional outlet for the expression of American patriotism and national pride. As Eliot Cohen's chapter explains, however, the gap between the civilian and military ways of life has widened in recent years, creating a grave risk of mutual incomprehension and disaffection that transcends public attitudes toward any particular war.

INDIVIDUALISM

Long before Tocqueville and ever since, foreign observers have been struck by Americans' faith—some would say *naïve and unwarranted* faith—in the power of individuals to shape their own destinies through their exercises of freedom. Americans, more than Europeans, believe that success in life is determined by their own efforts: two-thirds of all French, Germans, and Italians, compared to only one-third of all Americans, believe that success in life is determined by "forces outside their own control." In the taxonomy of liberty popularized by Isaiah Berlin, Americans have especially cherished "negative" liberty, understood as freedom from government restraint, rather than "positive" liberty, which imagines government as the source and shaper of moral community and guarantor of the resources necessary to develop individual capacity and social fulfillment.

This belief in individualism causes Americans to place an unparalleled emphasis on the notion of individual rights in every area of social life and, correspondingly, to be suspicious of group rights. It also causes Americans to disparage their governing institutions, especially Congress and the bureaucracy, even as they revere the constitutional system that has created these institutions. Ask any soldier for what he or she is fighting, and chances are they will say "to preserve or expand freedom." Ask immigrants what they want when they come here and almost all will mention freedom. When asked whether they "completely agree" that the government should provide a safety net, only one-third of Americans say "yes," compared to 60 percent or more in most European countries.

This ethos of individualism is manifested in almost all of the institutions and public policies discussed in this book. Religious pluralism, with a marked emphasis (even in Catholicism, to an extent) on decentralized administration, congregation-centered organization, and doctrines of individual access to Scripture and God, is probably the most important and historically continuous of these individualistic manifestations. But much the same pronounced individualism is also true, *mutatis mutandis,* of the American economy, education systems, public administration, health care system, litigation, law enforcement, and much, much more.

RELIGIOSITY

Surrounding and shaping American culture is a remarkably strong religious tradition and an inventive though sometimes repellent popular culture of religiosity. As Robert Wuthnow explains in his chapter, the relationship between religion and popular culture is a complex and, on the whole, generative and socially beneficial one.

America has many secularists, but a far higher percentage of its people attend religious services than in Europe (except for Ireland and Poland). Many scholars estimate that nearly half of all Americans attend religious services each week compared to 4 percent of the English and 5 percent of the French. Other scholars dispute the magnitude of the gap, arguing that fewer Americans actually go to church than the number who tell pollsters that they do. But no scholar disputes the fact that Americans are much more deeply involved with religion than are Europeans. Church leaders and their flocks have led almost all of the reformist causes in American history: abolition, women's suffrage, temperance, civil rights, opposition to unpopular wars, and environmentalism. Some mainstream religious groups tend to support liberal candidates and policies. Many other religious groups now support conservative presidential candidates, but this is only a recent development. Moreover, these conservative groups are divided politically by quarrels over abortion, gay rights, stem cell research, foreign policy, and many other issues.

One reason for this pronounced religiosity is that creating and sustaining churches was never in the hands of the federal government and only briefly in those of the first states; instead, religious development was promoted by spiritual entrepreneurs engaged in competitive marketing, vigorous proselytizing, and doctrinal and liturgical innovations. Immigration, moreover, has fortified this religious commitment throughout American history. Churches grew rapidly in membership even before non-English immigrants began to arrive in the second half of the nineteenth century. The earliest German immigrants tended to be non-observant Lutherans, but by the third generation they had acquired the churchgoing habits of their neighbors.

ENTERPRISE

Well over half of all Americans think that economic competition is desirable because it stimulates people to work hard. In comparison, only one-third of French and Spanish people agree. Sixty percent of Americans think that their children should be taught these values; only one-third of the British and Italians and one-fifth of the Germans agree. These values, historian Victoria de Grazia notes, have long been an essential part of America's quest for what President Woodrow Wilson called its commercial "conquest of the world," an ambition that de Grazia describes as "the rise of a great imperium with the outlook of a great emporium."[1]

This American belief in the virtues of competition and enterprise extends well beyond the economic sphere to almost all other areas of social life outside the family. (Sibling rivalry, of course, is hardly unique to American families.) This competitiveness and enterprise are evident, most obviously, in the economic sphere described by Benjamin Friedman, and in the health care system discussed by David Cutler and Patricia Keenan. But even more revealing is the fact that the entrepreneurial spirit is also conspicuous in the remarkably dynamic realms of popular culture and the mass media, as the chapters by Martha Bayles and by S. Robert Lichter explain, and in the intensely adversarial, sharp-elbowed, take-no-prisoners political culture that Jack Citrin analyzes. Remarkably, and perhaps inevitably, however, this bellicose, rambunctious political culture could not exist without a corresponding emphasis on compromise and conciliation.

Constitutionalism

If American culture has shaped its constitutional values, those values have in turn shaped its constitutional system and its other central institutions. The constitutional restraints on government action influence how the economy, the bureaucracy, the legal system, and the mass media operate. The Constitution's very first phrase affirms its establishment by "We the people," and the Bill of Rights and the earlier language of the Declaration of Independence rejected the views that Americans' liberties depended on the government's grace or consent, and that government could act in ways that affect their interests without their consent. Instead, they insisted that Americans—indeed, all people—possessed natural rights that preceded and constrained government authority.

The political system is presidential, not parliamentary, yet as Nelson Polsby shows, the U.S. Congress is almost certainly the most powerful legislature, both constitutionally and functionally, in the democratic world. Most members of Congress are elected on schedules that are to some degree independent of the presidential election and come from states and districts where local issues often influence the outcome more than does presidential popularity. Congress can vote down even the most important presidential proposals without causing a new election to be held, and when there is a new election, the support or opposition that legislative candidates receive from the president ordinarily counts for little. Congress, in short, is not a tool of the executive branch even when the president is from the same party that controls the House and Senate.

Like the enormous power of Congress to shape executive action, the authority of the federal and state courts to constrain the actions of both agencies and legislatures—and in a real sense, to make law—has long been a unique feature of the American constitutional system, one that some European constitutional courts have begun to emulate. Legal historian Lawrence Friedman shows how the expansive power of American judges in both private and public law has shaped a legal system that is remarkably accessible to the people (one reason for its litigiousness) and strongly oriented toward the creation and protection of individual rights at the expense of governmental and social claims. A striking example of this exceptionally expansive scope of individual rights is America's constitutional protection of speech in all of its myriad forms and contexts (except for pornography, "fighting words," and a few other narrow categories). More than any other country, U.S. law broadly protects expression of all kinds—not only political advocacy but speechlike behavior (e.g., picketing and message-bearing clothing), commercial advertising, and defamatory, indecent, abusive, and outrageous utterances as well.

As Donald Kettl emphasizes, the system of administrative law delegates enormous power and discretion to federal agencies under political conditions that make it unusually difficult—especially when compared to European state administrations—for bureaucratic officials to establish the democratic legitimacy of their actions. The constitutional system also leaves many of the most important public functions—education, land use, criminal justice, transportation, domestic relations, tort law, occupational licensure, and much more—in the hands of state and local governments. Beginning in the 1990s, a series of Supreme Court decisions imposed some constitutional limits on federal power, limits not enforced by the judiciary since the demise of the "Old Court" sixty years earlier. (One should not make too much of these decisions, which are fairly narrow in scope, can often be circumvented by Congress, and are offset by some other recent rulings that augment federal power at the expense of state authority—for example, over medicinal uses of controlled substances.

As Martha Derthick shows, political factors maintain this highly decentralized distribution of authority, even when the Constitution would permit a greater centralization of power. Her discussion of federalism emphasizes many of the reasons for this strong structural continuity. Justice Louis Brandeis's famous dictum that federalism creates "laboratories of democracy" that can foster innovation and experimentation on a smaller, and more readily reversible, scale helps to explain, among other things, the political and policy success of the 1996 welfare reform discussed by Gary Burtless and Ron Haskins, the different approaches to substance abuse policy described by Jonathan Caulkins and Mark Kleiman, and the school reform initiatives analyzed by Paul Peterson.

Not only can government choose what to do, people can make their residential choices among states based on these differences. People who want medical marijuana, tough environmental laws, same-sex marriage or civil unions, stem cell research, charter schools, strict law enforcement, English-only policies, or low taxes can decide to live in states or localities that have these policies; those who prefer the opposite can live elsewhere. James Q. Wilson's chapter explains how this localism has affected criminal justice and enforcement policies. Every district attorney, mayor, and governor, as well as many judges, are elected by their communities, and this solicitude for popular concerns has made the American response to crime stronger, swifter, and more incarceration-oriented than in the United Kingdom and Europe. Majorities support the death penalty in the United States, the United Kingdom, and Europe, but among democratic nations only in America (and Japan) does it exist, and here it exists in most states (although there are signs that some may repeal it).

Despite the structural, functional, and normative underpinnings of decentralization in America, a number of other forces push strongly in the opposite direction, militating in favor of more centralized authority. An increasingly national (indeed, global) market for products and services strengthens the argument for uniform regulation at the national level, minimizing state-by-state differences. Hence the intermittently successful campaign by business for federal tort reform. Also, multi-state externalities such as air pollution have prompted more centralized control systems, even where environmental regulators use decentralized market mechanisms to implement those controls. Campaign finance reforms and stronger, more ideologically polarized national parties are tending to nationalize electoral contests, which in turn can be expected to support more policy initiatives from Washington. And so forth.

The competition between a constitutional system that favors decentralized political structures, and some political, technological, and economic changes that tend to push authority toward the center, is a perennial contest with no readily predictable outcome. The competitive struggle among the states over the scheduling of their presidential primaries for the 2008 election is an example, as is the continuing debate over the funding of stem cell research. The chapters by Wilson, by Kleiman and Caulkins, and by Peterson illustrate how this competition plays out in the quite different policy domains of criminal justice, controlled substances, and education. What these and other chapters make clear, however, is that America's political and policy systems, like its economy and society more generally, remain far more decentralized than their European counterparts.

Economy

The American economy is unique among those of advanced democracies in achieving a sustained record of growth, job creation, technological innovation, capital investment, and a widespread distribution of ownership. Benjamin Friedman's chapter attributes these achievements to the remarkable flexibility and competitiveness of American enterprises and a largely unregulated, highly mobile labor market that imposes few constraints on firms and that rewards workers who can shift from dying industries to growth sectors. He also shows how the regulatory environment, compared with its more intrusive foreign counterparts, encourages entrepreneurship, new business formation, and job growth. Immigration also contributes to these economic strengths, albeit with some effect on low-skill wage rates.

Friedman's analysis, as well as the chapter on social policy and inequality by Burtless and Haskins, casts light on a more worrisome feature of the American economy: the pace and shape of social mobility. They show that the iconic Horatio Alger, rags-to-riches myth that has inspired so many Americans in the past may be increasingly just that: a myth. According to traditional indices, mobility in the United States today is not particularly high when compared with that in some European countries and may be declining over time. Although the accuracy of these mobility indices is distorted by the (hard-to-measure) impact of immigrants who presumably improve their lots in the United States, any decline in economic and social mobility would be a cause for grave concern.

Diversity

America is probably the most diverse society on earth—certainly the most diverse industrial one. This is true regardless of how one thinks about or measures diversity or which kind of diversity is under discussion. Ask a random group of Americans or foreign visitors to name the most distinctive aspects of American society, and diversity will be high on everyone's list. According to Orlando Patterson (himself an immigrant), America's embrace of diversity "finds no parallel in any other society or culture in the world today." Patterson's chapter on race in America emphasizes the tensions between viewing diversity as an essentially monolithic problem or instead unpacking it into a number of quite different issues affecting disparate groups and subgroups.

As Peter Schuck's chapter on immigration explains, American society has always been diverse. He notes historian Jill Lepore's report that "the percentage of non-native English speakers in the United States was actually *greater* in 1790 than in 1990."[2] Although America has not always relished this diversity—slaveholders, eugenicists, racists, homophobes, xenophobes, church establishmentarians, monolingual diehards, and many others opposed it on principle—it views diversity today as constitutive of the national mythos and underwrites this by welcoming more than 1 million legal immigrants each year (1.26 million in 2006), while tolerating another estimated 12 million undocumented ones. (New immigrants to Canada, a vast, thinly settled land seeking more people, constitute a much larger share of its much smaller population.)

Despite (or perhaps because of) this diversity, the American polity's enduring stability and unity remain the envy of the world. Today, many other polyglot nations—India, Indonesia, Russia, Nigeria, Turkey, South Africa, Sri Lanka, and even Canada—are at serious risk of fragmenting into ethnic shards. (Australia and Switzerland stand, so far, as notable exceptions.) Indeed, even strong unitary states like the United Kingdom, Spain, France, and China, and religiously homogeneous states like Belgium, are being roiled by militant demands for devolution or even full independence. The victory of the Scottish National Party in the spring of 2007 presages an increase in such demands in the United Kingdom. In sharp contrast, the United States has maintained its social and political cohesion, even achieving a kind of cultural coherence, though this is more debatable. Moreover, it has done so without sacrificing its economic, social, and cultural dynamism. By any standard, this represents an immense national achievement.

Two possible reasons for this achievement, compared with the more divisive systems that exist in many other countries, are the unquestioned primacy of the English language throughout the United States, even in much of the second immigrant generation and certainly in the third, and the long-standing American (and British, Canadian, and Japanese) preference for first-past-the-post electoral systems rather than the proportional representation (PR) that prevails in Europe. A recent study by political scientists Torben Iversen and David Soskice shows that, among seventeen large democracies, those that use PR are three times more likely than those using majority vote to have leftist governments that redistribute income from rich to poor. If there are only two major parties, middle-class voters will worry that voting for leftist parties will increase their taxes, and the policies supported by the parties will reflect their anxieties, whereas under PR, such voters will support parties that want to tax the rich and benefit themselves, knowing that they can change their voting habits if a government wishes to increase their own taxes.

Civil Society

Civil society—the array of groups and institutions that stand between the individual and the state—is the domain in which almost all people conduct their most important activities and cultivate their most meaningful relationships. This is particularly true in a liberal democratic nation like the United States that emphasizes individualism, voluntary associations, private markets, and limited government.

Perhaps the most striking, and puzzling, aspect of American life is that its civil society is extraordinarily robust in every respect—except the most important one, the family. This, of course, is no small exception. The family, after all, strongly influences individual values and character, which in turn determine the nature of both civil and political society. The chapter by Linda Waite and Melissa

Howe explains how the American family has changed and the growing challenges that it faces in light of economic, cultural, legal, demographic, and other developments.

But first consider the extraordinary strengths of American civil society. We have already noted the remarkable role that religious organizations play in mediating between the spiritual and communal yearnings of individuals and the shaping of cultural norms and public policies. As Arthur Brooks demonstrates in his chapter, Americans' private philanthropic giving—to secular causes as well as religious ones—is unmatched anywhere in the world not just in absolute terms but also as a share of income and wealth. These charitable donations, moreover, are made disproportionately by those with modest incomes. Private charity in the United States supports a vast array of non-profit organizations—schools, universities, hospitals, nursing homes, child welfare agencies, ethnic advocacy groups, museums, and a host of others—providing diverse social services to the needy and other members of the public. Local, regional, and national voluntary associations form constantly to pursue a bewildering variety of private and public interests, providing many more avenues for citizen participation in larger collective endeavors.

Many functions that in Europe are largely reserved to government are performed by private institutions in the United States. Peterson's chapter, for example, reveals how private institutions dominate higher education, while also playing a leading role in elementary and secondary education for elites and lower-income students alike. Much the same pattern prevails, Cutler and Keenan show, in the health care field—to the consternation of many health policy critics of the status quo who prefer a single-payer system, or at least a more centrally coordinated one.

The achievements of the ubiquitous non-profit sector in the United States, and the American public's relatively high degree of confidence in it, have prompted policymakers to initiate a large number of programs seeking to draw on the distinct advantages of both public authority and private incentives and innovation. These public-private partnerships exist in many different fields including housing and community development, scientific research, environmental protection, the integration of immigrants, public safety, and many areas of regulatory policy.

This upbeat picture of civil society, however, is seriously marred by the deep pathologies that afflict many low-income communities, pathologies that tend to corrode the integrity of civil society and contribute to the formation of a small but durable "underclass." A number of the chapters in this book—particularly those by Patterson, by Burtless and Haskins, and by Waite and Howe—help us assess the scale and possible causes of this underclass, particularly the disturbingly large and growing incidence of single-parent and specifically female-headed households. One can scarcely exaggerate the importance of this development, as it affects almost every aspect of American life—educational progress, public health, crime, substance abuse, mobility, racial and political attitudes, inequality, demography, morality, unemployment, and social values. The dismal trends in non-marital births, family dissolution, and children growing up without paternal guidance constitute America's single most urgent and (at least so far) intractable social problem.

Welfare State

Traditionally, the United States has been considered a "welfare state laggard" compared with Europe and Canada. This epithet (for so it is usually intended) highlights the absence of the kinds of universal health care programs, family allowances, and extended unemployment and other worker benefits established long ago in these other systems. Although the differences between the American and European social systems are indeed great, such comparisons are invariably simplistic and, as explained in the Burtless and Haskins chapter, miss some of the distinctive features of American social policy. In addition, developments in Europe suggest that those systems are beginning to cut back on public benefits for demographic and other reasons. These changes are reducing, but certainly not eliminating, the differences with the United States in the design of welfare state programs.

The most important feature of the American welfare state is its reliance on private provision of certain benefits through policy instruments whose costs are not wholly reflected on public budgets. Tax credits, tax subsidies, loan guarantees, regulatory mandates, and other incentives to private employers and providers finance health insurance, retirement pensions, unemployment compensation, worker's compensation, educational tuition support, and many other benefits provided directly by government in welfare states abroad. In addition, many social programs in the United States, most notably Medicaid and many worker benefits, are joint federal-state programs in which the states finance much of the cost. If these off-budget "tax expenditures" and non-federal payments were included in the tally, the American welfare state would be comparable to its foreign counterparts. Moreover, the largest and most important of these programs aimed at the poor—particularly Medicaid, food stamps, and the Earned Income Tax Credit—have expanded significantly not only over the last two decades but in recent years as well.

The American and European welfare states also differ in their political and policy responses to the growing fiscal burdens of these programs. These burdens are likely to be far more severe in Europe than here, largely because of more adverse demographic trends, higher existing tax rates, slower economic growth, and less flexible labor market and political structures. In the 1983 amendments to Social Security, the 1996 welfare reform law, and some other changes, the United States has begun to make the difficult political and programmatic adjustments to the more constrained fiscal environment, adjustments that the European systems have so far found it very difficult to undertake but can no longer avoid.

Demography

Perhaps no contemporary aspect of American life is more exceptional, when compared with other advanced democracies, than its demography—in particular its relatively high fertility rate and consequent population growth. Waite and Howe provide the numbers, and they are truly stunning. We suspect that this demographic exceptionalism has a great deal to do not only with immigrants, who bring their high fertility rates with them to the United States, but also (and relatedly) with the greater optimism and future orientation of Americans, which in turn may relate—doubtless in complicated ways—to its greater religiosity, discussed earlier. This population growth, whose magnitude will depend largely on the fertility trends among Latino immigrants, has immense implications for economic growth, family structure, the design of welfare state programs, popular culture, immigration, and many other of the institutions, practices, and policy debates analyzed in this book. It may also affect how the burgeoning America is viewed by the already declining and soon-to-shrink populations abroad, as sketched by Josef Joffe.

On the evidence of this book, then, we are convinced that America is indeed exceptional. But since all nations are distinctive in their own ways, and some of their features (like some of those in the United States) are inevitably unattractive, what of it? Our answer is that American exceptionalism helps explain some social patterns that would otherwise seem incongruous, even perverse. The individualism of the people, the productivity and flexibility of the economy, and the power of its popular culture feed mass consumerism, but this consumerism is tempered by deep patriotism and a strong commitment to civil liberties, even in times of war. The constitutionally constrained reach of the federal government limits the amount of money spent on welfare, but this limited government helps to encourage a strong interest in religion and an unparalleled commitment to private philanthropy and voluntary organizations providing a vast array of social services to the poor. Americans distrust many of their governmental institutions but venerate their

Constitution and the personal freedoms that it protects, freedoms that in turn create and shape those public institutions. Americans were once politically isolationist and racially intolerant, but the culture has transformed those views in so many ways that the great majority now acknowledge this country's responsibility to other parts of the world, readily accept and encourage racial and ethnic minorities, and—in the most telling sign of a tolerant, integrating society—interethnic and interracial marriage is on the rise.

Unlike what some foreign observers may think, this country is not an odd mixture of Paris Hilton, Pat Robertson, and robber barons. It is an astonishingly open society that from the beginning, and more than any other nation, has welcomed people from all over the world. Within a generation, the overwhelming majority of those immigrants and their children have become fully American and Anglophone, not residents of isolated ethnic enclaves. America's main problems today—a large underclass, the continuing isolation of many blacks, reduced economic mobility, a deeply polarized electorate, substance abuse among the young, many families in crisis, and a popular culture that is at once immensely creative and often debased—have many causes, but they are neither unique to America nor the result of collective decisions about how we ought to behave. They are the large and unfortunate costs of freedom, and freedom is America's watchword.

Notes

CHAPTER 1 The Political System

1. James Madison, *The Federalist* (no. 51).

2. Joseph Alsop, *FDR 1882–1945: A Centenary Remembrance* (New York: Viking Press, 1982), 154.

CHAPTER 2 Bureaucracy

1. For analysis of the historical foundations of American public administration, see Anthony M. Bertelli and Laurence E. Lynn, Jr., *Madison's Managers: Public Administration and the Constitution* (Baltimore: Johns Hopkins University Press, 2006).

2. U.S. Office of Personnel Management, *Demographic Profile of the Federal Workforce* (2004), at www.opm.gov/feddata/demograp/demograp.asp#summary.

3. United Kingdom, Cabinet Office, *Civil Service Statistics: 2004 Report,* at www.civilservice.gov.uk/management/statistics/reports/2004/diversity/index.asp.

4. Herbert Kaufman, "Emerging Doctrines of Public Administration," *American Political Science Review* 50 (December 1956), 1059–1073.

5. Woodrow Wilson, "The Study of Administration," *Political Science Quarterly* 2 (1887), 197–222.

6. Office of Personnel Management, *Biennial Report of Employment by Geographical Area,* Table 4 (2004), at www.opm.gov/feddata/geograph/table4.pdf.

7. Paul C. Light, "The Changing Shape of Government," *Brookings Policy Brief #45* (Washington, DC: Brookings Institution, February 1999), at www.brookings.edu/comm/policybriefs/pb45.htm.

8. James Q. Wilson, *Bureaucracy: What Government Agencies Do and Why They Do It* (New York: Basic Books, 1989).

9. Diane Vaughan, *The Challenger Launch Decision: Risky Technology, Culture and Deviance at NASA* (Chicago: University of Chicago Press, 1996).

10. *The Federal Register* is online at www.gpoaccess.gov/fr/index.html.

11. Martha Derthick, *Up in Smoke: From Legislation to Litigation in Tobacco Politics,* 2nd ed. (Washington, DC: Congressional Quarterly Press, 2004).

12. Robert Kanigel, *The One Best Way: Frederick Winslow Taylor and the Enigma of Efficiency* (New York: Viking, 1997).

13. David Osborne and Ted Gaebler, *Reinventing Government: How the Entrepreneurial Spirit Is Transforming the Public Sector* (Reading, MA: Addison-Wesley, 1992).

14. See Frederick C. Mosher, "The Changing Responsibilities and Tactics of the Federal Government," *Public Administration Review* 40 (1980), 541–548; Lester M. Salamon, "Rethinking Public Management," *Public Policy* 29 (1981), 255–275; and Donald F. Kettl, *Government by Proxy: (Mis?)Managing Federal Programs* (Washington, DC: Congressional Quarterly Press, 1988); and Lester M. Salamon, ed., *The Tools of Government: A Public Management Handbook for the Era of Third-Party Government* (New York: Oxford University Press, 2002).

15. Organization for Economic Cooperation and Development, *OECD in Figures: 2005 Edition* (Paris: OECD, 2005), at www.oecd.org/document/62/0,2340,en_2649_201185_2345918_1_1_1_1,00.html.

16. E. S. Savas, *Privatization: The Key to Better Government* (Chatham, NJ: Chatham House, 1987).

17. See, for example, Paul E. Peterson, *The Price of Federalism* (Washington, DC: Brookings Institution, 1995).

18. U.S. Senate, Committee on Homeland Security and Governmental Affairs, *Hurricane Katrina: A Nation Still Unprepared* (2006), 2.

CHAPTER 3   The Legal System

1. For the full story, see Stuart Banner, *How the Indians Lost Their Land: Law and Power on the Frontier* (Cambridge, MA: Harvard University Press, 2005).

2. There is a huge literature on the law of slavery; see, for example, Thomas D. Morris, *Southern Slavery and the Law, 1619–1860* (Chapel Hill: University of North Carolina Press, 1996).

3. For the story, see in general Lawrence M. Friedman, *Private Lives: Families, Individuals, and the Law* (Cambridge, MA: Harvard University Press, 2004).

4. On the history of the system, see Lawrence M. Friedman, *Crime and Punishment in American History* (New York: Basic Books, 1993).

5. The fullest treatment of this case is Don E. Fehrenbacher, *The Dred Scott Case: Its Significance in American Law and Politics* (New York: Oxford University Press, 1978).

6. Drunk driving laws have gotten tougher; but here the emphasis is on its danger to other people. Restrictions on smoking, too, are rooted in health considerations.

7. On the rise of no-fault, see Herbert Jacob, *Silent Revolution: The Transformation of Divorce Law in the United States* (Chicago: University of Chicago Press, 1988).

8. Lawrence M. Friedman, *Total Justice* (New York: Russell Sage Foundation, 1985).

9. The studies are John P. Heinz and Edward O. Laumann, *Chicago Lawyers: The Social Structure of the Bar* (Evanston, IL: Northwestern University Press,

1982); John P. Heinz et al., *Urban Lawyers: The New Social Structure of the Bar* (Chicago: University of Chicago Press, 2005).

10. Marc Galanter, "Planet of the AP's: Reflections on the Scale of Law and Its Users," *Buffalo Law Review* 53 (2006), 1369, 1383–1384.

11. Robert A. Kagan, *Adversarial Legalism: The American Way of Law* (Cambridge, MA: Harvard University Press, 2001).

12. See the discussion in Marc Galanter, *Lowering the Bar: Lawyer Jokes and Legal Culture* (Madison: University of Wisconsin Press, 2005), especially chapter 11.

13. See John Fabian Witt, *The Accidental Republic: Crippled Workingmen, Destitute Widows, and the Remaking of American Law* (Cambridge, MA: Harvard University Press, 2004).

14. On this, see Peter H. Schuck, *Agent Orange on Trial: Mass Toxic Disasters in the Courts* (Cambridge, MA: Harvard University Press, 1986).

15. See Alex Stone Sweet, *The Judicial Construction of Europe* (Oxford: Oxford University Press, 2004) on the use of the European Court of Justice by litigants and pressure groups.

16. See Arthur J. Sabin, *In Calmer Times: The Supreme Court and Red Monday* (Philadelphia: University of Pennsylvania Press, 1999).

CHAPTER 4   The Economic System

1. See chapter 14 in this volume.

2. Data on population and employment, from the Census Bureau, are for 2006.

3. Data on capital stocks and employment (in both cases for the non-farm business sector), valued at reproduction cost, are from the Bureau of Economic Analysis and the Bureau of Labor Statistics, respectively. Government, including the federal, state, and local levels, also employs 22 million people (not counting uniformed military personnel) and holds $8 trillion of assets; but calculating the effective capital/labor ratio for government is less straightforward, both because of the nature of what government does and because of the nature of government assets.

4. Data on employment (here including part-time employees) and output (actually, here represented by income) by industry, from the Commerce Department's National Income and Product Accounts, are for 2005. In these data agriculture also includes forestry, fishing, and hunting; transportation also includes warehousing; finance also includes insurance, real estate, rental, and leasing; and education and health care also includes social services. Especially in agriculture and construction, the numbers at work would be somewhat larger if the self-employed were included.

5. One may question, of course, whether the output produced by any given industry is "worth" the market price attached to it, and therefore whether productivity differentials based on output measured at market prices correspond

to genuine differences in how productive different workers are. The point is especially relevant here in that, because both education and health care are mostly produced in the non-profit sector, the "market" price is simply the cost of providing the services.

6. Data on firms by number of employees, from the Census Bureau, are for 2003. Data on firms' sales are for 2002.

7. See chapter 18 in this volume.

8. Cross-country comparisons of per capita income, from data published by the World Bank, are for 2005 (see *World Development Report 2007,* Table 1).

9. 2005 is the most recent year for which data on other countries' total output is available both on a purchasing-power basis and at market exchange rates.

10. The United Kingdom and China are sufficiently close in this respect to be easily within the range of uncertainty in measuring the usual national income and product data.

11. Data shown in Table 4.2 are for 2005 unless otherwise specified. Data on population age structure are from the World Bank.

12. Data on labor force participation are from the OECD.

13. Data on unemployment are from the OECD. The difference between the United States and the other G–7 countries in this regard has narrowed somewhat in recent years, as France and Italy in particular have reduced their unemployment rates. On average over the previous decade (1995–2004), unemployment in the United States was 5.1 percent of the labor force versus 7.8 percent on average across the other six countries.

14. Data on hours worked and productivity are from the Groningen website (www.ggdc.net).

15. Some part of this difference, however, may reflect the greater tendency of people elsewhere to work in the "underground"—that is, not officially recorded—economy. One recent set of estimates (for 2002–2003) found the size of the underground economy to be 8.4 percent of official GDP in the United States, versus percentages ranging from 12.2 in the United Kingdom to 25.7 in Italy, among the other G–7 countries; see Friedrich Schneider and Christopher Bajada, "An International Comparison of Underground Economic Activity," in Christopher Bajada and Friedrich Schneider, eds., *Size, Causes and Consequences of the Underground Economy* (Aldershot, UK: Ashgate, 2005), 73–106. Such activity is, by definition, difficult to measure. Other estimates for the United States range from 3.2 percent to 24.9 percent, with comparably large ranges for other countries as well; see Frank Schneider and Dominik H. Enste, *The Shadow Economy: An International Survey* (Cambridge: Cambridge University Press, 2002).

16. The data on output per hour worked shown in the last column of Table 4.2 are from the Groningen website. The values given, for 2005, are in 2006 dollars (EKS basis for comparability across countries).

17. Data on educational attainment, from the World Bank, are for 2000.

18. Data on U.S. graduation and enrollment rates are from the National Center for Education Statistics. The inclusion of resident non-Americans is one reason the 90 percent completion rate is as low as it is. In recent years an increasing number of students have also been entering college at older ages, and so the total percentage that receives at least some higher education at some point is well above two-thirds.

19. American education, however, is also highly heterogeneous—the primary responsibility lies with more than fourteen thousand local school boards—as is the American population, and so the results of that education are far from uniformly positive. Specifically, the lower part of the distribution probably produces more young adults who cannot effectively read or write or perform standard mathematical operations, and whose knowledge of science or history or even general information is clearly deficient, than is the case in most other advanced economies. On average, therefore, American students typically lag behind not just those from other G–7 countries but many others besides. An OECD study comparing thirty-one countries, for example, ranked the United States fifteenth in reading, nineteenth in mathematics, and fourteenth in science.

20. The labor quality index used here incorporates only directly measurable differences, such as years of education. The advantages of America's more general approach to education are omitted, as are the disadvantages of American students' weaker performance in mathematics and reading.

21. The estimates shown in Table 4.3 are from an updated version of Dale W. Jorgenson, "Information Technology and the G7 Economies," *World Economics* 4 (December 2003).

22. See again the very high labor productivity level in France shown in the final column of Table 4.2.

23. The index is reported in the OECD *Jobs Study* (1994), Part 2, Table 6.7. The comparisons are presumably partly ordinal.

24. Data on unionization and collective bargaining coverage, from the OECD, are for 2000.

25. See chapter 17 in this volume.

26. Data on the distribution of tax filers by marginal tax rates, from the IRS, are for 2003.

27. Alexis de Tocqueville, *Democracy in America* (New York: Vintage, 1990), vol. 2, 136, 137, 153.

28. This estimate, for 1995–2004, is from an updated version of Dale W. Jorgenson and Khuong Vu, "Information Technology and the World Growth Resurgence," *Scandinavian Journal of Economics* (December 2005).

29. Data on saving rates, from the OECD, are for 2005 (2004 in the case of Japan). Because conventionally measured saving rates exclude capital gains

(and losses), they usually understate the increase in either personal net worth or the net worth of a nation's economy as a whole. Moreover, this understatement is likely to be larger for the United States than for just about all other countries because Americans not only own more equity investments in business capital but also live in larger (and more valuable) houses—both assets that normally appreciate over time. For purposes of investment in new productive capital, however, what matters is the flow of saving in the conventional sense of income earned but not spent on either private or public consumption. Capital gains on appreciated assets are available for reinvestment on an individual basis but not in the aggregate.

30. Data on banking and securities markets, from the World Bank, are for 2004.

31. Data on family asset ownership are from the Federal Reserve Board, 2004 Survey of Consumer Finances.

32. See "Recent Changes in U.S. Family Finances: Evidence from the 2001 and 2004 Survey of Consumer Finances," *Federal Reserve Bulletin* (March 2006).

33. As of 1998 the top 1 percent of households owned 53.2 percent of the common stock held by all households other than that held via retirement accounts, and 47.7 percent including stock held in retirement accounts; see James M. Poterba, "Stock Market Wealth and Consumption," *Journal of Economic Perspectives* (Spring 2000).

34. Data on ownership of retirement accounts are again from the 2004 Survey of Consumer Finances.

35. Data on median income and mean income within each quintile are from the Census Bureau; 2005 is the latest year for which data are currently available.

36. Chapter 17 of this volume presents a detailed analysis of the rise in economic inequality and considers possible policy responses

CHAPTER 5 Federalism

1. By comparison, Australia has six states, Austria nine, Canada ten (called provinces), and Germany sixteen (called *Länder*). Other federal countries toward the high end are Mexico with thirty-one states and Switzerland with twenty-six cantons. See Ann L. Griffiths, ed., *Handbook of Federal Countries, 2002* (McGill-Queen's University Press for the Forum of Federations, 2002). In addition to its many general-purpose governments, the United States contains approximately thirteen thousand school districts and thirty-five thousand special districts that serve various purposes, such as the management of port facilities.

2. Cf. William S. Livingston, "Canada, Australia and the United States: Variations on a Theme," in Valerie Earle, ed., *Federalism: Infinite Variety in Theory and Practice* (F. E. Peacock, 1968), 94–141.

3. Letter, Hamilton to George Clinton, February 13, 1778, in Frederick C. Prescott, ed., *Alexander Hamilton and Thomas Jefferson* (American Book Company, 1934), 13. "Folly, caprice, a want of foresight, comprehension, and dignity

characterize the general tenor of their action," Hamilton wrote. The letter brims with outrage and disgust.

4. On Madison's use of the term "compound," see Number 51 in *The Federalist,* by Alexander Hamilton, James Madison, and John Jay (Modern Library, Robert Scigliano, ed., 2000), 333.

5. On the influence of American constitutionalism abroad, see Bernard Bailyn, *To Begin the World Anew* (Alfred A. Knopf, 2003), chapter 5.

6. Number 39 in *The Federalist*, 245.

7. Dual federalism is explored at length in Edward S. Corwin, *The Twilight of the Supreme Court* (Yale University Press, 1934).

8. 247 U.S. 251 (1918), in Alpheus T. Mason and William M. Beaney, eds., *American Constitutional Law* (Prentice-Hall, 1959), 280.

9. Woodrow Wilson, *The State,* rev. ed. (D. C. Heath, 1898), 501, 506.

10. *Facts and Figures on Government Finance, 1988–1989 Edition* (Johns Hopkins University Press for the Tax Foundation, 1988), 20.

11. Ibid., 32.

12. Stewart E. McClure: Chief Clerk, the Senate Committee on Labor, Education, and Public Welfare (1949–1973), Oral History Interviews, Senate Historical Office, Washington, D.C. The interview is available at http://www.senate.gov/artandhistory/history/oral_history/Oral_History_McClure.htm. The quotation is from interview no. 4, January 28, 1983, 110–111. See Gareth Davies, *See Government Grow: Education Politics from Johnson to Reagan* (University Press of Kansas, 2007), 11.

13. 74 U.S. 700 (1869).

14. Henry M. Hart, Jr., "The Relations between State and Federal Law," in Arthur W. Macmahon, ed., *Federalism: Mature and Emergent* (Doubleday, 1955), 194.

15. 312 U. S. 100 (1941).

16. Martha Derthick, "Roosevelt as Madison: Social Security and American Federalism," in *Keeping the Compound Republic* (Brookings Institution Press, 2001), 123–137.

17. I. L. Kandel, *Federal Aid for Vocational Education,* Carnegie Foundation for the Advancement of Teaching, Bulletin no. 10 (New York, 1917), 3–19.

18. The following discussion draws on G. Edward White, "Warren Court," in Leonard W. Levy, Kenneth L. Karst, and Dennis J. Mahoney, eds., *American Constitutional History: Selections from the Encyclopedia of the American Constitution* (Collier Macmillan, 1986 and 1989), 279–293.

19. Archibald Cox, *The Role of the Supreme Court in American Government* (Oxford University Press, 1976), 77.

20. Peter W. Low and John C. Jeffries, Jr., *Civil Rights Actions: Section 1983 and Related Statutes* 2nd ed., (Foundation Press, 1994), 721–722.

21. Ross Sandler and David Schoenbrod, *Democracy by Decree* (Yale University Press, 2003), 4.

22. For an extensive analysis of partial preemption and other federal regulatory techniques vis-à-vis the states, see Advisory Commission on Intergovernmental Relations, *Regulatory Federalism: Policy, Process, Impact and Reform* (Washington, DC, 1984), 70–92.

23. Cf. R. Shep Melnick, *Congress and the Supreme Court in a Partisan Era*, Policy Brief 5, Foundation for Law, Justice, and Society (University of Oxford, 2007). Available at www.fljs.org.

24. For a summary of the law, reactions to it, and problems in implementation, see Frederick M. Hess and Michael J. Petrilli, *No Child Left Behind: Primer* (Peter Lang, 2006).

25. Sheryl Gay Stolberg, "Testing Presidential Waters as Race at Home Heats Up," *New York Times,* March 26, 2006, section 1, 26, http://web.lexis-nexis. com/universe/document?_m=fc2bacfdeb30a8, accessed April 12, 2006.

26. Historically, schools in the United States have been financed mainly with local revenues, which were supplemented with state funds that had only moderately equalizing effects. Resource-poor districts typically spent less per pupil than rich districts, with differences that were often extreme. Beginning in the 1970s, school finance came under attack in both federal and state courts. In *San Antonio Independent School District v. Rodriguez* (1973), the U.S. Supreme Court declined to intervene. State supreme courts then became the principal site of action. Their decisions have contributed to a rapid growth in state spending for schools and to a substantial narrowing of the gap in interdistrict spending.

27. Barry C. Rabe, *Statehouse and Greenhouse: The Emerging Politics of American Climate Change Policy* (Brookings Institution Press, 2004).

28. Miriam Jordan, "States and Towns Attempt to Draw the Line on Illegal Immigration," *Wall Street Journal,* July 12, 2006, A1; Peter Whoriskey, "States, Counties Begin to Enforce Immigration Law," *Washington Post,* September 27, 2006, A1.

29. Karen Tumulty, "Where the Real Action Is . . .," *Time,* January 30, 2006, 50–53.

30. David Vogel, *Trading Up: Consumer and Environmental Regulation in a Global Economy* (Harvard University Press, 1995), 259.

CHAPTER 6   Political Culture

1. Rogers Smith, *Civic Ideals: Conflicting Visions of Citizenship in U.S. History* (New Haven, CT: Yale University Press), 1997.

2. See as a sample, Arthur Schlesinger, Jr., *The Disuniting of America: Reflections on a Multicultural Society* (New York: W. W. Norton), 1998; Todd Gitlin, *The Twilight of Common Dreams* (New York: Metropolitan Books, 1995); Gertrude Himmelfarb, *One Nation, Two Cultures* (New York: Vintage Books, 2001); James Davison Hunter, *Culture Wars: The Struggle to Define America* (New York: Basic Books, 1991).

3. Alan Wolfe, *One Nation after All* (New York: Penguin Books, 1999), and Morris Fiorina with Samuel Abrams and Jeremy Pope, *Culture War? The Myth of a Polarized America,* 2nd ed. (New York: Pearson Longman, 2006).

4. James Davison Hunter and Alan Wolfe, *Is There a Culture War? A Dialogue on Values and American Public Life* (Washington, DC: Brookings Institution, 2006).

5. Samuel Huntington, *American Politics: The Promise of Disharmony* (Cambridge, MA: Harvard University Press, 1983), 262.

6. T. Alexander Aleinikoff, "A Multicultural Nationalism?" *American Prospect* 36 (1998), 80–87.

7. David Fischer, *Albion's Seed: Four British Folkways in America* (New York: Oxford University Press, 1989), and Samuel Huntington, *Who Are We? Challenges to American National Identity* (Cambridge, MA: Harvard University Press, 2004).

8. James Thomas, "New Survey Paints Vivid Portrait of U.S. Latinos," US-INFO, December 8, 2006.

9. Jack Citrin, "The End of American Identity," in Stanley Renshon, ed., *One America?* (Washington, DC: Georgetown University Press, 2001), 285–307.

10. Morris Fiorina, Paul Peterson, Bertram Johnson, and D. Stephen Voss, *The New American Democracy,* 4th ed. (New York: Pearson Longman, 2005), 103.

11. Everett Ladd, *The American Ideology* (Storrs, CT: Roper Center for Public Opinion Research, 1994).

12. Harold Wilensky, *Rich Democracies* (Berkeley: University of California Press, 2002); Lane Kenworthy and Jonas Pontusson, "Rising Inequality and the Politics of Redistribution in Affluent Countries," *Perspectives on Politics* 3 (2005), 449–473.

13. Sidney Verba and Gary Orren, *Equality in America: The View from the Top* (Cambridge, MA: Harvard University Press, 1985).

14. Alberto Alesina and Edward Glaeser, *Fighting Poverty in the U.S. and Europe* (New York: Oxford University Press, 2004).

15. Paul M. Sniderman and Edward Carmines, *Reaching Beyond Race* (Cambridge, MA: Harvard University Press, 1998).

16. Peter Schuck, *Diversity in America* (Cambridge, MA: Harvard University Press, 2003), 170.

17. Seymour Martin Lipset and Gary Marks, *It Didn't Happen Here: Why Socialism Failed in the United States* (New York: Norton, 2000).

18. See James Q. Wilson and John Diulio, *American Government,* 10th ed. (Boston: Houghton Mifflin, 2006), 82–86, for a summary of these poll data and related arguments.

19. James Davison Hunter, "The Enduring Culture War," in Hunter and Wolfe, *Is There a Culture War?*, 25.

20. Wayne Baker, *America's Crisis of Values: Reality and Perception* (Princeton, NJ: Princeton University Press, 2005), 183–186.

21. Geoffrey Layman, Thomas Carsey, and Juliana Horowitz, "Party Polarization in American Politics: Characteristics, Causes, and Consequences," in Nelson W. Polsby, ed., *Annual Review of Political Science* 9 (2006), 67–81.

22. Martin Wattenberg, *Is Voting for Young People?* (New York: Pearson/Longman, 2007).

23. Marc Howard, "American Civic Engagement in Comparative Perspective," *Democracy and Society* 3, no. 2 (2006), 17–20.

CHAPTER 7   The Media

1. Thomas Jefferson, "Letter to John Norvell," 1807, in Andrew Lipscomb and Albert Bergh, eds., *The Writings of Thomas Jefferson,* vol. 11 (Washington, DC: Thomas Jefferson Memorial Association, 1907), 225.

2. Eric Burns, *Infamous Scribblers* (New York: PublicAffairs, 2006), 238.

3. Quoted in Michael Schudson, *Discovering the News* (New York: Basic Books, 1978), 111.

4. Harlan Stensaas, *The Rise of Objectivity in US Daily Newspapers* (Ph.D. dissertation, University of Southern Mississippi, 1986); cf. Donald Shaw, "News Bias and the Telegraph," *Journalism Quarterly* 44 (Spring 1967), 3–12.

5. Leo Rosten, *The Washington Correspondents* (New York: Harcourt Brace, 1937).

6. William Rivers, "The Correspondents after 25 Years," *Columbia Journalism Review* (Spring 1962), 5.

7. Rosten, *Washington Correspondents*, 191.

8. Rivers, "Correspondents after 25 Years," 5.

9. John Mueller, *War, Presidents, and Public Opinion* (New York: John Wiley and Sons, 1973).

10. Eric Larson, *Casualties and Consensus* (Santa Monica, CA: RAND, 1996).

11. Peter Braestrup, *Big Story* (New Haven, CT: Yale University Press, 1977); S. R. Lichter, "The Media and National Defense," in Robert Pfalzgraff and Uri Ra'anam, eds., *National Security Policy* (Hamden, CT: Archon, 1984).

12. Stephen Hess, *The Washington Reporters* (Washington, DC: Brookings Institution, 1981; S. Robert. Lichter, Linda Lichter, and Stanley Rothman, *The Media Elite* (New York: Hastings House, 1990), chapters 1–2.

13. David Halberstam, *The Powers That Be* (New York: Knopf, 1979); David Halberstam, "Starting Out to Be a Famous Reporter," *Esquire*, November 1981, 74; Henry Fairlie, "How Journalists Get Rich," *Washingtonian,* August 1983, 81–86; Joseph Kraft, "The Imperial Media," *Commentary,* May 1981, 39–42; John Johnstone, Edward J. Slawski, and William W. Bowman, *The Newspeople* (Urbana: University of Illinois Press, 1976); Dom Bonafede, "The Washington Press—Competing for Power with the Federal Government," *National Journal,* April 17, 1982.

14. Quoted in Christopher Arterton, "Campaign Organizations Confront the Media Political Environment," in James David Barber, ed., *Race for the Presidency* (Englewood Cliffs, NJ: Prentice-Hall, 1978), 6.

15. Kiku Adatto, "Sound Bite Democracy," research paper, Kennedy School Center of Press/Politics, Harvard University, 1990; Stephen Farnsworth and S. Robert Lichter, *The Nightly News Nightmare* (Lanham, MD: Rowman and Littlefield, 2007), 82–83.

16. Stephen Farnsworth and S. Robert Lichter, *The Mediated Presidency* (Lanham, MD: Rowman and Littlefield, 2006).

17. Joel Schwartz, David Murray, and S. Robert Lichter, *It Ain't Necessarily So* (New York: Penguin, 2002).

18. Cynthia Crossen, *Tainted Truth* (New York: Simon and Schuster, 1994), 19; William Tucker, *Progress and Privilege* (New York: Anchor Books, 1982); Gregg Easterbrook, *A Moment on the Earth* (New York: Viking, 1995); Raymond Bonner, "Crying Wolf over Elephants," *New York Times Magazine*, February 7, 1993.

19. Seymour Martin Lipset and William Schneider, *The Confidence Gap* (New York: Free Press, 1983), 403, 158–159.

20. Richard Noyes and S. Robert Lichter, *Good Intentions Make Bad News* (Lanham, MD: Rowman and Littlefield, 1995), chapter 4.

21. Data on TV news coverage from "The Media at the Millennium: The Networks' Top Topics, Trends and Joke Targets of the 1990s." *Media Monitor* 14, no. 4 (July/August 2000); data on homicide rates from FBI Uniform Crime Reports.

22. Doris Graber, *Processing Politics* (Chicago: University of Chicago Press, 2001); Doris Graber, *Crime News and the Public* (New York: Praeger, 1980); S. Robert Lichter, *Assessing Local Television News Coverage of Health Issues* (Washington, DC: Center for Media and Public Affairs, 1997).

23. Donald Kinder and Shanto Iyengar, *News That Matters* (Chicago: University of Chicago Press, 1989); Shanto Iyengar, *Is Anyone Responsible?* (Chicago: University of Chicago Press, 1994).

24. Benjamin Page, Robert Shapiro, and Glenn Dempsey, "What Moves Public Opinion?" *American Political Science Review* 81 (1987), 23–45.

25. Doris Graber, *Mass Media and American Politics* (Washington, DC: Congressional Quarterly Press, 2002), 174.

26. David Gergen, "Can We Trust the Media?" in Austin Ranney, ed., *The American Elections of 1984* (Washington, DC: American Enterprise Institute, 1985).

27. Quoted in Harry Stein, "How '60 Minutes' Makes News," *New York Times Magazine,* May 6, 1979, 76.

28. William Scheider and I. A. Lewis, "Views on the News," *Public Opinion* August/September 1985, 7; Lichter, Lichter, and Rothman, *Media Elite*, especially 39–43; S. Robert Lichter, "Consistently Liberal—But Does It Matter?" *Forbes Media Critic* Fall 1996, 26–39; on journalists' economic conservatism, see David Croteau, "Examining the 'Liberal Media' Claim," *International Journal of Health Services* 29, no. 3 (1999), 627–655.

29. S. Robert Lichter et al., *Nuclear News* (Washington, DC: Center for Media and Public Affairs, 1986); S. Robert Lichter and Stanley Rothman, "Elites in Conflict: Nuclear Energy, Ideology, and the Perception of Risk," *Journal of Contemporary Studies* (Summer/Fall 1985), 23–44.

30. S. Robert Lichter and S. Rothman, *Environmental Cancer—A Political Disease?* (New Haven, CT:Yale University Press, 1999); S. Robert Lichter and D. Murray, "Organochlorine Residues and Breast Cancer," *New England Journal of Medicine* 338, no. 14 (April 4, 1998) 988–991; S. Robert Lichter and Harrison G. Pope, "The Reporting of AIDS," *Journal of the American Medical Association* (October 13, 1989), 1949–1950; Mark Snyderman and Stanley Rothman, *The IQ Controversy* (New Brunswick, NJ:Transaction, 1990).

31. Farnsworth and Lichter, *Mediated Presidency*; D. Graber, "Kind Words and Harsh Pictures," in K. Lehmann-Schlozman, ed., *Elections in America* (Boston: Allen and Unwin, 1987); Marion Just, Ann Crigler, Timothy Cook, and Montague Kern, *Crosstalk* (Chicago: University of Chicago Press, 1996); Michael Robinson and Margaret Sheehan, *Over the Wire and on TV* (New York: Russell Sage Foundation, 1983); Maura Clancey and Michael Robinson, "General Election Coverage," in Michael Robinson and Austin Ranney, eds. *The Mass Media in Campaign '84* (Washington, DC: American Enterprise Institute Press, 1985).

32. In his book *Bias in the News* (Columbus: Ohio State University Press, 1976), Richard Hofstetter reported that Richard Nixon received more favorable media coverage than George McGovern in 1972. However, his analysis grouped statements about the candidates' viability (horse race news) with statements about their desirability for the office. Nixon led the race from start to finish, giving him a considerable advantage in favorable coverage as defined here. Robinson and Sheehan cited this problem as the rationale for separating these two dimensions in *Over the Wire and on TV.* Their work became the dominant model for scholarly content analysis of election news.

33. S. Robert Lichter, "Campaign 2004—Election Final: How TV News Covered the General Election Campaign," *Media Monitor* 18, no. 6 (November/December 2004), 1–6; S. Robert Lichter and Stephen J. Farnsworth, "Television Coverage of the 2004 Presidential Election," *Presidential Studies Quarterly* (in press).

34. S. Robert Lichter, *Government in and out of the News* (Washington, DC: Council for Excellence in Government, 2003).

35. Tim Groseclose and Jeff Milyo, "A Measure of Media Bias," *Quarterly Journal of Economics* 120 (2006), 1191–1237.

36. Rob Puglisi, "Take Control of the Political Agenda in 1992," *RTNDA Communicator* 45 (1991), 12.

37. Times Mirror Center for the People and the Press, "The Press and Campaign '92: A Self-Assessment," news release, December 20, 1992.

38. Times Mirror Center for the People and the Press, "The Press and Campaign: Part II," news release, November 15, 1992.

39. Project for Excellence in Journalism, "The State of the News Media 2005," www.stateofthenewsmedia.org/2005.

40. Farnsworth and Lichter, *Nightly News Nightmare,* chapter 6.

41. Jody Baumgartner and Jonathon Morris, "The 'Daily Show' Effect," *American Politics Research* 34 (2006), 341–367; Pew Research Center, "News Audiences Increasingly Politicized," survey report, May 2004. However, it appears that many young people are adding comedy shows to their news consumption rather than using them to replace traditional news shows. See Dannagal Young and Russell Tisinger, "Dispelling Late-Night Myths," *Harvard International Journal of News/Politics* 11 (2006), 113–134.

42. Simeon Djankov et al., "Who Owns the Media?" Harvard Institute of Economics, Research Paper 1919, April 19, 2001.

43. A "host" is an Internet service provider's direct connection to the Internet. The number of hosts indicates the level of Internet connectivity.

44. Paul Starr, *The Creation of the Media* (New York: Basic Books, 2004).

CHAPTER 8   Popular Culture

1. Lawrence Levine, *Highbrow, Lowbrow: The Emergence of Cultural Hierarchy in America* (Cambridge, MA: Harvard University Press, 1988), 2.

2. Alexis de Tocqueville, *Democracy in America,* trans. George Lawrence (New York: First Perennial Classics, 2000), vol. 2, part 1, chapter 9, 454–455.

3. John A. Kouwenhoven, *The Arts in Modern American Civilization* (New York: Norton, 1967), 15.

4. Ibid., 10, 66.

5. For an excellent recording of Foster songs in a variety of modern styles, hear the CD *Beautiful Dreamer* (Emergent, 2004).

6. Levine, *Highbrow, Lowbrow,* 64, 56, and chapter 1.

7. See John Strausbaugh, *Black Like You: Blackface, Whiteface, Insult and Imitation in American Popular Culture* (New York: Tarcher/Penguin, 2006), 62–63.

8. Eileen Southern, *The Music of Black Americans: A History* (New York: Norton, 1971), 104, 169.

9. Ibid., 269, 266.

10. Ibid., 365.

11. In the context of Louisiana, *Creole* typically refers to a group's linguistic inheritance, not its racial background. So there were both white and black Creoles, all of whom spoke the distinct language (not dialect) known as French Louisiana Creole.

12. S. Frederick Starr, *Red and Hot: The Fate of Jazz in the Soviet Union* (New York: Limelight, 1985), 31, 38–39.

13. Cook was a violinist trained at the Oberlin Conservatory, the Berlin Hochschule für Musik, and (with Antonín Dvořák) at the National Conservatory of Music. He was also the creator (with the poet Paul Laurence Dunbar) of a pioneering all-black musical, *Clorindy; or, The Origin of the Cakewalk*. In 1919 his Southern Syncopated Orchestra gave a command performance for King George V of England.

14. Ernst-Alexandre Ensermet, "Brecht and Jazz Visit Europe, 1919," in Robert Gottlieb, ed., *Reading Jazz: A Gathering of Autobiography, Reportage, and Criticism from 1919 to Now* (New York: Pantheon, 1996), 745–746.

15. "On the Music of the Gross," in Starr, *Red and Hot,* 90–91.

16. To Russell Lynes, a writer for popular magazines, whose famous essay "Highbrow, Lowbrow, and Middlebrow" appeared in *Harper's Magazine* in 1949, there was no question that "the jazz musician" was "a creative lowbrow." See Russell Lynes, *The Tastemakers* (New York: Grosset and Dunlap, 1954), 318.

17. The phrase has been attributed to James Baldwin, but the person most responsible for keeping it in circulation is the pianist Billy Taylor, whose tireless evangelism on behalf of jazz began decades before Wynton Marsalis came along. One could argue, as does jazz composer Bill Kirchner, that "America's classical music is classical music: Ives, Barber, Copland, Harris, Schuman, and so forth. Jazz is jazz—certainly not inferior or less substantial, but different." But that does not lower jazz's prestige. See my essay "What's Wrong with Being Classical?" in *Antioch Review* 57, no. 3 (Summer 1999), 318–326.

18. Dwight MacDonald, *Against the American Grain: Essays on the Effects of Mass Culture* (New York: Da Capo, 1983), 14.

19. For an extraordinary film capturing the ebullient and eclectic spirit of that year's festival, see Bert Stern, *Jazz on a Summer's Day* (Galaxy Productions, 1959).

20. For a fuller discussion of this vexed topic, see my essay "The Strange Career of Folk Music," in *Michigan Quarterly Review* (Spring 2005), 304–317.

21. Mike Gold, quoted in Judith Tick, *Ruth Crawford Seeger: A Composer's Search for American Music* (New York: Oxford University Press, 1997), 195. Hill, the legendary songwriter for the Industrial Workers of the World, added protest lyrics to hymns ("Nearer My God to Thee" became "Nearer My Job to Thee"), sentimental ballads ("Down by the Old Mill Stream" became "Down in the Old Dark Mills"), and Broadway hits ("Everybody's Doing It" became "Everybody's Joining It"). One of Dylan's early antiwar anthems, "With God on Our Side," takes its melody from the Irish protest ballad "The Patriot Game." And at Woodstock, when Country Joe sang his anti–Vietnam War song, "I-Feel-Like-I'm-Fixin'-to-Die," few fans realized that the tune came from Kid Ory's 1926 hit, "Muskrat Ramble."

22. This story is nicely fictionalized in the film *Songcatcher* (ErgoArts, 2000).

23. Personal communication, spring 1999.

24. Gene Bluestein, *Poplore: Folk and Pop in American Culture* (Boston: University of Massachusetts, 1994), 8–9.

25. Albert F. McLean, *American Vaudeville as Ritual* (Louisville: University of Kentucky Press, 1965), 19. For a fascinating look at vaudeville, see the hypertext Web site at the University of Virginia's program in American Studies: http://xroads.virginia.edu/~MA02/easton/vaudeville/vaudevillemain.html.

26. See Kathryn J. Oberdeck, *The Evangelist and the Impresario: Religion, Entertainment, and Cultural Politics in America, 1884–1914* (Baltimore: Johns Hopkins University Press, 1999), 87.

27. Quoted in Charles W. Stein, ed., *American Vaudeville as Seen by Its Contemporaries* (New York: Knopf, 1984), 17, 24.

28. Tocqueville, *Democracy in America,* 493.

29. Lawrence E. Mintz, "Humor and Ethnic Stereotypes in Vaudeville and Burlesque," *Melus* 21, no. 4 (Winter 1996), 20.

30. The classic portrait of the stock figures of both minstrelsy and Yankee humor can be found in Constance Rourke, *American Humor: A Study of the National Character* (New York: Harcourt, 1931).

31. Quoted in John Lowe, "Theories of Ethnic Humor: How to Enter, Laughing," *American Quarterly* 38, no. 3 (1986), 445.

32. Mintz, "Humor and Ethnic Stereotypes," 26.

33. Edward Rothstein, "At the Edge of Respectability, a Celebration," *New York Times* (November 19, 2005), 19.

34. See MPA Web site: www.mpaa.org/AboutUs.asp.

35. See Erik Barnouw, *A History of Broadcasting in the United States* (New York: Oxford University Press, 1966), and Asa Briggs, *The History of Broadcasting in the United Kingdom* (London: Oxford University Press, 1961).

36. Of course, it is also true that the number of radio stations tripled during that period and continued to rise during the 1960s and 1970s, as FM stereo technology became the transmission system of choice, and radio in general returned to the music-based programming of its pioneering years.

37. *Support for Tougher Indecency Measures, but Worries About Government Intrusiveness,* Pew Research Center for the People and the Press (April 19, 2005), 2.

38. Ibid., 2.

39. The classic American statement of this argument can be found in Alexander Meiklejohn, *Free Speech and Its Relation to Self-Government* (New York: Harper, 1948). For a more nuanced and up-to-date version, see the writings of Harry M. Clor, most recently *Public Morality and Liberal Society: Essays on Decency, Law, and Pornography* (Notre Dame, IN: University of Notre Dame Press, 1996).

40. This argument is most fully expressed in the many dissenting opinions of U.S. Supreme Court Justices Hugo Black and William O. Douglas.

41. One of the scholars defending 2 Live Crew was Henry Louis Gates, Jr., who argued that African-American culture has always contained a streak of raunchy humor. Why this was accepted as proof of the artistic seriousness of lyrics like "Suck my dick, bitch, till it pukes" is not clear. But the jury took the expert's word for it, and the group was acquitted. See Gates, "2 Live Crew, Decoded," *New York Times* (June 19, 1990), A23.

42. John Schwartz, "Shouting Porn! on a Crowded Net," *Washington Post* (March 30, 1997), C1, C4.

43. James Q. Wilson, "Violence, Pornography, and Social Science," *Public Interest* 22 (Winter 1971), 58, 61.

44. See Bureau of Economic Analysis Web site: www.bea.gov/international/intlserv.htm.

45. Remarks to ShoWest (trade exhibition for companies engaged in film exhibition and distribution) 2005, March 15, 2005, quoted in *Cultural Diplomacy and the National Interest* (Curb Center for Art, Enterprise, and Public Policy at Vanderbilt University), 24.

46. Quoted in Yale Richmond, *Cultural Exchange and the Cold War* (College Park, PA: Penn State University Press, 2003), 206.

47. *Changing Minds, Winning Peace,* Advisory Group to U.S. House of Representatives (2003), 21.

48. See my article "Attacks on Rap Now Come from Within," *Wall Street Journal,* April 28, 2005, D8.

49. Interview with author, April 26, 2005.

50. For a fascinating discussion of these trends, see *Arts and Minds,* the report of a conference held by the National Arts Journalism Program at Columbia University (2003).

51. *Global Unease with Major World Powers* (Washington, DC: The Pew Global Attitudes Project, June 27, 2007), 6. In the report, the phrase "U.S. cultural exports" is used interchangeably with the phrase used in the survey question: "American music, movies and television." It is perhaps indicative of America's low image in the world that Pew does not ask about any other, more prestigious cultural exports.

52. Ibid., 5.

53. Limited in scope but highly suggestive is a 2003 survey of teenagers in twelve countries (Saudi Arabia, Bahrain, South Korea, Mexico, China, Spain, Taiwan, Lebanon, Pakistan, Nigeria, Italy, and Argentina) that found a high correlation coefficient (+.526) between exposure to U.S. media and specific negative attitudes toward Americans. The authors suggest the following expla-

nation: "The depiction of Americans in media content as violent, of American women as sexually immoral and of many Americans engaging in criminal acts has brought many of these 1,313 youthful subjects to hold generally negative attitudes toward people who live in the United States." Melvin and Margaret Defleur, *Learning to Hate Americans: How U.S. Media Shape Negative Attitudes Among Teenagers in Twelve Countries* (Spokane, WA: Marquette Books, 2003), 74.

54. *Global Unease with Major World Powers,* 18.

55. *In the Blink of an Eye: A Perspective on Film Editing,* 2nd ed. (Beverly Hills, CA: Silman-James Press, 2001), 15. Much is best known for his work on *Apocalypse Now, The Godfather, The Unbearable Lightness of Being, The English Patient,* and *The Talented Mr. Ripley.*

56. "*Tantum series iuncturaque pollet, / Tantum de medio sumptis accedit honoris.* / "Such is the power of judgment, of knowing what it means to put the elements together in just the right way; such is the power of making a perfectly wonderful thing out of nothing much." David Ferry, trans., *The Epistles of Horace* (New York: Farrar, Straus and Giroux, 2001), 168–169.

57. Some recent examples of insightful work on global popular culture include: James Watson, ed., *Golden Arches East* (Stanford, CA: Stanford University Press, 1997), a study of McDonald's in South Korea, China, and other East Asian settings; and Victoria De Grazia, *Irresistible Empire* (Cambridge, MA: Harvard University Press, 2005), a history of the growth of consumerism in western Europe.

58. Chandra Mukerji and Michael Schudsen, "Introduction," in Chandra Mukerji and Michael Schudsen, eds., *Rethinking Popular Culture: Contemporary Perspectives in Cultural Studies* (Berkeley: University of California Press, 1991), 5.

59. Readers of a certain age, be advised that "mosh pit" is a term of art for the area in front of the stage where fans aggressively jostle one another and occasionally lift up one of their number to be passed hand-to-hand overhead. No longer in evidence at rock concerts is the activity known to previous humanity as dancing.

CHAPTER 9   The Military

1. All figures are drawn from the International Institute for Strategic Studies, *The Military Balance 2006* (London: Routledge, 2006).

2. For information on the evolution of the volunteer military, see Bernard Rostker, *I Want You! The Evolution of the All Volunteer Force* (Santa Monica, CA: RAND, 2006).

3. Ibid., chapter 1.

4. For a reasonably comprehensive list of U.S. military exercises, see www.globalsecurity.org/military/ops/ex.htm.

5. The Chinese military text "Unrestricted Warfare" is revealing in this vein.

6. Sean Naylor, *Not a Good Day to Die: The Untold Story of Operation Anaconda* (New York: Berkley Books, 2005), is a powerful description of this fight.

7. See Kevin Woods et al., *Iraqi Perspectives Project: A View of Operation Iraqi Freedom from Saddam's Senior Leadership* (Suffolk, VA: US Joint Forces Command, Joint Center for Operational Analyses, 2006).

8. Robert W. Komer, *Bureaucracy Does Its Thing: Institutional Constraints on U.S.-GVN Performance in Vietnam,* R-967-ARPA (Santa Monica, CA: RAND, 1972).

9. I have discussed this at some length in *Supreme Command: Soldiers, Statesmen and Leadership in Wartime* (New York: Free Press, 2002).

10. For a remarkably perceptive look, see Leonard Wong and Stephen Gerras, *CU@ The FOB: How the Forward Operating Base Is Changing the Life of Combat Soldiers* (Carlisle, PA: U.S. Army War College, Strategic Studies Institute, 2006).

11. Department of Defense, "Selected Manpower Statistics, FY 2005," http://siadapp.dior.whs.mil/personnel/M01/fy05/m01fy05.pdf.

12. U.S. Census Bureau, "Educational Attainment in the United States: 2005," www.census.gov/population/www/socdemo/education/cps2005.html.

13. This and other material drawn from the latest DOD data, Department of Defense, Office of the Under Secretary of Defense, Personnel and Readiness, "Population Representation in the Military Services," www.dod.mil/prhome/poprep2004/.

14. See his important book, *The Utility of Force: The Art of War in the Modern World* (New York: Alfred A. Knopf, 2007).

CHAPTER 10   Religion

1. G. K. Chesterton, *What I Saw in America* (London: Hodder and Stoughton, 1922); reprinted in *The Collected Works of G. K. Chesterton,* vol. 21 (San Francisco: Ignatius, 1990), 41–45.

2. *General Social Survey, 2004* (Chicago: National Opinion Research Center, 2004); electronic datafile; my analysis.

3. Office of the Press Secretary, "President Attends 54th Annual National Prayer Breakfast," White House (February 2, 2006), online at www.whitehouse.gov.

4. Oscar Handlin, *The Uprooted: The Epic Story of the Great Migrations That Made the American People* (New York: Grosset and Dunlap, 1951), 117.

5. H. Richard Niebuhr, *The Social Sources of Denominationalism* (New York: World, 1929).

6. Thomas Jefferson to Jacob Delamotta, September 1, 1820; reprinted in James H. Hutson, ed., *The Founders on Religion* (Princeton, NJ: Princeton University Press, 2005), 136–137.

7. Frederick Jackson Turner, *The Frontier in American History* (New York: Dover, 1996 [1893]), 35.

8. Sydney E. Ahlstrom, *A Religious History of the American People* (New Haven, CT: Yale University Press, 1972), xiv.

9. Robert N. Bellah, Richard Madsen, William M. Sullivan, Ann Swidler, and Steven M. Tipton, *Habits of the Heart: Individualism and Commitment in American Life*, 2nd ed. (Berkeley and Los Angeles: University of California Press, 1996), 221, 235.

10. Stanley Fish, "Our Faith in Letting It All Hang Out," *New York Times* (February 12, 2006).

11. Figures cited in this paragraph are from Ihsan Babgy, Paul M. Perl, and Bryan T. Froehle, *The Mosque in America: A National Portrait, A Report from the Mosque Study Project* (Washington, DC: Council on American-Islamic Relations, 2001); Edwin Scott Gaustad and Philip L. Barlow, *New Historical Atlas of Religion in America* (New York: Oxford University Press, 2000), 268–274; *Harvard Pluralism Project Directory,* online at www.pluralism.org.; James W. Coleman, *The New Buddhism: The Western Transformation of an Ancient Tradition* (New York: Oxford University Press, 2001); and Don Morreale, ed., *The Complete Guide to Buddhist America* (Boston: Shambala, 1998).

12. More information about this survey is presented in my book *America and the Challenges of Religious Diversity* (Princeton, NJ: Princeton University Press, 2005).

13. Robert Wuthnow, *Sharing the Journey: Support Groups and America's New Quest for Community* (New York: Free Press, 1994), 320.

14. John K. Fairbank, "Introduction: The Many Faces of Protestant Missions in China and the United States," in John K. Fairbank, ed., *The Missionary Enterprise in China and America* (Cambridge, MA: Harvard University Press, 1974), 8.

15. Dotsey Welliver and Minnette Northcutt, *Mission Handbook: U.S. and Canadian Protestant Ministries Overseas 2004–2006* (Wheaton, IL: Billy Graham Center, 2004).

16. This information is from annual reports and IRS 990 forms for the organizations mentioned.

17. Esther Kaplan, *With God on Their Side: How Christian Fundamentalists Trampled Science, Policy and Democracy in George W. Bush's White House* (New York: New Press, 2005), 1–2.

18. John C. Green, "The American Religious Landscape and Political Attitudes: A Baseline for 2004," Pew Research Center Report (2004); online at http://people-press.org.

CHAPTER 11   The Family

1. Arland Thornton and Thomas E. Fricke, "Social Change and the Family: Comparative Perspectives from the West, China and South Asia," in J. Mayone Stycos, ed., *Demography as an Interdiscipline* (New Brunswick, NJ: Transaction, 1989), 128–161, especially p. 130.

2. J. Lupton and James P. Smith, "Marriage, Assets, and Savings," in S. Gross-bard-Shechtman, ed., *Marriage and the Economy: Theory and Evidence from Advanced Industrial Societies* (Cambridge: Cambridge University Press, 2003).

3. John Mirowsky and Catherine E. Ross, *Social Causes of Psychological Distress* (New York: Aldine de Gruyter, 1989); Linda Waite and Maggie Gallagher, *The Case for Marriage* (New York, Doubleday, 2000).

4. L. Friedberg, "Did Unilateral Divorce Raise Divorce Rates? Evidence from Panel Data," *American Economic Review* 88 (1998), 608–627.

5. Matthew D. Bramlett and William Mosher, "Cohabitation, Marriage, Divorce and Remarriage in the United States" (Hyattsville, MD: National Center for Health Statistics, 2002).

6. Linda J. Waite and Lee A. Lillard, "Children and Marital Disruption," *American Journal of Sociology* 96 (1991), 930–953.

7. Teresa Castro Martin and Larry L. Bumpass, "Recent Trends in Marital Disruption," *Demography* 32 (1989), 509–520.

8. Bramlett and Mosher, "Cohabitation, Marriage, Divorce and Remarriage."

9. Kathleen Kiernan, "European Perspectives on Union Formation," in L. Waite, C. Bachrach, M. Hindin, E. Thomson, and A. Thornton, eds., *Ties That Bind: Perspectives on Marriage and Cohabitation* (New York: Aldine de Gruyter, 2000), 40–58.

10. J. Fields and L. M. Casper, "America's Families and Living Arrangements: March 2000," in *Current Population Reports* #P20–537, (Washington, DC: U.S. Census Bureau, 2003), especially Table A1.

11. U.S. Bureau of Labor Statistics and U.S. Bureau of the Census, 2006, "Annual Demographic Survey: March Supplement." Table HINC–05 (http://pubdb3.census.gov/macro/032006/hhinc/new05_000.htm).

12. T. W. Smith, "Attitudes Toward Sexual Permissiveness: Trends, Correlates, and Behavioral Connections," in A. S. Rossi, ed., *Sexuality Across the Life Course* (Chicago: University of Chicago Press, 1994), 63–97.

13. Edward O. Laumann, John H. Gagnon, Robert T. Michael, and Stuart Michaels, *The Social Organization of Sexuality* (Chicago: University of Chicago Press, 1994).

14. Dan Black, Gary Gates, Seth Sanders, and Lowell Taylor, "Demographics of the Gay and Lesbian Population in the United States: Evidence from Available Systematic Data Sources," *Demography* 37 (2000), 139–154.

15. Patrick Heuveline and Jeffrey Timberlake, "The Role of Cohabitation in Family Formation: The United States in Comparative Perspective," *Journal of Marriage and Family* 66 (2004), 1214–1230, especially Table 4, p. 1226.

16. Larry Bumpass and Hsien-Hen Lu, "Trends in Cohabitation and Implications for Children's Family Contexts in the United States," *Population Studies*

54, no. 1 (2000), 29–41. Similar patterns appear for cohabiting relationships in Canada. For example, see Zheng Wu and T. R. Balakrishnan, "Dissolution of Premarital Cohabitation in Canada," *Demography* 32 (1995), 521–532.

17. Kiernan, "European Perspectives on Union Formation," 40–58.

18. U.S. Bureau of the Census, "Population Profile of the United States, Dynamic Version," (2006) www.census.gov/population/pop-profile/dynamic/ LivArrChildren.pdf.

19. Rosanna Hertz, *Single by Chance, Mothers by Choice: How Women Are Choosing Parenthood Without Marriage and Creating the New American Family* (Oxford: Oxford University Press, 2006).

20. Kristin Anderson Moore, Susan M. Jekielek, and Carol Emig, "Marriage from a Child's Perspective: How Does Family Structure Affect Children and What Can We Do about It?" *ChildTrends Research Brief* (2002).

21. Sara McLanahan and Gary D. Sandefur, *Growing Up with a Single Parent: What Hurts, What Helps* (Cambridge, MA: Harvard University Press, 1994); Sandra L. Hofferth and Kermyt G. Anderson, "Are All Dads Equal? Biology Versus Marriage as a Basis for Paternal Investment," *Journal of Marriage and Family* 65 (2003), 213–232.

22. Bumpass and Lu, "Trends in Cohabitation," 29–41.

23. Ibid.

24. Patrick Heuveline, Jeffrey Timberlake, and Frank F. Furstenberg, Jr., "Shifting Childbearing to Single Mothers: Results from 17 Western Countries," *Population and Development Review* 29, no. 1 (2003), 47–71, especially p. 58.

25. William G. Axinn and Arland Thornton, "The Relationship Between Cohabitation and Divorce: Selectivity or Causal Influence?" *Demography* 29 (1992), 357–374.

26. Neil G. Bennett, Ann K. Blanc, and David E. Bloom, "Commitment and the Modern Union: Assessing the Link Between Premarital Cohabitation and Subsequent Marital Stability," *American Sociological Review* 53 (1988), 127–138.

27. The twenty-two countries are Australia, Austria, Belgium, Canada, Denmark, Finland, France, West Germany, Greece, Ireland, Italy, Japan, Luxembourg, Netherlands, New Zealand, Norway, Portugal, Spain, Sweden, Switzerland, the United Kingdom, and the United States. See Ronald R. Rindfuss, Karen B. Guzzo, and S. Philip Morgan, "The Changing Institutional Context of Low Fertility," *Population Research and Policy Review* 22 (2003), 411–438, especially pp. 411, 435.

28. Chris Wilson, "Fertility Below Replacement Level," *Science* 304 (2004), 207–208.

29. Amélie Quesnel-Vallée and S. Philip Morgan, "Missing the Target? Cor-

respondence of Fertility Intentions and Behavior in the U.S.," *Population Research and Policy Review* 22 (2003), 497–525, especially p. 516.

30. Peter McDonald, "Low Fertility and the State: The Efficacy of Policy," *Population and Development Review* 32, no. 3 (2006), 485–510.

31. Kellie J. Hagewen and S. Philip Morgan, "Intended and Ideal Family Size in the United States, 1970–2002," *Population and Development Review* 31, no. 3 (2005), 507–527, especially p. 513.

32. See also John Bongaarts, "The End of Fertility Transition in the Developed World," *Population and Development Review* 28, no. 3 (2002), 419–443.

33. Quesnel-Vallée and Morgan, "Missing the Target? Correspondence of Fertility Intentions," 497–525.

34. Table 1, U.S. Centers for Disease Control and Preventions (CDC), "Births: Final Data for 2004," *National Vital Statistics Reports* 55 (September 29, 2006).

35. U.S. Census Bureau, *Census 2000 Brief—The Foreign-Born Population: 2000* (Washington, DC: U.S. Census Bureau, 2003), www.census.gov/population /www/socdemo/foreign/reports.html.

36. William D. Mosher, Linda B. Williams, and David P. Johnson, "Religion and Fertility in the United States: New Patterns," *Demography* 29, no. 2 (1992), 199–214.

37. Ibid., especially Table 4, p. 209.

38. Mosher, Williams, and Johnson, "Religion and Fertility in the United States," 199–214, especially p. 207.

39. Rindfuss, Guzzo, and Morgan, "The Changing Institutional Context," 411–438, especially p. 416.

40. Heuveline, Timberlake, and Furstenberg, Jr., "Shifting Childbearing to Single Mothers," 47–71, especially p. 56.

41. Bumpass and Lu, "Trends in Cohabitation," 29–41; Heuveline, Timberlake, and Furstenberg, Jr., "Shifting Childbearing to Single Mothers," 47–71.

42. The countries (with the corresponding percentage of children born to a single mother) are Belgium (1.5 percent), Italy (2.2 percent), Switzerland (3.0 percent), Spain (3.1 percent), Finland (3.1 percent), France (4.3 percent), Hungary (4.4 percent), Czech Republic (5.4 percent), Sweden (5.5 percent), Slovenia (6.8 percent), Canada (8.3 percent), Latvia (8.8 percent), Poland (9.7 percent), New Zealand (12.6 percent), Austria (13.6 percent), Germany (15.2 percent), and the United States (16.2 percent). Heuveline, Timberlake, and Furstenberg, Jr., "Shifting Childbearing to Single Mothers," 47–71, especially Table 1, p. 56.

43. Hertz, *Single by Chance*.

44. Quesnel-Vallée and Morgan, "Missing the Target? Correspondence of Fertility Intentions," 497–525, especially p. 501.

45. Hertz, *Single by Chance*.

46. Ibid.

47. Black, Gates, Sanders, and Taylor, "Demographics of the Gay and Lesbian Population," 139–154.

48. Linda J. Waite, "Does Marriage Matter?" *Demography* 32, no. 4 (1995), 483–508.

49. The Population Division of the Department of Economic and Social Affairs, United Nations Population Division. 2000. "Replacement Migration: Is It a Solution to Declining an Ageing Population?" www.un.org/esa/population/publications/migration/migration.htm.

50. Rindfuss, Guzzo, and Morgan, "The Changing Institutional Context," 411–438, especially p. 416.

51. McDonald, "Low Fertility and the State," 485–510; Rindfuss, Guzzo, and Morgan, "The Changing Institutional Context," 411–438.

CHAPTER 12   Immigration

1. Rogers M. Smith, *Civic Ideals: Conflicting Visions of Citizenship in U.S. History* (New Haven, CT: Yale University Press, 1997).

2. Gerald L. Neuman, "The Lost Century of Immigration Law (1776–1875)," *Columbia Law Review* 93 (1993), 1833 ff.

3. Thomas Archdeacon, *Becoming American: An Ethnic History* (New York: Free Press, 1983), 168.

4. This paragraph and the one that follows draw on Peter H. Schuck, *Citizens, Strangers, and In-Betweens: Essays on Immigration and Citizenship* (Boulder, CO: Westview, 1998), 9–10. Supporting references are cited there.

5. Peter H. Schuck, "The Disconnect Between Public Attitudes and Policy Outcomes in Immigration," in Carol Swain, ed., *Debating Immigration: 21st Century Perspectives* (Cambridge: Cambridge University Press, 2007), 17–31.

6. The remainder of this section draws upon Schuck, *Citizens, Strangers, and In-Betweens,* 142–145.

7. See Robert Rector, "Senate Immigration Bill Would Allow 100 Million New Legal Immigrants over the Next Twenty Years," Web Memo #1076, Heritage Foundation, May 15, 2006.

8. The 2006 data in this section are drawn from Kelly Jefferys, "U.S. Legal Permanent Residents: 2006," Annual Flow Report, U.S. Department of Homeland Security, March 2007.

9. Meredith Kolodner, "Private Prisons Expect a Boom," *New York Times,* July 19, 2006, C1.

10. See generally, Peter H. Schuck and Rogers M. Smith, *Citizenship Without Consent: Illegal Aliens in the American Polity* (New Haven, CT: Yale University Press, 1985).

11. James P. Smith and Barry Edmonston, eds., *The New Americans: Economic, Demographic, and Fiscal Effects of Immigration* (Washington, DC: National Academy

of Science, 1997). For a discussion of the NAS and other studies on labor market and fiscal effects, see Michael J. Trebilcock and Matthew Sudak, "The Political Economy of Emigration and Immigration," *New York University Law Review* 81 (2006), 234, 269–276.

12. "Information on Criminal Aliens Incarcerated in Federal and State Prisons and Local Jails," GAO–05–337R, April 7, 2005; "Information on Certain Illegal Aliens Arrested in the United States," GAO–05–646R, May 9, 2005.

13. Peter H. Schuck and John Williams, "Removing Criminal Aliens: The Pitfalls and Promises of Federalism," *Harvard Journal of Law and Public Policy* 22 (2000), 367, 376–382.

14. See Ruben G. Rumbaut, Roberto G. Gonzales, Golnaz Komaie, and Charlie V. Morgan, "Debunking the Myth of Immigrant Criminality: Imprisonment Among First- and Second-Generation Young Men," http://contact. migrationpolicy.org/site/R?i=vhS06zFz8ttwehKjdrEprA. Indeed, immigration may be a major cause of the declining homicide rates since 1990. Robert J. Sampson, "Open Doors Don't Invite Criminals," *New York Times,* March 13, 2006, A15.

15. Email from Prof. Kristin Butcher, Dept. of Economics, Boston College, to author, March 6, 2006.

16. For two comparisons of the Borjas and Card approaches, see Christopher Jencks, "Who Should Get In?" *New York Review of Books,* November 29, 2001; and Roger Lowenstein, "The Immigration Equation," *New York Times Magazine,* July 9, 2006.

17. Ron Haskins, "Economic Mobility of Immigrants in the United States," Economic Mobility Project of the Pew Charitable Trusts, July 2007, 5–6.

18. Ibid., citing studies by Lerman and by Mark Rosenzweig.

19. Julia Preston, "Immigration Lawyers to Sue Over Change in Visa Policy," *New York Times,* July 6, 2007, A9.

20. See, for example, Peter H. Schuck, *Diversity in America: Keeping Government at a Safe Distance* (Cambridge, MA: Harvard University Press, 2003), chapter 4 and references there cited.

21. This paragraph draws on Schuck, *Diversity in America,* 110, and references there cited. For extensive discussion of bilingual education, see pp. 109–123 and references there cited.

22. See ibid., p. 208, and references there cited.

23. Roger Waldinger and Renee Reichl, "Second-Generation Mexicans: Getting Ahead or Falling Behind," www.migrationinformation.org/Feature/print.cfm?ID=382. See also George Borjas, "Making It in America: Social Mobility in the Immigrant Population," NBER Working Paper No. 12088 (2006) (predicting less mobility for Mexicans than for earlier groups).

24. See, for example, Michael Jones-Correa, *Between Two Nations: The Political Predicament of Latinos in New York City* (Ithaca, NY: Cornell University

Press, 1998); Mary C. Waters, *Black Identities: West Indian Immigrant Dreams and American Realities* (Cambridge, MA: Harvard University Press, 2001).

25. For a discussion of the multiculturalism issue in the United States, see Schuck, *Diversity in America,* 99–106.

26. The U.S. Commission on Immigration Reform recommended such a program in its final report, *Becoming an American: Immigration and Immigrant Policy* (Washington, DC: Government Printing Office, 1997), 26–58.

27. "Muslim Americans: Middle Class and Mostly Mainstream," Pew Research Center, May 22, 2007, http://pewresearch.org/pubs/483/muslim-americans.

28. Peter Skerry, "American Muslims Never Had to Unite—Until Now," *Washington Post,* January 5, 2003.

29. "Muslim Americans," Pew Research Center.

CHAPTER 13   Black Americans

1. U.S. Census Bureau News, "Texas Becomes Nation's Newest Majority-Minority State," August 11, 2005.

2. For more on this, see Orlando Patterson, *Rituals of Blood: Consequences of Slavery in Two American Centuries* (New York: Basic Books, 1989), chapter 1.

3. Patterson, *Rituals of Blood,* chapter 2.

4. Steven Hahn, *A Nation Under Our Feet: Black Political Struggles in the Rural South from Slavery to the Great Migration* (Cambridge, MA: Harvard University Press, 2003).

5. Jay Greene, "High School Graduation Rates in the United States," Manhattan Institute, Civic Report, November 2001.

6. U.S. Census Bureau, *Income Poverty and Health Insurance Coverage in the U.S.* (Washington, DC: U.S. Census Bureau, 2006).

7. Julia Isaacs, "Economic Mobility of Black and White Families," (Washington, DC: Brookings Institution and the Economic Mobility Project of the Pew Charitable Trusts, November 13, 2007.) Available at http://www.economicmobility.org.

8. Rakesh Kochhor, *The Wealth of Hispanic Households, 1996–2007* (Washington, DC: Pew Hispanic Center, 2004).

9. Melvin Oliver and Thomas Shapiro, *Black Wealth, White Wealth* (New York: Routledge, 1997), 5.

10. Ibid., 5.

11. Mikael Atterhog, "The Importance of Government Policies for Home Ownership Rates: An International Survey and Analysis" (Stockholm: Department of Real Estate and Construction Management, Working Paper no. 54, 2005), 13.

12. Debbie G. Bocian, Keith S. Ernst, and Wei Li, "Unfair Lending: The Effect of Race and Ethnicity on the Price of Sub-prime Mortgages," (Durham, NC: Center for Responsible Lending, 2006).

13. Center for Responsible Lending, "Subprime Lending: A Net Drain on Homeownership," CRL Issue Paper No. 14, March 27, 2007. Available at www.responsiblelending.org/pdfs/Net-Drain-in-Home-Ownership.pdf.

14. Mary Pattillo-McCoy, *Black Picket Fences: Privilege and Peril Among the Black Middle Class* (Chicago: University of Chicago Press, 1999).

15. Isaacs, "Economic Mobility of Black and White Families."

16. Tom Hertz, "Rags, Riches and Race: The Intergenerational Economic Mobility of Black and White Families in the United States," in Samuel Bowles, Herbert Gintis, and Melissa Groves, eds. *Unequal Chances: Family Background and Economic Success.* (Princeton: Princeton University Press and the Russell Sage Foundation, 2005.)

17. William Frey and Dowell Myers, "Racial Segregation in U.S. Metropolitan Areas and Cities, 1990–2000: Patterns, Trends, and Explanations" (Population Studies Center, University of Michigan, Report 05–573, April 2005), 18.

18. Ibid., 22.

19. William Easterly, "Empirics of Strategic Interdependence: The Case of the Racial Tipping Point," DRI Working Paper # 4, New York University, October 2005.

20. Bruce Western, *Punishment and Inequality in America* (New York: Russell Sage Foundation, 2006); U.S. Bureau of Justice Statistics, "Prison and Jail Inmates at Midyear," 2005, Table 13, U.S. Dept. of Justice, 2006.

21. U.S. Bureau of Justice Statistics, "Prison & Jail Inmates at Midyear," 2005, Table 13, U.S. Dept. of Justice, 2006.

22. Western, *Punishment and Inequality in America.*

23. Michael Tolnay, *Malign Neglect: Race, Crime and Punishment in America* (New York: OUO, 1995), 79.

24. Matthew Mamlett and William Mosher, "First Marriage Dissolution, Divorce and Remarriage: United States" (CDC: Advance Data, No. 323, May, 2001).

25. Patterson, *Rituals of Blood,* chapter 1.

26. For a recent review of this literature, see Robert Wagmiller, Jr., et al., "Economic Disadvantage and Children's Life Chances," *American Sociological Review* 71, no. 5 (2006), 847–849.

27. Sarah McClanahan and Gary Sandefur, *Growing Up with a Single Parent* (Cambridge, MA: Harvard University Press, 2006).

28. See James P. Smith and Barry Edmonston, *The New Americans* (Washington, DC: National Academy Press, 1997; Daniel Mammermesh and Frank D. Bean, eds. *Help or Hindrance? The Economic Implications of Immigration for African Americans* (New York: Russell Sage Foundation, 1998).

29. Roger Waldinger, *Still the Promised City? New Immigrants and African Americans in Post-Industrial New York* (Cambridge, MA: Harvard University Press, 1996).

30. Nelson Lim, "On the Backs of Blacks? Immigrants and the Fortunes of

African Americans," in Roger Waldinger, ed. *Strangers at the Gates: New Immigrants in Urban America* (Berkeley: University of California Press, 2001): 186–227.

31. Andrew Sum, Paul Harrington, and Ishwar Khatiwada, "The Impact of New Immigrants on Young Native-Born Workers, 2000–2005," Center for Immigration Studies, Backgrounder, September 2006.

32. Marsha Lillie-Blanton and Caya B. Lewis, "Policy Challenges and Opportunities in Closing the Racial/Ethic Divide in Health Care," Kaiser Family Foundation, 2005.

33. Gary Orfield and Chungmei Lee, "Racial Transformation and the Changing Nature of Segregation," The Civil Rights Project, Harvard University.

34. James Coleman, *Equality of Educational Opportunity* (Washington, DC: Government Printing Office, 1966; Christopher Jencks and Meredith Phillips, eds., *The Black-White Test Score Gap* (Washington, DC: Brookings Institution, 1998); David Card and Alan B. Krueger, 1996, "Labor Market Effects of School Quality: Theory and Evidence," NBER Working Papers 5450 National Bureau of Economic Research, Inc., http://ideas.repec.org/p/nbr/nberwo/5450.html.

35. John Skrentny, *The Ironies of Affirmative Action* (Chicago: University of Chicago Press, 1996).

36. Vincent Hutchings and Nichollas Valentino, "The Centrality of Race in American Politics," *Annual Review of Political Science* 7 (2004), 383–406; Nichollas A. Valentino, "Old Times There Are Not Forgotten: Race and Partisan Realignment in the Contemporary South," *American Journal of Political Science* 49 (2005), 672–678.

37. See William G. Bowen and Derek Bok, *The Shape of the River: Long Term Consequences of Considering Race in College and University Admissions* (Princeton, NJ: Princeton University Press, 1998); Alexandra Kalev, Frank Dobbin, and Erin Kelly, "Best Practices or Best Guesses: Diversity Management and the Remediation of Inequality," *American Sociological Review,* forthcoming.

38. Alexandra Kalev, Frank Dobbin, and Erin Kelly, "Best Practices or Best Guesses: Assessing the Efficacy of Corporate Affirmative Action and Diversity Policies," *American Sociological Review* 71 (2006), 589–917.

39. H. O. Duleep and S. Sanders, "Discrimination at the Top: American-Born Asian and White Men," *Industrial Relations* 31, no. 3 (1992), 416–432.

40. David Demo and Keith Parker, "Academic Achievement and Self-Esteem Among Black and White College Students," *Journal of Social Psychology* 127 (1987), 345–355.

CHAPTER 14   Education

1. Member Nations of the Organization for Economic Co-operation and Development, "Education at a Glance," 2006.

2. Alexis de Tocqueville, *Democracy in America,* vol. 1 (New York: Random House, 1945), 95.

3. Peter H. Schuck and Richard J. Zeckhauser, *Targeting in Social Programs: Avoiding Bad Bets, Removing Bad Apples* (Washington, DC: Brookings Institution, 2006).

4. *Tinker v. Des Moines Independent Community School* (1969).

5. Abigail Thernstrom, "Where Did All the Order Go? School Discipline and the Law," in Diane Ravitch, ed., *Brookings Papers on Education Policy* (Washington, DC: Brookings Institution, 1999), 299–326.

6. This topic is explored in Marty R. West and Paul E. Peterson, eds., *The School Money Trials* (Washington, DC: Brookings Institution, 2007).

7. William G. Howell and Paul E. Peterson, with Patrick Wolf and David E. Campbell, *The Education Gap* (Washington, DC: Brookings Institution, 2002).

CHAPTER 15   Health Care

1. Michael S. Kramer, et. al., "Registration Artifacts in International Comparisons of Infant Mortality," *Paediatric and Perinatal Epidemiology* 16, no. 1 (2002),16–22.

2. Robert S. Pritchard et al., "Influence of Patient Preferences and Local Health System Characteristics on the Place of Death. SUPPORT Investigators. Study to Understand Prognoses and Preferences for Risks and Outcomes of Treatment," *Journal of the American Geriatrics Society* 46, no. 10 (1998), 1242–1250.

3. About 40 percent of children who are uninsured are eligible for Medicaid, and additional children are eligible for coverage under the Children's Health Insurance Program (CHIP).

4. Institute of Medicine, *Care Without Coverage: Too Little, Too Late* (Washington DC: National Academy Press, 2002).

5. Lawrence Summers, "Some Simple Economics of Mandated Benefits," *American Economic Review* 79, no. 2 (May 1989), 177–183; Jonathan Gruber, "The Incidence of Mandated Maternity Benefits," *American Economic Review* 84, no. 3 (June 1994), 622–641.

6. Michael Chernew, David M. Cutler, and Patricia S. Keenan, "Increasing Health Insurance Costs and the Decline in Insurance Coverage," *Health Services Research* 40, no. 4 (2005), 1021–1039.

7. David M. Cutler, "Equality, Efficiency, and Market Fundamentals: The Dynamics of International Medical Care Reform," *Journal of Economic Literature* 40, no. 3 (September 2002), 881–906.

8. "Partial capitation" can occur in several ways. Some physicians are capitated for care used in the primary setting, medications, and non-emergency hospitalizations but not for emergency hospitalizations. Others are capitated for all costs but have reinsurance for very expensive patients. Still others have varying degrees of capitation depending on total spending in the practice as a whole.

9. For a summary, see David M. Cutler and Richard Zeckhauser, "The Anatomy of Health Insurance," in Anthony Culyer and Joseph P. Newhouse, eds., *Handbook of Health Economics,* vol. IA (Amsterdam: Elsevier, 2000), 563–643.

10. Sherry Glied, "Managed Care," in Culyer and Newhouse, *Handbook of Health Economics,* 707–753; Thomas McGuire, "Physician Agency," in Culyer and Newhouse, *Handbook of Health Economics,* 461–536.

11. Robert H. Miller and Harold S. Luft, "HMO Plan Performance Update: An Analysis of the Literature, 1997–2001," *Health Affairs* 21, no. 4 (July/August 2002), 63–86.

12. David M. Cutler, *Your Money or Your Life: Strong Medicine for America's Health Care System* (New York: Oxford University Press, 2004).

13. David M. Cutler, "Equality, Efficiency, and Market Fundamentals: The Dynamics of International Medical Care Reform," *Journal of Economic Literature* 40, no. 3 (September 2002), 881–906.

14. David M. Cutler, Mark McClellan, and Joseph P. Newhouse, "How Does Managed Care Do It?" *Rand Journal of Economics* 31, no. 3 (Autumn 2000), 526–548.

15. Ernst R. Berndt, Richard G. Frank, and Thomas G. McGuire, "Alternative Insurance Arrangements and the Treatment of Depression: What Are the Facts?" *American Journal of Managed Care* 3, no. 2 (1997), 243–250.

16. Robert H. Miller and Harold S. Luft, "HMO Plan Performance Update: An Analysis of the Literature, 1997–2001," *Health Affairs* 21, no. 4 (July/August 2002), 63–86.

17. Robert J. Blendon et al., "Common Concerns amid Diverse Systems: Health Care Experiences in Five Countries," *Health Affairs* 22, no. 3 (May/June 2003), 106–121.

CHAPTER 16   Criminal Justice

1. James Q. Wilson, "Crime and Punishment in England," *Public Interest,* no. 43 (Spring 1976), 3–25; James Q. Wilson, "Criminal Justice in England and America," *Public Interest,* no. 126 (Winter 1997), 3–14.

2. Joshua Rosenberg, *The Search for Justice* (London: Hodder and Stoughton, 1994), 275–291.

3. David P. Farrington, Patrick A. Langan, and Michael Tonry, eds., *Cross-National Studies in Crime and Justice* (Washington, DC: Bureau of Justice Statistics, 2004), iii–xiii, 1–74; Michael Tonry and David P. Farrington, eds., *Crime and Punishment in Western Countries, 1980–1999* (Chicago: University of Chicago Press, 2005).

4. Rosenberg, *Search for Justice,* 324–325.

5. Steven D. Levitt, "Why Do Increased Arrest Rates Appear to Reduce Crime: Deterrence, Incapacitation, or Measurement Error?" *Economic Inquiry*

36 (1998), 353–372; Steven D. Levitt, "The Effect of Prison Population Size on Crime Rates: Evidence from Prison Overcrowding Litigation," *Quarterly Journal of Economics* 111 (1996), 319–352; Daniel S. Nagin, "Criminal Deterrence Research," in Michael Tonry, ed., *Crime and Justice: An Annual Review of Research* (Chicago: University of Chicago Press, 1998); and Daniel S. Nagin, "Deterrence and Incapacitation," in Michael Tonry, ed., *The Oxford Handbook of Crime and Punishment* (New York: Oxford University Press, 1998).

6. William Spelman, *Criminal Incapacitation* (New York: Plenum, 1994); Thomas B. Marvell and Carlisle E. Moody, Jr., "Prison Population Growth and Crime Reduction," *Journal of Quantitative Criminology* 10 (1994), 109–140.

7. Thomas B. Marvell and Carlisle E. Moody, Jr., "Age Structure and Crime Rates: The Conflicting Evidence," *Journal of Quantitative Criminology* 7 (1991), 237–273; Steven D. Levitt, "The Limited Role of Changing Age Structure in Explaining Aggregate Crime Rates," *Criminology* 37 (1999), 581–597.

8. P. Mayhew and J. J. M. van Dijk, "Criminal Victimization in Eleven Industrialized Countries," *1996 International Crime Victims Survey* (Netherlands: Ministry of Justice, 1997).

9. Eric H. Monkkonen, *Murder in New York City* (Berkeley: University of California Press, 2001), 170–179.

10. Franklin E. Zimring and Gordon Hawkins, *Crime Is Not the Problem: Lethal Violence in America* (New York: Oxford University Press, 1997), 109–116.

11. For example, Steven F. Messner, Lawrence E. Raffalovich, and Peter Schrok, "Reassessing the Cross-National Relationship between Income Inequality and Homicide Rates," *Journal of Quantitative Criminology* 18 (2002), 377–395; Steven F. Messner and Richard Rosenfeld, "Political Restraint and Levels of Criminal Homicide," *Social Forces* 75 (1997), 1393–1416; Morgan Kelly, "Inequality and Crime," *Review of Economics and Statistics* 82 (2000), 530–539.

12. Steven D. Levitt, "The Changing Relationship Between Income and Crime Victimization," *Federal Reserve Bank of New York Policy Review,* September 1999, 87–98.

13. Steven F. Messner and Richard Rosenfeld, *Crime and the American Dream* (Belmont, CA: Wadsworth/Thomson, 2001), 25–26.

14. Alfred Blumstein and Richard Rosenfeld, "Explaining Recent Trends in U.S. Homicide Rates," *Journal of Criminal Law and Criminology* 88 (1998), 1175–1216.

15. Alfred Blumstein, Jacqueline Cohen, and Daniel Nagin, eds., *Deterrence and Incapacitation: Estimating the Effects of Criminal Sanctions on Crime Rates* (Washington, DC: National Academy of Sciences, 1978).

16. Jan Chaiken and Marcia Chaiken, *Varieties of Criminal Behavior* (Santa Monica, CA: RAND, 1982); John DiIulio and Anne Piehl, "Does Prison Pay?" *Brookings Review* (Fall 1991), 28–35.

17. The older studies of the death penalty as a deterrent were reviewed and rejected in Blumstein, Cohen, and Nagin, *Deterrence and Incapacitation*. Newer studies that claim to find a deterrent effect include Joanna M. Shepherd, "Murders of Passion, Execution Delays, and the Deterrence of Capital Punishment," *Journal of Legal Studies* 33 (2004):, 283–321; H. Naci Mocan and R. Kaj Gittings, "Getting off Death Row: Commuted Sentences and the Deterrent Effect of Capital Punishment," *Journal of Law and Economics* 46 (2003),453–478; Harold J. Brumm and Dale M. Cloninger, "Perceived Risk of Punishment and the Commission of Homicides," *Journal of Economic Behavior and Organization* 31 (1996), 1–11; Hashem Dezhbaksh, Paul H. Rubin, and Joanna M. Shepherd, "Does Capital Punishment Have a Deterrent Effect?" *American Law and Economics Review* 5 (2003), 344–376; Paul R. Zimmerman, "State Executions, Deterrence, and the Incidence of Murder," *Journal of Applied Economics* 7 (2004), 163–193. A critique of these studies is John J. Donohue and Justin M. Wolfers, "Uses and Abuses of Empirical Evidence in the Death Penalty Debate," *Stanford Law Review* 58 (2006), 791–845.

18. Francis T. Cullen, "Rehabilitation and Treatment Programs," in James Q. Wilson and Joan Petersilia, eds., *Crime* (Oakland, CA: Institute for Contemporary Studies, 2002), 253–289.

19. For example: Douglas Lipton, Robert Martinson, and Judith Wilks, *The Effectiveness of Correctional Treatment: A Survey of Evaluation Studies* (New York: Praeger, 1975).

20. Lee Sechrest, Susan O. White, and Elizabeth D. Brown, eds., *The Rehabilitation of Criminal Offenders* (Washington, DC: National Academy of Sciences, 1979).

21. Cullen, "Rehabilitation and Treatment Programs," 282.

22. Peter W. Greenwood, *Changing Lives: Delinquency Prevention as Crime-Control Policy* (Chicago: University of Chicago Press, 2006), 84–116.

23. See Peter H. Schuck and Richard J. Zeckhauser, *Targeting in Social Programs: Avoiding Bad Bets, Removing Bad Apples* (Washington, DC: Brookings Institution, 2006).

24. See Delbert S. Elliott, ed., *Blueprints for Violence Prevention* (Boulder, CO: Center for the Study and Prevention of Violence at the University of Colorado, 1997–1998). A brief survey of these program can be found in Peter W. Greenwood, "Juvenile Crime and Juvenile Justice," in Wilson and Petersilia, *Crime,* 98–103. See also Brandon C. Welsh and David P. Farrington, *Preventing Crime* (Berlin: Springer, 2006) and David P. Farrington and Brandon C. Welsh, *Saving Children from a Life of Crime* (New York: Oxford University Press, 2007).

25. On the national victim survey, see D. McDowall and B. Wiersema, "The Incidence of Defensive Firearm Use by U.S. Crime Victims," *American Journal of Public Health* 84 (1994), 1982–1984; on private surveys, see Gary Kleck, *Targeting Guns* (New York: Aldine de Gruyter, 1997), 147–89.

26. John R. Lott, Jr., *More Guns, Less Crime,* 2nd ed. (Chicago: University of Chicago Press, 2000), and citations therein to other studies that support his findings.

27. D. A. Black and Daniel Nagin, "Do Right to Carry Laws Deter Violent Crime?" *Journal of Legal Studies* 27 (1998), 209–219; I. Ayres and John J. Donohue III, "Shooting Down the 'More Guns, Less Crime' Hypothesis," *Stanford Law Review* 55 (2003), 1193.

28. Charles Wellford, John V. Pepper, and Carol V. Petrie, eds., *Firearms and Violence* (Washington, DC: National Academy of Sciences, 2005).

29. Philip J. Cook, Mark H. Moore, and Anthony A. Braga, "Gun Control," in Wilson and Petersilia, *Crime,* esp. 322–324.

30. Jan M. Chaiken and Marcia R. Chaiken, "Drugs and Predatory Crime," in Michael Tonry and James Q. Wilson, eds., *Drugs and Crime,* vol. 13 in *Crime and Justice: A Review of Research* (Chicago: University of Chicago Press, 1990), 203–239.

31. David Boyum and Peter Reuter, *An Analytic Assessment of U.S. Drug Policy* (Washington, DC: American Enterprise Institute, 2005); Robert J. MacCoun and Peter Reuter, *Drug War Heresies* (New York: Cambridge University Press, 2001).

32. Boyum and Reuter, *An Analytic Assessment,* 18.

33. Angela Hawken and Mark Kleiman, "H.O.P.E for Reform," *American Prospect,* April 20, 2007.

34. M. Harvey Brenner, "Influence of the Social Environment on Psychopathology," *Stress and Mental Disorder,* no. 161 (1979). His arguments were refuted in Philip J. Cook and Gary A. Zarkin, "Homicide and Economic Change: Recent Analyses of the Joint Economic Committee Report of 1984," *Journal of Quantitative Criminology* 2 (March 1986), 81–103. They also offer a broader critique of this research in Philip J. Cook and Gary A. Zarkin, "Crime and the Business Cycle," *Journal of Legal Studies* 14 (January 1985), 115–128.

35. Richard B. Freeman, "The Economics of Crime," in O. Ashenfelter and D. Card, eds., *Handbook of Labor Economics,* vol. 3 (New York: Elsevier, 1999); A. M. Piehl, "Economic Conditions, Work, and Crime," in Michael Tonry, ed., *Handbook of Crime and Punishment* (New York: Oxford University Press, 1998); European Committee on Crime Problems, *Economic Crises and Crime* (Strasbourg, Germany: Council of Europe, 1985).

36. Sara McLanahan and Gary Sandefur, *Growing Up with a Single Parent* (Cambridge, MA: Harvard University Press, 1994), 48–51, 137.

37. Shawn Bushway and Peter Reuter, "Labor Markets and Crime," in Wilson and Petersilia, *Crime,* 191–224, esp. 220.

38. Alfred Blumstein, "Racial Disproportionality of U.S. Prison Populations Revisited," *University of Colorado Law Review* 64 (1993), 743–760.

39. Studies that claim that a black murderer of a white victim is more likely to be sentenced to death than is a black murderer of a black victim include D. Baldus, C. Pulaski, and G. Woodworth, "Comparative Review of Death Sentences: An Empirical Study of the Georgia Experience," *Journal of Criminal Law and Criminology* 74 (1983), 661–753, and Raymond Paternoster and R. Braeme, "An Empirical Analysis of Maryland's Death Sentence System with Respect to the Influence of Race and Legal Jurisdiction," Department of Criminology, University of Maryland (2003). Studies that do not find such racial effects include Richard Berk, Azusa Li, and Laura J. Hickman, "Statistical Difficulties in Determining the Role of Race in Capital Cases," Department of Statistics, UCLA (2005).

40. Rand Corporation, *Promoting Cooperative Strategies to Reduce Racial Profiling,* chapter 9 (April 2004).

CHAPTER 17   Inequality, Economic Mobility, and Social Policy

1. Thomas Piketty and Emmanuel Saez, "Income Inequality in the United States, 1913–1998," *Quarterly Journal of Economics* 118 (February 2003), 1–39. Data updated through 2004 available at http://emlab.berkeley.edu/users/saez/TabFig2004prel.xls (accessed August 17, 2006).

2. The bottom panel ranks individuals according to their market income, so the household at the tenth percentile of the market distribution is not the same as the household at the tenth percentile of the distribution after taxes and transfers.

3. Nicholas Eberstadt, "The Mismeasure of Poverty," American Enterprise Institute, August 10, 2006.

4. Bruce D. Meyer and James X. Sullivan, "The Effects of Welfare and Tax Reform: The Material Well-Being of Single Mothers in the 1980s and 1990s," *Journal of Public Economics* 88 (2004), 1387–1420.

5. Congressional Budget Office, "Federal Spending on the Elderly and Children," July 28, 2000, www.cbo.gov/showdoc.cfm?index=2300&sequence=0 (accessed November 14, 2006).

6. U.S. Census Bureau, "Living Arrangements of Children Under 18 Years Old: 1960 to Present," www.census.gov/population/socdemo/hh-fam/ch1.xls (accessed August 18, 2006).

7. Sara McLanahan, Elisabeth Donahue, and Ron Haskins, "Introducing the Issue," *Future of Children* 15 (Fall 2005), 3–12; Paul R. Amato, "The Impact of Family Formation Change on the Cognitive, Social, and Emotional Well-Being of the Next Generation," *Future of Children* 15 (Fall 2005), 75–96.

8. George Borjas, *Heaven's Door: Immigration Policy and the American Economy* (Princeton, NJ: Princeton University Press, 1999), 28.

9. George J. Borjas and Rachel Friedberg, "The Immigrant Turnaround of the 1990s," Kennedy School Working Paper, Harvard University, August 2006.

10. U.S. Census Bureau, "Foreign Born Population of the United States: Current Population Survey, 2004, Detailed Tables, PPL–176," Table 5.11, www.census.gov/population/socdemo/foreign/ppl–176/tab05–11.xls.

11. Mark Rosenzweig, "Global Wage Differences and International Student Flows," *Brookings Trade Forum* (Washington, DC: Brookings Institution, 2006), Figure 4.

12. For evidence that including the estimated 1979 wages of those who migrated to the United States between 1979 and 1996 reverses the trend in wage inequality, see Robert Lerman, "U.S. Wage-Inequality Trends and Recent Immigration," *American Economic Review* 89 (May 1999), 23–28.

13. U.S. Census Bureau, *Alternative Poverty Estimates in the United States: 2003* (Washington, DC: U.S. Census Bureau, 2005), Table B–1.

14. Timothy Smeeding, "Poor People in Rich Nations: The United States in Comparative Perspective," *Journal of Economic Perspectives* 20 (Winter 2006), 69–90.

15. Isabel Sawhill and Sara McLanahan, "Introducing the Issue," *Future of Children* 16 (Fall 2006), 3–17.

16. Anders Bjorklund and Markus Jantti, "Intergenerational Mobility of Socioeconomic Status in Comparative Perspective," *Nordic Journal of Political Economy* 26 (2000), 3–33.

17. Robert Erikson and John Goldthorpe, "Are American Rates of Social Mobility Exceptionally High?" *European Sociological Review* 1 (May 1985), 1–22.

18. Bhashkar Mazumder, "Fortunate Sons: New Estimates of Intergenerational Mobility in the United States Using Social Security Earnings Data," *Review of Economics and Statistics* 87 (May 2005), 235–255.

19. Markus Jäntti et al., "American Exceptionalism in a New Light: A Comparison of Intergenerational Earnings Mobility in Nordic Countries, the United Kingdom and the United States." IZA Discussion Paper No. 1938 (Bonn, Germany: Institute for the Study of Labor, January 2006).

20. Congressional Research Service, *Cash and Noncash Benefits for Persons with Limited Income: Eligibility, Receipt, and Expenditures Data, FY2002–FY2004,* RL33340 (Washington, DC: Congressional Research Service, March 2006), 5.

21. U.S. House of Representatives, Committee on Ways and Means, *2004 Green Book* (Washington, DC: Government Printing Office, 2004), Section 13.

22. A few of these programs, primarily the Earned Income Tax Credit and the Child Tax Credit, are included in the spending analysis conducted by the Congressional Research Service referred to above.

23. U.S. House of Representatives, Committee on Ways and Means, *2004 Green Book,* Section 13; a table of EITC parameters is found on pp. 13–37.

24. Willem Adema and Maxime Ladaique, "More Comprehensive Measures of Social Support," OECD Social, Employment, and Migration Working

Paper No. 29, Net Social Expenditure, 2005 Edition (Paris: OECD, 2005), Chart 5 and Table 6.

25. Paul Fronstin, "Sources of Health Insurance and Characteristics of the Uninsured: Analysis of the March 2005 Current Population Survey," EBRI Issue Brief No. 287 (Washington, DC: Employee Benefit Research Institute, November 2005), Figures 2, 3, and 15; Craig Copeland, "Employment-Based Retirement Plan Participation: Geographic Differences and Trends, 2004," EBRI Issue Brief No. 286 (Washington, DC: Employee Benefit Research Institute, October 2005), Figure 1.

26. Gary Burtless and Christopher Jencks, "American Inequality and Its Consequences," in Henry J. Aaron, James M. Lindsay, and Pietro Nivola, eds., *Agenda for the Nation* (Washington, DC: Brookings Institution, 2003); Smeeding, "Poor People in Rich Nations."

27. Lars Osberg and Tim Smeeding, "'Fair' Inequality? Attitudes Toward Pay Differentials: The United States in Comparative Perspective," *American Sociological Review* 71 (June 2006), 450–473.

28. On average among the six nations other than the United States, 64 percent of adults strongly agreed that the government should guarantee a minimum standard. Everett C. Ladd and Karlyn H. Bowman, *Attitudes Toward Economic Inequality* (Washington, DC: American Enterprise Institute, 1998), 103–113, 118–123. See also Alberto Alesina and Edward L. Glaeser, *Fighting Poverty in the US and Europe: A World of Difference* (London: Oxford, 2004).

29. Ladd and Bowman, *Attitudes Toward Economic Inequality,* 118–122.

30. Michael B. Katz, *In the Shadow of the Poorhouse: A Social History of Welfare in America,* 2nd ed. (New York: Basic Books, 1996); James T. Patterson, *America's Struggle Against Poverty, 1900–1985* (Cambridge, MA: Harvard University Press, 1986); Walter I. Trattner, *From Poor Law to Welfare State: A History of Social Welfare in America,* 6th ed. (New York: Free Press, 1999); Martin Gillens, *Why Americans Hate Welfare: Race, Media, and the Politics of Antipoverty Policy* (Chicago: University of Chicago Press, 1999).

31. Daniel Patrick Moynihan, *The Politics of a Guaranteed Income: The Nixon Administration and the Family Assistance Plan* (New York: Vintage, 1973).

32. The sweeping 1996 legislation also reformed many other welfare programs including Supplemental Security Income, Child Support Enforcement, food stamps, Medicaid, the EITC, welfare benefits for non-citizens, child care, and others; Ron Haskins, *Work over Welfare: The Inside Story of the 1996 Welfare Reform Law* (Washington, DC: Brookings Institution, 2006).

33. Douglas J. Besharov and Caeli A. Higney, *Federal and State Child Care Expenditures (1997–2003): Rapid Growth Followed by Steady Spending* (Washington, DC: U.S. Department of Health and Human Services, May 2006).

34. Congressional Budget Office, *Policy Changes Affecting Mandatory Spending for Low-Income Families Not Receiving Cash Welfare* (Washington, DC: Congressional Budget Office, September 1998).

35. U.S. Bureau of Labor Statistics, ftp://ftp.bls.gov/pub/suppl/empsit.ceseeb1 .txt. Payroll employment climbed from 108.3 million in 1991 to 131.8 million in 2000. Over 12 million of the new jobs were created between 1996 and 2000.

36. Haskins, *Work over Welfare*, 332–363.

37. Timothy M. Smeeding, "U.S. Income Inequality in a Cross-National Perspective: Why Are We So Different?" in James A. Auerbach and Richard S. Belous, eds., *The Inequality Paradox: Growth of Income Disparity* (Washington, DC: National Policy Association, 1998), 203. Smeeding's calculations refer to absolute incomes received in the early 1990s. Comparisons of average per capita income are based on OECD estimates for 1997.

CHAPTER 18   Philanthropy and the Non-Profit Sector

1. Morris Berman, *The Twilight of American Culture* (New York: Norton, 2001), 33.

2. Tony Hendra, "The Cheney Files," The American Prospect, August 17, 2004, www.prospect.org/web/page.ww?section=root&name=ViewWeb&articleId=8365.

3. Alexis de Tocqueville, *Democracy in America,* ed., J. P. Maier, trans. George Lawrence (Garden City, NY: Anchor Books, 1969).

4. The data from this essay come from the following sources: Independent Sector, *The New Nonprofit Almanac and Desk Reference* (Hoboken, NJ: Jossey-Bass, 2002); U.S. Bureau of the Census, *Statistical Abstract of the United States* (Washington, DC: U.S. Government Printing Office; National Center for Charitable Statistics, www.nccs.urban.org (accessed July 14, 2006); Johns Hopkins Comparative Nonprofit Sector Project (see www.jhu.edu/cnp); *Giving USA 2005* (Giving USA Foundation, Center on Philanthropy at Indiana University, 2005); Center on Philanthropy Panel Study (COPPS), 2003 PSID (2003), in the Panel Study of Income Dynamics (PSID) Wave 32 Computer File, Ann Arbor, MI: ICPSR (http://simba.isr.umich.edu); Independent Sector, *Giving and Volunteering in the United States* (Washington, DC: Independent Sector (2001), www.IndependentSector.org; James Allan Davis, Tom W. Smith, and Peter V. Marsden, *General Social Surveys, 1972–2002: Cumulative CodeBook* (Chicago: National Opinion Research Center, 2002); International Social Survey Program (ISSP), Zentralarchiv für Empirische Sozialforschung, *International Social Survey Programme,* 1998; 2000 SCCBS, *Social Capital Community Benchmark Survey* (SCCBS), www.cfsv.org/communitysurvey/; Robert Wuthnow, *Arts and Religion Survey* [computer file] (Princeton, NJ: Gallup Organization [producer], 1999); U.S. Census, Population Division, International

Programs Center; National Election Studies (2002) [dataset] (Ann Arbor, MI: University of Michigan, Center for Political Studies [producer and distributor], 2002); Campbell Public Affairs Institute, 2004 Maxwell Poll on Civic Engagement and Inequality (Maxpoll), 2004, Maxwell Poll on Civic Engagement and Inequality [Computer File], Syracuse, NY: The Maxwell School at Syracuse University (www.maxwell.syr.edu/campbell/Poll/CitizenshipPoll.htm).

5. Lester M. Salamon, "The Resilient Sector: The State of Nonprofit America," in Lester M. Salamon, ed., *The State of Nonprofit America* (Washington, DC: Brookings Institution, 2002), 3–61.

6. Karen Woods, "Does American Charity Cheat the Tax Man?" *Acton Commentary* (January 18, 2006), Grand Rapids, MI.

7. Mark Dowie, *American Foundations* (Cambridge, MA: MIT Press, 2001).

8. Arthur C. Brooks, "The Effects of Public Policy on Private Charity," *Administration and Society* 36, no. 2 (2004), 166–185.

9. Henry Hansmann, "The Role of Nonprofit Enterprise," *Yale Law Journal* 89, no. 5 (1980), 835–898.

10. Burton A. Weisbrod, *The Voluntary Nonprofit Sector: An Economic Analysis* (Lexington, MA: Lexington Books, 1978).

11. Arthur C. Brooks, "Is There a Dark Side to Government Support for Nonprofits?" *Public Administration Review* 60, no. 3 (2000), 211–218.

12. Michael Rushton and Arthur C. Brooks, "Government Funding of Nonprofit Organizations," in Dennis R. Young, ed., *An Integrated Theory of Nonprofit Finance* (Lanham, MD: Lexington Books, 2006).

13. National Center for Charitable Statistics (NCCS), 2002.

14. Quoted in Waldemar A. Nielsen, *The Big Foundations* (New York: Columbia University Press, 1972), 311.

15. Janet Poppendieck, *Sweet Charity? Emergency Food and the End of Entitlement* (New York: Penguin, 1998), 6.

16. Peter L. Berger and Richard John Neuhaus, *To Empower People: From State to Civil Society* (Washington, DC: AEI Press, 1996 [1977]).

17. Berger and Neuhaus, *To Empower People,* 189.

18. James Q. Wilson, *The Marriage Problem: How Our Culture Has Weakened Families* (New York: HarperCollins, 2002).

19. Arthur C. Brooks, "Welfare Receipt and Private Charity," *Public Budgeting and Finance* 22, no. 3 (2002), 100–113.

20. Franklin D. Roosevelt, "Annual Message to Congress," January 4, 1935, Samuel Rosenman, ed., *The Public Papers and Addresses of Franklin D. Roosevelt,* vol. 4 (New York: Random House, 1938).

21. Mark Wilhelm, Eleanor Brown, Patrick Rooney, and Richard Steinberg, "The Intergenerational Transmission of Generosity" (working paper, Indiana University–Purdue University at Indianapolis, 2004).

22. Patrick Festy, "Looking for European Demography, Desperately?" Population Division, Department of Economic and Social Affairs, United Nations, 2000, www.un.org/esa/population/publications/popdecline/festy.pdf; "The Fertility Bust," *The Economist,* February 9, 2006, 50.

23. In some data, conservatives earn more than liberals, but differences are rarely large in either direction.

24. See also G. Jeffrey MacDonald, "Who Are the Nation's 'Cheapstates'? Try the Blue Ones," *Christian Science Monitor,* December 22, 2004.

25. Karen Paget, "Lessons of Right-Wing Philanthropy," *American Prospect* 9, no. 40 (1998), 89–96; James Piereson, "Investing in Conservative Ideas," *Commentary* 119, no. 5 (2005), 46–53.

26. Peter Collier and David Horowitz, *The Rockefellers, an American Dynasty* (New York: Holt, Rinehart and Winston, 1976), 48.

27. Arthur C. Brooks, *Social Entrepreneurship: A Modern Approach to Social Value Creation* (Upper Saddle River, NJ: Prentice-Hall, forthcoming 2008).

28. Robert D. Putnam, *Bowling Alone: The Collapse and Revival of American Community* (New York: Simon and Schuster, 2000).

29. Thorstein Veblen, "Survivals of the Non-Invidious Interest," in *The Theory of the Leisure Class: An Economic Study of Institutions* (New York: Macmillan, 1899), 334.

30. James Morgan, "Too Good to Be True? Altruism's Better for You," *The Herald* (UK), October 26, 2006.

31. This conclusion is the product of a two-stage least squares regression, in which income is regressed on a vector of demographics and a fitted value of charitable donations. This fitted value comes from a regression of donations on volunteer time plus appropriate demographics.

32. I infer causality through the use of Granger tests.

CHAPTER 19   Drug Policy

1. Manuel Eisner, "Crime, Problem Drinking, and Drug Use: Patterns of Problem Behavior in Cross-National Perspective," *Annals of the American Academy of Political and Social Science* 580, no. 1 (2002), 201–225.

2. See Jonathan P. Caulkins, Susan M. Paddock, Rosalie Liccardo Pacula, and James Chiesa, *School-Based Drug Prevention: What Kind of Drug Use Does It Prevent?* RAND MR–1459-RWJ (Santa Monica, CA: RAND, 2000).

3. B. Taylor and T. Bennett, "The International ADAM Program: Comparing Drug Use Rates Among Arrestees in the United States and England," National Institute of Justice Research Report (Washington, DC: National Institute of Justice, 1999).

4. Eisner, "Crime, Problem Drinking, and Drug Use," *Annals of the American Academy of Political and Social Science* 580, no. 1 (2002), 201–225.

5. Obtaining drug prevalence data that is comparable across nations is difficult, so the ensuing discussion compares the United States primarily with countries covered by the European Monitoring Centre for Drugs and Drug Addiction (EMCDDA) common data collection and reporting frameworks. In particular, we compare rates of use among the general young adult population, among school students, and among problem drug users. U.S. Household Survey data are typically reported for all people age twelve and over, but the EMCDDA custom is to focus on young adults, defined as spanning from the teen years up to age thirty-five. Table 19.1 shows that among this population and for a range of substances, U.S. use rates are all at the upper end of the range of values observed.

6. Comparisons among secondary school students are difficult because different countries survey different ranges of ages. However, if one averages the prevalence reported by the U.S. Monitoring the Future Survey for 8th, 10th, and 12th graders as an approximation to rates for thirteen-to-eighteen-year-olds, the U.S. does not stand out from the European pack. Except for the Netherlands, the higher prevalence rates among EMCDDA countries tend to be among countries that surveyed only older students, and the U.S. data for 8th, 10th, and 12th graders show, not surprisingly, that lifetime prevalence is much higher for seniors than for 8th graders. So there may be some non-comparability in ages covered in Table 19.2. EMCDDA do report some information specifically for fifteen-to-sixteen-year-olds concerning availability and age of first use of cannabis (http://stats05.emcdda.europa.eu/en/elements/eyetab03b-en .html). Comparable data from the U.S. Monitoring the Future data are not readily available, but among U.S. Household Survey respondents aged fifteen to sixteen who are in school, first use of cannabis occurring by age thirteen is much higher (12 percent versus the EMCDDA average of 4 percent), as are rates of having used cannabis many (forty-plus) times. The United Kingdom is the only country with rates close to those in the United States, consistent with the hypothesis that Anglo-American countries generally have high rates of problems associated with the transition from adolescence to adulthood. Also, far more of the fifteen-to-sixteen-year-olds in the United States described cannabis as being "fairly easy" or "very easy" to obtain (71 percent) than did EMCDDA respondents (average of 34 percent).

7. Such comparisons are fraught with inconsistencies in definitions and data collection methods (Kraus et al., 2003), but more careful comparisons of the United States and specific other countries support the general tenor of the comparison. For example, Furr-Holden and Anthony (2003) find that the household surveys identify rates of drug dependence in the United States that are two to three times those of the United Kingdom.

8. See Yih-Ing Hser, Maria Elena Stark, Alfonso Paredes, David Huang, M. Douglas Anglin, and Richard Rawson, "A 12-Year Follow Up of a Treated

Cocaine-Dependent Sample," *Journal of Substance Abuse Treatment* 30 (2006), 219–226; and Yih-Ing Hser, Valerie Hoffman, Christine E. Grella, and M. Douglas Anglin, "A 33-Year Follow-Up of Narcotics Addicts," *Archives of General Psychiatry* 58, no. 5 (2001), 503–508.

9. Philip J. Cook and Nataliya Khmilevska, "Cross-National Patterns in Crime Rates," in Michael Tonry and David P. Farrington, eds., *Crime and Punishment in Western Countries, 1980–1999* (Chicago: University of Chicago Press, 2005), 333.

10. A. Golub and Bruce B. Johnson, "A Recent Decline in Cocaine Use Among Youthful Arrestees in Manhattan, 1987 Through 1993," *American Journal of Public Health* 84, no. 8 (1994), 1250–1254.

11. Jonathan P. Caulkins, Doris A. Behrens, Claudia Knoll, Gernot Tragler, and Doris Zuba, "Modeling Dynamic Trajectories of Initiation and Demand: The Case of the US Cocaine Epidemic," *Health Care Management Science* 7, no. 4 (2004), 319–329.

12. See Alfred Blumstein and Jacqueline Cohen, "A Theory of the Stability of Punishment," *Journal of Criminal Law, Criminology, and Police Science* 63, no. 2 (1973):198–207; Alfred Blumstein and Allen Beck, "Population Growth in U.S. Prisons, 1980–1996," *Crime and Justice* 26 (1999), 17–61; and Jonathan P. Caulkins and Sara Chandler, "Long-Run Trends in Incarceration of Drug Offenders in the US," *Crime and Delinquency* 52, no. 4 (2006), 619–664.

13. See Jonathan P. Caulkins and Eric Sevigny, "How Many People Does the US Incarcerate for Drug Use, and Who Are They? *Contemporary Drug Problems* 32, no. 3 (2005), 405–428; and Eric Sevigny and Jonathan P. Caulkins, "Kingpins or Mules? An Analysis of Drug Offenders Incarcerated in Federal and State Prisons," *Criminology and Public Policy* 3, no. 3 (2004), 401–434.

14. EMCDDA data on treatment admissions from http://stats05.emcdda .europa.eu/en/elements/tditab02b-en.html. U.S. rates calculated using Treatment Episode Data Set (TEDS) data available online at www.icpsr.umich .edu/SAMHDA/das.html.

15. John G. Haaga and Peter Reuter, *The Limits of the Czar's Ukase: Drug Policy at the Local Level*, N–3171 (Santa Monica, CA: RAND, 1990).

CHAPTER 20   A Canvas, Not a Country: How Europe Sees America

1. As quoted in Jean Jules Jusserand, chapter 1, "Rochambeau and the French in America," *With Americans of Past and Present Days* (New York: Charles Scribner's Sons, 1916), online edition Bartleby.com, 2001, www. bartleby.com/238/.

2. "Member of Parliament Edmund Burke's Speech on Conciliation with America," March 22, 1775, www.gutenberg.org/dirs/etext04/burke10.txt.

3. John Winthrop, *A Modell of Christian Charity* (1630), Collections of the Massachusetts Historical Society (Boston, 1838), 3rd series, vol. 7, 47.

4. *The American Enemy: The History of French Anti-Americanism* (Chicago: University of Chicago Press, 2005), 24. The quotes by Talleyrand, Stendhal, and La Rochefoucauld are from pp. 41, 52, and 37.

5. "The Unloved American," *The New Yorker,* March 10, 2003, 34.

6. John Locke, *Second Treatise Concerning Civil Government,* chapter 5, section 49 (New York: The Liberal Arts Press, 1952), 29.

7. These differences between Europe and the United States should not be overdone. Arguably, the United States was ultimately completed by conquest, or a war of national unification, when the Union vanquished the Confederacy in 1865.

8. "Whose rule, his religion."

9. This is the message of Alexis de Tocqueville's *Democracy in America* (New York: Random House, Vintage Books, 1945) and of Louis B. Hartz's *The Liberal Tradition in America* (New York: Harcourt Brace and World, 1955).

10. On a more acute note: why, given the country's sizeable Arab-Islamic community (about 3 million), was the United States spared (so far) the curse of "homegrown" terrorism that has afflicted Europe, including Britain, in the aftermath of 9/11? Or the revolts that have erupted in the outer cities of France? It is not clear that U.S. law enforcement has been more efficient than Europe's. It is clear, though, that economic opportunity is far greater, and the road to citizenship and participation far shorter, than in Europe. A scholarship to an Ivy League school might just be more enticing than a terrorist career, and being different is a lot easier in the "universal nation" than in France, which has a hard time legitimizing identities that are not "French."

It may also be argued that the U.S. attracts a self-selected sample of Arabs and other Muslims, which is better educated and better off to begin with, hence better equipped to succeed and assimilate. This would certainly be true for the half-million Lebanese, the biggest group, who are also largely Christian. This raises the next question: why do the "best and the brightest" go to the U.S. rather than to Europe? And so back to the first answer: because of opportunity and openness.

11. Heinrich Heine; "Ludwig Börne: Eine Denkschrift" (July 1, 1830), *Sämtliche Schriften* (Munich: Hanser, 1976), vol. 4, 39.

12. As quoted in Günter C. Behrmann, "Geschichte und aktuelle Struktur des Anti-Amerikanismus, *Aus Politik und Zeitgeschehen,* July 21, 1984, 5.

13. G. F. W. Hegel, *Vorlesungen über die Philosophie der Geschichte,* in *Werke,* vol. 12 (Frankfurt: Suhrkamp, 1986), 112.

14. Thus the title of an essay in *Commonweal,* republished in Hannah Arendt, *Essays in Understanding, 1930–1945* (New York: Harcourt, Brace, 1993), 409–417.

15. Hannah Arendt, "The Threat of Conformism," in Arendt, *Essays in Understanding,* 437, 426 (first published in *Commonweal,* September 24, 1954).

16. A concept named after Frederick Winslow Taylor (1856–1915), the American inventor and engineer, whose time studies on the shop floor powerfully influenced the management of mass production throughout Europe.

17. "Anti-Americanism" should not be confused with opposition to particular American policies or presidents. It is the hostile stereotyping and denigration of America-as-such—its polity, culture, and morality. Next to denigration comes demonization—the obsessive, unfalsifiable idea that the United States is omnipotent and omnicausal, hence the main author of the world's afflictions.

18. Religion is "very important" to 59 percent of Americans, but only to 27 percent of Italians, 21 percent of Germans, and 11 percent of the French. Even in Poland, normally seen as the most religious country in Europe, only 36 percent opt for "very important." Pew Global Attitudes Project, "Among Wealthy Nations, U.S. Stands Alone in its Embrace of Religion," December 19, 2002, http://pewglobal.org/reports/display.php?ReportID=167.

19. Significantly, American Calvinism soon forsook "predestination" in favor of the quintessential American idea of self-salvation by way of hard work and/or hard prayer.

20. Former British settlements like Australia, New Zealand, and Canada fit the bill, as well. But all of them, Canada with its royalist and French roots in particular, are more "European" than American in their politics and culture.

21. Andrew Kohut and Bruce Strokes, *America Against the World* (New York: Henry Holt, 2006), 158.

22. Franz Müntefering, then chairman of Gerhard Schröder's Social Democratic Party, who would become vice chancellor, targeted "certain financial investors [who] do not care about the people whose jobs they destroy. They remain anonymous, have no face, and fall like locusts over companies. These they graze bare and then move on." As cited in "Die Namen der Heuschrecken," *Stern,* May 3, 2005, www.stern.de/politik/deutschland/539759. html. These were mainly American.

23. As quoted in "Onkel aus dem Westen," *Der Spiegel,* August 28, 2001, 29.

24. As cited in Josef Joffe and Elisabeth Niejahr, "Wie in einem Krämerladen," interview with chancellor candidate Edmund Stoiber, *Die Zeit,* July 25, 2002, 4. This was his response to the question: "So no *amerikanische Verhältnisse?*"

25. As quoted in Claire Trean, "Le réseau français de coopération internationale: 'Un atout face à la mondialisation' selon M. Jospin," *Le Monde,* July 25, 2001, http://acadmae.free.fr/LM/Jospin200107.htm.

26. "Wir schicken Soldaten, um sie einzusetzen," interview with *Die Zeit,* February 28, 2002, 3.

27. "Die Entdeckung Amerikas," April 1, 1997, 170.

28. Lion Feuchtwanger, *Die Geschwister Oppermann* (Berlin: Aufbau Taschenbuch Verlag, 2006, first published in 1933), 20–21.

29. Hubert Védrine (with Dominique Moisi), *Les cartes de la France à l'heure de la mondialisation* (Paris: Fayard, 2000), 29.

30. "Unsere Erneuerung: Nach dem Krieg—Die Wiedergeburt Europas," *Frankfurter Allgemeine Zeitung,* May 31, 2003, 33. Given the opaque, postmodernist style, the author has taken some liberties with the translation.

31. *Considérations sur la France,* chapter 7. Online French editions of University of Manitoba. As cited from http://cage.ugent.be/~dc/Literature/JMCF/JMCF07.html: "On ne saurait réunir plus de symptômes de faiblesse et de caducité." And: "Les établissements particuliers de l'Amérique anglaise ne m'inspirent aucune confiance." Given De Maistre's fondness for absolutism, this swipe probably was directed more against democracy than America.

32. Passed in 2002 in response to high-profile financial scandals, the act imposes rigorous new auditing, disclosure, and record-keeping duties on public companies.

33. Figures taken from www.tns-sofres.com/etudes/pol/030704_etats-unis_r.htm#5. Percentages do not add up to 100, as multiple responses were allowed.

34. World View 2002: European Public Opinion and Foreign Policy, www.worldviews.org/detailreports/europeanreport.pdf, 15.

35. Anti-Americanism: Causes and Characteristics, December 10, 2003, http://pages.zdnet.com/trimb/id214.html. Emphasis added.

36. "France Is Not a Pacifist Country," interview with *Time* (International), February 2, 2003, 31; Jacques Chirac, "French Leader Offers America Both Friendship and Criticism," *New York Times,* September 8, 2002, A9.

37. "Dann lasst uns streiten," interview with *Der Spiegel,* April 4, 2003, 53.

38. "The Last Word: Dominique de Villepin," *Newsweek* (International), December 15, 2003, 66.

39. "La France s'oppose à une nouvelle résolution de l'ONU," interview with *Le Figaro,* February 24, 2003, 3.

40. The Pew Global Attitudes Project, *American Character Gets Mixed Reviews* (Washington, DC: Pew Research Center, 2005), 30. Even America's best allies, the British—58 percent—want American power to be rivaled by another world heavyweight.

41. Harris Interactive / Financial Times, online interviews with about two thousand adults each in Britain, France, Germany, Italy, and Spain, conducted in August 2006. As cited in Angus Reid Global Monitor: Polls and Research: "Europeans See U.S. as Threat to Global Stability," September 5, 2006, www.angus-reid.com/polls/index.cfm/fuseaction/viewItem/itemID/13028.

42. I have listed a host of examples in the chapter on "The Rise of Americanism" in my *Überpower: America's Imperial Temptation* (New York: W. W. Norton, 2006).

43. Védrine, *Les cartes de la France,* 10.

44. Other trendsetters have not been idle. Sushi parlors are crowding in on McDonald's, and Japanese manga cartoons (or anime, the generic Japanese term) represented a $5 billion global market in 2006. But it might be argued that these new fads entered the world via the American portal—just as bagels (German-Jewish-East European) and pizzas (Neapolitan) did in the past.

45. Joseph S. Nye, *Bound to Lead: The Changing Nature of American Power* (New York: Basic Books, 1990), esp. p. 188 ff.

46. Kohut and Strokes, *America Against the World,* 195.

47. Robert Cooper, *The Breaking of Nations: Order and Chaos in the Twenty-First Century* (New York: Atlantic Monthly Press, 2003), 53.

48. See Arthur Brooks's contribution in this book (chapter 18), as well as his *Who Cares: The Surprising Truth About Who Is Charitable, Who Isn't, and Why It Matters for America* (New York: Basic Books, 2006).

49. Rachel Halloran, "Volunteering in the United States: Where We Stand," 2002, http://lmi.ides.state.il.us/lmr/winter_2002/volunteering.htm.

50. Kohut and Strokes, *America Against the World,* 102.

51. Tocqueville, *Democracy in America,* vol. 1, 131.

CHAPTER 21   Looking Back

1. Victoria de Grazia, *Irresistible Empire: America's Advance Through 20th-Century Europe* (Cambridge, MA: Harvard University Press, 2005), 3.

2. Jill Lepore, *A Is for American: Letters and Other Characters in the Newly United States* (New York: Alfred A. Knopf, 2002), 28.

Contributors

Martha Bayles teaches at Boston College and writes about the arts and cultural policy. She is the author of *Hole Our Soul: The Loss of Beauty and Meaning in American Popular Music* and *Ain't It a Shame? Censorship and the Culture of Transgression*. In 2008 her book about the cultural dimension of America's global image will be published by Yale University Press.

Arthur C. Brooks is the Louis A. Bantle Professor of Business and Government at Syracuse University's Maxwell School of Citizenship and Public Affairs. His books include *Who Really Cares: The Surprising Truth About Compassionate Conservatism* and *Social Entrepreneurship*.

Gary Burtless holds the John C. and Nancy D. Whitehead Chair in Economics at the Brookings Institution in Washington, D.C. He is the coauthor, editor, or coeditor of a number of books, including *Growth with Equity: Economic Policymaking for the Next Century*. Before coming to Brookings, he served as an economist in the U.S. Departments of Labor and Health, Education, and Welfare.

Jonathan P. Caulkins is a Professor of Operations Research and Public Policy at Carnegie Mellon University. His monographs about drug use and policy, published by the Rand Corporation, include *Mandatory Minimums; An Ounce of Prevention, a Pound of Uncertainty;* and *School-Based Drug Prevention*.

Jack Citrin is Heller Professor of Political Science and Director of the Institute of Governmental Studies at the University of California, Berkeley. Among his publications are *The Politics of Disaffection among British and American Youth; Tax Revolt: Something for Nothing in California; California and the American Tax Revolt;* and the forthcoming volumes *American Identity and the Politics of Multiculturalism* and *Public Opinion and Constitutional Controversy*.

Eliot Cohen is the Robert E. Osgood Professor of Strategic Studies at Johns Hopkins University's School of Advanced International Studies and founding director of the Philip Merrill Center for Strategic Studies there. He has written widely on defense policy and military history: his most recent book is *Supreme Command: Soldiers, Statesmen, and Leadership in Wartime.*

David Cutler is Otto Eckstein Professor of Applied Economics at Harvard University. He is the author of *Your Money or Your Life,* as well as many professional publications. Cutler worked on the Clinton health plan and has advised several presidential candidates on health policy.

Martha Derthick is the retired Julia Allen Cooper Professor of Government and Foreign Affairs at the University of Virginia. She is the author of *Keeping the Compound Republic: Essays on American Federalism* and the editor of *Dilemmas of Scale in America's Federal Democracy.*

Benjamin M. Friedman is the William Joseph Maier Professor of Political Economy at Harvard University. His most recent book is *The Moral Consequences of Economic Growth.*

Lawrence M. Friedman is the Marion Rice Kirkwood Professor of Law at Stanford Law School. He is the author or editor of more than two dozen books, including *A History of American Law; The Legal System: A Social Science Perspective;* and *Crime and Punishment in American History.* He is a past president of the Law and Society Association and a member of the American Academy of Arts and Sciences.

Ron Haskins is a senior fellow in the Economic Studies Program and co-director of the Center on Children and Families at the Brookings Institution, Washington, D.C., and senior consultant at the Annie E. Casey Foundation. He is the author of *Work over Welfare: The Inside Story of the 1996 Welfare Reform Law* and a senior editor of *The Future of Children.*

Melissa J. K. Howe is a doctoral candidate in sociology and a Resident Fellow at the Center for Gender Studies at the University of Chicago. Her dissertation, "Intergenerational Transmission of Gender Norms in Muslim American Families," focuses on mechanisms of acculturation in Chicago's Muslim immigrant communities.

Josef Joffe wears two hats. He is publisher-editor of *Die Zeit,* the German weekly. In his academic role, he is Senior Fellow of the Institute for International Studies at Stanford, where he also teaches in the political science department. His most recent book is *Überpower: The Imperial Temptation of America,* which has been translated into German and French.

Patricia Keenan is an Assistant Professor of Health Policy at Yale School of Medicine. Her recent articles include "The Graying of Group Health Insurance" and "Biotechnology and Medicare New Technology Policy."

Donald F. Kettl is the Robert A. Fox Leadership Professor in the Social Sciences at the University of Pennsylvania, where he directs the Fels Institute of Government. He has written *System Under Stress: Homeland Security and American Politics* and the forthcoming *The Next Government of the United States.*

Mark A. R. Kleiman is a Professor of Public Policy at UCLA. He has written *Against Excess: Drug Policy for Results* and the forthcoming *When Brute Force Fails: Strategy for Crime Control.*

S. Robert Lichter is a Professor of Communication at George Mason University, where he directs the Center for Media and Public Affairs and the Statistical Assessment Center. His most recent books (coauthored with Stephen Farnsworth) are *The Mediated Presidency* and *The Nightly News Nightmare.*

Orlando Patterson, a historical and cultural sociologist, is John Cowles Professor of Sociology at Harvard University. Author of many articles and books, including *Slavery and Social Death* (1982), *Freedom in the Making of Western Culture* (1991) (winner of the National Book Award for Non-Fiction), and *The Ordeal of Integration* (1997), he has also been Special Advisor for Social Policy and Development to the prime minister of Jamaica, a founding member of Cultural Survival, and a board member of Freedom House.

Paul E. Peterson is the Henry Lee Shattuck Professor of Government at Harvard University and the director of its Program on Education Policy and Governance. He is a Senior Fellow at the Hoover Institution and editor-in-chief of *Education Next: A Journal of Opinion and Research.* The author of *School Politics Chicago Style* and *The Politics of School Reform, 1870–1940,* he has also recently edited several books on education policy, including *Generational Change; No Child Left Behind?,* and *Choice and Competition in American Education.*

Nelson W. Polsby was until his death in 2007 a professor of political science at the University of California, Berkeley. He was the author of many books, including *How Congress Evolves; Congress and the Presidency;* and *Political Innovation in America.*

Peter H. Schuck is the Simeon E. Baldwin Professor at Yale Law School. He is the author of many books, including, most recently, *Diversity in America:*

Keeping Government at a Safe Distance; Meditations of a Militant Moderate: Cool Views on Hot Topics; Targeting in Social Programs: Avoiding Bad Bets, Removing Bad Apples (with Richard J. Zeckhauser); and *The Limits of Law: Essays on Democratic Governance.* Before joining the Yale faculty, he was an official in the U.S. Department of Health, Education, and Welfare and an attorney in private and "public interest" practice.

Linda J. Waite is the Lucy Flower Professor of Sociology and Director of the Center for Aging at the University of Chicago. She is the coauthor (with Frances Goldscheider) of *New Families, No Families?* and (with Maggie Gallagher) of *The Case for Marriage.* She is past president of the Population Association of America.

James Q. Wilson has been a Professor of Government at Harvard University and of Public Policy at UCLA. He now teaches at Pepperdine University. His books include *Thinking About Crime; Crime and Human Nature* (coauthored with Richard J. Herrnstein); and *On Character.* In 2003 he received the Presidential Medal of Freedom, the nation's highest civilian award.

Robert Wuthnow is Gerhard R. Andlinger '52 Professor of Social Sciences, Chair of the Sociology Department, and Director of the Center for the Study of Religion at Princeton University. He is the author of numerous publications, including *America and the Challenges of Religious Diversity* and *After the Baby Boomers: How Twenty- and Thirty-Somethings Are Shaping the Future of American Religion.*

Index

PublicAffairs is a publishing house founded in 1997. It is a tribute to the standards, values, and flair of three persons who have served as mentors to countless reporters, writers, editors, and book people of all kinds, including me.

I.F. Stone, proprietor of *I. F. Stone's Weekly*, combined a commitment to the First Amendment with entrepreneurial zeal and reporting skill and became one of the great independent journalists in American history. At the age of eighty, Izzy published *The Trial of Socrates*, which was a national bestseller. He wrote the book after he taught himself ancient Greek.

Benjamin C. Bradlee was for nearly thirty years the charismatic editorial leader of *The Washington Post*. It was Ben who gave the *Post* the range and courage to pursue such historic issues as Watergate. He supported his reporters with a tenacity that made them fearless and it is no accident that so many became authors of influential, best-selling books.

Robert L. Bernstein, the chief executive of Random House for more than a quarter century, guided one of the nation's premier publishing houses. Bob was personally responsible for many books of political dissent and argument that challenged tyranny around the globe. He is also the founder and longtime chair of Human Rights Watch, one of the most respected human rights organizations in the world.

·　　·　　·

For fifty years, the banner of Public Affairs Press was carried by its owner Morris B. Schnapper, who published Gandhi, Nasser, Toynbee, Truman, and about 1,500 other authors. In 1983, Schnapper was described by *The Washington Post* as "a redoubtable gadfly." His legacy will endure in the books to come.

Peter Osnos, *Founder and Editor-at-Large*

ELITES ?

25

36

191

(KUTOR   198

200

219

237

268

477

006